THE HOUR OF FATE

THE HOUR OF FATE

THEODORE ROOSEVELT, J.P. MORGAN,
AND THE BATTLE TO TRANSFORM AMERICAN CAPITALISM

SUSAN BERFIELD

BLOOMSBURY PUBLISHING
NEW YORK · LONDON · OXFORD · NEW DELHI · SYDNEY

BLOOMSBURY PUBLISHING
Bloomsbury Publishing Inc.
1385 Broadway, New York, NY 10018, USA

BLOOMSBURY, BLOOMSBURY PUBLISHING, and the Diana logo are
trademarks of Bloomsbury Publishing Plc

First published in the United States 2020

ISBN: HB: 978-1-63557-249-0; eBook: 978-1-63557-247-6

Library of Congress Cataloging-in-Publication Data is available

2 4 6 8 10 9 7 5 3 1

Typeset by Westchester Publishing Services
Printed and bound in the U.S.A. by Berryville Graphics Inc., Berryville, Virginia

To find out more about our authors and books visit www.bloomsbury.com
and sign up for our newsletters.

Bloomsbury books may be purchased for business or promotional use. For information on
bulk purchases please contact Macmillan Corporate and Premium Sales Department at
specialmarkets@macmillan.com.

To my family, always

CONTENTS

PROLOGUE

Leon Czolgosz hadn't worked in years. When he arrived in Buffalo on the last day of August 1901, he rented a room above John Nowak's saloon for two dollars a week. Czolgosz—slender, clean-shaven, brown-haired, blue-eyed, twenty-eight years old—survived mostly on milk and bread. He didn't talk much. He didn't stay long. He seemed to be one of those young men adrift in America's raw, roaring economic churn. One afternoon, he walked to Walbridge Hardware on Main Street and bought the most expensive handgun on display, a .32 caliber Iver Johnson automatic revolver, for $4.50.

Czolgosz's parents immigrated from Eastern Europe to the Midwest and then kept moving in search of work. His mother died when he was about ten. His stepmother seemed uncaring, his father distant. Czolgosz attended school when he could, worked a few hours here and there when he had to, and then, when he turned sixteen, followed his father's instructions to get a full-time job. Five years in classrooms made him the best educated of his seven siblings. Czolgosz eventually ended up at the Cleveland Rolling Mill, a steel wire factory with modern equipment and management. He could count on decent pay, steady hours, and tolerable physical demands. If all went well, Czolgosz might one day rise out of the working class.

Things didn't go well. In 1893, America sank into a depression, businesses shut down, and people across the country lost their jobs. Czolgosz was among them. When he was rehired, the company engaged in a brutal price war that resulted in lower wages. After Czolgosz joined a strike, he was fired and put on a blacklist. The only way he could work again was to wait for a new foreman to come in and then reapply under a fake identity. He chose the name Fred Nieman: Fred Nobody.

Everyone around him could see that he was unhappy, brooding, almost broken. He had been set back, as so many others had, and couldn't recover, and in this too he wasn't alone. Then he stopped trying. In 1898 he told his boss that he was unwell and had to quit.

His family had purchased a 55-acre farm—he had emptied his bank account to contribute—and it was there he took refuge. He tinkered in the barn but refused to help with the hard labor. He wouldn't eat with his family when his stepmother was home and took herbal remedies for ailments he wouldn't discuss. Reading the newspapers and Edward Bellamy's bestselling utopian novel, *Looking Backward: 2000–1887*, became preoccupying interests. Czolgosz called himself a socialist, sometimes an anarchist. In May 1901 he heard one of the most famous anarchists, Emma Goldman, speak in Cleveland and was so taken by her that he began to contemplate radical, violent, and, in his mind, heroic, action. First, though, he introduced himself. They exchanged a few words, and he made a good impression, but if he was expecting to be taken in, he would have been disappointed. All he came away with was a few books she recommended.

His family didn't know what to make of him, and he did not seem to know what to make of himself, either. "I never had much luck at anything, and this preyed upon me," Czolgosz later said. "It made me morose and envious." He desperately wanted to sell his share of the farm and leave his family behind. They gave him seventy dollars in July 1901, and he disappeared.

PRESIDENT WILLIAM MCKINLEY, well rested after a summer at home in Ohio, arrived in Buffalo on Wednesday, September 4, 1901, for the Pan-American Exposition. It was a months-long festival in a 350-acre park meant to showcase America as a flourishing and innovative nation, taking its rightful place as a world leader. The Expo featured a Fountain of Abundance and a Tower of Light, and each evening, hundreds of thousands of eight-watt lightbulbs illuminated the buildings, reflecting pools, and sculptures. It was the first massive display of electric power, generated by the alternating currents of nearby Niagara Falls. Inventors presented a new electric battery, a wireless telegraph, and a device called an akouphone that allowed the deaf to hear. A simulated trip to the moon on the spaceship *Luna* was so popular that afterward the creator patented the machine. Thomas Edison's film company captured it all.

The showmen organized the fairground to reflect the achievements of a modern, industrial America—as they understood it. Visitors to the midway could watch reenacted battles between Native Americans and U.S. soldiers. Organizers had brought entire indigenous families to live in faux villages. "Darkest Africa" was enclosed by a fence; across from it was the "Old Plantation." Only after activists, mostly black women, called on officials to do better, did the fair find room to display the books, art, and inventions of African Americans. "The Negro Exhibit" opened in a stifling convention center and received little attention from white journalists or the Expo's promoters. Some of those on display resisted and a few others protested that it was wrong, or racist, to treat humans as specimens. To most of the crowd, though, it was all just a spectacle.

"My fellow citizens, trade statistics indicate that this country is in a state of unexampled prosperity. The figures are almost appalling," McKinley said to a cheering audience of some fifty thousand mostly middle-class men and women gathered on the vast esplanade. "That all the people are participating in this great prosperity is seen in every American community."

McKinley had campaigned as "The Advance Agent of Prosperity" and often celebrated the country's good fortune. He was fifty-eight years old, charming and generous even to critics, a gracious envoy to the business class who was still considerate of other opinions. He had been easily reelected in 1900. His vice president for his second term was Theodore Roosevelt, who was young and energetic and popular with voters because he didn't seem beholden to the rich. Born into New York's privileged set, Roosevelt had become a civil service reformer, then a Rough Rider cavalryman in the Spanish-American War, then a crusading governor. The Republican establishment barely tolerated him. The vice presidency was supposed to diminish Roosevelt's power and keep him out of sight.

On McKinley's final day at the Expo, September 6, he planned to greet anyone who cared to meet him at the Temple of Music, an ornate domed building that could hold two thousand people. Many more than that were waiting outside late Friday afternoon. George Cortelyou, McKinley's personal secretary, had advised against a public reception, warning that the president would be too vulnerable. Twice Cortelyou tried to cancel it.

The weather was humid and heavy, and many in the queue held handkerchiefs and dabbed at their brows. Within the Temple, a musician played a Bach Sonata on one of the country's largest organs as McKinley entered through a back door. He took his place between Cortelyou and John Milburn, the president of the Expo. He noted how cool it was inside. He seemed eager. "Let them come," he said.

Attendants opened the front doors. National Guard soldiers paced in front of the entrance, and Secret Service agents and local police hovered. But no one noticed Czolgosz.

He had arrived at the Temple hours earlier and was near the front of the crowd, inconspicuous in his pressed gray suit, flannel shirt, and black string tie. "He appeared as a mechanic, a printer, a shipping clerk," an eyewitness noted later. Except for one detail: He had wrapped his right hand with a plain handkerchief, as if he were injured. Underneath, he gripped his revolver.

McKinley smiled and reached to shake Czolgosz's left hand. As Czolgosz stepped forward, he raised his right instead and fired two

President McKinley on his way to the Temple of Music, September 6, 1901, with John Milburn (left) and George Cortelyou (right)

bullets. The first grazed the president, but the second went deep into his abdomen, puncturing his pancreas and kidney and embedding somewhere beyond.

McKinley staggered. Cortelyou and Milburn steadied him, then eased him onto a chair. The man waiting behind Czolgosz—James Parker, an African American former constable from Georgia, now a waiter at an Expo restaurant—tackled him. Someone, a Secret Service agent or a soldier, grabbed the gun. In the melee it was hard to know who.

"I done my duty," Czolgosz said as the police and soldiers and men waiting in line hit and kicked him. Czolgosz was blood-spattered and unmoving. McKinley was half conscious. "Be easy with him, boys," he murmured. The police had to carry Czolgosz out before he was killed.

The president poked his fingers under his shirt. They came out bloody.

NEARLY FOUR HUNDRED miles away in New York City, everything seemed just as it should that afternoon as John Pierpont Morgan was about to leave work. The streets around his headquarters at 23 Wall Street were quiet. Trading on the stock market ended at three, and by four the big and the small who calculated, bought, sold, loaned, speculated, hedged, hustled, and bluffed had emptied their offices. Trains, ferries, and yachts carried them away to the suburbs. Summer was still in the air, but the cheerful ease of the wealthy on an unhurried Friday was about to end.

On Wall Street, Morgan had two nicknames: Jupiter and Zeus. He controlled the "coal roads" of Pennsylvania—the railroads and their anthracite coal fields supplying energy along the East Coast and out to Chicago and St. Louis. He controlled the Northern Pacific line and the New York Central, too. He wielded power in banks and financial institutions other than his own. When the U.S. government needed gold, Morgan provided it. He had funded Thomas Edison, consolidated General Electric, and sat on the company's board. He was a director at Western Union, the Pullman Palace Car Company, and Aetna Fire Insurance. If anything important was happening on Wall Street, Morgan was assumed to be behind it.

On the eve of McKinley's second inauguration, Morgan had announced the creation of the first billion-dollar American company, United States

Steel. It was a grandiose, thrilling, and frightening prospect. The corporation would be in charge of almost half of the country's steelmaking capacity and be worth double the entire federal government's revenues in 1900. McKinley was dazzled by Morgan, but the admiration wasn't mutual. In the financier's world, Washington was a second-rate power and its chief executive of limited use. Morgan explained as little as possible and confided nothing to McKinley. He said only that he assembled U.S. Steel to end ruinous price wars and compete in the global marketplace. He had done so by combining his company with it biggest rival, owned by Andrew Carnegie, and acquiring several smaller businesses.

And at 4:07 P.M. on September 6, 1901, Leon Czolgosz, a former employee of one of those smaller businesses, was firing a bullet into President McKinley's abdomen.

Morgan was among the last to leave his office that day. A courier had earlier delivered secret documents Morgan had been working to secure for months. They established a formal alliance with one of his few remaining adversaries. Their fight that spring had been public and bitter and costly. But he had won. It would be some time before the public would learn the news these documents affirmed. Morgan, who already controlled the world's largest company, would now control the second-largest, as well: a railroad behemoth called Northern Securities.

Morgan put on his silk hat, picked up his mahogany cane, tucked a box of cigars under his arm, and on his way out glanced at the ledger on a clerk's desk. He couldn't help himself. A reporter rushed in.

"We have a dispatch, Mr. Morgan, stating that an attempt has been made on the life of the president at Buffalo."

"What?" Morgan looked hard at the reporter, set down his cane and cigars, and grasped the man's arm. "What?"

The reporter said the president had been shot. This time the words registered.

"Is it serious?" Too early to know.

At 4:18 an electric ambulance brought McKinley to a hospital on the Expo grounds. He was pale, weak, aware enough to consent to immediate surgery.

In Manhattan, one of Morgan's sons-in-law, Herbert Satterlee, arrived at the firm's Wall Street headquarters to pick the elder man up as they had planned. They retreated inside the office. Morgan whispered to the sole executive still there, who went to call for a private account of the events in Buffalo. Fifteen minutes later he confirmed that McKinley had been shot twice. So much about Morgan seemed permanent and superior, but now as he sat at his desk, he appeared shaken and helpless.

Another reporter arrived to ask about the financial community's reaction to the shooting. "This is sad, sad, very sad news. It is very sad news, very sad," Morgan said. "No, I don't want to say anything. The news is very sad. There is nothing I can say at this time." Morgan and Satterlee slowly walked out of the office at five o'clock, climbed into a waiting carriage, and drove to the New York Yacht Club.

McKinley was put under the influence of ether by 5:20. Nine minutes later, the surgeon made his first cut. The team that operated on the president faced some challenges. Electricity brightened attractions throughout the Expo, but not the hospital. A doctor used a mirror to reflect the rays of the setting sun onto the operating table until someone could hook up a light. The hospital was well equipped to treat any minor health problem— over the summer the most common complaints had been digestive troubles and toothaches—but no one expected a retractor would be required for a life-threatening injury. "The greatest difficulty was the great size of President McKinley's abdomen and the amount of fat present," the surgeon later noted. He first inserted a finger and then his entire hand but couldn't find the second bullet. He cleaned the wounds, stitched them up, and sent a still unconscious McKinley to Milburn's home to recover.

In New York, newspaper staff stayed on the streets with brushes and crayons updating the bulletin boards set up along Park Row. Crowds swirled around them, pushing and shoving, stunned and nervous. People stood by the news tickers in hotel lobbies, or roamed Broadway, ducking into cafés and saloons for the latest word. Rumors percolated through the city: Morgan was making contingency plans. He was gathering the "chief bankers and capitalists on board his yacht and was holding a ways and means conference." He was summoning the presidents of the big banks to the Metropolitan Club. Or to the Fifth Avenue Hotel, to Delmonico's, to the Yacht Club.

Nothing of the sort. Morgan boarded his yacht, *Corsair*, with only Satterlee accompanying him. They cruised to Long Island in silence.

At seven, McKinley's doctors issued an update, which the president's secretary, Cortelyou, relayed to the public: "The patient stood the operation well. Pulse of good quality, rate of 130, condition at the conclusion of operation was gratifying. The result cannot be foretold. His condition at present justifies hope of recovery."

Some on the streets of Manhattan cheered, some kept an anxious silence. After President James Garfield had been shot in 1881, he had lingered, bedridden and uncomfortable, for more than two months before succumbing. The agitated crowds at the Waldorf-Astoria—many Wall Street brokers among them—remained until well past midnight.

ROOSEVELT TOO WAS four hundred miles from Buffalo that day, in Vermont, to give a luncheon speech to some thousand guests on a small island in Lake Champlain. He was changing his clothes, preparing to rejoin the men and women eager to shake his hand, and generally enjoying the hours as the center of attention when he was summoned to the phone around five thirty in the afternoon. He was told McKinley had been shot and had just entered surgery. "My God" was all the vice president could say. Tears filled his eyes. He couldn't bring himself to announce the news and asked one of the hosts to speak to the crowd.

He paced the room, murmured every now and then, kept his composure, and waited for word. Soon it came. The president's wounds weren't fatal, there didn't seem to be any complications, and he should recover. "That's good—it's good. May it be every bit true," Roosevelt said as he rushed to the veranda. He wanted to be the one to share the encouraging message.

Roosevelt didn't linger. A few minutes later, he boarded a guest's yacht to sail to the mainland. On the trip, in motion, doing something, he was a bit more talkative. He described McKinley as gentle and lovable: "Of all the men I have known in public life he was the last to excite animosity." Roosevelt arrived in Buffalo by train the next afternoon. Much of McKinley's cabinet and family—as well as Senator Mark Hanna, his confidant and campaign manager—were already there. Roosevelt told a friend he felt a hundred years old.

In Manhattan, the stock market had opened on time for its regular two-hour session that Saturday morning. Now Morgan did meet with the chief bankers. Wall Street suspected that he sent brokers on the floor to buy anything at whatever the price. "The financial situation is absolutely good," he said. "There is nothing to derange it. The banks will take care of that. Nobody need worry about that." Morgan knew that appearances mattered, his most of all. Afterward he kept to his schedule. He went down to the harbor to meet a railroad executive returning from a summer vacation in Europe. As Morgan waited for the ship to dock, a friend relayed the latest from Hanna. The president was doing as well as could be expected.

Before long, the president's condition seemed to improve. Doctors allowed only his wife, Ida, to see him, but provided regular reports. His mind was clear. He was resting well. He took a teaspoon of beef juice every hour. Then three. He had a few drops of whiskey and jokingly asked to smoke a cigar. Doctors considered using one of Edison's new X-ray machines to help locate the second bullet and recruited another doctor, whose height, weight, and fifty-six-inch girth matched the president's, to serve as a test subject. But they never tried out the X-ray on McKinley.

Two days after the shooting, doctors reported that the president was past the danger point. "Now everything will go on swimmingly," Hanna said. "We are going to have good times."

ALL THAT WEEK Morgan arrived at his office before eleven in the morning, sometimes by nine—early for him. Police had been watching 23 Wall Street ever since steel workers went on strike over the summer. Now at least six detectives stood at the main entrance at all times, while others stationed themselves throughout the financial district. Plainclothes officers kept an eye on the Yacht Club pier, where a launch would take Morgan to *Corsair* to sleep each night.

There was no credible threat to Morgan. Czolgosz—angry, desperate, ill—said he acted alone, and really he barely had a plan. But in an unsettled time, Morgan had to be protected. Through his companies and connections he controlled and influenced more money than any other person in America, maybe the world. He had partners and he had a son, but none could replace him. That summer, British investors had taken out life insurance policies on him, nervous about the more typical deaths that could come for a sixty-four-year-old man.

In Buffalo, the worry once so heavy seemed to evaporate. McKinley's sister and nieces returned home. Attorney General Philander Knox and Treasury Secretary Lyman Gage left for Washington. Hanna went back to Cleveland. "You may say that I am absolutely sure that the president will recover," Roosevelt told reporters. Then he left too.

Roosevelt set off on a hiking expedition with his family in a particularly remote part of the Adirondacks. He would climb the highest peak, eat lunch at Lake Tear of the Clouds, and stay at a cabin thirty-five miles from the nearest railroad and telegraph station and ten miles from a telephone.

Then, before daylight on Friday, September 13, McKinley's heart began failing. His pulse slowed. He could no longer eat. He became disoriented. Stimulants had no effect. Oxygen didn't help. Gangrene had developed along the path of the bullet and he was in septic shock. A flock of crows flying over the Milburn house had to be a bad omen. The doctors' bulletin came at six thirty that evening: "The end is only a question of time."

Morgan received updates in his office between meetings. Afterward he stayed busy, traveling uptown to the Union Club, to his yacht for a quick trip to see his daughter on Long Island, and back to the club.

At ten, Ida held her husband's hand, then left his bedside. McKinley's doctors discontinued the oxygen. At eleven, Morgan returned to the Yacht Club, where he told reporters that he had been on the phone with Buffalo, and the president would not live out the night. He had nothing more to say and boarded *Corsair*.

Roosevelt had rushed down ten miles of trails when he first got word of trouble, making it back to a lodge high in the hills as the last light was fading. Before midnight, he received another update: "The President appears to be dying and members of the Cabinet in Buffalo think you should lose no time coming."

Roosevelt began the moonless descent, in a horse-drawn carriage navigating narrow roads in the fog and mist of a mountain storm. He changed horses and drivers along the way rather than stop to allow the team to rest. Some six hours later he reached the North Creek train station, where another telegram was waiting.

"The President died at 2:15 o'clock this morning."

Roosevelt silently folded the paper and put it in his pocket. He was forty-two years old. He would be the youngest person ever to lead the nation. He had been headed toward the presidency almost since he entered public life. Now he would have to claim the office amid violence and grief.

Outside the mansion in Buffalo, storm winds howled. In New York, the streets and hotels and bars remained full and hushed, and the bells of Trinity Church rang out. The twenty-fifth president of the United States was the third to be assassinated in four decades.

A train, the fastest on the line, waited for Roosevelt at North Creek. He strode across the platform and boarded the private car. The locomotive traveled at a top speed of 60 miles per hour, through the rain-soaked night.

ON THE MORNING of Saturday, September 14, workmen arrived early at 23 Wall Street with two heavy boxes and a sewing machine. They stitched long streamers of black crape to drape over the building's marble facade. An immense American flag fluttered in the wind. Soon the city would be shrouded in black. The stock exchange was closed for the day, but still Morgan showed up for work. He was wearing a black suit instead of his usual gray.

At 1:30 P.M., Roosevelt reached Buffalo. "I was so shocked by the terrible news brought to me last night and by the calamity it entailed upon the country, as well as by the personal sorrow I feel, that I have had no time to think of plans for the future conduct of the office which has been so suddenly and sadly thrust upon me," he said to reporters, looking worn.

He went straight to the mansion of a friend, Ansley Wilcox, where Roosevelt decided to be sworn in. But first he had to pay his respects. He borrowed a coat and trousers from Wilcox and a hat from another friend. He had his boots polished, gathered a gold-topped cane and gloves, and told his military escort to stay behind. Roosevelt was alert to the moment. While he still could, he thought it best to appear a solitary figure, stripped of the presumptions of power.

McKinley's cabinet members, exhausted and distraught, were waiting for him at the Milburn house. "The President of the United States," someone called out as he entered. Roosevelt seemed barely to hear it. Doctors were performing an autopsy of the body, and Ida McKinley was too overcome to see Roosevelt. He stayed in the parlor and briefly conferred with Elihu Root, the secretary of war and a longtime friend from New York. Root urged him to convey a sense of stability—to the conservative men of McKinley's cabinet and to the nation. Roosevelt returned to the Wilcox home alone.

He chose a spot by the library window, where the afternoon sun was streaming in. Cabinet members circled around him. A federal judge stood opposite. Roosevelt summoned two dozen reporters angling for a view from the outside. The ceremony began.

Roosevelt straightened the lapels of his frock coat and steadied himself. "I wish to state that it shall be my aim to continue absolutely unbroken the policy of President McKinley for the peace, prosperity, and honor of our beloved country." He uttered the oath of office, his voice firm, his face stern, and his right arm fully extended. He bowed his head in silence for three full minutes. The sob of a passing woman pierced the room. Roosevelt stood up and signed the parchment declaring him president.

Reporters hounded Morgan for comment. "So many of the enterprises which he had started and the projects which he then had in hand depended on the continuance of peace and prosperity to bring them to success," his son-in-law wrote later. Notwithstanding the new president's words, Morgan "was afraid that Roosevelt was too temperamental, and that he would disturb the prosperity of the country by trying experiments."

From Morgan himself, the press got nothing but silence.

A MOB GATHERED around the prison calling for the assassin's death. "I did not feel that one man should have all this power while others have none," Czolgosz told his interrogators. "I am not afraid to die. We all have to die some time." He said the lecture by Goldman inspired his crime: "She set me on fire." Goldman was arrested in Chicago on September 10, questioned by police, brought before an assistant to Buffalo's district attorney, and after two weeks let go. She said she met Czolgosz only briefly—in Cleveland and in Chicago, where he had arrived uninvited two months later. The

Leon Czolgosz's police report

police said there was no plot. But Goldman alone defended Czolgosz as a "soul in pain." She became a pariah because of it.

Czolgosz's trial lasted barely two days. The jury deliberated for thirty minutes. On the morning of October 29, prison guards brought Czolgosz into the execution chamber. He was ashen, dressed in a gray shirt, prepared to speak his final words. "I shot the president because I thought it would help the working people and for the sake of the common people. I am not sorry for my crime," he said. The guards tightened the straps on his head and chin. At twelve minutes past seven, one thousand seven hundred volts of electricity shocked the body of Leon Czolgosz.

He was buried in an unmarked grave. His corpse was dissolved in carbolic acid.

PART I

CHAPTER 1

"The Storm Is on Us"

I n the first hours, days, and months of the new presidency, Roosevelt heard the same warning again and again. Be cautious. He heard it even as McKinley lay in bed on September 13, organs failing, death approaching. Douglas Robinson, a prominent businessman and Roosevelt's brother-in law, wrote from New York City: "I must frankly tell you that there is a feeling in financial circles here that in case you become President, you may change matters so as to upset the confidence, for the time at least, of the financial world, which would be an awful blow to everybody."

Immediately after he was sworn in, Roosevelt said what he was expected to. McKinley's cabinet—uniformly conservative, governed by the desire to "stand pat," and trusted to protect the privileges of America's wealthy—would become his. But McKinley's closest adviser, the one who perhaps needed the most assurance, was not in the Wilcox mansion to hear Roosevelt's promise. Mark Hanna had wept after seeing the dying president and was making preparations to bring the body to Washington.

Hanna was a well-to-do industrialist and senator from Ohio who, like most officials at the time, didn't consider one job a conflict with the other. He was among the most influential politicians in the country. He had helped bring McKinley to power, managing his presidential campaigns with a wary eye toward the populists in the West and a hand out to the money men in the East. He calculated potential contributions from

Ohio Senator Marcus Alonzo Hanna

the tycoons commensurate with their financial worth. No one had done that before. Political cartoonists called him Dollar Mark. A journalist described him as having "a cash-register conscience." He hated both caricatures. But the tycoons, the ultimate bottom-liners, didn't object to his methods. In return, Hanna promised a "safe" leader to shield them from political attacks. McKinley hadn't disappointed them.

Hanna wanted to make sure Roosevelt wouldn't either. He was wary of Roosevelt's obvious magnetism and seeming impetuousness. He considered Roosevelt unsafe, the most damning criticism of all. Hanna alone fought Roosevelt's nomination as the vice presidential candidate, giving way only at the last minute, when his support didn't matter. It was a humbling, infuriating snub. "Don't any of you realize there's only one life between that madman and the Presidency?" he pleaded.

"I am as strong as a bull moose and you can use me up to the limit," Roosevelt had told Hanna as the campaign got under way. He had traveled twenty-one thousand miles to visit twenty-four states and speak in front of some three million people, and in doing so he earned Hanna's grudging admiration. Hanna didn't have that kind of stamina. He was stout, stiff, and, at age sixty-three, in dubious health.

In Buffalo, Roosevelt and Hanna went for a brief walk along an empty street to take each other's measure. Hanna still called Roosevelt Teddy, knowing he disliked the nickname. Roosevelt called Hanna Old Man. Each had the power to check the other's ambitions and neither could be certain who would prevail.

On Monday, September 16, a special train provided by the Pennsylvania Railroad left Buffalo for the capital. McKinley's body lay in a glass observation car for the twelve-hour journey. Also aboard were Roosevelt, the cabinet he had just inherited, McKinley's family and intimate friends, and

President Roosevelt conferring with Senator Hanna in Buffalo

the press. The train traveled on tracks cleared of traffic, past station platforms crowded with people who came to mourn McKinley and glimpse his replacement. An anxious, bewildering sorrow pervaded.

Roosevelt could not remain silent among those men. At the suggestion of Herman Henry Kohlsaat—a businessman, publisher of the *Chicago Evening Post*, and presidential confidant—Roosevelt invited Hanna to share a meal. "That damn cowboy wants me to take supper with him, alone," Hanna grumbled. Of course he accepted.

Roosevelt reassured Hanna that he wanted the senator's support and would seek his counsel in the coming months. The senator promised to back the new president as long as he carried out the old policies. In Buffalo, Hanna had warned that he wouldn't necessarily support Roosevelt's nomination in 1904. This time he was even more blunt: "Do not think anything about a second term." Roosevelt didn't reply.

Hanna returned to his seat feeling relieved. "He's a pretty good little cuss, after all!"

When the train stopped in Harrisburg, Pennsylvania, Kohlsaat jumped out to scan the evening papers and gauge the mood of the country, which to him meant the financial community. Wall Street's leaders and followers were placated, he happily reported. An unchanged cabinet with unchanged priorities seemed a sufficient guarantee of stability. "The tremendous responsibility of his new position will have a quieting effect on him," one broker commented. "Mr. Roosevelt is a safe man, and there is no reason to fear anything that would happen under him as President," said a banker.

Morgan hadn't even mentioned Roosevelt: "President McKinley was a much beloved man, and his death is a great sorrow to the nation. While it was a great shock to all, I do not think business interests will be affected. Our Government is sound and prepared for great emergencies."

Roosevelt's train hurtled on toward Washington. "I don't care a damn about stocks and bonds," he told Kohlsaat, "but I don't want to see them go down the first day I am President!"

A military escort positioned McKinley's casket in the center of the Capitol rotunda, draped in an American flag, surrounded by wreaths, roses, and crosses. The funeral began at eleven on Tuesday morning. For an hour before, the official mourners, some seven hundred, filed slowly in and filled the chairs circling the casket. Morgan walked among former administration officials. Roosevelt took his place with the cabinet, close to McKinley's body. He struggled to remain composed as he spoke. His voice faltered, and once or twice he brought his handkerchief to his eyes. Hanna sat alone with his grief, silent, his face bowed in his hands. Ida McKinley was inconsolable and didn't attend.

That evening Roosevelt, Hanna, the cabinet, and the family traveled to McKinley's home in Canton, Ohio. His body was interred in a simple vault in a local cemetery. Hanna immediately began to raise the six hundred thousand dollars he deemed necessary to build a proper memorial.

The train returned to the nation's capital at 9:26 Friday morning, September 20, 1901. Police held back the small crowd waiting at the station as Roosevelt, compact and bristling with energy, bowed and hurried to his carriage. Fifteen minutes later, he arrived at 1600 Pennsylvania Avenue. There was no ceremony, no formalities, no callers to greet him. As Roosevelt crossed the portico, a guard swung open the front door, and the president strode in.

He greeted the staff, rode the elevator to the second floor, entered his private office, and began dictating responses to the hundreds of messages offering congratulations, hope, advice, admonishment. At eleven sharp, he took a seat at the head of a long wooden table and called for his first full cabinet meeting.

"It's a dreadful thing to come into the presidency this way," he wrote to a friend, "but it would be a far worse thing to be morbid about it."

BY THE TURN of the century, the domination of the West was complete. For more than a hundred years, the government of the United States had gobbled up the continent piece by piece, through war, through treaties brokered and broken, and through the violent enclosure of ranges that once sustained native nations. The frontier had been marketed to the American poor and rootless with promises of escape, reinvention, independence, vast resources, land for grabs. Now it was closed.

America's restless ambitions became mechanized and manufactured, pushing and pulling people from their farms and towns into factories, into cities, into a faster, sometimes freer, largely more codified life. With automobiles coming onto the streets, and electric lights and telephones being installed in homes, the American standard of living was improving. But many were also confused, uprooted, and surrounded by the unfamiliar. There were more roads and rail lines, more people and buildings, bigger farms, bigger corporations, bigger cities.

For those who stayed in place, the new rules and rhythms seemed determined by distant and abstract forces: technology controlled by private corporations, capital controlled by Wall Street, wages and prices controlled by industrialists. Those who left for the factories joined an industrial world where their productivity was measured and their safety often disregarded. If they were cheated or hurt, their options for recourse were scant. Almost half a million immigrants arrived in 1901, drawn by dreams of freedom and a better life, but they were unprotected, crowded into unhealthy tenements and some of the most unreliable jobs. The backlash against Reconstruction in the South—and pervasive racism throughout the country—meant many African Americans struggled to rise out of poverty with the promise of a fair deal unfulfilled. Women could work on the production lines, or in the sweatshops, but they earned considerably less than men, and most still couldn't vote.

New York was the wealthiest city in the country and becoming wealthier by the year. Between 1895 and 1900, ten families with fortunes from mining and manufacturing in the West and Midwest moved east. Together they were worth tens, maybe hundreds, of millions of dollars. Among them was William Clark, a senator and copper magnate from Montana, who was constructing a one hundred and twenty-one room home on Fifth Avenue. It included four art galleries, a swimming pool, and an underground rail line to supply heating coal. When Clark came across a bronze foundry whose work he liked, he bought it. Elsewhere on the avenue, descendants of the railroad tycoon Cornelius Vanderbilt lived in a row of mansions; they called one the Petit Château. Mrs. Astor's new residence featured a ball-room big enough for more than a thousand guests.

The figures were staggering. But these industrialists accumulated their wealth in ways most Americans could understand. They dug up something. They discovered something. They built something. The financiers backing the industrialists, as Americans were just learning, found their riches in the flow of money itself. They lent and borrowed capital, collected fees and commissions, created stocks, sometimes inflated, to sell to eager small-time investors. They helped concentrate the economy. Few people could avoid everyday encounters with monopolies: the companies that traded in oil, salt, meat, whiskey, starch, coal, tin, copper, lead, oil cloth, rope, school slate, envelopes, and paper bags were pooled, combined, controlled.

Morgan was the most influential of these businessmen. He wasn't the richest—by most counts John D. Rockefeller and Andrew Carnegie were—but that didn't matter; he was commanding in a way none could match. Wherever he sat became the head of the table. He was comfortable in his dominion, though never with his fame. He had an aristocrat's disdain for public sentiment and the conviction that his actions were to the country's advantage, no explanations necessary.

Roosevelt thought big business was not only inevitable but essential. He also believed it had to be accountable to the public, and Roosevelt consid-ered himself to be the public. Each presumed he could use his authority to determine the nation's course. Each expected deference from the other along the way.

Morgan and Roosevelt both knew privilege and loss, though they would have balked if anyone had pointed out their similarities. They were a generation apart, but that wasn't the only explanation for the essential differences in how they perceived their shared experiences.

Morgan in his sixties was physically intimidating: he had become a large man, with a square chin, thick chest and sturdy legs. Meeting his blazing dark eyes was like confronting the headlights of an express train bearing down on you, the photographer Edward Steichen said after shooting his portrait. But Morgan's defining feature was his diseased, bulging purple nose. He called it "part of the American business structure."

Portrait by Edward Steichen

Roosevelt was young and kinetic, a moralist and opportunist. He had a fighter's instinct for keeping opponents off balance and a showman's sense of drama. When he came to power, the possibility of social unrest seemed close. "The storm is on us," said a friend of both the president and the financier. Morgan didn't sense the energy and anger swelling up. Roosevelt grabbed it and tamed it. "I am not advocating anything very revolutionary," he said. "I am advocating action to prevent anything revolutionary." Morgan couldn't see that.

The president aimed to guarantee that, as America's prosperity took hold, the laws applied to the country's elite and its poor alike—to its agitated laborers, and its heralded capitalists. He wanted to assert the primacy of government over business. The financier thought that was needless, even dangerous: The country's strength accrued from capital, trade, economic efficiency. These were the provinces of businessmen, and Morgan their unofficial ruler. He required order and stability, along with political predictability, to assure America's growth and ascent to global power. To Morgan, the giant railroad and steel companies he was constructing would allow the country to compete in the world market and its citizens to benefit. The pace and scale of these operations shouldn't be cause for worry or resentment, and certainly not regulation.

"I am afraid of Mr. Roosevelt because I don't know what he'll do," Morgan reportedly said. "He's afraid of me because he does know what I'll do," Roosevelt replied.

Roosevelt and Morgan were bound for conflict. Roosevelt took office in the autumn, and before spring had arrived, he began the fight against corporate power that would mark the seasons of his presidency, though not always as he expected. By the next winter, he would be forced to turn to Morgan to help resolve a coal strike that could have brought despair to millions. Roosevelt defended the public interest; Morgan, the coal barons'. Roosevelt was a new kind of president. He believed American capitalism needed a guiding hand. So did Morgan. Each assumed it should be his own.

AT THE END of September, Morgan, two bishops, and several clergymen left New York aboard a private six-car train for a convention of the Episcopal Church in San Francisco. Morgan was a lay delegate and generous funder. Less than two weeks prior, a train carrying two presidents—one deceased, the other very much alive—had been granted absolute right of way on vacated tracks. Now Morgan would receive the same treatment. Other trains were shunted aside to allow him to speed across the continent in just four days, a record run. From the depot the travelers took a ferry across the Bay. Morgan and Bishop Henry Potter of New York took in the view, better enjoyed, they thought, with cigars. A deckhand apparently reminded them smoking wasn't allowed on board, and they blithely ignored him. Morgan had arranged to stay with his guests at a three-story mansion built by a railroad magnate atop a windy hill. Louis Sherry, Morgan's favorite New York caterer, was already there with French chefs and waiters.

From San Francisco, Morgan traveled up the coast to Oregon with intentions that were entirely less ecclesiastical in nature. In fact, his purpose had everything to do with those secret documents that had been delivered to his hands the very day that McKinley was shot. Now Morgan was bent on inspecting two properties, the Great Northern and Northern Pacific railroad lines, that were central to his plans to create his next great company. The financial world he so dominated suspected he was ready to strike again.

"All Wall Street was on tip-toe" in October, waiting for their Jupiter to return.

CHAPTER 2

The Best of Everything

B efore the Jupiter of Roman myth could become king of the sky and thunder, he had to overthrow his father in a mighty battle. Not so for the Jupiter of Wall Street. Morgan had trusted his father to set him on the right path and steer his career, and even when his father was overbearing, Morgan never mounted a challenge. The creator of the biggest companies the world had ever known was, himself, very much the creation of paternal influence. The young Morgan, once established, proved instinctively suited to the times in which he lived. It was an era of raucous, unfettered competition: chaotic capitalism that he would try to order.

John Pierpont Morgan was born in April 1837 into a wealthy family and inherited his father's European connections and tastes, along with part of his fortune. He grew up in the river town of Hartford, Connecticut, a thriving center of trade and, by necessity, insurance. John preferred to be called Pierpont, though schoolmates nicknamed him Pip. As the eldest of five and the only son to live past childhood, he was also entitled to a lifetime of moral education and cautionary advice from his father, Junius, and continual redirection when he strayed. His mother, Juliet, was troubled by depression and lived at a sullen remove from the family. She once scolded Pierpont for writing home too often.

Pierpont suffered physically as a child. For months before and after his first birthday he was so frequently overcome by convulsions that his parents feared he might not survive. In adolescence, he missed school because of sore throats, headaches, earaches, boils on his face, and ulcerated sores on his lips. When Pierpont was fifteen, his father sent him to the Portuguese Azores, hoping the warm climate would cure his rheumatic fever. He stayed there, with only a family friend and a doctor to check on him, for four months.

Junius moved Pierpont into and out of boarding and public schools—transferring him nine times in thirteen years—without explanation. Pierpont didn't complain. He was an indifferent student in most subjects other than math: "full of animal life and spirits . . . and not renowned as a scholar," one classmate later described him. Pierpont sought order in the only ways he could. He collected and organized, first stamps and autographs of Episcopal bishops and then his own accounts. When he traveled, he noted the latitude of his destination and the time of his arrival, and wherever he was he kept a leather-bound journal of daily expenses: paper and postage, ice cream and strawberries, beaver hats, silk gloves, buggy rides, opera tickets.

In 1854, the family moved to London after Junius accepted a partnership in the British office of the premier American private bank, run by George Peabody, to help direct European capital to the United States. Junius would one day take over, and he hoped Pierpont would do so after him: a Morgan dynasty.

Pierpont was seventeen. He had graduated from the English High School of Boston, which specialized in math, and was eager to begin his career. But Junius wanted him to learn French and German and enrolled him at a school near Lake Geneva. Pierpont considered the accommodations too sparse and the studies uninteresting. "Adapts himself very slowly . . . Answers back . . . sulky," the headmaster wrote of the new student. Outside the classroom, he was happier. He enjoyed the camaraderie of the other American students and soon made himself their unofficial leader. If they went on an expedition, he planned it; if they hosted a party, he arranged it. Taking charge would become a lifetime impulse—one, though, that Pierpont would have to curb around his father for years.

At the University of Göttingen, where Junius sent him next, Pierpont was such an exceptional math student that his professor thought he could one day join the academy. Neither Morgan considered that a suitable career path.

In 1857, Junius arranged a first job for Pierpont, as an unpaid clerk at a New York investment firm linked to his. It specialized in financing the railroads eager builders were haphazardly laying across America. The industry was all raw hustle. Lines overlapped each other or ran parallel, creating a tangle of tracks of different widths and trains running on different time clocks. Operators constructed as much as they could afford and then stopped, requiring passengers to regularly switch cars to complete their trips. When Abraham Lincoln traveled from Springfield, Illinois, to New York in 1860, he had to change trains four times (and take two ferries) over the course of four days.

Pierpont moved into the city's most fashionable neighborhood, around Union Square, and lived comfortably on the two hundred dollars his father sent every month. In exchange, Junius expected Pierpont to ignore the chance to make a quick profit in the stock market. But there were many chances. When Pierpont bought shares in a steamship company benefiting from a large government subsidy to carry mail, Junius disapproved. "Bring your mind quietly down to the regular details of business," he advised. Pierpont was to become a banker beyond reproach, trusted to handle other people's money and not speculate with his own. "Never under any circumstances do an act which could be called in question if known to the whole world," Junius wrote. Integrity would give the Morgans a competitive edge in America.

After Pierpont served as an apprentice for two years, Junius decided his son should resign. The firm's partners praised their clerk's "untiring industry," and suggested he would be even more successful if he approached colleagues with "suavity and gentle bearing" instead of impatience. Pierpont, recipient of regular job evaluations from his father, graciously accepted this one.

He may also have been distracted. He had fallen for Amelia Sturges, known as Memie, a bright, well-read, high-spirited member of his social circle. They planned a rendezvous in Europe that autumn. On their way home, Pierpont moped when the ship's captain seemed to take an interest in Memie. "One of my friends very *blue* all day. Disappeared from dinner very suddenly," she wrote in her diary. "No cry of Man Overboard so concluded he was all right." They were engaged in August 1860.

That November, Abraham Lincoln was elected president, and within half a year, the North and the South were at war. But Pierpont was happily preoccupied by Memie and the autumn wedding they were planning. He didn't even mind that Junius hadn't found the right firm for him yet. He tried some freelance work instead, helping to finance a controversial deal to supply the ill-prepared Union Army with five thousand Hall carbines, refurbished rifles left over at the end of the Mexican-American War in 1848. Pierpont didn't see the sale through but earned a generous commission for his efforts. A congressional committee called the entire transaction profiteering. The Supreme Court didn't. It ruled the government had to pay as promised, twenty-two dollars for each altered rifle originally priced at $3.50.

More troubling for Pierpont, Memie had taken ill with a severe, lingering cough. A week before the wedding, she was still unwell, vomiting and sleeping badly. She looked so thin that she decided to keep a veil over her face during the entire marriage ceremony. It took place in her parents' Manhattan home at ten in the morning on October 7, 1861, in front of a small group of friends and family. Two days later, the newlyweds left New York for a European honeymoon.

The couple consulted specialists in Paris, who determined Memie had tuberculosis: cause unknown, cure undiscovered. Pierpont didn't share the diagnosis with Memie, only the doctors' recommendations, which included rest and warm air as well as turpentine pellets, cod liver oil, and donkey's milk. Nothing helped. Not the roses and geraniums he brought or the apples he roasted, not the nightingales and canaries that sang in their hotel room. By December, Memie was too weak to stand. Pierpont asked his mother-in-law to cross the Atlantic as soon as she could and meet them in Nice. Memie's father had come to regard Pierpont as a hypochondriac and thought he might be exaggerating the danger of her condition, but he sent Memie's mother and brother over in January.

After they arrived, Pierpont relented to pressure from Junius and traveled to London to discuss business. By the time he could wrest himself away ten days later, Memie was much worse. She threw her arms around him when he arrived at her bedside, and just that took all her energy.

Pierpont stayed close to her throughout the day. At eight thirty the next morning, he was called from his bedroom to hers. She died moments later. They had been married four months.

BACK IN NEW York, Pierpont formed a business partnership with his cousin and hoped "constant occupation" would keep him from dwelling on his grief. His loss hung on him, and so did his regret. No one blamed Pierpont for failing to save Memie—except for Pierpont himself. His gaze intensified, his hazel eyes seemed to darken, and his constitution weakened again. In the days following her funeral that spring, sores appeared all over his body, a mild form of smallpox, and once he recovered, headaches would sometimes overcome him. Throughout those months, and for many afterward, Pierpont stayed in touch with Memie's parents and held on to her Bible. He acquired his first oil painting, of a fragile young woman, and hung it over the mantel in his library. He read poetry about lost love.

The Civil War provided opportunities to trade foreign exchange and new government bonds, and, eventually, offer railroad financing. But Pierpont exhausted himself and suffered new breakdowns of his nerves and body. "I am never satisfied until I either do everything myself or personally supervise every thing done even to an entry in the books," he wrote to his father in September 1862. Those periods of helplessness were also the only times when the pressure from Junius let up, and Pierpont was forced to relax his own exacting standards. His vigor returned by the next summer, and on behalf of his father's firm and his own, he was issuing short-term loans, brokering securities, and financing commodity trades. That year, he, like many men of means, paid a substitute three hundred dollars to take his place in the army. He went on to earn fifty-eight thousand dollars from his firm. Lincoln's salary that year was twenty-five thousand dollars.

Morgan back in New York after the death of his wife, Amelia Sturges Morgan, 1862

Pierpont supplemented his salary by manipulating the market for gold. He and a friend created an artificial shortage by shipping gold they had bought on credit to London. When prices in America went up, they sold, and each took a profit of sixty-six thousand dollars. Other Wall Street brokers admired the scheme. Junius was furious, believing Pierpont had been reckless and greedy and had violated the Morgan code of conduct. Junius at first threatened to cut professional ties, then decided instead to arrange for a senior partner to join his son in New York. For much of the next two decades, Pierpont would have to be the junior.

In March 1865, as the world watched the war draw down, Pierpont proposed to Frances Louisa Tracy. She was twenty-two; he was close to twenty-eight. They lived in the same neighborhood, worshipped at the same Episcopal church, occupied equally comfortable positions in Manhattan's social hierarchy. Fanny, as she was called, enjoyed attending the opera and concerts with him, and he enjoyed the idea of being married again. The nation was still in mourning for the slain President Lincoln when, on May 31, Pierpont and Fanny wed at St. George's Church. She gave birth to their first child, Louisa, nine months and ten days later.

They had three more children over the next seven years: John Pierpont Jr. (who always went by Jack), Juliet, and Anne. Fanny, too, could be overwhelmed by melancholy, but while Pierpont craved work and social distractions, she needed quiet. She wanted to move to the suburbs of New Jersey. He told her he couldn't survive there. Eventually, they began to create separate lives for themselves in different homes, cities, sometimes continents.

BY 1871, A new national optimism had taken hold, a confidence in an expanding economy of steel and oil and electric power, of perseverance and luck. It was a time that Mark Twain would soon call the Gilded Age. Americans paid to hear a lecture titled "The Aristocracy of the Dollar," and Walt Whitman was paid one hundred dollars to compose "Song of the Exposition" in celebration of the country's industrial strength. John Sherman, a Republican senator from Ohio, wrote to his brother, General William Tecumseh Sherman, of how the wealthy "talk of millions as confidently as formerly of thousands." With the massively popular serialized novel *Ragged Dick*, Horatio Alger's fictions of social mobility made it seem as if anyone who worked hard enough could elevate themselves. Personal thrift for some; stock market speculation for others.

Pierpont grew weary amid this thronging hopefulness. He was so strained by his dealmaking and worn out by his perfectionism that he wanted to retire at age thirty-three. His father refused to let him. Instead, Junius allowed Pierpont to take his family to Europe for a year.

When he returned, Pierpont started a new partnership with Anthony Drexel, head of a prominent Philadelphia banking family. Drexel, who was twelve years older than Pierpont, had a reputation sound enough to satisfy Junius. Drexel's name came first at the firm, and Junius still held sway, but Pierpont was permitted to manage the New York office. He had more authority than he was used to, which allowed him to reveal his vaulting ambition. But Drexel, Morgan & Company it was for the next two decades, until Drexel died and Morgan renamed the firm.

Drexel set Morgan up nicely. He paid more than nine hundred thousand dollars, in gold, for several lots on Wall Street. Number 23 sat at the intersection with Broad Street across from the New York Stock Exchange, and when Drexel purchased the land in 1872, no comparable property in any city in the world had been sold for more. The six-story building was known simply as "the Corner." It was constructed with white Vermont marble, a grand mansard roof, and statues representing Europe and America above the main entrance. Its interior was finished in black walnut and mahogany, with marble floors, steam heat, and, after Morgan financed Edison's electric company, six hundred lightbulbs. It was among the first buildings to be illuminated entirely by electricity. The firm rented out office space on the upper floors, and several railroad companies relocated their headquarters to take up residence there.

Morgan's days came to be consumed by the railroads: a sprawling, over-extended, indebted industry that was growing with careless speed and changing everything it touched. It absorbed more money, mostly from European investors, than any enterprise before and more natural resources than any other in America. Some 170 million acres of the country's public land would become the private property of the railroads, given, not sold,

The J. P. Morgan Building, 23 Wall Street, circa 1905

to them. Lincoln hoped transcontinental railroads would be a nation-building project after the Civil War. For every mile of track laid, the government awarded companies 12,800 acres, along with a bonus: any coal or iron underground.

Railroads relied on the labor of Chinese immigrants in the West and Irish, Italian, and Greek immigrants in the East. They first brought Scandinavian immigrants to the Midwest, then Eastern Europeans. The cars carried citrus, timber, cotton, grain, gas, pigs, cattle, mail, and mail order catalogs across the country. They advocated for public schools to create a ready supply of clerks. Their need for precise train schedules helped standardize time itself.

Railroads altered the geography of opportunity. Their lines determined which towns became impoverished and which prospered. Billings, Cheyenne, Tacoma, Reno: these were not places that would have otherwise attracted populations of any size. The companies' shipping rates, adjusted as owners saw fit, influenced the economics of small and big businesses. They handed out free passes to the politicians they hoped to sway. The railroads had a greater impact on people's well-being than the government, and though Americans might not have liked that feeling of dependence, they had to live with it.

The possibilities for making a name and a fortune were so extravagant and, initially, the oversight so minimal that railroads naturally attracted uninformed investors and unscrupulous brokers to take advantage of them. They sold overpriced stocks and bonds to build lines with little prospect of success. Owners bribed politicians, bought off journalists, pushed aside Native American tribes, and dismissed environmental concerns as a matter of business.

Safety precautions were especially lax. Tens of thousands of railroad employees died or ended up mangled every year. "It was taken as a matter of course that the men must of necessity be maimed and killed," wrote one railroad commissioner hoping to improve that record. Many of the railroads were built cheaply. Repairs weren't timely. Lines ran in both directions on single tracks with rudimentary signal systems. Men had to climb on top of freight cars traveling 20 miles an hour to activate the hand brakes. Then they had to jump to the next car to do it again. If the train lurched, they could tumble to the ground. A low overhead bridge could knock them out. Men linked or unlinked cars by maneuvering in between, and inevitably some fell underneath.

In Winona, Minnesota, one day in February 1873, E. Campbell, the engineer on a passenger train, didn't sound the alarm or apply the brakes when he saw a freight train on the tracks. The trains collided and both engines were smashed. Campbell jumped off in time. But J. C. Reilly, the baggage master, was badly burned when he fell onto the stove.

Conductor Arthur Lindsley lost his right arm after he was run over by a freight train at Janesville, Wisconsin, in April of the same year. Fireman R.

Construction of St. Paul, Minneapolis & Manitoba Railway, which became the Great Northern Railway, a key component of J. P. Morgan's planned railroad empire

Brown was killed in an accident at Vincent Station, Ohio, in July. In November, an employee named Amandas Hagerty was bent over the track repairing a switch at the Mauch Chunk station in Pennsylvania on a Wednesday afternoon. Maybe he heard the No. 4 passenger train backing in. Maybe he didn't. But he didn't have time to escape. Two wheels severed his body, and he died immediately.

The mere fact of working on the railroads shortened a man's life expectancy. But if a brakeman or switchman or fireman proved himself and managed to avoid injury, he figured his job was secure.

Then, in 1873, one of the Morgans' most prominent American rivals, Jay Cooke and Company, went bankrupt. Cooke, who had assembled his own army of agents to sell government bonds across the Union, was known as the financier of the Civil War. Afterward, he turned his considerable talents for promotion to the railroads. He would finance the construction of the Northern Pacific Railroad, meant to traverse the sparse, frigid lands of Minnesota, North Dakota, Montana, Idaho, and Washington. Cooke promised a temperate climate, tropical vegetation, and a broad fertile belt "within the parallels of latitude which in Europe, Asia, and America embrace the most enlightened, creative, conquering, and progressive populations." Instead, the land through which the Northern Pacific would pass was disparagingly called "Jay Cooke's banana belt." When wheat prices fell and farmers failed, trouble followed for Cooke. He couldn't find enough buyers for one hundred million dollars' worth of bonds. His firm went under, and the shock set off a series of bank failures that caused a panic on Wall Street and shut down the stock exchange for ten days.

Banks collapsed. Businesses failed. People lost their savings and their homes. By 1876, an uncounted number of adults were unemployed and underemployed, and tens of thousands roamed the country looking for food and work, sleeping in police stations when they could. The railroad men's expectation of lifetime positions was revealed as empty hope. Some tried to leave the country. Two hundred or so accepted work building a railroad in Brazil. After their ship sank off the coast of North Carolina, hundreds of other desperate men applied for the jobs.

The Long Depression ground on for six years, contributing to an international financial crisis. European investors lost six hundred million dollars in American railroad stocks. It was a scare for the Morgans. Pierpont's health faltered; he stopped exercising. Friction in the office sank him lower. Amid the dreariness, he tried again to retire in 1876, and, failing to secure permission from his father, left for a summer abroad that lasted until the following spring.

In July 1877, firemen and brakemen in Martinsburg, West Virginia, walked off the job in a spontaneous protest against the second wage cut in a year by the Baltimore & Ohio. Railway workers across the country joined them, stopping train traffic in Baltimore, Philadelphia, Pittsburgh, Chicago. They took control of switches, uncoupled rail cars, blocked trains, and set fire to railway buildings and bridges. Breweries and flour mills idled in St. Louis. Banks closed. Bridges burned.

In Pennsylvania, anthracite coal miners stopped digging. The railroads oversaw the mines and transported the coal. "Bread is what we are after and, sir, we have not had enough to keep our families from suffering say for nearly two years, and it is written that man should not live by bread alone," one miner told the governor after being granted an interview in his private rail car—an unusual gesture of conciliation. But to no avail. Coal fields flooded and steel mills shut down.

Executives called on state officials for help. "There are two military companies at Martinsburg, armed and supplied with ammunition," the governor of West Virginia replied to a Baltimore & Ohio vice president. But the local militia sympathized with the strikers. The governor called for federal intervention. "Please send in addition 100 men and two pieces of artillery," he said in a telegram to the secretary of war.

The military campaign against Native Americans out west had sapped the Army's coffers. Pierpont—whose firm held almost a million dollars of the Baltimore & Ohio's short-term debt, while his father's firm held another four million—offered to lend the federal government money to pay Army officers. The military moved into the cities, subdued the streets, and took control of the railroads and mines.

Pierpont assessed the credit risk. The Baltimore & Ohio's losses required it to take on longer-term debt, which he knew would be a hard sell. Instead, he and Junius organized a banking syndicate to buy and hold the railroad's bonds until circumstances changed. "Affairs for a time looked very critical and gave me much anxiety for many days and nights," Pierpont told one of his father's partners that August. It took years to sell all the bonds.

More than one hundred thousand workers around the country protested that summer of 1877. One hundred were killed and a thousand jailed. The public called it a rebellion; the government called it a riot. Later, it came to be known as the Great Upheaval.

In November, the country's business and political elite set aside any lingering worries and came together at Delmonico's Restaurant on Fifth Avenue to commend Junius for upholding the nation's credit and "honor in the commercial capital of the world." That capital was still London. The Morgans had become trusted advisers on both sides of the Atlantic, just as Junius had wanted. "A kind Providence has been very bountiful to us," Junius said. "And under this guidance, the future is in our own hands."

BY THE 1880s, business was humming again. The railroads comprised 80 percent of the listings on the New York Stock Exchange, brought in revenue about two times as great as the federal government's, and added an average of seven thousand miles of track each year. They couldn't all survive. But in their construction, promotion, and dissolution, they provided possibilities of all kinds. When William Vanderbilt wanted to secretly sell shares in the railroad his father, Cornelius, had built, Pierpont helped. Vanderbilt's nearly exclusive ownership of the New York Central was becoming a liability, likely to provoke either new restrictions or taxes. He wanted to avoid both. Pierpont persuaded the British investors he and his father had cultivated to buy the shares and give him the voting power, which meant he could take a seat on the company's board. He made half a million dollars in the process.

Pierpont's firm had also made a killing easing the Long Island Railroad into and out of bankruptcy. His most conspicuous deal involved helping sell forty million dollars' worth of Northern Pacific bonds in November 1880 so the company could lay down the final sixteen hundred miles of track required to reach the Pacific. It was the largest railroad bond offering in the country to date. Before the Panic of 1873, Jay Cooke's aggressive salesmanship on behalf of the Northern Pacific had helped inflate the railroad bubble in the first place. Now Pierpont was reaping the rewards. The Northern Pacific would become pivotal to his ambitions—and his conflict with Roosevelt.

New York thrived too. Plans were set for the city's most expansive apartment cooperative, a twelve-story redbrick Victorian Gothic pile on West Twenty-Third Street, with the top floor given over to artists' studios. It would be the tallest building in the city. (Later, it would become the Chelsea Hotel.) The Brooklyn Bridge was almost complete after more than a decade under construction. Luxury department stores opened on Broadway, and carriages lined the streets of Ladies' Mile.

Morgan's share of his firm's profits was eight hundred thousand dollars in 1880 and nearly one million the year after. He acquired his own notable address at 219 Madison Avenue, in a neighborhood where he already knew everyone. The brownstone was renovated to his uncompromising requirements: walnut doors at a new entrance on Thirty-Sixth Street; a stained-glass dome and stained-glass sliding panels opening onto the front hall; twin white oak staircases; a two-story safe in the butler's pantry. The mansion was the first private residence to rely completely on Edison's lights. Morgan installed a private telegraph wire connecting the house to 23 Wall Street. The telegraph was meant for business but proved useful at other times, including when he accidentally locked the family's French poodle in the wine cellar and carried off the key.

The drawing room took up the entire west side of the house, with a ceiling painted to look like a mosaic. The library was decorated with octagonal panels of allegorical figures representing History and Poetry, painted by Christian Herter, the premier interior designer of the time. On the shelves were Robert Burton's *Anatomy of Melancholy* from 1621, a copy of the John Eliot Indian Bible from 1663, sixty-six volumes on *Napoleon and His Generals*, and hundreds of other leather-bound treasures. Morgan wanted the best of everything—"Nothing but masterpieces," a friend said. "And he can afford to have them."

That year, Morgan also purchased his first yacht, *Corsair*. It was a 185-foot black-hulled steamer, the largest and most technically sophisticated in the country. His close friends began to call themselves the Corsair Club and Morgan himself the Commodore. During summer weekends, he

J. P. Morgan's home, 219 Madison Avenue, before 1903

would steam up the Hudson to Cragston, the country estate near West Point where his family lived in the hot months. There he maintained kennels for his show dogs, collies mostly; he liked to give their puppies as gifts, but only to those he held in the highest regard. On Sunday evenings he and his guests slept aboard the yacht so they could get under way at daybreak. By the time they arrived on the New Jersey side of the Hudson, a hearty breakfast was ready. As they finished, around nine, a launch pulled up alongside *Corsair* and everyone went ashore. Morgan's carriage waited to take him to 23 Wall Street.

He worked on the ground floor, in an office with glass walls, at a large desk, plain and businesslike. He kept the door open. Sometimes he could be seen swinging in his pivot chair, if anybody dared look. He usually had a long cigar, banded in gold, often unlit in his mouth or in his left hand. His Chesterfield topcoat and silver-tipped mahogany walking stick were set aside. Mr. Morgan, as everyone called him, attended to matters large and small: the daily flow of cash and accumulation of debt, the stream of potential dealmakers and advice seekers. He would concentrate intensely, maybe for a few moments, maybe for more, then arrive at a decision, dispatch instructions, and move on. That focus was his genius, but it was the genius of a monarch not a democrat. It kept him isolated, made him severe, and sometimes left him exhausted. Morgan said he could do a year's work in nine months, but not twelve. His impatience could be withering. When a church organist gathered the nerve to ask a favor, Morgan gave him a minute. "I'm struggling to . . ." the man stammered. "So am I," Morgan supposedly replied. "Keep struggling. Good day." Then he walked back to his desk.

Morgan became more than a banker in the 1880s. His transformation wasn't gradual, it was absolute, and it happened in a day. Morgan worried that European railroad investors were wearying of American imprudence, of accounting fictions and expensive rivalries that wasted their money. He made

J. P. Morgan, circa 1902

up his mind to remedy some "sore spots" in the industry. One of them ran right past his summer home. The West Shore line had been built to compete with the New York Central, operating parallel to it from New York City to Buffalo on tracks close enough to be visible. There wasn't enough freight traffic for two lines, though, so each reduced rates until the West Shore was insolvent and the Central was heading that way.

Morgan devised a plan whose legality might have made others hesitate, but he was willing to take the risk. He invited the railroad executives onto *Corsair* and didn't let them off until they came to an agreement to end their hostilities. If they didn't, they wouldn't get any more money from him. They ate a lovely lunch and smoked cigars as they sailed to Sandy Hook, New Jersey, then up the Hudson to West Point, where they could view the military academy high on the bluffs, and back again. "You must come into this thing now," Morgan said to the lone holdout, and then said little else. By day's end they had a deal. The Central would buy the West Shore out of bankruptcy. In exchange, the West Shore owners could buy from the Central's owners a line in Pennsylvania to combine with the one they already operated there. Because such a monopoly was unlawful in Pennsylvania, Morgan would step in as a proxy buyer.

That didn't fool everyone. The Pennsylvania Supreme Court eventually ruled against the merger, but by then the rivalries between the railroads

Theodore learned about a Roosevelt's responsibilities from his father, sometimes joining him on those Sundays. He wanted to be like his father, a man of consequence. Only after his father was gone did Theodore understand that he wanted to do even more. He wanted to govern.

Theodore Roosevelt was raised in a brownstone on East Twentieth Street with his younger brother, Elliott, and his sisters, Anna (nicknamed Bamie) and Corinne. Their mother, Martha Bulloch, had spent her childhood on a Georgia plantation with nineteen slaves, supported the Confederacy during the Civil War, pleaded with her husband not to fight in it, and, as Roosevelt later said, remained "entirely unreconstructed." She was warm but could be distant, often retreating to spas—or her bedroom—to quiet her nerves.

Theodore Roosevelt Sr. was a disinterested businessman and committed philanthropist who nonetheless enjoyed his inherited wealth. He paid for a substitute to join the Union Army, and during the Draft Riots the family was summering at a New Jersey beach. The Panic of 1873 didn't touch them directly; that was the year they moved into a grand new home on Fifty-Seventh Street. During the depression that followed, he tried a Knickerbocker form of politics, joining the Republican Reform Club to fight corruption in the civil service.

He was an exuberant presence. He romped around with his children, taught them to ride horses and take risks, and led the family on a year-long trip through Europe. He was especially attentive to his eldest daughter and son. Theodore admired his father above everyone else and dreaded disappointing him.

As a child, Theodore was frail, timid, and asthmatic—a "great little home-boy," his older sister Bamie called him. When he struggled to breathe, his father took him on late night carriage rides in the fresh air; his mother calmed him with stories. Theodore tried steam baths, quinine with iron, ipecac, coffee, cigars. He was a worry to his family. He seemed to crave the care. Theodore was educated at home and protected beyond it by Elliott, who was sixteen months younger but strong enough and charming enough for both of them.

When he was well, Theodore collected bugs, studied birds, learned about Charles Darwin, and read wilderness tales. As he turned twelve, with his father's urging, he began the very American act of self-creation. He lifted weights, swung on horizontal bars, bore down on a punching bag—trying, not entirely successfully, to build up his body. He boxed and wrestled with his brother. He adopted their father's motto, "Get action." It would eventually become an apt description of his whirling, turbulent energy. He would become a man of extreme enthusiasms and vitality. He read with near total recall, soaked up information from everyone he drew close, and then burst forth with opinions on the Byzantine Empire, the *Volsunga Saga*, Western irrigation, bird songs, the strenuous life. He never sat when he could stand. When provoked, he would thrust, and when he hit, he hit hard. Friends said he was steamed up, a swift and awful Chicago express, a wonder of nature.

But when Theodore entered Harvard at seventeen, he was still a scrawny, sheltered boy—and one with a snobbish sense of morality and outsized confidence. He boxed and wrestled there too, joined the exclusive Porcellian Club, served as vice president of the Natural History Society, and edited a literary magazine. Roosevelt was "forever at it," a classmate said. He was a curiosity, always pushing and straining and admonishing friends around him to do the same.

Then came anguish. His father, just forty-six, fell ill with stomach cancer. Theodore returned home from Cambridge as soon as he received word but was too late. "Have had a good square breakdown, and feel much better for it," he wrote in his diary in March 1878. And then a few days later: "Every now and then there are very bitter moments; if I had very much time to think I believe I should go crazy." So he kept moving, frenetically. By summer, he regained his "very buoyant temper." Corinne understood what that required: out in Oyster Bay, their Long Island home during the sweltering summer months, Theodore "loved to row in the hottest sun, over the roughest water, in the smallest boat."

Back at Harvard for his junior year, Theodore relied on a trust fund to provide him with an annual income of eight thousand dollars, more than the university president was paid. He was wealthy and he was busy, but he wasn't Harvard's model man. That was his classmate Robert Bacon: captain of the football team, boxing champion, president of the Glee Club, and the most handsome and agreeable man on campus, according to pretty

Theodore with Elliott, Corinne, and Edith Carow in Oyster Bay and at Harvard in his rowing outfit

much everyone. If asked to guess which of the two would one day be President of the United States, most people would not have picked the short, scrappy New Yorker.

Theodore hoped to graduate with distinction, but he had another preoccupation during those final years in Cambridge. He had fallen for Alice Hathaway Lee, nicknamed "Sunshine." She was tall and athletic, and hailed from a prosperous Boston family. "I have been in love with her for nearly two years now; and have made everything subordinate to winning her," he confided to a friend during his last semester on campus. He graduated in June 1880 and on October 27, his twenty-second birthday, he and Alice married. Elliott stood beside him as best man. That winter Theodore and Alice attended dinners at Mrs. Astor's, dances, theater parties, society balls. That spring, they embarked on a five-month trip to Europe, during which Theodore worked on his first book, *The Naval War of 1812.* Then they settled into the Roosevelt home on Fifty-Seventh Street with his mother and sisters.

Roosevelt began to reconsider his future. He had thought he would be a lawyer like one of his uncles, but realized he didn't want to serve corporate clients. He could have become a banker like Alice's father, or a civic-minded businessman like his own. But he wasn't interested in commerce, or money; the flow of currency didn't feel like power, as it did for J. P. Morgan. Roosevelt decided instead to become a public man, representing his home district in the state assembly in Albany. He would bring his morality and energy to an institution he believed didn't have enough of either. He expected to change society in the ways he had learned from his father, and he would need years to understand that to remedy the injustices of modern industrial life, being a Knickerbocker Roosevelt wasn't enough.

The twenty-first, known as the silk stocking district, was the wealthiest in the state but wasn't composed solely of the upper class. After securing the Republican nomination in a party caucus Roosevelt went to canvass for votes with two ward leaders. They walked into a saloon on Sixth Avenue near Fifty-Fifth Street, only blocks from his mother's home. The owner complained that his liquor license was too expensive. When he mentioned the price, about two hundred dollars, Roosevelt said: "Well, that's not right. I don't think you pay enough. I thought it would be at least twice as much!" After that, one of his handlers told him to "see to the college boys and his friends on Fifth Avenue, the society folks." They would take care of the other end.

The society folks—including many contemporaries of Roosevelt's father, such as the prominent attorneys Elihu Root (later to become President McKinley's secretary of war) and Joseph Choate—endorsed him. Roosevelt promised he "would obey no boss and serve no clique." He won 3,490 votes, his opponent 1,989.

On his first day as a legislator in the state capitol, in January 1882, Roosevelt burst through the door of the gilded chambers carrying a gold-headed cane and a silk hat. "Who's the dude?" asked a colleague. "What on earth will New York send us next?" an Albany reporter mumbled.

Roosevelt was twenty-three years old, stood five feet eight inches tall, and weighed about 140 pounds. His blond hair was slick and parted slightly off center. His mustache and sideburns were bushy. He dressed as if he were going to a Manhattan dinner party, with tight trousers that flared over his shoes. From his earliest days as a politician he wore thick gold-rimmed pince-nez that swung from a black silk cord. When he smiled, which was often, his teeth were everywhere. But it was his voice—high-pitched and percussive—combined with his habit of leaning forward as he spoke, arm outstretched, that colleagues and political cartoonists seized upon. "I do not speak enough from the chest so my voice is not as powerful as it ought to be," he wrote to his mother.

Roosevelt could be affable. He was definitely energetic and often imperious, certain he knew what was right and that his upbringing and education would convince others of that. He bored into issues and people. He sponged up details. Most mornings, he brought a stack of newspapers to breakfast at the Albany hotel that was his home during the week. "He threw each paper as he finished it on the floor, unfolded, until at the end there was on either side of him a pile of newspapers as high as the table for the servants to clear away," recalled one journalist.

Most of his colleagues in the assembly were farmers, small-town lawyers, merchants, mechanics, and tradesmen at least a decade older. A majority were Democrats. Politicians from both parties were willing to support legislation for a price or threaten regulation to get a corporate payoff. They were part of political machines that exchanged patronage and government assistance for votes on Election Day and traded favors and bribes afterward. To the victor belong the spoils.

Roosevelt began to peer into the workings of the New York elite, the politicians and judges and businessmen whose common cause was to entrench themselves in power and enrich themselves as a result. He called for an investigation of a judge accused of rigging the bankruptcy proceedings of the Manhattan Elevated Railway Company so that a notorious financier could take it over. Roosevelt's was a singularly unpopular project. The investigation was a whitewash, and his attempt to impeach the judge failed. "He was just like a jack coming out of the box," one of Roosevelt's closest friends in Albany said. "When they attacked him, he would fire back with all the venom imaginable. He was the most indiscreet guy I ever met."

As Roosevelt's first term was coming to an end, another uncle—a businessman who helped manage the family money—invited him out for lunch to share some advice. "He explained that I had done well in the Legislature," Roosevelt recalled. "But that I had gone far enough, and that now was the time to leave politics and identify myself with the right kind of people, the people who would always in the long run control others and obtain the real rewards." He would take on that inner circle at his peril, the older man warned. It was a flag before a bull.

Roosevelt didn't take the advice. In Albany, his social status and youth, and his "most refreshing habit of calling men and things by their right names," won attention. Which he enjoyed. He resolved to run again.

When he was reelected in the fall of 1882 with 67 percent of the vote, his colleagues chose to make him their leader. It didn't count for much since they didn't control the Assembly. But for a moment they were Roosevelt Republicans. Outside of his home state, he gained notice as "the rising hope and chosen leader of a new generation." He liked to hear that, too. "I rose like a rocket," he said. It didn't take long, though, before he sputtered. Roosevelt was unskilled at creating alliances, even temporary ones. He shouted and paced the aisles. He harangued. "I would listen to no argument, no advice. I took the isolated peak on every issue, and my people left me." He would learn to compromise, which he called being practical, and to work with men as they were: "I turned in to help them, and they turned to and gave me a hand. And so we were able to get things done."

Economic trouble began spreading through the country, brought on by railroads that were again spending wildly and factories that were producing more than customers required. Employers responded as they usually did, by cutting wages and then workers. The industrial depression would last three years. To help ease the hardship among Manhattan residents, the Assembly passed a bill to lower the fare on the elevated railway in the city by half, from ten cents to five cents. It was a priority for the legislators, but the new governor, Democrat Grover Cleveland, vetoed it. The law would violate the railway's contract with New York, he said. "The state must not only be strictly just, but scrupulously fair."

Roosevelt didn't have to say anything. He could have let Cleveland have the last, unpopular, word, but he spoke up anyway. He believed the owners of the railway had illegally acquired it out of bankruptcy, and he had wanted to punish them by reducing their profits, he said. "I have to confess I weakly yielded, partly in a vindictive spirit toward the infernal thieves and conscienceless swindlers who have had the elevated railroad in charge and partly in answer to the popular voice of New York." He was sympathetic to the demands for help, he said, but wanted to provide the right kind of help, a law that could withstand scrutiny. As for those thieves and swindlers in charge of the railroad, he said that "they belong to that most dangerous of all classes, the wealthy criminal class."

Roosevelt's quick turn was mocked and the veto criticized in the city—but that phrase stuck. Of course it did. The wealthy criminal class: It was a perfectly cutting comment on what many considered a bitter reality. It showed the emotion he was capable of invoking but may have signaled a more radical attitude than he was ready to act on. He was beginning to grasp the power of laying bare American nervousness, and even if sometimes his words were more satisfying than his deeds, he could set a new tone, high-minded and righteous.

After that legislative failure, Roosevelt began a more promising project. He worked with Cleveland to pass a civil service reform bill that awarded jobs based on merit, not connections. Their hope was to weaken the party machines that regularly undermined efforts at good governance and left immigrants in particular at the mercy of political bosses.

Harper's Weekly *cartoon of New York's reformers, Assemblyman Theodore Roosevelt and Governor Grover Cleveland*

Hundreds of thousands of immigrants lived in New York City's lower east side in the 1880s, crowded into tenements with no running water, infrequent electricity, and air infected with soot and smoke. Entire families worked long hours in perilous conditions at poverty wages right in their own living quarters. Among the most noxious were the cigar manufacturers, who often owned the tenements, too. Samuel Gompers, a cigar maker turned labor activist, lobbied

Albany to ban such work at home. Albany assigned a committee to investigate the situation. The representatives visited the tenements with Gompers, but Roosevelt was the only one to return there. He walked into a room shared by two families and a boarder. "The tobacco was stored about everywhere, alongside the foul bedding, and in a corner where there were scraps of food," he recalled. "The men, women, and children in this room worked by day and far on into the evening, and they slept and ate there."

The notion that government should legislate how business operated contradicted the laissez-faire principles of Roosevelt's class. He opposed bills to raise the minimum wage and increase the salaries of policemen and firemen. Restricting cigar manufacturers was a similarly unacceptable idea. "The respectable people I knew were against it," he said. Roosevelt decided he was for it. The conditions in those rooms were too dire to dismiss. At his urging, the Assembly passed a bill to prohibit cigar manufacturing in the tenements, the Senate agreed, and Cleveland signed

Child asleep in a tenement in New York City's Lower East Side

it into law. Less than a year later, the New York Court of Appeals ruled the ban itself unconstitutional.

It was the beginning of the end to Roosevelt's Knickerbocker conviction. "Of course it took more than one experience such as this Tenement Cigar Case to shake me out of the attitude in which I was brought up," he wrote. The meanness of daily work, with its coarse accounting of hours and pounds and miles, hadn't fully roused Roosevelt. He and his political colleagues didn't comprehend the gathering discontent. "We were as yet by no means as thoroughly awake as we ought to have been to the need of controlling big business and to the damage done by the combination of politics with big business."

In the early 1880s, one of the best-selling books was *Progress and Poverty*, in which a newspaper editor named Henry George argued that industrial capitalism imperiled democracy because it worsened the wealth gap. Progress enriched some and impoverished others: "It is as though an immense wedge were being forced, not underneath society, but through society," he wrote. "Those who are above the point of separation are elevated, but those who are below are crushed down." George's solution was to impose a single tax, on land, and abolish the rest. Roosevelt regarded that as immoderate, unfeasible. But he could see that something had to be done about the wedge.

OVER THE DECADE to come, Roosevelt's experiences—especially in his family world—would continue to shake his inborn assumption of stability and control. He would understand in the most personal way that the foundations on which a seemingly secure life was built could, all at once and without warning, collapse.

On February 13, 1884, Roosevelt arrived at the Assembly with cigars for his colleagues. (Some habits were hard to break.) He was midway through his third term, deep into an investigation of corruption in New York City, and had just become a father. An early morning telegram had brought the news: his wife had given birth to a daughter, also named Alice Lee. His child was healthy. His wife "only fairly well."

That afternoon another telegram arrived for him at the Assembly. Roosevelt suddenly looked worried. He rushed out of the chambers to the train station. Both his wife and his mother were seriously ill.

A dense fog settled over the Northeast and slowed Roosevelt's travel. The *New York Times* called it "suicidal weather . . . suggestive of death and decay in the dampness that fills the world." It was midnight when he finally reached his family's home on Fifty-Seventh Street. Elliott flung open the door. "There is a curse on this house!" he said.

Roosevelt climbed the stairs to Alice's bedroom on the third floor where she lay, barely conscious. As he knelt beside her, Bamie told him that Alice was suffering from Bright's disease, a chronic inflammation of the kidney that had gone undiagnosed. There was no cure.

At three in the morning, on the second floor of her home, with her children, Theodore, Bamie, Elliott, and Corinne, near, Martha Bulloch, forty-eight years old, died of acute typhoid fever. Alice died less than twelve hours later. She was twenty-two. Theodore drew a big black X on that page in his diary and wrote: "The light has gone out of my life." He rarely spoke of Alice again.

THE DAKOTA BADLANDS, a curious, forbidding wonder of timeworn rocks and water, held the last grassy stretches of a vanishing frontier. It was there that Roosevelt retreated in the summer of 1884. He needed its bleak expanses and raw, physical tests of endurance to chase away the depression bearing down on him. "Black care rarely sits behind a rider whose pace is fast enough," he wrote.

He built a house, bought several thousand cattle, and became a rancher. The Northern Pacific Railroad cut through the territory and, to encourage business, promoted the creation of a new beef industry beyond the Texan plains. Roosevelt wrangled horses and herded cows. He slept outside, hunted bears, bucks, grouse, rabbits. He killed for food and sport and trophies, and the bloody thrill of pursuit helped blot out his despair. Social conventions were scarcely observed, personal histories left unspoken. Roosevelt later wrote that he practiced the diplomacy of the Badlands: not uttering one word that could be avoided.

Roosevelt didn't entirely shed the privileges and inclinations of his old life. He wore a handmade buckskin shirt and chaps and alligator boots. His silver spurs were engraved with his initials, and his silver bowie knife came from Tiffany's. He began work on a book, *Hunting Trips of a*

Ranchman, in which he wrote of skylark songs and savage desolation, and dedicated it to "that keenest of sportsmen and truest of friends, my brother Elliott Roosevelt." He created a new constituency. He was the unofficial deputy sheriff of his surrounding region and official delegate to the powerful Montana Stockgrowers Association. As his melancholy receded, he was able to enjoy "perfect freedom," he wrote.

Still, he returned home. He had left his young daughter with Bamie, but there were other reasons to go east every few months. He had a political career to tend to, even though he frequently suggested, in public and in private, that it could already be over. Roosevelt's three terms in the Assembly ensured he would be a delegate to the Republican national convention in Chicago the summer of 1884 if he wanted. He did. "I realize very thoroughly the absolutely ephemeral nature of the hold I have upon the people," he said, "and a very real and positive hostility I have excited among the politicians." By the fall of 1886, Roosevelt was back in New York City. He was about to turn twenty-eight, tanned, hardened, and revived. Ready. But for what?

The Republicans needed a candidate for an office no Republican was likely to win: Mayor of New York City. Roosevelt's acquaintance Elihu Root had already turned the party down. Roosevelt said he'd campaign. His rivals were Abram Hewitt, a wealthy steel manufacturer with a reformist bent, and Henry George, who had decided to test his ideas at the ballot box.

The public was on edge. Divides were sharp. Earlier that year, on Saturday, May 1—May Day—three hundred fifty thousand workers around the country went on strike to demand an eight-hour workday with no pay cut. In New York, twenty-five thousand people marched along Broadway carrying torches.

Dramatic events in Chicago had rattled the whole nation. During the strike, the railroads were stalled, many businesses were unable to open and the stockyards were closed. The McCormick Reaper Works brought in strikebreakers, and police to defend them against the picketers. On May 3, as a crowd of strikers surged the factory gate at the end of the day, police fired. They wounded many and killed at least two.

Anarchists printed handbills in English and German—"Revenge! Workingmen, to Arms!!! They killed the poor wretches, because they, like you, had the courage to disobey the supreme will of your bosses"—and called for a meeting at Haymarket Square the next evening. Some two thousand people, the mayor among them, showed up to hear speeches that by all accounts were unobjectionable. By the time a more provocative speaker took the stage, it was late, a storm approached, the mayor had returned home, and only about three hundred people remained.

Then one hundred eighty policemen arrived in formation. A bomb exploded in their midst. The police fired into the crowd, wounding dozens and killing several. Sixty-seven officers were injured, many from friendly fire, and eight later died.

The prominent businessmen George Pullman and Marshall Field were among those who secretly funded the police investigation and the prosecution. Roosevelt, still in Medora in May, was unwilling to distinguish the strikers from the anarchists. He didn't support their cause or approve of their methods. Social disorder alarmed him, a violent response didn't. "My men here are hardworking, laboring men who work longer hours for no greater wages than many of the strikers," he wrote to Bamie. "I believe nothing would give them greater pleasure than a chance with their rifles at one of the mobs."

The police arrested anarchists around the city and charged ten with murder. A jury convicted the eight who stood trial. Four were hanged and one killed himself. (The other three were eventually pardoned by the governor of Illinois.)

In upstate New York that tumultuous year, a sixteen-year-old immigrant recently arrived from St. Petersburg, Russia, was unhappy at home, dissatisfied with her work as a seamstress, yearning for more. Then Emma Goldman read about the violence at Haymarket. It changed her life, propelling her to a career of radical political activism.

It was also that year that New York police charged a crowd during a strike by streetcar conductors, and men crawled away bloody from the beating. Mayoral candidate Henry George proclaimed: "We are beginning a movement for the abolition of industrial slavery." Abram Hewitt called him an anarchist and nihilist who wanted to start a class war. Neither of them said much about Roosevelt. But when he spoke for himself, he promised radical municipal reform. That wasn't much of a platform.

Roosevelt, for once, didn't care if he lost. He was showing his party loyalty. He was also secretly in love. He had reunited with Edith Carow, a family friend and childhood sweetheart long devoted to him. She enjoyed riding, hiking, and camping with him. She read nearly as energetically. In other ways she seemed his opposite—haughty, reserved, and socially unadventurous. She was more shrewd about money, almost as willful, and prepared to make a home with someone who could feel as restless as a "caged wolf." They were engaged for almost a year before they told anyone. Roosevelt was embarrassed to be remarrying so soon after Alice's death, a violation of Knickerbocker romantic convention. Edith didn't seem to share his concern.

On November 1, 1886, Roosevelt revealed to Henry Cabot Lodge, a friend and mentor in Boston, that he and Edith would soon marry. And then he sent another dispatch on Election Day: "Am badly defeated. Worse even than I feared."

Not too long after, he and Bamie set sail for London under the alias Mr. and Miss Merrifield. Elliott saw them off. Edith was waiting on the other side of the ocean. On December 2, on a misty morning, in front of only a few family members, they were married at St. George's Church in Hanover Square. Edith wore a lace gown and orange blossom veil. Theodore wore bright orange gloves.

Edith Kermit Carow Roosevelt, 1901

They toured Europe, returned to New York, and planned to live in the Oyster Bay home he had built for his first wife. He had changed the name from Leeholm to Sagamore Hill. Roosevelt had imagined himself a rancher and an author. He secured a contract to write a four-volume history, *The Winning of the West*. But his cattle business had failed after a harsh winter and he had lost at least half of his inheritance. Politics beckoned. During the presidential campaign of 1888, Roosevelt didn't hesitate to accept an invitation to travel to Illinois, Michigan, and Minnesota to speak on behalf of the Republican candidate, Benjamin Harrison. "I always genuinely enjoy it and act as target and marksman alternately with immense zest," he wrote to a friend.

After Harrison won, Roosevelt decided to establish himself in Washington. Lodge, then a congressman, lobbied the new president to appoint Roosevelt assistant secretary of state. Instead, Harrison named him to the Civil Service Commission, where the president hoped he could more easily contain Roosevelt's natural enthusiasm for improvement. The civil service included departmental staff throughout the government, such as postal workers, printing and customs officials, and those administering services for the Indian tribes. The commission was charged with filling these posts with merit-based hires, but it was an inefficient bureaucracy run in undemocratic ways. A place in the system was usually secured by connections and bribes rather than qualifications. Outside the power centers, people saw the civil service as a suspect enterprise, and its reform was a popular cause. A perfect realm to occupy Roosevelt.

In the spring after Harrison's inauguration, he moved to Washington. The city in 1889 was gracious and airy, surrounded by trees. Edith joined him that winter with their two young children, Ted and Kermit, as well as Theodore's firstborn, five-year-old Alice Lee, who Edith insisted live with them. Over the next few years, Edith would give birth to Ethel and

Pennsylvania Avenue, Washington, D.C., circa 1890s

Archibald and hold her own in a swirl of dinners, teas, dances, and rides with Washington's elite.

Roosevelt's mandate included oversight of only twenty-eight thousand of the one hundred forty thousand positions the Civil Service Commission managed, but he made the most of what power he had. President Harrison privately complained that Roosevelt "wanted to put an end to all the evil in the world between sunrise and sunset." Roosevelt in turn wrote to Lodge: "It is horribly disheartening to work under such a Chief. However, the very fact that he takes so little interest gives me a free hand to do some things."

Roosevelt's family spent the summer and early autumn at Sagamore Hill. Theodore's always attentive sisters were frequent, cheery guests. But their brother, Elliott, was a constant source of anxiety. For years, inexplicable seizures had plagued him, and he drank. Theodore and Bamie confined him to a mental hospital against his will, but whatever treatment he received for his alcoholism was ineffective. More galling to Theodore was that Elliott seemed unrepentant.

In the end, Theodore gave up on him, on the brother who had been a companion and protector and rival and now threatened to become a public scandal. Elliott had a wife, whose death brought him many dark nights; several mistresses; two surviving children he called his own (the elder was Eleanor Roosevelt) and one son he didn't. In August 1894, Elliott, too, would die, at age thirty-four. "Theodore was more overcome than I have ever seen him and cried like a little child for a long time," Corinne wrote.

Roosevelt headed west. He was grieving, ill, and frustrated. A couple of weeks before his brother's death, he had passed up a chance to run for New York City mayor again. Edith had insisted. Campaigning cost money and they were pinched, and if he lost, they'd have no income at all. Now, on the range, he desperately wished he had pushed aside her objections. He was sure he had given up his last opportunity for elected office.

CHAPTER 4

Railroad Nation

When white settlers first trekked to the southeast plains of Nebraska, they came for the salt marshes. They also found rolling prairies, river-carved valleys, and fertile soil. There were antelope, deer, and elk; maple, walnut, cottonwood, and fruit trees; blackberry vines. The Pawnee called the area around the salt creek Ká'it Kiicu'. A representative from a Pennsylvania salt company named it Lancaster in 1856. By 1860, some twenty-nine thousand people lived in the territory. After the federal government promised homesteaders 160 acres each, practically for free, tens of thousands more arrived, and Nebraska became a state in 1867.

The Pflug Brothers were among the first to open a store in the capital, Lincoln. They sold groceries, whiskey, and hardware. James Sweet set up the first bank in the first commercial building, and when he became state treasurer a few years later, he operated the treasury out of there too. The Bain Brothers sold clothes; the Bohanan Brothers sold meat; D. B. Cropsey sold real estate; R. R. Tingley sold drugs. An African American man called Moore ran the barber shop. New arrivals opened a saloon, a shoe store, a stone schoolhouse. The newspaper changed its name to the *Nebraska State Journal*, and in 1869 the University of Nebraska was founded. For all that, it was still frontier. Those seeking justice in the capital had only a couple of lawyers to rely on to settle disputes. The judge moonlighted as a merchant, and a milk house doubled as the city and county jail.

Lincoln had no major waterways, no oil or coal or iron deposits, no natural advantages other than its soil and its salt, and no one could figure out how to extract the salt profitably for long. The grasshoppers came in 1873, the floods came the next year. By then the railroads had come too, having determined that Lincoln did have one other natural advantage: its location. It was halfway between the industrial pole of Chicago—more than three hundred thousand strong, rapidly rebuilding and expanding after the Great Fire of 1871—and Denver, growing rich from Colorado's gold mines. Lincoln was perfectly situated between St. Louis, the nation's fourth-biggest city, and a tiny outpost in Montana that would become Billings, named for the railway president who selected it as a transportation hub for the state's agricultural produce.

The Burlington railroad was the first to lay tracks in Lincoln, in 1870, and over the next two decades would operate six lines out of the city. The company recruited people to eastern Nebraska and sold them land it had been given by the federal government. An advertisement from 1882 promised that twenty thousand merchants, farmers, artisans, and professional men could "testify that they are pleased with the country and climate, and that the soil cannot be excelled," and that the school system was wonderful as well. "The roads have reason to push the city, and they will do so," a resident of Lincoln wrote.

The Lancaster County courthouse was built in 1888. The next year, a young lawyer named William Jennings Bryan, who had moved to town from Illinois, became the first Democratic congressman elected in Nebraska.

By then Lincoln had a post office, a gas light company, paved roads, public water, a public library with five thousand volumes, and a telephone exchange with more than six hundred phones connected. Funke's Opera House was open. The Commercial Hotel became the city's biggest, with accommodations for three hundred guests. There were banks and businesses of all kinds that repaired locomotives, processed grain heading east from the country's western farmlands, packed pork and beef from the surrounding states, and sold farm equipment to them all. More than sixty trains arrived and departed daily.

The Burlington was owned by J. M. Forbes, a conservative financier in Boston who would eventually combine some two hundred separate railroad companies into the Chicago, Burlington & Quincy. It operated almost eight thousand miles of track stretching from Michigan across the Mississippi to the fertile plains of Iowa and Nebraska, up to the forests of Minnesota, out to the mines of Colorado and ranch lands of South Dakota and Wyoming. It connected almost every important commercial center between Chicago and the Rocky Mountains: St. Louis, St. Paul and Minneapolis, Kansas City, Lincoln, Denver, and Billings.

Far from Lincoln, on Wall Street, J. P. Morgan would one day formulate a plan to create something never seen before—a truly global transportation network. To do so, he would need a reputable Western railroad that reached into Chicago, and he set his sights on the Burlington. But he wouldn't be the only one who wanted it.

IN JANUARY 1889, AS Theodore Roosevelt was planning his move to Washington, Morgan summoned twenty-two Western railroad bosses, and the five private bankers who supplied their financing, to his home at 219 Madison Avenue. The meeting was too big to keep secret. Reporters hovered around the mansion, and one of the executives said, "The public are sure to think we are conspiring to do something that we ought not to do." Morgan still kept the doors closed.

They *were* conspiring, or at least Morgan hoped they would. The government had created the Interstate Commerce Commission in 1887 to supervise railroad rates, but it was proving ineffective. Competition—bitter and sometimes dishonest—was still unsettling the industry. The new law required companies to set reasonable prices and publicize them. Big shippers could still insist on lower rates, though, and the railroads themselves found ways to lure customers from rivals with illegal discounts. A company might employ a broker to sell its own tickets at half their value or it might post its official rate list in the woods where few would see it and then offer to carry freight for much less. Farmers could sometimes benefit—where a railroad had a monopoly, prices could be twice as high. Travelers could benefit—the fare from New York to Chicago was sometimes as low as one dollar.

Morgan's investors were suffering, though. Profits were diminishing, and with them the value of his clients' holdings and the soundness of his firm's credit. In 1888, the hundred or so biggest railroads did twenty million dollars more business than the previous year and made fourteen million dollars less. Small investors who weren't Morgan's clients were hurting too. "A number of innocent investors in railway stocks have been reduced to penury, and in some cases to actual destitution," the *New York Sun* said. "The gentlemen who have accomplished this magnificent result are still receiving large salaries; salaries which allow them to live in opulence."

Morgan couldn't let business rivalries bankrupt an industry so essential to the nation's promise—and to his position in the financial world. He decided to establish his own commission, the Interstate Commerce Railway Association, to encourage the railroad men to cooperate instead of compete. He wanted to fix prices, spread profits, and ensure dividends. He said nothing about their salaries.

The men he invited to his home were expected to follow his directions. He gave them a gracious welcome and brought them to his library, with its stained-glass windows, room-sized carpet, and mosaic-tiled fireplace. Then he got down to business. "The purpose of this meeting is to cause the members of this association to no longer take the law into their own hands when they suspect they have been wronged," he said. No more rebates, no more secret pacts, no more scalping tickets. They would give their word in a gentlemen's agreement.

When one of the gentlemen complained later about Morgan's interference in their roads, Morgan snapped: "Your roads? Your roads belong to my clients." Not all of them, however. The Burlington remained independent, able to pay its own way.

The agreement wouldn't last. The railroad men were too quarrelsome and suspicious, and, essentially, too competitive, to cooperate.

Newspapers tried to predict Morgan's next move. "Morgan began to be looked upon as a rescuer of investors, a solver of difficult financial problems," John Moody, the financial analyst, wrote. "And he stood alone in this regard." Morgan had become a national figure whose financial decisions had political consequences. This sudden scrutiny perplexed him. "I have done nothing except stop men fighting," he said. "I don't like to see men fighting. There is too much waste."

Morgan believed in free enterprise, but he thought business worked best when it operated on an industrial scale. He preferred alliances to rivalries, self-regulation over government regulation, and above all, order and stability. Some on Wall Street speculated that Morgan's solution to the railroad crisis would be to form a trust. This would have solved some of his problems. A trust relied on control through ownership; it was a legal means to force cooperation. Shareholders of competing companies would turn over their stock to trustees in exchange for certificates entitling them to dividends. Then these trustees could see that all the companies played nicely together. A trust wasn't technically a corporation. It didn't require a state license to exist. It wasn't—yet—subject to state regulation.

But trusts had come to represent everything skeptical, restless Americans feared about the influence of Wall Street, concentrated power, and income inequality. Trusts had enough influence over their markets to force suppliers to lower prices while charging customers more. Trusts could restrict production. They could sway politicians, providing campaign contributions and investment opportunities and using economic muscle when necessary.

Standard Oil was the trust par excellence. It combined fifty-two refineries spread over dozens of states and closed thirty-one of them within three years. Thousands lost their jobs and their businesses. In New York, where some competitors remained, Standard sold oil for ten and a half cents a gallon and still made a profit, while in Chicago, where none of its rivals survived, it charged nearly twenty cents. John D. Rockefeller said his company was efficient. Critics said it was untouchable. "The Standard has done everything with the Pennsylvania Legislature, except refine it," Henry Demarest Lloyd wrote in the *Atlantic Monthly*. His exposé, "The Story of a Great Monopoly," was so popular that the magazine reprinted the issue six times.

Standard Oil was hardly the only example of this kind of dominance. The Sugar Trust shut down seven of its eighteen refineries and merged eight others into larger plants. Thousands more lost their jobs.

But an uncertain regulatory environment made forming a trust a risky proposition now. Back in Washington, Senator John Sherman—financial statesman of the Republican Party—proposed a law to curb the political and economic might of these megacorporations. "The popular mind is agitated with problems that may disturb social order," he told his colleagues. He had a solution: an act of Congress to overpower monopolies. No problem "is more threatening than the inequality of condition, of wealth, and opportunity," Sherman said. "If the concerted powers of this combination are entrusted to a single man, it is a kingly prerogative, inconsistent with our form of government." Congressmen could believe as they chose, ally themselves with magnates as they saw fit, but they had to reckon with public hostility. The easiest way to get a rise out of an opponent—Democrat or Republican—was to accuse him of defending the trusts. Then, whether he believed it or not, he'd say something such as "They are abhorrent to me; they are malicious; they are destructive of the good of the country, and they ought to be destroyed."

Thirteen states—Iowa was first—wrote their own laws prohibiting combinations organized in order to raise prices or lower production. A few specifically banned trusts altogether. Sherman took a different approach. He used the broad language of the common law, old and well-established principles, to assure conservative senators that they weren't creating new rules but merely enabling the federal courts to apply existing standards to the new economy. The Sherman Antitrust Act declared illegal every contract, combination of companies, or conspiracy that restrained or monopolized interstate trade or commerce. And then, as the state laws did, it imposed criminal penalties: Those found guilty of forming such combinations were subject to fines of up to five thousand dollars and a year in jail. Those suffering losses because of the trusts could sue for triple damages. That was not a well-established principle.

The bill passed the Senate on April 8, 1890. Fifty-two senators voted for it, twenty-nine were absent, and Rufus Blodgett, a Democrat from New Jersey with ties to the railroads, voted against it. One senator—a cynic or a realist—said that his colleagues were interested only in the optics, in "some bill headed, 'A Bill to Punish Trusts' with which to go the country." The House passed the bill unanimously. President Harrison signed it into law on July 2, 1890.

But even as antitrust laws won support throughout the country, clever minds were hard at work devising ways around them. In 1889, Robert Green, the governor of New Jersey, asked a "cheerful, rosy-faced lawyer" if he had any ideas how the state might increase its revenues to pay off its Civil War debts. James Dill suggested New Jersey become a safe haven for big business by offering an alternative to the trust. The state could pass a sweeping law permitting one corporation to hold the stock of any other—an idea once considered a conflict of interest but that now, amid large-scale industrial development, seemed inevitable. New Jersey conjured the holding company into existence, a feat for which critics dubbed it a "traitor state."

Businessmen quickly realized how much they wanted to do business in New Jersey. They could create legal combinations that weren't strictly trusts but offered just as much control. Usually, a holding company would buy up small companies for more than they were worth, then issue new stock and sell it for more than it was worth. Investors had little information to go by and no protection against false optimism. Dill didn't suggest any new regulations to deal with that.

In 1892, Dill and Governor Leon Abbett, Green's successor, formed a company of their own, Corporation Trust, which provided firms based outside New Jersey everything they needed to establish residency in the state: a mailing address, safe deposit boxes, and the use of a tiny room in Dill and Abbett's office in Jersey City. Business was good for the state, which collected incorporation fees and franchise taxes, and for the governor and the lawyer. Dill once began a lecture at Harvard Law School: "I am the lawyer for a billion dollars of invested capital."

The Sherman Antitrust Act itself had weaknesses. It was a federal law that largely depended on states to enforce it by initiating legal proceedings against suspect organizations. But state attorneys general only sporadically challenged the offenders, and when they did they often lost. Companies took advantage of the ambiguities of the law, which didn't define trusts or monopolies or conspiracies or combinations; the biggest among them could rely on the best attorneys to help.

The state of Ohio did prevail over Standard Oil in 1892, and the company was ordered to end its trust agreement. But the court gave Rockefeller plenty of time to comply, during which he was able to purchase most of the remaining independent oil companies and incorporate as a holding company in New Jersey before the deadline.

Morgan and his lawyers took note.

ON FEBRUARY 20, 1893, the Philadelphia & Reading Railway Company went bankrupt. It had forty million dollars in capital and one hundred twenty-five million dollars of debt. "Fear irregularities and scandals," Morgan cabled a partner. His firm had bailed out the railroad before.

The Reading's collapse was the first signal of the trouble to come. In the next sixteen months, one hundred ninety-one other railroads failed. They operated almost forty-one thousand miles of track, represented one fourth of the country's rail system, and were worth two and a half billion dollars.

Though the memory was a generation old, the pain of 1873 had not lost its sting. People panicked, and institutions they once entrusted with their money seemed unsafe. In 1893, as many families, especially in interior towns, tried to withdraw their cash, they came up hard against a financial system that favored the East. Their money was on deposit in the cities, and the sudden demand for it forced the Eastern banks to call in loans made to farmers and small businessmen, causing cascading economic ruin that was highly regional in effect. One hundred fifty-eight national banks failed; one hundred fifty-three of them were in the West and South. Without access to credit, businesses had to shut down, steel mills went dormant, and farms lay fallow. Fifteen percent of the work force was unemployed.

Those workers were stranded. They had no unemployment insurance, no food or medical assistance from the government, and few charities to help them. People begged on the streets; some of the homeless were sentenced to hard labor as punishment. As the financial structure collapsed around them, an anger emerged that would define itself as anti-elite, anti-urban, anti–East Coast populism. Twenty years earlier, the country was just beginning to industrialize and the frustration at its failures and excesses was inchoate. By 1893, that frustration had a focus. It had leaders and it had enemies.

Many of the wealthy seemed oblivious. They raised money at Hard Times Balls, where the guest wearing the most convincing hobo costume won a sack of flour. "Everything here continues as blue as indigo," Morgan wrote that July. "Hope we shall soon have some change for the better, for it is very depressing and very exhausting." He spent that summer living mostly aboard his yacht.

The depression led to labor unrest. Workers at the Pullman Palace Car Company staged a strike that turned bloody. An Ohio businessman named Jacob Coxey led a march to Washington to protest the wealth gap. He called on the government to "heed the voice of despair and distress" coming up around the country. He had a specific suggestion: a Good Roads Bill, a five-

Private Pullman car

hundred-million-dollar program to create jobs for the unemployed and improve the nation's infrastructure. A thousand or so out-of-work men and women, white and black, from all over America, thought that sounded like a pretty good idea. They joined Coxey's Army in 1894 and headed to the capital to urge Congress to pass the bill.

To those with means, this looked like the beginning of an uprising. Officials in Chicago and Pittsburgh banned the marchers from entering their cities, and the Virginia militia burned their camp. Nonetheless, on May 1, Coxey's Army arrived in Washington. President Grover Cleveland ordered Treasury Department officials to arm themselves with rifles. Tens of thousands came out to watch as Coxey tried to read his bill on the Capitol steps. He was stopped by police, who then swung their sticks at the crowd. Everyone fled. Coxey and a co-leader were sentenced to twenty days in prison for damaging the congressional lawn.

Workers walked off the job at the Pullman factory outside Chicago later that month. They built the sleeping coaches the wealthy traveled in, decorated with thick carpeting, glass chandeliers, wood-paneled walls, and baroque, upholstered armchairs. More than eight thousand people lived in a company town built by George Pullman, in residences that reflected their status: apartments for unskilled workers, row houses for the foremen, modest Victorians for the executives, and, for visitors, a luxurious hotel named after his daughter Florence. Pullman oversaw the one church, which charged a rent so high it was unoccupied. Libraries around the country were often free to enter; Pullman required a membership fee at his. The company owned the bank and ran the stores. Pullman set the workers' rent and automatically deducted it from their paychecks. He thought he had built a model town. "It is not the American ideal," an economist pronounced in *Harper's* magazine after a visit. "It is benevolent, well-wishing feudalism."

As business contracted during the depression, Pullman laid off thousands of workers and cut the wages of those who remained. But he didn't lower their rents or the prices at his stores. After employees went on strike, railway men across the country, organized by the newly formed American Railway Union, refused to work on trains carrying the sleeping cars. More than two hundred thousand workers boycotted the railroads. The Baltimore & Ohio, the Northern Pacific, the Burlington, and most other lines were stalled. Carloads of bananas, strawberries, and cherries rotted on the tracks. Milk spoiled. Meat stank. Cities slowed.

President Cleveland—who had served one term, joined a New York law practice, and now was in the middle of his second—was already on edge from Coxey's march. Encouraged by railroad executives and his own attorney general, Richard Olney, Cleveland declared the strike a federal crime under the Sherman Antitrust and Interstate Commerce Acts. He deployed troops to end it. Simmering violence turned into riots and fires and gunshots and at least thirty dead. By August the strikers had been beaten down. Workers who weren't blacklisted returned to their jobs. The railway union had to disband, and one of its founders, Eugene Debs, went to jail, proclaiming that the union "put forth its efforts to rescue Pullman's famine-cursed wage slaves from the grasp of an employer as heartless as a stone, as remorseless as a savage and as unpitying as an incarnate fiend."

That summer a weary President Cleveland made a symbolic gesture. He established a federal holiday in honor of workers. On Monday, September 3, 1894, the country celebrated the first national Labor Day.

WHERE OTHERS SAW only turmoil, Morgan also saw opportunity. He had tried cajoling the railroad executives to view the industry as he did.

Now he could force them to. Before, he had tried to broker gentlemen's agreements, and now he could dictate the rules. Now he became Jupiter.

Among the lines that failed were some of the country's smallest and many of its largest, including the Northern Pacific, the Union Pacific, and the Baltimore & Ohio. Few could be abandoned altogether without destroying the towns they had helped establish. The railroads had to be reorganized. The railroad bosses, having amply demonstrated their inability to balance the books in the first place, weren't up to the job. Investors required the assistance of investment bankers.

Morgan became *the* railroad investment banker and much more than that. He was familiar with the industry's finances and trusted by those who would still have to fund the roads. His presence was reassuring and his confidence unyielding. He always kept his word, though he made as few promises as possible. He began to accumulate the troubled railroads, sort them out, and put them together into voting trusts, which involved persuading shareholders to transfer their stock and voting rights for several years to trustees he carefully selected. Then he put his people—and sometimes himself—on the boards and in the executive offices. The process became known as "Morganization." The result was incomparable commercial power with little accountability.

Morgan, in his fifties, also became his own man. Juliet and Junius were gone: she of a seizure when she was sixty-seven, he after a carriage accident in Monaco at age seventy-six. Anthony Drexel had died suddenly too. Morgan was now fully in command at 23 Wall Street, decisive, visible, and accessible. Though brusque with outsiders, he was convivial with his partners. But what he demanded of himself, he also required of them. The reorganizing work was complex: in one case, transferring companies and properties from a bankrupt system to a new one involved "executing two trustees' sales, one receivers' sale, ten foreclosure sales, six conveyances without foreclosure, and all manner of other contracts and agreements."

The partner Morgan relied on the most was Charles Coster, scrupulous and energetic, "a white-faced, nervous man, hurrying from meeting to meeting and at evening carrying home his portfolios," as one acquaintance recalled. Admirers of Coster called him Morgan's "right arm" and one of the "great organizing minds" on Wall Street. (In 1900, at age forty-seven,

Coster would succumb to pneumonia brought on by a bad cold and his state of constant exhaustion. An obituary noted that he was serving on fifty-nine corporate boards that year.)

Coster mastered the details. That allowed Morgan himself to master the men involved. "Probably it will not do for us to oppose Mr. Morgan, we would scarcely wish to do so unless really necessary," one banker said to another about a financing plan. Morgan gave a proposal a yes or a no, and he rarely explained why. His reserve was regal. His anger could be majestic. If a banker or broker declined to participate in one stock or bond offering, Morgan made clear no other opportunities would be coming.

Within five years, the Morganized railroads' stock and debt were worth more than two and a half billion dollars. They comprised thirty-three thousand miles, one sixth of the country's total. They earned about three hundred million dollars annually—the federal government's revenue in 1898 was about four hundred million.

As hard-up railroads were forced to reckon with their many deficiencies in the 1890s, the Burlington continued to prosper. It hadn't gone into debt building lines that went from nowhere to nowhere or went to somewhere that people could already travel to. The company maintained its tracks and locomotives. Happy customers said the CB&Q stood for "the Cheapest, Best and Quickest." It didn't need to be Morganized.

But Morgan wanted it. And so did two rival railroad barons: James J. Hill, and Edward H. Harriman.

Hill had built the Great Northern, which started at Lake Superior and ended in Seattle, with deliberate thrift and brutal efficiency. He never sought land grants from the government, but benefited from them nonetheless. During the Long Depression, he bought up failed lines that had taken advantage of federal and state help, and he added to them when money was easy to obtain. He promised that the cars on the Great Northern were among the best available—the diners and sleepers finished in polished oak, the observation car decorated with rich carpets, ornate lamps, and intricate wrought-iron details. His railroad would become among the most profitable in the Northwest. He didn't need Morgan the way other railroad executives did.

Hill was short and stocky, blind in his right eye, and long-haired at a time when most men weren't. Raised on a farm in Ontario, he moved to

Pounding the last spike of the Great Northern Railway, near Scenic, Washington, in the Cascade Mountains, January 6, 1893

America as a teen, started out as a steamboat agent, and was a multimillionaire by the time he was forty. He joined Morgan's private resort on Jekyll Island, a strip of land ten miles long and one mile wide off the coast of Georgia, and Morgan's Metropolitan Club, off Fifth Avenue.

Hill built a mansion on a bluff in St. Paul, Minnesota, for his wife, Mary, and their ten children. They shared forty-two rooms and thirteen bathrooms designed with the latest technology—hot and cold running water and showers with adjustable pressure. Hill insisted on a private telephone system and electrical plant. The grounds included a cave to grow mushrooms. The entire property was guarded and alarmed and cost Hill more than nine hundred thousand dollars. The municipality of St. Paul spent only six hundred thousand to build its Kasota stone courthouse and city hall in 1889. The bill for the St. Paul Union Depot, where Hill's trains would stop along their journey to Seattle, came to a paltry one hundred twenty-five thousand.

James J. Hill

Hill was like a lot of other rich men when it came to money. He wanted to make sure he was paying as little as possible but still getting everything he wanted. During the Panic of 1893, he ordered his operating chief to lay off workers and reduce the day laborers' wage to a single dollar. "There will be plenty of men to work at those rates," he said. Someone sent hate mail to Hill's home in response: "It would be a fitting climax if you should be taken by your employees and *hung* by the neck till dead, from one of the triumphal arches so recently erected at the expense of the very people you are now defrauding of their hard earnings."

Hill kept track of everything: grudges, slights, affronts, mistakes. He bullied other executives, second-guessed his own, cursed, kicked doors, and once shattered a desk. He had a nervous habit of playing with a handful of rough stones he carried in his pocket. He didn't trust politicians—or most of Wall Street's statesmen—to do right by the railroads. He also knew he couldn't ignore Morgan.

That's because Morgan controlled the Northern Pacific, the railroad once financed by his rival Jay Cooke. After its first bankruptcy, the Northern Pacific fell into the hands of a new owner, Henry Villard. But he, too, failed. The company foundered yet again in 1893, and desperate investors pleaded with Morgan to step in. He and Coster refinanced the company's debt, replaced its executives, and hoped to reduce competition in the northwest.

So did Hill. In May 1895, after two years of negotiations, Morgan and Hill completed a merger of their two railroads that would put Hill in charge of operating both. It was a risky move, and lawyers for both men weren't sure they could defend the deal in court. They hoped they wouldn't have to. But Hill ignored their advice and arranged for a shareholder to test the legality of combining two competing lines. A Minnesota Circuit Court judge ruled that the deal could stand. Instead of accepting that victory, Hill pushed the case to the Supreme Court for the ultimate validation. He

A construction crew at Hill's St. Paul mansion, 1891

didn't win it. In March 1896, the court ruled that the merger put "the public at the mercy of the corporation."

Now the two partners knew for certain that they had to be craftier. Right after the decision came down, Hill crossed the Atlantic aboard the *Lucania* and Morgan crossed on his new yacht, still called *Corsair*. (He had traded up for a bigger model.) They met in a mansion on St. James's Place to sign the "London memorandum," an accord to aggressively protect the interests of both the Great Northern and Northern Pacific. A shadow merger. Hill and his allies bought shares in the Northern Pacific from Morgan, enough to make them the largest group of investors in the company. Morgan kept control over the voting trust and kept his men at the Northern Pacific. He wanted to maintain appearances and reward loyalty. "You will have to be as wise as a serpent and as harmless as a dove," a friendly banker advised Hill.

One failed railroad seemed impenetrable even to Morganization: the Union Pacific, the first transcontinental line. The company allowed its tracks to disintegrate and its subsidiaries to remain tangled. The federal government demanded the company make good on its debt, with interest that had accrued over thirty years. Morgan called the Union Pacific "two streaks of iron rust across the plains" and walked away. It was a big mistake.

Edward H. Harriman took over the Union Pacific. For financing, he turned to James Stillman, the president of National City Bank—otherwise known as the Standard Oil Bank, with deep reserves of Rockefeller money. Harriman had started his career in 1870 as a stockbroker, with a seat on the New York Stock Exchange (purchased with a three-thousand-dollar loan from his uncle) and a small office down the street from Morgan's. He made money during panics in the market and invested in small, troubled railroads. He was usually called furtive. His "was the genius of the conqueror," a colleague said. "He was brusk [*sic*], short-tempered, with extraordinary faculty for doing the very thing, rubbing people the wrong way." Harriman said he couldn't change. "They will have to take me as I am or drop me."

Among those he rubbed the wrong way was Morgan. Harriman thwarted one of Morgan's railroad reorganizations and later tried to block another. Morgan considered him a "punk."

Harriman spent tens of millions to upgrade and expand the Union Pacific. The line had become "bold, energetic, and a dangerous rival" to the Great Northern, a newspaper editor and friend of Hill's wrote.

TWO YEARS INTO the depression—amid bank failures, fear that the country's paper currency could be worthless, and a run on gold, which backed the dollar—the Treasury's reserves were dangerously low. The government usually kept one hundred million dollars' worth of gold available; by February 1895 it had less than forty-five million and was losing two million dollars a day. A fractious Congress couldn't find a solution. It seemed not only possible, but unavoidable, that the government itself would have to declare insolvency.

Morgan thought he could prevent that. He had quietly suggested to Treasury officials that the government sell bonds directly to him and his syndicate of buyers rather than to the public, which he said would take too long and might not be successful. In exchange, Morgan would give the

Treasury the hundred million in gold it required. All that was left to be decided were the specific terms.

When rumors of the deal reached Wall Street brokers, they wanted to be involved too. Morgan refused. "It was absolutely impossible for more than one party to negotiate," he later said. "It would only have made competition." He dismissed anyone else's ability to pull off the sale: "They could not do it." When journalists heard about Morgan's proposal, they accused President Cleveland of letting the money men profit at the expense of the nation.

Cleveland reconsidered. John Carlisle, the secretary of the treasury, told Morgan he was ending their discussions. The administration would rely on Congress to authorize gold bonds to sell directly to the public instead. "We consider situation critical, politicians appear to have absolute control," Morgan cabled his London office.

Morgan decided to speak with the president himself. He traveled to Washington on Monday, February 4. At his side was one of his firm's bright-eyed new hires: Robert Bacon, Theodore Roosevelt's Harvard classmate and friend. When Bacon had been employed by a Boston brokerage firm that handled Morgan's business, Morgan had come to appreciate his charm, tact, and industriousness—the financier had "fallen in love," one of the firm's partners said—and insisted on having the young man near him. At first Bacon was reluctant to accept the job offer, but Morgan persisted, and in 1894 he succeeded in poaching Bacon away to New York. Before Bacon left Boston, his mentor offered advice: "Don't overwork like Coster just because you can and like to do it. He is wonderful—and unwise—to do so."

Morgan and Bacon arrived in the capital uninvited. President Cleveland wished they would just go away and sent one of his closest advisers, Secretary of War Daniel Lamont, to the railroad station to try to persuade them

Robert Bacon, a partner in J. P. Morgan's firm and a friend of Roosevelt's

to. Lamont told them Cleveland didn't want to meet and wouldn't consider a private bond sale. "I have come down to see the president," Morgan told Lamont. "And I am going to stay here until I see him."

Late that evening, Morgan talked to Attorney General Olney, who talked to President Cleveland, who relented. Cleveland, the first Democrat elected after the Civil War, had been an almost model Republican on most issues. Morgan had no quarrel with him. Morgan's counsel, Francis Stetson, had been Cleveland's law partner and was a frequent, confidential visitor to the Executive Mansion. He later became known as Morgan's own attorney general.

At nine thirty the next morning, Morgan arrived at the Executive Mansion with Bacon and Stetson on either side. Another New Yorker was already there. August Belmont, representative of the Rothschilds, the powerful British bankers, had been working with Morgan on the bond plan. The president sat them all in the corner of his library. And then he ignored them as he conferred with his own men.

White House and Treasury Building, 1890s

Eventually, Cleveland walked over to them. Morgan, as was his habit, got to the point. He told the president that demands from New York could empty the treasury reserves that very day. They had no more time to negotiate. "Have you anything to suggest?" Cleveland asked. Morgan did. To avoid the wait for Congress to approve the deal, he said, the loan could be considered a purchase of coin rather than a sale of bonds, an obscure legal loophole that granted the president the right to make the deal on his own.

"I never was so excited in my life as at the interview," Morgan told a friend. "Everything depended on my changing Mr. Cleveland's mind. When I went into the room, I had an unlighted cigar in my hand; as I arose from the chair to go, I had no cigar but saw on the floor a little pile of snuff." Cleveland begrudgingly agreed to Morgan's plan, insisting, though, that the government would be fine with just sixty-five million. Then the president pulled a box of cigars from his desk and asked Morgan to stay while he dictated a note to Congress.

The plan worked. But when Morgan refused to reveal his profits on the deal—about three hundred thousand dollars—Cleveland's fellow Democrats excoriated him. It was bad enough that Morgan, king of Wall Street, had extended his command to the heartland. Now he was giving instructions to Washington.

Morgan believed the country's financial and business structure should be controlled, and propped up when necessary, by the country's financial and businessmen. They knew best. Or really, he knew best. He alone could protect the national interest, the soundness of America's reputation, and even though he had a singular personal interest in doing so, he expected Americans to trust his motive. His patriotism called him to act. A "fascinating and lucrative patriotism," one Wall Street broker said.

In his world, when there was a problem, Morgan could call men together in a drawing room or on his yacht. In the rest of the world, the growing antagonism toward the rich was a problem Morgan couldn't understand. He didn't want to adjust to it. When asked about it, he sometimes quoted his first father-in-law, Jonathan Sturges: "If God had intended that you should be the steward, he would probably have given you and not me the wealth."

CHAPTER 5

The Invisible Empire

Manhattan, a June night, 2 A.M.: A man emerges from the Union League Club on Fifth Avenue, pulls up the collar of his coat, lowers the brim of his slouch hat, and sets off east on Forty-Second Street. It is Theodore Roosevelt, out to check on his police officers.

In 1895, after six years on the Civil Service Commission, Roosevelt had decided his work was done. He had stuck it out through Harrison's term and into Cleveland's too. Roosevelt took on an egregiously corrupt postmaster from Harrison's hometown of Indianapolis; exposed wrongdoing in the prominent Baltimore post office; and encouraged promotions based not on favor but achievement. His greatest contribution may have been bringing ample public attention and his own private stores of energy to a once unproductive commission.

He cast about for a position back in New York City, with the thought of one day becoming a senator. The newly elected mayor suggested he start as street cleaning commissioner. After some gentle pressure from Roosevelt's friends, the mayor offered him a position as a police and health commissioner instead. In the new role, his nighttime inspections became a cherished part of his routine. He usually invited a reporter along. On this June night, he came across three officers talking in front of a saloon, and others eating, sleeping, and chatting up a prostitute. Roosevelt couldn't find their supervisor anywhere.

The consequences of these impromptu reviews weren't uniform: Some officers received warnings, some paid fines, and some started to work their beats. "These midnight rambles are great fun," Roosevelt said. Roosevelt is "the biggest man in New York," a newspaper said.

The street patrols showed Roosevelt the city of shadows. His health inspections revealed the city of gloom, of darkened rooms and stale air. "My whole work brings me in contact with every class of people in New York, and I get a glimpse of the real life of the swarming millions," he wrote to Bamie. One of his frequent companions was Jacob Riis, the photojournalist whose groundbreaking report about New York City's slums, *How the Other Half Lives*, had been published in 1890. Shortly afterward, Roosevelt visited the *Evening Sun* office where Riis worked and left his card with a note on the back: "I have read your book and I have come to help." Roosevelt was working on the Civil Service Commission then, so there wasn't much he could do, but the two became friends. Five years later, as health commissioner, Roosevelt saw that living conditions for the working poor were unimproved since then, or even since his time as legislator, when his fact-finding missions among tenement dwellers had first challenged his perspective on the underclass.

His political pronouncements became more forceful. "There is not in the world a more ignoble character than the mere money-getting American, insensible to every duty, regardless of every principle, bent only on amassing a fortune," Roosevelt wrote in a magazine article in 1895. "These men are equally careless of the workingmen, whom they oppress, and of the State, whose existence they imperil."

As president of the commission, Roosevelt condemned rotten tenements and took on abusive landlords. He insisted on requiring an exam, instead of a bribe, for entry into the police force. He refused to consider religious or political affiliations for appointments. He put new officers on probation and gave on-the-spot promotions for heroism. He also bickered with the three other commissioners; he rarely thought they moved quickly enough. "The actual work is hard; but far harder is the intense strain," he wrote to Bamie. "I have the most important, and most corrupt, department in New York on my hands."

Bribes, payoffs, kickbacks, shakedowns, tips, protection: there were many ways to describe the shady transactions that police instigated to supplement their salaries. Proprietors paid something extra to open a brothel, run a gambling operation or a grocery store, sell fruit on the streets. They paid to keep their saloons open on Sundays. That violation was particularly lucrative and brazen, and ending it was personal for Roosevelt. Elliott had died an alcoholic just a year earlier. When Roosevelt began enforcing the law, the businesses lost a sizable amount of their weekly profits. Some newspapers and their readers regarded the crackdown as too harsh, and German Americans, many among them regular patrons on Sundays, their one day off, defected to the Democrats.

This placed Roosevelt in direct conflict with Thomas Platt, the head of the Republican Party in New York. "Easy Boss" Platt, as he was usually known, enjoyed national recognition and the backing of Morgan and Wall Street. Thin and pressed-looking in his early sixties, Platt was soft-spoken but tenacious, and Roosevelt's actions had infuriated him. "As for my being a United States Senator, I have, as I wrote you, just about as much chance of being Czar of Russia," Roosevelt told Lodge.

One Sunday morning in January 1896, Roosevelt was granted a meeting with Platt, at the Fifth Avenue Hotel, where he lived, just across from Madison Square Garden. The police commissioner had heard some disturbing rumors. The party boss confirmed them. Albany was combining the counties around Manhattan into one great city—New York City—with a municipal police leadership that wouldn't include Roosevelt. The Republicans' primary goal was to gerrymander as wide a swath as possible; abolishing Roosevelt's commission in the process was an additional benefit. Roosevelt would be removed from his position in two months. He thought he had more time. "We got along very well, in an entirely pleasant and cold-blooded manner," he recounted to Lodge. "They intend to legislate me out in about 60 days." But after the *New York Times* published an investigative series called "The Republican Plot to Oust Roosevelt," Platt backed down. If Roosevelt tipped off the paper, he kept it to himself.

ONE-HUNDRED-DEGREE HEAT SCORCHED the city in the summer of 1896. As many as one thousand three hundred people from the tenements died. Most of the victims suffered heat stroke and dehydration. A few, seeking fresher night air and escape from their stifling rooms, fell from their roof tops in their sleep. The body count was as high as if a cholera epidemic had swept through. Horses collapsed by the thousands, making it impossible to transport all the carcasses to the rendering plants on Barren Island. Many of the beasts rotted on the streets. "They added a genuine flavor of pestilence," Roosevelt wrote.

The mayor didn't call an emergency meeting until nine days had passed. One health commissioner promised to at least make sure the streets were hosed down regularly. Roosevelt announced that he himself would help distribute ice from the police stations. A monopoly was keeping the price of ice artificially high. Giving it away was an unusual gesture—a handout from the government—and an implicit rebuke of the nation's governing philosophy. "While the people should patriotically and cheerfully support their Government," President Cleveland said, "its functions do not include the support of the people."

But as the 1896 presidential race kicked off amid the backlash from Morgan's bailout plan, Roosevelt wasn't the only politician interested in renegotiating the compact between the government and the people. At its national convention that summer, Cleveland's Democratic Party backed William Jennings Bryan, the fiery thirty-six-year-old populist from Lincoln, Nebraska. He was tall and dark-eyed and had a voice that could reach the last rows. He was called the Great Commoner. He advocated using silver as a legitimate currency alongside gold to help Westerners out of their financial troubles. "Free Silver" would expand the money supply, creating inflation and higher prices for crops and livestock. Farmers and ranchers could pay off their debts with cheaper dollars. Miners could mint their supply of silver bullion into coins. "You come to us and tell us that the great cities are in favor of the gold standard; we reply that the great cities rest upon our broad and fertile prairies," he said to his critics. "Burn down your cities and leave our farms, and your cities will spring up again as if by magic; but destroy our farms and the grass will grow in the streets of every city in the country." Bryan brought the speech to a dramatic end. He stretched out his arms, lowered his head, and said: "You shall not crucify mankind upon a cross of gold." The crowd swelled with shrieks and cries and cheers.

Bryan traveled the country with his wife, Mary, and few of the usual political pretensions. He wore easy-to-clean alpaca suits and string ties and snacked on radishes. He spoke to a total audience of some five million people. He was mesmerizing and inspiring, and the Republican candidate knew he would be no match on the trail. William McKinley was fifty-three years old, a Civil War veteran from Ohio whom many still called Major. He had been a lawyer, a congressman, and a governor. His two daughters had died young, and his wife, Ida, had been unwell ever since. Voters knew that McKinley was responsible for Ida's care, but that wasn't the only reason he decided to campaign from his front porch in Canton. "I might just as well put up a trapeze on my front lawn and compete with some professional athlete as go out speaking against Bryan," he said.

McKinley appealed to the desire for stability and unity after the upsets of the 1893 depression. He promised to protect American enterprise by maintaining the gold standard and restoring high tariffs. He offered a conciliatory vision of American opportunity. "All of us want good times, good wages, good prices, good markets, and then we want good money, too," he said. Bryan didn't think that was possible. For Wall Street and the business community, there was really no choice. If McKinley was refusing to go out on the campaign trail, then they would bring the campaign trail to him. The railroads cooperated to offer discounts that allowed three quarters of a million people—men mostly, but some women—to hear the Republican candidate. A Democratic newspaper sneered that it was cheaper to travel to Canton than to stay home.

Poster from William McKinley's 1896 presidential campaign

Meanwhile, James Hill introduced McKinley's campaign manager and fellow Ohioan Mark Hanna to the east coast magnates who might help with finances. J. P. Morgan, Hill's business partner, contributed, and so did Andrew Carnegie. John D. Rockefeller, a childhood friend of Hanna's, donated a quarter of a million dollars in corporate funds and wrote a personal check for twenty-five hundred. In total, Hanna raised three and a half million dollars—three million of it in New York and proceeded to direct the most expensive campaign the country had ever seen. It included more than a hundred million pieces of literature, printed in ten languages; parades and fairs; and a silent film, *McKinley at Home*, that debuted in New York and then was screened in theaters across the country.

Roosevelt, with an eye toward his own political future, had introduced himself to Hanna that summer. Roosevelt wasn't always the best judge of people, but his description of the businessman from Cleveland was just right—"a good natured, well meaning, coarse man, shrewd and hard-headed but neither very farsighted nor very broad-minded." Someone, he thought, who must be handled with care. Roosevelt offered to join those already out stumping for McKinley. Hanna knew that Roosevelt's vigorous presence would counter Bryan's and so off went Roosevelt.

In the last days of the campaign, tens of thousands of people—merchants, brokers, brewers, railroad men, electricians, lawyers, and grocers—paraded along the main thoroughfares of their cities in a remarkable demonstration of support. They were marching for gold.

On November 3, 1896, McKinley won the election with 51 percent of the vote.

Roosevelt worried that he might end up unemployed if he remained in New York, a "melancholy spectre" and "idle father, writing books that do not sell." A more promising future lay in Washington. Since he had written *The Naval War of 1812*, Roosevelt thought he might make an ideal assistant secretary of the Navy. Friends had already been lobbying on his behalf.

McKinley agreed to appoint Roosevelt to the position he sought, but wanted Boss Platt's approval first. "He has been a disturbing element in every situation," Platt said. But if McKinley wanted to put Roosevelt somewhere, the Navy would be a safe spot.

Roosevelt was returning to Washington.

MCKINLEY WAS INAUGURATED in March, Roosevelt arrived in late April, and by the end of May the two were taking afternoon buggy rides around the city. During the summer, Roosevelt's boss retreated from the city's heat, leaving his assistant secretary in charge. "I am having immense fun running the Navy," Roosevelt wrote to a friend. Through the autumn and winter of 1897, newspaper stories of Spain's brutal rule in Cuba convinced many that America should help the revolutionaries fighting for independence. Some believed increasing humanitarian assistance on the island would be sufficient; others warned that military intervention could be required. Roosevelt was first among them. He argued that the Navy needed to better prepare for the possibility and carried on a campaign of persuasion at the White House. But McKinley wasn't ready to join the battle.

On the evening of February 15, 1898, a mysterious explosion destroyed the battleship *Maine*, which the U.S. Navy had sent to Havana Harbor to protect American lives and property. Investigations never determined exactly what happened; most likely it was some sort of accident. But Roosevelt—cheered on by Joseph Pulitzer and William Randolph Hearst's newspapers—said the sinking was a provocation that couldn't be ignored. "The defective imaginations of many good people here, the limited mental horizon of others, and the craven fear and brutal selfishness of the mere money-getters, have combined to prevent us from doing our duty," he wrote. The time had come to go to war, expand America's reach, and upset the imperial order.

For Roosevelt, the pull of the war—of physical tests, of action—was irresistible. He was thirty-nine years old. The previous November, Edith had given birth to their fifth child, Quentin, then had been sick all winter, and was recovering from surgery for an abscess near her hip. Their two eldest sons were also unwell. But Roosevelt would not be dissuaded. He quit the Navy and got permission to help raise a volunteer cavalry unit for what John Hay, then ambassador to England, called "a splendid little war." Some thousand men turned out by May. New York clubmen and Harvard men seeking adventure, cowboys eager to fight, merchants, clerks, brokers, and cops: the Rough Riders. Roosevelt had himself named lieutenant colonel. He sported the same khaki uniform as his commanding officer; he wore a blue polka-dotted bandana, too, like many of the other recruits. But he did carry some distinctly irregular gear: a Stetson hat with two pairs of glasses sewn into it, a revolver salvaged from the *Maine*, an officer's saber with a sharkskin hilt, and a custom-made Winchester carbine. His regiment didn't have to rely on standard equipment, either. The Rough Riders fought with a pair of Colt machine guns, provided by two of the millionaire soldiers.

For another millionaire, hard at work tending to his railroad investments, the conflict was a mere inconvenience. "I knew that if we had war, that would be the last of Havana cigars," Morgan told a friend. "I had somebody in Washington ready to cable me of the declaration of war. I received my cable before it was made public." That gave him time to drive to every cigar store in Manhattan that sold his favorites and buy them all.

He did make one sacrifice toward the war effort: *Corsair*. The Navy was purchasing the yachts of the wealthy and converting them to gunboats to fill out its fleet. Morgan "tried to put them off in every way and offered to build a vessel for the Government," his son-in-law wrote. But there wasn't time for that. The Navy paid Morgan two hundred twenty-five thousand dollars, and his second *Corsair* became the USS *Gloucester*. Within a month, Morgan had commissioned an even bigger third *Corsair*.

At the front, Roosevelt complained of the military's blunders and inefficiency. The ships were overcrowded. Few men had been able to bring their horses across to the island. There were supply-line shortages of food, water, and ammunition. The heat was brutal. Malaria, yellow fever, and typhoid were rampant. In the battle for San Juan Heights, seventeen of his men died and eighty-six were wounded. Yet Roosevelt charged up Kettle Hill and became a war hero.

When he returned to New York later that summer, Platt was waiting with an offer to nominate him as governor of the most populous state in the nation, prosperous from trading, manufacturing, and Wall Street stock making. Platt's opinion of Roosevelt was unchanged—and when the greater New York City of Platt's hopes did come into existence that year, the first police chief did away with many of Roosevelt's reforms. But Platt was desperate. The current occupant of the office, Republican Frank Black, faced accusations of corruption. Roosevelt had a sterling reputation in that regard; if he ran, the party could proclaim to voters that "every thief will be caught and punished, and every dollar that can be found will be restored to the public treasury."

In early October 1898, eight thousand, maybe ten thousand people pressed into Carnegie Hall and out onto the wet streets to see the war hero launch his campaign. Rough Riders marched down the main aisle. Magnificently dressed women and suited men cheered. Mark Hanna occupied a box seat and didn't once look away from Roosevelt. "A soft, easy life is not worth living, if it impairs the fiber of brain and heart and muscle," the candidate said. "We must dare to be great."

Roosevelt was running against another Knickerbocker, former judge Augustus Van Wyck, and it turned out to be a closer race than the Republicans expected. In the final days of the campaign, the state party head told Platt and Roosevelt that he needed more money. Platt made a list of six contributors, with Morgan at the top, and said each would give ten thousand dollars. Roosevelt protested: "I cannot accept contributions from the men you mention. Really, I must decline." Platt reminded him who was running the campaign and what was at stake, then headed down to Wall Street.

ON SUNDAY, JANUARY 1, 1899, Governor Roosevelt stood alone on the veranda of the Executive Mansion in Albany's bitter night cold. He had stayed out late, still exuberant over his victory, bubbling with plans and talk, and returned to his new home on Eagle Street to find it dark, silent, and locked. When he couldn't rouse the watchman, Roosevelt smashed one of the large front windows to get in.

The next morning, thousands of people stood in the snow along the procession route to the just-completed state capitol. Roosevelt rode there in a sleigh. At 11:15 A.M. he walked into the Assembly chamber, which had been decorated in red velvet embroidered with gold, bowed to his wife, waved to his children, then sat behind a mahogany desk and turned his attention to the ceremony. Roosevelt had been sworn in as governor in a small event two days before. Now he gave his first speech. "Under no form of government is it so necessary thus to combine efficiency and morality, high principle and rough common sense, justice and the sturdiest physical and moral courage, as in a republic," he said. This would be his governing code: optimistic, forceful, unnerving to critics. At a reception that afternoon, he shook hands with six thousand guests.

The next day he began the practice of inviting reporters into his office for fifteen minutes in the morning and afternoon to gossip and chat. He won their confidence despite only occasionally answering their questions. His aim, he wrote later, was to break down the secrecy that allowed the "invisible empire" of politicians and high capitalists to thrive.

By the end of the legislative session in April, Roosevelt had signed bills that promised stricter regulation of working conditions in the tenements, gave factory inspectors more authority and resources, and restricted state employees' labor to eight hours a day.

He also alienated New York's Republican establishment, along with its financial backers, by supporting a proposal to curtail corporate privileges by imposing a franchise tax. If companies received rich concessions from the state—to supply utilities such as gas or elevated railways—they should pay taxes on their revenue. That, Roosevelt said, would "even things up."

As the debate got under way in the legislature, Morgan's deputies made what they considered a reasonable request: an exemption for the New York Central Railroad, one of the largest in the northeast. The Vanderbilts still owned a significant part of it, but most knew that Morgan controlled it. Roosevelt confided to a friend: "I like Pierpont Morgan and his partner Bacon is my classmate and close friend, but of course I cannot consider that in connection with this bill."

After Roosevelt pushed the bill through, Platt suggested that he had undermined his chances to be renominated for governor—a contest still more than a year away. "I had heard from a good many sources that you were a little loose on the relations of capital and labor, on trusts and combinations, and, indeed, on those numerous questions which have recently arisen in politics affecting the security of earnings and the right of a man to run his own business in his own way," Platt wrote. Roosevelt replied that as Republicans they should set themselves "as resolutely against improper corporate influence on the one hand as against demagogy and mob rule on the other." Platt had said all he needed to. Several corporations, "howling like mad" at Roosevelt, challenged the legality of the tax measure. (In 1903 the law would be upheld by the Supreme Court.)

As the century was drawing to a close, an astonishing era of corporate expansion was beginning. Manufacturing plants combined, incorporated, and sold stock to a newly credulous public. So did railways: sixty-seven million dollars' worth in 1898 and shares valued at one hundred seven million dollars in 1899.

To farmers it seemed that they had more opportunities to sell their produce to distant buyers but less control over their futures. Factory workers were free from the unpredictability of droughts and pests but left to defend themselves against the danger and drudgery of industrial jobs and the irascibility of bosses who could fire them or cut their pay with little explanation. President McKinley touted the nation's burgeoning prosperity, but in the great scramble for a foothold, the striving middle classes—clerks and managers, teachers, and foremen—also felt forgotten as their independence dimmed. Many were unsettled by the arrival in their cities and towns of migrants from southern and eastern Europe. Anti-immigrant racism gained purchase.

"Would you mind giving me a hint about trusts? I have been in a great quandary over them," Roosevelt wrote to a friend in Kansas during the summer of 1899. "I do not intend to play a demagogue. On the other hand, I do intend to, so far as in me lies, see that the rich man is held to the same accountability as the poor man, and when the rich man is rich enough to buy unscrupulous advice from very able lawyers, this is not always easy." The Supreme Court was skeptical of executive power, and Congress uneasy about extending a president's authority to the world of business. The trusts were a quandary that McKinley was willing to set aside. His populist opponents made it into a cause.

Roosevelt wrote letters and talked to business leaders, politicians, journalists, academics, historians. By the time he gave his second annual message as governor, in January 1900, he had refined his position on the trusts. He advocated government regulation, the right to intervene against monopolies, and the authority to demand corporations publicly report their earnings. It was an ambitious agenda, well received by the public, and unlikely to be fulfilled by the state legislature.

Roosevelt hoped he would have a second term as governor to make good on these promises. Circumstances—man-made and natural—prevented that. Platt recognized the limits of his control over Roosevelt. "I can't do what I want with him, he is willful as Hell," he told a friend. When Vice President Garret Hobart died in November 1899, Platt saw a chance to remove the governor who had become a liability and a threat. He pushed Roosevelt as McKinley's running mate for the 1900 campaign. As vice president, Roosevelt would have no power and no constituency.

"All the big-monied interests that make campaign contributions of large size and feel that they should have favors in return, are extremely anxious to get me out of the State," Roosevelt wrote to Lodge. He called the vice presidency an "irksome, wearisome place where I could do nothing," and told Platt he would rather be a professor of history.

That spring of 1900 Roosevelt set himself the task of dissuading McKinley and Hanna from considering him for the job. It was easier than he thought. "I think you are unduly alarmed," Secretary of State Hay wrote to one of Roosevelt's friends who had passed along his objections. "There is no instance on record of an election of Vice-President by violence, and I think people here are looking in quite another direction." After Roosevelt himself went to Washington, Hay wrote of his visit: "He came down with a sombre resolution thrown on his strenuous brow to let McKinley and Hanna know once and for all that he would not be Vice-President, and found to his stupefaction that nobody in Washington except Platt had ever dreamed such a thing."

But to many outside Washington, Roosevelt wasn't impetuous or capricious; he didn't seem beholden or bought. He wasn't a crank, he was a reformer. A cowboy. A Rough Rider. As Republicans prepared for their national convention in Philadelphia that June, they couldn't deny the enthusiasm for Roosevelt.

McKinley thought it unseemly to involve himself in a decision meant to reflect the will of the convention. Roosevelt would be there, among New York's delegates. Platt had already seen to that. He kept up the pressure on the other states to support Roosevelt's nomination, aided by Republican senators hostile to Hanna and eager to see his stature diminished.

In the days before the convention, Alton B. Parker, chief justice of the New York Court of Appeals, came for dinner at the governor's mansion in Albany. Edith asked what to expect in Philadelphia. "You will see your handsome husband come in and bedlam will at once break loose, and he will receive such a demonstration of applause . . . as no one else will receive," Parker told her. Roosevelt wouldn't be able to refuse a place on the

Republican ticket. "You disagreeable thing," Edith interrupted. "I don't want to see him nominated for the vice-presidency."

When Roosevelt entered the Hotel Walton at a brisk march, through two massive stone arches and into the lobby, the crowd milling around came to. "T.R.'s name was on every lip," a friend recalled. Some delegates already wore McKinley-Roosevelt campaign buttons. The June days in Philadelphia were hot, and the hotel's corridors swarming. Bands blared. Delegations paraded from floor to floor. For a while Roosevelt sat at the window of his corner room, enjoying the breeze as he read the *The Works of Flavius Josephus*.

On Monday, June 18, Roosevelt called a press conference in his room, the unofficial headquarters of his unwelcome campaign. So many journalists and supporters crowded in that some stood on the bed. Roosevelt thanked the delegates for an honor he would rather not accept. He pleaded with them to respect his judgment that he could do more for the party as governor than as vice president. But he did say that the vice presidency was "well worthy of the ambition of any man in the United States." Those closest to Roosevelt knew he had conceded. Decode his message and it revealed Roosevelt's promise not to snub the party leaders, even as some wished they could do just that to him.

Nearly fifteen thousand people gathered in the Convention Hall on the morning of June 21, boisterous, shouting, already celebrating. McKinley's position was assured. In keeping with precedent, he remained in Washington at the Executive Mansion. Roosevelt strode in at ten o'clock wearing a neat black cutaway coat, dark striped trousers, a blue necktie, and a delegate's badge. Cheers and outstretched hands prodded him as he made his way to where his fellow New Yorkers waited. Moments later, Hanna arrived to equally loud applause. He approached Roosevelt, put an arm on his shoulder and whispered into his ear. Roosevelt nodded. Hanna, certain his party was making a grievous mistake, smiled and waved to the crowd.

On stage, Ohio senator Joseph Foraker nominated McKinley for president. Roosevelt listened to the speech, foreboding on his face. When he rose to his feet at the conclusion, he remained silent, hands in his pockets. Foraker called him to the stage to second the nomination. He stood unsmiling amid the thrum of enthusiasm in the audience. He began

Opening of the Republican National Convention, June 1900.

his speech by condemning the Ice Trust, with which he had tangled during New York City's heat wave of 1896. "That's right, Teddy!" delegates yelled in response. Later in his speech, Roosevelt previewed a campaign theme: "We did not promise the impossible . . . [that] there would come prosperity to all men; but we did say that each man should have a better chance to win prosperity than he had ever yet had." Then, as whoops and applause filled the hall, he smiled.

Roosevelt returned to his seat, waving to the crowd along the way. He caught a glimpse of Edith, sitting in a gallery box, wearing a pink gown, pearl necklace, and black hat with feathers, the "cynosure of all eyes," one reporter wrote. He smiled again. When the crowd finally quieted, the head of Iowa's delegation nominated Roosevelt as vice president. All around him men threw their hats into the air, raised their state flags, pulled out banners with his name, and came roaring to their feet. The only female delegate on the floor, identified in the papers as Mrs. William Henry Jones from

The "chair" Roosevelt used as a delegate from New York

Salt Lake City, presented Roosevelt with roses. He bowed as he accepted them. The band played what had become his theme song, "A Hot Time in the Old Town Tonight," and delegates marched past Roosevelt, who sat imperturbable. Of the 926 delegates at the convention, 925 voted for Roosevelt to be the Republican nominee for vice president. He abstained.

After the convention, Hanna wrote to McKinley: "Your duty to the country is to live for four years."

IN OCTOBER, SHORTLY before the election, Morgan and Hill boarded *Corsair* one evening for an overdue reconciliation. Morgan was frustrated with Hill. He didn't get along with Morgan's man at the Northern Pacific, Charles Mellen, and the feeling was mutual. After a meeting in St. Paul in February 1900, Mellen reported back confidentially to New York: "You know how difficult it is to get anything tangible from Mr. Hill in connection with any matter. He does not write me, but prefers to conduct his negotiations by personal interview, and his memory is treacherous regarding what transpires." The situation was made worse by Coster's death that March; one of his many roles at Morgan's firm had been to make sure Hill didn't interfere too much in the Northern Pacific.

That fall, when a friend suggested to Morgan that Hill probably wanted to repair their relationship, Morgan replied: "Yes, I should think he would." They talked until two in the morning.

They decided to extend their not-so-secret, not-technically-illegal railroad system eastward to Chicago, where both lines could connect to the New York Central. That would give them a route from coast to coast.

Chicago at the turn of the century had a population of 1.7 million, making it the second-largest city in the nation after New York. The five biggest meat packers operated in Chicago. So did iron and steel mills, breweries, and food companies. Chicago was home to the two most important mail order catalog companies, Montgomery Ward and Sears, Roebuck, and its publishing and printing industry was second only to New York's. William Wrigley had given up on baking soda and sold chewing gum instead. Frank Lloyd Wright worked in an architectural studio connected to his home in the suburb of Oak Park. Jane Addams opened Hull House as a social services agency.

The Northwestern lines wouldn't build their way to Chicago; they would buy their way in. Hill decided that he and Morgan needed to acquire the Burlington—independently run, publicly held, and uninterested in expanding further on its own. Securing those eight thousand miles of track would lead to one of the most contentious corporate battles the public had ever witnessed. That's because Harriman, who owned the railroad that dominated the Southwest, decided he needed the Burlington too.

CHAPTER 6

Buy at Any Price

The wedding was scheduled for three thirty on the afternoon of Thursday, November 15, 1900. Spectators congregated in the streets and park near the church two hours before, in such a crush that a police squad was called to hold them back. St. George's, the largest Episcopal chapel in New York, with seats for two thousand, was full. Morgan accompanied his eldest and favorite daughter, Louisa, down the aisle as an organist played the Lohengrin Wedding March. Pierpont was tall, but Louisa might have been just a little taller.

She wore a white satin dress with Alençon lace so elaborate the technique required ten years of training to master. Her veil was held in place with orange blossoms and a large spray of diamonds. Her corsage was surrounded by a diamond sunburst and brooch. Her father bought the wedding gown with her during a spring trip to Europe. He selected her bouquet (lilies of the valley, white roses, and orchids), all the decorations, and the guests (drawn from the social register and political elite). Louisa, thirty-four and involved in charitable work none of the papers bothered to describe, had long ago ceded the privilege of making her own decisions. Her husband, Herbert Satterlee, a thirty-seven-year-old lawyer, learned to accept his father-in-law's singular munificence. Morgan told Herbert he intended to provide Louisa with a ten-thousand-dollar-a-year allowance even after they married. That about equaled Herbert's salary as a lawyer. He told Morgan that wouldn't be necessary. "I tried to head him off, but it was no use!" Herbert reported back to Louisa. She got her allowance. Morgan also gave the couple a country home on the Hudson near his. Later, he would build Louisa and Herbert a city home near his as well.

Morgan invited six hundred of the wedding guests to the family's mansion at 219 Madison Avenue for the reception. Some chose to use the servants' entrance to avoid the press of people in the grand foyer. Morgan had anticipated the crowd. He'd had a large ballroom built on an empty lot behind his home. Its floor was carpeted in royal red, the walls were the same color, and on them hung eight tapestries depicting the story of the sun god Apollo. The ceiling was covered with pleated cream-colored cloth that formed a sunburst. Strings of electric bulbs were suspended from it.

Neapolitan orchestras played ragtime and opera. Morgan was seen issuing instructions to the staff of waiters he hired from Sherry's, the city's finest restaurant. Herbert and Louisa stood in the drawing room to receive the guests: Rockefellers, Astors, and Vanderbilts; Secretary of War Elihu Root and his wife, Clara; Chauncey Depew, once the president of the New York Central Railroad, now a senator. James Hill couldn't be there but sent Louisa bear, otter, and sable skins from the Northwest.

By seven in the evening the party was over. Morgan threw a white silk shoe in celebration as the newlyweds left for their honeymoon. The ballroom would likely be demolished before they returned.

The wedding took place just nine days after the 1900 presidential election. The people had again voted for McKinley over Bryan. Morgan invited the president and his wife, both of whom declined to attend. He also invited the new vice-president-elect and his wife. Only Edith, it seems, considered accepting.

In early December, Roosevelt—finishing his term as governor of New York—planned a banquet of his own. It was in honor of Morgan. Roosevelt wanted to show his appreciation for the banker's support in the presidential campaign.

My dear Mr. Morgan,

I will have the dinner at the Union League Club, Saturday, December 29th at 8 pm. With great regard,

Sincerely yours, Theodore Roosevelt.

P.S. I inclose [sic] an invitation to your son. I have always known him as "Jack" and I am not certain whether he is J. Pierpont Morgan Jr. or not.

He was still Jack.

Roosevelt also sent a note to Root, who had just finished a term as president of the club. Roosevelt asked Root to attend the dinner, which he said "represents an effort on my part to become a conservative man, in touch with the influential classes, and I think I deserve encouragement. Hitherto I have given dinners only to professional politicians or more or less wild-eyed reformers. Now I am hard at work endeavoring to assume the Vice Presidential poise." Root offered encouragement but sent regrets. He said he had too much work to complete in Washington.

Located on Fifth Avenue and Thirty-Ninth Street, just blocks from Morgan's own residence, the Union League Club was a fanciful mix of red brick and brownstone, gables, columns, chimneys and balconies. Louis Tiffany, the artist and glassmaker, helped design the interior. Membership was limited. The admission fee was, for all concerned, an insignificant three hundred dollars and annual dues a mere seventy-five. The rules were strict: no tipping, no card games, no smoking pipes, no women (except on Fridays and Saturdays before five).

Roosevelt's father and Morgan's first father-in-law helped found the club during the Civil War. Roosevelt was admitted when he was an assemblyman and managed his early political career from its rooms. He would soon serve as a vice president of the club as well.

On the evening of the twenty-ninth, an exhibit of modern painters hung in the art gallery, featuring Thomas Moran's just-completed *Shoshone Falls on the Snake River*. The meal, the twenty-one guests, the surroundings—the familiar comforts of a privileged world—seemed to acknowledge Morgan's rightful place atop it.

Around the country a sense of wonder at America's prosperity—the gross national product had increased almost 30 percent in McKinley's first term—mixed with a quickening sense of inequity. Businessmen saw a rosy future uninterrupted by "vexatious" legislation. On Wall Street, investors were alert. More than twelve hundred companies were bought up in 1899, and a thousand or so more in 1900, enriching their owners and shareholders in the process. Rumors of railroad deals kept trading brisk. Now the new year was bearing down, and with it, new and aggressive moves from within the House of Morgan.

On March 3, just before Roosevelt stepped into the vice presidency, a new company, U.S. Steel, captured almost as much attention. Morgan had assembled the conglomerate—capitalized at $1.4 billion, incorporated in New Jersey—in parallel to his efforts to combine railroads. It was responsible for more than half the country's steel production and almost one hundred fifty thousand workers. Speculators went mad for the stock. Orders came from global centers of commerce, and from hundreds of American towns. So many checks and pledges poured into 23 Wall Street that the firm had to hire extra clerks to handle the mail. Millionaires came in person to ask to get into the syndicate. Many government officials—Republican senators in particular—were also tied up in Morgan's steel enterprise, the *World* wrote in an editorial. "Mr. Morgan's power over the Senate is more sinister than his power over Mr. McKinley. With the President he is simply an adviser, whose advice is usually heeded. With the Senate Mr. Morgan can exert the rude might of Money."

"Pierpont Morgan is apparently trying to swallow the sun," Henry Adams, the well-known historian and gossip, wrote to a friend. Adams seemed merely amused. "America is good enough for me," Morgan reportedly told one paper. "Whenever he doesn't like it, he can give it back to us," the editor replied.

The new year brought a new face at 23 Wall Street as well. Just days after U.S. Steel opened for business, George Perkins officially joined the firm. He and Morgan had met in 1900, when Perkins, thirty-eight at the time and a senior executive at New York Life Insurance, had approached the financier for a contribution to a campaign to save the Hudson River

Palisades. (The fundraising drive was then-Governor Roosevelt's idea.) It was good timing. Morgan wanted something from Perkins as well. Morgan promised to provide the full amount to the Palisades project on one condition—that Perkins come work for him.

"Take that desk over there," Morgan said, pointing to an empty one among the partners'.

"I have a pretty good desk up at the New York Life," Perkins answered.

That position, and some degree of independence, was important enough to Perkins that Morgan reluctantly agreed to let him keep it when he finally did join the firm two months later. The only request Morgan refused to honor was to give Perkins's secretary, Mary Kihm, a desk. Morgan didn't allow women to work at the bank. Perkins set her up in a rented office nearby instead.

Perkins didn't care much about promoting stocks and bonds. He was interested in creating the political environment he believed necessary to achieve the corporate efficiency he demanded. Like Morgan, he thought the surest route to profitability was to centralize power and cooperate with would-be rivals. Competition seemed so wasteful. Perkins would become Morgan's strategist, mediator, lobbyist, and publicist as the firm entered into increasingly sensitive public negotiations and private reorganizations. Perkins, who had run his family's grocery store, would earn more than a million dollars some years, and yet Morgan left him cold. "I began life sorting lemons," he wrote a friend. "I have been doing it ever since."

George Perkins, Morgan's "secretary of state"

On March 11, 1901, at the end of Perkins's first week at Morgan & Co., Vice President Roosevelt sent him a telegram of congratulations and greetings to his boss. As with the Union League dinner, Roosevelt still intended to stay in the good graces of Wall Street's most influential man. Morgan seemed at the height of his powers, unshakable. But his railroad deals—the juddering pistons driving him and his firm forward—were about to give Wall Street an unexpected shock.

THAT SAME MONTH, the president of the Burlington Railroad accepted Hill and Morgan's third offer for the company. They had started at one hundred forty dollars a share and shook hands at two hundred. "It was the only price at which it could be bought and we had great difficulty in getting it at that," Morgan said. They did receive one concession: the Burlington accepted bonds rather than cash.

Soon afterward, Jacob Schiff, the head of the firm Kuhn, Loeb & Co., asked to speak with Morgan. Wall Street's anti-Semitism was unabashed and mostly unquestioned; Schiff was one of the few Jewish bankers Morgan seemed to respect. Still, Robert Bacon and not Morgan would be the one to take the meeting.

Schiff did business with both Harriman and Hill. They were among the most prominent railroad tycoons, and if he could avoid having to choose one over the other he would. But when it came to the Burlington, they were opposed, and he was on Harriman's side. Harriman had bid for the Burlington in 1899 but was refused; then he tried to gain control in the open market but couldn't find enough stockholders willing to sell. Now Schiff argued that, to keep the peace, Morgan and Hill should sell Harriman one-third of the rail line. He would pay cash. Bacon said it was too late. Schiff told Bacon his rebuff was a "grave mistake," and Harriman's Union Pacific "would have to protect itself." Bacon didn't seem worried.

In early April, just weeks after U.S. Steel had gone public and McKinley had taken the oath of office again, Morgan boarded the White Star Liner the *Teutonic* with his sister and a female friend. A plain-clothed police escort accompanied them to the gangway. Morgan and his guests settled into first-class staterooms, and then they were off to Europe. At 23 Wall Street, Bacon and Perkins, on the job for just a month, were in charge of business.

Harriman and Schiff made one more attempt to get in on the Burlington deal. On Easter Sunday, April 7, Hill was dining at the Madison Avenue home of George Baker, the head of First National Bank and one

Edward H. Harriman

of the richest men in the country. At midnight they planned to board a train to Boston to complete the purchase of the Burlington. As they finished their meal, Harriman and Schiff showed up. Hill again turned down Harriman's offer, and Harriman again threatened to retaliate. "Very well, then, this is an invasion of Union Pacific territory, a hostile act, and you will have to take the consequences," he said. He wasn't done. He and Schiff jumped into the carriage with Hill and Baker and were still talking as the men walked onto the platform at Grand Central. Hill and Baker hurried onto the train and headed north.

On April 14, Hill returned to St. Paul briefly before heading out west with two important Great Northern shareholders and two company executives. He wanted to show off his railroad. "Papa has had another busy day. No let up," Hill's wife, Mary, wrote in her diary of his Sunday at home.

"We see by papers that Papa is hurrying back from the Coast," she wrote on Thursday. *The Minneapolis Journal* reported that as soon as Hill and his party had arrived in Seattle, he had immediately wired St. Paul that he wanted "fast time" home. The tracks were cleared and the three-car train— "President Hill's magnificent car, made of steel throughout, a baggage car and a strong engine"—would stop only for coal and water. Normally the eighteen-hundred-mile route required sixty-six hours to traverse. They made it in just under forty-six hours, breaking all Great Northern records, the paper noted. When the train reached a top speed of 85 miles an hour, the vibrations of the engine made it impossible for the fireman to stand, so he sat down to shovel the coal.

As Hill stepped onto the platform in St. Paul, his secretary gave him a coded telegram from Daniel Lamont—Cleveland's former secretary of war was now a Northern Pacific executive: "Is it Louisa Pomegranate to Comport Hopingly Nursery Wooden?" It was a request that Hill return to New York to conclude the Burlington deal.

While Hill traveled out west and Morgan acquired a Raphael Madonna in Paris, Harriman and Schiff secretly bought up shares in Northern Pacific. This was their revenge. Hill and Morgan had effective control over the Northern Pacific, but they didn't own a majority of the shares. That was common practice among railroad executives and their bankers, and Morgan in particular had never found it necessary to own a company outright in order to exert influence. No one around Morgan—and certainly not the man himself—believed a raid on a Morgan company in the open market would succeed. They couldn't imagine who would dare. Harriman dared.

The Northern Pacific's stock price rose as a result of the stealth purchases, but that didn't surprise anyone at 23 Wall Street. U.S. Steel had begun operations, investors were optimistic, speculators were busy. "A stream of excited customers, of every description, brought their money down to Wall Street, and spent their days in offices near the Stock Exchange," the financial journalist Alexander Noyes wrote. "The newspapers were full of stories of hotel waiters, clerks in business offices, even doorkeepers and dressmakers, who had won considerable fortunes in their speculations."

Bacon and the Northern Pacific board decided to cash in and sold some of the railroad's stock. Morgan's firm unwittingly sold a million dollars' worth, too.

"The reckoning comes from an unexpected cause," Noyes wrote, "at the moment when the public and the speculators have reached the conclusion that it can never come."

VISITORS, "INCLUDING A multitude of women in spring costumes," filled the galleries of the New York Stock Exchange when the gong rang out at three in the afternoon on Friday, April 26. Many old members who hadn't been there for years were on the floor. When trading ended, they all cheered. It was the last day of business in the thirty-five-year-old building. The exchange needed a bigger space that reflected the country's new global financial dominance.

Business resumed Monday in temporary quarters in the New York Produce Exchange, a five-minute walk away. Workmen installed four hundred fifty phones and dozens of cables in preparation.

Signs of exuberance were everywhere. The price of seats on the floor had increased from one hundred seventy-five dollars to three hundred in a matter of days. Tuesday, April 30, was the first session in which stock transactions had ever totaled more than three million shares. By Thursday, so much stock was trading hands that specialists had to work late, some through the night, to record all the transactions.

Still, something didn't seem quite right. Bacon began to suspect that Harriman and Schiff were behind the purchases of Northern Pacific stock. He cabled Morgan that they might be seeking a seat or two on the board, a prospect that alarmed no one at the firm.

But Hill was alarmed. He had come to New York and on Friday, May 3, went to Schiff's office, conveniently located a few floors below his. Schiff told him everything. He and Harriman owned 50 percent of Northern Pacific's stock, both common and preferred shares. They intended to combine the railroads Hill and Morgan controlled with those Harriman owned. Hill could run the whole system if he abandoned Morgan and added his stock to theirs. Harriman promised to stay out of his way. Hill didn't give the idea a moment's thought. He had built the Great Northern and negotiated for the Burlington, and there was no way he was giving up either without a fight.

"They actually had the gall to suppose that I would consider such a proposal," he wrote to a friend. Hill turned down the offer. But he accepted Schiff's invitation to dinner that evening at his home high on Fifth Avenue.

Then Hill went straight from 27 Pine Street to 23 Wall Street to warn Bacon and Perkins. They summoned every assistant in the office to count shares to determine if Hill and Morgan had really lost the Northern Pacific. As they scoured the record books, Hill recalled an unusual provision of the company charter they might use to thwart Harriman. The dread in the office briefly lifted. Harriman and Schiff had bought 50 percent of Northern

Pacific's stock, but they held more preferred shares than common shares. Both had voting rights, but at Northern Pacific common shares gave their owners more control. The board of directors had the power to essentially null the preferred stock come the first of the year. And the directors were almost all Morgan men. A new board was supposed to be elected on the first of October 1901. If Morgan and Hill could gain a majority of the common stock, they could keep control of the board, which could then retire the preferred shares.

It wasn't an elegant solution—and would likely be challenged in the courts—but it seemed the only way to prevent Harriman from taking over.

Now they needed to buy common shares. For permission to do so, Bacon had to interrupt his boss's vacation. He sent a telegram to Morgan—codenamed Flitch—seeking approval to purchase one hundred fifty thousand more shares of Northern Pacific. This was the first Morgan was hearing of the raid and he was growling mad. He dictated a curt reply in code: Buy at any price. Starting Monday, they would.

Before then, Schiff would again attempt to end the hostilities. Hill arrived for Friday night dinner with the banker, his wife, Therese, and their children. Once his family left the room, Schiff said he and Harriman would stop buying Northern Pacific stock if Hill made Harriman a director of the Burlington. Hill trusted Schiff but not Harriman. They talked for hours, and when Hill finally left it was close to midnight. He made no promises.

Harriman called Schiff's office the next morning to instruct him to buy forty thousand shares of Northern Pacific's common stock before the exchange closed at noon. Harriman seemed to have discovered the loophole, too. With that last batch, he could be assured of control even if the company's board took the drastic action of doing away with the preferred stock he had been accumulating. Schiff was at Temple Emanu-El when he received a note with Harriman's message. He ignored it. He never explained why. He didn't seem to understand how vulnerable their position was. Certainly Hill had been careful not to give Schiff any indication that he had found a flaw in their plan. "We are letting the enemy think they have control," Hill wrote to a friend and investor.

Hill and the House of Morgan could afford no more miscalculations. Hill cabled his friends in England to hold onto their Northern Pacific stock. But Bacon was frantic over the possibility that more shares might inadvertently slip away. "Damn it, Bacon, don't worry," Hill told him. "My friends will stand without hitching."

Meanwhile, Bacon contacted Jack Morgan, who ran the firm's London operations: "Most important you or friends should not sell NP common at any price without consulting JPM."

"What is happening?" Jack wrote back.

On Monday, May 6, Morgan & Co. sent Jim Keene, a notorious stock manipulator, into the market to secure the shares it needed to retain control of the Northern Pacific. By Tuesday, the exchange was teeming with Keene's brokers, some of whom were buying Northern Pacific shares that, it turned out, didn't exactly exist. The price increased so sharply—it had been trading at one hundred ten on Saturday and by Tuesday had reached one hundred forty-nine—that traders were selling the stock short. That is, they were selling stock they didn't yet own, expecting that later, as shares flooded the market in response to demand, they could purchase what they needed at a lower price—thus making good on their commitment and making a profit. But traders discovered there was little stock to borrow and almost none to buy. And the price was not falling.

Speculators had to liquidate their shares of other companies to pay for the borrowed Northern Pacific shares. By Wednesday, May 8, the entire exchange was crashing. Many investors stayed in town long after the market's close to gossip and glean what information they could at the Waldorf-Astoria, the preferred public gathering spot for the Wall Street elite. They had borrowed money at staggering rates of interest and paid small fortunes to borrow the stock. "The air was thick with rumors, with tobacco smoke, and with the fumes of various fluids which the brokers, bankers and financiers were consuming in order to steady their nerves," one reporter wrote. Loss, maybe ruin, were waiting for them.

The Produce Exchange, with its arched windows and stained-glass skylight high above the floor, usually felt bright with promise. Thursday, May 9, was a day of shadows and despair. At a quarter past eleven, a single share of Northern Pacific stock reached the shattering price of one thousand dollars. Then somewhere, someone heard the music slowing and understood what would happen when it stopped. Somewhere, someone decided to get ahead of the impending crash. Suddenly, the price of Northern Pacific shares dropped four hundred dollars in a single trade.

Everyone rushed to sell. Men who were strong enough threw smaller ones out of their way. They elbowed themselves back into the crowd, grabbed coats and collars, and pushed on.

At one in the afternoon, prices were still dropping. The value of Morgan's U.S. Steel fell by half. A second's delay could mean thousands of dollars lost. Traders were desperate as their riches vanished and brokers helpless as their customers' investments shrunk by the moment. The spectators in the gallery were escorted out. A rumor spread that uniformed guards might be required to protect brokers on the floor from being attacked by distressed customers.

At a quarter past two, Schiff's firm and Morgan's tried to still the chaos by announcing they wouldn't expect brokers to deliver Northern Pacific stock due the next day. That wasn't enough.

Morgan had been enjoying the spa treatments and sulfur baths at the Grand Hotel in Aix-les-Bains when he received word of the panic. He had no choice and he hated having no choices. He had to give up on his holiday there. Morgan traveled to the Paris office, and sent word to Bacon to end the trouble with a settlement—otherwise he would return to New York to do so himself. In the meantime, he remained in contact with his partner, dictating telegrams early in the morning from his bed. Later, sitting in a Parisian park, he looked deep in thought. He was said to be in a "snarling mood."

On May 10, as he instructed, Hill, Harriman, and Schiff agreed to accept one hundred fifty dollars for a share of Northern Pacific stock to allow short sellers to clear their accounts. That still wasn't enough. A good part of Wall Street was technically insolvent for a couple of hours that day. Morgan directed that six million dollars be available for immediate loans, New York banks offered another twenty million, and no firm went bankrupt. This was little comfort to the many small investors who wouldn't recover as easily. "The spell was broken," said the *Commercial and*

Vol XLV No 2317   10 Cents a Copy

HARPER'S
WEEKLY

A JOURNAL OF   CIVILIZATION

NEW YORK   MAY 18, 1901

THOSE LAMBS WERE GETTING TOO "CHESTY"

"Those lambs were getting too 'chesty,'" Harper's Weekly *cover after the May 1901 stock market panic*

Financial Chronicle. Speculative fortunes could be unmade as quickly as made. "Belief in the invulnerability of any such movement is therefore a delusion," the paper warned. Some called it the hysteria of stock gamblers.

The Panic of 1901 was the biggest market crash in a century. Many held Morgan responsible for allowing a fight among tycoons to wreak public havoc. Undaunted, he resumed his European vacation once the panic subsided. In June, he dined at Windsor Castle with the new king, Edward VII.

In New York, amidst the worst of the frenzy, Hill remained in his office. It had no stock ticker, no telephone, just a box of expensive cigars on his desk and a few pictures of locomotives on the walls. From there he told reporters: "All I can do is to liken it to a ghost dance. The Indians began their dance and don't know why they are doing it. They whirl about until they are almost crazy. It is so when these Wall Street people get the speculative fever. Perhaps they imagine they have a motive in that they see two sets of powerful interests which may be said to be clashing."

A few days later, he said that the Great Northern was "quite able to skin its own rabbits," and denied that he and Morgan were working together. But both he and one of Schiff's partners, Otto Kahn, said that none of this would have—could have—happened if Morgan had been in town. He would have detected trouble sooner and put an end to it faster. "We are all a little ashamed of ourselves," Kahn admitted. Hill admitted nothing.

"We appreciate very much all you have done for us in this miserable business," Bacon cabled Jack Morgan in mid-May.

BY THEN, ROOSEVELT had long left Washington for Sagamore Hill, his home on Long Island's Oyster Bay, intending to return to his new job in

October. He joked that as vice president he had "taken the veil." He thought political oblivion waited for him. He considered studying the law while in office to prepare for it.

But first, summer with Edith and the children. Marshes, beaches, pastures, and woods spread over 89 acres. Winter wrens, great crested flycatchers, yellow-billed cuckoos, and ruby-crowned kinglets. A library with southern light. A gun room facing north over the bay. No electricity. Rocking chairs on the veranda. "I am rather ashamed to say that I am enjoying the perfect ease of my life at present," he wrote to William Howard Taft, who was about to become the colonial governor of the Philippines. "I am just living out in the country, doing nothing but ride and row with Mrs. Roosevelt, and walk and play with the children; chop trees in the afternoon and read books by a wood fire in the evening."

THE METROPOLITAN CLUB was the most luxurious social club in New York, constructed during the depression of the 1890s at a cost of almost two million dollars on land once owned by Consuelo Vanderbilt, before she became the Duchess of Marlborough. Morgan was its first president. On May 31, 1901, after weeks of negotiations, Bacon, Hill, Harriman, and Schiff met in the club's private dining room to sign a truce. Morgan's firm would create a new board of directors for the Northern Pacific that included Harriman. Hill would run the Great Northern, Northern Pacific, and Burlington lines with "uniform methods of management and accounting." The rivals were making peace.

On July 4, Morgan returned to the United States aboard the *Deutschland*. He had been in Europe for three of the most tumultuous months on Wall Street. When the ship docked at Hoboken, *Corsair* was waiting to ferry him up the Hudson to Cragston, his country estate. So were reporters. "Mr. Morgan as is his custom was most outspoken—on subjects that are not connected with the business world and that he can discuss without danger of anybody knowing what he proposes to do," his son-in-law noted.

Two weeks later, Morgan announced the new board members of the Northern Pacific, a company he had refinanced twice and defended at the cost of his public reputation. Hill, of course, would be a member and, said Morgan, "We will put Mr. Harriman on this board, and Mr. Schiff, too, to show them we are not afraid of them."

Morgan kept quiet about what else he and Hill proposed to do—set up a holding company to protect the railroads from anyone else, or even Harriman himself, who might try again to seize control. The larger the company, the more difficult it would be to secure a majority of it. New Jersey beckoned, with its promises to fast track applications, impose few burdens, and provide "freedom from undue publicity."

But first, Morgan and Hill had to placate Harriman. He had embarrassed and almost outmaneuvered them, and they still regarded him as an impetuous outsider. As Harriman suspected he would, Morgan instructed the board to implement his plan of last resort. Preferred shares had to be converted to common by January 1, 1902. Morgan and Hill's control of the Northern Pacific wouldn't be certain until Harriman handed over the paper proxies for his shares.

Morgan invited Hill and Harriman to Bar Harbor on *Corsair* to persuade the adversaries to set aside their complaints and antagonisms. Harriman invited Hill to Arden, his sprawling estate in New York. On September 1, at Arden, Harriman finally agreed to surrender the proxies. Within a week a courier arrived at 23 Wall Street to deliver them.

These were the secret contents of the package Morgan received on the morning of Friday, September 6. That afternoon, President McKinley was shot.

ROOSEVELT HADN'T SEEMED the vice presidential type. That summer, as he considered his future, a friend said: "I would not like to be in McKinley's shoes. He has a man of destiny behind him." Destiny arrived sooner and with more force than anyone expected. Those first days in power, among his confidants, Roosevelt was voluble, vehement. He walked faster than usual. He was already anxious that the compromises required to secure a second term would be too great: "I rather be a full President for three years than half a President for seven years."

Morgan carried on as planned. He took his trip to the west coast for the Episcopal Church convention in San Francisco (and to inspect his railroad properties). When he returned to Wall Street in late October, he directed a holding company—Northern Securities—be formed for the stock of the Northern Pacific, Great Northern, and Burlington lines. Morgan brushed off concerns that the new company might violate anti-trust laws. Maybe he regarded the Sherman Act as inconsequential, largely unenforceable, a sop to an ill-informed public. Maybe he assumed Roosevelt did too. But his lawyers were worried. "What do you want to do?" one said. "Do you want to go to jail?"

Complicating matters was the fact that Morgan's favored partner was unwell. The May panic had strained Bob Bacon. Overworked since Coster's death and clashing with Perkins, he had suffered a nervous breakdown. Morgan granted him a year's leave, and on November 6, Bacon sailed for Europe. (When he returned to New York at the end of 1902, he resigned from Morgan & Co. Including the sabbatical, he had lasted eight years.)

On the night of November 11, 1901, Harriman, Hill, and Perkins gathered at the Corner long after normal business had concluded. They haggled over the final details of their arrangement. Sometime past two in the morning, the men got into their carriages and stole into the moonless night.

At noon on November 13, the Northern Securities Company was incorporated in Trenton. Morgan signed the eighty-thousand-dollar check for the filing fee himself. That afternoon, the company held its first board meeting; Hill was elected chairman and presented with a twenty-dollar gold piece. He gave the coin to his wife. "Smithy very habitation," he wrote in code to a friend. "Situation very gratifying."

CHAPTER 7

The State of the Union

T he Roosevelt family—six children aged three to seventeen and their stilts, roller skates, bicycles, their guinea pig named Admiral Dewey, their Manchester terrier, Jack, and Tom Quartz the cat—packed up at Sagamore Hill and moved into the Executive Mansion. Ike Hoover, the chief usher, called it "the wildest scramble in the history of the White House."

They found themselves in a glorious Victorian relic: drafty and fusty with ornate but uncleaned ceiling frescoes, elaborate but fraying wallpaper, imposing furniture, bad plumbing, and little privacy. The family quarters were on the same floor as the executive offices. "Edie says it's like living over the store!" Roosevelt told a friend. The Executive Mansion in 1901 didn't yet reflect the aspirations of its chief occupant: to lead a government with a vitality equal to the nation's. Roosevelt soon changed its official name to the White House, and by summer, he and Edith had selected Charles McKim, the architect who designed Columbia University, to renovate it.

Roosevelt settled into a routine. He ate breakfast with his family and lunch with Edith and several guests, often invited at the last minute. Congressmen and cabinet members who had come on appointment, friends who were in town, the academics, writers, reformers, labor leaders, occasional businessman, explorers, and big game hunters whom he invited to visit—they all waited as the table was configured to fit everyone. Dinner invitations were only slightly more formal.

Among his early guests was Booker T. Washington, the head of the Tuskegee Institute and the first African American man to be invited to dine at the White House. Roosevelt wanted to talk about political appointments in the South and the black vote; the next day Southern racists were so enraged some called for his impeachment. Nothing came of it, but Roosevelt didn't extend another dinner invitation to Washington.

Evenings included Roosevelt's sort of family time. "I play bear with the children almost every night, and some child is invariably fearfully damaged in the play; but this does not seem to affect the ardor of their enjoyment," the president wrote to Alice, who was about to make her society debut and was often with friends in New York.

Roosevelt consumed nearly a gallon of sweetened coffee a day along with generous portions of plainly prepared food: chicken, fish, or a chop, soup, biscuits with currants called Fat Rascals. "The Roosevelts lived in middle-class simplicity," one regular guest said. The household was boisterous, and Roosevelt—caffeinated, exclaiming, often completing others' sentences—was the most animated of them all. He commanded the table and the room. Roosevelt said that his entire salary, a substantial fifty thousand dollars a year, went to funding their social life, which otherwise wasn't provided for in any White House budget. He relied on Edith to figure out how to make all the ends meet.

Most mornings, he dispatched with dozens of visitors in the reception room near his second-floor office. He gave each a handshake, a welcome, and an abrupt reminder to skip any formalities. No compliments, either, or they'd hear: "Never mind that. Come to the point." He responded in a loud voice to whispered requests he didn't want to honor or judgments he didn't think fair. If he had a spare moment, he turned to a book.

In the late afternoons, he often went riding on Bleistein. He named the horse for the friend—a businessman in Buffalo and fellow member of the Mason Lodge—who responded to his request for a suitable mount. "I want him to be big and powerful . . . with good manners and afraid of

President Roosevelt with the cabinet he inherited, clockwise: Lyman Gage, Philander Knox, John Long, James Wilson, Ethan Hitchcock, Charles Smith, Elihu Root, and John Hay, November 16, 1901

nothing," Roosevelt wrote. "There must be no chance of his misbehaving himself, as the President must not take the position of 'broncho buster.'" When Edith joined him, they would make a show of driving in a carriage engraved with the presidential initials to the city's edge, where their horses were waiting. They galloped through the hills of Maryland and Virginia. When Roosevelt rode with friends, he followed a different protocol. They all mounted their horses at the side door of the White House. Roosevelt protested that he didn't need bodyguards during these afternoon excursions—he carried his own revolver—but the Secret Service, and Edith, eventually prevailed.

He took vigorous cross-country jaunts through Rock Creek Park with visiting dignitaries and friends. He ordered the White House lawn trimmed and a rolled dirt tennis court constructed outside the executive offices. He trained with wrestlers, boxers, and jujitsu masters and often shared amused accounts of his mishaps: swollen bruises, bloody gashes, sopping wet and muddy clothes, stiff and sore limbs.

"He has made a splendid impression on public opinion," said Secretary of State John Hay, calling him "a young fellow of infinite dash and originality." Roosevelt charged the presidency with a new velocity. The world was speeding up, and he was a man of his time.

ROOSEVELT'S PERSONAL BARBER arrived at the White House just before lunch, as he did most days, to give the president a shave. Roosevelt perched in a straight-backed armchair, a Tiffany lamp next to him, in a small room between his office and that of his secretary. With shaving cream on his face and a razor close, he often gossiped with journalists or held informal, off-the-record press conferences. Sometimes he dictated letters. Rarely did he keep still.

This particular afternoon he was preoccupied, alone, quiet. It was Wednesday, November 13, 1901. Pierpont Morgan had just announced that the controversial takeover fight for the Northern Pacific had been settled. He didn't say how, not yet. But if Morgan revealed that a business dispute had ended in a deal, that usually meant it had gone according to his instructions.

Roosevelt and the nation learned the details of that deal hours later: a four-hundred-million-dollar railroad colossus called Northern Securities.

Now it seemed as if a small group of the very wealthy, concentrated in the precincts of Wall Street, could issue decrees and determine the destinies of the most important parts of the nation's economy. They pulled the strings, everyone else jumped. Americans were skeptical of these men, discontent with these vast rearrangements, and felt unable to stop them.

Roosevelt said nothing. But after his shave on that November day he ate lunch with his attorney general, Philander Chase Knox.

Roosevelt showed Knox the just-finished draft of his first state of the union speech. His predecessors had relied on cabinet members to write passages that did little but recount accomplishments. He intended to use this address to set the agenda for his unexpected presidency. A clerk would read his words, all twenty thousand of them, to Congress on Tuesday, December 3. An anxious nation waited.

In the early weeks of autumn, Roosevelt had devoted much of his time to writing the address, especially the language describing the central economic concern of the moment—the shadowy power of industrialists and bankers who were accumulating wealth at astounding rates with little government supervision.

Roosevelt wanted to assert Washington's supremacy over this secretive system and assure those venturing to find their places in the modern economy that he would be their champion. He needed to carefully calibrate his tone to appeal to progressives and conservatives. He wanted to arouse confidence and understanding, not suspicion or antagonism. He hoped for mutual agreement that the country required new rules for a new century: that the government must be able to regulate businesses, hold businessmen to account, and promise to be fair. Roosevelt had to mediate between the assumptions of the past and the hopes for the future. He had to consider his principles and the circumstances. Most of all, he had to strive for the possible.

Allies, supporters, Republican leaders, and Wall Street and railroad executives all sought to influence Roosevelt in the first months of his presidency. He didn't turn anyone away. In every job Roosevelt had held, he had gathered information and opinion, sought preapproval when he could. Hanna had known only of Roosevelt's swagger, not his hard practicality. Now Hanna thought he saw something fresh and promising in Roosevelt's method— an indication of maturity and pliability. "President Roosevelt is a different man than he was a few weeks ago," the senator declared to the *New York Times*. "The new and great responsibilities that have been so suddenly thrust upon his shoulders have given him equipoise and conservatism . . . I believe that he will live up to the expectations of his dearest friends."

Among the first of those dearest friends to visit Roosevelt in October happened to be emissaries from the House of Morgan. George Perkins, slick, energetic, and charming, and Roosevelt's classmate from Harvard, Robert Bacon (in his last weeks on the job before his escape to Europe) arrived with a message: Leave business matters to the businessmen. Perkins and Bacon counseled the president to "sit back in the harness." Great combinations of business and wealth perturbed the nation, but Perkins said

Roosevelt need only offer platitudes. Before long both Perkins and Bacon would have seats on the board of the newest of those perturbations, Northern Securities.

After they left, Roosevelt wrote to his brother-in-law Douglas Robinson. Although Roosevelt was fond of Bacon and Perkins, they were nonetheless, "arguing like attorneys for a bad case, and at the bottom of their hearts each would know this . . . if he were not the representative of a man so strong and dominant a character as Pierpont Morgan."

Transparency was the first order of business. Roosevelt wanted the government to have the right to inspect the workings of big companies. "Knowledge of the facts—publicity," then regulation through federal legislation. Perkins argued that Morgan's companies were already voluntarily disclosing their earnings and losses. Perkins wants us to "accept the publication of what some particular company chooses to publish, as a favor, instead of demanding what we think ought to be published from all companies as a right," Roosevelt wrote to Robinson.

Soon after, Roosevelt also found himself in the company of two of the railroad tycoons most personally involved in the May panic. James Hill invited himself to dinner on November 1, ostensibly to discuss his railroads' value in the West. At eleven, he, Roosevelt, and Secretary of State Hay were still talking. The president himself contacted Harriman, whom he had known for years. Harriman was a Republican campaign donor with a particular interest in New York state politics. On November 12, the day before Harriman, Hill, and Morgan announced the formation of Northern Securities, Roosevelt wrote to Harriman, thanking him for sending the first volume of a scientific exploration of Alaska's coast that he had funded. Roosevelt also took the opportunity to invite Harriman to dinner in Washington to "talk over various matters." Harriman didn't take the president up on the offer right away.

In the speech he was still busily revising, Roosevelt called the railroads a "public servant," obliged to serve all customers fairly. But he said he would leave it up to Congress to determine the precise means of regulating rates.

Hanna read his copy of the president's message in New York, where he was staying at the Waldorf-Astoria. Hanna replied with a handwritten four-page letter that began, "I have been thinking (hard) about that portion of your message regarding 'Trusts.'"

In addition to Hanna's jobs as senator and industrialist, he also served as the first president of the National Civic Federation, a group of business and labor leaders who believed in the right of workers to organize but wanted to soften what they considered the unions' rough tactics. Hanna argued for inaction on their behalf. "We can hold our power in politics as long as we can retain the confidence of this element," he wrote of union members. "They are not worried over the 'Trusts' question and I do not believe they want to see it made a political issue."

Hanna believed that industrial efficiency required regulatory guarantees and the consolidation of power and resources. Protecting the right of workers to organize also meant protecting the right of capital to organize. (The courts held the inverse to be true: if trusts could be prosecuted under the Sherman Act, then unions could be too.) Big Labor was inextricably linked to Big Business, and Hanna was for both. But he failed to convince Roosevelt.

Hanna, like his friend Perkins, was also concerned about Roosevelt's demand that companies disclose financial information to the government. "The inquisition feature is most objectionable," he wrote at the end of his letter. "I see dynamite in it." Roosevelt kept that feature in.

During his final weeks of preparation, Roosevelt also read the speech to members of his cabinet and sent sections of it to newspaper editors. Many warned the president that what they saw as government interference in the conduct of business could endanger America's expanding affluence. "You have no conception of the revolt that would be caused if I did nothing," Roosevelt replied to Paul Dana, the conservative editor of the *New York Sun*. "The message has been prepared in collaboration with Knox, I have gone over it carefully with Root and have submitted it to the most influential Senators and to at least a dozen prominent businessmen. I am very sorry to disagree with you."

KNOX AND ROOT—ELIHU Root, the secretary of war—were Roosevelt's closest advisers in his inherited cabinet. Roosevelt liked them, trusted them, but didn't always rely on them. They were corporate attorneys: Knox was intimately familiar with the most formidable industrialists of the time;

Root, with the financiers. They would serve their new client. But they would test the scope of the country's trust laws only if he asked.

Knox was just five and a half feet tall, clean-shaven and well appointed. When he first arrived from Pittsburgh in the spring of 1901 to serve in McKinley's cabinet, reporters in the capital noted how fine his horses were and how beautifully he dressed, down to the pearls in his cuffs. His habit of seesawing back and forth on his toes seemed to hint at some hesitation, and the droop of his eyelids suggested a certain lassitude. Critics dubbed him

Attorney General Philander Knox, circa 1902

Sleepy Phil, but in fact Knox was alert, confident, quick-stepping, charged with energy. When he argued in court, he was precise, unemotional. "One of our more highly finished domestic products," as a journalist described him.

Knox had come to the late President McKinley's attention as a student. In 1870, McKinley was a county prosecutor in Ohio and college debate judge. Knox was a champion debater. McKinley was impressed enough to offer him career advice: become a lawyer. Knox, already planning to do just that, went on to become among the best-known and best-paid attorneys in Pittsburgh. His practice was so lucrative that he turned down McKinley's first offer to become attorney general in 1897. Pittsburgh by then was gathering its industrial might, powered by steel, controlled by Andrew Carnegie, his right-hand man, Henry Clay Frick, and the banker Andrew Mellon. All three were Knox's clients.

Knox occupied a comfortable position among the city's elite. When Mellon and Frick were interested in buying a controlling stake in the Pittsburgh National Bank of Commerce in 1881, Knox helped. He was not just their lawyer, he was also one of the bank's directors. When Mellon organized the Union Trust Company, he put Frick and Knox on the board. Knox joined Frick's regular Thursday night poker game and an exclusive hunting club outside Johnstown, Pennsylvania. Knox's professional expertise would soon be called on by some of the club's members.

Sixteen of them had built cottages in the woods around an unused reservoir with a dam. The club modified the structure and was supposed to maintain it, but in 1889, after torrential rains, the dam broke, flooding the town below and killing more than two thousand residents. The Red Cross led the relief effort in Johnstown. Knox defended his friends against claims from the flood's survivors, arguing that the dam's collapse was an act of God. An engineers' report concluded negligence. But no judge or jury held anyone responsible or awarded the survivors any compensation. Some families received donations from club members. Carnegie built a new library in the town. No one there thought any of that was enough.

Knox would have other occasions to fight on behalf of these magnates. Early in the summer of 1892, as Knox was administering the merger of several firms into Carnegie Steel and Carnegie himself was vacationing in Scotland, Frick built a fence three miles long and twelve feet high around the Homestead Steel Works. He topped the fence with barbed wire and cut out holes for rifles. On June 29, he locked out the thirty-eight hundred workers after their union refused to accept proposed wage cuts. Frick claimed that a slowing economy and falling prices made the reductions necessary. He was also eager to crush a labor organization that he considered too sure of itself. When the workers still wouldn't accept lower wages, he fired them all.

The men surrounded the idled mill and sealed off the town of Homestead, established by Carnegie along a bend of the south bank of the Monongahela River, about six miles upstream from Pittsburgh. The town and the mill had prospered together; conflicts had been negotiated, compromises made. Frick wasn't interested in conducting business that way.

He secretly hired three hundred armed guards from Pinkerton's, the private police force that provided intelligence to the Union Army and, afterward, muscle to companies that wanted to break strikes. The agency told the guards their assignment wasn't dangerous. They would be protecting property. They didn't need to know where. They were also, thanks to Knox's efforts, supposed to be operating under the auspices of the county sheriff once they arrived. The sheriff had ordered the workers to give up their protest outside the mill, and when they didn't he counted on the Pinkertons to enforce his command. The Pinkertons arrived by riverboat in the early morning darkness of July 6. The steelworkers were prepared to repel anyone who tried to enter Homestead without their permission. Thousands of men, women, and children from the town—armed with bricks, clubs, shotguns, revolvers and Civil War muskets—joined them on the riverbank. Someone fired a first shot. The Pinkertons and the Homesteaders plunged into a battle: Sharpshooters on the barges. Men barricaded on land. Bullets, scrap metal, and cannon balls flying in the smoke and powder. By the end of the day, seven steelworkers and three guards had died. The wearied and fearful Pinkertons raised a white flag. They were marched through the town—harassed, threatened, poked and prodded along the way—until they reached the Opera House, where they were held until they could safely depart the area by train. The townspeople burned their barges.

Frick did not surrender, though. He prevailed on the governor to call in eighty-five hundred National Guardsmen—armed with the latest rifles and two Gatling guns—to retake the town and mill and protect strikebreakers. The troops remained in Homestead for three months.

On July 23, Frick returned to his office in Pittsburgh after lunch with a friend. Alexander Berkman, a stern and single-minded anarchist, was waiting. Berkman wore a new gray suit, purchased with funds from his sometime lover, Emma Goldman. He posed as the head of a New York employment agency eager to supply Frick with strikebreakers.

As soon as Berkman was admitted in, he drew a revolver, and fired three shots. The first two hit Frick's neck and lodged in his shoulders, one bullet on the right, the other on the left. A colleague in the room grabbed Berkman's wrist as he fired again. That bullet hit the ceiling. Frick, bloody and stunned, helped knock his assailant to the ground. Berkman managed to pull from his pocket a handmade dagger with a twelve-inch blade and gash Frick's legs. It took a blow to the head with a hammer and a gun aimed at him before Berkman gave up. Frick survived the assassination attempt. Berkman, twenty-one years old, was found guilty of attempted murder and sentenced to twenty-two years in prison.

In late November, the steelworkers called off the strike and returned to the mill on the company's terms. Their leaders were blacklisted. Carnegie Steel eliminated five hundred jobs, cut wages, and imposed twelve-hour workdays.

Knox argued that the rioting strikers could be prosecuted for treason because they had violently resisted the sheriff's orders. "This case will attract as much, if not more interest, than did the famous trial of Aaron Burr," Knox said after filing charges. "The [union's advisory] committee took the law in their own hands, ignoring the government of the state. We think this constitutes treason." The court thought otherwise, and no indictments were brought against the workers.

In 1901, the businessmen and financiers who benefited from Knox's exertions again eagerly supported his nomination as attorney general. Carnegie and Frick both took credit for it. Carnegie described Knox as a "veritable little giant." Labor groups opposed Knox's candidacy almost as vigorously, but Knox explained that in helping to break the Homestead strike he was simply acting on behalf of his client. That client went on to sell his company to Pierpont Morgan, who turned it into U.S. Steel in March 1901. By April Knox had another client, the president.

McKinley didn't test the skills of his attorney general. In his nomination acceptance speech, McKinley included a passage about trusts carefully written by Hanna. Trusts are "dangerous conspiracies against the public good and should be made the subject of prohibitory or penal legislation," McKinley said, believing that voters, generally satisfied with a growing economy, would wait for appropriately measured, likely ineffective legislation. But McKinley never proposed any legislation. He didn't bring any antitrust cases. He and Knox seemed content to wait until some egregious illegality forced them to act, confident they would win. The *New York Evening World* described the attorney general as a "distinguished practitioner" of "trust lawlessness."

Five months later, Knox was working for a new president he didn't really know and wasn't sure he could trust. But in spite of everything, the forty-eight-year-old Knox (the cabinet's youngest member) quickly fell in with the even younger Roosevelt. They often rode together on the forested paths winding through Rock Creek Park. Knox liked fast horses as much as Roosevelt did. The president called his attorney general his "playmate." Knox also became Roosevelt's dispassionate confederate in the fight to make the domineering businessmen the lawyer once worked for—and still admired—yield to the government he now served. He would enforce the laws to benefit his client just as before he had tried to bend them. Knox was always eager to demonstrate his ingenuity.

Secretary of War Elihu Root, circa 1902

Root was already one of Roosevelt's trusted advisers. As a lawyer in New York, he had represented and vouched for Roosevelt during his campaigns for mayor and governor. In 1898, the press raised legitimate questions about Roosevelt's eligibility to run since he had been residing in Washington. Root answered with enough force to help Roosevelt secure the nomination.

Root provided the same service to New York publishers and the state and city governments, as well as the Sugar Trust, the Lead Trust, the Whiskey Trust, the Watch Trust, the Rockefellers' Standard Oil Company, and at least six railroad companies.

McKinley appointed Root as secretary of war with a mandate to curtail the corruption and inefficiencies, jealousies and spite, that weakened the department during the Spanish-American War. Root was also supposed to improve the department's colonial administration of the Philippines and Cuba. After his first day in Washington, in July 1899, he wrote to a friend: "I feel like a cat just about to walk along a wall with broken bottles on the top." Roosevelt himself would gladly have undertaken the assignment, but McKinley never offered it to him.

Root was fourteen years older than Roosevelt and kept an almost paternalistic eye on him in the White House. Root was athletic and witty. He loved good horses and cigars. He and Roosevelt shared meals, afternoon rides, and some of the same friends, but none of the same opponents. Root was a problem solver; his was an ordered, impersonal mind. To him, inequity was a matter of math, and changing the formula demanded the utmost precision. He didn't think Roosevelt was the one who should try. Roosevelt said that when dealing with the trusts, he used Knox as the driving force and Root as the brake.

THE FIFTY-SEVENTH CONGRESS—REPUBLICAN-CONTROLLED, with four newcomers in the Senate and none the press deemed noteworthy in the House—opened on Monday, December 2. Many found extravagant flower arrangements on their desks, tributes from constituents, maybe reminders from donors, and most asked that the bouquets be removed and brought to their homes. The new senator from South Dakota received an arrangement so large it took two men to carry it in and then, presumably, out again. The room had been redecorated in their nine months' absence: the new carpet was green with gold figures; the desks were replaced, the chairs reupholstered. Families and visitors mingled, roll call was taken, and then Congress adjourned until it was time to hear the president's message.

A cold rainstorm blew through Washington the next morning but nearly every seat in the congressional chambers and the public galleries was filled. Just after noon, Octavius Pruden, the president's assistant secretary, pulled up at the House in a monogrammed carriage carrying Roosevelt's speech—eighty pages, silk-lined, bound in brown morocco, gold-stamped "Message in Congress." Roosevelt insisted the speech be printed rather than handwritten. He wanted the text available so that everyone listening could easily follow along, which they did, and so that it could be sent in advance to editors around the country and in Europe who would report on it right away, which they did.

The clerk of the House took his place behind a mahogany desk. In a voice purposely devoid of emotion, he began reading aloud. The first sentence, bold and direct, caused a stir: "The Congress assembles this year in the shadow of a great calamity." McKinley's speeches had been stilted; Roosevelt knew how to grab attention. In that first section, he gave tribute to McKinley. "The blow was not aimed at tyranny or wealth. It was aimed at one of the strongest champions the wage-worker has ever had,"

Roosevelt said. "His one anxiety in every crisis was to keep in closest touch with the people—to find out what they thought and to endeavor to give expression to their thought, after having endeavored to guide that thought aright."

Roosevelt condemned the assassin and his creed. "Anarchy is no more an expression of 'social discontent' than picking pockets or wife-beating," he said. "For the anarchist himself, whether he preaches or practices his doctrines, we need not have one particle more concern than for any ordinary murderer. He is not the victim of social or political injustice. There are no wrongs to remedy in his case."

The speech, more than two hours long, required several clerks in the House and Senate to take turns reading. Few of the men and women who had secured seats in the galleries walked out for a smoke or a snack. The audience listened and learned Roosevelt's rhythms—a rebuke to business, a warning to labor, a promise, a caution, balance. Here was a president who trusted his instincts, had called mere money-getting Americans curses to the country, and called himself a practical man—who dined with Morgan, who conferred with Hanna—laying out his governing philosophy about American capitalism. He sought a narrow rail.

America's new wealth wouldn't have been possible without big business, Roosevelt said, but now was the time to control those corporations benefiting only a privileged few. "The captains of industry who have driven the railway systems across this continent, who have built up our commerce, who have developed our manufactures, have on the whole done great good to our people," he said. America was becoming a global power, citizens were enjoying a better standard of living than they ever had. No president would jeopardize that.

Roosevelt encouraged Americans not to begrudge business success or envy the moneyed class, even as he conceded that the economy's boons and burdens were shared unequally. In prosperous times some would accumulate more and in times of adversity some would suffer more: "The capitalist may be shorn of his luxuries; but the wage-worker may be deprived of even bare necessities."

He heard the American people's cries that the giant corporations seemed above the law, too big to be restrained, too powerful to be punished. Should they be prohibited altogether? Roosevelt said Americans were too sensible to want that. Instead, they believed that combinations should be "supervised and within reasonable limits controlled." He did, too.

Many farmers, laborers, and entrepreneurs who once regarded Washington's power with suspicion, if not fear, now appealed to the national government as the only authority that could control the combinations taking hold of the economy. "Great corporations exist only because they are created and safeguarded by our institutions; and it is therefore our right and our duty to see that they work in harmony with these institutions," Roosevelt said.

"The old laws, and the old customs which had almost the binding force of law, were once quite sufficient to regulate the accumulation and distribution of wealth," Roosevelt said. "Since the industrial changes which have so enormously increased the productive power of mankind, they are no longer sufficient."

The national government should assume the power of regulation and supervision over the trusts, he said. "It has in practice proved impossible to get adequate regulation through State action." Trusts didn't confine their business to a single state. They operated across boundaries, and often they didn't operate at all in the state where they were chartered. Washington had to step in.

Roosevelt promised the government would be rational, practical, and resolute. Its rules would be uniform. He even said "it is probable that supervision of corporations by the National Government need not go as far as is now the case with supervision exercised over them by so conservative a State as Massachusetts, in order to produce excellent results."

The government would begin by requiring companies to disclose financial information usually kept private. Roosevelt urged Congress to create a Department of Commerce and Industries, led by a cabinet secretary, and within it a Bureau of Corporations to take on these new responsibilities. "Publicity is the only sure remedy which we can now invoke."

Roosevelt turned his attention from capital to labor. "If the farmer and wage-worker are well off, it is absolutely certain that all others will be well off too," he said. He called on the government to offer eight-hour workdays to its employees and for all government contractors to ensure work was done under fair conditions. He supported the law excluding Chinese laborers—they were willing to work too cheaply, he said—and proposed changing broader immigration laws to require "proper proof of personal capacity to earn an American living and enough money to insure a decent start under American conditions." He hoped to decrease the competition for jobs that gave rise to so much bitterness in American industrial life and to "dry up the pestilential social conditions" in the cities. He didn't, however, suggest that employers pay decent wages.

But in tone and substance Roosevelt's speech was, as one paper, noted "more devoted to business and fruitful, practical suggestions on every-day affairs than we have ever seen in a President's message." Roosevelt promised the working class, and signaled to big business, that the government would not be a spectator in the new economy.

The audience in the gallery cheered. Roosevelt, in the family's quarters at the White House, clapped when he learned of the response. Investors, reacting only to Roosevelt's praise of industrialization and already familiar with his plans to seek more disclosure, sent the stock market soaring. Some of their Republican allies in the Senate admitted that "the young and supposedly impetuous President had discussed the trust question with rare discrimination," reported the *Chicago Daily Tribune*. Which is why others among the Democrats would have preferred that he "had dipped his pen in vitriol before he started to write about the trusts."

In all of his twenty thousand words, the president hadn't once mentioned Northern Securities or referred to the Sherman Antitrust Act.

One paper described the president's moderated approach as "conservative and yet progressive, constructive and not destructive," and the message as like Roosevelt himself: "thoughtful, vigorous, well written and markedly individual."

That evening, Roosevelt hosted a celebratory dinner for the Republican leadership, who nonetheless remained uneasy about what their young, publicity-seeking president might do.

Afterward, Roosevelt dispatched Knox to Florida, publicly ordering him to rest in the southern warmth—and privately instructing him to review recent business combinations to see if any defied the antitrust law. Knox was to tell no one, not even other officials, and especially not

Root. "This is not a Cabinet secret," the president said to his attorney general. Roosevelt didn't want to be dissuaded, and he didn't want to give Wall Street any warning, other than the traces of his public declarations so far.

Knox sent a telegram to the president from St. Augustine on December 11 about the case that would shake Wall Street and its sovereign power: "It is desirable that you and I should first determine some important points relative to scope of action. If you are to take legislative responsibility. All its bearings must be carefully considered. The intervening time is not being wasted. Am giving it constant consideration to the end that your wishes with which I am in full sympathy can be creditably executed."

CHAPTER 8

Rival Operators

P hilander Chase Knox emerged from seclusion on February 10, 1902. He had returned from his vacation in Florida still uncertain he could persuade the courts that Northern Securities had defied the law by its very existence. Roosevelt urged him to keep working until he could argue that it had. Knox promptly canceled all his appointments and retreated to his mansion on K Street.

Roosevelt promised Americans that the government—*his* government—could limit the dominion of business. Northern Securities seemed an ideal example. It comprised three lines and some eighteen thousand miles of track that stretched from Seattle to Chicago—routes cattlemen, farmers, and miners relied on, and businessmen, clerks, and politicians traveled on. The men at its head had put their own interests well above any public interest in May, producing a stock market panic, and then had done so again in November with Northern Securities' imperious founding. If Morgan, Hill, and Harriman expected "to profit by the governmental impotence," as Roosevelt put it, they were in for a shock.

Congress's initial attempt to oversee the railroads through the Interstate Commerce Commission was compromised from the start. The regulatory agency—the country's first—was created in 1887 because of the outrage over price fixing and political favoritism by the railroads. But the commission's decisions were subject to review by unsympathetic courts. When shippers complained about railroad rates, they had to be prepared for costly legal fights against some of the best attorneys in the country. "The Commission . . . is, or can be made, of great use to the railroads," Attorney General Richard Olney, a railroad lawyer himself, later said. "It satisfies the popular clamor for a government supervision of the railroads, at the same time that supervision is almost entirely nominal."

Olney—born in Massachusetts, educated at Brown and Harvard—had come to Grover Cleveland's attention as he considered a second campaign for president in 1892, and the only wonder was that they hadn't become acquainted earlier. Their country estates, at Buzzards Bay and Falmouth, were just a few miles apart. After Olney accepted Cleveland's offer to run the Department of Justice, he continued to give legal advice to the Burlington Railroad and receive a salary for it.

In 1895, the Supreme Court seemed to repudiate Congress's second attempt to limit big business, the Sherman Antitrust Act. The court refused to break up the holding company, incorporated in New Jersey, that controlled 98 percent of the country's sugar refineries. In the Knight case, as it came to be known, the court determined that the exchange of stock, and consolidation of competitors, used to create the Sugar Trust was legal under New Jersey law and that the government didn't have the right to regulate the manufacturing of local products—that, too, was the province of the states.

The trust, however, didn't confine its business to New Jersey. It sold sugar throughout the country and had a near complete hold on the supply. If he had been of a mind to, Olney could have advanced that argument before the Court. But he didn't make any claims for federal jurisdiction, having inherited a case that relied on a law he didn't think should be enforced against companies. He had, however, invoked the Sherman Act during the Pullman strike, claiming the railway union was a combination created to hinder trade. After the government's defeat in the Knight case, Olney wrote: "I have taken the responsibility of not prosecuting under a law I believed to be no good."

The lone voice of dissent on the Court belonged to John Marshall Harlan, a Republican from Kentucky, who was still on the bench in 1902. Knox studied Harlan's argument, hoping to incorporate it into his own.

Harlan argued that his fellow justices' narrow interpretation of the law was better suited to a preindustrial America where interstate commerce was naturally restricted by geography. Their reasoning left the federal government "in such a condition of helplessness that it must fold its arms and remain inactive while capital combines, under the name of a corporation, to destroy competition, not in one state only, but throughout the entire country." The only power that can protect the public from companies that want to control the production of such essentials as sugar, salt, flour, cotton, even oil, Harlan wrote, is national power.

Knox brought a fourteen-page typed document to the White House that Monday, February 10. He was ready to take on Northern Securities. "These views are submitted with a full appreciation of the startling consequences which would flow from their adoption by the courts and of the vigorous and possibly successful opposition with which they will be met," he wrote. "I see no reason, however, why the responsibility should not, in the present instance, be thrown upon the courts." The brief was coolly reasoned and sufficiently optimistic, and Knox was even more reassuring in person, telling the president, "If you instruct me to bring such a suit, I can promise you we shall win it."

BY THAT POINT, Knox was not the only one crafting a legal challenge to Northern Securities. In November, shortly after its creation was publicly announced, Governor Samuel Van Sant of Minnesota had declared that Northern Securities was an obvious violation of the state's antitrust law. "It should and will be a fight to the finish."

The state had assented to Hill's plan to combine the Great Northern and Northern Pacific five years earlier. Hill's ill-advised determination to test that merger in the Supreme Court had proved disastrous then; now suspicion of trusts had grown and the Great Northern's general counsel warned his boss not to aggravate the situation while Van Sant considered his options. The lawyer sent a coded cable to Hill that translated: Don't do anything rash.

Hill had expected the citizens and politicians in the Northwest to be grateful. He had built up the region, protected it from the predations of

Harriman, even sided with the most influential banker in the world. Yet now legislators talked about living under the yoke of capitalistic domination. Sold into commercial slavery. They said the merger silenced competition. That even if rates remained steady the mere possession of such power to control them was a menace to the country. "All I ask is fair play," Hill said. "Let time determine whether the public will be benefited or injured by what we have done and will continue to do."

Hill didn't wait. In December he, his son (his assistant at the company), and a Northern Pacific lawyer began a covert campaign to influence the press to support the Northern Securities merger. "You should spend Forty or Fifty or Seventy-five thousand, if necessary, to good advantage. Get this going as rapidly as you can," Hill told him. When those efforts proved ineffective, they considered sponsoring a challenger to Governor Van Sant. "Such a man could swing the papers better than the Railroads as the press would take more kindly to supporting a politician than backing a railroad." That didn't work either.

In early January, as Knox was reviewing antitrust law, the Minnesota attorney general applied to the Supreme Court to file a case of its own against Northern Securities. Knox reviewed those files too. If Minnesota won the right to bring a case directly to the Court, that would bolster the federal government's. If the state lost, as seemed more likely, then the federal government would have even greater reason to act. Washington—Roosevelt—would come to the defense of the aggrieved.

Hill spoke at a convention in Fargo a few days later. Three thousand farmers and ranchers gathered at the opera house gave him a standing ovation. They might oppose Northern Securities, but they still appreciated his resourcefulness. "Remember that whatever helps you helps the railroad, and whatever hurts you or restricts your growth, restricts the growth of the railroad serving you," he told them. "We will always prosper together or be poor together."

A FEROCIOUS STORM swept into New York City late on Monday night, February 17, 1902. The early evening was calm, and at nine the sky was still clear, but by midnight the wind was gusting. Snow came down in blinding clouds at four in the morning, and when New Yorkers began to wake a few hours later, nine inches of snow had already fallen. Giant drifts piled up and in some cases were flung against house walls, windows, and doors. Street cleaners struggled to keep up. Until the tempest subsided in the afternoon, streetcars were stalled, suburban trolleys were out of service, and trains were delayed.

Yet commerce in the city of three and a half million continued. Snow shovels—hardwood and steel-edged—were on sale for twenty-five cents. Men's fur gloves were going for $3.75, almost half price, at Siegel-Cooper, the six-floor department store downtown. Uptown, Bloomingdale's offered fifteen-dollar women's seal plush jackets for $8.90 on clearance and Persian lamb fur coats for thirty-nine dollars. Stores advertised American and German flags for those planning to celebrate George Washington's birthday and the arrival later in the week of the kaiser's representative, Prince Henry.

The New York Stock Exchange opened for business on time. Enough brokers showed up to work, and it turned out to be a pretty good day. Stock prices mostly went up. That was a noticeable improvement, the *New York Times* noted, after weeks of enforced inactivity as financial firms waited to see what Roosevelt might do about the trusts. Speculation in the stocks of the Sugar Trust and the Copper Trust contributed to the market's performance that day. The paper called their price rises manipulation, warning that "being equal mysteries, they are equally dangerous."

Morgan's U.S. Steel Company held its first annual shareholders' meeting that Monday, in an unpretentious room in an office in Hoboken, New Jersey. About forty people showed up, many of them newspaper reporters. As George Perkins promised Roosevelt, the company made a show of opening its financial records to any of its investors. A man who claimed ten shares said he'd like to "copy from the books," and was permitted to. "The most striking thing about the whole proceeding was the apparent openness of it all—the willingness of the management to reveal the inside workings of the trust," the *New York Times* reported. At the close of the meeting, the shareholders elected Morgan, Perkins, John D. Rockefeller, Henry Frick, and Marshall Field, among others, to the board of directors.

Morgan had been communicating with Charles Mellen, the president of the Northern Pacific, in secret for weeks. Mellen heard that, in the

governor's annual message that month, Van Sant planned to call for legislation of railroad rates. Mellen worried that the unpopularity of the
Northern Securities merger—and, he claimed, of James Hill himself—
made this more likely. "I assume you want success, or rather, in this
instance, immunity, and the method is not so important as the result,"
Mellen wrote from St. Paul. He had already spent five thousand dollars
on lobbyists. Now he told Morgan he would require "unlimited use of
money" to overcome both the resentment toward Hill and the states' tight-
ening control of the railroads. When pressed, Mellen said twenty-five
thousand dollars would be sufficient. While the governor seemed incorruptible, some on his staff might be more amenable to financial incentives.
"All right, do whatever is necessary," Morgan replied on the eighteenth.

Hill testified in a shareholder suit against Northern Securities that he
regarded as frivolous. He said he didn't mean to be evasive, but mostly he
was. Afterward, he sent a telegram to his wife, Mary, who was in New
York: "All well here. How are you?"

These were the last moments of the old order—protected, conniving,
banal. The presumptions of the nineteenth century were about to give way.

IN WASHINGTON, ROOSEVELT ate breakfast with Hanna that Tuesday
morning. "What do you think about the Northern Securities Company?"
the president asked. He didn't know that soon after the company came
into existence, Hanna invested in it. The senator had obtained some shares
from Hill, but he wanted more. "I am so on the outside that I don't get a
chance at such things while I am 'serving the Country,'" Hanna wrote to
Perkins. "I wish you would look 'a little out' for me." Perkins did. When
Roosevelt asked about Northern Securities, Hanna confidently said it was
the "best thing" for the Northwest.

Later that day, Hanna traveled by train to New York, and Roosevelt
held his weekly cabinet meeting at the White House. Knox didn't say a
word about Northern Securities when he updated his colleagues about his
department's work. Roosevelt didn't ask.

Morgan was at home the next evening, hosting a dinner for several
business associates. As the men took their places in the dining room,

Morgan was called to the telephone. A journalist shared some
unnerving news from Wash-
ington. The president had asked
his attorney general to prosecute
Northern Securities for violating
the Sherman Act. Morgan
returned to the table in a state of
"appalled dismay," a journalist
later recounted. Roosevelt should
have warned him, Morgan grumbled. They could have worked out
a deal in private.

Roosevelt at his desk in the White House, 1902

Presidents didn't keep secrets
from the captains of industry, and the House of Morgan had never before
been surprised by the White House. Morgan traded in confidences and negotiated on shared assumptions. He had considered Roosevelt a gentleman.
Now he called the president a "lunatic." Roosevelt had changed the rules on
the sly. For someone whose view of the world was as unvarying as Morgan's,
there was hardly a greater affront. Morgan would never forgive him.

The dinner at Madison Avenue ended abruptly. No one lingered in the
library and smoked expensive Cuban cigars. Morgan didn't play his usual
game of patience once the guests left. Consumed by indignation, he
conferred with his partners and attorneys in his grand study through the
night. Their meetings continued at 23 Wall Street the next day.

By then the official statement from Knox was public. It was brief,
lawyerly, bloodless. But it was enough. The attorney general believed that
Northern Securities should be dissolved. This was the first time since 1895
that the government had invoked the antitrust law against such a prominent company. As word filtered out from Washington, some in the financial district insisted the reporters must have it wrong.

Hanna got the news in the parlor car of a train returning him to the
capital. The messenger was John Griggs, McKinley's first attorney general.
Griggs had news of his own: He now represented Northern Securities.
Hanna was so shocked by Roosevelt's secrecy and bewildered by Knox's

willingness to bring charges that he couldn't say a word. He felt old. Secretary of State Hay was perturbed. When Roosevelt wasn't around, he called the Sherman Act "an idiotic law which had been wisely allowed to remain dormant." Root believed he had been betrayed. He expected Roosevelt to seek his counsel.

Lawyers for Northern Securities promised a long legal fight. "We do not propose to be made scapegoats of by President Roosevelt, Attorney-General Knox or anyone else," they said. "There are many other instances of existing mergers which have been entirely overlooked by the President. But they will all have to join us in this fight."

One Minnesota paper noted that railroad officials were angry about the lawsuit—and the more authority they wielded, the angrier they seemed. Railroad employees were more appreciative of the attempt to hold their bosses to account. Roosevelt defended "the interests of the people in whatever way they may be threatened," the editorial said. He also acted with due regard for his own reputation.

On February 19, James Hill was suddenly ill with a severe cold and confined to his bed, in his mansion overlooking the Mississippi River Valley. The next day, though, he was feeling well enough to accomplish a number of things. He wrote to an associate in London assuring him that if Northern Securities were somehow forced to dissolve, he and Morgan could still maintain control by selling shares to their friends. He wrote to Hanna that the political situation in the Northwest, particularly in his home state, was worrying and that he hoped to see the senator when he was in Washington the next week. And he threatened the president and attorney general that "if they do fight they will have their hands full, and will wish they had never been born before they get through." The president had some choice words for Hill, expressed privately. "He detests me, but I admire him," Roosevelt said. "He will detest me much more before I have done with him."

The men who traded, speculated, and shorted thousands of dollars of stocks, who measured success in hundreds of thousands and dreamed in millions were "dazed, incredulous and indignant." They described Roosevelt's attack as a "thunderbolt out of a clear sky," unreasonable, beyond comprehension, dangerous, theatrical. One broker was ready to bet a thousand dollars that Roosevelt wouldn't receive the nomination for the presidency in 1904. A banker close to Morgan's firm sneered: "The business of the country appears to be conducted in Washington now."

When the gong sounded to open trading on the New York Stock Exchange on Thursday, February 20, brokers scrambled to sell shares, especially in railroad companies. It was the busiest first hour of the year. "Not since the assassination of President McKinley has the stock market had such a sudden and severe shock," noted the *New York Tribune*. One investor complained to the attorney general about his potential losses. "There is no stock ticker in the Department of Justice," Knox replied. By midmorning, Morgan & Co. was buying stock in Northern Securities— which hadn't yet been admitted into the exchange but was being traded in the "curb market"—to keep the price up and prevent brokers and investors from panicking. It kept close watch on the exchange of U.S. Steel's shares, too.

In Washington, in the waning light of late afternoon, Knox and Roosevelt went for a two-hour ride in Knox's carriage, drawn by two of his finest horses.

MORGAN DISPATCHED PERKINS, his "secretary of state," to meet with the president in Washington on Friday, February 21. His brief: to reason with Roosevelt. As improbable as it seemed to most everyone else who knew the president, inside the House of Morgan there was hope that they might still have time to reestablish the old order. Knox had announced he would file a lawsuit, but he hadn't yet done so. Maybe Perkins and Roosevelt could come up with alternatives to the prosecution of Northern Securities. Maybe they could strike some kind of deal. Maybe Roosevelt would back down.

It was a short conversation.

That evening, Perkins met Hanna at the hotel where they were both staying. The Arlington was then the most elegant and exclusive in Washington, located down the block from the White House. Perkins asked him why he hadn't warned anyone at the firm about the possibility of a lawsuit. How could he, Hanna replied, since he had no warning himself. Then it was Perkins who was perplexed. During their discussion, Roosevelt told

Perkins that he had "consulted" Hanna the day before the announcement. Hanna probably gave more thought to how much he ate for breakfast that morning than how to respond to the casual question about Northern Securities. "I'm sorry for Hill," Hanna said, "but just what do you gentlemen think I can do?"

Morgan, who was due at the White House Monday evening for a state dinner in honor of the German prince, decided to confront the president directly. He and six associates arrived in the capital in a private train on Saturday. Ice, sleet, and slush had slowed their journey, and they were "in an ulcerated state of inflammation," noted Henry Adams, who knew the Wall Street men well. They, too, headed to the Arlington. Morgan was an investor in the hotel and kept a suite of rooms there designed according to his specifications.

Dinner was at the Corcoran House, the grand palazzo on Lafayette Square, the most fashionable blocks in Washington, with views of the White House. Morgan's host was Chauncey Depew, the senator from New York who had been president of the New York Central Railroad and still served on the boards of some fifty transportation companies. Like many in Congress, he was renting.

The guests were members of Morgan's informal cabinet, the "Corsair Club." Members discussed anything other than the businesses that made them so wealthy, Depew explained to a reporter. The only other rule: never reveal anything more than that.

The Corsairs sat at a great square table in the oak-paneled dining room. Two months earlier, Depew had organized a bachelor party for himself in the same room, and Roosevelt was among those who had celebrated with the senator. But now the "whole party was black," Adams wrote, and Morgan was in a mood.

At ten o'clock, the phone rang. It was the president. He asked the thirteen men to come to the White House. No one could refuse such an invitation, but still they had to cajole Morgan into going. As snow fell, they traveled the few blocks to the White House in cars and carriages and entered the otherwise quiet mansion. Roosevelt greeted them formally, and they responded with chilly politeness. Among them were two senators, the secretary of war, and William Rockefeller. They were the establishment, barbed with privilege, unused to being challenged, uncomfortable being summoned. They had all watched Roosevelt rise—Morgan and Rockefeller had even helped fund some of his political campaigns. None had suspected that he would move against them so suddenly. Hanna and Root believed they had successfully convinced the new president not to.

The gathering lasted an hour and it seems that no one mentioned the lawsuit on everyone's mind or acknowledged the obvious tension between the irrepressible president and their ill-tempered commodore. Everyone knew their relationship was, at best, one of utility. They could cooperate when necessary; otherwise, they could avoid one another. Roosevelt wrote he'd rather have a political career that "ended with a failure than the career of Pierpont Morgan," and the thought of spending the day on a yacht with him or any of the other New York money men filled Roosevelt "with frank horror"—not that any had extended an invitation. Morgan was no more eager to spend the day with Roosevelt. They didn't have to like each other. But they had never clashed openly. Now the president had struck the king of Wall Street with "an awful blow square in the face."

As Depew left the White House with his dinner guests, a reporter asked if they had discussed Northern Securities. "No. Not a word of it," he said. "It was a social call."

The next morning, Morgan returned to the White House, a somber figure amid Washington residents enjoying the first bright sun in weeks. Morgan, cold-eyed, fierce, peremptory, still expected to convince Roosevelt to back down. When he met the president, Knox was by his side. As soon as they had taken their seats, Morgan began to speak. He demanded to know why Roosevelt hadn't warned him.

"This is just what we did not want to do," said Roosevelt.

"If we have done anything wrong," Morgan replied, "send your man to my man and they can fix it up."

Commodore Morgan, circa 1890s

"That can't be done."

"We don't want to fix it up," Knox interjected. "We want to stop it."

"Are you going to attack my other interests, the Steel Trust and the others?"

"Certainly not," said Roosevelt, "unless we find out that in any case they have done something that we regard as wrong."

After Morgan left, Roosevelt marveled at the financier's impudence. "That is the most illuminating illustration of the Wall Street point of view," he said to Knox. "Mr. Morgan could not help regarding me as a big rival operator, who either intended to ruin all his interests or else could be induced to come to an agreement to ruin none." "Theodore laughs at Pierpont," Adams wrote, "and Pierpont acts like a sulky child."

Morgan was fuming when he returned to his hotel suite. He composed an indignant, threatening letter to Roosevelt, but his lawyer persuaded him not to send it. No one, though, would be able to convince Morgan that "Roosevelt was anything other than a double-faced demagogue," a friend wrote. Those close to him who believed otherwise learned to avoid mentioning the president's name at all.

The Supreme Court signaled the next morning that it had come to a decision about Minnesota's antimonopoly lawsuit against Northern Securities. Morgan entered the north wing of the Capitol (where the Court sat before it had a building of its own) and walked into the chambers as the session was already under way. He took a seat, reserved for lawyers, in the front. Directly across from him were the nine judges. As both Knox and Morgan's own attorneys had expected, the Court declined to consider the case for lack of jurisdiction and sent it back to the Minnesota court: a brief victory for Morgan.

Washington's attention turned to the visit of Prince Henry. He was in the United States to receive and launch the emperor's racing schooner, the *Meteor III*, and to present a friendlier image to the new administration than his more bellicose brother could. That evening the Roosevelts would host their first state dinner. Theodore and Edith—as well as Alice, who would christen the *Meteor*—prepared for more than a month for the occasion.

Earlier in February, Roosevelt had written to Nicholas Murray Butler, the president of Columbia University, about the prince's visit. Roosevelt told him that in order to avoid upsetting any of their business friends—by choosing one over the other "as the big representative man of New York" for the banquet—he had selected the only person no one would complain about: Pierpont Morgan.

Morgan had accepted the offer. Now, in a fit of pique after the Northern Securities lawsuit was announced, he wanted to decline the dinner invitation. But he grudgingly attended. The seventy guests—men only, and among them Adolphus Busch, the millionaire St. Louis brewer, as well as Knox, Root, and Hanna—gathered just before eight in the East Room. Edith had supervised the decorations. The chandeliers were entwined with Southern smilax, and strands of it hung from the ceilings, braided with strings of electric lights. Silver candelabra with pink shades lit the table. The Marine band played "Hands Across the Sea" by John Philip Sousa and a selection from Richard Wagner's "Grand Fantasia." The meal began with oysters on the half-shell and Baltimore terrapin and ended with ice cream. At ten, Roosevelt led his guests to the Red Room for coffee, beer, and cigars.

Two days later, Morgan was back in New York, hosting a lunch at Sherry's Restaurant for the prince and more than a hundred of the city's business leaders. At the end of the hour-long meal, he rose from his seat next to the guest of honor to offer four toasts. The first was to President Roosevelt. Everyone stood and drank in silence.

"I AM A little concerned over some of the things I hear from New York," Roosevelt wrote to the editor of the *Sun* in early March. "It is very important we should not lose this fall." Roosevelt was referring to the midterm elections and had underlined the word "very." His attack on the trusts brought him all manner of compliments and unequivocal promises of support—except from his home state of New York, where, Roosevelt feared, Wall Street's influence exceeded Washington's.

In the weeks after Morgan and Perkins failed to dissuade the president from following through on his threat, the House of Morgan urged the White House to at least spare the financier the humiliation of being named in the lawsuit and called on to testify in public. Faith in Morgan, they said, was vital to the nation's financial standing. Roosevelt, with an eye on the upcoming elections, wavered. He asked Knox if it was necessary to include Morgan in the suit. "Well, Mr. President, if you direct me to leave his name out I will do it," the attorney general said. "But I want to say that in that case I will not sign my name to the bill."

Knox prepared the formal complaint against Northern Securities to be filed March 10. Morgan was named as one of the defendants.

At five that afternoon the United States District Attorney for Minnesota, Milton Dwight Purdy, walked into the Federal Court House in St. Paul carrying a stack of documents. Construction had just been completed and the formal opening was still weeks away. But the five-story, pink granite building—with turrets, gables, steeply peaked roofs and two towers—provided a dramatic setting that suited Knox and Roosevelt. Purdy climbed the four flights of marble stairs and presented the brief. At just that moment, word went out that the government had filed its lawsuit against Northern Securities. The city where Hill had lived for almost fifty years would be the first to hear of it, just as Knox had planned.

Knox's detailed complaint was printed in full in papers around the country, including in the *St. Paul Globe*, which featured it on the front page. "The Northern Securities Company was not organized in good faith," the petition stated. It was a conspiracy to restrain trade. Knox argued that if the government failed to prevent the combination of the Great Northern and Northern Pacific railroads, the holding company would have monopoly power, could destroy any competition, and would show how to circumvent the Sherman Act through this sort of "corporate scheme." Knox declared that "all transcontinental lines, indeed the entire railway systems of the country, may be absorbed, merged, and consolidated, thus placing the public at the absolute mercy of the holding corporation."

"It really seems hard," Hill wrote to a friend, "that we should be compelled to fight for our lives against the political adventurers who have never done anything but pose and draw a salary." He alone among Morgan's associates considered the attack on Northern Securities a personal insult. He had built the Great Northern, traveled the rails, monitored the trains, supervised the employees. Morgan maintained his control from a distance.

Hill had read the petition in New York, where he was supposed to attend a shareholder meeting. He didn't bother to suppress his fury. "When we get through with the charge against us its own father won't know it," he told a local reporter. *The Minneapolis Journal* reprinted the remarks with the headline JAMES J. SEEMS TO TALK MUCH MORE FREELY IN NEW YORK THAN IN MINNESOTA.

Morgan and his family left New York soon afterward, taking a private train to his private club on Jekyll Island. There he could be temporarily lulled by Gulf stream breezes, a semitropical climate, palmettos and magnolias, and the assurance that "no unwanted foot ever touched the island." It was a wonderful place to hide. Members hunted (deer, quail, and wild turkey), fished, and golfed, but Morgan usually smoked, talked with his friends, or played solitaire. A one-hundred-twenty-five-room clubhouse was the center of social life on the island. Next to it was what might have been the country's first condominium, called the Sans Souci; Morgan's apartment was on the third floor, William Rockefeller's on the second. Morgan didn't found the Jekyll Island Club, but after a few years it was said there were only three ways to gain admission: by marriage, inheritance, or ties to Morgan.

A private train brought the family to Washington on March 20. Morgan met Hanna for lunch, still hoping to find a way to settle his Northern Securities trouble. No luck. Instead, when he returned to New York, Morgan was served a subpoena to testify in another suit against the holding company. A messenger from the law firm called at No. 219 in the evening, sending word that he had a personal message from Morgan's own attorney, Francis Stetson. It was a ruse. "A very questionable expedient," Morgan's son-in-law, Satterlee, called the deception.

A disgruntled Northern Pacific shareholder named Peter Power had filed a complaint in Minnesota about the stock exchange plan Morgan and Hill had devised to create Northern Securities. Hill had offered few details when he testified in February. Morgan considered the suit more nuisance than threat, but Stetson believed the financier could provide testimony compelling enough to swing public opinion their way.

Morgan never gave speeches, only rarely made public toasts, and even less frequently spoke to journalists. The chance to hear him speak in the open, about one of his most controversial deals, drew so many people that the Circuit Court room in the Manhattan Post Office Building filled to capacity in minutes. The hearing, presided over by a special examiner appointed by the Minnesota court, was scheduled to begin at eleven thirty on Wednesday, March 26. Morgan arrived fifteen minutes late. As soon as he saw the photographers hovering around the table where he was supposed to sit, he asked that they be banned from the room altogether. The U.S. marshal had them escorted out.

Morgan answered questions for three hours, in a chair beside the table full of his lawyers. When he wasn't talking, he turned his back on them and looked out the window. At one point, when he couldn't provide even an estimate of how many Northern Pacific shareholders there were at the end of 1900, he assured George Lamb, the opposing attorney, that he wasn't trying to dodge the question. "There is nothing under heaven connected with the transaction that I know that I won't tell you," he said. "And I will tell you how to get the rest." That prompted laughter from everyone, including Morgan himself. When Lamb asked what Morgan's firm was paid for organizing a Northern Pacific stock deal, the financier replied, "Nothing whatever." Apparently sometimes "things had to be done for nothing." That also amused those in the room. As did Morgan's characterization of a transaction worth twenty-six million dollars as not such a big deal.

Morgan recounted his official history of Northern Securities, describing it as a way to maintain "moral control," not practical control, over the Great Northern and Northern Pacific. When Lamb suggested that because the two railroads together purchased a third (the Burlington) they would be less inclined to compete, Morgan replied: "Not necessarily." That too should have elicited a few surprised chuckles among the audience, but the papers didn't mention any. What did please Morgan, at least, was his own definition of a so-called community of interest: "That a certain number of men who own property can do what they like with it." And what they wanted to do was avoid profit-draining conflict. The free market meant freedom to cooperate and organize.

When Lamb asked again why Morgan wanted to form a holding company, he answered bluntly, heedless of the temper of the country. The convulsions of the May panic had been unsettling—to him. He noted only briefly the effect on ordinary investors. "I wanted it so that I could go to Europe and not hear the next day that somebody had bought it for the Boston and Maine, or I don't know what other company," he said. "There is no interest that I know of today that can control the Northern Securities Company." He argued that he and Hill and Harriman had not agreed to maintain rates or restrain competition. "It never entered my head," Morgan said. Yet it was definitely a possibility.

At the conclusion of his testimony, Morgan said he was leaving for Europe in a week and wouldn't be available to answer further questions. If any other subpoenas were coming his way, he asked to be served at his office, not his home.

The conflict between the House of Morgan and the White House, and the uncertain prospect of stricter regulation of one of the country's biggest industries, rattled investors. "Wall Street is in a desperate state of mind," Henry Adams wrote, adding that Morgan and Hanna insisted their allies in the cabinet, Root and Hay, remain there "until they have worked Roosevelt into a harness." Hanna himself complained that Roosevelt's actions hurt his company's business as a coal and iron ore broker. Customers hadn't placed a single order beyond November.

But the House of Morgan kept itself busy. In April, Perkins negotiated to buy stock in a rail line that ran parallel to one the firm already controlled and planned to create another holding company for the railroads. "The lawyers say there is absolutely nothing to prevent this being done," he wrote to Morgan.

By then Morgan had crossed the Atlantic on the White Star Line, and for the first time, he had ordered his yacht to sail over as well. When he arrived at Southampton, a private railway carriage brought him to London, where he began making deals to create an international shipping line. While he was in the city, he also hinted that he was interested in plans to extend its subway. On the street peddlers sold a "License to stay on the Earth," signed "J. Pierpont Morgan." The cost: a penny.

Roosevelt, too, was traveling. He and Edith had gone to South Carolina for another exposition, this time in Charleston. Their day began with a military parade from their hotel to the fairgrounds; thousands lined up along the route and crowded onto porches and at windows to see Roosevelt,

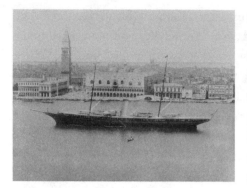

Morgan's yacht, Corsair, *in Venice*

a president from whom 90 percent of them differed politically. Another ten thousand were waiting for him in the auditorium. He dressed for the occasion, wearing what a local paper described as "a well-fitting Prince Albert, cut rather high in the neck and buttoned closely, showing only a small section of a turndown collar and a blue and white four in hand tie."

He spoke about the need for national supervision of the richest corporations as well as the most powerful labor unions. "Our astounding material prosperity, the sweep and rush rather than the mere march of our progressive material development, have brought grave troubles in their train," he said. And then, more forcefully than he had in his annual message, he argued the inequities couldn't be solved by the policies of the demagogue who raves against wealth and incites hatred. Or by following "those who fear to recognize injustice and to endeavor to cut it out because the task is difficult or even—if performed by unskilful hands—dangerous."

Then the Roosevelts walked through the 250-acre expanse, with its Woman's Building and "Negro" Building, its Cotton Palace, sunken garden, and race course. Marine guards, following the new protocol for presidential visits, closed the buildings to the public.

As Knox and his colleagues at the Justice Department began to prepare their case against Northern Securities, Roosevelt took every opportunity to present their side to the public and the press. In May, he wrote to Knox asking him to meet with a friend, the correspondent from the *Times* of London. "I want him to have a talk with you, because in New York he lives at the Metropolitan Club and meets largely the gentlemen who since the merger suit cross themselves at the mention of our names." On July 4, at a banquet hosted by Knox in his hometown of Pittsburgh, Roosevelt said that the country's new economic and social problems would be solved with legislation from the governments of the cities, states, and the nation—and that the laws must be upheld for each person, rich or poor, big or small, strong or weak. "The most important department of civilized government is the Department of Justice. Think what it means!"

At that very moment, two hundred fifty miles to the east in Pennsylvania's coal country, tens of thousands of miners were also demanding that the nation honor its commitment to justice even as the coal barons denied it. Their fight would become one of the greatest labor actions in American history, and would redefine Roosevelt's presidency in the months ahead.

PART II

CHAPTER 9

Anthracite

T ectonic plates collided, folded, and deformed the Appalachian region two hundred and fifty million years ago, and the Great Dying decimated primitive life: the end of the Paleozoic Era. Above were the Ridge-and-Valley mountains of northeastern Pennsylvania and, far beneath the surface, the metamorphosis of forested swamps into a dense, glinting, almost purely carbon rock: anthracite coal.

The men who mined the anthracite coal probably never knew this. They knew that natural forces twisted narrow veins of coal between thicker layers of rock and if they wanted to get at the coal they needed to create a force of their own.

They had to plunge into darkness—chilly, damp, echoless, coal-dusted darkness—until sometimes they were two thousand feet underground, below the water line, beyond anything familiar. Once at the bottom, they might have to walk three miles of tunnels, braced with creaking timber, home to colonies of rats, wide enough only for a mule and a cart to pass through, to reach the owner's subterranean "office." They'd hang their identification tags on a pegboard. That way their bosses would know where to look for them, just in case. They'd follow passageways that might be named Primrose or Peach Orchard into the chambers they'd been assigned. They'd take their time drilling holes into the rock and placing squibs—handmade, powder-filled fuses—inside. Then they'd set off an explosion.

Geology created the coal. Harmful vapors hid in the seams around it. Fire bosses checked the mines at five every morning, but chemistry could still surprise the men.

They probably couldn't identify the chain reactions that caused the accidents. But the miners knew that "firedamp" could be ignited by an exposed lamp wick or triggered by a spark from a pickax. "Blackdamp," in small amounts, caused suffocating dullness and numbness, and in large amounts death. They knew that "whitedamp" was odorless and impossible to detect and inhaling even a small amount could kill a miner. That's what the canaries were for.

They knew all the ways they could die. Mines could collapse, rocks could fall, water could rise. The dust and damp and explosive powder could turn their lungs black. They knew the whistle that signaled the start of work, and the one that signaled an end. In 1901, the warning whistle would blow three or four times a day in the three hundred forty-six mines that held almost all of the nation's anthracite. Twelve hundred men were injured that year and another five hundred miners died. The bodies were claimed by families who might or might not have set aside money to bury them, and only some employers might help. But if the miner had immigrated recently, alone, and hadn't made friends, the corpse would be donated to a medical school and dissected.

Coal's shadow hung over northeastern Pennsylvania. The anthracite was concentrated in four hundred and eighty square miles across five counties. By 1901, one hundred forty-seven thousand miners, including some twenty-four thousand boys, worked there. In the 1840s, Frederic Church's painting *Rapids of the Susquehanna* depicted the region's untamed nature; the landscape painter George Inness captured the railroads cutting through the Lackawanna Valley in the 1850s. By the end of the century, the hillside forests were mostly gone, the streams filled in, the ground shattered—so that every storm meant a flood—and the towns blackened by soot. More than one billion tons of anthracite coal had been broken loose from the earth in eighty years, almost all of it by hand.

America's industrialization depended on the coal. Anthracite was more efficient than charcoal; in many places it was more plentiful than wood. It burned hotter and cleaner than either. Anthracite made possible stronger grades of iron and steel, which made stronger rails, which allowed for heavier locomotives, which made interstate trade on the transcontinental railroads possible. Anthracite generated steam for those locomotives and for manufacturing glass, textiles, ceramics, and chemicals. In other words, anthracite powered the quest to expand westward. It also warmed the homes, offices, and schools of a distant America, urban and modern.

All natural resources are political, and here too anthracite was of decisive consequence. A fight between the miners and the mine owners would come to roil Roosevelt's presidency.

Coal-breaking machines, housed in hundred-foot-high black buildings, marked the land of Schuylkill and Lackawanna and Carbon counties. That's where the youngest and the oldest worked. They were all called breaker boys. The coal was hauled up to the top of the tower, crushed between powerful rollers into marketable pieces, and poured down chutes. The boys, crouched on planks across the coal slides, stopped the tumble with their feet and picked out the slate. At the bottom, the coal dropped into a railway freight car to be transported to Boston, New York, Philadelphia, and Washington, leaving behind the grinding noise and choking dust.

The breaker boys were supposed to be at least twelve years old. Many began working when they were eight. Fake birth certificates were provided by mine inspectors, signed by parents desperate for their sons' wages, notarized for twenty-five cents, and accepted without question by company supervisors. The boys were paid about seventy cents for ten hours of work—enough to buy a dozen eggs and a pound of butter.

Next to the breakers were heaps of culm, the wasted rock, where women and girls foraged for tiny pieces of discarded coal that the boys missed.

The breaker boys graduated to jobs belowground when they were (or could claim they were) fourteen. Boys loaded coal onto carts after the explosions, boys opened the doors for the approaching carts, boys ran alongside the carts to keep them on track or slow their momentum, boys drove the mules that carried the carts filled with coal from the deepest veins. Two years of experience underground, and enough English and preparation to

Breaker boys picking slate, circa 1913

Coal breaker, Scranton, Pennsylvania

pass a twelve-question test about mine safety, qualified a boy to become a digger. If a boy couldn't pass the test, he could sign up for a correspondence class, or, as a last resort, simply buy a certificate.

Everything in the anthracite counties had a price, and a cost. The companies controlled a natural resource whose limits they couldn't be sure of. The first to dig weren't thinking about the next century anyway. They started with the better, easier deposits first, took as much as possible, sold as much as they could, and accepted the falling prices that competition sometimes brings. As they depleted those seams, they had to spend more to extract what remained. Small independent operators eventually had to sell out to the bigger companies. These were backed by the railroads, which in the 1860s and 1870s had plenty of financial supporters, including the U.S. government. By 1874, most of the coal land in northeastern Pennsylvania was controlled by the railroads. By 1900, most of the railroads were controlled by Pierpont Morgan.

The conditions were perfect for a powerful cartel to form. After the labor unrest of the 1870s and early attempts at unionization, the coal bosses wanted to hire workers who wouldn't challenge their authority. They recruited miners from central and eastern Europe, often more than they could fully employ, so that the men ended up working intermittently for less money in hazardous conditions. That had the effect of depressing all wages. The men called it "mining the miners." Then owners lowered production and raised prices. Some of the earlier generations, resentful or retired, moved away. By 1902, at least half of the anthracite miners were immigrants from Slavic countries; by some counts they spoke fourteen different languages and dialects.

They were the new working poor, each month calculating how to support their families. The old high-priced "pluck-me" company stores had officially closed, only to be handed over to the relatives of favored foremen or superintendents. Shopping there wasn't compulsory, if a miner didn't care about losing a rich vein or the days to mine it. As one striker recounted, the superintendent might ask: "Do you know that my wife's brother George has a store?" A day or two later, if the miner's wife hadn't shown up at George's store, the miner might hear that the promising spot was no longer his. Then the miner would stop in to tell the superintendent that his wife had tried George's store and liked it better than where she had shopped before. "Brother-in-law George had the right kind of stuff," and of course they were willing to pay a few cents more for it.

The miners' biggest complaint about these arrangements was that they had no choice about where to purchase the black explosive powder they needed to do their jobs: a twenty-five-pound keg, enough to last a week, cost the companies one dollar and the miners as much as two dollars and seventy-five cents. The companies argued that having control of the supply allowed them to regulate the quality.

Families could manage on five or six hundred dollars a year, if they could make that much. Many didn't. They'd spend ten dollars and fifty cents a month to rent a home for their family of six and four dollars on the coal to heat it. Groceries—butter, eggs, potatoes, cabbage, flour, and sugar—cost twenty-two dollars; the butcher got another six. That would leave seventeen dollars a month for clothes, church dues, and insurance fees of two dollars and twenty cents, medicine if they needed it, savings if they could afford it. They had to consider the possibility that the next month they might earn less.

JOHN MITCHELL FIRST entered a mine when he was twelve years old. His mother had died—he never knew how—and his father had been crushed to death by a team of runaway horses. He was living, unhappily and in poverty, with his stepmother and her new husband in Braidwood, Illinois. It was 1882.

A farmer had discovered deposits of soft bituminous coal in the fields of northeastern Illinois two decades earlier, and Braidwood had become a coal town, attracting immigrants from Italy, Ireland, Scotland, and Germany. Their houses were made of cheap wood; the streets and paths were like swamps when it rained. Dogs, hogs, and sheep roamed the business district, which consisted of a few general stores and banks, a newspaper office, and eighty saloons.

The exuberance of discovery set in motion the same cycle in Illinois as it had in Pennsylvania, as it would over again throughout the country. Companies removed as much as they could, too much, then competed

Breaker boys waiting to be paid, Archbald colliery, Lackawanna County, 1890

Underground first aid station for anthracite miners

fiercely for markets and customers by lowering prices. They compensated by lowering wages and reducing the number of days miners could dig. During the first two years Mitchell was underground—as his stepfather's apprentice—miners were forced to accept two pay cuts, and in 1884 the state government reported that many mining families spent more to get by than they could earn.

Mitchell, along with many Braidwood miners, joined the local union. Unlike most of them, he saw the union as a potential career path out of the mines. It took ten years and two major confrontations. The first, a preemptive lockout in 1889, left many Illinois miners homeless, hungry, and sick, and after eight months they agreed to give up their union membership as well as 20 percent of their wages to get their jobs back. The second was a strike in 1894, one year into the depression and just before the Pullman workers walked off their jobs and Coxey's Army marched to Washington. The coal strike was organized by the newly created United Mine Workers of America. More than one hundred twenty-five thousand of the one hundred fifty thousand or so bituminous coal miners around the country stopped working. Five states, including Illinois, called in their militias, igniting outbursts of violence. When strikers blockaded coal trains, lawyers arrived with restraining orders, and federal troops came to enforce them. Hard-coal miners kept digging, as did some soft-coal miners, and two months after the strike began, the leaders called it off. Mitchell participated in the first action and lost his job after the second.

He was twenty-four. He had a wife, Kate, and a son, Richard. They all lived in her father's home in Spring Valley, Illinois. Mitchell was shy and barely educated, but he was remedying that. He read newspapers and joined an "athletic club" for coal miners who preferred to drink and debate. He became close friends with an influential Catholic priest who guided his intellectual development. He cast his vote for the Populist candidate in the 1894 midterm elections (who lost). Like many young miners, Mitchell was lean and muscular, with the eyes of an older man. He kept his hair neatly combed and his clothes clean. He accumulated facts and statistics and spoke carefully. He seemed to have good judgment. He was preparing for a life outside the mines.

His first opportunity came in 1894, when he was offered an unpaid job as an organizer for the United Mine Workers. Mary Harris Jones joined the union as an organizer around then, too. At fifty-seven years old, she would soon be known as Mother Jones. Later she was called "the most dangerous woman in this country." By contrast, Mitchell was the mediator, eager to win approval from the powerful men he would work with and against. He admired their material success, desired their comforts, but set out in a direction that could only leave him grasping. He was a contradiction, a mystery even to himself.

Mitchell won his first union election two years later. He had a low-level position, secretary-treasurer in a subdistrict in Illinois, with no salary. But his expenses were paid. It was a difficult time. Union membership had fallen below ten thousand after the failed strikes and few of those miners paid their dues. The organization was nearly bankrupt. Around the country, millions were unemployed. Three hundred miners in Spring Valley were so hard up they offered to work for no pay at all if the coal companies provided their families with food, fuel, and clothing.

In 1897, conditions were still desperate, and a new union president called for bituminous miners around the country to stop working on July 4. Within days production nearly stopped in Indiana, Ohio, and northern Illinois. The union sent Mitchell to southern Illinois, where some bituminous deposits had recently been discovered. He walked from camp to camp trying to persuade the men to join the strike. This time, unlike in 1894, operators didn't call in replacement workers. Many of them—including Mark Hanna, in his capacity as an industrialist in Cleveland—realized that acquiescing to one of the miners' demands, standardized wages, might help stabilize the industry. Violence was minimal, and the Illinois governor refused some sheriffs' requests to call out the state militia. Thousands of people sent food and clothes to the miners, and the American Federation of Labor held rallies to raise money. In September, the operators offered a compromise and the union accepted.

During the strike, Mitchell listened to the miners, kept their spirits up, maintained order, and became a local hero. He gained confidence and ambition, and at its conclusion, with a push from his mentor, he won the vice presidency of the union. He moved to Indianapolis, some two hundred fifty miles from his family. Eight months later, President McKinley asked the president of the United Mine Workers to become a member of the new Industrial Commission. Mitchell was appointed acting president of the union in October and was elected president of the United Mine Workers in January 1899. He was twenty-eight years old. The union had fifty-five thousand members and a nearly hundred-thousand-dollar budget. Among his hopes was to draw a fifteen-hundred-dollar annual salary.

Mitchell's new job was demanding: he was building a national organiza-tion out of quarrelsome officials and clamorous miners with the goal of negotiating contracts and upholding them peacefully. He traveled constantly. The pay he deemed insufficient. Nine months in, he considered quitting. "My personal interests would be best served by my retirement," he wrote a friend, "as I can secure employment which would not only be conge-nial, but would pay a much higher salary than is paid me by the miners."

Mitchell was eager to propel himself into the middle class one way or another. He looked into becoming a silent partner in a hardware store or starting a tobacco manufacturing company. But he soon realized that he could take advantage of opportunities that came his way on the job. When he decided to take a vacation in California, he asked for free passes from the coal and railroad officials he knew. He acquired a taste for cigars, and an expensive gold ring with six small diamonds. After talking with several politicians on a trip to the capital, he wrote to his brother, Robert, "Have just returned from Washington, DC where I had the pleasure of meeting and conversing with that renowned statesman, Mark Hanna, as well as many senators and congressmen of National fame." Robert, a miner out west in Washington, was not impressed.

It was the beginning of the American century, and coal was the all-American source of energy. Mitchell seized the moment. His union now included ninety-three thousand members, most of whom who worked in small bituminous mines in West Virginia, Illinois, Indiana, and Ohio. There were another one hundred forty-seven thousand miners just one state over. If he wanted to increase the size and influence of the union, he had to bring the union to Pennsylvania.

Six railroads controlled more than 96 percent of the anthracite coal there; the Reading, out of bankruptcy and planning to expand, was the most influential. Mitchell knew that a few men in a few corporate offices in New York and Philadelphia determined how much coal to produce, how much to charge, and how much to pay the miners. He knew he would be taking on Big Capital and the Biggest Capitalist, Pierpont Morgan. He also knew that in 1900 President McKinley would be running for a second term.

John Mitchell, president of the United Mine Workers of America

He and the union he represented "cared nothing for one party or another," Mitchell said. But one party cared more than the other about industrial peace that year: "We [have] learned that the Republican administration were very desirous of having all labor disputes settled before the campaign opens, and particularly in the mining regions." If he could build up the union until it was big enough to threaten the Republicans' coveted economic stability, the miners would be in a much stronger position.

Mitchell prepared to face the coal bosses as their workers were being recruited by his organizers. It was stressful, and in March, Mitchell suffered a physical breakdown that might have been exacerbated by heavy drinking. He called it "extreme nervousness." A week in a hotel in Chicago under the care of a doctor seemed to help.

Union men moved from town to town in Pennsylvania's anthracite counties, held meetings open only to those who knew the password, signed up some nine thousand members, and encouraged many more to at least consider the possibility that miners could unite to challenge the coal monopoly.

Many were skeptical at first. Two years earlier, some three hundred anthracite miners, most of them Eastern European, joined a strike, raised an American flag, and marched toward the town of Lattimer, Pennsylvania, where they hoped to shut down operations. They were protesting their low wages and miserable living conditions. The sheriff called in the

Coal and Iron Police. A small scuffle—and an impulsive order to shoot—left at least nineteen unarmed miners dead and thirty-two wounded. The aftermath revealed the ethnic tensions among the miners—and the public. Many noted that English-speaking strikers wouldn't have faced such a violent end, and others were just as sure that the eastern Europeans must have instigated the confrontation. No officer was convicted in what became known as the Lattimer massacre.

In 1900 ethnic prejudice and antagonism still simmered among some miners, and Mitchell worried they might not hold together during a strike. He told the miners to blame their bosses, not each other, for their low wages. "The coal you dig isn't Slavish or Polish or Irish coal, it's coal."

That summer, the union's campaign was explicit: it boasted that over the years it had won pay increases of as much as 50 percent for some bituminous miners. That made membership, and its obligations, more appealing. The anthracite miners hadn't received a wage hike since 1880.

In September, from a shabby room at the Old Valley Hotel in Hazleton that served as his headquarters, Mitchell decided it was time to act. There were enough miners on the rolls. He would test their resolve. He sent telegrams to the presidents of the anthracite railroads requesting that the miners' complaints about wages and working conditions be submitted to arbitration. He asked each executive to respond by the end of the day. They responded with hostile silence. Mitchell called for a strike to begin five days later, on September 17, 1900.

At least eighty thousand anthracite miners stayed home that Monday. Within two weeks almost all the mines were shut down. Their grievances—the artificially high cost of their explosive powder and the goods they purchased from the company stores, their reduced workdays, the improper weighing of the coal they dug, their unpredictable wages tied to the market price of coal—stirred voters of all political leanings. The miners' ability to keep the peace also won them supporters.

It was campaign season. Bryan promised "equal rights to all and special privileges to none." McKinley promised a full dinner pail. Roosevelt was giving speeches out west, as he had promised Hanna, though his schedule was more grueling than he expected. "I have had a very hard trip," he wrote from Denver to his sister Corinne. "I have had half a dozen first-class horseback rides. Otherwise I do nothing but fester in the car and elbow to and from stagings . . . I have not the slightest idea how the election is coming out, but at any rate I am doing my part as hard as I can."

McKinley left it to Hanna—his campaign manager, head of the Republican National Committee, spokesman for the financial powers, and dominant force in the National Civic Federation dedicated to industrial peace—to try to secretly end the strike. Creating trade agreements between workers and owners made sense to him. Cooperation was more profitable than confrontation. Mitchell would come to agree.

The anthracite coal bosses were harder to convince. They considered Mitchell a self-serving, ill-informed interloper whom they could wait out, and through September they remained fiercely uninterested in discussing the demands of their employees. Then they heard from Hanna. He invited them to a meeting at Pierpont Morgan's office in New York. That was an invitation they couldn't ignore. Hanna told them "that if the strike was not settled it would extend to Ohio, Indiana, and Illinois, and the election of Mr. McKinley and Mr. Roosevelt would be endangered." The operators, led by George Baer, the president of the most important of the railroads, the Reading, reluctantly agreed to settle the strike.

They offered a 10 percent wage increase through April 1, 1901, and promised to reduce the price of the explosive powder and abolish the sliding pay scale. The miners didn't win everything they wanted. None of companies acknowledged Mitchell or the union. But the miners understood the concessions as a tacit recognition of their power. They declared victory, and on October 29 returned to work. Then they voted to make every October 29 a holiday, Mitchell Day.

Mitchell became a national figure, with more than a hundred fifty thousand miners under his command and a political alliance with one of the most powerful men in the country. Hanna described Mitchell as a responsible and trustworthy labor leader. Mitchell called Hanna "the Captain" and visited him at home in Cleveland. Mitchell also went on a "jollification tour" of anthracite country. He happily accepted a gold medal, a gold-headed cane, a silver cup, and two candelabra from grateful miners and local business owners. The value of these gifts "could not be less than one thousand dollars!" he wrote to a friend.

Mitchell looked for other ways to make extra money. He thought about selling large framed photos of himself to the miners and setting up a "John Mitchell" cigar company. The most lucrative opportunity, though, was a job offer from an insurance firm in Philadelphia. Mitchell could become a vice president, with a salary of four thousand dollars a year and an annual bonus of one thousand dollars-worth of stock. It took him a full year to turn down the position.

WILLIAM MCKINLEY AND Theodore Roosevelt defeated William Jennings Bryan and Adlai Stevenson on November 6, 1900. As Hanna prepared for McKinley's second term, with an ambitious new vice president hovering in the background, his political instincts failed. He didn't notice the coal barons' glowering resentment. They felt they'd been forced to compromise for the sake of political expediency. They wouldn't do so again.

Three weeks after the March inauguration—as Morgan was preparing to leave for Europe and James Hill was making plans for their new purchase, the Burlington—the miners' wage agreement was close to expiring. Mitchell wrote a desperate note to Hanna. He had invited the coal executives to talk with union representatives about maintaining the higher wages beyond April and, again, they had ignored him. If Hanna could arrange a meeting, Mitchell was confident they "could reach an understanding which would be satisfactory to all concerned and would not necessarily mean any loss of dignity on the part of the railroad presidents." Hanna replied that he was "only too happy to do anything."

Doing anything usually required Morgan. Hanna visited 23 Wall Street to discuss the matter. Morgan wasn't as opposed to unions as the coal executives were. Like Hanna he believed it inevitable that workers would organize. He suggested that if Mitchell could keep his men in line for a year—no local strikes, no day-long boycotts—the union might win recognition from the coal operators.

The coal companies quietly extended the wage increases for another year, until April 1902. But by summer, the local union leaders were reporting that the companies were violating the agreements. The miners were agitated, and Mitchell was too. He didn't want another strike so soon. Through the autumn and early winter he held on to the hope that he wouldn't have to lead one. Pressure-testing the previous year's fragile victory would be risky; perhaps the assassination of McKinley, and the nation's unease in the ensuing transition, also factored into his calculations.

In February 1902, two months before the already broken agreement would officially end, Mitchell got a chance to appeal directly to Morgan to broker talks. They met on February 26, the same day the king of Wall Street hosted lunch for the prince of Germany. Morgan was friendly and courteous and, as Mitchell recalled, said: "If the railroad presidents were wrong he would not sustain them, if the miners were wrong, he would not help them." The financier assured the labor leader he would "do what was right when the opportunity for action came." But he also said that he could not order the coal presidents to meet Mitchell.

Afterward, Ralph Easley, the energetic founder of the National Civic Federation, told Mitchell not to worry about Morgan's refusal to take command of the situation. Eventually everything would work out. Mitchell wanted to believe him.

Mitchell had joined with Hanna, believed in industrial capitalism, and thought of himself as a conservative. Radicals accused him of chloroforming the class consciousness of workers. And still he couldn't persuade the coal executives to talk with him. "I fear that unless I can get a rest I am going to break down altogether," Mitchell wrote. "I do not know what trouble I have. But I suffer constantly with my lungs and my heart, and during the past week or so I had intense pains across my back."

He pressed on, asking the coal operators to meet with a union committee representing the mine workers. This time he received an answer. "We will endeavor to correct every abuse, to right every wrong, to deal justly and fairly with [the men we employ] . . . Beyond this we cannot go," wrote George Baer, the Reading Railroad president. "There cannot be two masters in the management of business." A month later, in late March, Mitchell sent another round of telegrams to the coal presidents, and again Baer replied. "Always willing to meet our employees to discuss and adjust any grievances. I had hoped that my letter clearly expressed our views."

Finally, in late April, the National Civic Federation persuaded the executives to meet with Mitchell after all. They gathered at the headquarters of the Central Railroad of New Jersey, a subsidiary of the Reading.

A restaurant catered lunch, and for forty-five minutes the railroad presidents and the miners' representatives talked and ate. Two boxes of perfecto cigars arrived. That seemed auspicious. Mitchell presented the union demands. No response. Then the executives announced that they would rather go bankrupt than surrender to the union. It seemed they had come only to assess the strength of their opponent.

The miners again pressed for action. Mitchell again suggested arbitration. Baer insisted that the operators must be free to run their businesses without interference from the unions. Or politicians who couldn't understand the complications of coal mining. Rumors spread that, as they had done in 1901, the companies had been stockpiling anthracite and enough bituminous to run their locomotives until winter.

"Anthracite mining is a business, and not a religious, sentimental or academic proposition," Baer wrote in reply to Mitchell's final telegram on May 8. And despite being a businessman to his core, Baer was willing to lose money to make his point.

Mitchell believed Hanna was now frustrated enough to support a strike, and that the growing suspicion of big business among Americans would help his effort. But he was anxious about the trouble and suffering to come for the miners. Two days later, he wrote a letter to Mother Jones, who was organizing miners in West Virginia. "I am of the opinion that this will be the fiercest struggle in which we have yet engaged," he said. "It will be a fight to the end, and our organization will either achieve a great triumph or it will be completely annihilated."

CHAPTER 10

On Strike

Whistles pierced the May morning at the anthracite coal mines. Expectancy hung in the air. In Coaldale, Carbondale, Shamokin, Panther Creek, and the other towns in northeastern Pennsylvania, more than one hundred forty-seven thousand men and boys heard the whistle calling them to work. They ignored it. The miners knew the hurt the strike would bring: payless days, rationed food, untreated illnesses, possibly eviction. "Our boys are not expecting automobiles and membership cards in clubs of every city," said one of the strikers. "But they want their fathers to earn enough to keep them at school."

Their union leader knew the ripple effects of the strike would also bring deprivation to the eastern cities and their poor first. He felt responsible.

The presidents of the coal companies seemed unconcerned. They were reportedly playing golf in the early days. They called the strikers foolish and inconsiderate. "They have no tangible grievances . . . We will let them fight it out," said one. "We are confident they will regret their action and be glad to resume work on the old terms," said another. Later, George Baer, their unofficial leader, said: "These men don't suffer. Why, hell, half of them don't even speak English."

But the strike that began that May morning would reveal itself to be much more than a protest for fair wages and treatment, more than a faceoff between labor and capital. It was a confrontation between a past where power was concentrated and a future where it was shared.

Baer represented the past, where a man like him answered only to his conscience, his God, occasionally to his wife. He was a fourth-generation Pennsylvanian, a college dropout, bookkeeper, Civil War officer, and country lawyer by the age of twenty-eight. The Philadelphia & Reading Railroad, built to carry anthracite coal to Philadelphia and its port, hired him as its "confidential counsel" in 1870. Baer also worked for one of the railroad's smaller competitors. His first task was to help the Reading acquire it.

Baer reported to the railroad's ambitious president, who wanted the Reading to control the entire anthracite industry. Pennsylvania prohibited that—railroads couldn't legally own and operate coal mines—but a loophole allowed railroads to own a subsidiary that owned mines. The Philadelphia and Reading Coal and Iron Company was born.

Baer earned a generous salary from the railroad, five thousand dollars a year, which allowed him to become a real estate developer and industrialist at the same time. No one at the company complained when he served as a prosecutor for the Commonwealth as well. After violent conflicts in the coal region in the 1870s, he helped convict twenty Irish miners—suspected members of the Molly Maguires secret society—of murder and other crimes. They were hanged.

Baer came to Pierpont Morgan's attention in 1893. The economy was depressed. The Reading had expanded wildly and was bankrupt for the third time in thirteen years. Baer was crucial to its Morganization. In 1901 he engineered a merger with the Reading's biggest rival, the Central Railroad of New Jersey. Morgan rewarded Baer by naming him president of the company in April of that year. Baer—sharp-eyed, religious, and a fervent capitalist—became the most important executive in the anthracite industry.

George Baer, circa 1886, when he was the lawyer for the Philadelphia & Reading Railroad Company

In the first days of the strike, Baer and the other coal executives called in five thousand Coal and Iron Police to guard the collieries—the mines and breakers and the land in between. They feared vandalism by the strikers and violence against the men the companies hired to replace them. The strikers paraded through the streets carrying homemade banners: "We are slaves now but John Mitchell will soon set us free." John Mitchell urged them not to provoke the security forces standing by with their Winchester rifles. Mother Jones led her own parade of women armed with mops and brooms and tin pans to harass anyone heading to work in the mines. She knew she made Mitchell nervous.

The companies paid five thousand dollars to the Pennsylvania treasury, one for each soldier, to create a state-sanctioned private militia to do their bidding. Mostly untrained and often undisciplined, the men received $2.50 a day, about $70 a month if they lasted that long. They lived behind barricades in basic accommodations. On patrol they were surrounded by hostile strikers. Many left as soon as their contracts permitted. The coal companies began to recruit soldiers who had just returned from the Philippines, where they had been fighting against nationalist guerrillas seeking independence. The coal operators expected men hardened in brutal colonial warfare to be more resilient.

A paramilitary force bankrolled by the coal companies on one side; enforcers threatening miners who broke ranks on the other. Violence seemed inevitable. Mitchell worried that no matter how it began, it would only hurt the miners' cause. The union issued rules of conduct: Don't carry weapons, or mops; don't hang effigies, or otherwise threaten the men who still want to work. Don't set fires at the collieries so they can't work. Definitely don't throw stones at the Coal and Iron Police and don't kidnap them either.

The miners didn't always follow the rules. One of Mitchell's district secretaries had to rescue five new policemen, grabbed by strikers moments after they stepped off the train outside Hazleton. He made sure the men returned home to Philadelphia without any trouble. He didn't want to have to do that again. Miners who tried to work could find their porches dynamited or their names on tombstones.

On June 5, three weeks into the strike, the Coal and Iron Police shot Charles McCann in the chest as he approached a mine they were protecting outside Wilkes-Barre. McCann was only twelve. Men had been tearing down the fence and setting small fires, and McCann's involvement, if any, was unclear. An angry crowd of some three thousand gathered. The police chief sent in reinforcements. Everyone was on edge. Four of the Coal and Iron Police were arrested by the official police, and the other guards on duty said they would leave if they could get out safely. McCann was taken to a hospital and survived.

After the shooting, strikers hung an effigy of Morgan and pelted it with stones. Morgan, who was in Europe attempting to combine six shipping lines into one company, chose to not get involved in the strike. He expected the coal executives to deal with their own employees.

Heavy rains fell over coal country that June. The untended mines began to flood. Avondale, where one hundred eight men and boys had died in a fire in 1869, threatened to cave in. The No. 11 was filling with water after unskilled workers broke the pumps, and even an offer of five dollars a day to fix them wasn't enough to entice skilled workers to break the strike.

Colliery No. 5 at Nanticoke became known as Fort Susquehanna. The coal company's man on the ground was Lieutenant Jones, a veteran of the war in Cuba and graduate of Yale. He requested a moat, barbed wire, stockades, a thousand feet of heavy fire hose, eighty armed men, and a small battalion of professional photographers. They were supplied with huge cameras and plenty of flashlight powder and ordered to capture images of anyone attempting to attack the coal fort.

Bituminous miners in West Virginia, Alabama, and Michigan walked off their jobs in support, and sentiment seemed to grow for a national strike. "I view with *alarm* the talk of a sympathetic strike," Hanna wrote Mitchell. Many of the soft-coal miners had a contract with their employers, negotiated by the union and backed by Hanna's National Civic Federation. Mitchell urged them not to break it. Hanna did more than that. He sent men posing as union representatives into the coal fields to persuade the union members not to go back on their word.

Eventually, Mitchell suggested the soft-coal miners instead create a relief fund for the hard-coal miners. He was already leading enough strikers to command attention. He thought reaching further could be dangerous.

"One thing at a time, and not all things at once, is the way a better state will be ushered in," Mitchell said.

The anthracite miners, many among them Catholics, had the support of priests in the area. Intellectuals around the country backed the miners, as did much of the press, which featured stories of the strikers on its front pages. Mitchell remained cautious, which infuriated such organizers as Mother Jones and gave comfort to such politicians as Hanna. Mitchell thought that was a fair trade.

He set up headquarters in the Hotel Hart in Wilkes-Barre, a modest brick building in the center of the city, next to the Lackawanna rail depot. Wilkes-Barre had been made wealthy by coal but by 1902 no longer relied on it. Ninety-six companies operated nearby, including Hazard Wire Rope, Sheldon Axel Works, Vulcan Iron Works, Stegmaier Brewing, W. B. Lace Manufacturing. Women working in the lace factory earned about one hundred ninety-five dollars a year. Men who worked in any of the other factories earned four hundred ninety-two dollars—about as much as a miner did, if he worked a full year—but with less chance of being injured or killed on the job.

Mitchell was the calm center of the strike. He usually dressed in a high-collared shirt with a black tie and long frock coat that made him look like a priest. "I will say that we do not desire to make any city a victim or have any person suffer because of our quarrel with the coal companies," he said. He listened to the miners' complaints, and he praised them for maintaining the peace. Someone wrote a song, "On Johnny Mitchell's Train," about the husbands and sons who left coal country to find temporary work elsewhere:

I'm an honest union laborin' man,
And I'll have you understand,
I'll tell you just the reason why
I left the mining land.

It was Baer and Morgan done it,
And for they'll repent,
For we don't intend to work a tap,
Till we get the ten percent.

A month into the strike—as railroads and factories began to conserve their coal supplies—it looked as though the new kind of leader in Washington might get involved. Several people suggested how: just as Roosevelt had taken on Morgan's railroad combination for violating the Sherman Act, Roosevelt could order Attorney General Knox to prosecute Morgan's coal cartel for the same offense. The decision would be just as popular in the East as going after Northern Securities was in the West. Or Roosevelt could ask the Board of Trade and Transportation to help resolve the strike. George Perkins, in his second year at the House of Morgan (and still speaking with the White House, despite the ongoing legal battle), suggested Roosevelt do neither. Taking action would be a fatal mistake, he said. He told Roosevelt he was going to give Knox the same advice. No need. Knox had already come to the same conclusion. Roosevelt replied that he had no intention of doing anything just yet.

But that wasn't exactly the case. He ordered Carroll Wright, his secretary of labor, to investigate the grievances of the miners and claims of the operators and push them to arbitrate. Wright was a lawyer, statistician and bureaucrat. He had some experience. President Cleveland had asked him to lead a commission to investigate the claims of the Pullman strikers and managers in 1894. Wright dispatched deputies to the coalfields while he went to New York to meet with Mitchell and the coal presidents. He quickly came to a stark conclusion: "There is no confidence existing between the employees and their employers, and that suspicion lurks in the minds of everyone and distrust in every action on either side." He didn't believe anyone was misrepresenting facts. But they drew radically different conclusions from them.

The anthracite miners should be allowed to form their own union, he wrote in his report, rather than join the United Mine Workers, which already represented the bituminous coal miners. The executives had convinced Wright that the two kinds of coal competed in the marketplace and that bituminous, which was easier to transport and better suited for pig iron and steel mills, had the advantage. Mitchell couldn't advocate for both, they said. But the anthracite miners should be allowed to bargain collectively, have their grievances heard by a conciliation committee, and see their coal weighed by two inspectors, Wright concluded. The companies should experiment for six months with a nine-hour workday instead of ten. In exchange, the miners had to promise not to intimidate those who didn't want to join the union.

Baer told Wright his recommendations would lead to ruin. "We can help to destroy the prosperity of the country by meeting the foolish demands of those who are asking for more than it is in our power to give."

Roosevelt sent the report to Knox: "I like its tone greatly, but I am not certain what can be accomplished by publication," Roosevelt told him. The president had no legal sway, and he didn't like to be ignored. Knox—who as a corporate lawyer had tried to prosecute the Homestead strike leaders for treason and as attorney general was wary of testing constitutional limits—advised him not to make it public. By the end of the summer, though, Roosevelt was frustrated enough to release the report. Knox released a note of his own. "The Executive had no power whatever to take action in the matter."

VIOLENCE ERUPTED IN Shenandoah in the early evening of July 30. Several thousand miners stood in a picket line that ran past the Reading railroad station in the southern part of town. They were on the lookout for men who had broken the strike and gone to work in the mines. Maybe they were looking for trouble, too. Either way, three men came near, walking on the tracks, accompanied by a sheriff's deputy and carrying bundles under their arms. The miners tugged at the bundles. Overalls, tools and dinner pails tumbled out. The men were employees of the Reading railroad company, coming from the West Shenandoah colliery where they had inspected a broken pump. "Scabs!" the strikers shouted as they began throwing stones, beating and kicking the repairmen. The deputy pulled out his revolver and fired shots over the miners' heads, but they didn't turn back. They hurled rocks through the windows of the rail depot as the men retreated inside. When the deputy's brother, a hardware store owner named Joseph Beddall, tried to make his way to the depot with weapons and ammunition, the miners attacked.

A light engine pulled into the back of the station to rescue the three company men. Two scrambled on; the third, George Good, got one foot inside when a striker grabbed the other. The deputy sheriff shot the striker in the leg, then, with Good, jumped aboard. The train, bombarded by stones, maybe even bullets, started out of the station.

Police fired into the crowd of strikers. Hundreds of bullets flew. At least twenty miners and five policemen were injured in what became known as the Bloody First Ward riot. Joseph Beddall—skull fractured, nose broken, body beaten—was rushed to the hospital. He died two days days later.

Sheriff S. Rowland Bedall, Joseph's uncle, sent a desperate telegram to Pennsylvania governor William Stone just after seven o'clock that night: "Bloodshed and riots in this county, property destroyed, civilians killed and injured. Situation beyond my control. Troops should be sent to Shenandoah immediately."

The governor called in the Pennsylvania National Guard. By the next morning, fifteen hundred infantrymen surrounded Shenandoah and patrolled the nearby towns on horseback. "All along the valley great piles of culm surmounted by huge breakers marked the sites of the collieries. The machinery for the most part was silent . . . The huge steel cars were standing empty, and the works deserted save for an occasional Coal and Iron policeman, who stood, armed with a Winchester, solitary and undemonstrative," Stewart Culin, a private from Philadelphia, wrote of his first days in the valley. "We frequently galloped through the village streets . . . Everywhere the people looked clean, with clean white shirts and dresses that contrasted strangely with the pall of blackness that enveloped the country."

The guardsmen eventually set up camps throughout the region, installed phones lines and plumbing, and settled in for a stay of who knew how long. Their arrival proved a boon to business. The commissary bought meat and smoked fish (one brigade spent $4,118 for a month's worth), calfskin shoes (1,200 pairs for $2,532.81), and wool blankets (three hundred for $993). Captain Livingston V. Rausch hired horses for his regiment at a cost of $960 a month. The men were well fed and provided for, but they didn't earn very much. Most were paid $1.50 a day. They would remain in coal country until early winter, an occupying force that helped keep a sullen calm among the strikers. The total cost to the state for their deployment was $993,856.46—every penny accounted for in a hundred-twenty-two-page report.

The coal barons expected that the riot would turn public opinion   and Roosevelt—their way. Mitchell was worried about that, and everything else, too. He didn't feel well and he couldn't sleep. Some said he was drinking. In 1901 the miners had won most of what they wanted after a month and a half. The strikers had already been out of work for almost twice that long in 1902. The coal executives swore they wouldn't surrender to political pressure again, and they didn't think much of Hanna, Mitchell's political ally, either. "I am fully convinced the strike would have collapsed had the operators at this time opened their mines and invited the strikers to return," Mitchell later wrote.

But three weeks after the violence, Baer turned public opinion against the coal barons all on his own. He had received a letter from a concerned citizen pleading with him, as a good Christian, to settle with the miners. Someone else might have at least offered some hope of conciliation. Not Baer. He was confident his intransigence was not only good for business in the long term, but morally correct. "The rights and interests of the laboring man will be protected and cared for—not by the labor agitators, but by the Christian men to whom God in His infinite wisdom has given the control of the property interests of the country," he wrote. His reply was made public, widely mocked (though not by Mitchell), and stirred resentment against him, Morgan, and the other men who controlled the nation's economy. That they believed they did so by divine right seemed the ultimate arrogance to the Americans at their mercy.

The coal companies were facing a financial disaster, but they tried to keep up appearances. A group of strikers climbed the stockade at the Avondale colliery one August night to investigate reports that one hundred cars of coal had been brought up from the mine. That seemed unlikely. They discovered that the cars were filled with dirt and only sprinkled with coal on top.

Baer nonetheless insisted that the striking miners would soon give up. They faced the hard prospect of a freezing winter without wages and only dwindling funds to sustain them.

Coal miners evicted from company-owned housing during strike, northeast Pennsylvania, 1902

The day before Baer riled the late summer calm, Morgan returned to New York aboard the luxury liner *Oceanic*. He had enjoyed an invigorating four months. He cruised from Venice down the Dalmatian coast on *Corsair*, attended the coronation of King Edward VII in Westminster Abbey, and hosted grand dinner parties at Princes Gate, his London home. He had spent lavishly on art. And to top it all off, he had created the International Mercantile Marine, "the beginning of an ultimately vast combination of shipping interests," he explained to George Parkin, a fellow passenger, who was in charge of setting up the Rhodes Scholar program. Morgan felt comfortable enough at his private dining table aboard the ship to speak freely. Parkin said he had been enthralled with Morgan's idea that "combination will progress, growing wider and greater all the time."

The *Oceanic* belonged to the White Star Line, which now belonged to Morgan's new trust. He treated the ship as if it were his own. Before departing England, he brought aboard food from his estate: boxes of melons, hothouse grapes, peaches, nectarines, bottles of cream, eggs and butter. He also came with his folding card table and silver box containing two packs of cards.

Morgan left America before the coal strike began and was frustrated that it hadn't been resolved before his return. Reporters boarded the *Oceanic* as it was held in quarantine and no one—not even Morgan—was allowed to depart. They entered his stateroom. A bodyguard stood nearby. Morgan was replacing his yachting cap with a flat-top English derby. He looked bronzed and hearty, they noted, and his skin seemed healthy. But he was still gruff. "There's one thing I want above everything else, and that is to keep my name out of the papers," he told them. "I'll be at my office every day but I'll not have any opinion to express." Why not, one reporter ventured. "Why should I?" snapped the financier. "I don't know anything about the coal strike. How should I settle it? I don't know a thing about the situation."

That, of course, wasn't true. Perkins had kept him apprised of the situation. In early June, Perkins had told Morgan that as the possibility of the bituminous miners joining the strike seemed more likely, he had conferred with Hanna about how to keep them on the job. "We did hit on some plans that will be helpful," Perkins wrote, and "are watching every move in the strike very very carefully and if we see any indications of serious complications we will not hesitate to ask you to step in and suggest some way of compromise." Perkins assured Morgan that the strike hadn't affected stock prices. "Unless something entirely new and unforeseen turns up in connection with it, it will not be much of a factor unless it should run on much longer than is expected," he wrote in his June 23 report. In his last update at the end of July, just hours before the violence in Shenandoah, Perkins suggested the strike could be coming to an end. "I am very anxious to have this whole matter settled, if possible, before you get home, so that you will not have to be bothered with it." If it wasn't settled, Perkins went on, "Mitchell and the miners generally have great confidence in your fairness and would be almost willing to leave the entire case in your hands." That would turn out to be an overly generous assessment of both men's inclinations.

The strike—and the owners' unyielding stand—was exposing capitalism's weaknesses and encouraging a hard cynicism about its practitioners. Morgan didn't understand that these fissures would last beyond the strike. He saw idle men and unworked mines and thought it a waste. He imagined he could find a fair solution. But when he met with Baer and the others at Delmonico's, he didn't impose or even suggest a way out. He would rather they come up with their own. Morgan preferred not to get involved in such messy situations.

The coal executives didn't want him to either. And none of them wanted Roosevelt to get involved. But inaction always vexed Roosevelt. He was almost ready to test the limits of his presidential power.

On August 21, the day that Baer's letter was published, Roosevelt wrote a note to his attorney general asking again why the government couldn't challenge the legality of the coal cartel. "What is the reason we cannot proceed against the coal operators as being engaged in a trust? I ask because it is a question continually being asked of me." The reason, Knox told him, again, is that the railroads had shrewdly organized the coal companies' cooperation, making prosecution difficult under the Sherman Act. He wanted to wait for the ruling on the Northern Securities case before proceeding. Not the answer Roosevelt wanted. But he also understood that a legal solution, if there was one, would come too late.

Midterm elections were about ten weeks away. Roosevelt and his advisers worried that the strike could hurt the Republican Party. He set off on a six-hundred-mile campaign tour through New England to make sure it didn't. He kicked off the tour with a speech in Providence, Rhode Island, on the steps of City Hall, in front of twenty thousand people. His subject: the trusts. Steam and electricity helped create America's industrial economy, its great cities, prosperity for many, fortunes for a few. Now, he said, the dominion of massive business combinations must be restrained by law. "Some governmental sovereign must be given full power over these artificial, and very powerful, corporate beings," he said. "In my judgment this sovereign must be the national government."

And a few days later in Massachusetts, he leaned over a balcony rail, left arm sharp on his hip, and said to the citizens of Lynn: "All law must be so administered as to secure justice for all alike—a square deal for every man, great or small, rich or poor." Roosevelt wasn't the first to talk of a "square deal," but once he used the phrase, it became his, and he employed it to its fullest, at a New York State Fair, in front of a crowd that included African Americans in Butte, Montana, in a letter to Knox. He would come to call it his "favorite formula."

Roosevelt, in Lynn, Massachusetts, promises, "a square deal for every man, big or small, rich or poor"

The president tells a crowd in Providence, Rhode Island, that the federal government must have power over corporations.

John Mitchell entering Shenandoah, Pennsylvania, 1902

Roosevelt traveled from Lynn to Boston, while some three hundred miles to the south, Hanna arranged for Perkins and Mitchell to meet in Philadelphia. Perkins suggested to the union leader the same thing he had to his boss—that Morgan oversee an investigation into working conditions in the anthracite fields and persuade the operators, as only he could, to accept the findings. All Mitchell had to do was send the miners back to work immediately and agree to be bound by the conclusions for three years.

Mitchell respected Hanna, Perkins, and, most of all, Morgan. But the operators' threats—to resign if forced to arbitrate, to ask for more troops, to call for the prosecution of the union on antitrust grounds—had toughened the strikers. Mitchell had collected about three million dollars in union assessments and donations to help them survive the winter. The miners knew they were making history.

Mitchell declined the offer.

CHAPTER 11

"Catastrophe Impending"

It was just after breakfast on the last day of Roosevelt's New England campaign tour. He was on his way to the Pittsfield Country Club by hired carriage to give a speech. The horse-drawn coach was open to the early September Berkshires air, about two hundred yards from its destination. Roosevelt always sat on the right in a carriage; the governor of Massachusetts, Winthrop Murray Crane, took the spot to his left. George Cortelyou sat opposite; the man who had been by President McKinley's side when he was shot was now Roosevelt's senior secretary, essentially his chief of staff. William Craig, Roosevelt's personal Secret Service agent, perched next to the driver.

All five heard the ring of a trolley bell behind them. Strange. The road was supposed to be clear. Crane turned to wave a warning to the driver. Craig stood up, raised his arm as if to hold off the inevitable, and yelled, "Oh my God!"

"It came down upon us like a flash," Roosevelt said later that day. The trolley hit one of the four horses. The animal collapsed and died. In the next instant, a collision of metal on metal. Roosevelt, Cortelyou, and Crane were hurled forty feet to the side of the road. Passengers in the trolley screamed.

A doctor riding in another carriage jumped out and helped Roosevelt get to his feet. The president was bloody and bruised and looked unsteady.

But he broke away and said, "No. I'm not hurt." He told the doctor to look after the others. Cortelyou was dazed by a severe blow to the back of his head. Crane was shaken but had only a few scratches. Their driver had been dragged by the other horses but survived. Craig had fallen straight across the trolley tracks and been crushed to death.

Holding a handkerchief to his face, Roosevelt walked to the smashed carriage and the stopped trolley. He knelt beside Craig's body. "This is the most damnable outrage I ever knew," the president yelled at the trolley driver. "If you lost control of your car, there is some excuse, but if you tried to pass us, disregarding all our warnings, you ought to be punished." He would be. Motorman Euclid Madden pleaded guilty to manslaughter and served a six-month sentence in jail. Some said the trolley was traveling 30 miles an hour at the point where the carriage route crossed the tracks. Some said Madden was trying to beat the president to the country club. Madden insisted the trolley wasn't going faster than normal and blamed Roosevelt's driver for the accident.

Had the collision occurred at a slightly different angle, Roosevelt would have been killed. As it was, his lips were bleeding, his face swollen, his right eye blackened, and he had hurt his left leg badly.

Roosevelt accompanied the men carrying Craig's body to a home across the street. He made sure it was properly covered and that the family was notified. After half an hour he left. He stopped where he was supposed to stop during the day, but he didn't make any speeches. He told those waiting that the man who had protected him for the past year had died. Craig was the first Secret Service agent to be killed on duty.

By evening Roosevelt was with Edith aboard the presidential yacht, the *Sylph*, on the way home to Oyster Bay. "The bruise on my face is no more than a man might get in a polo game or any other sport in which he might unskillfully engage," Roosevelt said. But a man had died and the president could have. Messages of sympathy, support, and relief arrived from the German emperor, the French president, the Cuban president, the Persian shah.

One day at Sagamore Hill with his family and then Roosevelt was off on a southern tour, stopping in Chattanooga, Tennessee, to address the twenty-first annual convention of the Brotherhood of Locomotive Firemen. The Brotherhood initially provided members insurance in case of disability, or

Roosevelt's carriage after a collision with a trolley in Pittsfield, Massachusetts

death, and later advocated for better working conditions and wages. It was a union, not a secret society. But the brotherhood seemed to imitate one. It was led by a grand master and grouped into lodges, and was open only to white men. Roosevelt overlooked their racism and praised their "rugged virtues," their willingness to meet danger on the job. He said he admired their collective effort and individual enterprise. "I believe emphatically in organized labor," he told them. "The worth of an organization depends upon its being handled with the courage, the skill, the wisdom, the spirit of fair dealing . . . and the wise self-restraint which . . . your Brotherhood has shown."

On September 15, back at Sagamore Hill, Theodore and Edith hosted a garden party, with cookies and raspberry lemonade for anyone in Nassau County who wanted to stop by. Eight thousand people came. Theodore shook hands with them all. The next day he hosted a smaller gathering. Five senators, including his friend Henry Cabot Lodge and his sometime supporter Mark Hanna, came to discuss the Republican Party's prospects in the upcoming midterm elections. "I have grave and delicate questions to meet," Roosevelt wrote to Secretary of State John Hay afterward. "I was glad to find that all of them, including Senator Hanna, thoroughly approved of my position on the trusts." Thoroughly might have been stretching it. The men behind the trusts thought Hanna was their best hope to replace Roosevelt, and Hanna didn't discourage them. He was too smart a politician to believe he had a real chance to become president, and his position as head of the Republican National Committee suited him better anyway. But a shadowy campaign on his behalf backed by the promise of big money might help recover some of his lost prestige.

In the meantime, Hanna had been calling on the House of Morgan to help settle the coal strike and fund the elections. He wasn't getting far with either effort. The miners had received millions of dollars to help them through the forbidding winter and wouldn't resume work without winning some concessions from the operators. Morgan remained uninterested in making that happen. Hanna also would have heard the rumors that Morgan might use his influence to flip the House of Representatives to a few reliably friendly Democrats, just to irk Roosevelt.

"TOMORROW I TAKE up the burden again and start off for a three weeks' nerve-shattering trip," Roosevelt wrote to Hay. But he loved it. And the trip seemed to start off well. Huge crowds gathered in Cincinnati's Music Hall. "We do not wish to destroy corporations. We wish to make them subserve to the public good," he told an audience of enterprising citizens. "All individuals, rich or poor, private or corporate, must be subject to the law of the land." In Detroit, he reviewed a military parade with Red Cross founder Clara Barton, steamed along the river, stayed in the Cadillac Hotel, and spoke to veterans of the Civil War and Spanish-American War. "We are optimists," he said. "We know there are dangers ahead and evils to fight and overcome, but we feel to the full the pulse of the prosperity which we enjoy."

A bruise on the president's left shin, the only one that remained after the trolley accident, swelled and throbbed. He asked Cortelyou if all his bruises had healed. They had. One night in Cincinnati, Roosevelt asked to delay dinner by thirty minutes so he could rest, "a most unusual request," a reporter noted later. When he thought no one would notice, he limped a little. Finally, he admitted to his doctor that walking had become painful. Cortelyou had overseen McKinley's medical care after he was shot in Buffalo. He would do the same for this president. Roosevelt had to ask: Are these the best surgeons?

Cortelyou scheduled an operation to drain an abscess for the next afternoon at a hospital in Indianapolis. Before then: an overnight train to Indiana, a speech at City Hall in Logansport and another in front of six thousand people at Tomlinson Hall in the capital; a consultation with the surgeon before lunch at the Columbia Club; a few words to those gathered outside, possible only if Roosevelt leaned heavily on the balcony.

Roosevelt was a patient at St. Vincent's for four hours. The surgery took place in a private operating room on the fifth floor. Doctors cleaned the injured area with carbolized soap and water and numbed it with a local anesthetic. Curious, Roosevelt asked to see the aspirator, the device the surgeons would use to drain his wound. The pus they suctioned off was clean. The president's blood wasn't poisoned.

By five, he was recovering in Room 52. He ate some toast, soft-boiled eggs, and fruit, drank some tea. By half past seven, he was ready to leave. Four Pullman porters carried Roosevelt one block from the hospital to the train. Like almost all Pullman porters they were African American. If passengers called them George, after the company founder, they were still required to respond. Secret Service agents and local police surrounded the stretcher so no one could see the president under a blanket up to his chin.

Cortelyou canceled the rest of his trip out west.

"My leg was attended to just in time, as (in strictest confidence) there had begun to be trouble with the bone," Roosevelt wrote to Lodge two days later.

EDITH WAS OVERSEEING a five-hundred-thousand-dollar renovation of 1600 Pennsylvania Avenue that summer and autumn that included expanding the residence and switching from gas light to electric. A new West Wing was intended to be big enough for the president, thirty-eight assistants, and the press. Roosevelt's private office, with olive burlap walls and matching curtains, had plenty of bookshelves, comfortable chairs, a divan, and a portrait of Abraham Lincoln over the fireplace mantel. Near his desk he would hang a sonnet written years earlier by Kansas senator John James Ingalls and sent to Roosevelt by his widow. It was called "Opportunity."

> *Master of human destinies am I . . .*
> *I knock unbidden once at every gate!*
> *If sleeping, wake—if feasting, rise before*
> *I turn away. It is the hour of fate . . .*

When he returned to Washington in late September, Roosevelt lived in the temporary White House, a mansion at 22 Jackson Place. The four-story house had been owned in the 1880s by one of the wealthiest congressmen in the country. William Scott, a Democrat from Erie, Pennsylvania, made his fortune in coal, iron, railroads, and the stock market. His obituary noted that he once made two million dollars on a single trade. His daughter, who had a mansion of her own nearby, leased the house, furnished, to the government.

Roosevelt, confined to a wheelchair, worked from a bright and airy dining room on the first floor, looking onto Lafayette Square and beyond that the White House. Only the mahogany table used for cabinet meetings had been brought over. Otherwise, Cortelyou, the press, and the usual assortment of guests and visitors occupied the parlors, while the Roosevelt family took over the second and third floors when they were in town.

For four days everything was fine, but then Roosevelt developed a slight fever and his left leg became inflamed. That afternoon, in his bedroom, surgeons applied cocaine as an anesthetic, cut open his wound, scraped an abrasion from the bone, and drained more pus. Afterward he seemed in good spirits, reading in his wheelchair, talking with Edith, dismissing the fuss over what he considered trivial. His doctors said there was still no evidence of blood poisoning.

Roosevelt worried more about other matters. Earlier that month, local officials made a startling announcement: There wasn't enough coal to run the Washington Monument's new electric elevator for the thousands of tourists who visited every month. Unscrupulous businessmen in cities throughout the Northeast and Midwest were buying most of the remaining supply of anthracite and charging four times the normal price. The Post Office threatened to shut down, and public schools warned they might not be able to remain open past Thanksgiving. Steel mill owners in Pennsylvania told their workers to prepare for mass layoffs. In Milwaukee, men stole wooden beer kegs from saloons to burn as fuel, and in Stamford, thrifty housewives resorted to using dried horse chestnuts to cook. Even a wealthy railroad executive was unable to secure sufficient coal to heat his home in Greenwich and had to order his hickory trees cut down instead.

Toward the end of September, Hanna went to New York to try again to mediate. He met secretly with Morgan, who finally said he would help broker a truce. He was frustrated enough by the coal executives' stubbornness to act himself. Then Hanna met with John Mitchell. The financier and the labor leader could come to an agreement, Hanna believed. But when the senator went to Philadelphia to discuss the idea of arbitration with George Baer, he "absolutely refused to entertain it. You can see how determined they are," Hanna wrote to Roosevelt. "It looks as if it was only to be settled when the miners are starved to it."

No president had ever shown much sympathy to workers on strike. Rutherford Hayes sent federal troops to quell the national railroad strike in 1877. Grover Cleveland sent troops to break the Pullman strike in 1894. If strikers seemed out of control, Roosevelt would send troops too. He worried about unrest wherever it might emerge.

But the anthracite region wasn't out of control. Roosevelt made clear to Hanna he thought the coal presidents should make some "slight concession."

The general public did too. Debating and literary societies, labor unions, religious congregations, political and reform clubs, good government organizations, social service charities: they all wanted the coal companies to settle. Prominent citizens—in business, law, religion, and the press—urged the miners, operators, and federal government to end the conflict. In New York, ten thousand people rallied in Madison Square in support of the strikers.

Roosevelt was restless, fretful. He knew he would be blamed for remaining idle while Americans suffered. "There is literally nothing, so far as I have yet been able to find out, which the national government has any power to do in the matter," he wrote to Lodge. The senator from Massachusetts told the president that Republicans in his state were advocating for nationalization of the mines. "That it would be a good thing to have national control, or at least supervision, over these big coal corporations, I am sure," Roosevelt responded. "I am at my wits' end how to proceed."

Prices increased at laundries, bakeries, cafés, restaurants. Landlords raised the rent on apartments. Hotels charged more for rooms. Landowners sold their timber. In Chicago, residents tore out wooden paving from their streets to use as fuel. Railroads gave their employees old crossties to burn. Trolley lines limited service. Manufacturers had to get by with sawdust in their furnaces. Many inserted delay clauses into their contracts.

There was an alternative—soft coal—though it came with costs. Elevated trains, drawn by steam locomotives, began to use it in New York City. So did some businesses. Dark smoke and cinders settled onto clothes, got into lungs, and filled the air so full of soot and thick haze that the Brooklyn Bridge was obscured.

Families used asbestos coal bricks soaked in oil for cooking, and on the Lower East Side, residents burned coconut shells purchased from candy manufacturers, fifteen cents for 60 pounds. The health commissioner reported a notable increase in the death rate from pneumonia and other respiratory diseases because homes and other buildings weren't warm enough and the air was polluted.

Roosevelt worried about a winter of misery, of sickness, starvation, and darkness. People might freeze to death; others could riot. He understood how panic could outrun reality. Lawlessness would demand force. He wouldn't take the chance of it leading to social upheaval. If other workers went on strike too, the nation could face a crisis that he feared could be almost as serious as the Civil War. So much suddenly seemed fragile.

The president shared his concerns with Massachusetts governor Crane. He had been in the trolley accident that fall, but that wasn't why Roosevelt was conferring with him. He was a businessman (the family company was Crane's Paper) and earlier that year he had helped defuse a strike by the Teamsters. He and Roosevelt began to consider the options. Elihu Root, the former corporate lawyer serving as secretary of war, recognized that the president was going to do *something*, so he had better lend a hand. Knox, the former corporate lawyer serving as attorney general, came around, "as he always does in such cases," Roosevelt later wrote. "The course or policy having been decided he did his very best to make it successful."

Someone—not Roosevelt—needed to apprise Morgan. They decided that someone should be Root. He went to New York with a message from the president. Radical action could be necessary unless the operators "wake up" to the dangers of a prolonged strike. "I am thoroughly awake and will do what I can," the president said.

On the last day of September, Baer expressed confidence that the strike would be over—on his terms—before winter. "The strike will not be settled either, but will end in the return of the miners to work," he said. Mitchell, in Philadelphia, was just as resolute. "We have not underestimated the strength of our opponents," he said. "We have not overestimated our own power of resistance."

The People's Gas Light and Coke Company in Chicago calculated that its coal supply would run out in twenty days, leaving three hundred fifty thousand businesses and residences in the dark. The New York State Democratic Convention, with ten thousand delegates in attendance, backed a call for Roosevelt to take over the mines. Business leaders affected by the coal shortage agreed that the government should step in. "The operators do not seem to understand that the present system of ownership, or at least of management in the anthracite fields, is on trial," Roosevelt wrote to a friend.

The time had come.

"I should greatly like to see you on Friday next, October 3rd, at eleven o'clock am, here in Washington, in regard to the failure of the coal supply, which has become a matter of vital concern to the whole nation," Roosevelt telegraphed the six biggest owners of coal mines. "I have sent a similar dispatch to Mr. John Mitchell, President of the United Mine Workers of America." Roosevelt had decided to use the force of his personality to try to broker a compromise, and just like that, decades of alliance between government and industry came to an end. Roosevelt saw two sides and inserted himself in between. He became the first president to try to mediate between big business and labor.

The miners in Pennsylvania celebrated with a boisterous parade. Morgan was quoted as saying, "The plan to have these gentlemen meet the President and confer about the situation is a most admirable one." But the enraged coal operators hatched a plan of their own.

MITCHELL WAS THE first to arrive at 22 Jackson Place on the morning of October 3. The streets were crowded with residents and journalists eager to get a glimpse of the former miner leading one hundred forty-seven thousand strikers, and the powerful executives who had been unwilling to compromise with him. Mitchell looked fatigued and, briefly, nervous. He was accompanied by the union's three district officials from Pennsylvania: Thomas Duffy, Thomas Nichols, and John Fahy. Mitchell wore his usual starched white collar and on this day added a black frock coat, Prince Albert style, and a fedora. Duffy wore a "total abstinence" badge in solidarity with the eight thousand men in District No. 7 who pledged not to drink while on strike.

They had rolled into town in the smoking car of a commercial train around one in the morning, checked into their hotel, and slept. In the morning, they ate breakfast with Samuel Gompers, the activist who years ago had taken Roosevelt to see the deprivation among New York City cigar workers; now he was leader of the American Federation of Labor and vice president of Hanna's Civic Federation. Mitchell and his deputies took a public trolley to Lafayette Square.

Baer and the five other coal executives came down the night before in two luxurious private Pullman coaches. They slept in the cars, parked on tracks just outside the city, guarded by private detectives. In the morning, the cars were run down to the Baltimore & Ohio station. They ate breakfast, read the newspapers, chatted and smoked, and afterward, for exercise, walked the length of the cars on the station platform.

When will you leave for the White House, a reporter asked Baer. "We will get to the White House exactly at 11 o'clock. There will be no trouble about that," he responded. "But when will we get away? That is the question we would like to have an answer to." At ten forty-five they took two private carriages to Lafayette Square.

They traveled together to show the president, and the public, that they were united and shared the same concerns: the disruption to their business and the disorder caused by the strikers. Being summoned to the capital by the president on forty-eight hours' notice had inconvenienced and annoyed them. They understood what Roosevelt wanted—as much anthracite on the market as quickly as possible—but not what he would do to get it. Nonetheless, they were confident they could withstand Roosevelt's hectoring. That morning, with Baer in the lead, they strode past the waiting throngs and into the mansion. They considered their presence a generous gesture to an interfering president whose motives they distrusted.

"You will have to excuse me, gentlemen, I can't get up to greet you," Roosevelt said as they entered. He was wearing a blue striped robe and sitting in a wheelchair with his left leg propped up. With him were labor secretary Carroll Wright, Knox, and Cortelyou. Roosevelt was energetic and eager. Baer, he remarked later, was belligerent from the start, while Mitchell, sensing a historic opportunity to establish his standing, and that of the labor movement, was conciliatory. The ten men from Pennsylvania sat in hard-backed wooden chairs around Roosevelt, Mitchell on his left.

His voice booming in the confines of the room, Roosevelt began the meeting. "I speak for neither the operators nor the miners, but for the general public," he said. "The urgency, and the terrible nature of the catastrophe impending over a large portion of our people in the shape of a winter fuel famine impel me, after much anxious thought, to believe that my duty requires me to use whatever influence I personally can to bring to an end a situation which has become literally intolerable." He asked that they resume operations immediately and settle their claims later. He threatened them: "I am constrained urgently to insist that each one of you realize the heavy burden of responsibility upon him. We are upon the threshold of winter with an already existing coal famine, the future terrors of which we can hardly yet appreciate. The evil possibilities are so

Roosevelt meeting with John Mitchell, his deputies, and the anthracite coal barons at 22 Jackson Place

far-reaching, so appalling, that it seems to me that you are not only justified in sinking but required to sink for the time being any tenacity as to your respective claims." He appealed to their patriotism: "Meet the crying needs of the people."

Mitchell quickly stood up and said, "I am impressed with the gravity of the situation. We feel that we are not responsible for this terrible state of affairs." He spoke in a measured tone intended to reassure everyone in the room. "We are willing to meet the gentlemen representing the coal operators to try to adjust our differences among ourselves." That's what he had wanted all along. If those talks weren't successful, Mitchell asked Roosevelt to set up an arbitration panel to rule on the miners' complaints about their low pay, long hours, and dangerous working conditions. "If the gentlemen representing the operators will accept the award or decision of such a tribunal the miners will willingly accept it, even if it is against their claims."

Baer sat silently, every glance forbidding. The coal operators had never acknowledged Mitchell's hold over the union men or their grievances, and even though Roosevelt expected them to do so now, they refused. Roosevelt asked the men to consider his plea and Mitchell's proposal, and return to Jackson Place at three that afternoon. They filed out of the room without a word. It was twenty minutes past eleven.

Mitchell and the three other representatives returned to their hotel, where the prix fixe lunch was a bargain. The coal executives retreated to their cars, blinds drawn, doors locked and guarded. A stenographer stood by while they drafted their responses, each alone in his own compartment. They ate a buffet lunch cooked with wood and soft coal. No anthracite was available.

Roosevelt took a few minutes to reply to a telegram he had just received from Seth Low, the mayor of New York City. The temperature had dropped. Residents needed anthracite to keep warm and they didn't have any. The mayor also sent a pamphlet, *The Coal Mines and the Public*, that argued the federal government should seize the coal mines, and maybe the railroads, too. Roosevelt didn't offer any opinions about the coal operators to Low. He only wrote: "What they will do when they come together I do not know."

When they resumed the meeting that afternoon, Baer took his seat across from Roosevelt. He barely waited for a greeting before standing up to reject every approach Mitchell had suggested. The executives would not consider anything other than the miners' surrender. The president should not have presumed otherwise, said the man who had claimed a divine right to control a limited resource. The strikers were responsible for the coal shortage. "Mitchell's men dynamite bridges and tracks, mob trainmen, and by all manner of violence try to prevent its shipment to relieve the public," he said.

Baer grew more agitated, pointing a finger at the president and at one moment pounding his fist on the table so loudly people outside the room heard it. He insulted the very idea of the conference. "The duty of the hour is not to waste time negotiating with the fomenters of this anarchy and insolent defiance of law, but to do as was done in the war of the rebellion, restore the majesty of law, the only guardian of a free people, and to reestablish order and peace at any cost," he said. He offered a final taunt: "Free government is a contemptible failure if it can only protect the lives and property and secure the comfort of the people by compromising with the violators of law and the instigators of violence and crime." And finished with a word of sarcasm: "We decline to accept Mr. Mitchell's considerate offer to let our men work on terms he names."

The other coal executives stood to read their statements, exaggerating the violence and crime—dozens killed, brutal assaults, washeries burned, gangs roaming—to the four men most able to determine the truth. "Are you asking us to deal with a set of outlaws?" one said. If the president wanted to get involved, he should prosecute the United Mine Workers under the antitrust law and send in federal troops to protect those who wanted to work in the mines.

Roosevelt was determined to keep his temper and not be drawn into a quarrel over accusations coming from either side. It couldn't have been easy for him, but he did restrain himself. When the operators finished, he gave them one last chance to cooperate, hoping their bombast was a negotiating tactic, knowing it wasn't. He sternly asked again if they would consider trying to resolve the miners' claims as operations resumed. They answered with a resounding no. No, they wouldn't offer any other proposals. No, they wouldn't ever come to a settlement with Mitchell. No, they didn't need the president to tell them how to manage their business. The conference was over. At five o'clock, Baer and the other executives hurried out of the room.

The union officials stayed behind. Roosevelt saw that the miners trusted Mitchell—he was reasonable and pragmatic, unwavering and sympathetic. He could sit among the rich and the powerful. Now the president warned the labor leader to control his men. "I explained in the most friendly way to Mitchell and his companions that I most earnestly hoped they would do everything in their power to put a stop to violence. I explained that violence meant they would inevitably lose."

Outside, reporters swarmed the usually talkative Mitchell, but he could only deliver the news that there was no settlement. Later he found a few more words. "The coal operators have neither regard for their former employees nor for the public, which is suffering so much for lack of fuel."

Roosevelt remained stunned and seething in the dusky parlor. He had not edged the men any closer to a resolution. Mitchell "behaved with great dignity and moderation," he wrote. "The operators, on the contrary, showed extraordinary stupidity and bad temper." Their insolence was meant to dishearten him, and make it impossible for Mitchell to hope for anything better. "The language used by the operators at the conference was exquisitely well calculated to prevent any kind of yielding on the part of the miners." They had intended to show Mitchell and the miners that not even the president could help them, and they had succeeded.

"Well, I have tried and failed," Roosevelt wrote that evening to Hanna, who was in Cleveland. "I would like to make a fairly radical experiment . . . I must now think very seriously of what the next move shall be. A coal famine in the winter is an awful ugly thing."

Roosevelt had just been rebuffed. Hanna had been rejected in September. Roosevelt could only turn back to Mitchell. If Mitchell called off the strike, the president would appoint a commission to investigate and try to address the miners' complaints. Mitchell politely refused. The president had sent Wright to investigate conditions in June and nothing had come of it. Hanna asked Gompers to persuade Mitchell to reconsider the president's offer, but Gompers replied that he couldn't "advise Mr. Mitchell accept a proposition so elusive and unpromising."

Five months of struggle had not wore down the strikers. After the conference and more requests from the operators, Governor Stone sent in the rest of the National Guard to protect miners who wanted to work. The soldiers took their positions in front of the collieries and on the railroad bridges. But few miners showed up.

Roosevelt proposed the "radical experiment" he had earlier hinted at. He ordered the head of the Army to draw up plans to take control of the anthracite mines. Ten thousand soldiers were at the ready. Roosevelt intended to wait until Governor Stone asked for help to maintain order. Then he would send in Major General Schofield, who could be counted on to follow orders, whatever they were. Having once helped President Cleveland put down the Pullman strike, this time Schofield would take over the mines. "I only wanted a method of getting the army in," Roosevelt said later. "Then I would run the situation as I thought it ought to be run."

It would be an unprecedented expansion of presidential power. Root and Knox wouldn't approve. But the operators had attacked him and the office he held. Roosevelt prepared to hit back. "I have been so indignant with the mine-owners that it has been difficult to control myself in reference to them," Roosevelt wrote to his friend Jacob Riis.

One morning, the president mentioned his scheme to a leading Republican politician, James Watson. The representative was alarmed: "What about the Constitution of the United States? What about seizing private property for public purposes without due process?" Roosevelt took hold of Watson's shoulder and almost shouted: "The Constitution was made for the people and not the people for the Constitution." Then he let the rumor spread that he planned to take over the mines.

Winter was closing in. The nation was uneasy. Soldiers stood ready. On Dundee Island, in New Jersey, a band of fifty men and women, using nothing but little wagons and bags carried away several tons of coal from parked railroad cars.

When a New York City dealer was able to procure a small amount of coal to sell to the very poor at cost, more than five thousand people lined up to buy ninety cents' worth of anthracite, carrying the nuggets home in buckets, wrapped in cloth, and even putting them next to their children in baby strollers.

Fifteen hundred manufacturers reported that they would soon have to shut down their factories because their coal supplies were exhausted. Representatives of the National Association of Manufacturers met with Mitchell in Buffalo and the coal executives in Philadelphia. "We wish to learn from Mitchell what is the least the miners will take, and then see the operators and find out the most they will offer," one member explained. "This is a purely business move. No politics in it whatever." No matter. Still no settlement.

The governor of New York, Benjamin Odell, met with Baer and the others. Baer did not appreciate the offer of assistance. "We will not accept political advice or allow the interference of politicians," he told the man who represented seven million Americans.

As almost every big paper east of Chicago printed stories about the impending "coal famine," even Mark Twain interjected himself into the swirling anxiety and published a letter to the secretary of the treasury:

> Sir: Prices for customary kinds of Winter fuel having reached the
> altitude which puts them out of the reach of literary persons in

straitened circumstances, I desire to place with you the following order: forty-five tons best old dry Government bonds, suitable for furnace, gold 7 per cents, 1864, preferred. Twelve tons early greenbacks, range size, suitable for cooking. Eight barrels seasoned 25 and 50 cent postal currency, vintage of 1866, eligible for kindlings.

Please deliver with all convenient dispatch at my house, in Riverdale, at lowest rates for spot cash, and send bill to your obliged servant, Mark Twain, Who will be very grateful and will vote right.

The operators had asked Morgan to let them fight it out with the strikers, but he never thought the strikers would last this long. After the Washington conference, Morgan announced that he would buy fifty thousand tons of coal from Wales, transport it on International Mercantile Marine ships, and distribute it for free to New York City's poor. He would likely spend half a million dollars. It was an unsubtle reminder to the coal executives that he was losing patience.

Roosevelt made one final attempt to end the strike without force. He turned to Morgan, the only man who could control Baer and the coal executives. The only man who hadn't really tried. By now, it seemed that even Morgan was embarrassed by Baer's intransigence and arrogance. He feared the public hostility toward the coal industry might spread to his other, more profitable companies. Most of all, he worried about disorder. Morgan, too, wanted to resolve the crisis before the unyielding November cold arrived.

CHAPTER 12

The Corsair Agreement

October 11, 1902. Choking smoke and fog pressed down on New York City; residents called it a Pittsburgh gloom. The sun hadn't broken through by the time offices and stores opened. The elevated trains and trolleys kept their headlights on. Morgan waited aboard his yacht, *Corsair*, shrouded in the Hudson River. Few other places afforded him the privacy he sought, especially on this Saturday morning.

All the news was disturbing. Brooklyn's courts were out of coal. The King's County Hospital and Almshouse were down to their last two days' worth. Schenectady schools, which educated four thousand students, were closed. Mount Vernon bought two thousand oil-soaked railroad ties from the New Haven line in hopes of keeping classrooms warm until the holidays. Janitors banked the furnaces promptly at three every afternoon. Night school was canceled.

The manager at the Siegel Cooper emporium warned that to conserve energy he might have to confine business to the first floor of his building's six floors. Without new supplies, half the businesses in Harlem would have to close down, said a shop owner: "It will mean another French Revolution."

In Pennsylvania's anthracite counties, the National Guard built stockades topped with barbed wire, "pens" for those caught in any violence. The coal executives, still unable to persuade miners to break the strike and return to work—even for an extra two dollars a day—demanded more protection. "They seem to want a soldier at the door of every house in the coal region," Brigadier General John Gobin said. He didn't ask for additional men. Newspapers published rumors that Governor Stone might declare martial law or the federal government might take over the mines.

Garrisoned at his headquarters in Wilkes-Barre, Mitchell was tired and depressed. He had gained prestige in Washington and the operators had lost public support. The miners are "standing firm as the rocks of Gibraltar," he said. But he didn't how to bring the strike to an end.

Roosevelt anxiously considered his options. Usually when he needed to distract himself, he rode hard or tramped miles, anything to sweat and strain. But his leg was still healing and he wasn't able to exercise. So he turned to his other favorite activity, reading, and asked the Librarian of Congress to select books for him. "It has been such a delight to drop everything useful—everything that referred to my duty—everything, for instance, relating to the coal strike and the tariff, or the trusts, or my power to send troops into the mining districts, or my duty as regards summoning Congress—and to spend an afternoon in reading about the relations between Assyria and Egypt; which could not possibly do me any good and in which I reveled accordingly."

Senator Lodge, normally restrained and often on the side of management, wrote to the president about the coal operators. "Such insolence and arrogance coupled with stupidity I have never seen," he said. "I firmly believe Morgan is behind them. He is playing with fire." Roosevelt didn't immediately reply.

It was October 11, the one hundred fifty-third day of the strike, and Morgan agreed to try to end it. Secretary of War Root, unflappable and pragmatic, was a regular conduit between Washington and Wall Street. He thought Roosevelt "needed a little help" and had told the president he saw a way for the executives to break the impasse without humiliation. Roosevelt "very violently" approved of Root's plan. When Root sent a note to Morgan suggesting the two talk, Morgan immediately got on the phone to make arrangements.

Both the president and the financier trusted Root far more than they trusted each other. As for the coal executives, they had already denounced the president, at least two governors, and several senators for interfering in their business. Root decided he might do better acting as a private citizen. He took a day's leave from his official role to travel to New York.

It was a precarious time for Morgan. The federal government's case against Northern Securities was in the lower courts, and he didn't want another lawsuit charging that he controlled a coal monopoly too. He had to consider the possibility that Roosevelt wasn't bluffing about sending soldiers to take control of the mines. He also expected that, however hard he worked to end the strike, the president—who had already claimed the part of mediator—would take the credit for any success. Morgan was mostly fine with that. He had become the uncomfortable object of public fascination and resentment and didn't care to bring any more attention to himself.

Root arrived early Saturday morning and made his way to the Union League Club, where a reporter found him hard at work on a large breakfast. Root said he was in the city to register to vote in the November congressional elections. By ten, though, he was on his way to the Thirty-Fifth Street pier, where *Corsair* was docked. A launch waited to take him to the 304-foot vessel with its glimmering black hull, graceful clipper bow, and stores of vintage wine, specially blended tea, and Morgan's favorite Cuban cigars.

"Root saw Pierpont Morgan, found that Pierpont Morgan was alive to the seriousness of the situation, and impressed upon him the imminence of the danger," Roosevelt wrote afterward. Root and Morgan conferred for almost five hours. They drafted an eight-page document, which Root wrote in pencil on ivory-colored *Corsair* stationery, crossing out words as they went along. They intended to leave no doubt that the statement reflected only the coal operators' point of view. It condemned "the reign of terror" in the anthracite fields. It recognized "the urgent public need of coal." It gave no ground to the union. But it ended with the creation of a presidential commission to arbitrate the disputed issues among the owners and their employees. It was in substance the idea that Mitchell had proposed, Roosevelt had supported, and the executives had rejected. It was the form that mattered. "It was a damned lie, but it looked fair on paper," Root said later. He had understood what Morgan hadn't—that the appearance of compromise could be more powerful than compromise itself.

Commodore Morgan and private citizen Root hoped to leave the yacht undetected. Morgan ordered the launch to drop them at a different pier, but their carriage was delayed, or their driver confused, and for twenty minutes they stood in the rain, surrounded by reporters. Morgan ignored their questions; Root evaded them.

Finally, the two reached the Union Club. Root stayed only briefly, then caught the 4:25 train back to Washington. Severe rainstorms slowed the trip, though, and he didn't arrive until after eleven. Too late even to visit Roosevelt.

Morgan remained at the club, accompanied by George Perkins and guarded by attendants who turned away everyone but two coal executives. Word of a possible settlement passed from the club to the Wall Street crowd at the Waldorf-Astoria and beyond. Morgan and Perkins left around nine and slept on the yacht, leaving the reporters at shore's edge.

Sunday: more launches, more secret meetings on *Corsair*. Reporters called the coal operators at home, visited their offices. None could be found until that evening, when Baer left Philadelphia, on a special train. Morgan had called him to New York, and he wasn't happy about it. "You know as much about it as I do," he grumbled to a reporter.

It would be a brief talk. Morgan would force the executives to face bitter facts. They had a right to conduct business as they pleased. But not if it led to ruin. Or a government takeover. They were not mining coal, the cold was coming, and they had no reasonable solution. Roosevelt, they all agreed, could be unpredictable. It was time to end the strike on their terms, while they still could.

In Washington, Root reported to Roosevelt the details of what he called the "little memorandum." As they waited for Morgan to confirm the coal operators' acquiescence, Roosevelt wrote a letter to Ted, who was at boarding school. "I can now get about on crutches . . . Mother goes home tomorrow. She says she is leaving *me* to take care of *Ethel*; I have gloomy forebodings that after a brief struggle *Ethel* will take care of *me*." Roosevelt's youngest daughter had recently turned eleven.

Edith was returning to the Sagamore Hill estate, which stretched along the bay and into the forests of Long Island, to close their home for the winter. Full-time residents were gathering wood. Farmers were cutting down apple trees past their prime. One even tore down his fences. Cords of wood from large trees were sold for seven dollars; hard dry oak could bring ten. Scrub pine, ordinarily useless, had become worth something—anything that could be burned as fuel had.

Sand doused with kerosene generated enough heat to cook. So did porous terra cotta bricks soaked in oil. City residents used them to warm their homes, and no pile on any street was safe. A newspaper cartoon pictured Morgan in his nightgown and slippers peering down into his basement: "How would Morgan feel if he had to get up at 6 o'clock in the morning and yell down elevators for his oiled bricks?"

On that Monday afternoon, October 13, Fanny Simon was buried. She was a washerwoman supporting five children on her own, and she couldn't work if she didn't have fuel. She used her savings to take advantage of a supply of cheap coal for the poor. Fifteen cents for a 35-pound pail, and who knew how long it would last? She went back and forth from the depot to her sixth-floor apartment on the Lower East Side carrying 70-pound bags on her shoulders. The next day she died of internal bleeding, brought on, the doctor said, from the physical strain. Other families in the tenement paid for her funeral, but none could take in her children. They were sent to an orphanage.

Morgan left 23 Wall Street later than usual that Monday. He was on his way to the Union Club when reporters caught up to him and asked about the coal conferences that seemed to take up most of his day. "What do I know about coal?" he snapped as he got into this cab and drove away.

But of course Morgan knew a great deal. He knew that all six coal operators had, at last, agreed to arbitration. Under pressure from Roosevelt's threats and Morgan's influence, they required less than forty-eight hours to realize this was the most dignified conclusion they could expect to one of the most disruptive industrial actions the country had experienced. "If the solution which I proposed to Morgan had been sent by the President it would certainly have been rejected," Root wrote later. "But when the operators were afforded an opportunity to propose the solution themselves, Morgan was able to carry it through." The conflict between the coal companies and the union was not over, though; it had merely entered a new phase. Determined to press their advantage, the operators insisted on detailing the composition of the five-person commission that the president was to appoint. No labor representative was among them.

That left Mitchell in an awkward position. The miners would have a chance to speak of their troubles, but no union official on the arbitration board to hear them. The president invited Mitchell to Washington to discuss the proposal, and Mitchell arrived with one goal: to persuade him to push back against the barons. He wanted Roosevelt to add a labor representative to the commission and, because many of the miners were Catholic, a representative of the Church, as well. The strikers would object to the plan otherwise, and Mitchell didn't know how he could prevail upon them.

Late that evening, Morgan committed a surprising act of diplomacy. He presented the Corsair Agreement to Roosevelt in person. He arrived in Washington around ten, accompanied by his other favorite partner, Robert Bacon—back from his medical leave, but now in his last months with Morgan's firm. They picked up Root. And they went to see the president. Morgan still felt betrayed by Roosevelt's claims on his empire. Roosevelt still believed that Manhattan was the country's most "troublesome insular possession." Yet they set aside their mutual suspicion and antagonism to cooperate as the country faced the potential devastation of a winter without coal.

They spoke in the cabinet room of the temporary White House for ninety minutes. Roosevelt was told that the coal barons had very specific ideas of the kind of men he should appoint to the commission. That didn't go over too well. He resolved to deal with the owners' demands later.

Just before midnight, Morgan, Root, and Bacon emerged onto Lafayette Square. Reporters gathered around, desperate to find out if the strike was over. Instead of rushing past them as he usually did, Morgan stopped. He struck a match, lit his cigar, and smiled. Then he walked on. Inside his residence, Roosevelt was giddy with relief. Cortelyou released the agreement, addressed to "the public," at one in the morning.

"It was a concession," one of the coal executives said later that day, "but not to the miners. It was a concession to humanity."

Morgan and Bacon returned to Jersey City on the Royal Blue Express Tuesday afternoon. As they walked to the ferry that would take them across

J. P. Morgan and Robert Bacon,
1902

the Hudson River, Morgan bought the New York papers. He took a seat toward the front of the ferry. He appeared nervous. Instead of opening the pages, he asked one of the reporters following him: "What is the latest news from the coal fields?" When he heard that some miners weren't pleased with the terms of the agreement, he became concerned. "I hope they do accept. I think it will be for their own good to accept," he said. "But of course I can't tell what they will do."

Everything now depended on the selection of the arbitration commission. The owners would have to make another concession, or two, before Mitchell and the strikers would accept their proposal. The coal road presidents had stipulated that the commission include "a businessman active in coal mining and selling," which sure sounded as if the coal executives wanted one of their own on the arbitration panel. Mitchell argued the board wouldn't be impartial without a labor representative. Roosevelt promised to do everything he could so that "justice will be done the miners regardless of the railroad presidents." Frank Sargent, the former grand master of the Brotherhood of Locomotive Firemen who was serving as Roosevelt's immigration commissioner, said he was confident both sides could come to a compromise: "I believe that we have seen the beginning of the end of the strike."

Or maybe it was the end of the beginning. Bacon returned to the White House with Perkins on Wednesday evening to discuss how to accommodate Mitchell without angering the operators. Roosevelt had men in mind for each of the five designated positions on the commission as well as the two Mitchell pressed for. The president wasn't expecting a difficult conversation. Bacon and Perkins were friends. Everyone, it seemed, wanted the men back in the mines and anthracite back on the market. So he hobbled off across Lafayette Park to dinner at the home of John Hay, arriving "under cover of the darkness," the secretary of state wrote. "He began talking at the oysters and the pousse-café found him still at it."

At ten Roosevelt re-appeared at 22 Jackson Place. Bacon and Perkins were waiting. The discussion didn't go smoothly. "The operators were balking," and Bacon and Perkins were "both of them nearly wild," Roosevelt later recounted. The operators could accept a prelate on the commission but refused to allow a labor official. They would withdraw their offer to arbitrate if Roosevelt insisted. Morgan couldn't persuade them otherwise. Mitchell wouldn't relent.

At eleven they were still at a standoff. Bacon and Perkins pleaded with Roosevelt to force Mitchell and the miners to capitulate. They said the operators never would.

Finally, at midnight, movement. Bacon mentioned that the operators wouldn't object to Roosevelt's exercising latitude in his appointments as long as he stuck to the categories they set out. One was "a man of prominence, eminent as a sociologist." Roosevelt had an idea. "I instantly said that I should appoint my labor man as the 'eminent sociologist,'" Roosevelt later recounted. That night E. E. Clark, the head of the brotherhood of railway conductors, became an "eminent sociologist."

Roosevelt was astounded and relieved that operators accepted this semantic sleight of hand: "The mighty brains of these captains of industry had formulated the theory that they would rather have anarchy than tweedledum, but if I would use the word tweedledee they would hail it as meaning peace." Bacon and Perkins called Morgan in New York and Baer in Philadelphia for their approval. The commission was complete.

"These names are accepted by the operators and I now most earnestly ask and urge that the miners likewise accept this commission," Roosevelt telegrammed Mitchell. "It is a matter of vital concern to all our people and especially to those in our great cities who are least well off that the mining of coal should be resumed without a day's unnecessary delay."

It would take a little longer than a day. "Gentlemen, if you consider that we are deserving of congratulations I will gladly accept them now," Mitchell told the reporters gathered at Hotel Hart. But that was premature, too. Mitchell couldn't assume sole authority for calling off the strike. He had asked for arbitration on behalf of the members of his union, and now they should share in the final responsibility of accepting it. This would be the ultimate test of the strikers' loyalty to him. What they couldn't know, not yet, was that he placed as much faith in his new political allies as he did in them—maybe more. Mitchell's prestige depended on satisfying both these constituencies.

He called a convention of delegates from all three of the anthracite districts on October 20 in Wilkes-Barre. Mitchell looked haggard at the start, but he promised to answer every question they put to him. That took the better part of two days. Would the strikers be discriminated against? No. Would they all get their jobs back? Maybe not. But the union would take care of them and help them find other work. Would they receive back wages if they did? He hoped so. In the end, he promised that "this proposal will secure to the anthracite mine workers and those dependent upon them a greater measure of justice than they could attain by continuing the conflict . . . [and] a greater degree of justice than they have enjoyed in the past." The strikers—eager for a steady income and the resumption of their daily routines—chose to believe him, and on October 21, they voted to accept the Corsair Agreement.

The headlines were big and bold. Roosevelt was called a statesman, his mediation a welcome approach, his commission impartial and expert. He had already been celebrating. "I feel like throwing up my hands and going to the circus," he wrote. He would go on a bear hunt in Mississippi instead. He knew he didn't deserve all the credit: "I am being very much overpraised by everybody, and although I suppose I like it, it makes me feel uncomfortable too."

Roosevelt was generous with his own praise. "Late last night when it became evident that we were going to get a commission which would be accepted by both sides I remarked, 'Well, Uncle Mark's work has borne fruit,'" he wrote to Hanna, who didn't like being called Uncle Mark.

The president also knew that even as he had created a new role for the federal government in labor disputes, he couldn't have done so without the biggest of the titans: Morgan. In the moment—and even more so, as the years went on—Roosevelt considered his intervention in the strike one of the great achievements of his presidency.

He made clear his gratitude to Morgan. "My dear sir," Roosevelt wrote in a letter, "let me thank you for the service you have rendered the whole people. If it had not been for your going in to the matter I do not see how the strike could have been settled at this time, and the consequences that might have followed upon its being unsettled when cold weather set in are in very fact dreadful to contemplate. I thank you and congratulate you with all my heart."

Morgan apparently never sent a reply.

The men went back to the anthracite mines on October 23. The strike had lasted one hundred

Anthracite Coal Strike Commission in Pennsylvania, 1903

sixty-four days. It cost thirty thousand dollars a day to keep the Pennsylvania National Guard in the field. It cost the mines and railroads some seventy-four million dollars and their public standing. It cost the miners twenty-five million in lost wages. "One great trouble was that the little world in which the operators moved was absolutely out of touch with the big world that included practically all the rest of the country," Roosevelt wrote to his sister Bamie.

The arbitration commission met at the White House on October 24 and began its work soon afterward. It would set conditions for the one hundred forty-seven thousand miners to produce one of the nation's most vital commodities for the next three years—through the 1904 presidential election.

AT A BANQUET in Mitchell's honor, hosted by the union at the Hotel Hart in Wilkes-Barre, the labor leader received an expensive gold watch and a gold medallion with his initials set in diamonds. On Mitchell Day, October 29, supporters gave him more gifts. One hundred thousand people in towns across anthracite country came out to celebrate. Parades of miners marched down main streets. People said he could be elected the next leader of the American Federation of Labor or the governor of Illinois.

Mother Jones offered no compliments. She believed the strikers should have stayed out of the mines until the union won recognition. Mitchell had been close. Then Roosevelt, Hanna, Root, and Morgan played him. "Flattery and homage did its work with John Mitchell," she wrote. Mitchell publicly thanked Roosevelt and Morgan. He had confidence in the powerful, which made politicians admire him and, later, made workers distrust him.

Yet in the late fall of 1902 he was famous and adored. He considered going on a speaking tour to cash in "while the iron is hot and the public is interested," as a friend advised. But he thought he could probably make more by writing about the strike. *McClure's*, one of the nation's most popular magazines, would pay him five hundred dollars to publish his own account of the strike. And it would be easier. He was weary: of the attention, the scrutiny, and "the terrible nervous strain" of the strike. He wanted to rest.

That wouldn't be possible for a while. The commissioners were coming to town.

Mitchell rented two floors of a house in Philadelphia and hired investigators, economists, researchers, publicists, and secretaries to prepare the miners' case. He needed bodies and stories. He needed information—statistics on wages and hours to start, but also the costs of living, the costs of mining, production, and distribution, the top line and the bottom line.

Mitchell submitted the miners' demands in early November: a 20 percent increase in wages for contract miners (who were paid by the ton), a 20 percent reduction in the hours for everyone else—and union recognition. Mitchell hadn't given up on that after all. The coal executives declared the three demands arbitrary and unreasonable. But it wasn't up to them now.

The Anthracite Coal Strike Commission began hearings November 14 at the Lackawanna County Court House in Scranton. No one was on trial, exactly, but there were two opposing sides and they both lawyered up. Witnesses—five hundred fifty-eight of them, including Mitchell and Baer—were sworn in and cross-examined. Their testimony came to more than ten thousand pages.

The workers recited a litany of injuries they were never compensated for, hours they couldn't count on, wages never paid in cash. They spoke of debt, and of death. Over the days, as the men and women of coal country presented evidence, it came to seem as if the system in which they labored could best be described as feudal.

Andrew Chippie, twelve years old and "no taller than a yardstick," was a breaker boy. His father died in the mines indebted to the company for $54.95, the equivalent of a good month's wages. The company allowed Andrew, his three younger siblings, and his mother to live in their company house rent-free for eighteen months. But once Andrew could work, the company could collect the rent. Andrew earned four cents an hour, and now, after working sixty-four hours over six weeks, he owed the company $88.17. "You weren't getting ahead very fast, were you," remarked Judge George Gray, one of the commission members.

James Gallagher was sixty years old and had worked in the mines all his life; for almost eighteen of those years, everything he earned—except for fifty dollars—went to paying rent at his company-owned home and provisions at the company-owned store. When one of the union lawyers asked if he had ever been hurt, Gallagher answered: "A man is never hurt in the mines unless he is half-killed." When he was asked how many times he had been half-killed, he said twice. "Then you were killed entirely," Judge Gray said after the laughter subsided. "No, it was this way," Gallagher explained. "The first half was healed before I got the second."

Henry Coll summed up his twenty-nine years underground: leg and fingers broken, ribs smashed, skull fractured, half-blind. "I lost my right eye, and I can't see out of the glass one much," he told the commission. He had more to say. He had served on the miners' relief committee, been evicted, and forced to move into a house in such poor condition that his kids got sick. His wife, already ill, died two days later. "She died?" Judge Gray repeated. She died. No one cross-examined Coll.

Officially, the commission would not recognize Mitchell as president of a union whose existence the coal operators refused to acknowledge. But he gave testimony nonetheless. In his forty-three-minute-long opening statement, Mitchell argued that the miners "have as much right to select spokesmen to act for them, to present their grievances, to manage their affairs as have the stock holders of any one of the anthracite coal companies." Mitchell rejected the idea of inherent friction between management and workers. He reminded the commission that his union had honored contracts made with the bituminous coal companies. His union wanted peace. His union wanted harmony. His union could be trusted. It was his union that conferred with the president, that sent the men back to the mines, that agreed to accept the findings of the commission. "The wealth and the future of the nation are not measured by its palaces and millionaires," he concluded, "but rather by the enlightened contentment and prosperity of its millions of citizens, [who] constitute the bone and sinew of our land."

He remained on the witness stand for four days of cross-examination. He wasn't known for his sense of humor, but it turned out he had one. A lawyer for the operators expressed a sudden concern that the cost of increased wages for the miners would lead to prices unaffordable to the most vulnerable. "If you demand an increase and [the companies] have no profits where are they going to place it except upon the bowed backs of the poor?" he asked. Mitchell suggested an alternative: "They might put it on the bowed backs of the rich."

In January, the hearings moved to Philadelphia to accommodate the operators' schedules. They spoke of violence. They named the dead: Luigi Vanassa, William A. Duryea, Drummond Klinger, Joseph Beddall, John Lineheart, William Purcell, Daniel Sweeney, Patrick Sharp, C. M. Brush, Sistieno Castelli, James Winstone, Joseph Gillis, John Mullen, Anthony Colson, William Durham.

The noted journalist Ray Stannard Baker investigated the circumstances of some of their deaths for *McClure's* that month. The men's stories revealed the bitter toll of the strike—the sense of betrayal and confusion in the coal communities, the anger and fear that Mitchell tried to tamp, Roosevelt had to weigh, and the coal operators hoped to exploit.

James Winstone lived in Olyphant, an unusually prosperous mining town of six thousand people. Winstone was a more than usually prosperous miner. He was forty-eight years old, a husband and father of three. He owned the best home in the best neighborhood. Winstone had been a treasurer in the Lackawanna Accident Fund and, for a while, an official with the United Mine Workers. But he had voted against the strike. He thought anyone who worked hard could get ahead, as he had.

Once the strike began, he stopped working in the mines and found a job elsewhere that paid less. Eventually he returned home. He wasn't eligible for assistance, the union told him, since he could mortgage his home. He didn't want to mortgage his home. He went back to the mines. Threatening crowds gathered in front of his home in the mornings and evenings as he went to and from work.

On the morning of September 25, Winstone and his son-in-law were beaten by men with clubs. His son-in-law survived, but Winstone died a few hours afterward. The attackers escaped by train to Hoboken but were caught, brought back to Scranton, and jailed. They were Winstone's neighbors.

Anthony Colson was still alive. And he was called John. He was an engineer, the best position at any colliery. He didn't believe in the strike, but he joined it. After a month, he went back to work and lived in a railcar close to the mine. He was safe there, though his wife was turned away at stores, and yelled at on the streets, and feared their home would be blown up. He was headed there one night to help pack up and move his family when he was beaten, robbed, and left for dead. "He might better be dead, for he's brought disgrace on the name," his mother said. "He deserved all he got. He wasn't raised a scab." John's father had retired, his six brothers stayed out of the mines until Mitchell told them to return. By then the entire Colson family's finances were so circumscribed that John's father had to go back. His face was scarred blue from a powder explosion. He was blind in one eye. Now he was doing a boy's work in the mines, turning a fan for seventy-five cents a day.

Mitchell apologized for the intimidation, the assaults, the deaths. He said the union didn't condone violence, hadn't organized it, and wanted the men responsible for it punished.

Baer gave the closing speech in front of a full courtroom. He argued that the only monopoly in the anthracite fields was the union itself, which broke man-made laws and forced men to surrender their God-given right to work. He described mining, the deep underground, explosive work of it, as an unskilled trade that more men than necessary wished to be paid to undertake. "What does that indicate? Why, that labor there is attractive," he said.

He spoke, again, of God's creation of the world. It would be idle to speculate why "He should have stored the fuel deep down in the bosom of the earth and compelled men to bore through solid adamant to reach the hidden treasure, and dig it in darkness and danger," Baer said. "This is the way He did create the world and it is in this world we live." To the admittedly perplexing question of "why one man should be strong, happy and prosperous, and another weak, afflicted and distressed," Baer offered an answer: "To teach the power of human endurance and the nobility of a life of struggle."

He spoke, in his final moments as a witness, of his own place in God's plan. "It is entirely possible that a new order of men could create a new order of things," he said. They should try somewhere else, like the Philippines. Until then, he suggested that those who wanted to give advice "but do not know how to do things themselves" resist interfering in his affairs. "For the time being we have surrendered, not to the Mine Workers, but to this Commission, our reasonable, rightful control of the complicated business we are managing."

Baer's assertions—narrow-eyed, contemptuous, self-serving—were extraordinary even for him, a last public howl of protest at a changing world. Roosevelt had described Baer and the other coal barons' defiance as "a condition of wooden-headed obstinacy and stupidity." Roosevelt wasn't in the room, though. Mitchell was, and Mitchell walked over to Baer and shook his hand.

The audience gasped. Mitchell had said capital and labor should be allies. He said he believed in class harmony, not conflict. He thought he could be the bigger man. So he shook Baer's hand.

The commission agreed to cut the miners' workday from ten to nine hours and awarded a retroactive 10 percent wage increase to the miners, admitting that a 10 percent price increase in coal was likely. The commission did not recognize Mitchell's union. That, it said, was beyond the scope of its mandate. But the report stated that all workers had the right to join unions and that employers would ultimately benefit from collective bargaining. It would help train union representatives to be more businesslike. The commission created a permanent six-member board of conciliation to rule on disputes between the miners and their employers.

Both sides could, and did, consider the conclusions a victory. Mitchell said he was pleased to win a wage increase. The coal presidents said they were gratified that Mitchell didn't win recognition for his union. Hanna reportedly declared that "the era of labor strikes is drawing to an end." Roosevelt said the commissioners did a great job and invited them to dinner at the White House.

Morgan said nothing.

Mitchell—raised in poverty, educated on the job—had proven himself capable of leading one hundred forty-seven thousand men in a fight for their dignity and then sealing peace with a handshake. He didn't see a future in politics, though; he was more interested in business. He invested in a bituminous coal mine, Carbon Hill in Virginia, in the autumn of 1902 and helped found the Egyptian Powder Company the next year. These were surely conflicts of interest, but no one knew about his arrangements at the time.

He became an editor and columnist at a new labor-friendly paper in Chicago called *Boyce's Weekly*, which paid him an annual salary of at least a thousand dollars. To boost its popularity, he wrote a letter to Andrew Chippie, the breaker boy who had come to national attention with his testimony, to encourage him to work as a newsboy, and draw in subscribers, in his free time. "Many a wealthy man got his start in life as a newsboy," he told Chippie. Not at *Boyce's Weekly*, though. The paper went under in September 1903.

Mitchell had already been enjoying other perks of the job. Ralph Easley of the National Civic Federation invited him to a business dinner with George Perkins during the strike and promised a show afterward. "'When Knighthood was in Flower' with Julia Marlow [sic] is a lovely thing," Easley wrote. Mitchell attended a National Civic Federation banquet in New York City during the commission's hearing. Hanna greeted him as John.

He wore a new silk hat and expensive tailor-made suits. He developed a paunch. His face got puffy. It could have been from eating to excess. It could have been from drinking to excess. Mitchell came to resemble the moneyed executives he admired.

AS THE ARBITRATION commission was hearing testimony in Scranton, Northern Securities lawyers were preparing briefs for the circuit court in St. Louis. Roosevelt hoped the judges wouldn't take too long to rule. The presidential election would test the détente between Roosevelt and Morgan. The president expected to win the lawsuit, but timing was everything; he wanted a victory that the public would remember, and that Wall Street would have forgotten, by the time Election Day rolled around. Investors still seemed to prefer Hanna, who continued to insist that he would not challenge Roosevelt. "Rot all rot," he told a reporter who brought news of his alleged desire for the presidency. Hanna really wasn't interested in the presidency. He was interested in unnerving the president.

In the capital, there was a more immediate concern. Coal soot was ruining the Washington Monument. During the strike, businesses—and even the government—had burned soft coal in violation of the city's smoke code. Until regular shipments of anthracite resumed, the city wasn't enforcing the regulation. The particular problem for the monument was dense black smoke from a huge nearby chimney belonging to a railway and

Roosevelt reading his annual message to his cabinet before sending it to Congress, composite photo, 1902: "We draw the line against misconduct, not against wealth"

electric company. Misty weather was helping it adhere to the marble obelisk. When an employee reached out to wipe the small windows at the top, the clean spot was visible from the ground. It would take spring wind and rain to completely dissolve the soot.

CHAPTER 13

Rich Man's Panic

At midnight a spark of electricity sent its impulse from the Naval Observatory in Washington through a thousand telegraph wires around the country. A murmuring anticipation on the streets of the capital gave way to cheers, whistles, tin horns, cowbells, firecrackers, and gunshots.

The new year began with a sense of bigness. The Treasury had a surplus of some fifty million dollars—and an extra eighty million dollars' worth of gold locked in its vaults. Congress repealed all war taxes. Unemployment was dropping. Companies raised wages, though sometimes workers had to go on strike first.

Broadway was bright and noisy at midnight. A hundred thousand people stamped and hoped and shed their complaints, though not all of them. "Down with the Trusts," forty people yelled into handmade megaphones. Earlier that day, Pierpont Morgan's firm had presented bonuses to its one hundred thirty or so employees that reportedly equaled their annual salary. Northern Securities had just reelected its board of directors and promised a stock dividend.

It was 1903. The anthracite coal miners were back underground in Pennsylvania. The wound on Roosevelt's leg was healed. The renovation of the White House was nearly complete. On January 1, Cabinet secretaries, Supreme Court justices, members of Congress, commanders from the

Army, Navy, and Marines, the diplomatic corps, the press corps, and some seven thousand of the citizen corps paraded through its doors. The Marine band accompanied them.

The president and his wife stood in front of a bay window in the Blue Room. A colonial blue silk with a gold border covered the parlor walls. The furniture was upholstered in blue satin with a gilt fleur-de-lis pattern. Edith wore a gown of ecru lace spangled with silver over pale blue mousseline de soie. She kept on her white suede gloves. He was dressed more somberly, in a frock suit and gray tie—no gloves. Roosevelt shook everyone's hand. "De-lighted." "I'm glad to see you." "Well, how are you?" "Ever so glad to see you." Again and again, and he seemed to mean it.

The entire first floor was open to the public: the Red Room, the Green Room, the East Room, the expanded dining room. The heads of four bears and four deer from Roosevelt's favorite taxidermist—along with that of a great moose from Alaska—hung on the walls. The image of an eagle was carved into the mahogany table.

New Year's Day was sunny. The only one likely disappointed by that was Charles Maxwell, who had overseen a six-month effort to electrify the White House that included the installation of thirty-one miles of wire, three thousand incandescent bulbs, three crystal chandeliers in the East Room alone, two telephone systems (one public, one private), and a security system. But on that Thursday, no one needed to turn on the lights.

Maxwell's project cost ninety-five thousand dollars. The budget for the entire renovation was half a million dollars. Completely worth it, some Washingtonians thought, to end the national humiliation of having a White House that was cramped, grimy, and outdated.

Time itself seemed to be accelerating. By early 1904, Henry Ford would set a land speed record for automobiles of 91.37 miles an hour, and the Wright brothers would pilot the first motorized flight. Americans' daily lives became more streamlined: Michael Owens would patent a fully automated glass-bottle-making machine. Roberta Lawson and Mary McLaren would patent the tea bag.

The president's year began with a rush of business. There was a lot he wanted Congress to accomplish before its session ended March 4. Congress wasn't used to such presidential interest and insistence. Roosevelt and

Attorney General Knox were pushing a bill to create a Department of Commerce and within it a Bureau of Corporations empowered to investigate companies' finances. Another bill they backed would ban the rebates railroads gave their biggest customers and fine both for violations. Another would speed up antitrust litigation.

"This week I have been as busy as I possibly could be," Roosevelt wrote to his son Kermit in mid-January. "My exercise has for the most part been confined to singlestick with General Wood in the evenings . . . I pass my days in a state of exasperation, first, with the fools who do not want to do any of the things that ought to be done, and, second, with the equally obnoxious fools who insist upon so much that they cannot get anything." Three days later, he wrote to his son Ted that he had to stop singlestick with General Wood because his right arm had been "badly battered." The doctor said Roosevelt had a slight fracture. Roosevelt said he didn't.

The president was frustrated through January and right into February. He was coming hard up against the limits of his executive power. He could wheedle, bargain, and bully, but he still had to wait for Congress to vote on legislation. And then he had to trust the courts to enforce it.

The bill proposed by Stephen Elkins, a Republican senator from West Virginia, to end railroad rebates faced little resistance. The railroads' practice of favoring large companies had infuriated farmers and small business owners for years. Ida Tarbell's groundbreaking investigation into Standard Oil's power and corruption exposed how crucial obtaining those discounts—called "Rockefeller's rebates"—was to the company's success. By 1903, though, big customers demanded cash rebates that cost the railroads millions. They were ready to back a government solution to an expensive problem they couldn't fix on their own. Corporations didn't oppose the legislation, either. They expected to find other ways to secure special treatment from the railroads.

The Expedition Act would help hold big business to account, and passing it was crucial if the fate of Northern Securities was to be determined before the end of Roosevelt's term. The law would send appeals of antitrust cases directly to the Supreme Court. That sounded like a terrible idea to the lawyers and lobbyists representing the trusts. The system—lengthy waits, procedural obstruction, judicial confusion—worked to their advantage. If they could no longer ignore the Sherman Antitrust Act, then they could at least stall its application. Northern Securities' men in Washington whispered suggestions about how best to achieve that. But in this case, their advice went unheeded.

Congress was also debating what information it should demand from corporations, what it should make public and what penalties it could impose when it found wrongdoing. Roosevelt didn't like the tenor of the discussion. He thought it was too harsh. He had two requirements, both controversial. He wanted to reserve for the president the authority to decide which financial details to publicize. That was a power that could easily corrupt, which is why Roosevelt thought it should belong to the president, and members of Congress preferred it remain in the agency. Roosevelt also wanted executives to believe the rules were fair—not vindictive—so they would adhere to them instead of immediately trying to subvert them. He consulted his friend George Perkins, Morgan's partner, to make sure they were. James Dill, the lawyer who did so much to make New Jersey a corporate safe haven, gave Roosevelt some tips too. "But as soon as the business interests showed any symptoms of acquiescence," Roosevelt wrote to a friend, "certain individuals have at once asserted that the legislation was bad, because they did not want it unless it frightened the corporations!"

Roosevelt employed all his powers to define the terms of the debate. He leaned on his friends in the Senate to support the law as he wanted it and griped to his friends in the press about corporate interference to sabotage it. He said, for effect, that John D. Rockefeller himself sent telegrams to certain Republicans reminding them who they really represented. This was not, strictly speaking, true, but the publicity did help neutralize the pressure to craft a more punitive measure. It was true that Standard Oil remained opposed to any new government bureau with too much authority over companies. Standard Oil sent three lawyers to Washington to make that clear. Senator Nelson Aldrich, whose youngest daughter was married to Rockefeller's only son, advised the Standard men to depart before they made matters worse.

That left Roosevelt with only one complaint. He didn't like the name Congress wanted to give the new department. "For heaven's sake do try to get the words 'and labor' out of the Department of Commerce Bill," he wrote to Senator Hanna. "The title is cumbrous, misleading and slightly ridiculous."

On February 14 the Department of Commerce and Labor was created. That month the Elkins Act and the Expedition Act went into effect too. Roosevelt got most of what he wanted. Knox got half a million dollars to start up what would become the antitrust division of the Justice Department. Perkins got one of the pens the president used to sign the commerce bill. George Cortelyou, who would lead the new department, got the other.

During the legislative season, the Gridiron Club, run by Washington correspondents, hosted an annual dinner at which they lampooned the rich and powerful people they wrote about. Sometimes the subjects even showed up. This time, surprise of surprises, Morgan made an appearance. On Saturday evening, January 31, he and Hanna, along with two hundred others, mingled in the Arlington Hotel's banquet hall. Roosevelt was invited, as always, but had to attend a dinner for his cabinet.

Morgan sat to the right of the club's new president, the British ambassador to the left. Roses and orchids were on every table, along with terrapin, English mutton, Philadelphia squab, ice cream, champagne, and cigars. Club members performed skits between the courses. Morgan wasn't among the speakers—that would be too much to hope for—but he was the unwitting star of the evening.

The Wall Street office of P. J. Morgan & Co., Busters and Boosters was the setting for the final performance. "The thing that worries the old man is what we had better do about a president," said one employee.

"President of what? President of the Board of Aldermen?"

"President of the United States."

"Oh, I thought it was something important."

"Well, it is important if the old man is anxious about it."

No one seemed to enjoy that more than the old man himself. The next morning Morgan reportedly told Hanna—his preferred presidential candidate for 1904—that he "had the time of his life."

"Beginning to like newspaper men at last?" Hanna said.

"I can say that I like newspaper men quite as much as they like me, but of all the dinners I ever sat down to, the Gridiron Club dinner last night takes the palm."

Morgan stopped back in Washington about six weeks later on his way home from a trip to Cuba, where he met the president, toured the island, and no doubt bought up his favorite cigars. In Havana, he stayed with a prominent shipping executive. In Washington, he stayed at the Arlington, as he usually did, without registering, which he rarely did. Morgan visited a few senators and the treasury secretary to press for lower import duties on art. Much of his European collection remained in London because bringing it to New York could cost him three million dollars in taxes.

When he returned to the hotel with Hanna, the clerk told Morgan: "The White House wants you." Morgan reportedly smiled and replied, "Tell the White House I haven't come in yet." He went off with Hanna, and only a while later allowed the clerk to notify the White House that he was in. He met with Roosevelt alone for thirty minutes. It was the first time they had been together unaccompanied in years, maybe ever. The government's case against Morgan's railroad company would soon begin in a lower court. The two men would have nothing to say to each other about that. It could be that they discussed America's treaty with Cuba, which included the lease of Guantánamo Bay, or the anthracite coal strike commission's report, which the president was expecting any day. But neither said anything publicly about that half hour, not then and not later.

THE MARSHAL REQUESTED extra security guards to keep order in the St. Louis courtroom on Wednesday, March 18. Every seat was taken. A special panel of four federal circuit court judges was ready to hear some of the highest-paid corporate lawyers in the country defend their most important clients. The trial of Morgan, Hill, and their company, Northern Securities, was about to begin. The question before the court: With its eighteen thousand miles of railroad track along the Northern Pacific, Great Northern, and Burlington lines, was Northern Securities too powerful to be allowed to exist? It was either a monopoly that had to be broken up no matter how cleverly it had been put together, or just another New Jersey holding company, one of thousands registered every year.

John Griggs, fifty-three years old, sharp-nosed, with gray hair and sideburns, led Morgan's legal team. As governor of New Jersey in 1896, he had been an unwavering creature of the Republican machine. As attorney general under McKinley for three years, he had declined all opportunities but one to enforce the Sherman Antitrust law. (That one was a case against a combination of coal producers and shippers in West Virginia and Ohio, which the government won.) Griggs said he didn't want to waste the government's money or humiliate its lawyers with other cases sure to lose. Northern Securities was his chance to prove that he had been right all along.

James Montgomery Beck, more than a decade younger than Griggs, was assistant attorney general. He had dark hair and wore thick round glasses and a large ruby ring. He was languid and suave, so boyish and slight that at first the courtroom audience didn't recognize him as the government's lawyer. This was his final appearance on its behalf. The following month he joined the New York law firm that had advised Harriman in his attempted hostile takeover of Northern Pacific.

Congress passed the Expedition Act just in time. Knox had filed the case against Northern Securities in St. Paul a year earlier, and it was moved to St. Louis, where the four judges could hear the proceedings sooner. No witnesses would be called. Testimony from Morgan, Hill, and other executives was already on the record. The judges didn't need to be told that a speedy decision would be best. Their opinion would be delivered back in St. Paul. The appeal would go straight to the Supreme Court. The final verdict on the most important antitrust case in two administrations would be handed down well before the Republican and Democratic national conventions in the summer of 1904.

Beck went first. "Few cases have been presented to any court which affected corporate interests to such magnitude, and still fewer which more vitally concern the welfare of the American people," he said. He began at ten in the morning on that Wednesday and spoke until almost four in the afternoon, stopping only for a court-ordered two-hour lunch break. Griggs summed up the defense on Friday. Why are we here, he asked. This company didn't deserve to be punished. The Sherman Act doesn't forbid "the natural process of unification."

Beck argued that Northern Securities combined two competing transcontinental railroads and was a "virtual merger," no matter what Morgan and Hill called it. He criticized New Jersey for its "reckless sale of corporate privileges to secure petty fees." He told the courtroom that the method of creating a monopoly could be ingenious. It could be indirect. But it would still be illegal. He said the Sherman Act could be invoked even though prices on the three lines hadn't increased. They always could be. Northern Securities, he said, was a monopoly whose powers were "infinite in scope, perpetual in character, vested in the hands of a few," and may be exercised "by methods secret even to stockholders."

Griggs asserted that the combination of Morgan's Northern Pacific and Hill's Great Northern and their purchase of the Burlington line created a new commercial empire in the Northwest that benefited everyone. They weren't monopolizing trade but "strengthening, augmenting and extending the trade and business of the two companies in both transcontinental and worldwide competition." He parsed the difference between rivalry and hostility. The Great Northern and Northern Pacific had experienced a little of the former and none of the latter. "Competition can be and is carried on between individuals and corporations, not only without rancor and jealousy but in a spirit of friendliness and with a mutual desire to promote good relations," he said. "The law does not forbid that."

Beck concluded that "however public spirited the purposes of the defendants in forming this merger may have been, and whatever its resultant good or evil, it is enough for present purposes to say that it clearly violates existing law."

Griggs reminded the judges that whatever influence Morgan and Hill desired to wield over the two rail lines, they already possessed before the merger. The consequences of their combination were not "pernicious but beneficial and should be marked with public approval rather than by legislative and governmental obstruction."

IN THE WEEKS after the trial, Morgan had more on his mind than the future of Northern Securities. There was trouble in the stock market, enough trouble that he gave a rare interview to the *New York Times* at the end of March. He spoke in public only when he needed to. The reason was always the same: to impart confidence to investors and creditors. The optimism of early 1903 was dimming, that sense of bigness began to seem a deception. American companies were building and extracting and smelting their way to industrial power. That was real, grounded, sometimes excessive, often inescapable. Then there was Wall Street, where combining those companies and selling the new stock to eager investors depended on imagining the ledgers would always tilt in their favor.

Not at all, Morgan said. "Not only is there prosperity everywhere, but the promises are of a continuation of that prosperity for a long time to come." Any decline in stock prices was a temporary matter. "The general pessimistic talk indulged in not alone in foreign but in local circles is in no sense justified by the facts." The problem, if that's what critics wanted to call it, was simple. "There are in the market many undigested securities."

Undigested securities: That was a new one. Morgan meant to defend the many recent public offerings of stock, often created by the mergers and acquisitions he promoted. They weren't overvalued, speculative, or unwarranted. They just hadn't been digested by the public yet. Even Hill seemed doubtful. He suggested later that the stocks were "indigestible."

ROOSEVELT LEFT WASHINGTON at nine in the morning on April 1 in a fully electrified private six-car train. He would live on it for almost all of his nine-week, fourteen-thousand-mile speaking tour. He would visit one hundred fifty cities in twenty-five states and give some two hundred speeches about regulating trusts, improving relations between employers and workers, being a good citizen, the dignity of labor, the coal strike commission, the Philippines, tariffs, irrigation, roads, industrial life, prosperity. Sometimes he spoke to crowds so large that those on the edges couldn't hear him. They could see him, though, and he hoped that would be enough to impress them.

He said the trip would be a "terrific strain," but he also knew it would be the last one for a while. Once the 1904 election season began, he would be confined closer to home. Sitting presidents didn't stump for themselves— that would be unseemly—they sent out proxies instead. So he would take advantage of the bully pulpit while he could. "I did not 'divine' how the people were going to think," he wrote later. "I simply made up my mind what they *ought* to think, and then did my best to get them to think it."

Roosevelt would be away from the capital longer than any of his predecessors, though Congress would be gone too. He would travel with a smaller entourage, but it still included executives from Western Union and the Pennsylvania Railroad, which provided the train and printed a booklet mapping the president's route. Roosevelt's private car, the Elysian, would be plenty comfortable. It contained three state rooms, an observation parlor, two living rooms, a dining room, and a room for his attendants. A Pullman conductor would drive the locomotive and a Pullman butler would look after the president.

George Cortelyou, once Roosevelt's senior secretary and adviser and now head of the new Commerce and Labor Department, came to see him off at the Sixth Street station. "How can I leave you here with those horrible trusts?" Roosevelt joked. "Do not let them hurt you while I am away."

The train traveled over tracks owned by the railroads Roosevelt and his attorney general had accused of monopoly power. How could it not? The president himself would be in St. Paul just days before the lower court's verdict on the Northern Securities case. He would also be in Chicago, Evanston, Milwaukee, Minneapolis, Sioux Falls, Fargo, Bismarck, Medora (near his old ranch), and Jamestown. Roosevelt said his trust legislation was "meant to do square justice to each man, big or little, and to ensure, as far as by legislation we can secure, that he will do fair justice in return." The message went over well in the Dakotas.

In between stops he read the forty books he ordered for the trip, among them: *The Work of Wall Street* (written by the editor of the *Wall Street Journal*), *Some Ethical Phases of the Labor Question* (written by his own labor commissioner), *The Citizen in His Relation to the Industrial Situation*, by Morgan's friend Bishop Henry Potter, as well as *Biography of a Prairie Girl* by Eleanor Gates and a Booth Tarkington love story set in the early days of the Mexican-American War. An eclectic list, as usual, gathered from friends, family, and the Librarian of Congress.

On April 8, Roosevelt arrived in Livingston, Montana, just north of Yellowstone National Park. He came over Morgan's Northern Pacific line.

The railroad's president, Charles Mellen, rode in his private car fifteen minutes ahead of Roosevelt's to make sure the track was clear.

Yellowstone, the country's first national park, was established by President Grant in 1872 and turned over to the Army to administer. The city of Livingston was founded a decade later by the Northern Pacific. The last spike of the line was hammered into place in 1883 some two hundred miles away. Back then, Livingston had a depot, a casino, some saloons. And it had Yellowstone, which spanned more than three thousand square miles, sat on a volcanic caldera, and offered iridescent geysers. Still, as James Hill later said, "You might put a railroad in the Garden of Eden, and if there was no one there but Adam and Eve it would be a failure." By 1884, the Northern Pacific was advertising trips to the park with a story, "Alice's Adventures in the New Wonderland." Soon Livingston had tourists, too.

Roosevelt hoped he wouldn't see any of them. He was taking a vacation in Yellowstone, hiking, riding, studying—not hunting—the big and

Roosevelt in Yellowstone Park, 1903

small game. Every once in a while even he needed to be unobserved, to retreat into the wilderness. He'd been to the park twice before, when he lived in the west and then with Edith a few years into their marriage. "I am back in my own country again," he said to Major John Pitcher, the superintendent of Yellowstone.

This time Roosevelt was accompanied by the poet and naturalist John Burroughs. R. A. Waagner, better known as "The Duke of Hell Roaring," and Billy Hofer, a dead shot and longtime friend of the president, were their guides. No one else traveling with Roosevelt joined them. The reporters would have, but he didn't invite them. They had to wait on the train, under instructions not to enter the park; if they tried, they'd be arrested and kept in the guard house until the president returned.

Roosevelt set up headquarters at Major Pitcher's home. From there he could stay in touch by phone with his personal secretary, William Loeb, who was also stationed on the train. When the first ruling on Northern Securities came, he wanted to know.

HILL RETURNED FROM Europe aboard a luxury liner on April 9. He wore an ordinary Ulster coat and an old brown slouch hat and hoped not to be noticed. No luck. He looked so unassuming he stood out. As journalists crowded in, Hill—controlling micromanager Hill—tried to appear nonchalant about the fate of the company he had spent twenty years building. "No man knows less about the condition of business than I do at this moment," he said when asked about the trial. "It is strange how absolutely ignorant of affairs a man can become in five weeks' time." He rushed off into the New York morning, leaving his bags for an employee to collect.

At noon the four judges walked into the main courtroom of the circuit court of appeals in St. Paul. With twenty-foot ceilings, a stained glass skylight, and marble walls, it was an impressive setting for such a critical decision. A crowd waited.

The judges' verdict was unanimous. The merger between the Great Northern and Northern Pacific placed the control of both "in the hands of a single person, to wit, the Securities company," and "destroyed every motive for competition between the two roads," they said. They had upheld the antitrust law against the most powerful financier in the world. Northern Securities was illegal and had to be disbanded.

Roosevelt, on his campaign trip that he didn't call a campaign trip, could claim a victory for all those spread across the plains and prairies. His bark had a bite. "The courts can be educated, just as the public can be educated," he later wrote to Knox.

The government's victory "reaffirms the right of the people to be free from the slavery of monopoly," one of Beck's colleagues said. The government's victory was "revolutionary," Griggs said. He meant that no one was safe from Washington's prying reach. The government's victory "was like a thunderbolt out of a clear sky to Wall Street," the *Minneapolis Journal* said.

Morgan and Hill were shocked. No company as notable as theirs had ever been brought to heel by the courts. Publicly, Morgan said the decision "will not rest where it is." In his office, he turned to his longtime counsel, Francis Stetson, and said: "You will have a pretty job, unscrambling the eggs and putting them into their shells and getting them back to the original hens." Morgan's son, Jack, sent a telegram from London: "We hear with greatest surprise and chagrin of the Northern Securities decision . . . and feel sure that you will be able in some way to nullify its bad effect."

Hill couldn't conceal his bitterness. He said the court ruled that having power to compete globally "is a crime, and that he who exercises it is a criminal." Then he paused. "I now here plead guilty to that crime."

He and Morgan holed up at 23 Wall Street the next day. They had never been fond of one another. Hill was explosive, Morgan glacial. Theirs was a partnership of convenience that had become unexpectedly inconvenient. But now they were united in a common cause. Northern Securities appealed to the Supreme Court, which scheduled the case for a final review in December.

"If this decision is upheld by the Supreme Court—but I am confident that it will not be—no less than 85 percent of the railway systems of the United States will be up in the air. All the work of the last seven years will have to be done all over again," Hill said. In private, he was more distraught. "The decision itself is so unreasonable that if carried out it would undo the work of a hundred years and leave the country in a state of financial chaos," he wrote. Hill had a secret last-resort plan. If he and Morgan couldn't own the Burlington together, he would buy Morgan's share. That would help protect his railway system from any unwanted competition. "What the Northern Pacific loses, the Great Northern gains" was the way one of Hill's executives put it.

If this decision is upheld, railroad men will at least know where they stand, Morgan said, and "will probably find good ways to see that properties are operated economically and profitably." Hill was riling up investors; Morgan needed to steady them. If the government put an end to holding companies like this one, he and the railroad men would find another way to work together. In a contest of wits, of dodges and feints and single-minded determination, he was confident Wall Street would outmaneuver Washington.

Morgan's few public words weren't enough, though. Coal companies might be prosecuted under the antitrust act; their shares fell. The Union Pacific and Southern Pacific might be forced apart; their shares fell. The Pennsylvania Railroad's stake in the Baltimore and Ohio might be illegal; their shares fell. Morgan's U.S. Steel and International Mercantile Marine bonds fell to their lowest prices ever. Northern Securities lost 8 percent of its value in one day.

Morgan was forced to delay his annual trip to Europe.

On the bright side, he was in New York on April 17 for his sixty-sixth birthday. His wife was in California, but some of the family were there, and that morning Morgan, ruler of Wall Street, had a frolic with his grandkids. They gave him a poem: "Who eats his morning codfish balls / while twenty people pay him calls / and we go rushing through the halls? Our Grandpa."

During the next week, Morgan sent in brokers to buy stocks from panicky investors. He propped up as many companies as he could, starting with two of his own. He lent his name to confer stability, and it helped—for a while.

WHEN THE PRESIDENT emerged from Yellowstone, he got more good news. The government had won an injunction against the Beef Trust. He congratulated Knox again. "My dear sir, I wonder if you realize what a great work you have done, how proud I am of you and how grateful to you?" By then, as everyone expected, Northern Securities had filed an appeal with the Supreme Court.

Two weeks in the park seemed to have mellowed Roosevelt. He wrote to William Howard Taft, still off in the Philippines as governor: "I have certainly tried my hardest to be a decent President and to act up to the principles I have for many years advocated. On the whole I think I have succeeded fairly well; but I haven't any idea whether any considerable portion of my fellow citizens do or do not accept this pleasant view . . . I am entirely aware that I have had a first-class run for my money, and that whatever comes I am ahead of the game."

Roosevelt toured California, for the first time, in May. He was enthralled. "I congratulate you upon your fruit farms, your orchards, your ranches, upon your cities, upon your industrial and agricultural development, but above all, I congratulate you upon the quality of your citizenship," he said. California seemed enthralled back. The president is "a man who has made his way in the world by the force of will and earnestness," said one reporter who also noted that if you didn't know Roosevelt was president, "You would size him up as an athletic professor of German or a boxing instructor with a taste for literature."

When Roosevelt visited Los Angeles, he watched a procession of floats and flowers, Rough Riders on their horses, and Chinese dressed in their finest traditional robes. No one commented on Roosevelt's support for extending the Chinese Exclusion Act, which first closed the country to Chinese immigrant laborers in 1882 and later required Chinese residents to register with the government and carry the certificates at all times.

The Secret Service seemed to be on especially high alert. They asked police to jail John Czolgosz, the younger brother of McKinley's assassin, as a precaution. John, like many young men, had come west a year earlier. He was working as a cook in a local tamale factory.

San Francisco's welcoming committee planned a military parade and banquet so extravagant it had to raise twenty-six thousand dollars to fund them. The only company that seemed unwilling to contribute cash was the Southern Pacific railroad, controlled by Harriman. The general manager said his line would carry the president through the state without charge. Legislators and soldiers could travel for free to the city. That would cost about six thousand dollars, and he figured that was a sufficient donation.

Five hundred people attended the Golden Banquet at the Palace Hotel on Tuesday, May 12. The hall glittered. Roosevelt sat on a blue and gold chair at a sixty-foot table. When the orchestra played "A Hot Time in the Old Town Tonight," he stood up and sang loudly. Other guests joined in and he looked so happy that the orchestra played the song again. At night's end he received a golden cup big enough to hold a quart of champagne.

By the weekend, he was in Yosemite with the naturalist and conservationist John Muir for three snowy days of camping. He told the organizers he wanted "a roughing trip."

This time, when he emerged from the wilderness, he turned fierce. The Ohio Republican convention was coming up. Ohio was the home of Senator Hanna, the man who notably didn't want Roosevelt to be vice president in 1900. The man who had been sparring with him for control of the Republican Party ever since. The man Wall Street hoped would deny Roosevelt the presidential nomination in 1904. "You know, as well as I do, what Wall Street does when men try to kick," Henry Adams wrote to a friend. "It is a war, now, to the last dollar . . . I am quite sure that not a dollar can be got for Theodore's campaign."

Roosevelt and Hanna had developed a working relationship over the previous three years. They agreed more often about labor than capital. They both believed that employees should have some say on the job and employers should have some limits. They respected each other, but they still had reservations about each other. They showed their respect and usually concealed their reservations.

In May, the other senator from Ohio, Joseph Foraker, tried to create a rift between them by calling on the state's delegates to endorse Roosevelt as the presidential candidate, a full year before the national convention. Doing so would put an end to speculation about Hanna's intentions on the White House, speculation that unsettled the current occupant more than any other political intrigue. A challenge from someone close to New York's financial elite was an urgent threat. This gave Hanna an advantage over Roosevelt, one of the few he still had. So Hanna said publicly that he didn't think it was necessary to go on the record so early. Roosevelt told him it was, and this time Hanna didn't protest. Just days after his first statement, he issued a second brief announcement that concluded: Roosevelt "will be the logical candidate of his party in 1904." Not exactly a rousing affirmation, though enough of a public acknowledgement of Roosevelt's power over the senator and the party to satisfy Roosevelt and embarrass Hanna.

Afterward, Roosevelt told Hanna that his initial reluctance "was everywhere accepted as the first open attack on me . . . that it was really an attack by the so-called Wall Street forces on me, to which you had been led to give reluctant acquiescence." Roosevelt almost apologized. "I hated to do it because you have shown such broad generosity . . . it was particularly painful for me to be put, even temporarily, in a position of seeming antagonism to you."

Privately, he wasn't apologizing for anything. "I decided that the time had come to stop shilly-shallying, and let Hanna know definitely that I did not intend to assume the position, at least passively, of a suppliant to whom he might give the nomination as a boon," Roosevelt wrote to Henry Cabot Lodge. "I rather expected Hanna to fight, but made up my mind that it was better to have a fight in the open at once than to run the risk of being knifed secretly." It didn't take much to provoke Roosevelt in a personal contest, sometimes it took nothing at all, and once he felt in peril, he pounced. Then he tidied things up with his opponent as best he could and moved on.

Near the end of his trip, Roosevelt gave what he considered the two best speeches of the two hundred or so. "This is not and never shall be a government either of a plutocracy or a mob," he said in Spokane. "No man is above [the law] and no man is below it. The crime of cunning, the crime of greed, the crime of violence, are all equally crimes . . . This is a government of the people; including alike the people of great wealth and of moderate wealth, the people who employ others, the people who are employed, the wageworker, the lawyer, the mechanic, the banker, the farmer."

On a return visit to Butte, Montana, he said: "I have the right to challenge the support of all good citizens and to demand the acquiescence of every good man. I hope I will have it; but once for all I wish it understood that even if I do not have it I shall enforce the law." He spoke to members of various unions that day but his real audience was in New York.

Roosevelt told Lodge he had been inspired by the "knock down and dragout fight with Hanna and the whole Wall Street crowd," and he wanted them to understand "that if they so desire they shall have all the fighting they wish." No one doubted that.

Then he pivoted. Roosevelt and his daughter Alice attended the June 10 wedding of Hanna's only daughter. Ruth Hanna was marrying Joseph Medill McCormick, heir to the *Chicago Tribune*. Roosevelt was among those who signed their marriage certificate.

After the ceremony, as the guests mingled at Glenmere, Hanna's Cleveland mansion, Roosevelt turned the talk to politics. He asked Hanna to serve again as chair of the Republican National Committee. The offer was a sign of his trust, and his lingering suspicion. Hanna hesitated. The job would be a strain, his health was poor, and he anticipated a difficult reelection campaign for his own Senate seat. Also: After being teased for his "back-action-double-spring-feat" over Roosevelt's endorsement, Hanna was a little sore. If Hanna didn't accept, the president would conclude he still didn't have the senator's full support, and every moment of uncertainty gave Hanna a last bit of influence. Maybe the convention delegates would rebel against the president. Or maybe the gloom on Wall Street would aggravate fears that Roosevelt was unreliable.

Any confidence that Morgan's pep talk gave investors didn't last long. New Jersey Governor Murphy reported in April that the state had been forced to dissolve more than nine hundred trusts and corporations that hadn't paid their annual taxes. Another one hundred twenty or so had been put into receivership over the past year. Some had failed honestly, others were frauds from the start.

By early June, shares were trading at the same low prices they had during the panic in May 1901. Anxiety can feed on less. Maybe Morgan had been wrong. The problem wasn't that the country was producing too much coal, iron, food or clothing. Or that good money had gone into factories and mines, real estate and homes, bridges and tunnels. The economy was expanding. Everyone agreed on that. The problem was that the Wall Street men were manufacturing too many securities. Financiers had rushed to buy industrial plants at inflated prices, wasted money on excessive underwriting fees to consolidate or reorganize them, and then tried to sell the stock to the public. The public wasn't buying.

This time, it was the insiders, the "infatuated millionaires" who suffered. The Rich Man's Panic in the stock market that summer halved the value of Morgan's other great trust, U.S. Steel. The company, which employed nearly one hundred fifty thousand people, reduced wages. When Morgan returned from his art-collecting travels in Europe, he was forced to deny reports that his shipping company, International Mercantile Marine, was in such financial trouble that it would have to be reorganized. "There is no crisis in the affairs of the company," he said as the *Oceanic* neared land. He said he felt refreshed after his six-week trip. Passengers said he had been "much more democratic than is his custom" on the Atlantic crossing. He spent time on deck. Some even described him as affable.

That wouldn't last. By July, the International Mercantile Marine had docked some of its ships and reduced operating expenses to a minimum. The Pennsylvania Railroad's yards were crowded with empty cars. Banks canceled credit and bankers warned Roosevelt of widespread agitation. Morgan, the unofficial chief banker, put together a reserve of fifty million dollars, just in case.

Roosevelt blamed the crash on Morgan, and Morgan blamed it on Roosevelt. "The financial situation here looks ugly," Roosevelt wrote to Lodge in August. "The panic is due chiefly, almost solely, to the speculative watering of stocks on a giant scale in which Pierpont Morgan and so many of his kind have indulged during the last few years. Of course, if the panic spreads so as to affect the business world I shall have to pay for it." Later in the month, he wrote to his sister Bamie that many excellent businesspeople believed his attitude toward the trusts and his creation of an agency to supervise the trusts were responsible for the stock market's collapse. Roosevelt described that as "about as intelligent as that it was due to the procession [*sic*] of the equinoxes or the position of the Great Bear at three o'clock in the morning."

The fall equinox came. The panic wore itself out, and stock prices slowly began to rise. The Great Bear receded.

Roosevelt resumed his consultations with the many excellent businesspeople who criticized him. It was a way to demonstrate good will and diminish Hanna's power as the conduit between Washington and New York. He even reached out to Morgan. "Mr. Perkins tells me you may pass through Washington this fall. If so, I should much like to see you to talk over certain financial matters," Roosevelt wrote in early October. "I should like extremely to have an interview with you on the subject but, at the moment, it is absolutely impossible for me to leave owing to the absence of Mr. Perkins and the serious condition of affairs in this city," Morgan replied. "There is no hurry whatever," Roosevelt wrote back. "I wished to speak to you about certain matters of financial legislation, but it would probably be better to wait until Congress has assembled for the special session after November 9." They never met.

"The Triumph of the Bear in the Wall Street Arena," Puck *magazine cover, June 1903, amid the Rich Man's Panic*

Hanna spent a summer month resting on a friend's yacht. The vacation seemed to help restore enough vigor that he could campaign for Republican legislators in Ohio's state elections. The assembly would vote to give him another term. Right after Hanna was reelected senator, businessmen in New York began to raise money to make him president. Soon they had one hundred thousand dollars, a pledge of another two hundred fifty thousand, and the promise of much more later. The state's governor, Benjamin Odell, let them know he would support Hanna too.

Hanna still didn't want to take on Roosevelt. Morgan invited Hanna to spend Thanksgiving at his Madison Avenue mansion so he could try one last time to persuade the senator to do so. Challenging an unsafe president, Morgan suggested, was Hanna's duty. Hanna didn't respond. Then Morgan turned to Hanna's wife, Augusta, and said her husband would be easily nominated "if only he would give the word." She told Morgan her husband would never give the word.

Later, at the Waldorf-Astoria, when reporters asked Hanna if he could be quoted saying that Roosevelt would be the candidate, Hanna replied: "You can say what you damn please." Then he laughed, rapped his cane on the floor, and limped away. Hanna made only one promise to Morgan and the others: he would not advocate for Roosevelt's nomination before the national convention in June. That would give Morgan and the others time to find a suitable candidate. The Supreme Court would rule on Northern Securities before then, and if the company prevailed maybe Roosevelt would be more amenable in a second term. Morgan wasn't placated. No matter if the company won or lost, if Roosevelt remained in office, the time will come, he said warily, "when all business will have to be done with glass pockets."

It had been a disappointing year, financially, for Morgan. The panic had been costly. When he closed his firm's books for 1903, he had to record a loss of more than three and a half million dollars—some two million from his shipping company alone. Still, he celebrated his admission into the secretive Zodiac Club that dark winter. Only twelve men, all wealthy connoisseurs of food and wine, were invited to participate. Each received an astrological call sign and was expected to host a dinner on the last Saturday of the month. Morgan became Brother Libra and planned his first meal at the private apartments of his favorite chef, Louis Sherry. The centerpiece was a roast suckling pig. "It was a very congenial group into which Mr. Morgan fitted like the last piece of a cut-out puzzle," noted his son-in-law.

On the evening of December 4, Roosevelt invited Hanna to the White House. The senator finally was ready to give the president an answer: Hanna declined the offer to stay on as chairman of the Republican National Committee for the 1904 election. Roosevelt would have to find other ways to keep Hanna close. Charm and humor usually worked. Roosevelt wrote to Hanna the next day that his private secretary had told the press the ninety-minute talk was "a most pleasant interview" and that relations between the two were as friendly as ever. "Now do come around here often so that the sensation-mongers may get tired of wondering if anything dark and sinister is met by the visits!" Hanna replied right away. "I will try to see you often enough to keep 'tab' on each other."

CHAPTER 14

"The Supreme Law of the Land"

A s the Northern Securities case sped toward the Supreme Court, Roosevelt and Knox and Morgan and Hill all knew one man would play an outsized role in determining the result: John Marshall Harlan. He was over six feet tall, red-haired before he went bald, a Southerner married to a Northerner. His very name was a sort of predestination, recalling John Marshall, fourth chief justice of the Supreme Court and one of the original architects of the American system of constitutional law. Harlan, a Kentucky native, attended law school at Transylvania University in Lexington—known as the Harvard of the West—and joined his father's legal practice. He ran an unsuccessful campaign for Congress in 1859 and rejoined his father's firm.

Harlan came from a slave-owning family. Well before he was born, his father had a son, Robert, with an enslaved woman; the two boys were raised in the same home and remained close after they both left it. In 1848, when Robert Harlan was thirty-two years old, he bought his own freedom with a five-hundred-dollar bond. He went on to become a businessman, civil rights activist, and eventually a Republican politician.

John Marshall Harlan's views on race evolved, but only so far. He was a border-land progressive and very much a man of his time. Harlan organized and led a regiment for the Union during the Civil War because he

Justice John Marshall Harlan,
circa 1890

opposed secession. Slavery, though, he defended. He argued that abolition violated property rights and promised to resign from the army if President Lincoln signed the Emancipation Proclamation. When Lincoln did, Colonel Harlan didn't. Not right away. But soon after, his father died, and Harlan left the military to take over the family law practice and resume his political career. He served as Kentucky's attorney general from 1863 to 1867.

The Ku Klux Klan and other white supremacist groups began a campaign of terror against blacks in Kentucky during those Reconstruction years. The arson, beatings, and lynchings—and the Democrats' tolerance of the postwar racist violence—turned Harlan to the party of Lincoln. Like Lincoln, he believed blacks should have legal and political equality, even if he didn't consider blacks social equals. Before he regarded the federal government as a potential threat to the legal autonomy of a state. Now he considered state jurisprudence subordinate to federal jurisdiction. He explained his philosophical change simply: "Let it be said that I am right rather than consistent."

Harlan ran for governor as a Republican twice and lost twice. He warned that monopolies could become powerful enough to control Kentucky politics and he proposed a tax on income, rather than property, to pay the state's Civil War debts. His influence was such that at the Republican national convention of 1876 he could swing the Kentucky delegation to Rutherford B. Hayes. The Democratic candidate was Samuel Tilden, governor of New York. The presidential campaign was hostile, disputed, and marred by voter suppression, and the winner was eventually determined by compromise.

Hayes rewarded Harlan by nominating him to the Supreme Court. Harlan, who was forty-four, had only ever served as a county judge. That didn't matter to Hayes. "Is Harlan not the man?" he wrote. "Of the right age—able—of noble character—industrious—fine manners, temper, and appearance. Who beats him?" Over the next several decades, Harlan, in his opinions and dissents, would shape many presidencies—especially the twenty-sixth.

Harlan, the Southerner, was the only justice who believed in civil rights for blacks. In 1857, in the Dred Scott decision, the Court had denied citizenship to African Americans, whether they were slaves or free. A quarter century later, it had to consider four prosecutions under the Civil Rights Act of 1875, which banned discrimination in places of public accommodation. The Court ruled the statute was unconstitutional. Eight justices concluded that railroads, inns, or any public places of amusement were private enterprises that could serve, or refuse to serve, potential customers as they chose. Justice Harlan disagreed. "Today it is the colored race which is denied, by corporations and individuals wielding public authority, rights fundamental in their freedom and citizenship," he wrote in his 1883 opinion. "At some future time, it may be that some other race will fall under the ban of race discrimination."

As Harlan struggled to finish his dissent, his wife, Malvina, put on his desk the inkstand once owned by Roger Taney, author of the Dred Scott decision, as inspiration. "It was, I think, a bit of 'poetic justice,'" she wrote. Afterward, Harlan confessed to Hayes "some surprise" that he found himself alone in his opinion. It would not be the last time.

On June 7, 1892, Homer Adolph Plessy bought a first-class railroad ticket for a fifty-mile trip around Lake Pontchartrain in Louisiana. He didn't expect to reach his destination. Plessy, mixed race and light-skinned, took a seat in the coach reserved for whites. He intended to be arrested. The railroad managers knew that.

A law enacted in 1890 by the mostly Democratic state assembly required railroads to provide "equal but separate" accommodations for those of different races. Louisiana wasn't the first state to reimpose racial segregation on railroads after the Civil War. Tennessee was. Florida, Mississippi, and Texas followed. Then came Louisiana with its "act to promote the comfort of passengers." By the summer of 1892, Georgia, Alabama, Arkansas, and Kentucky had put in place discriminatory statutes of their own.

The Louisiana railroads didn't support the Jim Crow law, mostly because of the cost of providing separate cars. When the conductor asked Plessy to move, he said he was comfortable where he was. A private detective escorted him off the train, arrested him, and, briefly, jailed him in New Orleans.

Four years later, the Supreme Court ruled on *Plessy v. Ferguson*. It upheld the Louisiana Jim Crow law. Only one justice dissented. In his argument, Harlan put forth two antagonistic claims: one, of legal equality for all Americans; the other, of white superiority. "The white race deems itself to be the dominant race in this country. And so it is in prestige, in achievements, in education, in wealth and in power," he wrote in May 1896. But "Our Constitution is color-blind, and neither knows nor tolerates classes among citizens. In respect of civil rights, all citizens are equal before the law." Toward the end of his opinion, he felt compelled to state again the certainty of America that many continued to deny: "The destinies of the two races in this country are indissolubly linked together, and the interests of both require that the common government of all shall not permit the seeds of race hate to be planted under the sanction of law." In 1896, though, as Democratic legislatures in the South disenfranchised blacks, and seventy-eight people were lynched, Harlan's lone voice on the Court barely registered.

Harlan also stood apart when it came to the other pressing issue of the 1890s—the gathering power in the hands of a few. Presidents of both parties nominated to the Supreme Court men who tended to believe, as Harlan once did, that federal power shouldn't necessarily supersede states' rights, that capital should be favored over labor, that the rich—and their propery—should be protected. The Justices couldn't always be counted on to side with business, but they often did.

Melville Fuller managed the campaign of Lincoln's Democratic opponent, became one of Chicago's leading attorneys, and took over as chief justice in 1888. Fuller looked like Mark Twain, if Mark Twain were only about five feet tall. Fuller used a stool so his feet wouldn't dangle from his chair in the courtroom. He was witty and gracious and often invited the other justices to hold their weekly conference in his mansion. It was his idea that they all shake hands at the start of every session.

David Brewer of Kansas had represented railroad and banking clients and served on state and federal courts for almost two decades before joining the Court in 1890. By the time Edward White of Louisiana took a place on the bench in 1894, he stood close to six feet tall and weighed 250 pounds. Some thought that made him look like a judge. White grew up among the sugar-growing Louisiana elite and fought for the Confederacy. After the war, he practiced corporate law and served on the state's supreme court and as a senator. Rufus Peckham was a New York lawyer and judge, a Democrat, and a friend of Morgan, Vanderbilt, and Rockefeller. When he took a seat on the Supreme Court in 1896 he gave up most public engagements so he could maintain the secluded life he believed a judge required. Yet he kept his investments and his position as trustee of Mutual Life Insurance Company of New York.

These were some of the men who would interpret the new Sherman Antitrust Act. While it gave the government broad jurisdiction over private economic power, it left the specifics of how to apply that authority to the courts. "All that we, as lawmakers, can do is to declare general principles," Senator Sherman said in 1890. The law was "experimental," even its advocates said.

In the year after President Harrison signed the antitrust act, his attorney general didn't issue any special instructions to the states on how to enforce it and didn't initiate any cases of his own. Tennessee was the first to test the law. The state charged that the Nashville Coal Exchange was a cartel of mine owners and coal dealers that fixed prices and restrained trade in an attempt to monopolize the market. The judge agreed, and the companies didn't appeal. *Jellico Mountain Coal* was one of the government's few victories in those early years.

The government lost its next case. A circuit court ruled in 1892 that the Trans-Missouri Freight Association—an agreement among eighteen competitive railroads to fix rates—didn't restrain trade because it kept those rates low and actually aided commerce by regulating traffic. Railroads shouldn't be subject to antitrust rules anyway, the court said, because they were already regulated by the Interstate Commerce Act. Critics noted the commission had little power to enforce its regulations.

Five years later the Supreme Court reversed the decision, made price-fixing illegal, and helped refine the language of the antitrust act. "The statute, in declaring illegal every combination in the form of trust or otherwise, or conspiracy in restraint of trade or commerce, does not mean what the language used therein plainly imports," the justices said. "It only means to declare illegal any such contract which is in unreasonable restraint of trade, while leaving all others unaffected." So now the courts would only punish those companies whose anticompetitive deals seemed *unreasonable*.

Only one state attorney general was willing to take on the most unreasonable of all the monopolies, Standard Oil. And in that case, the Ohio supreme court ordered the company to dissolve its holdings only to see the trust reorganize in New Jersey. (Standard Oil was eventually forced to break up in 1911.)

It wasn't until 1894 that the first major case against a national monopoly reached the Supreme Court. The Knight case, as the government's prosecution of the Sugar Trust was called, exposed other ways to parse the law and complicate enforcement. Every justice on the court except Harlan determined that the Sugar Trust was legal. In his dissent, Harlan showed how the government might have won, and Philander Knox studied this argument as he prepared the case against Northern Securities. Roosevelt himself later wrote of the Knight case: "This decision left the National Government, that is the people of the Nation, practically helpless to deal with the large combinations of modern business."

ROOSEVELT'S FIRST NOMINEE to the Supreme Court, Oliver Wendell Holmes Jr., seemed to understand what the president wanted. Holmes was seventeen years older than Roosevelt—sixty-one when he joined the Court in the fall of 1902—but came from the same social class and held some of the same grudges against it.

Both had been born into aristocratic families, Holmes in Boston, and grew up with famous fathers. Holmes Sr. was a physician and essayist whose friends included Ralph Waldo Emerson and Henry Wadsworth Longfellow. They both studied at Harvard and belonged to its secretive Porcellian Club. They both chose to fight in wars they could have avoided. Holmes left Harvard his senior year to enlist in the Union Army. He served three years, was wounded three times, and kept the bullet that surgeons extracted from his chest and the bullet that tore through his neck. Roosevelt and Holmes wrote books, read history, liked to talk. They were both romantics. "Life is a roar of bargain and battle," Holmes said.

They both were friends with Henry Cabot Lodge, the former Harvard history professor who had become a politician. Holmes stood by Lodge and Lodge stood by Roosevelt when they backed an unpopular Republican presidential candidate in 1884 out of party loyalty. Roosevelt appreciated loyalty. In 1895, when he served as New York City's police commissioner and Holmes was a Massachusetts Supreme Court judge, Holmes impressed him again. Holmes gave a Memorial Day speech called "The Soldier's Faith," in which he said that the joy of life is "to ride boldly at what is in front of you, be it fence or enemy; to pray, not for comfort, but for combat." He could have been describing Roosevelt.

The rumblings of discontent across America disturbed Holmes, though maybe not in the way Roosevelt imagined. Holmes held that judges should not be bound by personal ties to race or class. He understood the relationship between workers and their bosses as a competition. Employees wanted to earn as much as they could; employers wanted to pay as little as they could. He regarded the organization of rival businesses as inevitable and beneficial, and the organization of labor as a legitimate response. He had little personal sympathy for workers, but he ruled for them. When his fellow justices agreed a local strike could be stopped by injunction, Holmes dissented. "Free competition means combination," he wrote in 1896. "Combination on the one side is patent and powerful. Combination on the other is the necessary and desirable counterpart, if the battle is to be carried on in a fair and equal way."

He wasn't a reformer, nor was he a progressive. He believed the world's population would naturally grow faster than the means to sustain it, so the survival of the nation depended on weeding out the unfit. He was more cynical than Roosevelt judged, more independent than Roosevelt expected. Holmes later wrote he "loathed most of the things I decided in favor of."

Holmes became chief justice of the Massachusetts supreme court in 1899. He instituted one change right away: he asked the judges to wear black robes again, as the justices on the nation's Supreme Court did. Justice

Horace Gray, who was from Massachusetts, offered to lend his as a sample for the tailor.

Gray was in poor health and close to retirement. McKinley planned to replace him with a Massachusetts judge who wasn't Holmes. But after Roosevelt suddenly became president, Holmes thought he might get Gray's seat on the Supreme Court after all. Lodge recommended him to Roosevelt.

Holmes was hopeful. He told a cousin he had to withdraw from a business venture and wrote to friends in London that he might soon be moving to Washington. But Roosevelt took his time. In February 1902, Gray suffered a stroke. Roosevelt still wasn't ready to name Holmes. Now he had to consider that whoever he nominated could swing the court in the Northern Securities case. Roosevelt wanted to select a judge who shared his principles, as Gray did, a partisan in the highest sense, he said.

That summer Roosevelt reviewed Holmes's judicial record. "I am glad when I can find a judge who has been able to preserve his aloofness of mind so as to keep his broad humanity of feeling and his sympathy for the class from which he has not drawn clients," the president wrote to Lodge. Roosevelt approved of Holmes's labor decisions, especially since they had been "criticized by the big railroad men and other members of large corporations."

Justice Oliver Wendell Holmes, circa 1903

The president invited Holmes to Oyster Bay for a job interview. When Holmes arrived one evening in late July, Roosevelt wasn't there. He had gone sailing in the Long Island Sound, fog had settled over the water, and he had to camp overnight. Holmes ate dinner with Roosevelt's kids, instead, entertaining them with Civil War stories.

The next morning Holmes—tall, thin, prominent mustache—charmed Roosevelt too. Roosevelt flattered Holmes. The president "said just the right things and impressed me far more than I had expected," the judge wrote to a friend.

Roosevelt offered the seat to Holmes right then, and Holmes accepted.

On December 8, 1902, Holmes took his place on the far right end of the courtroom bench. The next day, he and the other justices celebrated Harlan's twenty-five years on the Supreme Court. He had served longer than any of them. Roosevelt spoke at the banquet at the Willard Hotel. He didn't praise Harlan for his dissents on the court. He praised Harlan as a Southerner who fought for the Union, a civil dissent of sorts. The president said publicly what he had already stated privately—that judges "must be great constructive statesmen." He reminded them of the court's history and duty. "In not one serious study of American political life will it be possible to omit the immense part played by the Supreme Court in the creation, not merely the modification, of the great policies through and by means of which the country has moved on to its present position."

Justice Brewer teased Harlan, saying he "goes to bed every night with one hand on the constitution and the other on the bible, and so sleeps the sweet sleep of justice and righteousness." Harlan taught a Sunday Bible study class for men and he could summon a moral indignation in the courtroom that the other judges didn't always appreciate. When he issued his dissent to the 1895 decision to strike down an income tax law, he banged his hand on the bench, shook his fingers at his colleagues, and scowled at the chief justice.

At age sixty-nine, Harlan still chewed tobacco, kept his face clean-shaven, chatted with train conductors and passengers on his daily

The Supreme Court of the United States

Justices of the Supreme Court, from left to right: Oliver Wendell Holmes, Rufus Peckham, Henry Brown, John Marshall Harlan, Melville Fuller, David Brewer, Edward White, Joseph McKenna, and William Day. Harper's Weekly, *1903*

commute, played baseball and sang at bar association picnics, and told Civil War stories. He was also still in debt. "The whole situation is so deadly mortifying," he had written back in Kentucky in 1880. The situation hadn't improved. Most Supreme Court justices found their salaries were sufficient; in 1902 each earned about twelve thousand dollars. Harlan didn't. For two decades the justice taught at what became George Washington University, "a position which, in spite of the arduous work it entailed, he felt compelled to retain," his wife, Malvina, said. He was paid two thousand dollars a year. Even with the extra income, the family lived beyond their means. Vacations, debutante balls, European educations. A huge home in Washington, which his sons helped finance, with portraits of John Marshall, Thomas Jefferson, John Jay, and Alexander Hamilton lining the entrance hall. At the foot of the stairs, a bust of Harlan himself. Maybe his secret financial troubles made him sensitive to the country's wealth gap. Maybe they made him more self-righteous.

Toward the end of January 1903 the Roosevelts hosted a reception for Congress and the judiciary. Holmes had become friendly with Justice White by then and noted that he had quickly left for some reason. "Some reason" was the presence of several African Americans. Other Southerners bolted too. Harlan stayed.

The next month Roosevelt nominated his second Supreme Court judge. William Day had practiced criminal defense and corporate law in Canton, Ohio. He had also been involved in local Republican politics. Of course he knew William McKinley. As president, McKinley appointed Day assistant secretary of state, secretary of state, and then a judge on the Court of Appeals for the Sixth Circuit. He was a reliable "constructive statesman," as Roosevelt preferred.

But he wasn't Roosevelt's first choice. William Howard Taft was. In October 1902, amid the coal strike and after Holmes's seat was secure, Roosevelt had tried to persuade Taft to give up his position as colonial governor of the Philippines and come home. "I do think it of the very highest consequence to get you on the Supreme Court," Roosevelt said. "I am not at all satisfied with its condition—let us speak this only with bated breath and between you and me. I think we need you there greatly." Taft was ambivalent. He wanted the position but also believed he was needed in the Philippines. His wife and brothers had other plans for him. They believed Taft could be president one day and advised him to turn down the lifetime appointment to the court.

Early in that year's session, with Day soon to join Holmes and Harlan on the bench, the Supreme Court ruled unanimously that Congress had the constitutional authority to unilaterally alter treaties with Native American tribes. Justice White described them as "wards of the government" and said Congress possessed "full administrative power" over tribal property. Harlan's notion of civil rights only extended so far. "It is the Dred Scott decision No. 2," Pennsylvania senator Matthew Quay said in disgust. "Except that in this case the victim is red instead of black."

The justices heard commercial disputes, personal injury suits against railroads, questions of taxes, contracts, wills, insurance policies, and bankruptcies. They ruled on trademark, patent, and copyright conflicts. They considered cases that tested the federal government's power over the states. Holmes found the questions arising "from every part of our great empire," exciting to contemplate. More often than not, the judges were in agreement.

They usually held conferences on Saturdays in a room below the chamber, windowless, with walls hazed by cigar smoke. Sometimes they went to Chief Justice Fuller's home. The conversations were mostly congenial. But Harlan and Holmes didn't like one another, and when they disagreed, Harlan could get excitable, insistent, close. Holmes never did. He called Harlan "my lion-hearted friend." He also compared Harlan's mind to "a powerful vise the jaws of which couldn't be got nearer than two inches of each other." But not when Harlan was alive. If Harlan ranted, Holmes interrupted, "That won't wash." If Harlan continued, Fuller might joke, "Still I keep scrubbing and scrubbing.'"

Work was engrossing for Holmes. Political life in the capital—a small, gossipy town full of people angling for power—was complicated. "It seems as if everybody smiled and lied," he wrote. "One realizes the possibility of having enemies—which one rather thought a romantic fiction in Boston. But here rivalries—envies—ambitions—grow fierce." Holmes wished to remain detached. He said he never read a newspaper while serving on the Supreme Court. As a resident of Washington, he couldn't vote in presidential elections.

Yet he and his wife, Fanny, quickly joined the Roosevelts' social circle. Fanny had been a recluse in Boston, but in Washington she shone. The Holmeses were clever and well-read. The justice could charm any woman. Fanny would watch, bemused. "Washington is full of famous men and the women they married when they were young," she said to Roosevelt one night. He howled with laughter. Henry Adams, a chatty, sometimes scathing companion, shared Fanny's disdain. He called her "our only social success" and wrote that for Edith, "who is victim to the whole mob of Judges, Cabinets and Senates, with wives, the Holmes's are a joy."

The Holmeses enjoyed the attention. "We are on top of the wave," the justice wrote to a friend in early 1903. He invited Edith to the Supreme Court to hear his opinion in a copyright case. He said he admired the way her husband gave everyone he spoke to the full magnetic force of his attention.

"Surely you must know without my telling it how immensely both of you have added to the enjoyment of the 'sire and siress' this winter," Roosevelt wrote to Holmes as official Washington closed for the summer. When the justice returned to the city, the Northern Securities case—eight thousand pages of transcripts, briefs, and arguments and the chance to decide the most public case of the Roosevelt administration—would be waiting. "I feel very proud of having had the chance to appoint you."

EDITH ROOSEVELT AND Lillian Knox sat together in the Ladies' Gallery overlooking the crowded Supreme Court chambers. Fanny Holmes was there too. The room, two stories high and semicircular, decorated in crimson and gold, was designed to evoke a Parisian amphitheater. People lined the hallways of the Capitol in the hours before the trial. They claimed every single red-velvet-upholstered seat. The late arrivals stood. Everyone waited for the show.

It began at half past noon on Monday, December 14, 1903. The justices would finally determine whether Pierpont Morgan and James Hill had broken the law. If their railroad company could regulate commerce or if the government could regulate it. A New Jersey law made corporations like Northern Securities. Could the federal law unmake them?

The railroads' influence seemed unbounded; now the justices would determine whether these already massive corporations could continue to consolidate power. By 1903 their combined stock value represented one-eighth the wealth of the country. They employed more Americans than any other enterprise. They carried passengers whose numbers equaled almost half the world's population. Tens of millions of people had a stake in the outcome of the trial.

John Johnson presented Morgan and Hill's appeal. Johnson was sixty-two years old and among the top lawyers in the country. He had turned down a seat on the Supreme Court, twice. He had turned down an offer from McKinley to be attorney general. Johnson turned down all sorts of other invitations—to attend dinners, make speeches, pose for photographs. He didn't even join the American Bar Association.

He collected paintings, as Morgan did, and not just the Old Masters, either. He bought as he pleased, and he hung the paintings where he pleased—on the backs of doors, at the foot of beds, on the ceiling of his home in Philadelphia.

Johnson had defended the Sugar Trust in the Knight case. He served as counsel for the Pennsylvania Railroad, the New York Central, and Morgan's U.S. Steel. He was always available when Morgan, or Hill, needed him. For the Northern Securities case, he was available for a reported five hundred thousand dollars. "There was no polish or adornment to his arguments," one colleague said. "Johnson goes straight to the point and hits it hard." That afternoon Johnson appeared cheery and optimistic.

Knox spoke for the government. Northern Securities was the first case he argued before the Supreme Court as attorney general. He was part of the attraction. But he wouldn't turn the trial into a spectacle. He rarely gestured or raised his voice. He seemed solemn.

Johnson was intense and Knox grounded; Johnson was Philadelphia and Knox, Pittsburgh. Both attorneys wore striped trousers, gray ascots, waistcoats, and cutaway morning coats.

Both had reason to be hopeful. The circuit court had ruled unanimously against Morgan and Hill in April. Four months later, a district judge heard the case that Minnesota's attorney general first tried to bring to the Supreme Court and ruled for Morgan and Hill. He said that Northern Securities couldn't be punished for having the power to suppress competition between the Great Northern and Northern Pacific unless it had actually used that power. As far as he was concerned, Northern Securities hadn't committed an offense. Johnson would attempt to persuade the Supreme Court of that. Johnson and Knox had the same advantage: the Court's wide discretion to interpret the language in the Sherman Antitrust Act.

Griggs, who lost the earlier trial for Northern Securities, filed a brief and sat with the company lawyers. But he didn't speak. Beck, who won the case for the government and relocated to a Wall Street firm, sat in the audience.

Johnson argued that the Northern Pacific and the Great Northern—and the line they owned together, the Burlington—had no agreement, contract, combination, or conspiracy to restrain competition. Recall the panic of May 1901, Johnson implored, when the two lines' rival, the Union Pacific, got control of the majority of Northern Pacific stock. "What was to be done?" Johnson asked as he paced the chamber, swinging his glasses on the end of their string. "Remain quiet and allow these people who were waiting like the fox under the tree for something to drop and let them have the prize, or to protect that alliance?" They couldn't remain quiet when the fox was Edward H. Harriman.

That's why Morgan and Hill created Northern Securities, he said. It was a device to hold their prize. It was the only way to protect the roads from a hostile takeover and compete as a global rail and shipping company. All that accomplished just by transferring stock: Individuals can transfer their shares; corporations should have the same rights as individuals.

The case, he said, wasn't about commerce at all. It was about private property. Either way, Northern Securities hadn't stifled commerce. It had expanded commerce. Now manufacturers could send flour from the Mississippi Valley to China, two thousand miles by rail and fifty-seven hundred miles by ship, all on lines controlled by Morgan and Hill, for eighty cents a barrel. Transporting a barrel of flour to New York on other railroads, a distance of less than fifteen hundred miles, cost fifty-five cents. Johnson leaned on these impressive figures to argue that the merger had made the Morgan, Hill, and Harriman lines more efficient and more able to absorb lower rates. Of course he avoided mentioning another possibility: that the size of the Northern Securities network meant its railroads were better able to absorb losses, and they were underpricing their services in hopes of weakening smaller lines.

Knox reminded the Court that the government chartered the Northern Pacific in 1864, authorized it to construct a transcontinental railroad, and gave it 43 million acres of the people's land. Morgan and Hill destroyed the independence of the Northern Pacific by bringing it under the domination of the Great Northern. Morgan had testified that he and Hill had formed a "community of interest," meaning "a certain number of men who own property can do what they like with it." That was their right, they said. Knox said otherwise: the Court has the power to prohibit such behavior.

After the May panic, Morgan wanted to create a company large enough that nobody else could ever take control of it. He had said so. The laws of New Jersey made it possible. Northern Securities had a value of four hundred million dollars, and Morgan believed that if his stock "was not safe there, it was not safe anywhere." Call it a merger, a combination, a pool, a conspiracy, a consolidation, a contract, a securities company. No state, not even New Jersey, "can construct a creature and endow it with immunity to defy the supreme law of the land," Knox said.

The Great Northern and Northern Pacific had pooled their stock. They had no reason to compete now; the dividends would likely decrease if they did. "The object of business is gain," Knox said. "And when the gains of competitive enterprises are combined and arbitrarily divided, competition is destroyed."

Knox argued that the power of a monopoly is not only that it can fix rates, high or low. "It means also getting the commerce which was conducted by many into the hands of the few," he said. "It means that new lines can be brought into existence to meet new needs only if the combination wills it so." It means that "the entire railway systems of the country may be absorbed, merged, and consolidated." No corporation should have that much power, the former corporate lawyer insisted.

On Tuesday, December 15, in the late afternoon, the Supreme Court adjourned. The justices would take the next few months to determine what the law would allow.

Morgan and Hill worked in their offices during the two-day trial. They had the "most sublime confidence" that the justices would come down on their side, a friend of Hill's said. Meanwhile, Hill announced that the Burlington railroad would not give away a 1904 calendar. The half million farmers and businesspeople along its routes who had hung up the calendar every year for the past ten would be disappointed. But Hill didn't want to spend the money.

Roosevelt worked in the White House. He met with representatives from the Arizona and New Mexico territories. Both advocated to be declared two separate states, not one. He met with several of his cabinet members. His friend Jacob Riis, the urban reformer, came to visit. The skies were clear, the temperature below freezing. He toured shanties and tenements just blocks from official Washington but ignored by many of its residents.

"Already I begin to hear the echos of the great speech," Roosevelt wrote to Knox about his argument before the Court. "Mrs. Roosevelt says she was so absorbed that even the close air of the cubby-hole where she and Mrs. Knox sat, couldn't make her lose interest for a moment." In the coming months, there was politics to attend to and businesses still to run. But there was nothing more to say about Northern Securities. Roosevelt and Knox and Morgan and Hill had to wait.

CHAPTER 15

The Ruling

Mark Hanna was sick with the flu. On Tuesday, December 15, the second and final day of the Northern Securities trial, he was in bed in Washington. He still had a fever and chills later in the week, but he insisted on going to New York for a meeting with business and labor leaders. He then traveled to Cleveland for Christmas, a twelve-hour trip that he made in the private car of the president of the New York Central Railroad. Hanna worked in his company's office for a week, talked with politicians in Chicago until midnight, gave a speech in Columbus after the state assembly reelected him senator, and pressed on as if he were healthy.

But he hadn't changed his mind about challenging Roosevelt. A group of railroad executives told him: "Stop making presidents and become one yourself." Hanna told them, once again, that he would not become one.

He returned to Washington in the middle of January, showed up at the Senate for half a week, and stayed in his bed at the Arlington Hotel for the second half. His doctor gave him morphine for a toothache, stimulants for exhaustion, sedatives for anxiety. Maybe he was suffering from more than the flu. He looked weary but assured friends he was fine.

On January 30 he ignored the doctor's advice, dressed for the evening, and joined hundreds of politicians, businessmen, and journalists downstairs at the hotel's banquet hall for a Gridiron dinner. Hanna usually carried a small cane and often limped. Everyone knew he suffered from rheumatism and no one thought it unusual that he sat during the reception. But he didn't eat or drink or give the speech he had prepared. When someone asked how he was feeling, he replied: "Not good."

Otherwise he tried to keep up appearances. He laughed during the skits, especially when the actors now and then shouted "Hurrah for Hanna," echoing his presidential boosters. Roosevelt attended the dinner too and laughed along with Hanna. Roosevelt said a few words about "public questions and public men," words that club rules forbade reporters to repeat. At one in the morning, the stragglers left. Hanna had returned upstairs, where he occupied the entire second floor.

He didn't like to complain, he said, but his hands felt like ice and every nerve ached. Four days later, a specialist diagnosed typhoid fever. It wasn't necessarily fatal. But Hanna was sixty-six, smoked a dozen of his own brand of cigars every day, and exercised only when he couldn't avoid it. He summoned his family and took to his bed.

Roosevelt came to visit the next morning, Friday, February 5. Hanna was asleep. "You touched a tender spot, old man, when you called personally to inquire after me this a.m. I may be worse before I can be better, but all the same such 'drops' of kindness are good for a fellow," Hanna wrote in pencil to the president. "Indeed it is *your* letter from your sick bed which is touching, not my visit. May you soon be with us again, old fellow, as strong in body and as vigorous in your leadership as ever," Roosevelt wrote back. Hanna never saw the president's reply.

Doctors sent out bulletins with Hanna's temperature and pulse. Roosevelt's updates came by phone. Hanna received oxygen and saline injections and as a last resort saline with some brandy. But his pulse became weaker. He spoke a few words to his family, then fewer.

Hanna's deathwatch began. Friends gathered in the hotel lobby, reporters stood outside. Everyone waited. His doctors said it wouldn't be long. But time seemed to slow at the Arlington.

By Monday, February 15, the bulletins arrived every fifteen minutes or so. Trading on the stock market was tentative. Many investors and brokers had hoped Hanna would be president. His decline temporarily blunted them. But they didn't panic. If they could anticipate a shift in power or prospects, they didn't fear it as much.

The capital was gray, cold. After sixteen inches of hard snow fell on the city in January, and some still remained on the streets in February, commissioners asked Congress to create a permanent fund, some ten thousand dollars would do, for snow and ice removal. In Chinatown, residents celebrated the Lunar New Year with tea, wine, cigars, oranges, incense, candles, and red envelopes filled with a little cash.

Buffalo Bill Cody visited the White House that Monday. So did delegates from the National Women's Suffrage Association; the president, who never took up the issue, invited Edith, who never pressed him to. Ohio's governor, Myron Herrick, a protégé of Hanna's, stopped by on his way to the Arlington. Hanna's doctors suspected he had contracted typhoid from drinking contaminated water in Columbus in January. Herrick told Roosevelt how terrible he felt about that.

Roosevelt walked over to the Arlington around three and stayed with Hanna's family for fifteen minutes. When he returned to the lobby, he told the crowd that the senator was near his end.

At 6:40 that evening, an hour after the winter sun set, Hanna died.

He made a president and the president helped make him powerful. He ran a company and accumulated a fortune. He tried to reconcile employers and employees. John Mitchell said the death was a "well-nigh irreparable loss" to the labor movement. Morgan said Hanna "understood all kinds of human nature." A colleague said the old order had passed away too.

Hanna served as a director of three banks and a railroad. He held significant shares of the Cleveland Electric Railway, the American Shipbuilding Company, and the Pittsburgh Coal Company. He owned the Euclid Opera House in Cleveland and vacation homes in Georgia and Maine. He had earned five thousand dollars a year as a senator. In the end, he reportedly left his family an estate worth some seven million, one of the biggest ever filed in probate court up to that point (though that might have been only because other wealthy men underestimated the value of their holdings). His estate was also one of the first compelled to pay a state inheritance tax, sixty thousand dollars. Governor Herrick signed the law in 1904—and asked the legislature to repeal it two years later because it was so unpopular.

"Hanna's death has been very sad," Roosevelt wrote to Root the next day. "He resolutely declined to be drawn into the position which a smaller man of meaner cast would inevitably have taken; that is, the position of antagonizing public policies if I was identified with them." Roosevelt admired Hanna even as he maneuvered, publicly, privately, and mercilessly, to limit the senator's influence.

Root had resigned as secretary of war by then. He was exhausted, and his wife wanted to return to New York. "I have missed, and shall miss, Root dreadfully," Roosevelt wrote to his son Ted, who was in his third year at Groton School in Massachusetts. "He has been the ablest, most generous and most disinterested friend and advisor that any President could hope to have." As Root's replacement, Roosevelt appointed William Howard Taft, who had finally agreed to leave the Philippines and be thrust into national politics. "Taft is a splendid fellow," Roosevelt continued, "but as Mother says, he is too much like me to be able to give me as good advice as Mr. Root was able to do because of the very differences of character between us."

The president was more expansive when he spoke with the journalist Walter Wellman, saying that Root "is the greatest man who has appeared in the public life of the country, in any position, on either side of the ocean, in my time." Roosevelt said Root was so great he could take the place of the great secretary of state John Hay or the great attorney general Philander Knox. But probably neither one could take his. After the article was published, Roosevelt realized how that sounded. He apologized to Knox and Hay, denied speaking to Wellman on the record, and promised if he had spoken to Wellman he hadn't used those exact words. "I feel that the service you have rendered in connection with the Northern Securities suit, and in connection with your entire attitude toward organized labor on the one hand, and great corporate wealth on the other, has been such as no other man, at this time, could have rendered, or could render, in your place," he wrote Knox. "I have shown this letter to Root."

Root spent one of his last evenings in Washington at the Gridiron dinner. Then he moved to New York and resumed his private practice. He accepted an offer to advise Morgan's firm and Morgan himself. He told Morgan and his other clients he wouldn't lobby the government on their behalf. He still earned one hundred thousand dollars in fees his first year, more than ten times his salary as secretary of war.

Root had another important job—advocating for the president in New York. Someone had to. The rumors were getting outlandish. Apparently some frustrated businessmen, "the Big Interests," a friend called them, hired psychologists to analyze Roosevelt's public statements and actions, looking for evidence that he was too unbalanced to be president.

Wall Street's opposition to Roosevelt wasn't public, but its leaders' murmurings of dissent influenced the men one notch down who looked to them for advice or standards or loans. They whispered that Roosevelt was dangerous, that his agitation against corporations and communities of interest would harm them. He shouldn't be allowed to control Wall Street. Wall Street had to control him. But Wall Street was in disgrace in early 1904. People had become cynical about the excessive speculation and constant promotion of dodgy stocks. If Wall Street was against Roosevelt, many people would be for him.

Roosevelt understood this and intended to capitalize on it.

Root's New York friends organized a dinner in early February at the Union League Club to welcome him home. He used the occasion to defend the president. Two hundred fifty-five guests crowded into the banquet hall, among them industrialists and investors and lawyers worried that the president would continue to impede their preferred way of conducting business. Cornelius Bliss—member of the Jekyll Island Club and president of the Union League—sat next to Root. John Griggs sat at the head table too. Morgan was supposed to be there but declined at the last minute.

"I am told he is not popular here in the city of his home. I am told that some people say he is not safe," Root said of the president. "He is not safe for the men who wish to prosecute selfish schemes to public detriment." The man the audience probably trusted more than any other Roosevelt intimate told them they were wrong in language they would understand. "I say to you that he has been, during the years since President McKinley's death, the greatest conservative force for the protection of property and our institutions in the city of Washington." How? By enforcing the law and promising fair treatment for every citizen.

Root didn't discuss the president's efforts to settle the anthracite coal strike, a controversial topic in the room. Root played a role in that, but they could forgive Root. He didn't take the strike's leader into his confidence as Roosevelt had. He didn't seem to encourage the strikers, as they believed Roosevelt had.

Root urged them to look beyond their immediate concerns. "There are some things to be thought of besides the speculation of the hour," he said. "There is the greater onward march of American institutions, there is the development of our social system." The old way will spark class resentment and social upheaval. Roosevelt's way will ensure "the great toiling mass of the American people shall feel that laws are just and justly administered; that every boy has his chance for the future."

To an audience of capitalists who believed they had one responsibility and only one—profit—Root spelled out a multitude of other obligations. They must be "fair to the consumer, fair to the laborer, fair to the investor," Root said. "Never forget that the men who labor cast the votes, set up and pull down governments."

When he finished, the men he hoped to persuade applauded. Some stood and waved their linen napkins over their heads. They were cheering for Root and the prosperous country, enlightened institutions, and hopeful future he described. Griggs, the Northern Securities lawyer, suggested Root could be president. Root had no desire to be president.

"You want to send a gold watch, or a diamond necklace, or a house and lot or any other little thing that occurs to you to your former Secretary of War at once," Governor Franklin Murphy of New Jersey wrote to Roosevelt afterward.

Roosevelt did thank Root. "The evil [in New York] had gone very deep and the effects were becoming noticeable far from the original center," he wrote. Root's speech would exorcise the evil. Newspapers had covered it, and the Union League Club was publishing it. Word would spread that Roosevelt was safe.

But the president was still anxious about his election prospects. Really, the president was just anxious. He had been cooped up in the White House during the howling winter, only able to chase off his doubts during a few icy walks in Rock Creek Park and hurried rides around the Washington Monument.

A jujitsu master trained Roosevelt three afternoons a week, and the close combat seemed to improve his spirits. It also helped him lose weight before the campaign season. Roosevelt practiced with whomever he could get his hands on: Taft, Loeb, the Japanese naval attaché, his sons, assorted visitors. "My right ankle and left wrist and one thumb and both great toes are swollen sufficiently to more or less impair their usefulness, and I am well mottled with bruises elsewhere," Roosevelt wrote to Ted. "Still I have made good progress, and since you have left they have taught me three new throws that are perfect corkers." He was down 20 pounds, to a solid 200, by May. The political rebukes of Roosevelt continued; a few newspapers criticized his spending. Roosevelt didn't like to be criticized about anything, but being accused of extravagance was especially galling. Part of Roosevelt's appeal, particularly out west, was that he had shaken off his privilege.

Roosevelt wrote a letter to Lawrence Abbott, the publisher of the popular *Outlook* magazine, defending himself and suggesting Abbott might do the same in print. The cost of the new tennis court, where Roosevelt and his children played—his children better than he—"has been trivial," less than four hundred dollars, he said. He hadn't even asked for the new stable. That was the doing of the public buildings superintendent who said the horses became sick in the old one. "I pay the butcher, baker and grocer at Washington just as I do at Oyster Bay," he said, and have "people whom I like lunch or dine with me at the White House." Who could protest that? As for the biggest expense of all, both the Republicans and Democrats in Congress "agreed that it was absolutely necessary" to expand the White House. "Only a yahoo could have his taste offended" by the renovations.

Among those still dining at the White House were Oliver Wendell Holmes and Fanny, along with the rest of the group Henry Adams called "our family circle." Holmes and the Supreme Court justices were debating the Northern Securities case. Newspapers reported each day that passed without a verdict. Roosevelt counted too. "All I can do is hope," he said. The decision could render his presidency a success or a disappointment, and for now he could do nothing. He knew not to ask Holmes about the deliberations, but he felt confident in his friend.

"The moral effect is incalculable," Knox had telegraphed Roosevelt after the government won a fraud case against a silk importer who evaded tariffs. "May our luck hold out."

THE MORNING OF Monday, March 14, 1904, was cold and windy. Snow was expected later in the week. Despite the wishes of the justices, news that they had reached a ruling had leaked out. When they filed into the domed chamber at noon, staff had brought in extra chairs, and still people stood in the back and in the hallway. The justices took their places at the bench, nine men, eight marble columns framing them. Chief Justice Fuller sat in the middle, a gilded eagle with outspread wings high on the wall behind him. Harlan was on his right, and beyond Harlan, Holmes.

Attorney General Knox sat directly in front of the justices. Taft and Lodge arrived together. Other congressmen left their own deliberations to join the audience.

Roosevelt remained at the White House entertaining guests for lunch. Among them were William Roscoe Thayer, an author who watched Roosevelt with a biographer's eye; the Austro-Hungarian ambassador and his wife; John Hay, who opposed Roosevelt's initial decision to take on the magnates; and Cardinal James Gibbons, who prayed Roosevelt would win the presidential election.

The courtroom fell silent as Justice Harlan announced Case Number 277. The evidence, he said "shows a violation of the act of Congress." And then, a little later: No scheme or device "could more effectively and certainly suppress free competition."

The government had won. The crowd murmured, and reporters rushed to cable the news to their editors. It wasn't clear until Harlan reached the end of the opinion, an hour and twenty minutes later, just how close the decision had been—five to four. After Harlan delivered the majority opinion, Justice David Brewer added an important caveat. Then came not one dissent, but two: one from Justice Edward White—and the other from Justice Holmes.

Four opinions. It was an unusual airing of legal, and partisan, particulars. It was also an unusual opportunity to address a rapt audience and one man specifically, the president, who sat beyond the courtroom. The political significance of Case 277 was undeniable.

In the fourteen years since Congress had passed the Sherman antitrust law, the Supreme Court had used it to shield the Sugar Trust and livestock exchanges it deemed not to be engaged in interstate commerce. Three times it had ordered cartels to break up: In 1897 the justices determined the Trans-Missouri Freight Association was illegally setting rates among fifteen railroad companies. Ditto for the Joint Traffic Association in 1899. That same year, the justices also determined that six companies had come together for the explicit purpose of bid rigging and fixing unreasonably high prices in the Addyston Pipe and Steel case. The justices were united in the Addyston case and remained divided about the railroad associations. Holmes was not on the bench for any of those arguments.

During the Northern Securities conference, Harlan and Holmes took opposite sides. Six other justices were equally split. Brewer alone was undecided. He consistently opposed the government's attempts to have a say in business affairs and legislate that every big merger created a monopoly. But he said he might be willing to agree that this specific merger had violated the law.

Harlan wrote an argument in favor of the government, not knowing whether it would be a majority opinion or a dissent. Brewer was not persuaded. Then the chief justice asked Holmes and White to write opinions and give them to the other judges. He hoped that Holmes would convince Brewer. "Yours will hit him between wind and water," Fuller wrote to the associate justice. It didn't. Brewer sided with Harlan, but wrote his own opinion.

"If such combination be not destroyed, all the advantages that would naturally come to the public under the operation of the general laws of competition, as between the Great Northern and Northern Pacific Railway Companies, will be lost," Harlan read in the courtroom, "and the entire commerce of the immense territory in the northern part of the United States between the Great Lakes and the Pacific at Puget Sound, will be at the mercy of a single holding corporation, organized in a State distant from the people of that territory."

He gave voice to a popular sentiment that others on the bench were reluctant to acknowledge. Many people believed they needed to be protected against "the exactions" of monopolies by the "strong arm of the National

Government," he said. "Undoubtedly, there are those who think that the general business interests and prosperity of the country will be best promoted if the rule of competition is not applied. But there are others who believe that such a rule is more necessary in these days of enormous wealth than it ever was."

The Sherman Act intended to "brush away all obstructions to the freedom of interstate commerce," he said, which meant that every contract and merger that restrained commerce must be forbidden, and "that must be, for all, the end of the matter if this is to remain a government of laws, and not of men."

He mentioned the man who didn't believe in the rule of free competition. Morgan knew what Northern Securities was designed to accomplish and what it had accomplished, Harlan said. And the court ruled that was illegal.

Justice Brewer agreed, but he wanted to refine the court's stance. He argued that only unreasonable restraint of trade should be prohibited. Northern Securities was unreasonable. Not every merger would be. "I have felt constrained to make these observations," he wrote, "for fear that the broad and sweeping language of the opinion of the court might tend to unsettle legitimate business enterprises, stifle or retard wholesale business activities, encourage improper disregard of reasonable contract and invite unnecessary litigation."

Holmes read his dissent, the first time he had done so since he took his seat on the bench. "When his voice, refined and clear, rose in the Court Room you could hear a pin drop & his sentences were as incisive as the edge of a knife," Fuller wrote of Holmes's performance that day. "Great cases like hard cases make bad law," Holmes said. "For great cases are called great, not by reason of their real importance in shaping the law of the future, but because of some accident of immediate overwhelming interest which appeals to the feelings and distorts the judgment. These immediate interests exercise a kind of hydraulic pressure which makes what previously was clear seem doubtful, and before which even well settled principles of law will bend."

Holmes argued that the intent of the merger between the two northwestern railroad lines was undoubted. It was to end competition between them. But the Sherman Act does not apply to Northern Securities, he said, because Hill and Morgan were partners who should be allowed to determine if they had exhausted their ability to compete profitably. Cooperation of this kind was not just inevitable, Holmes believed, but essential to creating efficient and stable businesses: someone had to win in the economy of scale. Not every big company violated the antitrust law by its very existence; only those that contrived to keep out competitors could be punished.

He insisted that Harlan's interpretation, taken to its logical extreme, would "disintegrate society so far as it could into individual atoms." Congress doesn't have the power to write a law so radical. "It would be an attempt to reconstruct society."

White made a similar argument. The government doesn't have the "power to limit the quantity and character of property which may be acquired and owned," he said. Controlling stock wasn't the same as controlling commerce. If the Court deemed that it was, the government would be endowed "with the arbitrary power to disregard the great guaranty of life, liberty and property and every other safeguard upon which organized civil society depends." That, he said, would be repugnant.

Case 277 concluded at 2:45 P.M., and the justices left for lunch.

Within thirty minutes of Harlan's opening words, the decision was on the ticker tape in Morgan's office. As for Roosevelt, he received word of the victory when the Associated Press reached him by phone. He was elated. Anyone could hear that in the punch of his voice, even as he uncharacteristically declined to comment right then.

Roosevelt was also brimming with relief and ambition. He had shown that he could take on the richest of men and hold them accountable, not to the bottom line or to investors, but to the public. It was the first time the government stood up so squarely for farmers and workers, clerks and shop owners, everyone who felt that the system was rigged. Roosevelt beat back the system—and he did so just eight months before the presidential election.

The only blow to Roosevelt that day was one he never anticipated and wouldn't be able to fully forgive. His friend, Justice Holmes—whom he put on the bench, invited to his home, joked and deliberated with—hadn't come down on his side. Holmes was the only Republican to join the three Democrats on the Court in dissent. This didn't seem a sign of principle, or duty, but weakness. "I could carve out of a banana a judge with more backbone than that," Roosevelt later said of his first Supreme Court pick.

Knox drove straight to the White House. The president congratulated his attorney general with the full force of his enthusiasm. Even in this moment, though, Knox remained reserved. "The danger of uncontrolled personal power in railway management has been averted," he said. Roosevelt must have wanted to say so much more, but he knew he shouldn't gloat. So for the rest of the afternoon, he expressed his utter happiness to everyone who walked through the White House in just a few words, slapping their backs and clapping his hands.

The Supreme Court gave Morgan and Hill thirty days to dissolve Northern Securities. If they didn't obey, criminal prosecution could lead to a fine of five thousand dollars and one year in prison for each. Locking up men as prominent as Morgan and Hill, though, still seemed an extraordinary breach of protocol and expectation, one that Holmes, at least, regarded as absurd and even Roosevelt likely would have resisted.

Morgan puffed on his cigar and said nothing as reporters gathered at his office on Wall Street. His losses were evident. Six months of secret negotiations to create the second-largest company in the world: wasted. The prospect of earning tens of millions of dollars from a globe-spanning transportation system: a dream. But above all, he had lost the prerogative to conduct business exactly as he thought best.

"Northern Securities Co. decision almost as bad as possible," Morgan's son, Jack, in town from London, telegraphed his office. "But it does not destroy value of properties involved. Dissenting opinions very strong and by best men."

Hill was defiant. Separately, the railroads would still be plenty profitable, he said. "The properties of the Northern Securities Company are still there. They are as good as ever." When a reporter asked about rumors that he would try to operate Northern Securities under a Canadian charter, he became peevish. "We have as much notion of incorporating a company in Mars or the moon as in Canada," he said.

Headlines in papers around the country celebrated the Supreme Court decision:

MERGER IS KNOCKED OUT. GETS SOLAR PLEXUS BLOW

MORGAN'S RAILROAD TRUST AN OUTLAW

MERGER DECISION PEOPLE'S TRIUMPH

"People will love him for the enemies he has made," one paper wrote. "It cannot now be said that the Republican Party is owned by the trusts. It cannot now be said that Mr. Roosevelt is controlled by them."

The Supreme Court "has practically renominated President Roosevelt and by this declaration of war against all industrial combines has all but insured his re-election," a Republican leader in Congress said. "The decision means more to the people of our country than any event since the great civil war," said Minnesota Governor Van Sant, whose early case against Northern Securities had been turned down by the Supreme Court. "The decision speaks for itself," said John Johnson, the Northern Securities lawyer. "The decision marks a radical change in public policy toward corporations," the columnist W. W. Jermane wrote in the *Minneapolis Journal*. Wall Street would give a good deal to know just what the president plans to do and when, he added.

Wall Street, or at least the men willing to speak for the investor class, said there was no cause for alarm. Alarm could lead to losses, maybe panic. When investors quivered anyway, "protective supporting orders," especially for Northern Securities, came in to hold up the stock market. Everyone knew where the orders came from.

Attorney General Knox, whose critics once called him the "hireling of the plutocrat and the instrument of everything that was odious to the common people," had accomplished what his enemies predicted he would never even attempt. Afterward he helped calm the money men he had helped antagonize. Which trust would be next? The Tobacco Trust, the Coal Trust, the Steel Trust? Knox told journalists it didn't seem necessary to promise that the government "does not mean to run amuck." But, there, he did.

The government's case against the Beef Trust—six meatpacking companies that fixed prices in half the country—was on its way to the Supreme Court. "Would not it be well to have some statement made as to what has been done about the beef trust, so that people will be advised?" Roosevelt wrote to Knox. "Sometimes things of this kind ought to be hammered in."

That challenge to the industrial order was the only one the government cared to make for a while. Northern Securities was a sweeping victory won by a narrow margin. When someone at a Gridiron dinner joked that the government prevailed by a vote of four and five-eighths, Justices Harlan and Brewer laughed the loudest. But Brewer, whose five-eighths support was crucial, might not swing its way next time. It looked as if during an election year the Justice Department's half-million-dollar antitrust budget wouldn't be zeroed out.

Roosevelt, his administration, and his party preferred it that way. They had enough to celebrate. The regular Tuesday cabinet meeting "resolved itself into a jollification over the merger decision," said one paper. "Republicans from all directions and in all official stations felicitated the President," reported another. The Northern Securities verdict confirmed the government's power to defend the public interests when they conflicted with corporate interests. Voters would know that. To encourage their appreciation of the administration's efforts on their behalf, Senator Lodge suggested the government printing office make available twelve thousand copies of the entire court proceeding.

In the weeks after the verdict, Justice Harlan got fan mail from people around the country. "Your opinion will do more to restore confidence to the whole country than any decision which has been rendered for many years," wrote one lawyer. Justice Holmes got the cold shoulder. "I have had no communication of any kind with [the president] upon the matter," he wrote to a friend. "If he should take my action with anger I should be disappointed in him and add one more to my list of cynicisms where before was belief. But I have such confidence in his great heartedness that I don't expect for a moment that after he has had time to cool down it will affect our relations. If however his seeming personal regard for us was based on the idea that he had a tool the sooner it is ended the better—we shall see."

Roosevelt did invite the Holmeses to the White House that spring and eventually his anger did cool. But so did their relationship. "The merger business is a grand mess," Henry Adams wrote after a dinner with them both. "Holmes should have been an ideal man for the bench," Roosevelt said later. "As a matter of fact he has been a bitter disappointment."

ON MARCH 21, ONE week after the court ordered Northern Securities to dissolve, Hill informed the attorney general that the company would comply without question or delay. The next day, Hill and his erstwhile rival Harriman were reported leaving Morgan's office at 23 Wall Street "arm in arm and apparently in the best of spirits." Neither would comment beyond saying that they had come to a perfect understanding of how best to break up.

That was either premature on Hill's part or deceptive on Harriman's. In early April, Harriman sued Northern Securities, alleging that Morgan's plan to divide the company's stock violated his rights. Northern Securities had been created by an exchange of stock. Those who owned shares of Northern Pacific and those who owned shares in the Great Northern turned them over to Morgan and received shares in Northern Securities instead. Now Morgan wanted to give back to Northern Securities share-holders stock in both the Great Northern and Northern Pacific regardless of which company they had originally invested in.

His proposal would leave Harriman with stakes in both railroads, but without a controlling interest in either. Harriman didn't think that was fair. His raid on Northern Pacific in 1901 ended when he had enough shares to influence the company. He wanted all of them back.

He didn't get them. He asked the Justice Department to intervene in the case, but Knox declined. Roosevelt thought he might have to be involved, because of a fluke of timing. The U.S. district court set to hear the argument had lost its judge and Roosevelt had to appoint a new one. He wanted someone "absolutely fair and square as between the public on one hand and both the Harriman and Morgan interests on the other, and as between the Harriman and Morgan interests," he said. "Next in importance to *having* him this, comes having him such a man that the public will *recognize* that he is this."

He wrote that to Root, who was defending Morgan in the case. Roosevelt was so certain of Root's rectitude that confiding in him didn't seem like a conflict of interest. In the end, the judge Roosevelt selected didn't hear the Northern Securities case. The judge who did ruled against Morgan—and Root appealed. That wasn't a surprise to Roosevelt but he still wished for a speedy end to the company, its charter torn up, its board of directors dismissed, its name spoken only as a warning. He had to wait. It wasn't until March of 1905 that Root argued the case before the Supreme Court. The judges allowed the company to adopt Morgan's redistribution plan. Northern Securities dissolved.

Morgan and Hill retained their original stakes in the railroads, which critics said still left them with too much power. They could devise a gentlemen's agreement, and Harriman would happily join them. But without the holding company—the device that protected those shares from rivals or uncooperative investors—they lost total control. Harriman lost interest, sold his stock at an opportune moment, and made a profit of fifty-eight million dollars.

The economic benefits of the decision weren't immediately obvious to most Americans. Rates on the rail lines hadn't increased—and Morgan and Hill could maintain any efficiencies if they chose to. But in every other way, the implications of the ruling were powerful, restorative, even if only symbolic. "A moral tonic," one official called it. He meant to disparage. Roosevelt considered that praise. "You must have a due regard for opportunism in the choice of the time and method in making the attack," he later said.

IN APRIL 1904, just days after Harriman first complained about Morgan's stock plan, Morgan boarded the *Oceanic*—once anyone with a camera had been asked to leave the gangplank and he had denied to the remaining journalists that he was relocating to London. He sailed to Europe with his youngest daughter, Anne, and several friends for a two-month vacation.

In May, Roosevelt wrote to Ted: "I am having a reasonable amount of work and rather more than a reasonable amount of worry. But after all life is lovely here . . . I do not think that any two people ever got more enjoyment out of the White House than Mother and I."

Knox resigned as attorney general in June. Senator Quay from Pennsylvania had died in office and the governor had asked Knox to replace him. Knox, maybe wearying of his client, maybe ready to depart after his victory, didn't hesitate to accept. But it didn't look good. Some suggested that the corporate powers who had recommended Knox for the job as attorney general under McKinley had removed him from it. Roosevelt wrote that "stanchest [sic] of props had suddenly been taken away from me." Knox's imminent departure from the Department of Justice relieved investors. Stock prices rose. Knox reminded Wall Street that "President Roosevelt's antitrust policies are his own."

CHAPTER 16

A President in His Own Right

On the first day of summer, 1904, nearly a thousand delegates and their alternates—four women among them—arrived in Chicago for the Republican national convention. They set aside private antagonisms, professional jealousies, differences in temperament, tempo, and policy, to come together to nominate a candidate for president. They shared one reluctant conviction: the party needed Roosevelt more than he needed the party.

Roosevelt remained at the White House during the convention as presidents were supposed to. Idle moments usually frustrated him, but now he enjoyed the brief interlude between the angling and needling of the past few months and the fight to come. His was a mind at peace. The letters he wrote that Tuesday, June 21 sighed with appreciation:

> Dear Ted: Mother and I had a most lovely ride the other day, way up beyond Sligo Creek to what is called North-west Branch, at Burnt Mills, where is a beautiful gorge, deep and narrow, with great boulders and even cliffs.
>
> Dearest Ethel: The garden here is lovely. A pair of warbling vireos have built in a linden and sing all the time. The lindens, by the way, are in bloom, and Massachusetts Avenue is fragrant with them.

Dear Kermit: It is a wonderful privilege to have been here and
  to have been given the chance to do this work, and I should
  regard myself as having a small and mean mind if in the event
  of defeat I felt soured at not having had more instead of being
  thankful for having had so much.

Roosevelt had tipped the scales back toward ordinary Americans, and
many were devoted to him. He was an insurgent within his own party, but
the people supported him so the party endorsed him. He reached over the
heads of politicians to promise a square deal for all. Roosevelt's approach
toward big business—selective prosecutions, unexpected interventions, jabs
and nudges and sidesteps—unnerved the magnates. But they discovered
he was practical. He wouldn't endanger the country's prosperity. He was
an insurable risk. He was so popular they couldn't find anyone who could
defeat him.

Theodore and Edith surrounded by their family, from left to right:
Quentin, Theodore Jr., Archie, Alice, Kermit, and Ethel, 1903

"Dear Kermit: Tomorrow the National Convention meets, and barring a cataclysm I shall be nominated. They don't dare to oppose me for the nomination and I suppose it is hardly likely the attempt will be made to stampede the Convention for any one."

Roosevelt was right, and since he was right and everyone knew he was right, he demanded loyalty and unity among the delegates. He swarmed the convention with friends to keep everyone in line. He vetted speeches. He dictated the party platform: "In the enforcement of the laws [Roosevelt] has shown not only courage, but the wisdom which understands that to permit laws to be violated or disregarded opens the door to anarchy, while the just enforcement of the law is the soundest conservatism." All those delegates and politicians, so many lawyers among them, together for three days with nothing to argue over. The convention was a rubber stamp. "Certainty produces no excitement," New York senator Chauncey Depew said. "It is difficult to excite a man who has a good dinner, and who doesn't need to feel any worry about breakfast," the *New York Times* said. Let's have some music, New York's lieutenant governor said. He paid a band to play at the state's convention headquarters, hoping "to throw something like ginger into affairs."

Twenty-dollar entrance tickets—featuring an in memoriam image of McKinley—sold for five dollars, and still the auditorium was about one-third empty on Tuesday morning when Root opened the convention. His voice didn't carry far, but that wasn't the problem it might have been. He reviewed the administration's achievements, starting with the ones he had the least to do with, money and trusts. The Department of Justice is protecting "men of small capital . . . against the crushing effect of unlawful combinations," he said, while reminding men of large capital that "no investment in lawful business has been jeopardized, no fair and honest enterprise has been injured." He hoped Americans would not want this new responsibility "transferred to unknown and perchance to feeble hands."

An immense oil painting of Mark Hanna hung above the platform: a tribute, a rebuke, a sign of defiance. An American flag covered Roosevelt's portrait, set on an easel on the stage. A sergeant at arms was supposed to unveil it at a suitably dramatic pause in Root's speech, but he missed his cue. The moment might have been diminished anyway. Roosevelt's portrait

Hanna's image looms over the 1904 Republican National Convention

was estimated by reporters to be one-sixth the size of Hanna's. The sena-tor's friends seemed to have commandeered the decorations committee.

"Our president has taken the whole people into his confidence," Root said in conclusion. "All except the members of the National Committee," a member of the National Committee said quietly.

There were other asides, small gestures of resistance. At a dinner one delegate made a toast: "Here's to Roosevelt, the insistent candidate, whom nobody wants." The New Yorkers at the table set down their glasses and refused to drink.

At the end of the first day some delegates proposed adjourning after the second day. Party leaders insisted they remain for the third. Then offi-cials from the St. Louis World's Fair announced that three special trains would bring delegates and visitors there Thursday evening. They'd get free rail tickets and free admission to the Expo, where they could see one hundred forty models of automobiles and an "airship" contest and get their first taste of a new drink called Dr. Pepper. It was incentive enough; the delegates stayed.

By eleven in the morning on Thursday, June 23, the Coliseum in Chicago was filled. The National Committee sold every available seat, more than an acre of them, making some fourteen thousand dollars, and doormen let people in to stand. Some ten thousand people waited. Bright sun beamed through the skylit arched ceiling.

Frank Black, the one-term governor of New York cast aside for Roosevelt in 1898, walked onto the stage. Black distrusted Roosevelt and thought he cared more about popularity than justice, but as head of the New York delegation he couldn't refuse to nominate him. He did so with the choice words of a man whose ire had been provoked long ago. Black spoke first of the parties themselves. "Both believe in the equality of all men," he said. "The difference is that the Democratic Party would make every man as low as the poorest, while the Republican Party would make every man as high as the best." He insisted that the Democrats were disorganized and divided and admonished Republicans to "never interrupt the enemy while he is making a mistake."

Of the candidate himself, Black said: "He is not conservative, if conservative means waiting till it is too late. He is not wise, if wisdom is to count a thing a hundred times when once will do." William Allen White, Kansan, newspaper editor, friend of Roosevelt, said the speech was full of "rhetorical icicles."

When Black finally, officially, nominated Roosevelt as the Republican presidential candidate, the crowd applauded and cheered for some twenty minutes. That was about as long as Black spoke. They kept at it, almost mindlessly, celebrating themselves as much as, and maybe more than, their leader.

Next, Joseph Cannon, speaker of the House of Representatives and chairman of the convention, carried onto the stage a torn flag from Lincoln's time. More cheering. Cannon held up the hand of George Knight, a California lawyer and super delegate who said in a booming voice that Roosevelt "hypnotizes obstacles, looks them in the eye and overpowers with self-conscious honesty of purpose." Cannon held up the hand of William Bradley, the former governor of Kentucky, who said: "They tell us that he

Roosevelt's control of the convention was unchallenged: "All in favor of the nomination will say aye!"

cannot be trusted, but the people know that one who does a right thing at the right time and in the right way is entitled to vast, implicit confidence." Cannon did not hold up the hand of Harry Cummings, the first African American councilman of Baltimore, which did not go unnoticed in the hall. Cummings said of Roosevelt: "With a vision unclouded by bias or prejudice he sees through the outer clay, clad in different hues, the man within."

When it came time to vote, every single delegate, nine hundred ninety-four in all, supported Roosevelt.

At the White House he received dispatches every ten minutes or so from a phone set up in the basement of the Coliseum. On that Thursday afternoon he was chatting with Alice, Edith, and her sister Emily on the South Portico after lunch. The view of the Potomac River was calming, and Roosevelt seemed relaxed.

When his secretary brought him the final ballot count, Roosevelt rose to his feet, grinning and self-possessed. He knew this moment was coming. He had probably known since Hanna's death in February, maybe before, that he would prevail over his party. But now his success was real, and it could be measured.

Edith and Alice kissed him on the cheek, the younger children moved in closer, and then he was in motion. His other important constituency, the press corps, was waiting in his office.

He passed around a box of cigars. "Don't tell Carrie Nation," he joked. He tilted back in a big armchair at his desk, laughed at a cartoon of himself, and gossiped with the correspondents "not as President of the United States, not as the standard bearer of a great political party, but as Theodore Roosevelt, the man and friend," a *New York Times* reporter wrote. But that was all. The correspondents swore to keep their "executive sessions" with Roosevelt to themselves.

Roosevelt got everything he wanted, except his vice president. He preferred Robert Hitt, an agreeable, seventy-year-old congressman from

Illinois with foreign policy expertise. The nomination went instead to Indiana senator Charles Fairbanks, fifty-two years old, an insider during the McKinley administration. He was stern-looking, with a comb-over and a thick, droopy mustache. He didn't mix with the delegates, who called him "the human iceberg." His main qualification seemed to be that he had the confidence of the New York tycoons, especially Harriman, who was an important fundraiser. Fairbanks had friendly relations with the railroads. And he had a fortune from his legal practice that he could contribute to the campaign. He was at odds with Roosevelt in most matters.

They did have one thing in common. Fairbanks didn't campaign for the nomination. He didn't even seem to want it, but said he would accept the will of the convention. He sounded a lot like Roosevelt in 1900. When Roosevelt sent a telegram of congratulations, Fairbanks responded with barely disguised resignation: "To be named by the convention as your associate in the great campaign that is before us is a distinction which I greatly appreciate." Roosevelt understood. He wrote back later in the day to acknowledge the vice presidential trap: "No man should take it who is not fit to be President, and it is not always easy to induce those who are fit to accept it."

That Thursday evening in Chicago, delegates from Fairbanks's home state rented a baby elephant from a local circus, hoping he would parade with it down Congress Street. Fairbanks wouldn't get near the animal. "That wouldn't be dignified," he said. Around him, the bars filled with delegates drinking down the highball reserves before heading to the St. Louis fair—the ineluctable end of the thirteenth National Republic Convention.

Secretary of State Hay wrote in his diary on Friday: "The President was not specially elated—it was too clear a walk-over."

ROOSEVELT'S DEMOCRATIC OPPONENT was Judge Alton Parker of New York. He was reserved on the bench, formal and uncharismatic in person, rooted in Gilded Age customs. Those in his home state knew him to be friendly to business and irritated by the press. Those outside New York barely knew him. Aside from a shared habit of exercise, Parker was the president's opposite in almost every way.

Parker, who was fifty-two, had managed Democratic campaigns, turned down an offer from Grover Cleveland to be assistant postmaster general in Washington, returned to the law, and in 1897 was voted in as chief judge on the New York Court of Appeals. He was the first Democrat to prevail in any election in New York in six years. That got the party's attention.

It got Roosevelt's attention too. "The judge at once loomed up as a Presidential possibility, and was carefully groomed for the position by the New York Democratic machine, and its financial allies in the New York business world," he wrote. Roosevelt became friendly with the judge when he served as governor in 1899. It was Parker who told Edith her husband would certainly be nominated for the vice presidency, and it was Parker who gave Roosevelt advice on studying the law once he assumed the office. Parker even promised that when Roosevelt was ready, he would arrange for the vice president to take the bar exam privately.

Hanna heard about the judge during his many trips to New York. After his last one, in December 1903, he told a friend that Parker would be the Democrat's choice. The judge's main appeal: he was unobjectionable.

That was important because as Black emphasized in his speech in Chicago, the Democrats were divided and disorganized. Conservatives in the party planned to wrest it from the control of William Jennings Bryan, their candidate in the past two elections. Populist, prairie-inspired Bryan—the galvanizing speaker, the ardent believer in ending the gold standard—pushed the party into the twentieth century. The old establishment wanted to push it back.

Their first choice had been Cleveland, the only Democrat elected president, twice, in the thirty-nine years after the Civil War. He was pro-business and pro-gold, fiscally conservative, generally cautious. Morgan, who bailed out the Treasury during Cleveland's second term, would back him again. Cleveland might be the one Democrat who could beat Roosevelt. Even Roosevelt considered him a singularly qualified opponent.

In January 1904, Cleveland's daughter, Ruth, died at age twelve from diphtheria. Cleveland had just returned to public life in February when H.H. Rogers, an executive at Standard Oil, ran into him at a funeral. "I never saw him look better," Rogers wrote to a friend. "He has lost a lot of flesh; his complexion was clear; his eyes as bright as possible. It is astonishing the hold he has on the American people." Maybe he would consider running again.

Definitely not. Cleveland announced he would not seek the nomination; and he would not accept it if offered. "Don't mention me" at the convention, he told delegates.

That left an opening for William Randolph Hearst, the forty-one-year-old New York publisher famous for his sensationalism, his wealth, and his marriage to a showgirl after affairs with other showgirls. He hoped to succeed Bryan as the "radical" choice. He was antitrust, even though he was building a newspaper trust of his own. He spent much of his first term in Congress thinking about a presidential campaign. Few among the party's leaders supported his self-proclaimed candidacy. Bryan didn't like him and never endorsed him.

Bryan didn't support Parker either. "Where does he stand on the trust question? Does anybody know?" Bryan asked a crowd at Cooper Union in June. The Democratic Party platform suggested that the majority opinion in the Northern Securities case was wrong, he said. If Parker got to make even one appointment to the Supreme Court, he could "change that decision and throw a bulwark about every private monopoly that would require years and years for you to get about or get over."

That didn't matter. Parker won the nomination on the first ballot, 679 votes to Hearst's 181. Parker didn't excite the delegates gathered in St. Louis in early July—he wasn't even there—but he unified them, which brought its own satisfaction. Parker's running mate was Henry Gassaway Davis, an eighty-one-year-old former senator from West Virginia who didn't look older than sixty and whose primary qualification was the fortune he had built from his political connections. Party leaders counted on his pliancy and campaign contributions.

As the delegates gathered for the closing session, their new candidate surprised them. The Democrats had tried to ignore the contentious issue of the nation's currency: that is, should the party support adding a silver standard, as Bryan wanted, or stick with the gold standard, as Wall Street insisted. "I regard the gold standard as firmly and irrevocably established," Parker wired the chairman. "As the platform is silent on the subject, my views should be made known to the Convention, and if it is proved unsat-isfactory to the majority, I request you to decline the nomination for me at once."

His views were made known and proved compatible with the majority, which hadn't included Bryan. They wouldn't change the platform—that would only alienate Bryan's Western and Southern supporters—but they wouldn't change their nominee, either. Parker's stance finally gave the dele-gates, and the press, cause for enthusiasm. He showed some nerve in just the way the eastern money men admired. He transformed himself "from a nobody into a somebody," Lodge wrote to Roosevelt. "He has become a very formidable candidate and opponent," Roosevelt replied. "For instead of being a colorless man of no convictions he now stands forth to the average man—and this at an astonishingly small cost—as one having convictions compared to which he treats self-interest as of no account."

Conservatives called Parker a courageous and principled leader. Demo-crats left St. Louis July 10 to begin the campaign against Roosevelt "not in gloom and fear, but in hope and confidence," Cleveland said.

Their optimism lasted exactly one month. On August 10, Parker welcomed hundreds of people to his farm in the small Hudson Valley town of Esopus to hear his acceptance speech on his lawn in the pouring rain. Local guests arrived by road sodden and muddy. The Democratic Committee came by boat along the Hudson River, scrambled up a steep hill, crossed a grassy slope, and arrived at Rosemount "breathless, wet to the knees and weary with unfamiliar exercise." Parker pulled out typewritten pages but didn't refer to them during most of the next hour, leaving listeners to marvel at how long he spoke and how little he said. What he did say about big business appealed more to potential donors than to voters: Roosevelt had gone too far in attacking the trusts. Let the states find remedies for the problem. Parker unintentionally delivered his biggest applause line at the end, when he promised not to seek a second term as president.

It was a nineteenth century address by an uninspiring orator who had been out of politics for almost two decades. Even his campaign manager thought he'd be out of politics again by the end of the year. Once excitable editors could only suggest that Parker would be a safe, rather than a strenuous, president. Hopes were dampened, chilled, clouded, dulled: reporters couldn't resist rainy-day adjectives. One gold telegram made Parker a somebody. One unremarkable speech turned him back into a nobody.

Parker did have two notable financial backers. James Hill and the coal baron George Baer—Roosevelt's bruised adversaries—contributed to a campaign that few others wanted to be part of. Hill recognized the challenge of selling his candidate to the public. "If Parker should be elected, there should be little danger of any bad legislation or extravagant administration," he wrote. "The country probably would be better off and the question arises: will the voters realize this?"

Party leaders stumped for Parker, half-heartedly. Parker himself stayed home, as McKinley had, hoping voters would come to him. But Esopus wasn't Canton and Parker wasn't McKinley. Few people visited. By autumn, the presidential candidate seemed to be fading from public view. When he went to his campaign headquarters in New York City, some workers didn't even recognize him.

There was but one issue at stake in the election: Roosevelt himself.

As president, he was supposed to remain quiet while others—often Root and Knox, sometimes Taft and Hay—defended his administration and touted his accomplishments. He did what decorum would allow. He suggested venues, reviewed speeches, and debriefed his proxies afterward. Knox should speak to serious audiences in small arenas. Fairbanks could appeal to the Methodists. Taft should go to Maine—and go on the offensive. "Attack Parker," Roosevelt instructed. "Show that his proposals are insincere."

Roosevelt gave control of the daily operation of his campaign to Cortelyou, his handpicked replacement for Hanna as chairman of the Republican National Committee. At the White House, Cortelyou rationalized operations, instituted protocols for visitors, set up the press room. He started up Roosevelt's Department of Commerce and Labor. He was dependable, cultivated, enterprising. He would also become controversial.

As campaign manager, he worked in an office in the Metropolitan Life Building on Madison Avenue, a location that suggested comfort with the corporate world. Cortelyou—slicked-back hair, sharp nose, round glasses—projected a new cool efficiency.

He had to. He had a demanding client who didn't have enough to occupy him that summer. "I wonder whether President McKinley bothered Hanna as I am bothering you!" President Roosevelt wrote him.

He suggested Cortelyou hire someone to handle the journalists who came into the headquarters with questions. Roosevelt worked the press too. When the *New York Times* reported that Hill had promised to contribute some four hundred thousand dollars to the national Democratic Party, Roosevelt ordered the campaign to circulate the story widely. Roosevelt also tried to link the Democratic Party to Standard Oil—still among the most reviled corporations in the country—after the *Wall Street Journal* suggested its executives might back Parker.

The president flattered and chastised newspaper and magazine editors about their coverage and took them into his confidence about issues he chose to ignore during the campaign. The suppression of black voters in the mostly Democratic controlled South "by force, by fraud, by every species of iniquity," made him indignant, he wrote to Lyman Abbott, the editor of the *Outlook*. The Republican Party platform favored reduced representation in Congress for any state that unconstitutionally limited voting rights. Roosevelt didn't amplify that in the one public speech he

George Cortelyou, Roosevelt's personal secretary, first head of the Commerce and Labor Department, and chairman of the Republican National Committee

gave, to accept the nomination, in late July: "Our policy is to do fair and equal justice to all men, paying no heed to whether a man is rich or poor; paying no heed to his race, his creed, or his birthplace." He wouldn't go further than that. He believed he had "nothing to gain and everything to lose by any agitation of the race question" in a campaign season. He didn't say anything about discrimination against immigrants, either.

He didn't involve himself in a brutal crackdown on striking miners in Cripple Creek, Colorado. At the companies' insistence and with their financial help, the governor called in the state militia. Troops beat the strikers, deported them from Colorado, and harassed their supporters. Union leaders asked the president to intervene. In August, Roosevelt asked his labor secretary to investigate and left matters there. But the fiasco carved a fissure in the foundation of union strength.

Mostly that summer Roosevelt brooded. "I wish I were where I could fight more offensively," he told Lodge. "I always like to do my fighting in the adversary's corner." Conservatives attacked him for inviting John Mitchell to a meal at the White House and becoming an honorary member of the Brotherhood of Locomotive Firemen. Populists attacked him for meeting with railroad executives. "While I am in the White House its doors will swing open as easily to wageworkers as to capitalists, and no more easily," he wrote to the House Speaker.

Roosevelt worried that his Wall Street support, tepid as it was, could still be held against him. He worried, too, that his Wall Street support wasn't strong enough to ensure that he carried his home state and that a Republican won the governor's race.

Hill was doing his best to ensure the Democrats took New York. He suggested he would donate one hundred thousand dollars to the state election campaign if Daniel Lamont—the vice president of the Northern Pacific railroad and Grover Cleveland's secretary of war—received the nomination for governor. The *New York Times* endorsed Lamont, while the *Brooklyn Daily Eagle* reported he didn't want to be a candidate. The Democratic Party agreed he shouldn't be, and Lamont didn't try to persuade them otherwise.

Roosevelt begged Root to run for the seat, but Root turned him down. He was representing Northern Securities in its fight against Harriman over how to break up the company. He couldn't return to public office before he argued the case at the Supreme Court. The Republicans would have to find someone else. "The thing to do is to strain every nerve to bring the result aright," Roosevelt said.

The prospect of Northern Securities lingering on as Morgan and Harriman tussled in the courts frustrated Roosevelt. Then another complication emerged. Root suggested that Northern Securities might not comply with the Supreme Court's order to stop paying dividends to its shareholders. He said among those hurt would be several hundred women and a half dozen colleges—Dartmouth alone owned shares worth half a million dollars. The Justice Department would have to consider contempt charges if Northern Securities disobeyed the order, but the new attorney general, William Moody, seemed hesitant.

Roosevelt lashed out, not at Moody or Root, but at the nearest man, Cortelyou. "To give any color for misrepresentation to the effect that we were now weakening in the Northern Securities matter would be ruinous," he wrote in mid-August. "I look back upon it with great pride, for through it we emphasized in signal fashion, as in no other way could be emphasized, the fact that the most powerful men in this country were held to accountability to the law. Now we must not spoil the effect of this lesson."

Cortelyou defended himself. "I think I have a fair degree of moral fiber, certainly enough to measure up to the requirements of this Northern Securities case," he replied. "There was no weakening, no letdown, no desire or attempt to do a thing out of harmony with your position." Roosevelt liked that spirited rebuttal, he told Cortelyou, and he backed down.

Root backed down, as well, after Moody told him the government would object to any attempt by Northern Securities to distribute dividends. Roosevelt bore no grudge against Root—new job, new responsibilities. "He was in honor bound to do all he could for his clients," Roosevelt wrote to Moody. He was still irritated, though. "It is the Hills and the Morgans who perpetrate the wrong," he said. "It is . . . the small folks . . . who pay most heavily when the wrong has been righted."

Morgan summered on *Corsair*, cruising from the Long Island Sound to Bar Harbor. Alice Roosevelt, twenty years old and more or less on her own, summered with the wealthy on Long Island's North Shore and in

Newport. That set weren't Morgan's crowd, but they too "regarded Father with suspicion and dislike," she wrote. "Trust busting was not exactly a war cry to rally their support." Still they issued invitations, still she accepted. She saw their skepticism up close and it worried her too, right up until Election Day. "I was holding my thumbs," she said.

By fall, back at work, the Eastern financiers assessed Parker's dismal August and seemed to accept the inevitability of his defeat. Money doesn't like to back a loser. The Republican Party was still conservative, even if the president wasn't, and that now seemed better than the alternative. As even the *New York Sun* had to admit in its pithy endorsement: "Theodore! with all thy faults—"

Cornelius Bliss, the Republican National Committee's longtime treasurer, began soliciting contributions from Roosevelt's new supporters. Bankers, industrialists, and dealmakers all welcomed the prominent New York merchant to their offices. He knew what they wanted from Washington, what they feared from Roosevelt, since he himself shared many of their views. "I think he always felt that I was too radical a man and did not entirely approve, and sometimes very much disapproved of the things that I advocated," Roosevelt later said. Morgan, on the other hand, could say that his "relations with Mr. Bliss were of a very intimate character." Bliss had worked with Morgan's father. "Consequently, when they wanted anything they always sent Mr. Bliss to me." In September, despite his personal dislike of Roosevelt and resentment at the president's hostile stance, Morgan gave Bliss one hundred thousand dollars, in cash. Andrew Carnegie, retired from his steel company and among the richest men in the world thanks to Morgan, contributed ten thousand to the campaign. Carnegie's former executive, Henry Frick, put in fifty thousand. George Perkins, the conduit between Roosevelt and Morgan, kicked in. So did the oil executive H. H. Rodgers.

None announced their donations, and the campaign had no legal obligation to report them. But word got out, and suspicions were raised. Big money must be supporting Roosevelt because his collectors promised favors or threatened retaliation. Cortelyou got the worst of it. As the head of the Commerce and Labor Department, he had access to companies' private financial information and power to investigate wrongdoing. Now he was accused of blackmailing the trusts.

Joseph Pulitzer, the reform-minded, Democrat-leaning publisher of the *New York World*, wrote his third open letter criticizing the Republican campaign. He printed ten questions on two pages of the Saturday, October 1, edition, expected to be read by hundreds of thousands of people, accusing Cortelyou of promising protection to corporate contributors.

1. How much has the beef trust contributed to Mr. Cortelyou?

How much have the paper, coal, sugar, oil, tobacco, steel and insurance trusts contributed? How about the national banks?

10. How much have the six great railroads contributed to Mr. Cortelyou?

A *New York Times* editorial published that same Saturday claimed that thanks to Cortelyou, the men of the trusts believe "they are buying, not the Presidency, but the President." The editors called his appointment as chairman of the national committee a "national disgrace" and asked, "Why does Theodore Roosevelt, honest, upright, incorruptible man that he is, allow his stainless reputation to be thus compromised?"

Parker kept silent on the subject at first. He had Hill and Baer on his side. He had August Belmont, too, the New York banker who was financing the construction of the city's subway system. He contributed as much as a quarter of a million dollars to Parker's campaign.

Roosevelt assumed his opponent's people were behind the attacks on his campaign manager. "Cannot our papers and our orators hit back as savagely as possible?" he wrote to Cortelyou. "If it is deemed advisable I am perfectly willing when the time comes to appear in the campaign myself . . . I should like to get at Brother Parker and his associates."

Cortelyou promised that the next Roosevelt administration would be "unhampered by a single promise of any kind." That wasn't nearly savage enough for Roosevelt. But he kept silent in public, at first.

Corporate contributions to the Republican National Committee had slowed by the end of September. Roosevelt's triumph over Parker seemed assured. The president didn't take that for granted, and he still worried about Republican prospects in New York. The candidate for New York governor, Frank Higgins, didn't arouse much enthusiasm and withered under criticism that he was a product of the political machine. "I earnestly hope that Higgins takes the aggressive," Roosevelt said. The state party was having financial trouble, too. It expected to receive two hundred thousand dollars from the national committee, and apparently the national committee didn't have the cash.

"In view of the trouble over the State ticket in New York I should very much like to have a few words with you," Roosevelt wrote to Harriman on October 10. When he didn't hear back right away, he considered the optics—Harriman was a railroad tycoon guilty of antitrust violations, an important New York fundraiser, a sometime friend and irregular correspondent. "You and I are practical men," he wrote in a second letter to reframe the request. "If you think there is nothing special I should be informed about, or no matter in which I could give aid, why of course give up the visit for the time being."

They met on October 20. Afterward, Harriman told friends that the national campaign was short of funds promised to New York. "They are in a hole," Harriman said, "and the President wants me to help them out."

With assistance from Bliss, Harriman raised a quarter of a million dollars in days. He contributed fifty thousand himself. Bliss gave five thousand. Perkins offered another thirty thousand. Frick agreed to donate another fifty thousand. So did Morgan. He wasn't surprised that the Republicans weren't satisfied with his original hundred-thousand-dollar contribution. "Gratitude has been rather scarce in my experience," he said.

Roosevelt later insisted he never knew Morgan contributed to the campaign. But in late October he found out that Bliss had persuaded John Archbold, the top executive at Standard Oil, to donate one hundred thousand dollars. "We do not want to make this contribution unless it is thoroughly acceptable and will be thoroughly appreciated by Mr. Roosevelt," Archbold told the treasurer. Bliss apparently smiled and said the company "need have no possible apprehension on that score." It was a vague statement open to interpretation but good enough for Archbold. He gave Bliss the money, in thousand-dollar bills.

Roosevelt was furious. He accepted corporate donations, however large, as long as they didn't seem to compromise him. But taking money from Standard Oil could. Once Ida Tarbell had revealed its economic and political power, people expected legal scrutiny to follow. It would begin with Cortelyou's Department of Commerce and Labor. "We cannot under any circumstances afford to take a contribution which can be even improperly construed as putting us under an improper obligation," Roosevelt wrote to Cortelyou on October 26. "They shall not suffer in any way because we refused it, just as they would not have gained in any way if we had accepted it. But I am not willing that it should be accepted, and must ask that you tell Mr. Bliss to return it."

On October 27, Roosevelt telegraphed Cortelyou: "Greatly desire that before leaving for Washington request contained in my letter of yesterday be complied with." He wrote Cortelyou a letter that same day: "I greatly wish to see you in person. Please come on at the earliest opportunity; but have the contribution returned immediately." In a memo, he said journalists told him Archbold and Standard Oil preferred Parker and only contributed to Roosevelt because they feared retaliation. On the twenty-ninth he wired Cortelyou again: "Has my request been complied with? I desire that there be no delay."

The money was never repaid. The campaign had already spent it and didn't have the funds to spare. Roosevelt said he didn't know that, but apparently he did. The letters, the telegram, the memo—they were a way to revise the historical record. Alice called them his "posterity letters."

Cortelyou did return one corporate donation, one hundred thousand dollars given by the Tobacco Trust—which the government was about to prosecute.

The country's business elite gave and raised about 70 percent of the Republican campaign funds. In total, the party collected almost $2.3 million dollars, less than what it had in 1900 and in 1896 but more than its rivals. The Democrats had barely a million dollars to work with, and the party ended the campaign in debt.

Roosevelt was pragmatic and conflicted about political money. He both sought it and resented it. "Corporation cunning has developed faster than the laws of nation and state," Roosevelt told a reporter. "Sooner or later, unless there is readjustment, there will come a riotous, wicked, murderous day of atonement . . . These fools in Wall Street think they can go on forever! They can't!"

AUTUMN IN THE capital brought small joys. The foliage in Rock Creek Park was "a perpetual delight," Roosevelt told Kermit. A dinner with a dignitary from France was a pleasure. "The President talked with great energy and perfect ease the most curious French I ever listened to," Hay noted in his diary. "It was absolutely lawless as to grammar and occasionally bankrupt in substantives; but he had not the least difficulty in making himself understood."

Then, on Saturday, October 22, another accident. Roosevelt's horse put a foot through a rotten plank on a bridge. The horse somersaulted; the president landed on his head, skinned his forehead, wrenched his neck and shoulders. Hay saw Roosevelt the next day, "badly bunged about the head and face," he wrote. "The President will of course outlive me, but he will not live to be old."

DANIEL LAMONT—NORTHERN PACIFIC executive, briefly considered a candidate for governor, born in the same town as Parker—visited his friend in mid-October. He told Parker he would lose.

"Well, old fellow," he declared, "they have got you licked, but I want you to go on and keep a stiff upper lip and make your fight, and I do not want it to break your heart."

"What do you mean by that?" Parker asked.

"It is all underwritten, and there is no show for you."

"I am not going to break my heart," Parker said.

Lamont told him that the trust magnates backed Roosevelt's campaign, with Roosevelt's knowledge, maybe even at his urging.

The Democratic National Committee told Parker that he could still win. The next day they said so publicly. They called Cortelyou's fundraising "either indecent or immoral." No one dared accuse the president directly. Not yet.

Parker came down from Esopus for the final week of the campaign. He brought a typewriter, throat spray, and drafts of six speeches. He didn't go far. He went on a stumping tour of New York, New Jersey, and Connecticut. At Madison Square Garden, he said the Republicans' fundraising was "nothing short of scandalous." At Cooper Union, he insisted that the Department of Commerce gave Roosevelt extraordinary powers and required extraordinary faith that he wouldn't abuse them.

Parker pushed, and Roosevelt wanted to push back. "I should feel an intolerable humiliation if I were beaten because infamous charges had been made against me and good people regarded my silence as acquiescence in them," he wrote to Cortelyou. "I think it would be in keeping with my character to end the campaign with one slashing statement."

He did. "The statements made by Mr. Parker are unqualifiedly and atrociously false," Roosevelt said. How could the administration that prosecuted Northern Securities and settled the anthracite coal strike behave as corruptly as Parker accused? It was unfathomable. "I shall see to it that every man has a square deal, no less and no more," he promised.

Fifty or so correspondents gathered in the office of Roosevelt's private secretary. Parker was making his last appearance, in Brooklyn, and everyone expected he would provide evidence of his charges against Cortelyou. A special wire carried the speech directly to the White House. When everyone in the room read the last sheet they agreed that Parker no longer had a chance. He had presented no evidence.

"Did you ever see such a flat fall-down as Parker's effort to answer my statement?" Roosevelt wrote to Knox. Gleeful probably isn't a strong enough word to describe how Roosevelt felt.

ROOSEVELT LEFT WASHINGTON on a private midnight train to cast his ballot on November 8 in Oyster Bay. At Jersey City he took a tugboat across New York harbor to Long Island City, and from there resumed the trip by rail. Roosevelt chatted, read, and finally, briefly, relaxed. Edith and Alice remained at the White House; women could vote for president only in Colorado, Idaho, Utah, and Wyoming.

Roosevelt arrived to a waiting crowd, shook as many hands as he could, and eventually walked into Fisher's Hall, above a Chinese laundry on Main Street. There he received ballot No. 164.

Parker drove his buckboard from Esopus to Kingston by a back road and voted an hour later. Then, as he usually did on Election Day, he went to the dentist.

Roosevelt was back at the White House by six thirty. William Loeb set up a telephone in the Red Room to keep track of the returns. Edith invited members of the cabinet, their wives, and a few close friends for "a little feast which can be turned into a festival of rejoicing or into a wake as circumstances warrant." She still liked to tease her husband.

By the time Roosevelt and company sat down to dinner at half past seven, his election was assured. Shortly after came more good news. The searchlight at the top of the Times Building flashed a steady white light to the west, and another to the north. It was a signal: Frank Higgins had won the New York governor's race, and Roosevelt had won his home state. Roosevelt strode up and down the room, arms waving, eyes glinting, energy surging: "How they are voting for me! How they are voting for me!"

Roosevelt claimed 56 percent of the popular vote, more than any other candidate ever had. He won 7.6 million votes to Parker's 5.1 million and 336 votes of 476 in the Electoral College. The Democrats won the Southern states as well as Maryland and Texas. The Republicans won everywhere else. The so-called radical Democrats voted for Eugene Debs, representing the Socialist Party, or for Roosevelt, or they didn't vote at all. "Have swept the country by majorities which astound me," Roosevelt cabled Lodge.

He took Edith aside and said, "I am no longer a political accident."

When Hay arrived at the White House a little after nine, the Red Room was full of people, Roosevelt in the midst of them with his hands full of telegrams. Parker had sent his moments earlier: "The people by their votes have emphatically approved your administration and I congratulate you." Roosevelt turned to Hay and said, "I am glad to be President in my own right."

The president received more than eight thousand notes and telegrams of congratulations. If Morgan sent one, Roosevelt didn't keep it.

Morgan's secretary noted in his appointment book that November 8 was Election Day. But he wasn't scheduled to attend any election night parties. The only entry is a late-afternoon meeting with two friends, Katherine Godkin, the widow of *The Nation*'s founder, and James Bryce, a British politician who later served as ambassador to America. Morgan was also negotiating to buy a Cincinnati rail line for the Erie Railroad—a deal in which he later admitted he was "badly bitten"—and a residence on Madison Avenue for Jack and his wife, Jessie—a deal worth more than one million dollars that he was entirely happy with. Maybe he was hoping to be knighted by the Italian government after returning one of his acquisitions, an embroidered ceremonial robe from the thirteenth century, preserved in the Ascoli Cathedral until it was stolen in 1902. He wouldn't be. But to show its gratitude, the city of Ascoli commissioned a marble bust of Morgan for its palace and named an avenue after him.

ROOSEVELT CALLED REPORTERS into the Executive Office late on elec-tion night. They gathered in a semicircle around him, expecting relieved banter, maybe a boast or a suggestion of what was to come. Instead, he made a promise that was perplexing and unnecessary, and that he would almost immediately come to regret. "I am deeply sensible of the honor done me by the American people in thus expressing their confidence in what I have done and have tried to do," Roosevelt began. When he took the oath of office on March 4, 1905, he would consider it the beginning of his second full term as president. He wouldn't run for a third. He could have. But he was riled over the insinuations and sometimes public insults about his tight grip on power, the command he had over the Republican Party. So he stated in the most definite terms that he would relinquish his hold: "Under no circumstances will I be a candidate for or accept another nomination."

When Edith heard, she flinched. Later she told a friend she would have done everything she could to dissuade her husband. He probably discussed the idea with her, as he did with other confidants, in the abstract. As in maybe, at some point, I should declare that I won't be a candidate in the next election. But no one expected him to announce his retirement from political life on the evening of his victory. He would only be fifty years old as his time in the White House ended. He later told his friend H. H. Kohlsaat that he would cut off his hand if he could take back those words. But he didn't take them back. Not then.

He thundered on. "Of all possible oligarchies I think an oligarchy of colossal capitalists is the most narrow-minded and the meanest in its ideals. I thoroughly broke up this connection, so far as it existed," he wrote to a friend that December. He also wrenched his thigh, again, and burst a blood vessel in his left eye while boxing, an injury that would eventually cause him to lose sight. Bad luck, he said.

The new year began with a dinner organized by Morgan, then a trip out west, mediation between Russia and Japan to end a worrisome war, and his inauguration.

The dinner, at the Arlington Hotel in early January, was meant to gather political and financial support for the American Academy in Rome. Morgan drew up the guest list, and what could he do other than place Roosevelt at the head table with him? They shook hands and joined in the toasts, and if anything more passed between them, neither revealed it.

Saturday, March 4, was sunny and blustery. Flags snapped, men pulled down their hats, women clutched their coats close. Washington was swarming. Thirty Rough Riders accompanied Roosevelt to the inaugural ceremony. Justice Harlan, in his flowing black robe, led his colleagues to their seats in front of the Capitol. Roosevelt's family sat nearby, among them his twenty-year-old niece Eleanor and his twenty-three-year-old fifth cousin Franklin, who would marry a few weeks later. People stood on the terraces and on the dome itself. Boys climbed trees for a better view.

Roosevelt had worn a borrowed suit when he first took the oath of office in Buffalo. This time, he wore a frock coat and trousers tailored from the finest black wool—the same material McKinley had chosen for his inauguration, supplied by the same Massachusetts family. Roosevelt wore something unusual, too: a heavy gold ring with a strand of Lincoln's hair. Hay, who had served as Lincoln's assistant private secretary, requested the clipping immediately after his death and later mounted it under glass on the ring. Now he had the initials of the two presidents engraved on the band before presenting the

Roosevelt and his party watching the inaugural parade

ring to Roosevelt the night before the inauguration. It was the ailing elder statesman's final commendation. Roosevelt told Hay the ring would remind him to "put human rights above property rights."

Roosevelt's inaugural address was to the point, much of it carried away by the wind, but applauded nonetheless. "Modern life is both complex and intense, and the tremendous changes wrought by the extraordinary industrial development of the last half century are felt in every fibre of our social and political being," he said. "The conditions which have told for our marvelous material well-being, which have developed to a very high degree our energy, self-reliance, and individual initiative, have also brought the care and anxiety inseparable from the accumulation of great wealth in industrial centres."

Maybe two hundred thousand people watched at least part of the three-hour inaugural parade down Pennsylvania Avenue. Harriman viewed it from the comforts of the Corcoran Building, where New York senator Depew rented a room with big glass windows for the occasion. George Perkins reserved three rooms at the New Willard Hotel; William Randolph Hearst took the best four.

James Hill remained in St. Paul, and George Baer stayed in Philadelphia. John Mitchell was listening to the grievances of bituminous coal miners in Birmingham, while Mother Jones had already gone to Chicago to discuss forming a more radical union for all workers. Emma Goldman was in New York, finally emerging from a despair brought on by her vilification after McKinley's assassination.

Knox, of all people, could not be there to witness Roosevelt's proud day; instead, he was in Florida, recovering from a bad case of the flu. But Root was in Washington. He had argued on behalf of Morgan and Hill at the Supreme Court on Wednesday and Thursday and on Friday turned down the president's offer to administer the construction of the Panama Canal.

Roosevelt stood for most of the three hours in the viewing stand while everyone else sat. It was just his kind of American pageant. "It really touched me to the heart," he said. Some thirty-five thousand soldiers, National Guardsmen, Filipino and Puerto Rican scouts, anthracite coal miners, cowboys, Native American chiefs, farmers, Oyster Bay residents, and Harvard Republicans marched by, representing "everybody and everything," Roosevelt said. When he saw someone he knew, he shouted out a greeting.

The Inaugural Ball, held in the Pension Building, attracted some six thousand guests, including most members of Congress and the diplomatic corps. Oliver Wendell Holmes and Fanny attended. George Cortelyou and his wife, Lily, were there. Most members of Congress and the diplomatic corps came. The room—high-ceilinged, with Corinthian columns supposed to be among the tallest in the world—resembled an Italian garden. A diffuse warm light flattered everyone. Outside, a crush of people waited for the president. Theodore and Edith promenaded around the room, Charles and Cornelia Fairbanks behind them. Edith wore a shimmering blue satin gown—made in America—with ostrich feathers and gold embroidered medallions so heavy that after five minutes, she was ready to sit. She and the president slowly climbed a staircase to join their family and friends in a private room. Then the dancing could begin below.

By midnight, the family and their guests were back in the White House, where they drank a toast to the president's health and so enjoyed the moment, wrote Edith, that they "could hardly bear to say 'goodnight.'"

On Monday, the Supreme Court unexpectedly announced its final decision about Northern Securities, with no dissent, directing the company to break up along the lines proposed by Morgan, not Harriman. The great railroad monopoly, with its vast profits and plans, was officially crushed, overpowered by Roosevelt's Justice Department. By then, Morgan, nervous about his health and feeling a bit melancholy, had set sail on his annual trip to Europe. He wouldn't return until July.

Roosevelt presented his cabinet to Congress for approval and over the next few days met with African American religious leaders, Railsplitter Republicans from Toledo, and Geronimo. He drafted six letters. He was on the crest, and after would come the hollow, he wrote, but he "had accomplished something worth accomplishing . . . The farmers, lumbermen, mechanics, ranchmen, miners, of the North, East and West, have felt that I was just as much in sympathy with them, just as devoted to their interests, and as proud of them and as representative of them, as if I had sprung from among their own ranks."

Roosevelt wrote letters for posterity. He created a symbol of his presidency for posterity, too. Commemorative inaugural medals were a tradition, and he received one back in 1901. But for his 1905 ceremony, he rejected that design in favor of something more distinguished, something modern. He commissioned the renowned sculptor Augustus St. Gaudens to craft a medallion nearly three inches in diameter, to be cast by Tiffany in a limited edition. The one for the president himself to keep was minted in gold. Its front showed Roosevelt in stark raised profile with the Latin motto ÆQVVM CVIQVE. Its meaning: A square deal for everyone.

Epilogue

Dozens of men huddled in Pierpont Morgan's study—standing, sitting, smoking, sweating. The west room of his library had not yet been completed to his satisfaction by that evening in November 1907. But the effect was already grand. The ceiling was made of panels taken from a Renaissance palace. Red silk, designed with the insignia of an ancient Sienese banking family, covered the walls. And Morgan—seventy years old, a January depression behind him, a cold brought on by exhaustion bothering him—was still commanding. No one could leave until he allowed them to. He had locked the library's bronze-paneled doors and put the key in his pocket.

The financial system was in crisis. Trust companies, essentially unsupervised banks, were failing, and they were threatening other institutions on their way down. The fearful, and there were many of them, were rushing to withdraw their savings. Morgan had raised money to help, and the government had contributed funds, but it wasn't enough. The men in the study had to prevent chaos.

Wall Street had blamed Roosevelt's stance toward business for undermining confidence in the first place. In response, the president turned the taunt back on Wall Street: "It may well be that the determination of the Government (in which, gentlemen, it will not waver) to punish certain malefactors of great wealth has been responsible for something of the trouble." If only, he said, because those he had provoked would risk turmoil to discredit him.

At 4:15 in the morning of that Sunday, November 3, Morgan presented a statement that committed each of the trust company presidents to providing a share of a twenty-five-million-dollar rescue loan. "There you are gentlemen," he said. Then he gestured to their unofficial leader, "There's the place, King, and here's the pen." Edward King signed, the others followed, and Morgan unlocked the door at 4:45 A.M.

The panic subsided. People first praised Morgan for this stark display of power and then condemned him for it. Roosevelt was criticized for allowing Morgan to profit from it. But the bailout would be one of the last times Morgan would exert his influence so publicly. Over the following years, he worked on a system to regulate the money supply—but he worked in private. And though he still loomed in the national imagination, he was ever more clearly a man out of his time. The country was leaving him behind.

As 1908 was drawing to a close, Morgan declined to speak at a dinner in his honor—"Money Talks But Morgan Doesn't" was the headline in the Chicago paper the next day. But he did talk to friends that evening, and they were happy to repeat to the *New York Times* the advice Morgan said he had received from his father long ago: "There may be times when things are dark and cloudy in America, when uncertainty will cause some to distrust and others to think there is too much production, too much building of railroads, and too much development in other enterprises. In such times, and at all times, remember that the growth of that vast country will take care of all." Years after Morgan first heard those words, and despite much evidence to the contrary, he still believed them.

The biggest piece of evidence that Morgan was only partially right— that growth created its own problems, which government could help solve—was Roosevelt himself. The president's impassioned campaign against "the men of swollen fortune" began soon after his second inauguration. "Their success sets up a false standard, and so serves as bad example for the rest of us," he had said that summer. A few months later, in his annual message to Congress, he had continued: "There can be no delusion more fatal to the Nation than the delusion that the standard of profits, of business prosperity, is sufficient in judging any business or political question."

Roosevelt had pushed a progressive legislative agenda to deal with those business and political questions—senators had pushed back hardest on behalf of the railroads. But the Hepburn Act gave the Interstate Commerce Commission new authority over railroad rates. The Meat Inspection and Pure Food and Drug Acts were the first significant consumer protection laws. Interstate railroads were held responsible for some workers' injuries under the Employers' Liability Act. New child labor regulations went into effect in the District of Columbia. And corporate campaign contributions were banned. Roosevelt proposed an eight-hour workday for public employees, stronger protection of unions, and federal licensing for corporations. He recommended a federal income tax and an inheritance tax on the wealthy. That was a particularly unpopular idea in Congress.

After the Northern Securities suit had concluded, the White House had backed away from further direct confrontation with the House of Morgan. George Perkins, Morgan's "secretary of state," had come to an agreement with Roosevelt's commissioner of corporations. Robert Bacon had regained his health and accepted the job of assistant secretary of state under Elihu Root, who had finished up his work for Morgan and rejoined Roosevelt's administration. Morgan's son-in-law Herbert Satterlee would even briefly serve as assistant secretary of the Navy.

But Morgan's railroads—four companies that controlled thousands of miles of track—were now subject to unaccustomedly strict government supervision, and his executives had acknowledged the administration's authority over strategic business decisions that might violate antitrust law. Morgan spent more time traveling Europe or ensconced in his study—his son and the other younger partners called it the uptown branch—than he did working at 23 Wall Street.

Hill, who turned seventy in 1908, was almost ready to leave one of his sons in charge of the Great Northern. Harriman was in poor health, nearer to death than he knew. John Mitchell, whose reputation had been damaged by the failed strike in Colorado four years earlier, had struggled as workers and employers became less conciliatory, not more, in a standardizing economy. He found himself without a constituency, lost a power struggle against more radical union leaders, and was forced out that year. A decade of unsuccessful attempts to secure the wealth he so desired would follow and break him. These antagonists and protagonists of Roosevelt's first term in office, the men he infuriated, elevated, and parried with, occupied less of his attention by the end of his second. Morgan, though, remained very much on his mind, and he on Morgan's.

Roosevelt could have run for president again. He was popular, a celebrity really, a man whose compelling performance did as much, maybe more, than his actual accomplishments to start balancing the scales. "The fight was really for the abolition of privilege," he wrote later. It wasn't over. But in 1908, he kept his promise to let someone else lead it.

After Roosevelt's handpicked successor, William Taft, won the election, Morgan telegraphed: "I wish to express to you my heartfelt congratulations on to-day's splendid results." His London office telegraphed 23 Wall Street: "Hope now we can have peace quiet and good business."

In his last days in the White House, Roosevelt wrote to a friend, "I have done my work; I am perfectly content; I have nothing to ask; and I am very grateful to the American people for what they have done for me . . . My future is in the past, save as I may do the decent work that every private citizen can do." Of course he would eventually try to do more than that again. But on March 4 of 1909, he returned home to Sagamore Hill. Less than three weeks later, he left to hunt in Africa.

ONE OF MORGAN'S favorite portraits, painted to express his intensity rather than his severity (and to deflect attention from his inflamed nose), now hangs over the enormous fifteenth-century mantel piece in his study. The solid steel bank door to the vault, where he once kept medieval manuscripts, is open. The room is regal, intimidating, almost chilling. It feels removed even from the hum of East Thirty-Sixth Street. There is nothing modern about it.

Rooms like it exist, or existed, in buildings as majestic as Morgan's Library in cities around the country. Many were built, as his was, during a reign of imperial capitalism when a few men—always men—controlled enormous resources, generated vast wealth, passed it to their heirs, and sometimes put it to use for the public good along the way. Museums, hospitals, foundations, universities, and libraries carry their names. That's one legacy of the one percent.

The other was the progressive moment that temporarily checked their power. The tycoons of the early twentieth century believed that capitalism generally, and their businesses specifically, could be self-correcting. The low wages, dangerous working conditions, high prices, uncomfortable dependence, and the fear, anger, and confusion among ordinary Americans, showed that it wasn't. The reforms, when they came, seemed too late to some, too timid to others—and too radical to Wall Street.

But they set a precedent for government oversight and a moral tone that helped soothe an agitated nation. America, Roosevelt said, must not be "the civilization of a mere plutocracy, a banking-house, Wall-Street-syndicate civilization." Material well-being, yes, and also "the sense of having so lived that others are better and not worse off."

Concentrated wealth, often the result of corporate domination, causes the kind of economic inequality that can undermine powerful societies. It challenges the notion of democracy; politics seems rigged in favor of the rich and influential. It can leave people feeling helpless and desperate. Roosevelt said making change could be dangerous but doing nothing could be fatal.

Capitalism doesn't stay reformed, though. It adjusts. New capitalists bring different ideas and methods, some bend the system toward equality, some toward excess. In 1902, coal mining profited a few; today, data mining does. Americans worry that companies intrude too deeply into private life, and use what they glean for purposes that are never fully brought to light. Big companies occupy central roles in the lives of consumers but don't always put the public's interests first and don't reliably benefit their workers. They can charge high prices or use low ones to push out smaller competitors. They might not invest in basic services or fund innovation. Sometimes they perpetuate racial inequity. Politicians can be swayed by their donations, or threats.

Corporate power is concentrated, again, and so is privilege. The top one percent of American households own thirty-two percent of the nation's wealth. It buys them private fire fighters, concierge health care, a separate system of college admissions and jobs afterward. It has created a new Gilded Age, and now, another progressive moment striving to hold capitalism and corporations to account.

Roosevelt believed the best way to do that was through regulation. He believed that government oversight was more effective than litigation, and he was convinced that he knew how best to wield that authority over business. Regulators, though, can become too close to the industries they are supposed to watch over. Sometimes their next job is in industry. And rules can have unintended consequences: They can be disruptive, they can be dodged. In Roosevelt's time, the federal government didn't collect income tax; now the nation's complicated tax code can be used as a shield, or to reward the highest earners. A president as autocratic as Roosevelt could be—as wrong as he could be—seems even more worrisome when autocrats are taking over democracies around the world. But the ideal remains the same: an economy that works for everyone.

America in the twenty-first century is a nation of vast and specific interests, diverse and complex. Few use the word "malefactors" anymore, as Roosevelt did. But his warning against "mere plutocracy" could hardly be more current. The notion of a square deal sounds quaint. But the battle to make American capitalism more fair rages just as furiously.

ACKNOWLEDGMENTS

Writing a book was a joyful strain in almost every way. Writing a note of thanks at the conclusion is pure joy. I'll start with my agents, Larry Weissman and Sascha Alper, who helped me see, and shape, the story I wanted to tell. They've offered years of counsel, close reading, and lively conversation. Ben Hyman smartly guided me, helped untangle parts of the manuscript, and found ways to deepen the story. He did so with immeasurable skill and unfailing kindness and calm. He has been an ideal collaborator. Morgan Jones provided insightful comments and, with Akshaya Iyer, anxiety-reducing production help. Emily Fisher arrived full of smart ideas about how to share the book. The enthusiasm of Cindy Loh, Nancy Miller, Laura Keefe, Marie Coolman, and many others at Bloomsbury, has been sustained and sustaining.

I'm indebted to many authors for their superb books about the two men at the center of *The Hour of Fate*, especially Jean Strouse, Doris Kearns Goodwin, H.W. Brands, David McCullough, Ron Chernow, and the late Edmund Morris. I appreciate the assistance and encouragement of the curators at the Morgan Library and the historians at the Theodore Roosevelt Center, as well as at other essential archives. Heidi Schultz was an exacting and energetic fact-checker. Jenna West and Michael Burke provided crucial research assistance. And Jane Yeomans generously gave her valuable time to help me find the evocative images on the book's pages.

At Bloomberg News, Bob Blau has offered unstinting enthusiasm, sharp-minded observations, and more understanding and opportunities than I could have hoped for. John Micklethwait, Reto Gregori, Tim Quinson, and Kristin Powers encouraged me, facilitated my book leave, and sent me off with reassuring words. Joel Weber, Dan Ferrara, Flynn McRoberts, Jim Aley, and Jeremy Keehn, and pretty much everyone else, supported this book right from the start. Over the years, I've been privileged to work with other terrific magazine editors who helped give me the confidence to undertake a project like this: Josh Tyrangiel, Ellen Pollock, Bryant Urstadt, and Emily Biuso foremost among them. Ann Morison gave me my first chance long ago. Steve Shepard, Joyce Barnathan, and many others on Businessweek's 43rd floor pushed me forward.

My book leave wouldn't have been nearly as productive and enriching were it not for the Jonathan Logan Family Foundation and the Logan Nonfiction Fellowship at the Carey Institute for Global Good. Carly Willsie and Josh Friedman run the program with unmatched acumen and ambition. The fellows that autumn of 2018 were uniformly inspiring and among the most careful, considerate readers I've come across. Pat Evangelista, Amy Dockser Marcus, Meg Kissinger, and Stobo Sniderman not only improved my writing while we were together, they continued to do so after we parted. Our kinship has been an unexpected and delightful gift, and I'm eager to give back.

I'm lucky to also have a community of longtime friends who reinvigorate and embolden me. Motoko Rich and Drake Bennett somehow found time to offer comments on the manuscript that were wonderfully perceptive and delivered in the most generous way. Claudia Kalb, Kimberly McCreight, and Alison Singh Gee encouraged me as only other authors can. Current and former colleagues Sheelah Kolhatkar, Brad Stone, Josh Green, Devin Leonard, Cam Simpson, Monte Reel, Bob Kolker, Nisid Hajari, Paul Barrett, and Ashlee Vance showed me how journalists become authors. Anu Heda, Art Jones, Julie Feldman-Abe, Amy Harmon, Erin Elder, Dune Lawrence, Charlie Herman, my Park Slope, Hong Kong and Los Angeles clans, and my Bloomberg colleagues, all warmly supported me during these past four years. Elaine Merguerian and Rick Morris and Eden Pontz and Doug Harsch graciously invited my daughter, and sometimes my husband, to their homes when I needed ours to myself. Thanks to all of you, and the many others, whose kind words and deeds and generous spirits have buoyed me. I hope to do the same for you again.

My family—big-hearted, inspiring, full of laughter—is a constant source of love and fortifying confidence: My parents, Janet and Mort, who let me find my way in the world knowing I had a place to return to; my sister, Amy, and brother, Michael, his wife, Holly, and their sons, Benjamin and Isaac, who travel the world with me; Phyllis and Nathan Shmalo, Sue and Jeff Brown, and the Brewers, who have extended themselves again and again; and the irrepressible Cohens who have stayed connected from coast to coast.

And most of all, thank you to Tim and Olivia, the first and last faces I see every day, the ones who challenge, nourish, humor, and cheer me. Tim read chapters aloud to me, asked all the right questions, and helped me find the answers. He keeps me energized. Olivia keeps me grounded. She proved to be an excellent barometer of my state of mind and a comfort when it was shaky. Best of all, she and Tim were involved with this project from beginning to end. They gave me the time and space to do what I've always wanted to—and they've given me so very much more.

SELECTED BIBLIOGRAPHY

BOOKS

Abbott, Lawrence F. *Impressions of Theodore Roosevelt*. Garden City, NY: Doubleday, Page & Company, 1922.

Adams, Henry. *Letters of Henry Adams, 1892–1918*. Edited by Worthington Chauncey Ford. Boston, MA: Houghton Mifflin Company, 1938.

———. *The Letters of Henry Adams*. Vol. 5, 1899–1905. Edited by J. C. Levenson et al. Cambridge, MA: Belknap Press, 1988.

Allen, Frederick Lewis. *The Great Pierpont Morgan: A Biography*. New York, NY: Harper & Row, 1949.

———. *The Lords of Creation: The History of America's 1 Percent*. New York, NY: Harper & Row, 1935. (Republished: Open Road Media, edited by Mark Crispin Miller 2014.)

Apple, R. W., Jr. "The Case of the Monopolistic Railroadmen." In *Quarrels That Have Shaped the Constitution*, revised edition, edited by John A. Garraty, 175–92. New York, NY: Harper Perennial, 1987.

Avrich, Paul. *The Haymarket Tragedy*. Princeton, NJ: Princeton University Press, 1984.

Azzarelli, Margo L. and Marnie Azzarelli. *Labor Unrest in Scranton*. Charleston, SC: The History Press, 2016.

Bacon, Robert and James Brown Scott, eds. *Miscellaneous Addresses by Elihu Root*. Cambridge, MA: Harvard University Press, 1917.

Barron, Clarence W. *More They Told Barron: Conversations and Revelations of an American Pepys in Wall Street, the Notes of the Late Clarence W. Barron*. Arthur Pound and Samuel Taylor Moore, eds. New York, NY: Harper & Brothers, 1931.

Bartoletti, Susan Campbell. *Growing Up in Coal Country*. New York, NY: Houghton Mifflin Harcourt, 1996.

Beschloss, Michael. *Presidential Courage: Brave Leaders and How They Changed America, 1789–1989*. New York, NY: Simon & Schuster, 2007.

Bishop, Joseph Bucklin. *Theodore Roosevelt and His Time: Shown in His Own Letters*. Vols. 1 and 2. New York, NY: Charles Scribner's Sons, 1920.

Blum, John M. *The Republican Roosevelt*. 2nd ed. Cambridge, MA: Harvard University Press, 1977.

Bocock, John Paul. *Character Sketch of Mr. Morgan, 1900–1909*. Unpublished manuscript. Pierpont Morgan Library.

Brady, Tim. *His Father's Son: The Life of General Ted Roosevelt Jr.* Berkley, CA: New American Library, 2017.

Brands, H. W. *T. R.: The Last Romantic*. New York, NY: Basic Books, 1997.

———. *American Colossus: The Triumph of Capitalism, 1865–1900*. New York, NY: Anchor Books, 2010.

Brecher, Jeremy. *Strike!* Revised edition. Oakland, CA: PM Press, 2014.

Briggs, Lloyd Vernon. *The Manner of Man That Kills: Spencer—Czolgosz—Richeson*. Boston, MA: The Gorham Press, 1921.

Bryan, William Jennings. *Speeches of William Jennings Bryan*. Introduction by Mary Baird Bryan Vol. 1. New York, NY: Funk & Wagnalls, 1909.

Budiansky, Stephen. *Oliver Wendell Holmes: A Life in War, Law, and Ideas*. New York, NY: W. W. Norton & Company, 2019.

Butler, Nicholas Murray. *Across the Busy Years*. New York, NY: Charles Scribner's Sons, 1939.

Byron, Joseph. *New York Life at the Turn of the Century in Photographs*. New York, NY: Dover Publications, Inc., 1985.

Cadenhead, I. E., Jr. *Theodore Roosevelt: The Paradox of Progressivism*. Woodbury, NY: Barron's Educational Series, 1974.

Campbell, Edward G. *Reorganization of the American Railroad System, 1893–1900*. New York, NY: AMS Press, 1938.

Cannadine, David. *Mellon: An American Life*. New York, NY: Alfred A. Knopf, 2006.

Carosso, Vincent P. and Rose C. Carosso. *The Morgans: Private International Bankers, 1854–1913.* Cambridge, MA: Harvard University Press, 1987.

Cashman, Sean Dennis. *America in the Gilded Age: From the Death of Lincoln to the Rise of Theodore Roosevelt.* 3rd ed. New York, NY: New York University Press, 1984/1993.

———. *America Ascendant: From Theodore Roosevelt to FDR in the Century of American Power, 1901–1945.* New York, NY: New York University Press, 1998.

Chaplin, Heman W. *The Coal Mines and the Public: A Popular Statement Of The Legal Aspects of the Coal Problem.* Boston, MA: J. B. Millet Co., 1902.

Charles River Editors. *Eugene V. Debs: The Life and Legacy of America's Most Famous Socialist Political Leader.* Amazon Digital Services, 2018.

Chernow, Ron. *The House of Morgan: An American Banking Dynasty and the Rise of Modern Finance.* New York, NY: Simon & Schuster, 1990.

Cordery, Simon. *Mother Jones: Raising Cain and Consciousness.* Albuquerque, NM: University of New Mexico Press, 1960.

Cordery, Stacy. *Theodore Roosevelt: In the Vanguard of the Modern.* Belmont, CA: Wadsworth Publishing, 2002.

———. *Alice: Alice Roosevelt Longworth, from White House Princess to Washington Power Broker.* New York, NY: Viking, 2007.

Corey, Lewis. *The House of Morgan: A Social Biography of the Masters of Money.* New York: G. H. Watt, 1930.

Cornell, Robert J. *The Anthracite Coal Strike of 1902.* Washington, D.C.: Catholic University of America Press, 1957.

Cowan, Geoffrey. *Let the People Rule: Theodore Roosevelt and the Birth of the Presidential Primary.* New York, NY: W. W. Norton & Company, 2016.

Creighton, Margaret. *The Electrifying Fall of Rainbow City: Spectacle and Assassination at the 1901 World's Fair.* New York, NY: W. W. Norton & Company, 2016.

Croly, Herbert David. *Marcus Alonzo Hanna: His Life and Work.* New York, NY: The Macmillan Co., 1912.

————. *The Promise of American Life*. New York, NY: The Macmillan Co., 1912.

Culin, Stewart. *A Trooper's Narrative of Service in the Anthracite Coal Strike, 1902*. Philadelphia, PA: George W. Jacobs & Co., 1903.

Cushman, Clare. *The Supreme Court Justices: Illustrated Biographies, 1789–2012*. 3rd ed. Thousand Oaks, CA: CQ Press, 2013.

Dalton, Kathleen. *Theodore Roosevelt: A Strenuous Life*. New York, NY: Random House, 2002.

Debs, Eugene V. *Debs: His Life, Writing and Speeches*. Chicago, IL: Press of Geo. G. Renneker Co., 1908.

Donald, Aida. *Lion in the White House: A Life of Theodore Roosevelt*. New York, NY: Basic Books, 2007.

Dublin, Thomas and Walter Licht. *The Face of Decline: The Pennsylvania Anthracite Region in the Twentieth Century*. Ithaca, NY: Cornell University Press, 2005.

Dunn, Arthur Wallace. *From Harrison to Harding: A Personal Narrative, Covering a Third of a Century, 1888–1921*. Vols. 1 and 2. New York, NY: G. P. Putnam's Sons, 1922–23.

————. *Gridiron Nights: Humorous and Satirical Views of Politics and Statesmen as Presented by the Famous Dining Club*. New York, NY: Frederick A. Stokes Co., 1915.

Eitler, Anita Torres. *Philander Chase Knox: First Attorney-General of Theodore Roosevelt, 1901–1904*. Abstract of a dissertation, Washington, D.C.: Catholic University of America Press, 1959.

Foner, Philip S. *History of the Labor Movement in the United States*. Vol. 3, *The Policies and Practices of the American Federation of Labor, 1900–1909*. New York, NY: International Publishers, 1964.

————. *The Great Labor Uprising of 1877*. New York, NY: Pathfinder Press, 1977/1997.

Frey, Juliet, ed. *Theodore Roosevelt and His Sagamore Hill Home*. National Park Service. Oyster Bay, NY: Sagamore Hill National Historic Site, 2007.

Galambos, Louis. *The Public Image of Big Business in America, 1880–1940: A Quantitative Study in Social Change.* Baltimore, MD: Johns Hopkins University Press, 1975.

Garraty, John A. *Right-Hand Man: The Life of George W. Perkins.* New York, NY: Harper & Brothers, 1957.

Glück, Elsie. *John Mitchell, Miner: Labor's Bargain with the Gilded Age.* New York, NY: John Day Company, 1929.

Goldfield, David. *America Aflame: How the Civil War Created a Nation.* New York, NY: Bloomsbury Publishing, 2011.

Goldman, Emma. *Living My Life.* New York, NY: Alfred A. Knopf, Inc., 1931.

Goodwin, Doris Kearns. *The Bully Pulpit: Theodore Roosevelt, William Howard Taft, and the Golden Age of Journalism.* New York, NY: Simon & Schuster, 2013.

———. *Leadership in Turbulent Times.* New York, NY: Simon & Schuster, 2018.

Grondahl, Paul. *I Rose Like a Rocket: The Political Education of Theodore Roosevelt.* Lincoln, NE: University of Nebraska Press, 2004.

Gould, Lewis L. *The Presidency of Theodore Roosevelt.* 2nd ed. Lawrence, KS: University Press of Kansas, 1991/2011.

———. *Theodore Roosevelt.* New York, NY: Oxford University Press, 2012.

———. *Reform and Regulation: American Politics from Roosevelt to Wilson.* 3rd ed. Prospect Heights, IL: Waveland Press, Inc., 1996.

———. *Edith Kermit Roosevelt: Creating the Modern First Lady.* Lawrence, KS: University Press of Kansas, 2013.

Haeg, Larry. *Harriman vs. Hill: Wall Street's Great Railroad War.* Minneapolis, MN: University of Minnesota Press, 2013.

Hagedorn, Hermann. *Roosevelt, Prophet of Unity.* New York, NY: Charles Scribner's Sons, 1924.

Hale, William Bayard. *A Week in the White House with Theodore Roosevelt.* New York, NY: G. P. Putnam's Sons, 1908.

Harbaugh, William Henry. *Power and Responsibility: The Life and Times of Theodore Roosevelt*. Oxford, UK: Oxford University Press,1975.

Harlan, Malvina Shanklin. *Some Memories of a Long Life, 1854–1911*. New York, NY: Modern Library, 2002.

Hawley, Joshua David. *Theodore Roosevelt: Preacher of Righteousness*. New Haven, CT: Yale University Press, 2008.

Hay, John. *Letters of John Hay and Extracts from Diary*. Vol. 3. Edited by Louisa Hay. Washington, D.C: 1908 (printed but unpublished).

Hayes, A. B. and Samuel D. Cox. *History of the City of Lincoln, Nebraska: With Brief Historical Sketches of the State and of Lancaster County*. Lincoln, NE: State Journal Company, 1889.

Helferich, Gerard. *An Unlikely Trust: Theodore Roosevelt, J. P. Morgan, and the Improbable Partnership That Remade American Business*. Guilford, CT: Lions Press, 2018.

Hidy, Ralph W. et al. *The Great Northern Railway: A History*. Cambridge, MA: Harvard Business School Press, 1988.

Hindman, Hugh D. *Child Labor: An American History*. Armonk, NY: M. E. Sharpe, Inc., 2002.

Hofstadter, Richard. *The Age of Reform*. New York, NY: Vintage Books, 1955.

Holmes, Olver Wendell, Jr. *The Essential Holmes: Selections from the Letters, Speeches, Judicial Opinions, and Other Writings of Oliver Wendell Holmes, Jr.* Edited by Richard Posner. Chicago, IL: University of Chicago Press, 1992.

Holton, James L. *The Reading Railroad: History of a Coal Age Empire*. Vol. 2, *The Twentieth Century*. Laury's Station, PA: Garrigues House, 1992.

Horner, William T. *Ohio's Kingmaker: Mark Hanna, Man and Myth*. Athens, OH: Ohio University Press, 2010.

Hovey, Carl. *The Life Story of J. Pierpont Morgan: A Biography*. New York, NY: Sturgis & Walton Company, 1911.

Howells, William Dean. *A Hazard of New Fortunes*. New York, NY: Harper & Brothers, 1890.

Irons, Peter. *A People's History of the Supreme Court: The Men and Women Whose Cases and Decisions Have Shaped Our Constitution*. New York, NY: Penguin Books, 2006.

Isaacson, Walter, ed. *Profiles in Leadership: Historians on the Elusive Quality of Greatness*. New York, NY: W. W. Norton & Company, 2010.

Janosov, Robert A. et al. *The "Great Strike": Perspectives on the 1902 Anthracite Coal Strike*. Easton, PA: Canal History and Technology Press, 2002.

Jeffers, H. Paul. *Commissioner Roosevelt: The Story of Theodore Roosevelt and the New York City Police, 1895–1897*. New York, NY: John Wiley & Sons, Inc., 1994.

Jenks, Jeremiah Whipple. *The Trust Problem*. New York, NY: McClure, Phillips & Co., 1903.

Jessup, Philip C. *Elihu Root*. New York, NY: Dodd, Mead & Company, 1964.

Johns, A. Wesley. *The Man Who Shot McKinley: A New View of the Assassination of the President*. Cranbury, NJ: A. S. Barnes & Co., 1970.

Jones, Eliot. *The Anthracite Coal Combination in the United States, with Some Account of the Early Development of the Anthracite Industry*. New York, NY: Harvard University Press, 1914.

Jones, Mary "Mother." *The Autobiography of Mother Jones*. Chicago, IL.: Charles H. Kerr & Co., 1925.

Josephson, Matthew. *The Robber Barons*. New York, NY: Houghton Mifflin Harcourt, 1962.

Jusserand, J. J. *What Me Befell: The Reminiscences of J. J. Jusserand*. Amazon Digital Services, Endeavour Compass, 1933/2015.

Katzman, David M. and William M. Tuttle. *Plain Folk: The Life Stories of Undistinguished Americans*. Urbana, IL: University of Illinois Press, 1982.

Kazin, Michael. *A Godly Hero: The Life of William Jennings Bryan*. New York, NY: Anchor Books, 2007.

Kelly, Jack. *The Edge of Anarchy: The Railroad Barons, the Gilded Age, and the Greatest Labor Uprising in America*. New York, NY: St. Martin's Press, 2018.

Kennan, George. *E. H. Harriman: Railroad Czar.* Vols. 1 and 2. New York, NY: Houghton Mifflin Company, 1922.

Klein, Maury. *The Life and Legend of E. H. Harriman.* Chapel Hill, NC: University of North Carolina Press, 2000.

Kohlsaat, H. H. *From McKinley to Harding: Personal Recollections of Our Presidents.* New York, NY: Charles Scribner's Sons, 1923.

Kohn, Edward P. *Hot Time in the Old Town: The Great Heat Wave of 1896 and the Making of Theodore Roosevelt.* New York, NY: Basic Books, 2010.

———. *Heir to the Empire City: New York and the Making of Theodore Roosevelt.* New York, NY: Basic Books, 2014.

Kolko, Gabriel. *The Triumph of Conservatism: A Reinterpretation of American History, 1900–1916.* New York, NY: Free Press, 1963.

———. *Railroads and Regulation, 1877–1916.* Princeton, NJ: Princeton University Press, 2015.

Krause, Paul. *The Battle for Homestead, 1880–1892.* Pittsburgh, PA: University of Pittsburgh Press, 1992.

Lamoreaux, Naomi R. *The Great Merger Movement in American Business, 1895–1904.* Cambridge, MA: Cambridge University Press, 1985/1988.

Latham, Frank Brown. *The Great Dissenter: John Marshall Harlan, 1833–1911.* Spokane, WA: Cowles Book Co., 1970.

Lawrence, William. *Pierpont Morgan.* Memoir of John Pierpont Morgan (1837–1913): written in the form of a letter to Herbert L. Satterlee, dated January 6, 1914. Unpublished Manuscript. Pierpont Morgan Library.

Leech, Margaret. *In the Days of McKinley.* New York, NY: Harper & Brothers, 1959.

Lepore, Jill. *These Truths: A History of the United States.* New York, NY: W. W. Norton & Company, 2018.

Letwin, William. *Law and Economic Policy in America: The Evolution of the Sherman Antitrust Act.* Chicago, IL: University of Chicago Press, 1956.

Leupp, Francis E. *The Man Roosevelt: A Portrait Sketch.* New York, NY: D. Appleton & Co., 1904.

Licht, Walter. *Working for the Railroad: The Organization of Work in the Nineteenth Century*. Princeton, NJ: Princeton University Press, 1987.

Lindsey, Almont. *The Pullman Strike: The Story of a Unique Experiment and of a Great Labor Upheaval*. Chicago, IL: University of Chicago Press, 1943.

Lloyd, Caro. *Henry Demarest Lloyd, 1847–1903: A Biography*. New York, NY: G. P. Putnam's Sons, 1912.

Lorant, Stefan. *The Life and Times of Theodore Roosevelt*. New York, NY: Doubleday, 1959.

Lowry, Edward G. *Washington Close-Ups*. Boston, MA: Houghton Mifflin Company, 1921.

Lundberg, Ferdinand. *America's 60 Families*. New York, NY: Vanguard Press, 1937.

Lutz, Tom. *American Nervousness 1903: An Anecdotal History*. Ithaca, NY: Cornell University Press, 1991.

Mann, William J. *The Wars of the Roosevelts: The Ruthless Rise of America's Greatest Political Family*. New York, NY: HarperCollins, 2016.

Martin, Albro. *James J. Hill and the Opening of the Northwest*. St. Paul, MN: Minnesota Historical Society Press, 1976.

Matkosky, Greg and Thomas M. Curra. *Stories from the Mines*. Scranton, PA: University of Scranton Press, 2006.

McCabe, James Dabney. *The History of the Great Riots*. Philadelphia, PA: National Publishing Company, 1877.

McCaleb, Walter. *Theodore Roosevelt*. New York, NY: Albert & Charles Boni, 1931.

McCullough, David. *Mornings on Horseback: The Story of an Extraordinary Family, a Vanished Way of Life, and the Unique Child Who Became Theodore Roosevelt*. New York, NY: Simon & Schuster, 2001.

McFarland, Philip. *Mark Twain and the Colonel: Samuel L. Clemons, Theodore Roosevelt, and the Arrival of a New Century*. Lanham, MD: Rowman & Littlefield, 2012.

McGerr, Michael. *A Fierce Discontent: The Rise and Fall of the Progressive Movement in America, 1870–1920*. New York, NY: Oxford University Press, 2003.

Merry, Robert W. *President McKinley: Architect of the American Century*. New York, NY: Simon & Schuster, 2017.

Miller, Donald L. and Richard E. Sharpless. *The Kingdom of Coal: Work, Enterprise, and Ethnic Communities in the Mine Fields*. Easton, PA: Canal History and Technology Press, 1998.

Miller, Nathan. *Theodore Roosevelt: A Life*. New York, NY: William Morrow, 1992.

Miller, Scott. *The President and the Assassin: McKinley, Terror, and Empire at the Dawn of the American Century*. New York, NY: Random House, 2011.

Mitchell, John. *Organized Labor: Its Problems, Purposes and Ideals, and the Present and Future of American Wage Earners*. Philadelphia, PA: American Book and Bible House, 1903.

Moody, John. *The Masters of Capital: A Chronicle of Wall Street*. New Haven, CT: Yale University Press, 1921.

Morris, Charles and Edward S. Ellis. *Our National Leaders of 1904: The Official Non-Partisan Handbook for the American Voter*. Springfield, MA: Hampden Publishing Co., 1904.

Morris, Edmund. *The Rise of Theodore Roosevelt*. New York, NY: Random House, 1979.

———. *Theodore Rex*. New York, NY: Modern Library, 2001.

———. *Colonel Roosevelt*. New York, NY: Random House, 2010.

Morris, Sylvia Jukes. *Edith Kermit Roosevelt: Portrait of a First Lady*. New York, NY: Modern Library, 1980/2001.

Mowry, George E. *The Era of Theodore Roosevelt, 1900–1912*. New York, NY: HarperCollins College Division, 1968.

Mutch, Robert E. *Buying the Vote: A History of Campaign Finance Reform*. New York, NY: Oxford University Press, 2014.

Myers, Gustavus. *History of the Great American Fortunes*. Vol. 3, *Great Fortunes from Railroads*. Chicago, IL: Charles H. Kerr & Co., 1911.

Nasaw, David. *Andrew Carnegie*. New York, NY: Penguin Press, 2006.

Nelson, Scott Reynolds. *A Nation of Deadbeats: An Uncommon History of America's Financial Disasters*. New York, NY: Vintage Books, 2013.

Norris, Frank. *The Octopus: A California Story*. New York, NY: Viking Penguin Inc., 1901/1994.

Novick, Sheldon M. *Honorable Justice: The Life of Oliver Wendell Holmes*. Lexington, MA: Plunkett Lake Press, 1989.

Noyes, Alexander Dana. *Forty Years of American Finance: A Short Financial History of the Government and People of the U.S. since the Civil War, 1865–1907*. New York, NY: G. P. Putnam's Sons, 1909.

———. *The Market Place: Reminiscences of a Financial Editor*. Boston, MA: Little, Brown and Company, 1938.

Oberholtzer, Ellis Paxon. *Jay Cooke: Financier of the Civil War*. Vol. 2. Philadelphia, PA: George W. Jacobs & Co., 1907.

Painter, Nell Irvin. *Standing at Armageddon: A Grassroots History of the Progressive Era*. New York, NY: W. W. Norton & Company, 1987/2008.

Pak, Susie J. *Gentlemen Bankers: The World Of J. P. Morgan*. Cambridge, MA: Harvard University Press, 2013.

Penrose, Charles. *George B. Cortelyou (1862–1940): Briefest Biography of a Great American*. Newcomen Society in North America, 1955.

Perry, Peter R. *Theodore Roosevelt and The Labor Movement*. Thesis, California State University, Hayward, 1991.

Phelan, Craig. *Divided Loyalties: The Public and Private Life of Labor Leader John Mitchell*. Albany, NY: SUNY Press, 1994.

Pickenpaugh, Roger. *McKinley, Murder and the Pan-American Exposition: A History of the Presidential Assassination, September 6, 1901*. Jefferson, NC: McFarland & Co., 2016.

Platt, Thomas Collier. *The Autobiography of Thomas Collier Platt*. Compiled and edited by Louis Lang. New York, NY: B. W. Dodge & Co., 1910.

Pringle, Henry. *Theodore Roosevelt: A Biography*. New York, NY: Harvest/HBJ, 1956.

Przybyszewski, Linda. *The Republic According to John Marshall Harlan*. Chapel Hill, NC: University of North Carolina Press, 1999.

Putnam, Carleton. *Theodore Roosevelt: A Biography*. Vol. 1, *The Formative Years, 1858–1886*. New York, NY: Charles Scribner's Sons, 1958.

Pyle, Joseph G. *The Life of James J. Hill*. New York, NY: Doubleday, 1917.

Rauchway, Eric. *Murdering McKinley: The Making of Theodore Roosevelt's America*. New York, NY: Hill & Wang, 2003.

Rhodes, James Ford. *The McKinley and Roosevelt Administrations, 1897–1909*. New York, NY: The Macmillan Company, 1922.

Richards, John Stuart. *Early Coal Mining in the Anthracite Region*. Charleston, SC: Arcadia Publishing, 2003.

Riis, Jacob A. *How the Other Half Lives: Studies Among the Tenements of New York*. New York, NY: Charles Scribner's Sons, 1890.

———. *Theodore Roosevelt: The Citizen*. New York, NY: The Macmillan Company, 1904.

———. *The Making of an American*. New York, NY: The Macmillan Company, 1922.

Risen, Clay. *The Crowded Hour: Theodore Roosevelt, the Rough Riders, and the Dawn of the American Century*. New York, NY: Scribner, 2019.

Roberts, Peter. *The Anthracite Coal Industry: A Study of the Economic Conditions and Relations of the Cooperative Forces in the Development of the Anthracite Coal Industry of Pennsylvania*. London: Macmillan & Co., 1901.

———. *Anthracite Coal Communities: A Study of the Demography, the Social, Educational and Moral Life of the Anthracite Regions*. New York, NY: Macmillan & Co., 1904.

Robinson, Corinne Roosevelt. *My Brother Theodore Roosevelt*. New York, NY: Charles Scribner's Sons, 1921.

Roosevelt, Theodore. *The Autobiography of Theodore Roosevelt*. Middletown, DE: Seven Treasures, 2009 (prepared from 1920 edition, Charles Scribner's Sons).

———. *Letters from Theodore Roosevelt to Anna Roosevelt Cowles, 1870 to 1918*. New York, NY: Charles Scribner's Sons, 1924 (reprint: Kessinger Publishing, 2010).

————. *Ranch Life and the Hunting Trail.* New York, NY: The Century Company, 1888.

————. *The Roosevelt Policy: Speeches, Letters and State Papers, Relating to Corporate Wealth and Closely Allied Topics.* Vols. 1 and 2, edited by William Griffith. New York, NY: Current Literature Publishing Company, 1919.

————. *The Letters of Theodore Roosevelt.* 8 vols. Edited by Elting E. Morison. Cambridge, MA: Harvard University Press, 1951–54.

————. *Theodore Roosevelt's Letters to His Children.* Edited by John Bucklin Bishop. New York, NY: Charles Scribner's Sons, 1919.

Roosevelt, Theodore and Henry Cabot Lodge. *Selections from the Correspondence of Theodore Roosevelt and Henry Cabot Lodge, 1884–1918.* New York: Da Capo Press, 1971.

Rosenthal, Michael. *Nicholas Miraculous: The Amazing Career of the Redoubtable Dr. Nicholas Murray Butler.* New York, NY: Columbia University Press, 2015.

Satterlee, Herbert L. *J. Pierpont Morgan: An Intimate Portrait, 1837–1913.* New York, NY: Macmillan, 1939.

Schiller, Elizabeth Ann. *James Brooks Dill: Father of the Trusts.* PhD dissertation, Seton Hall University, 2009.

Sherman, William Tecumseh and John Sherman. *The Sherman Letters: Correspondence between General and Senator Sherman from 1837 to 1891.* Edited by Rachel Sherman Thorndike. London: Charles Scribner's Sons, 1894.

Shoemaker, Fred C. *Alton Parker: The Images of a Gilded Age Statesman in an Era of Progressive Politics.* Thesis, Ohio State University, 1983.

Siegfried, John J. and Michelle Mahony. "The First Sherman Act Case: Jellico Mountain Coal, 1891." In *The Antitrust Impulse: An Economic, Historical and Legal Analysis*, edited by Theodore P. Kovaleff. Armonk, NY: M. E. Sharpe, Inc., 1994.

Sinclair, Andrew. *Corsair: The Life of J. Pierpont Morgan.* New York, NY: Little Brown, 1981.

Steffens, Lincoln. *The Autobiography of Lincoln Steffens.* New York, NY: Harcourt, 1931/1959.

Stern, Clarence A. *Resurgent Republicanism: The Handiwork of Hanna.* 1968 ed. Ann Arbor, MI: Edwards Brothers, 1963.

Stoller, Matt. *Goliath: The 100-Year War Between Monopoly Power and Democracy.* New York, New York: Simon & Schuster, 2019.

Strouse, Jean. *Morgan: American Financier.* New York, NY: Random House, 1999.

Sullivan, Mark. *Our Times: The United States, 1900–1925.* Vol. 1, *The Turn of the Century.* New York, NY: Charles Scribner's Sons, 1927.

———. *Our Times: The United States, 1900–1925.* Vol. 2, *America Finding Herself.* New York, NY: Charles Scribner's Sons, 1930.

Taft, William Howard. *The Anti-Trust Act and the Supreme Court.* New York: NY, Harper & Brothers, 1914.

Tarbell, Ida M. *The History of the Standard Oil Company.* Vol. 1. New York, NY: McClure, Phillips & Co., 1904.

Thayer, William Roscoe. *The Life and Letters of John Hay.* Vol. 2. Boston, MA: Houghton Mifflin Company, 1915.

———. *Theodore Roosevelt: An Intimate Biography.* Boston, MA: Houghton Mifflin Company, 1919.

Trachtenberg, Alan. *The Incorporation of America: Culture and Society in the Gilded Age.* New York, NY: Hill & Wang, 1982/2007.

Twain, Mark. *Mark Twain's Correspondence with Henry Huttleston Rogers, 1893–1909.* Edited by Lewis Leary. Oakland, CA: University of California Press, 1969.

Wagenknecht, Edward. *The Seven Worlds of Theodore Roosevelt.* London: Longmans, Green and Co., 1958.

Ward, James A. *That Man Haupt: A Biography of Herman Haupt.* Vols. 1 & 2. Historical Dissertations and Theses, Louisiana State University, 1969.

Warne, Frank Julian. *The Slav Invasion and the Mine Workers: A Study in Immigration.* Philadelphia, PA: J. B. Lippincott Co., 1904.

Watts, Sarah Lyons. *Order Against Chaos: Business Culture and Labor Ideology in America, 1880–1915.* New York, NY: Greenwood Press, 1991.

Wert, Jeffery D. *Civil War Barons: The Tycoons, Entrepreneurs, Inventors, and Visionaries Who Forged Victory and Shaped a Nation.* New York, NY: Da Capo Press, 2018.

Wexler, Alice. *Emma Goldman: An Intimate Life.* New York, NY: Pantheon Books, 1984.

Wheaton, James Otis. "The Genius and the Jurist: A Study of the Presidential Campaign of 1904." Unpublished dissertation, Stanford University, June 1964.

White, G. Edward. *Oliver Wendell Holmes, Jr.* New York, NY: Oxford University Press, 2006.

White, Richard. *Railroaded: The Transcontinentals and the Making of Modern America.* New York, NY: W. W. Norton & Company, 2011.

———. *The Republic for Which It Stands: The United States during Reconstruction and the Gilded Age, 1865–1896.* New York, NY: Oxford University Press, 2017.

White, William Allen. *The Autobiography of William Allen White.* 2nd ed., revised and abridged, edited by Sally Foreman Griffith. Lawrence, KA: University Press of Kansas, 1946/1990.

———. *Masks in a Pageant.* New York, NY: The Macmillan Co., 1928.

Wiebe, Robert H. *The Search for Order, 1877–1920.* New York, NY: Hill & Wang, 1967.

———. *Businessmen and Reform: A Study of the Progressive Movement.* Cambridge, MA: Harvard University Press, 1967.

Williams, R. Hal. *Realigning America: McKinley, Bryan, and the Remarkable Election of 1896.* Lawrence, KS: University Press of Kansas, 2010 (Kindle).

Winkler, John K. *Morgan the Magnificent: The Life of J. Pierpont Morgan, 1837–1913.* New York, NY: Vanguard, 1930.

Wister, Owen. *Roosevelt: The Story of a Friendship, 1880–1919.* New York, NY: The Macmillan Co., 1930.

Wolraich, Michael. *Unreasonable Men: Theodore Roosevelt and the Republican Rebels Who Created Progressive Politics.* New York, NY: Palgrave Macmillan, 2014.

Wood, Frederick S., ed. *Roosevelt as We Knew Him: Personal Recollections of One Hundred and Fifty of His Friends and Associates*. Philadelphia, PA: John C. Winston Co., 1927.

Wu, Tim. *The Curse of Bigness: Antitrust in the New Gilded Age*. New York, New York: Columbia Global Reports, 2018.

Yarbrough, Tinsley E. *Judicial Enigma: The First Justice Harlan*. New York, NY: Oxford University Press, 1995.

Zacks, Richard. *Island of Vice: Theodore Roosevelt's Quest to Clean Up Sin-Loving New York*. New York, NY: Anchor Books, 2012.

Zinn, Howard. *A People's History of the United States*. New York, NY: Harper-Collins, 1980/2013.

Zinn, Howard and Anthony Arnove. *Voices of a People's History of the United States*. New York, NY: Seven Stories Press, 2004.

ARTICLES

Archibald, James F. J. "The Striking Miners and Their Families." *Collier's Weekly* 30, no. 2 (October 11, 1902): 6.

Baer, George F. "Argument of George F. Baer before the Anthracite Coal Strike Commission." Clarence Darrow Digital Collection. University of Minnesota Law Library (February 12, 1903), www.moses.law.umn.edu/darrow/documents/Baer_Argument_Cropped_Opt.pdf.

Baker, Ray Stannard. "The Great Northern Pacific Deal." *Collier's Weekly* 28, no. 9 (November 30, 1901): 14–15.

———. "The Right to Work." *McClure's* (January 1903).

Bikle, Henry Wolf. "The Northern Securities Decision: A Review." *American Law Register* 52, no. 6, Volume 43 New Series (June 1904): 358–80.

Blackman, Joshua et al. "Justice John Marshall Harlan: Professor of Law." *George Washington Law Review* 81, no. 4 (July 2013): 1063–1134.

Burke, James Francis. "Philander Chase Knox." *American Bar Association Journal* 7, no. 11 (1921): 621–23, www.jstor.org/stable/25710700.

Channing, Walter. "The Mental Status of Czolgosz: The Assassin of President McKinley." *American Journal of Insanity*, LIX, no. 2, (October 1902).

Connelly, Scott. "The Greatest Strike Ever." Pennsylvania Center for the Book, Spring 2010, https://www.pabook.libraries.psu.edu/literary-cultural-heritage -map-pa/feature-articles/greatest-strike-ever.

Coolidge, L. A. "Attorney General Philander Knox, Lawyer." *The American Monthly Review of Reviews: An International Magazine* 26 (July–December 1902): 345.

Crane, Stephen. "In the Depths of a Coal Mine." *McClure's* III, no. 3 (August 1894).

Cutting, Robert. "The Northern Securities Company and the Sherman Anti-Trust Law." *The North American Review* 174, no. 545 (April 1902): 528–35.

Dalton, Kathleen. "Theodore Roosevelt, Knickerbocker Aristocrat." *New York History* 67, no. 1 (January 1986): 39–65.

Darrow, Clarence. "Johnny McCaffery: The Breaker Boy." Clarence Darrow Digital Library (December 1902), www.moses.law.umn.edu/darrow/documents /Johnny_McCaffery_Breaker_Boy.pdf.

———. "Documents Relating to the Anthracite Strike of 1902." Clarence Darrow Digital Collection. University of Minnesota Law Library, www.moses .law.umn.edu/darrow/trials.php?tid=12.

Dorsey, Leroy G. "Theodore Roosevelt and Corporate America, 1901–1909: A Reexamination." *Presidential Studies Quarterly* 25, no. 4, Perceptions of the Presidency (Fall 1995): 725–39.

Filene, Peter G. "An Obituary for 'The Progressive Movement.'" *American Quarterly* 22, no. 1 (Spring 1970): 20–34.

Gardner, Mark Lee. "Cowboys and Millionaires: How Teddy Roosevelt's Rough Riders bonded as brothers before leaving to fight in the Spanish-American War," *True West*, April 15, 2016.

Garner, James Wilford. "The Northern Securities Case." *The Annals of the American Academy of Political and Social Science* 24, The Government in Its Relation to Industry (July 1904): 125–47.

Goin, Peter and Elizabeth Raymond. "Living in Anthracite: Mining Landscape and Sense of Place in Wyoming Valley, Pennsylvania." *The Public Historian* 23, no. 2 (Spring 2001): 29–45.

Goodman, Bonnie K. Presidential Campaigns & Elections Reference, Overview & Chronologies: 1904, www.presidentialcampaignselectionsreference.wordpress .com/overviews/20th-century/1904-overview/.

Gordon, David. "Swift & Co. v. United States: The Beef Trust and the Stream of Commerce Doctrine." *The American Journal of Legal History* 28, no. 3 (July 1984): 244–79.

Grossman, Jonathan. "The Coal Strike of 1902—Turning Point in US Policy." *Monthly Labor Review* (October 1975). U.S. Department of Labor, www.dol .gov/general/aboutdol/history/coalstrike.

Hamilton, Virginia Van der Veer. "Review of Edward Douglass White: Defender of the Conservative Faith by Robert B. Highsaw." *Reviews in American History* 10, no. 1 (March 1982): 105–08.

Hannon, Michael. "Anthracite Coal Strike of 1902." Minneapolis, MN: University of Minnesota Law Library, 2010, www.moses.law.umn.edu/darrow /trialpdfs/Anthracite_Coal_Strike.pdf.

Hepp, John. "George Frederick Baer." Working paper, Wilkes University, 2012. Uploaded to Research Gate September 2017: www.researchgate.net/publication /319620655_George_Frederick_Baer.

Hutchison, Phillip. "The Harlan Renaissance: Colorblindness and White Domination in Justice John Marshall Harlan's Dissent in Plessy v. Ferguson." *Journal of African-American Studies* 19 (September 2015): 426–447.

James, Scott C. "Prelude to Progressivism: Party Decay, Populism, and the Doctrine of 'Free and Unrestricted Competition' in American Antitrust Policy, 1890—1897." *Studies in American Political Development* 13 (Fall 1999): 288–336.

Juergens, George. "Roosevelt and the Press." *Daedalus* 111, no. 4, Print Culture and Video Culture (Fall 1982): 113–33.

Knies, Michael. "'I Have Dreamed of It at Night': Trying to Prevent the 1902 Anthracite Strike: John Mitchell and the National Civic Federation."

Proceedings of the Canal History and Technology Symposium 27 (March 15, 2008): 43–80.

———. "Voting for a Strike? The Shamokin Convention and the 1902 Anthracite Strike." *Proceedings of the Canal History and Technology Symposium* (2006): 5–29.

Lauver, Fred J. "A Walk through the Rise and Fall of Anthracite Might." *Pennsylvania Heritage Magazine* 27, no. 1 (Winter 2001).

Leighton, George Ross. "Shenandoah, Pennsylvania: The Story of Anthracite Town." *Harper's Magazine* (January 1937).

Lemann, Nicholas. "Why Big Business and Big Government Haunt America." *New Yorker* (March 28, 2016).

Lewis, Alfred Henry. "Owners of America: Pierpont Morgan." *Cosmopolitan Magazine* XLV, no. 3 (August 1908): 250–62.

Maclean, Annie Marion. "Life in the Pennsylvania Coal Fields with Particular Reference to Women." *American Journal of Sociology* 14, no. 3 (November 1908): 329–51.

Meyer, Balthasar Henry. "A History of the Northern Securities Case." *Journal of Political Economy* 15, no. 3 (Mar. 1907): 182–83.

Mitchell, John. "Speech at the Mitchell, Darrow, Lloyd Reception, 1903." Clarence Darrow Digital Library, www.moses.law.umn.edu/darrow/documents/Speech_Mitchell_Darrow_Lloyd_Reception_1903.pdf.

Moffett, Cleveland. "The Overthrow of the Molly Maguires." *McClure's* (1894): 90–100.

Moody, John and George Kibbe Turner. "The Masters of Capital in America: Morgan, the Great Trustee." *McClure's* 36, no. 1 (November 1910).

———. "The Masters of Capital in America: The Multimillionaires of the Great Northern System." *McClure's* 36, No. 2 (December 1910): 123–40.

———. "The Masters of Capital in America: The Inevitable Railroad Monopoly." *McClure's* (January 1911): 334–52.

Morris, Elizabeth Catherine. "John Mitchell: The Leader and the Man." *Independent* (December 5, 1902): 3073–78.

Nelson, Henry Loomis. "The War on the Northern Pacific." *Harper's Weekly* XLV, no. 2318 (May 25, 1901).

Nichols, Francis H. "Children of the Coal Shadow." *McClure's* 20 (November 1902–April 1903).

Patterson, George Stuart. "The Case of the Trans-Missouri Freight Association." *University of Pennsylvania Law School* (May 1, 1897).

Peterson, Nancy. "Jim Hill: Railroad Builder and Visionary." *Wild West Magazine* 15, no. 2 (August 2002): 22–29.

Pratt, Sereno. "The President and Wall Street." *The World's Work* 7 (Novembner 1903–April 1904).

Reynolds, Robert. "The Coal Kings Come to Judgment." *American Heritage* 11, no. 3 (April 1960).

Roosevelt, Theodore. "Practical Politics: Third Installment of 'Chapters of a Possible Autobiography.'" *Outlook* (April 26 1913): 917–94.

———. "The President's Message." *Collier's Weekly* 28, no. 9 (October–March 1901–02): November 30.

———. "True American Ideals." *The Forum* (February 1895): 743–50.

Schmidt, Robert. "Labor Violence and the Industrialization of Northeastern Pennsylvania, 1871–1902." *Anthracite Unite*, August 15, 2008.

Southwick, Leslie. "A Judge Runs for President: Alton Parker's Road to Oblivion." *Green Bag* (Autumn 2001): 37–50.

Spahr, Charles B. "The Miners' Strike: Impressions in the Field." *Outlook* 71 (May 31, 1902): 321–25.

Steffens, Lincoln. "Governor Roosevelt—As An Experiment." *McClure's* (June 1900).

———. "The Overworked President." *McClure's* (April 1902).

———. "A Labor Leader of Today: John Mitchell and What He Stands For." *McClure's* (August 1902).

Strouse, Jean. "The Unknown J. P. Morgan." *New Yorker* (March 29, 1999).

Thompson, Charles. "Plessy v. Ferguson: Harlan's Great Dissent." *Kentucky Humanities*, no. 1 (1996). Reprinted: Louie D. Brandeis School of Law Library, www.louisville.edu/law/library/special-collections/the-john-marshall-harlan -collection/harlans-great-dissent.

Wagner, Richard H. "A Falling Out: The Relationship between Oliver Wendell Holmes and Theodore Roosevelt." *Journal of Supreme Court History* 27, no. 2 (June 28, 2008).

Walker, John Brisbane. "The World's Greatest Revolution." *Cosmopolitan Magazine* (April 1901).

Walker, John Brisbane. "Pierpont Morgan, His Advisors and His Organization." *Cosmopolitan Magazine* XXXIV, no. 3 (January 8, 1903): 247.

Warne, Frank Julian. "John Mitchell: The Labor Leader and the Man." *American Monthly Review of Reviews: An International Magazine* 26, no. 154 (November 1902): 556–60.

———. "Miner and Operator: A Study of Labor Conditions in the Anthracite Coal Fields." *Outlook* 82 (1906): 634.

———. "The Anthracite Coal Strike." *The Annals of the American Academy of Political and Social Science* 17 (January 1901): 15–52.

Wellman, Walter. "The Inside History of the Great Coal Strike." *Collier's Weekly* 30, no. 3 (October 18, 1902): 6–7, 27.

———. "How The President Settled the Strike." *Collier's Weekly* 30, no. 5 (November 1, 1902): 6.

———. "The Settlement of the Coal Strike." *Colliers Weekly* 30, no. 5 (November 1902).

———. "Elihu Root: A Character Sketch." *American Monthly Review of Reviews* (January 1904).

Westin, Allen F. "John Marshall Harlan and the Constitutional Rights of Negroes: The Transformation of a Southerner." *Yale Law Journal* 66, no. 5 (April 1957): 637–710.

Weyl, Walter E. "The Man the Miners Trust." *Outlook* 82 (March 24, 1906): 657–62.

———. "The Man the Miners Trust." *The American Monthly Review of Reviews* 33 (1906): 604.

White, William Allen. "Hanna: A Character Sketch." *McClure's* 15 (November 1900).

———. "Theodore Roosevelt." *McClure's* 18 (November 1901): 40–47.

———. "Platt." *McClure's* (December 1901): 145–52.

Wiebe, Robert H. "The Anthracite Strike of 1902: A Record of Confusion" *The Mississippi Valley Historical Review* 48, no. 2 (September 1961): 229–51.

Wilgus, Horace LaFayette. "The Northern Securities Decision." *Michigan Alumnus* 10 (1904): 316–23.

Wolff, Gerald W. "Mark Hanna's Goal: American Harmony." *Ohio History* 79 (Summer–Autumn 1970): 138–151.

Woodward, C. Vann. "Plessy v. Ferguson: The Birth of Jim Crow." *American Heritage* 15, no. 3 (April 1964).

Wright, Carroll. "Report to the President On Anthracite Coal Strike." *Bulletin of the Department of Labor* no. 43 (November 1902).

Zane, Jay R. "The Bloody First Ward—Part II: Shenandoah, Schuylkill Co, PA." Lithuanian Global Resources (October 14, 1998).

GOVERNMENT DOCUMENTS

"Report to the President on the Anthracite Coal Strike Commission." Clarence Darrow Digital Collection, University of Minnesota Law Library. (May–October 1902), www.moses.law.umn.edu/darrow/documents/Report%20Anthracite%20Comm.pdf.

"Proceedings of the Anthracite Mine Strike Commission." Reprinted from the *Scranton Tribune 1902–03*. Clarence Darrow Digital Collection, University of Minnesota Law Library, www.moses.law.umn.edu/darrow/documents/Proceedings_Anthracite_Strike_Cropped_OPT_Fina_OCR.pdf.

"Partial List of Acts of Violence of Intimidation During the Anthracite Strike of 1902." Clarence Darrow Digital Collection, University of Minnesota Law

Library, www.moses.law.umn.edu/darrow/documents/Partial_List_Violence _Intimidation_Optimized_Cropped.pdf.

Report of the Adjutant General of Pennsylvania. Harrisburg, PA: State Printer (May 31, 1902–December 31, 1903), https://babel.hathitrust.org/cgi/pt?id=md p.39015076666604;view=1up;seq=7.

Historical Statistics of the United States, 1789–1945. U.S. Department of Commerce, 1949, www2.census.gov/library/publications/1949/compendia/hist_stats_1789 -1945/hist_stats_1789-1945-front.pdf?.

U.S. Senate Hearings 1913. *Campaign Contributions: Testimony Before a Subcommittee of the Committee On Privileges and Elections, United States Senate, Sixty-second Congress, third session.* Pursuant to S. Res. 79, S. Res. 386, S. Res, 418. Vol. 1 and 2 (June 14, 1912–February 25, 1913]). Washington: Government Printing Office.

The Federal Antitrust Laws with Amendments: List of Cases Instituted by the United States. U.S. Department of Justice. Washington, D.C.: July 1, 1916, www .catalog.hathitrust.org/Record/100471077.

U.S. Congress, *Congressional Record.* 57th Cong., Special Session of the Senate., 1902. Vol. 35, pt. 8: 415.

MISCELLANEOUS

"A Miner's Story." *Independent,* 1902, www.ehistory.osu.edu/exhibitions/gildedage /content/MinersStory.

"Documents Relating to the Anthracite Strike of 1902." University of Minnesota, www.moses.law.umn.edu/darrow/documents/Documents_Relating_to _Anthracite_Strike_1902.pdf.

"Republican Party Platform of 1904." June 21, 1904, UC Santa Barbara American Presidency Project, www.presidency.ucsb.edu/node/273323.

Official Guide To The Louisiana Purchase Exposition: At The City Of St. Louis, State Of Missouri, April 30th to December 1st, 1904. Compiled by M. J. Lowenstein. Louisiana Purchase Exposition Company, 1904.

NOTES

PROLOGUE

ix   **Leon Czolgosz:** Details of his stay in Buffalo draws from A. Wesley Johns, *The Man Who Shot McKinley*, 13 and 49; Scott Miller, *The President and the Assassin*, 6.

ix   **Czolgosz's parents:** Details of his early and working life in Lloyd Vernon Briggs, *The Manner of Man That Kills*, 289, 296, 303–04; Walter Channing, *The Mental Status of Czolgosz*, 5, 12–13, 29; Eric Rauchway, *Murdering McKinley*, 166–67.

x   **His family had purchased:** This account of his life on the family farm draws from Briggs, *Manner of Man That Kills*, 306; Rauchway, *Murdering McKinley*, 169; Channing, *Mental Status of Czolgosz*, 40.

x   **In May 1901:** Johns, *The Man Who Shot McKinley*, 35; Emma Goldman, *Living My Life*, 194.

x   **"I never had":** "The Assassin Makes a Full Confession," *New York Times*, September 8, 1901; Johns, *The Man Who Shot McKinley*, 121–22.

x   **They gave him:** Rauchway, *Murdering McKinley*, 176.

xi   **afterward the creator:** Ron Miller, "In 1901, You Could Pay 50 Cents to Ride an Airship to the Moon," *Gizmodo*, May 31, 2012, io9.gizmodo.com/in-1901-you-could-pay-50-cents-to-ride-an-airship-to-t-5914655.

xi   **The showmen:** Details of the response to the Expo from Margaret Creighton, *The Electrifying Fall of Rainbow City*, 119–25, 273; Barbara A. Seals Nevergold, "'Doing the Pan': The African-American Experience at the Pan-American Exposition 1901," *Afro-Americans in New York Life and History* 12, no. 1 (2004); Andrew R. Valint, "Fighting for Recognition: The Role African Americans Played in World Fairs," (thesis, Buffalo State College, 2011).

xi   **"My fellow citizens":** Last Speech of William McKinley, Delivered at the Pan-American Exposition at Buffalo, September 5, 1901, 58th Congress, 2d Session, Senate Document no. 268, Government Printing Office, 1904.

xi   **On McKinley's final day:** Account of shooting draws from Johns, *The Man Who Shot McKinley*, 20, 89, 91, 94–6; Richard H. Barry, *The True Story of the Assassination of President McKinley at Buffalo* (1901), 12–13, 26; "Acted as a

Hero," *Washington Evening Star*, September 7, 1901, 1 and "James B. Parker: The Man Who Knocked the President's Assailant Down," *Washington Evening Star*, September 11, 1901, 6.

xiii **Trading on the stock market:** "Confidence in Financial Circles," *New York Times*, September 7, 1901, 3.

xiii **He controlled:** Ray Stannard Baker, "J. Pierpont Morgan," *McClure's* 17, no. 6 (October 1901): 512; "The Power of J. Pierpont Morgan," *Newton (Kansas) Journal*, January 19, 1900, 6.

xiv **The corporation would:** Jean Strouse, *Morgan: American Financier*, 404.

xiv **Be worth double:** *Historical Statistics of the United States, 1789–1945*, 296.

xiv **A courier had earlier:** Albro Martin, *James J. Hill and the Opening of the Northwest*, 427.

xiv **Morgan put on:** Morgan's reaction described in "Leaders of Finance Amazed," *New York Times*, September 7, 1901, 3; "Financiers Shocked," *New York Tribune*, September 7, 1901, 5; Alexander Dana Noyes, *The Market Place: Reminiscences of a Financial Editor*, 215.

xv **McKinley was put under:** Details of the operation drawn from "The Case of President McKinley," *Boston Medical and Surgical Journal* (now *New England Journal of Medicine*) CXLV, no. 17 (October 12 1901): 451–57; "Report of the Medical Department of the Pan-American Expo, Buffalo 1901," *Buffalo Medical Journal*, December 1901.

xv **In New York:** Details drawn from "How the News was Received in New York," *New York Times*, September 7, 1901, 2; "Leaders of Finance Amazed."

xv **Nothing of the sort:** Herbert L. Satterlee, *J. Pierpont Morgan: An Intimate Portrait, 1837–1913*, 363.

xvi **"The patient stood":** "Hoping for Recovery," *New York Tribune*, September 7, 1901, 1.

xvi **"My God":** "Mr. Roosevelt En Route," *New York Times*, September 7, 1901, 1.

xvi **He paced the room:** Details of Roosevelt's reaction and statements from "Vice President's Sorrow," *New York Times*, September 8, 1901, 1; "Mr. Roosevelt Gets Reassuring News," *New York Times*, September 8, 1901, 1.

xvii **"The financial situation":** "Banks Ready to Help," *New York Tribune*, September 8, 1901, 4.

xvii **He went down:** "Morgan Greets Friend," *New York Tribune*, September 8, 1901, 4.

xvii **Before long:** Details of McKinley's early progress drawn from "Great Hope for the President," *New York Times*, September 9, 1901, 1; "Still on the Mend,"

Washington Evening Star, September 11, 1901, 1; "The Case of President McKinley," 456; "Confidence and Joy at the Milburn Residence," *New York Times*, September 10, 1901, 1; "President's Double Tested the X-Rays," *Buffalo Enquirer*, September 10, 1901, 7.

xvii **"Now everything":** "Senator Hanna Is Happy," *New York Times*, September 10, 1901.

xvii **All that week:** "Detectives Guard J. P. Morgan," *New York Tribune*, September 8, 1901, 4.

xvii **That summer:** Baker, "J. Pierpont Morgan."

xviii **In Buffalo:** "Confidence and Joy at The Milburn Residence," *New York Times*, September 10, 1901, 1.

xviii **"You may say":** "The Fourth Day at the Milburn Residence," *New York Times*, September 11, 1901, 1.

xviii **Then, before daylight:** "The Case of President McKinley," 457.

xviii **A flock of crows:** Johns, *The Man Who Shot McKinley*, 158.

xviii **Morgan received updates:** "Morgan's Movements," *New York Times*, September 14, 1901, 3.

xviii **Roosevelt began:** Details of his trip to Buffalo from Theodore Roosevelt Papers: Scrapbooks, 1895–1910; Personal; vol. 1, 1901, Library of Congress; Edmund Morris, *Theodore Rex*, 3–11.

xix **Outside the mansion:** Johns, *The Man Who Shot McKinley*, 157.

xix **On the morning:** Details from "The City Draped in Black," *New York Tribune*, September 15, 1901, 3; "City Shows Its Grief with Crepe and Flags," *Brooklyn Daily Eagle*, September 15, 1901, 7; "Morgan Changes His Suit," *Brooklyn Daily Eagle Sun*, September 15, 1901, 5.

xix **"I was so shocked":** "No Time to Think," September 15, 1901 article in unidentified paper, Theodore Roosevelt Papers: Scrapbooks, 1895–1910; vol. 1, Library of Congress, and widely reported.

xix **He went straight:** Morris, *Theodore Rex*, 12–13.

xx **He chose a spot:** Details of swearing in from "Oath of Office Taken," Theodore Roosevelt Papers: Scrapbooks, 1895–1910; vol. 1, 1901, Library of Congress; "Roosevelt Now President," *New York Tribune*, September 15, 1901; report by Frederick A. McKenzie, unidentified newspaper, Theodore Roosevelt Papers: Scrapbooks, 1895–1910; vol. 1, 1901, Library of Congress; Morris, *Theodore Rex*, 14–15.

xx **"So many of the enterprises":** Satterlee, *J. Pierpont Morgan*, 362–63.

xx **"A mob gathered":** Johns, *The Man Who Shot McKinley*, 121.

xx   **"I did not feel"**: "The Assassin Makes a Full Confession." At least one author questions the accuracy of the full confession, but these sentiments are reported in Johns, *The Man Who Shot McKinley*, 123, citing the notes of a court stenographer.

xx   **Goldman was arrested**: Goldman, *Living My Life*, 201, 207; Alice Wexler, *Emma Goldman: An Intimate Life*, 106.

xxi   **"Soul in pain"**: Emma Goldman, "The Tragedy at Buffalo," *Free Society*, October 1901.

xxi   **"I shot the president"**: Details of Czolgosz's death and burial from "Assassin Czolgosz Is Executed at Auburn," *New York Times*, October 30, 1901, 1; Rauchway, *Murdering McKinley*, 79.

CHAPTER 1: "THE STORM IS ON US"

3   **"I must frankly"**: Douglas Robinson to Roosevelt, September 13, 1901. Theodore Roosevelt Papers, Library of Congress.

3   **"stand pat"**: Mark Sullivan, *Our Times: The United States, 1900–1925*, vol. 2: 377.

4   **"cash-register conscience"**: William Allen White, "Hanna," *McClure's* (November 1900).

4   **"Don't any of you"**: Arthur Wallace Dunn, *From Harrison to Harding: A Personal Narrative, Covering a Third of a Century, 1888–1921*, vol. 1: 335.

4   **"I am as strong"**: Roosevelt to Hanna, June 27, 1900, Theodore Roosevelt Papers, Library of Congress.

4   **He had traveled**: "Roosevelt Ends His Tour," *New York Times* November 3, 1900, 2.

4–5   **On Monday**: "Speeding through Mourning Land," *Minneapolis Journal*, September 16, 1901; "Martyr President Borne to Capital," *New York Times*, September 17, 1901.

5   **At the suggestion of**: Details of Roosevelt's meal with Hanna from H. H. Kohlsaat, *From McKinley to Harding*, 101–03; Edmund Morris, *Theodore Rex*, 16; James Ford Rhodes, *The McKinley and Roosevelt Administrations*, 218. Roosevelt later unconvincingly denies inviting Hanna to dinner, while Hanna confirms it. But Roosevelt does acknowledge the substance of their conversations in a letter to Lincoln Steffens, June 24, 1905, *The Letters of Theodore Roosevelt*, ed. Elting Morison, vol. 4: 1254–55.

5–6   **"The tremendous responsibility" and "Mr. Roosevelt"**: "Feverish Excitement at Waldorf-Astoria," *New York Times*, September 14, 1901, 3.

6   **"President McKinley":** "No Peril Ahead, Says Morgan," *New York Evening World*, September 14, 1901, 2.

6   **"I don't care a damn":** Kohlsaat, *From McKinley to Harding*, 105.

6   **Morgan walked:** Details of funeral in "At Work in the Rotunda," *Washington Times*, September 16, 1901, 2; "Nation Bids Its Dead Farewell," *Chicago Tribune*, September 18, 1901, 3; "Fitting Tribute to the Nation's Dead: Scene in the Rotunda," *Dayton Evening Herald*, September 17, 1901, 1.

6   **Hanna immediately:** McKinley's Tomb, National Park Service website, www.nps.gov/nr/travel/presidents/mckinley_tomb.html.

6   **The train returned:** "At the White House," *Evening Star*, September 20, 1901, 1. "Knows No Section," *Evening Star*, September 21, 1901, 1.

7   **"It's a dreadful thing":** Roosevelt to Henry Cabot Lodge, September 23, 1901, *Selections from the Correspondence of Theodore Roosevelt and Henry Cabot Lodge*, vol. 1: 506.

7   **Almost half a million:** Lewis L. Gould, *The Presidency of Theodore Roosevelt*, 34.

7   **Between 1895 and 1900:** "Western Wealth Enriches New York," *St. Paul Globe*, January 21, 1900, 20; "Senator Clark's New Home Causes a Suit," *New York Times*, December 11, 1901; Lindsay Turley, "Streetscapes: William A. Clark Mansion," Museum of the City of New York, 2018, www.mcny.org/story/william_clark_mansion.

9   **Meeting his blazing:** John A. Garraty, *Right-Hand Man*, 89.

9   **"Part of the":** Andrew Sinclair, *Corsair: The Life of J. Pierpont Morgan*, 192.

9   **"The storm is on us":** Henry Adams, in Paris, to Secretary of State John Hay, October 1, 1901, *Letters of Henry Adams*, ed. J. C. Levenson et al., vol. 5: 300.

9   **"I am not advocating":** Speech at Symphony Hall, Boston, August 25, 1902 in *The Roosevelt Policy: Speeches, Letters and State Papers, Relating to Corporate Wealth and Closely Allied Topics*, ed. William Griffith, 1: 47.

9   **"I am afraid":** Alfred Henry Lewis, "Owners of America III: J. Pierpont Morgan," *Cosmopolitan* XLV, no. 3 (August 1908), 250–60.

10   **At the end of September:** "Episcopal Prelates, Clergy and Laymen Assemble To-day for Triennial General Convention in Trinity Church," *San Francisco Call*, October 2, 1901, 1, 5; "Takes Big Party to San Francisco," *Chicago Tribune*, September 27, 1901, 9.

10   **"All Wall Street":** "Morgan Busy with NP War," *New York Evening World*, October 28, 1901, 10.

CHAPTER 2: THE BEST OF EVERYTHING

11   **John Pierpont Morgan:** I am indebted to Jean Strouse's *Morgan: American Financier* for its clear-eyed, comprehensive, and insightful account of Morgan's personal and professional lives. In the paragraphs that follow, I've noted original documents and other sources.

11   **by necessity, insurance:** Morgan's grandfather, Joseph Morgan, co-founded Aetna Insurance Company.

12   **"Full of animal life":** Jean Strouse, *Morgan: American Financier*, 35, citing J. B. Burbank letter to Herbert Satterlee, April 4, 1914, The Pierpont Morgan Library.

12   **He collected and organized:** Frederick Lewis Allen, *The Great Pierpont Morgan*, 12, 13, 18.

12   **Paper and postage:** Account book, personal expenses 1857–1858, Pierpont Morgan Library.

12   **"Adapts himself":** Strouse, *Morgan*, 55, citing Edouard Silling letter to Junius Morgan, February 21, 1855, Pierpont Morgan Library, Mabel Satterlee Ingalls collection.

13   **When Abraham Lincoln:** Richard White, *Railroaded: The Transcontinentals and the Making of Modern America*, 2.

13   **"Bring your mind":** Strouse, *Morgan*, 77, citing letter from Junius Morgan to Pierpont Morgan, March 25, 1858, Pierpont Morgan Library.

13   **"Untiring industry":** Strouse, *Morgan*, 83–84, citing letter from Sherman Duncan to Pierpont Morgan, September 24, 1859, Pierpont Morgan Library.

14   **"No cry":** Strouse, *Morgan*, 85.

14   **A controversial deal:** "The Astounding Disclosures of the Van Wyck Investigation," *Lancaster Examiner*, December 25, 1861, 3; "Pierpont Morgan Not Napoleon of Finance," *Greenville News*, January 6, 1913, 4.

15   **"Constant occupation":** Strouse, *Morgan*, 105–06, citing Morgan letter to his cousin, James Goodwin, March 21, 1862, Pierpont Morgan Library.

15   **He acquired:** "The Rise of the Morgan Dynasty," *Current Literature* XLIX, 1910; Carl Hovey, *The Life Story of J. Pierpont Morgan*, 28.

15   **"I am never":** Strouse, *Morgan*, 107, citing Pierpont Morgan letter to Junius Morgan, mid-September, 1862, George Peabody Papers, Phillips Library, the Peabody Essex Museum.

15   **Lincoln's salary:** Harry E. Pratt, *Personal Finances of Abraham Lincoln* (Lakeside Press, 1943), 124.

16 **Americans paid:** David Goldfield, *America Aflame: How the Civil War Created a Nation*, 843–44.

16 **One hundred dollars:** Karen Wolfe, "Song of The Exposition," in J. R. LeMaster and Donald D. Kummings, eds., *Walt Whitman: An Encyclopedia* (New York: Garland Publishing, 1998) via the Walt Whitman Archive.

16 **"Talk of millions":** Goldfield, *America Aflame*, 836, citing John Sherman letter to his brother, Gen. Tecumseh Sherman, November 10, 1865, *The Sherman Letters: Correspondence between General and Senator Sherman from 1837 to 1891*, ed. Rachel Sherman Thorndike, 258.

17 **He paid:** "The Great Architectural Change in Wall Street," *New York Times*, March 17, 1872, 3; Dan Rottenberg, *The Man Who Made Wall Street: Anthony J. Drexel and the Rise of Modern Finance* (Philadelphia: University of Pennsylvania Press, 2001), 102–04.

17 **It absorbed:** Larry Haeg, *Harriman vs. Hill: Wall Street's Great Railroad War*, 6.

17 **Some 170 million:** White, *Railroaded*, 24–25.

18 **For every mile:** White, *Railroaded*, 23; Sean M. Kammer, "Land and Law in the Age of Enterprise: A Legal History of Railroad Land Grants in the Pacific Northwest 1864–1916," (dissertation University of Nebraska, Lincoln, 2015).

18 **These were not:** John C. Hudson, "Towns of the Western Railroads," *Great Plains Quarterly*, Winter 1982, 41–54.

18 **They handed out:** Ralph W. Hidy, *The Great Northern Railway*, 130.

18 **Tens of thousands:** Senate Committee on Interstate Commerce Hearings on Automatic Couplers and Power Brakes, 1890, 41.

18 **"It was taken":** L. S. Coffin, "Safety Appliances on Railroads," *The Annals of Iowa* 5, no. 3, (1903): 561–82.

19 **In Winona:** "Railroad Accidents," *Star Tribune*, February 6, 1873, 4.

19 **Conductor Arthur Lindsley:** "Conductor Arthur Lindsley," *Mower County Transcript*, April 3, 1873, 1.

19–20 **Fireman R. Brown:** "Fireman and Brakeman Killed," *Star Tribune*, July 18, 1873, 4

20 **Amandas Hagerty:** "A Man Killed," *Carbon Advocate*, November 29, 1873.

20 **"within the parallels":** Ellis Paxon Oberholtzer, *Jay Cooke*, 313.

20 **Two hundred or so:** Howard Zinn, *A People's History of the United States*, 243; "Wreck of the Metropolis," *New York Tribune*, February 1, 1878, 1; "Other Accounts of the Wreck," *New York Times*, February 1, 1878, 1; "The Feeling at Philadelphia," *New York Times*, February 2, 1878, 1.

21 **"Bread is":** James Dabney McCabe, *The History of the Great Riots*, 1877, 202.

21   **"There are two":** McCabe, *Great Riots*, 20.

21   **"Please send in":** McCabe, *Great Riots*, 31.

21   **Pierpont—whose firm:** Vincent P. Carosso, *The Morgans: Private International Bankers, 1854–1913*, 229.

21   **"Affairs for a time":** Carosso, *The Morgans*, 230, citing Morgan letter to Walter H. Burns, August 24, 1877.

22   **"Honor in the":** Carosso, *The Morgans*, 190; "Early Life and Rise to Power of J. Pierpont Morgan," *Hartford Courant*, 10.

22   **"A kind Providence":** Strouse, *Morgan*, 178.

22   **Railroads comprised:** Figures for 1885, listings, Mary O'Sullivan, "The Expansion of the U.S. Stock Market, 1885–1930: Historical Facts and Theoretical Fashions," *Enterprise & Society* 8, no. 3, (2007): 495; revenue, *Historical Statistics of the United States, 1789–1945*, prepared by the Bureau of the Census, 1949, 201, 296; track added, Haeg, *Harriman vs. Hill*, 7.

22   **Pierpont's firm:** Details of the two deals in Carosso, *The Morgans*, 246, 250; "A Gigantic Syndicate," *Scranton Republican*, November 30, 1880, 1.

23   **He accidentally:** Herbert L. Satterlee, *J. Pierpont Morgan, 1837–1913*, 235.

23   **On the shelves:** Strouse, *Morgan*, 229; Joseph F. Sabin, Catalogue of the Library of Mr. J. Pierpont Morgan (New York, 1883).

23   **"Nothing but masterpieces":** John Paul Bocock, *Character Sketch of Mr. Morgan 1900–1909*, 11, Pierpont Morgan Library.

24   **On Sunday evenings:** Satterlee, *J. Pierpont Morgan*, 334.

25   **"I'm struggling to":** "J. Pierpont Morgan Dies in Rome," *Buffalo Evening News*, March 31, 1903, 10.

25   **"Sore spots":** Hovey, *Life Story*, 104.

25   **Morgan devised a plan:** Details from Hovey, *Life Story*, 113–15; Andrew Sinclair, *Corsair: The Life of J. Pierpont Morgan*, 63–66; Strouse, *Morgan*, 248–49.

26   **"Let the":** Carosso, *The Morgans*, 265, citing letter from Junius Morgan to Pierpont, December 29, 1887.

CHAPTER 3: A PUBLIC MAN

27   **"Theodore Roosevelt was":** Roosevelt's early years are wonderfully reconstructed in many books. I draw mostly from: Edmund Morris's *The Rise of Theodore Roosevelt*, David McCullough's *Mornings on Horseback*, Kathleen

Dalton's *Theodore Roosevelt: A Strenuous Life*, Carleton Putnam's *Theodore Roosevelt: The Formative Years*, and Roosevelt's own autobiography. The specific sources for quotes are cited.

27 **"Maniacal benevolence":** McCullough, *Mornings on Horseback*, 28, quoting John Hay.

28 **"Entirely unreconstructed":** Theodore Roosevelt, *The Autobiography of Theodore Roosevelt*, 12.

29 **"Forever at it":** William Henry Harbaugh, *The Life and Times of Theodore Roosevelt*, 21.

29 **"Have had a good":** McCullough, *Mornings on Horseback*, 187.

29 **"Very buoyant temper":** McCullough, *Mornings on Horseback*, 189.

29 **"Loved to row":** Corinne Robinson, *My Brother Theodore Roosevelt*, 90.

29 **Relied on a trust fund:** Lewis L. Gould, *Theodore Roosevelt*, 6; "Will of Theodore Roosevelt," *New York Times*, February 17, 1878.

29 **Robert Bacon:** John Winkler, *Morgan the Magnificent*, 147, and H. W. Brands, *T. R.: The Last Romantic*, 61.

30 **"I have been in love":** Roosevelt to Henry Davis Minot, February 13, 1880, *The Letters of Theodore Roosevelt*, ed. Elting Morison, vol. 1: 43.

31 **After securing:** Roosevelt's first political outing is recounted in Lawrence Abbott, *Impressions of Theodore Roosevelt*, 41; Harbaugh, *Life and Times*, 28; Paul Grondahl, *I Rose Like a Rocket*, 66, and elsewhere with slightly different wording but the same meaning.

31 **The society folks:** A note in Morison, *Letters* 1: 55; "Pamphlet recommending Theodore Roosevelt as member of the New York State Assembly," Theodore Roosevelt Collection, Harvard College Library.

31 **"Would obey no boss":** Carleton Putnam, *Theodore Roosevelt*, 248, citing *New York Herald*, November 1, 1881.

31 **"Who's the dude":** Morris, *Rise of Theodore Roosevelt*, 144, citing John Walsh in *Kansas City Star*, February 12, 1922.

31 **"What on earth":** Putnam, *Theodore Roosevelt*, 250, quoting Edgar Murlin of the *Tribune*.

32 **"I do not speak":** Roosevelt to Martha Bulloch Roosevelt, February 20, 1883, Morison, *Letters* 1: 60.

32 **"He threw each paper":** Putnam, *Theodore Roosevelt*, 273–74, quoting William Hudson of the *Brooklyn Daily Eagle*.

32 **Politicians from both:** Roosevelt, *Autobiography*, 43.

32 **"He was just like a jack":** Putnam, *Theodore Roosevelt*, 273, quoting Isaac Hunt, an assemblyman from Jefferson County.

33 **As Roosevelt's first term:** Roosevelt (*Autobiography*, 47) describes the concerned older man as a family friend. Morris (*The Rise of Theodore Roosevelt*, 158) identifies him as Roosevelt's uncle, James A. Roosevelt. It's likely that in his later years Roosevelt wanted to protect the reputation of his deceased uncle.

33 **"Most refreshing habit":** Morris, *Rise of Theodore Roosevelt*, 160, citing *New York Times* editorial, April 6, 1882, 4.

33 **"The rising hope":** Morris, *Rise of Theodore Roosevelt*, 168.

33 **"I rose like a rocket":** Roosevelt to his son Ted Roosevelt, October 20, 1903, *The Letters of Theodore Roosevelt*, ed. Elting Morison, vol. 3: 634–35.

33 **"I would listen":** Jacob Riis, *Theodore Roosevelt: The Citizen*, 58–59.

33 **Economic trouble:** Carroll Wright, *Industrial Depressions: The First Annual Report of the Commissioner of Labor, March 1886* (Washington, D.C.: Government Printign Office: 1886), 78.

33 **"The state must not":** Grondahl, *I Rose Like a Rocket*, 108.

34 **"I have to confess":** Grondahl, *I Rose Like a Rocket*, 108–09.

35 **"The tobacco was stored":** Roosevelt's quotes are all from his article, "Practical Politics," *Outlook*, April 6, 1913.

36 **"It is as though":** Henry George, *Progress and Poverty: An Inquiry into the Cause of Industrial Depressions and of Increase of Want with Increase of Wealth; The Remedy* (New York: D. Appleton & Co., 1879), 9.

36 **"Only fairly well":** February 13 telegram to Dora (Dolly) Watkins, Morison, *Letters* 1: 65.

37 **"Suicidal weather":** Putnam, *Theodore Roosevelt*, 384, citing "The Weather," *New York Times*, February 13, 1884, 4.

37 **"There is a curse":** Putnam, *Theodore Roosevelt*, 386.

37 **"Black care":** Theodore Roosevelt, *Ranch Life and the Hunting Trail*, 59.

37 **Roosevelt later wrote:** Roosevelt, *Autobiography*, 59.

37 **He wore:** McCullough, *Mornings on Horseback*, 320.

38 **"Perfect freedom":** Roosevelt to Henry Cabot Lodge, August 24, 1884, Morison, *Letters* 1: 79–80.

38 **"I realize":** Roosevelt to Simon Newton Dexter North, editor of *Utica Morning Herald*, April 30, 1884, Morison, *Letters* 1: 66.

38 **The public:** This account of unrest draws from Paul Avrich, *The Haymarket Tragedy*, 200–10 and other sources as cited.

39 **"My men here":** Roosevelt to Anna Roosevelt, May 15, 1886, Morison, *Letters* 1: 100.

39   **In upstate New York:** Alice Wexler, *Emma Goldman: An Intimate Life*, 30–31; 35–37. Emma Goldman, *Living My Life*, chapter 1.

39   **New York police charged:** "Rioters Get Broken Heads," *New York Sun*, June 6, 1886, 2.

39   **"We are beginning":** Richard Brookheiser, "1886: The Men Who Would Be Mayor," *City Journal*, Autumn 1993.

40   **"Caged wolf":** Roosevelt to Anna Roosevelt from Medora, May 15, 1886, Morison, *Letters* 1: 101.

40   **Would soon marry:** Morison, *Letters* 1: 115.

40   **"Am badly defeated":** Theodore Roosevelt and Henry Cabot Lodge, *Selections from the Correspondence of Theodore Roosevelt and Henry Cabot Lodge*, vol. 1: 50.

40   **Edith wore:** Sylvia Jukes Morris, *Edith Kermit Roosevelt*, 100.

40   **But his cattle business:** Roosevelt in Medora to Anna Roosevelt, April 16, 1887, Morison, *Letters* 1: 126–27.

40–41   **"I always genuinely enjoy":** Roosevelt to Cecil Spring Rice, November 18, 1888, Morison, *Letters* 1: 149.

42   **"Wanted to put an end":** Harbaugh, *Power and Responsibility*, 79.

42   **"It is horribly":** Roosevelt and Lodge, *Selections from the Correspondence* 1: 116.

42   **Theodore and Bamie:** Details of Elliott's struggles with addiction—and his family—drawn from William J. Mann, *The Wars of the Roosevelts*.

42   **Two surviving children:** Elliott Bulloch Roosevelt Jr. died from diphtheria in 1893 at age three.

42   **"Theodore was more overcome":** Mann, *The Wars of the Roosevelts*, 96.

CHAPTER 4: RAILROAD NATION

43   **When white settlers:** Jon Farrar and Richard Gersib, "Nebraska Salt Marshes: Last of the Least," Environmental Protection Agency and Nebraska Game and Parks Commission, July 1991.

43   **The Pawnee:** American Indian Research Studies Institute Dictionary Database.

43   **The Pflug Brothers:** This account of Lincoln's early days comes from A. B. Hayes and Sam Cox, *History of the City of Lincoln, Nebraska*, 149–55.

44   **More than three hundred thousand:** "Economic Geography," The *Electronic Encyclopedia of Chicago*, Chicago Historical Society, 2005.

44   **The Burlington Railroad:** "The Making of the Burlington," Speech by W. W. Baldwin, Burlington Vice President, July 2, 1920, 12, Reprinted from *Professional Engineer Magazine*, Library of Knox College.

44   **An advertisement:** Nebraska land sales advertisement, 1882; "The Emigration to B&M Lands in Eastern Nebraska," in *CB&Q: Building an Empire*, The Newberry Collection.

44   **"The roads have reason":** Hayes and Cox, *Lincoln, Nebraska*, 66.

45   **The Burlington was owned:** Details in this paragraph from Baldwin speech.

45   **In January 1889:** "They All Mean Business, the Railroad Trust Will Be Formed Very Soon," *New York Times*, January 8, 1889, 2; "Rules Against Rate Cutting," *Inter-Ocean*, January 11, 1889, 1–2.

45   **"The public are sure to":** Carl Hovey, *The Life Story of J. Pierpont Morgan*, 140.

45   **Farmers could:** "Freight Rates in the West," *Weekly Republican Traveler*, January 3, 1885, 3.

45   **Travelers could:** Andrew Sinclair, *Corsair: The Life of J. Pierpont Morgan*, 59.

46   **In 1888:** Hovey, *Life Story of J. Pierpont Morgan*, 126–27.

46   **"A number of innocent investors":** "They Meet To-day," *New York Sun*, January 8, 1889, 4.

46   **"The purpose of this meeting":** Hovey, *Life Story of J. Pierpont Morgan*, 139; John K. Winkler, *Morgan the Magnificent*, 109, 111.

46   **"Your roads":** The original source of this often-quoted line is Morgan's obituary in the *Wall Street Journal*, April 1, 1913.

46   **"Morgan began to be":** John Moody, *Masters of Capital: A Chronicle of Wall Street*, 25.

46–47   **"I have done nothing":** Winkler, *Morgan the Magnificent*, 101.

47   **A trust relied on:** Wayne D. Collins, "Trusts and the Origins of Antitrust Legislation," *Fordham Law Review* 81, no. 5, article 7, 2013.

47   **Standard Oil was:** Henry Demarest Lloyd, "The Story of a Great Monopoly," *Atlantic Monthly*, (March 1881).

47   **Reprinted the issue:** William Letwin, *Law and Economic Policy in America*, 69.

48   **"The popular mind":** "Trusts," John Sherman Speech to Senate, March 21, 1890. Published by Library of the University of Wisconsin.

48   **"They are abhorrent to me":** Letwin, *Law and Economic Policy*, 58, citing "A Debate about Trusts," *New York Times*, March 2, 1888, 2.

48   **Thirteen states:** Details about state antitrust laws from Collins, "Antitrust Legislation," 2336–37; Letwin, *Law and Economic Policy*, 51–53.

48   **Fifty-two senators:** Congressional Record, vol. 21 Part 4, 51st Congress, 3153; Steven Lavender, "Senator Rufus Blodgett: The Sherman Anti-Trust Act's Lone Dissenter," *American Journal of Legal History*, November 11, 2013.

48   **One senator:** Senator Orville Platt, a Republican from Connecticut, cited in Letwin, *Law and Economic Policy*, 53.

49   **"Cheerful, rosy-faced lawyer":** Frederick Lewis Allen, *The Great Pierpont Morgan*, 128–29.

49   **"Traitor state":** Gary Giroux, *Business Scandals, Corruption, and Reform: An Encyclopedia* (Greenwood, 2013), 388; Lincoln Steffens, "New Jersey: A Traitor State Part II—How She Sold Out the United States," *McClure's* 25, no. 1 (May 1905).

49   **Dill and Governor:** Elizabeth Ann Schiller, "James Brooks Dill: Father of the Trusts," 21.

49   **"I am the lawyer":** Mark Sullivan, *Our Times: The United States, 1900–1925*, vol. 2: 318.

49   **The Sherman Antitrust Act:** This history and analysis draws from Letwin, *Law and Economic Policy*, 100–03; Schiller, "James Brooks Dill," 19–20.

50   **"Fear irregularities":** Vincent P. Carosso, *The Morgans*, 379.

50   **One hundred and ninety-one:** Interstate Commerce Commission statistics, cited in Carosso, *The Morgans*, 363.

50   **One hundred and fifty-eight:** Alexander Dana Noyes, *Forty Years of American Finance*, 193.

50   **Fifteen percent:** Gary Richardson and Tim Sablik, "Banking Panics of the Gilded Age," www.federalreservehistory.org/essays/banking_panics_of_the _gilded_age#footnote1.

50   **People begged:** Jon Grinspan, "How a Ragtag Band of Reformers Organized the First Protest March on Washington," *Smithsonian Magazine*, May 2014.

50   **Hard Times Balls:** Grinspan; "Hard Times Party," *Nevada State Journal*, February 8, 1894, 3; "Hard Times Balls—What the Boys Say," *Atchison Daily Champion*, January 17, 1895, 2.

51   **"Everything here":** Jean Strouse, *Morgan: American Financier*, 324.

51   **"Heed the voice":** Details about Coxey's March from Jack Kelly, *The Edge of Anarchy*, 29–31; Lucy Barber, *Marching on Washington: The Forging of an American Tradition* (Berkeley, CA: University of California Press, 2004), 33, 36.

51   **More than eight thousand:** Details about the company town from Richard Ely, "Pullman: A Social Study," *Harper's Weekly* (February 1885): 452–66.

52   **More than two hundred thousand:** Details from Kelly, *Edge of Anarchy*, 109, 123.

52 **Simmering violence:** Howard Zinn, *A People's History of the United States*, 281.

52 **"Put forth its efforts":** Eugene V. Debs, "Proclamation to American Railway Union," June 1, 1895 in *Debs: His Life, Writing and Speeches*, 292.

53 **Among the lines:** Details of Morgan's reorganization efforts from Ron Chernow, *The House of Morgan*, 66–69.

53 **"Executing two trustees' sale":** Allen, *The Great Pierpont Morgan*, 68.

53 **"A white-faced":** Description of Coster from Moody, *Masters of Capital*, 33; "Obituary: Charles H. Coster," *New York Tribune*, March 14, 1900, 4; Carosso, *The Morgans*, 365.

54 **"Probably it will not do":** Carosso, *The Morgans*, 381.

54 **Within five years:** Details from John Moody and George Kibbe Kibbe, "The Masters of Capital in America: Morgan, the Great Trustee," *McClure's* 36 (November 1910), 23; Chernow, *House of Morgan*, 67; *Historical Statistics of the United States, 1789–1945*, prepared by the Bureau of the Census, 1949, 296.

54 **"Cheapest, Best and Quickest":** Ralph W. Linroth, interview about his 2016 book, *A History of the CB&Q Quincy Branch: The Northern Cross Route Quincy to Galesburg*, in *Quincy Herald-Whig*, January 10, 2016.

54 **Hill had built:** Ralph W. Hidy, *The Great Northern Railway*, 121.

54 **Hill was short:** Description of Hill from Winkler, *Morgan the Magnificent*, 160; Albro Martin, *James J. Hill and the Opening of the Northwest*, 428.

55 **Hill built a mansion:** Details from Barbara Ann Caron, "James J. Hill House: Symbol of Status and Security," Minnesota Historical Society, Summer 1997; Union Depot, history, www.uniondepot.org/history.

55 **Hill was like:** Details from Richard White, *Railroaded: The Transcontinentals and the Making of Modern America*, 425; Martin, *James J. Hill*, 411–16.

56 **"It would be":** A. Freeman letter to Hill, August 7, 1893, cited in Martin, *James J. Hill*, 416.

56 **He bullied:** Details here from Larry Haeg, *Harriman vs. Hill*, 28, 107.

56 **Hill ignored:** Martin, James J. Hill, 447–49; "Cannot Combine," *Minneapolis Star Tribune*, March 31, 1896, 1.

57 **"London memorandum":** Details from Martin, *James J. Hill*, 455; Carosso, *The Morgans*, 385.

57 **"You will have to be":** Martin, *James J. Hill*, 455, citing letter from Henry W. Cannon to Hill, February 26, 1896.

58 "Two streaks": Chernow, *House of Morgan*, 88, citing John Kobler, *Otto the Magnificent: The Life of Otto Kahn* (New York: Scribner, 1989), 23–24.

58 "Was the genius": Otto Kahn speech reprinted in his autobiography, *Of Many Things: Being Reflections and Impressions on International Affairs, Domestic Topics and the Arts* (New York: Boni & Liveright, 1926), 107–44, cited in Henry Pringle's Notes, Theodore Roosevelt Collection, Harvard College Library.

58 A "punk": Larry Haeg, *Harriman vs. Hill*, 42.

58 "Bold, energetic," Joseph G. Pyle, *Life of James Hill*, vol. 2: 112.

58 Morgan thought: Accounts of Morgan's negotiations and meetings in Strouse, *Morgan: American Financier*, 341–47; Hovey, *Life Story of J. Pierpont Morgan*, 172–92; Allen, *The Great Pierpont Morgan*, 85–95.

59 "It was absolutely": Hovey, *Life Story of J. Pierpont Morgan*, 191.

59 "We consider": Strouse, *Morgan: American Financier*, 342.

59 "Fallen in love": James Brown Scott, *Robert Bacon: Life and Letters* (Garden City, NY: Doubleday, Page & Company, 1923), 70.

59 "Don't overwork": Ibid., 71.

60 "I have come down": Herbert L. Satterlee, *J. Pierpont Morgan*, 286.

61 "Have you anything": Hovey, *Life Story of J. Pierpont Morgan*, 178.

61 "I was never so excited": William Lawrence, *Pierpont Morgan*, unpublished biography, 108.

61 Three hundred thousand dollars: Strouse, *Morgan: American Financier*, 350.

61 A "fascinating": Gustavus Myers, *History of the Great American Fortunes*, vol. 3: *Great Fortunes from Railroads*, 226.

61 "If God had intended": Lawrence, *Pierpont Morgan*, 57; his insights into Morgan on this matter, 108.

CHAPTER 5: THE INVISIBLE EMPIRE

62 A man emerges: For description that follows, H. Paul Jeffers, *Commissioner Roosevelt: The Story of Theodore Roosevelt and the New York City Police, 1895–1897*, 105–12; "Roosevelt as a Roundsman," *Evening World*, June 7, 1895, 2.

62 His greatest contribution: *The Letters of Theodore Roosevelt*, ed. Elting Morison, 1: 444 includes an author's note summarizing popular positive and negative opinion of Roosevelt's time on commission as both being too extreme.

62 On this June night: Jeffers, *Commissioner Roosevelt*, 105–08, and Richard Zacks, *Island of Vice: Theodore Roosevelt's Quest to Clean Up Sin-Loving New York*, 94–97.

63 **"These midnight rambles"**: Roosevelt to Anna Roosevelt Cowles, June 23, 1895, Morison, *Letters* 1: 463.

63 **"The biggest man"**: Morris, *The Rise of Theodone Roosevelt*, 521, citing *Chicago Times Herald*.

63 **"My whole work"**: Roosevelt to Anna Roosevelt Cowles, June 23, 1895, *Letters from Theodore Roosevelt to Anna Roosevelt Cowles*, 157–58.

63 **"I have read your book"**: Jacob Riis, *Theodore Roosevelt: The Citizen*, 131.

63 **"There is not"**: Roosevelt, "True American Ideals," *The Forum*, 743–50, February 1895.

63 **"The actual work"**: Roosevelt to Anna Roosevelt Cowles, May 19, 1895, *Anna Roosevelt Cowles Letters*, 155.

64 **Elliott had died:** Zacks, *Island of Vice*, 122, makes this connection.

64 **This placed Roosevelt:** Description of Platt and this encounter with Roosevelt draws from Zacks, *Island of Vice*, 159, 211; Morris, *The Rise of Theodone Roosevelt*, 534–40.

64 **"As for my being"**: Roosevelt to Henry Cabot Lodge, October 3, 1895, *Selections from the Correspondence of Theodore Roosevelt and Henry Cabot Lodge, 1884–1918*, vol 1: 183.

64 **"We got along"**: Roosevelt to Lodge, January 19, 1896, *Selections from the Correspondence* 1: 210.

64 **One hundred-degree heat:** Description of the heat wave draws from Edward P. Kohn, *Hot Time in the Old Town Town: The Great Heat Wave of 1896 and the Making of Theodore Roosevelt*, 55–56, 87–88, 92, 102. Kohn notes that official temperatures were often taken high above the sweltering streets and never inside the tenements.

65 **"They added"**: Roosevelt to Anna Roosevelt Cowles, August 15, 1896, *Anna Roosevelt Cowles Letters*, 190.

65 **"While the people"**: Second Inaugural Address of Grover Cleveland, Saturday, March 4, 1893.

65 **"You come to us"**: "Cross of Gold" speech, July 8, 1896, Democratic National Convention in Chicago, *Speeches of William Jennings Bryan*, 238–49.

65 **The crowd swelled:** Michael Kazin, *A Godly Hero: The Life of William Jennings Bryan*, 61, citing "A Bryan Cyclone," *New York World*, July 10, 1896, 2.

66 **Bryan traveled:** Kendrick A. Clements, "Secretary of State William Jennings Bryan," *Nebraska History* 77 (1996): 167–76; Louis Koenig, "The First Hurrah," *American Heritage* (April/May 1980).

66 **Five million:** Kazin, *A Godly Hero*, 68.

66   "I might just": Kazin, *A Godly Hero*, 66, citing Stanley Jones, *The Presidential Election of 1896* (Madison: University of Wisconsin, 1964), 277

66   "All of us want": R. Hal Williams, *Realigning America*, citing Joseph P. Smith, *McKinley: The People's Choice* (Repository Press, 1896), 38.

66   For Wall Street: John A. Garraty, "Bryan: The Progressives, Part 1," *American Heritage* (December 1961).

66   The railroads cooperated: Robert W. Merry, *President McKinley: Architect of the American Century*, 140; Margaret Leech, "The Front Porch Campaign," *American Heritage* (December 1959).

66   James Hill introduced: Details about Hanna as campaign chairman and fundraiser from Herbert David Croly, *Marcus Alonzo Hanna: His Life and Work*, 219–20; Robert E. Mutch, *Buying the Vote*, 22–24; Williams, *Realigning America*, 137; William T. Horner, *Ohio's Kingmaker: Mark Hanna, Man and Myth*, 187, 198; Jonathan Auerbach, "McKinley at Home: How Early American Cinema Made News," *American Quarterly* (December 1999).

67   "A good-natured": Roosevelt to Lodge, July 30, 1896, *Selections from the Correspondence* 1: 227.

67   In the last days: "As Seen in Wall Street," and "Marching in the Ranks," *New York Times*, November 1, 1896, 3; "Parades in Other Cities," *New York Sun*, November 1, 1896, 4.

67   "Melancholy spectre": Jeffers, *Commissioner Roosevelt*, 248, citing Maria Longworth Storer, *Theodore Roosevelt the Child*, private printing.

67   "He has been": Thomas Collier Platt, *The Autobiography of Thomas Collier Platt*, 541.

67   Afternoon buggy rides: Merry, *President McKinley*, 187.

68   "I am having": Roosevelt to Bellamy Storer, August 19, 1897, Morison, *Letters* 1: 655.

68   Roosevelt was first: Morris, *The Rise of Theodore Roosevelt*, 621; Clay Risen, *The Crowded Hour: Theodore Roosevelt, the Rough Riders, and the Dawn of the American Century*, 40, 43.

68   "The defective imaginations": Roosevelt to Brooks Adams, March 21,1898, Morison, *Letters* 1: 797–98.

68   "A splendid little war": Hay to Roosevelt, July 27, 1898, *Life and Letters of John Hay*, ed. William Roscoe Thayer, vol. 2: 337.

68   Some thousand men: Details of the Rough Riders drawn from Risen, *The Crowded Hour*, 74–75; Roosevelt to Corinne Roosevelt Robinson, May 5, 1898, Morison, *Letters* 2: 823–24.

68 **He sported:** Risen, *The Crowded Hour*, 92–93, 95; Mark Lee Gardner, "Cowboys and Millionaires," *True West*, April 15, 2016; Roosevelt to Leonard Wood, May 10, 1898, Morison, *Letters* 2: 829–30.

69 **"I knew that":** William Lawrence, *Pierpont Morgan*, 59.

69 **"Tried to":** Herbert L. Satterlee, *J. Pierpont Morgan: An Intimate Portrait*, 324.

69 **Roosevelt complained:** Roosevelt to Lodge, June 10, 1898, Morison, *Letters* 2: 837–38 and June 12, 1898, 840–41; Roosevelt to his sisters Corinne and to Anna, June 12, 1898, Morison, *Letters* 2: 839.

69 **In the battle:** Risen, *The Crowded Hour*, 214; Roosevelt to Douglas Robinson, July 19, 1898, Morison, *Letters* 2: 854–55; Roosevelt to Lodge, July 31, 1898, Morison, *Letters* 2: 861–62.

69 **"The first police chief":** Zacks, *Island of Vice*, 358, 364–65.

69 **"Every thief":** Nathan Miller, *Theodore Roosevelt: A Life*, 311, citing Chauncey Depew of the New York Central Railroad.

69 **In early October:** "Cheer for Roosevelt," *New York Times*, October 6, 1898, 1–2; "Big Rally Opens Campaign," *New York Tribune*, October 6, 1898, 1–2.

70 **Platt made a list:** Description of the back and forth in Platt, *Autobiography*, 538; Jean Strouse, *Morgan: American Financier*, 436.

70 **On Sunday:** Description of the night in "Roosevelt a Housebreaker," *New York Tribune*, Tuesday, January 3, 1899, 1.

70 **The next morning:** "Inauguration at Albany," *New York Tribune*, Tuesday, January 3, 1899, 1.

70 **"Under no form":** "Gov. Roosevelt Is Inaugurated," *New York Times*, January 3, 1899, 1.

70 **The next day:** Morris, *The Rise of Theodore Roosevelt*, 728.

71 **"Invisible empire":** Theodore Roosevelt, *The Autobiography of Theodore Roosevelt*, 154; Morris, *The Rise of Theodore Roosevelt*, 729.

71 **By the end:** William Henry Harbaugh, *Power and Responsibility: The Life and Times of Theodore Roosevelt*, 121; Morris, *The Rise of Theodore Roosevelt*, 735.

71 **"Even things up":** Francis Leupp, *The Man Roosevelt: A Portrait Sketch*, 279.

71 **"I like Pierpont Morgan":** Roosevelt to Joseph Bucklin Bishop, March 22, 1900, Morison, *Letters* 2: 1238.

71 **"I had heard":** Roosevelt, *Autobiography*, 166–67.

71 **"As resolutely":** Roosevelt to Platt, Morison, *Letters* 2: 1005.

71 **"Howling like mad":** Kathleen Dalton, *Theodore Roosevelt: A Strenuous Life*, 185, citing Roosevelt to John Coyle, May 15, 1899, Morison rejected letters, Theodore Roosevelt Collection, Harvard College Library.

71 **So did railways:** Alexander Dana Noyes, *Forty Years of American Finance*, 290.

72 **President McKinley touted:** George Mowry, *The Era of Theodore Roosevelt, 1900–1912*, 122.

72 **"Would you mind":** Roosevelt to Charles Frederick Scott, August 15, 1899, Morison, *Letters* 2: 1060.

72 **By the time:** Harbaugh, *Power and Responsibility*, 123; Roosevelt to Kohlsaat, August 7, 1899, Morison, *Letters* 2: 1045; Roosevelt to Root asking to get opinion of Attorney General Griggs, Morison, *Letters* 2: 1105.

72 **"I can't do":** Brands, *T.R.: The Last Romantic*, 389.

73 **"All the big-monied interests":** Roosevelt to Lodge, February 3, 1900, Morison, *Letters* 2: 1166.

73 **"Irksome, wearisome place":** February 2, 1900, letter to Anna Roosevelt Cowles, Morison, *Letters* 2: 1159.

73 **Professor of history:** Joseph Bucklin Bishop, *Theodore Roosevelt and His Time: Shown in His Own Letters*, 136.

73 **"I think you are":** Bishop, *Theodore Roosevelt and His Time*, 137.

73 **"He came down":** John Hay to Henry White, June 15, 1900, Thayer, *Life and Letters of John Hay* 2: 342; Miller, *Theodore Roosevelt*, 339; Henry Pringle, *Theodore Roosevelt: A Biography*, 170.

73 **"You will see":** Sylvia Jukes Morris, *Edith Kermit Roosevelt*, 204; Frederick Wood, *Roosevelt as We Knew Him*, 72–75.

74 **"T. R.'s name":** Nicholas Butler, *Across the Busy Years*, 227.

74 **For a while:** Corinne Roosevelt Robinson, *My Brother Theodore Roosevelt*, 196. She identifies the book as the *History of Josephus*.

74 **On Monday:** description from Butler, *Across the Busy Years*, 231–35; Roosevelt's speech, Morris, *The Rise of Theodore Roosevelt*, 764.

74 **Nearly fifteen thousand:** Description of nomination is from several articles in *Evening World*, June 21, 1900.

75 **The only female delegate:** "Several Women Delegates," *St. Louis Post Dispatch*, June 16, 1900, 3.

76 **"Your duty":** Merry, *President McKinley*, 444, citing Hanna letter to McKinley, June 24, 1900.

76 **In October:** Albert Bigelow Paine, *George Fisher Baker: A Biography* (New York: The Knickerbocker Press, 1920), cited in Vincent Carosso Papers, The Pierpont Morgan Library.

76 **"You know how difficult":** Mellen to Coster, February 21, Confidential letter, Vincent Carosso Papers, The Pierpont Morgan Library.

76　**When a friend:** The friend was the banker George Fisher Baker. The quote comes from Paine, *George Fisher Baker.*

76–77　**Chicago at the turn:** Details from "Economic Geography," Electronic Encyclopedia of Chicago, Chicago Historical Society, www.encyclopedia .chicagohistory.org/pages/409.html.

CHAPTER 6: BUY AT ANY PRICE

78　**The wedding was:** Details of the ceremony and reception drawn from Jean Strouse, *Morgan: American Financier,* and accounts in "Miss Morgan's Wedding," *New York Times,* November 16, 1900; "Street Filled by the Curious," *Cincinnati Enquirer,* November 16, 1901, 7; "Wedding of Wealth," *Boston Globe,* November 16, 1900, 5.

78　**Alencon Lace:** "Alencon Lace: Intangible Cultural Heritage," Unesco, ich.unesco.org/en/RL/craftsmanship-of-alencon-needle-lace-making -00438.

78　**Her father bought:** Herbert L. Satterlee, *J. Pierpont Morgan, 1837–1913,* 342, 344.

79　**"I tried to":** Details of Morgan's beneficence from Jean Strouse, *Morgan: American Financier,* 388–90.

79　**Morgan invited:** "Wedding of Wealth," *Boston Globe.*

79　**The guests:** "Miss Morgan's Wedding," *New York Times*; "Flowers Nod Glad Welcome to This Bride," *New York Press,* November 16, 1900, Satterlee scrapbook, Pierpont Morgan Papers, The Pierpont Morgan Library.

79　**He sent Louisa:** Albro Martin, *James J. Hill and the Opening of the Northwest,* 463.

79　**Edith may have:** The *New York Times* ("Miss Morgan's Wedding,") includes Edith on the guest list, but Sylvia Jukes Morris (*Edith Kermit Roosevelt*) makes no mention of her attending, nor do any other contemporaneous accounts.

80　**"My dear Mr. Morgan":** Roosevelt to Morgan, December 5, 1900, Theodore Roosevelt Papers, Library of Congress.

80　**"Represents an effort":** Roosevelt to Root, December 5, 1900, Theodore Roosevelt Papers, Library of Congress.

80　**Located on Fifth Avenue:** Details from "In New Quarters," *New York Sun,* March 5, 1881; 1901 Union League Club Annual Report; Henry Bellows, *Union League Club History*; "Lost Union League Clubhouse," daytoninman hattan.com.

80   **Morgan's first father-in-law:** Jonathan Sturges, father of Morgan's first wife, Amelia Sturges

81   **Gross national product:** Simon Kuznets, *Capital in the American Economy: Its Formation and Financing* (Princeton, NJ: Princeton University Press, 1961), 557–58.

81   **"Vexatious" legislation:** "The Financial Situation," *New York Sun*, December 31, 1900, 7.

81   **More than twelve hundred:** Lewis L. Gould, *Reform and Regulation: American Politics from Roosevelt to Wilson*, 16.

81   **It was responsible:** Strouse, *Morgan: American Financier*, 404; employment number, Craig Phelan, *Divided Loyalties: The Public and Private Life of Labor Leader John Mitchell*, 135; Philip S. Forner, *History of the Labor Movement in the United States*, 78.

81   **Orders came from:** Alexander Dana Noyes, *The Market Place: Reminiscences of a Financial Editor*, 191.

81   **So many checks:** John Winkler, *Morgan the Magnificent*, 197–98.

81   **"Mr. Morgan's power":** "J. Pierpont Morgan Dazzles Mr. McKinley," *The World*, March 9, 1901.

81   **"Pierpont Morgan is":** Henry Adams to Elizabeth Cameron, February 11, 1901, *Letters of Henry Adams*, vol. 5: 199.

81   **"America is good enough":** Mark Sullivan, *Our Times: The United States, 1900–1925*, vol. 2: 355 citing *The Commoner*, owned by William Jennings Bryan.

81   **George Perkins:** Details of Morgan's hiring of Perkins in John Garraty, *Right-Hand Man*, 83–89; Strouse, *Morgan: American Financier*, 409–11; Description of his role at the firm in Robert H. Wiebe, *The Search for Order, 1877–1920*, 182.

82   **"I began life":** Garraty, *Right-Hand Man*, 158.

82   **Telegram of congratulations:** Roosevelt to Perkins, March 11, 1901, Theodore Roosevelt Papers, Library of Congress.

83   **"It was the only":** Joseph Pyle, *The Life of James Hill* 2: 122: Larry Haeg, *Harriman v. Hill: Wall Street's Great Railroad War*, 88–89.

83   **Harriman had bid:** George Kennan, *E. H. Harriman: Railroad Czar*, vol. 1: 287; Haeg, *Harriman v. Hill*, 77–78.

83   **"Grave mistake":** Haeg, *Harriman v. Hill*, 64, citing Cyrus Adler, *Jacob H. Schiff, His Life and Letters* (New York: Doubleday, Doran and Co., 1928), vol. 1: 105.

83   **Morgan boarded:** "J. Pierpont Morgan Sails," *New York Times*, April 4, 1901, 8; "Morgan Sails for Europe," *New York Tribune*, April 4, 1901, 6.

83 **Harriman and Schiff made:** Details of the evening from Kennan, *E. H. Harriman*, 296–97; Haeg, *Harriman v. Hill*, 106–07.

84 **"Papa has had":** Sunday, April 14, entry in Mary Hill's diary, Mary T. Hill Papers, Minnesota Historical Society.

84 **"Fast time":** "Hill Hurries Home," *Minneapolis Journal*, April 19, 1901, 6; "Ride of JJ Hill," *Minneapolis Journal*, April 22, 1901, 6.

85 **"Is it Louisa":** Daniel Lamont in New York to Hill, James J. Hill Papers, Minnesota Historical Society.

85 **"A stream of":** Alexander Dana Noyes, *Forty Years of American Finance*, 300–01.

85 **Bacon and the Northern Pacific:** Haeg, *Harriman v. Hill*, 135, 152.

85 **"The reckoning comes":** Noyes, *American Finance*, 303–04.

85 **Visitors "including a multitude":** Details of the move and the exuberance from "Stock Exchange Goodbye," *New York Sun*, April 27, 1901, 10; "Moving Day on Exchange," *New York Tribune*, April 28, 1901, 6; New York Stock Exchange Brief Chronology; "Exciting Scenes in the Stock Exchange," *New York Times*, May 2, 1901.

86 **Schiff told him everything:** Some details of the meetings and communications that Friday and Saturday differ slightly. This account draws mostly from Vincent P. Carosso Papers, The Pierpont Morgan Library; Strouse, *Morgan: American Financier*; and Haeg, *Harriman v. Hill*. For this first part, specifically: Carosso, *The Morgans: Private International Bankers, 1854–1913*, 475; Strouse, 422; Haeg, 154–58.

86 **"They actually had":** Martin, *James J. Hill*, 501, citing letter to Lord Mount Stephen in London.

87 **Codenamed Flitch:** Carosso, *The Morgans*, 436; other details of the telegram and Morgan's response from Strouse, *Morgan: American Financier*, 423; Haeg, *Harriman v. Hill*, 165; Winkler, *Morgan the Magnificent*, 189.

87 **Schiff would:** Haeg, *Harriman v. Hill*, 158–59; Maury Klein, *The Life and Legend of E. H. Harriman*, 231.

87 **Harriman called:** All accounts agree on the call but offer different explanations for Schiff's decision not to place Harriman's order.

87 **"We are letting them":** Hill to Lord Mount Stephan, May 8, 1901. Typed correspondence, James J. Hill Papers, Minnesota Historical Society.

88 **"Damn it":** George Baker biography in Vincent Carosso Papers, The Pierpont Morgan Library.

88 **Bacon contacted:** Morgan Telegrams, Vincent Carosso Papers, The Pierpont Morgan Library.

88   **On Monday May 6:** Description of the panic from Haeg, *Harriman v. Hill*, 170–72, 184; Ron Chernow, *The House of Morgan: An American Banking Dynasty and the Rise of Modern Finance*, 92–93; Winkler, *Morgan the Magnificent*, 161; Frederick Lewis Allen, *The Great Pierpont Morgan*, 197; Ray Stannard Baker, "The Great 'Northern Pacific Deal,'" *Collier's Weekly*; "Northern Pacific Leads Bear and Bull Panic," *St. Paul Globe*, May 9, 1901; "Market Falls and Panic Soon Reigns," *New York Times*, May 10, 1901; "Swirling Maelstrom of Speculation," *New York Herald*, May 10, 1901; "The Northern Pacific Settlements Effected," *New York Times*, May 11, 1901; *Commercial and Financial Chronicle*, May 11 and May 18, 1901.

88   **Air was thick:** "Wall Street Features Not on the Ticker," *Chicago Tribune*, May 9, 190, 4.

89   **Dropped four hundred dollars:** Chernow, *The House of Morgan*, 92.

89   **The value of:** Andrew Sinclair, *Corsair: The Life of J. Pierpont Morgan*, 135.

89   **Morgan had been enjoying:** Allen, *The Great Pierpont Morgan*, 172; Strouse, *Morgan: American Financier*, 417.

89   **He remained in contact:** "Morgan to Sail Next Wednesday; Leaves on Teutonic for This City, He Says in Paris—in Angry Mood," *New York Evening World*, May 11, 1901, 3; "Mr. Morgan Is Silent," *New York Times*, May 12, 1901, 3; Strouse, *Morgan: American Financier*, xi.

89   **A good part:** Noyes, *American Finance*, 307.

89   **"The spell was broken":** *Commercial and Financial Chronicle*, May 11, 1901.

90   **In a century:** Chernow, *The House of Morgan*, 92.

90   **In New York:** Details and Hill quotes from "Wall Street Operations A Notorious Scandal throughout the Nation, Says James J. Hill," *New York Herald*, May 19, 1901, James J. Hill Papers, Minnesota Historical Society.

90   **Both he:** "Wall St. Smiles Again," *New York Sun*, May 11, 1901; "His Own Treatment for Mr. Hill," *New York Herald*, May 13, 1901.

90   **"We appreciate":** Carosso, *The Morgans*, 477, citing Private Telegrams, May 18, 1901.

91   **"Taken the veil":** Roosevelt to Leonard Wood, March 27, 1901, Morison, *Letters*, 3: 30–31.

91   **Eighty-nine acres:** Details of Sagamore Hill from Juliet Frey, ed. "Theodore Roosevelt and his Sagamore Hill Home," National Park Service, 2007.

91   **"I am rather ashamed":** Roosevelt to Taft, April 26, 1901, Morison, *Letters*, 3: 68–69.

91   **The Metropolitan Club:** metropolitanclubnyc.org.

91   **"uniform methods":** Martin, *James J. Hill*, 504–06.

91 **"Mr. Morgan":** Herbert L. Satterlee, *J. Pierpont Morgan: An Intimate Portrait*, 360.

92 **"We will put":** Martin, *James J. Hill*, 508.

92 **"Freedom from":** Balthasar Henry Meyer, "A History of the Northern Securities Case," 239.

92 **Morgan invited Hill:** Haeg, *Harriman vs. Hill*, 227–29.

92 **"I would not like":** William Roscoe Thayer, *Theodore Roosevelt: An Intimate Biography*, 156–57, quoting Charles Washburn, a college friend of Roosevelt's.

92 **"I rather be":** Nicholas Murray Butler, *Across the Busy Years*, 312–13.

93 **Morgan brushed off:** Strouse, *Morgan: American Financier*, 427.

93 **Complicating matters:** John Moody, *The Masters of Capital: A Chronicle of Wall Street*, 345; James Brown Scott, *Life and Letters of Robert Bacon*, 102.

93 **On the night:** Baker, "The Great 'Northern Pacific Deal'"; Morris, *Theodore Rex*, 59–60.

93 **Morgan signed:** *New York World*, November 14, 1901.

93 **Hill gave:** Mary Hill diary, Wednesday, November 13, 1901. Mary T. Hill Papers, Minnesota Historical Society.

93 **"Smithy very":** James J. Hill Papers, Minnesota Historical Society.

CHAPTER 7: THE STATE OF THE UNION

94 **Their guinea pig:** Information about the Roosevelt family pets from National Park Service, www.nps.gov/thrb/learn/historyculture/the-roosevelt-pets.htm.

94 **"the wildest":** Irwin Hoover, excerpt of memoir, *Forty-two Years in the White House*, in "The Roosevelts Move Into the White House, 1901," EyeWitness to History, www.eyewitnesstohistory.com (2003).

94 **Victorian relic:** James Goode, *The White House Album: The Theodore Roosevelt Years*, White House Historical Association; "Victorian Ornamentation: 1873–1901," www.whitehousemuseum.org/special/renovation-1873.htm; "Theodore Roosevelt Renovation: 1902," www.whitehousemuseum.org/special/renovation-1902.htm; Nathan Miller, *Theodore Roosevelt: A Life*, 359.

94 **"Edie says":** William Allen White, *The Autobiography of William Allen White*, 176.

94 **Charles McKim:** The architect also designed Morgan's Library.

94 **Roosevelt settled:** William Allen White, *Masks in a Pageant*, 310; Miller, 426–27.

95   **Among his early:** Morris, *Theodore Rex*, 52.

95   **"I play bear":** Theodore Roosevelt to Alice Roosevelt, November 29, 1901. *The Letters of Theodore Roosevelt*, ed. Morison, vol. 3: 203.

95   **The Roosevelts lived:** White, *Autobiography*, 176.

95   **Roosevelt said:** Aida Donald, *Lion in the White House: A Life of Theodore Roosevelt*, 169.

95   **"Never mind that":** Weldon Fawcett, "President Roosevelt at Work," *Lesley's Weekly*, undated. Theodore Roosevelt Papers: Scrapbooks, 1895–1910; Personal; vol. 1, Library of Congress.

95   **"I want him":** Roosevelt to Austin Wadsworth, September 14, 1901; Roosevelt to George Bleistein, October 29, 1901, Theodore Roosevelt Papers, Library of Congress.

96   **Roosevelt protested:** "Roosevelt Armed in His Daily Rides with the Revolver That He Carried at San Juan," May 30, 1901, unidentified clipping in Theodore Roosevelt Papers: Scrapbooks, 1895–1910; vol. 1, 1901, Library of Congress.

96   **He ordered:** Maureen Dowd, "The Ultimate Tennis Club," publication unidentified, in Theodore Roosevelt Collection, Harvard College Library.

97   **"He has made":** John Hay to Henry Adams, September 19, 1901, Tyler Dennett, *John Hay: From Poetry to Politics* (Dodd, Mead & Company, 1934), 343.

97   **"A young fellow":** John Hay to Lady Jeune, September 14, 1901, William Roscoe Thayer, *The Life and Letters and Diary of John Hay* 2: 266.

97   **Roosevelt's personal barber:** Morison, *Letters* 3: 401 provides the name of the barber, Delaney.

98   **Roosevelt had to mediate:** This relies on the characterization of Roosevelt in Mowry, 114. He calls Roosevelt "a skillful broker of the possible."

98   **"President Roosevelt":** "Mr. Roosevelt a Changed Man," *New York Times*, September 26, 1901.

98   **"Sit back":** Roosevelt to Douglas Robinson, October 17 1901, Morison, *Letters* 3: 177.

99   **"Arguing like":** Roosevelt to Douglas Robinson, October 4, 1901; Morison, *Letters* 3: 159–60.

99   **"Knowledge of the facts":** Roosevelt's First Annual Message, December 3, 1901.

99   **"Accept the publication":** Roosevelt to Douglas Robinson, October 4, 1901; Morison, *Letters* 3: 159–60

99   **James Hill invited:** Note from George Cortelyou to James Hill, October 29, 1901, James J. Hill Papers, Minnesota Historical Society.

99 **"Talk over various matters":** Roosevelt to Edward Harriman, November 12, 1901, Theodore Roosevelt Collection, Library of Congress.

99 **"I have been":** Mark Hanna to Roosevelt, November 10, 1901. Theodore Roosevelt Papers, Library of Congress.

100 **"You have no":** Roosevelt to Paul Dana, November 18, 1901. Morison, *Letters* 3: 200.

101 **"Knox was just":** Details from "Kate Carew Has a Spirited Chat with the Attorney General about His Hobbies, His Law, His Horses, Hunting, and Fishing," *The World*, March 20, 1904: Morris, *Theodore Rex*, 62; L. A. Coolidge, "Attorney General Knox, Lawyer," *McClure's* 19 (May 1902), 473.

101 **"One of our":** Edward G. Lowry, *Washington Close-Ups*, 194.

101 **Knox had come:** Details from Albert Beveridge, "Philander Chase Knox, American Lawyer, Patriot, Statesman," *Pennsylvania Magazine of History and Biography* XLVII, no. 2 (1923); J. B. Morrow, "Talks with Big Ones," *Los Angeles Times*, October 14, 1906; "Secretary Knox and the Steel Trust," *New York American*, January 12, 1912.

101 **Knox helped:** David Cannadine, *Mellon: An American Life* (New York: Vintage Books, 2008), 106.

102 **Sixteen of them:** Details of the flood's aftermath from David McCullough, *The Johnstown Flood* (New York: Simon & Schuster, 1968), 258, 264.

102 **Early in the summer:** Account of the Homestead strike, and Knox's role in particular, from Paul Krause, *The Battle for Homestead, 1880–1892*, 3, 26–37, 310; Howard Zinn, *A People's History of the United States*, 277, David Nasaw, *Andrew Carnegie*, 428–48.

103 **Gatling guns:** *Official Documents, Comprising the Department and Other Reports Made to the Governor, Senate and House of Representatives of Pennsylvania*, 1892, 116–17.

103 **On July 23:** Details from Paul Avrich and Karen Avrich, *Sasha and Emma: The Anarchist Odyssey of Alexander Berkman and Emma Goldman* (Cambridge, MA: Belknap Press, 2012), 65–67.

104 **"This case will":** Krause, *Battle for Homestead*, 271, citing *Pittsburgh Dispatch*, October 1, 1892.

104 **"Veritable little giant":** "Carnegie Says He Recommended Knox," *New York Tribune*, January 12, 1912; Krause, *Battle for Homestead*, 272; Ferdinand Lundberg, *America's 60 Families*, 64.

104 **"Dangerous conspiracies":** William Horner, *Ohio's Kingmaker: Mark Hanna, Man and Myth*, 270–71.

104 **"Distinguished practitioner":** Larry Haeg, *Harriman vs. Hill: Wall Street's Great Railroad War*, 105, citing "What He Will Be There for," *New York Evening World*, March 30, 1901, 6.

105 **"Playmate":** Morris, *Theodore Rex*, 61–62.

105 **As a lawyer:** Philip C. Jessup, *Elihu Root*, vol. 1, 184.

105 **"I feel like":** Ibid., 222.

105 **Athletic and wiry:** Description from Walter Wellman, "Elihu Root: A Character Sketch."

106 **Roosevelt said that:** Roosevelt to Nicholas Murray Butler, August 29, 1903, Morison, *Letters* 3: 580–81.

106 **Many found:** "Senate and House Organized Yesterday" and "Desks Loaded with Floral Tributes," *New York Times*, December 3, 1901.

106 **Just after noon:** Morris, *Theodore Rex*, 70–71; 1901 Annual Message of the President, Office of the Historian, Department of State.

107 **Few of the men:** Walter Wellman, "All Praise Message," *Chicago Record-Herald*, December 3, 1901, in Theodore Roosevelt Papers: Scrapbooks, 1895–1910; Personal; vol. 1, Library of Congress

109 **"More devoted to business":** "The President's Message," *Salt Lake Tribune*, December 4, 1901, 4.

109 **"The young":** "Message Shows Hand of Master," *Chicago Daily Tribune*, December 4, 1901, 1.

109 **"Had dipped":** "Washington Comment on the Message," *New York Times*, December 4, 1901.

109 **"Conservative and":** "The Message," *Inter-Ocean*, December 4, 1901, 6.

110 **"This is not":** Mark Sullivan, *Our Times: The United States, 1900–1925*, vol. 2. 413.

110 **"It is desirable":** Philander Knox to Roosevelt, December 11, 1902, Theodore Roosevelt Papers, Library of Congress.

CHAPTER 8: RIVAL OPERATORS

111 **Some eighteen thousand:** The miles of track that Northern Securities controlled varies slightly by source. The company itself claims almost twenty thousand miles in corporate filings and nineteen thousand in court filings. Larry Haeg, *Harriman vs. Hill: Wall Street's Great Railroad War*, 300, cites an independent estimate of the three lines that excludes side and double tracks and comes to eighteen thousand miles.

111 **"To profit":** Theodore Roosevelt, *The Autobiography of Theodore Roosevelt*, 235.

112 **"The Commission":** Richard Olney to Charles E. Perkins, December 28, 1892, cited in Daniel Carpenter and David A. Moss, eds. *Preventing*

Regulatory Capture: Special Interest Influence and How to Limit It (Cambridge University Press, 2013), 6.

112 **Legal advice:** "Richard Olney," Clarence Darrow Digital Collection, University of Minnesota Law Library, moses.law.umn.edu/darrow/photo .php?pid=79.

112 **If he had been:** Analysis of Olney's stance from William Letwin, *Law and Economic Policy in America*, 117–22.

112 **"I have taken":** Richard Olney to his secretary, the day after the Supreme Court defeat, cited in Letwin, *Law and Economic Policy*, 121.

112 **"In such a condition":** Harlan dissent, United States v. E.C. Knight Company (no. 675). Decided January 1, 1895.

113 **"These views are submitted":** Philander Knox Memo to President Roosevelt, February 10, 1902, Philander Knox Papers, Library of Congress.

113 **"If you instruct me":** Morris, *Theodore Rex*, 89, citing Walter Wellman, "All Praise Message," *Chicago Record-Herald*, March 16, 1904.

113 **"It should be":** "Ripple in Wall Street," *Minneapolis Journal*, November 18, 1901, 7.

113 **The lawyer sent:** The message in code read "The occurring benignant dwindle and no clump justiday by sewers conclusible that can be construed into an amazement in watered of tragedy liable." James J. Hill Papers, Minnesota Historical Society.

114 **Legislators talked:** "Van Sant's Stand Widely Discussed," *Minneapolis Journal*, November 19, 1901, 1; "Morganizing the North Pacific," *Baltimore Sun*, November 14, 1901, 4.

114 **"All I ask":** Hill statement to *St. Paul Globe*, which he owned, December 22, 1901, James J. Hill Papers, Minnesota Historical Society.

114 **"You should spend" and "Such a man":** December 7 and 9, 1901 communication between James Hill to L. W. Hill, James J. Hill Papers, Minnesota Historical Society.

114 **"Remember that":** "President Hill Talks at Fargo," *Duluth Evening Herald*, January 10, 1902.

114 **A ferocious storm:** Details of storm, "City Buried under Snow," *New York Times*, February 18, 1902. Details of sales from newspaper advertisements.

115 **Three and a half million:** Summary of Vital Statistics, City of New York, 2010. New York City Department of Mental Health and Hygiene, Table P1, 4, http://www.nyc.gov/html/records/pdf/govpub/655ias_2010_final_population_ &_mortality.pdf.

115   **The New York:** "Market Movement," *New York Times*, February 18, 1902.

115   **Morgan's U.S. Steel Company:** "The Steel Trust Meeting," *New York Times*, February 18, 1902.

115   **Morgan had been:** Vincent Carosso Papers, in Pierpont Morgan Papers, The Pierpont Morgan Library.

116   **"All well here":** James J. Hill Papers, Minnesota Historical Society.

116   **In Washington:** Details of the president's breakfast with Mark Hanna and his interest in Northern Securities stock from Martin, *James J. Hill and the Opening of the Northwest*, 514–15; Morris, *Theodore Rex*, 89; John A. Garraty, *Right-Hand Man: The Life of George W. Perkins*, 158.

116   **Morgan was:** Morgan's reaction to the news has been variously accounted in Allen, *The Great Pierpont Morgan*, 176; John K. Winkler, *Morgan the Magnificent: The Life of J. Pierpont Morgan, 1837–1913*, 220–22; Mark Sullivan, *Our Times: The United States, 1900–1925*, vol. 2, 412–13.

117   **"Appalled dismay":** Sullivan, *Our Times*, vol. 2, 412.

117   **Roosevelt should have:** Sullivan, *Our Times*, vol. 2, 412–413; Henry Adams to Elizabeth Cameron, February 24, *Letters of Henry Adams*, ed. J. C. Levenson et al., 346–47.

117   **"Lunatic":** Winkler, *Morgan the Magnificent*, 222.

117   **The dinner:** "President's Action Startles Wall Street," *New York Times*, February 21, 1902.

117   **Hanna got the news:** Martin, *James J. Hill*, 514.

118   **"An idiotic":** J. J. Jusserand, *What Me Befell: The Reminiscences of J. J. Jusserand* (Kindle edition).

118   **"We do not":** "Big Railroads in Merger Suit," *Evening World*, February 21, 1902.

118   **"The interests of":** "Duty Called Roosevelt," a *New York Times* editorial reprinted in *Minneapolis Journal*, February 21, 1902, 1.

118   **James Hill was:** Haeg, *Harriman vs. Hill*, 250, 253–54; "Federal Fight on Merger," *New York Times*, February 21, 1902; Letters from James J. Hill Papers, Minnesota Historical Society; "If they do" in "Hill Talks Fight," *Minneapolis Journal*, February 21, 1902.

118   **"He detests me":** Jusserand, *What Me Befell* (Kindle edition).

118   **The men who:** Details on Wall Street reaction from "President's Action Startles Wall Street," *New York Times*, February 21, 1902; *The Literary Digest*, XXIV, no. 9, March 1, 1902, 277–78; "Market Demoralized," *New York Times*, February 21, 1902; "Merger Arouses Federal Lion," *Minneapolis Journal*,

February 20, 1902, 2; "Knox Suit Hurts Stocks," *New York Tribune*, February 21, 1902.

119 **"There is no":** James Frances Burke, "Philander Chase Knox," *American Bar Association Journal* 7, no. 11 (November 1921): 621–23; Morris, *Theodore Rex*, 90.

119 **Two-hour ride:** "At the White House," February 20, 1902 in Theodore Roosevelt Papers: Scrapbooks; vol. 2, Library of Congress.

119 **Morgan dispatched:** There are many accounts of these few days and many slight variations among them, almost all concerning the order of events. The timing of Perkins's meeting with the president and with Hanna are confirmed by Morison's chronology (vol. 4, appendix II) and newspaper accounts ("Merger Case Discussed with President," *Washington Times*, February 22, 1902), though it differs from Martin, *James J. Hill*, 514–15.

120 **He had "consulted":** Martin, *James J. Hill*, 515.

120 **"I'm sorry for Hill":** William Henry Harbaugh, *Power and Responsibility: The Life and Times of Theodore Roosevelt*, 160.

120 **Morgan, who was:** The timing—though not the substance—of the Corsair dinner and Morgan's private meeting with Roosevelt also varies across accounts. This one relies Morison's chronology, notes from Henry F. Pringle (*Theodore Roosevelt: A Biography*, 1931,) the contemporaneous letters of Henry Adams, and newspaper accounts (including "City Isolated by Ravages of Storm," *Washington Times*, February 22, 1902). Gerald Helferich (*An Unlikely Trust: Theodore Roosevelt, J. P. Morgan, and the Improbable Partnership That Remade American Business*, 2018) reviewed some of the same material and provides the same chronology.

120 **"in an ulcerated":** Henry Adams to Elizabeth Cameron, February 23, 1902, Levenson, *Letters of Henry Adams* 5: 345.

120 **Dinner was:** Details from "Millionaires Dine," *Washington Times*, February 23, 1902, 2; Balthasar Meyer, "A History of the Northern Securities Case," 240.

120 **Two months earlier:** "Depew Gives a Farewell Dinner," *Philadelphia Inquirer*, December 8, 1901.

120 **"the whole party":** Henry Adams to Elizabeth Cameron, February 24, 1901, Levenson, *Letters of Henry Adams* 5: 346–47.

120 **At ten o'clock:** Morris, *Theodore Rex*, 90–91; Adams writes that the president called and the party had to persuade Morgan to accept the invitation. The *New York Tribune* provides the time of the call but reports that Depew initiated the meeting.

121 **"With frank horror"**: Roosevelt to Cecil Spring Rice, July 3, 1901, Morison, *Letters* 21 108.

121 **"An awful blow:** Henry Adams letter to Elizabeth Cameron, February 24, 1902; Levenson, *Letters of Henry Adams*, 346–47.

121 **"Not a word"**: "Morgan at White House," *New York Tribune*, February 24, 1902.

121 **The next morning:** Jean Strouse, *Morgan: American Financier* 440, notes that Morgan was accompanied by Senators Hanna and Depew.

121 **He demanded:** Joseph Bucklin Bishop, *Theodore Roosevelt and His Time: Shown in His Own Letters*, vol. 1: 184–85. Bishop's retelling of the meeting is based on Roosevelt's recollection and wasn't made public at the time. In September 1902, a paper reported, without identifying a source, that Roosevelt had told Morgan: "I am neither a bull nor a bear in Morgan stock. I am President of the United States, and am sworn to execute the law." The quote was first published in "Roosevelt Defies Morgan; Will Enforce Trust Law," *Inter-Ocean*, September 29, 1902, 1, and was widely reprinted.

122 **"Theodore laughs"**: Henry Adams letter to Elizabeth Cameron, February 24, 1902; Levenson, *Letters of Henry Adams*, 346–47.

122 **He wrote:** Winkler, *Morgan the Magnificent*, 222.

122 **"Roosevelt was anything"**: William Lawrence, *Memoir of John Pierpont Morgan*, 34–35.

122 **Morgan entered:** "Minnesota Loses Merger Case," *Washington Times*, February 25, 1902, 4.

123 **"As the big"**: Roosevelt to Nicholas Murray Butler, February 1, 1902. Theodore Roosevelt Papers, Library of Congress.

123 **Two days later:** "Meets Industries' Captains," *New York Tribune*, February 27, 1902, 1.

123 **"I am a little"**: Roosevelt to Paul Dana, editor of *Sun*, March 3, 1902, Theodore Roosevelt Papers, Library of Congress.

124 **"Well, Mr. President"**: Morris, *Theodore Rex*, 92; "Secretary Knox and the Steel Trust," *New York American*, January 12, 1912, in Knox clippings, Library of Congress.

124 **At five:** Details from "Merger Papers Filed," *St. Paul Globe*, March 11, 1902, 1 and 3; Letwin, *Law and Economic Policy*, 213 and 215, for Knox's plans.

124 **"The Northern Securities Company"**: "Railroad Combination Attacked in Courts," *New York Times*, March 11, 1902.

124 **"It seems really hard"**: James Hill to D. Willis James, March 8, 1902, James J. Hill Papers, Minnesota Historical Society.

125 **"When we get through"**: "Hill Will Force the Fighting," *Minneapolis Journal*, March 12, 1902, 1.

125 **Morgan and his family:** Details of the trip and the island from Herbert L. Satterlee, *J. Pierpont Morgan: An Intimate Portrait, 1837–1913*, 376–77; "Follow the Rich to Jekyll Island," *Washington Post*, March 27, 1983; Samuel M. Williams, "A Millionaire's Paradise," *Munsey's Magazine* 30, no. 5 (February 1904); "Men of Means, San Souci Markers," Historic Markers Across Georgia, www.waymarking.com/waymarks/WMGRC9_Men_of _Means_Sans_Souci_Jekyll_Island_GA.

125 **"A very questionable"**: Satterlee, *J. Pierpont Morgan*, 377.

125 **A disgruntled:** "Northern Securities Suit: JP Morgan to Testify Before the Commission To-day," *New York Times*, March 26, 1902; "Attitude of Northern Securities Witnesses," *New York Times*, March 28, 1902, "Morgan Defends Holding Company," *New York Times*, March 27, 1902; Morgan Testimony, Pierpont Morgan Papers, The Pierpont Morgan Library. Clippings from George W. Perkins Sr. Papers, Columbia University Libraries. *Landmark Briefs and Arguments of the Supreme Court of the United States: Constitutional Law*, eds. Philip B. Kurland and Gerhard Casper, 15, Northern Securities Co. v. United States, 193 US 197, Arlington, Virginia: University Publications of America, 1975. The judge ruled in favor of Northern Securities. Power turned out to be a dummy plaintiff and received a brief prison sentence.

127 **"Wall Street"**: Henry Adams to Elizabeth Cameron, April 6, 1902, Levenson, *Letters of Henry Adams* 5: 367 and April 7, 1902, in *Letters of Henry Adams, 1982–1918*, ed. Worthington Chauncey Ford, 385.

127 **"The lawyers say"**: George Perkins to Pierpont Morgan, May 12, 1902, George W. Perkins Sr. Papers, Columbia University Libraries.

127 **By then:** Details in this paragraph from Satterlee, *J. Pierpont Morgan*, 380–81.

128 **"Well-fitting"**: This and other details of his visit from *The Watchman and the Southron*, April 16, 1902; Anthony Chibarro, *The Charleston Exposition* (Charleston, SC: Arcadia, 2001).

128 **"Our astounding"**: "National Supervision of Great Combinations of Capital and Labor," April 9, 1902, *The Roosevelt Policy: Speeches, Letters and State Papers, Relating to Corporate Wealth and Closely Allied Topics*, ed. William Griffith, 25–27.

128 **"I want him"**: Roosevelt to Philander Knox, May 6, 1902, Morison, *Letters* 3: 258.

129 **"The most"**: *Pittsburg Dispatch*, July 5, 1902, included in www.theodore -roosevelt.com/trspeechescomplete.html.

CHAPTER 9: ANTHRACITE

133 **Tectonic plates:** W. E. Edmunds, *Coal in Pennsylvania*, 2nd ed. (2002); Pennsylvania Geological Survey, 4th ser., Educational Series 7, 8–9, 28; Thomas Dublin and Walter Licht, *The Face of Decline: The Pennsylvania Anthracite Region in the Twentieth Century*, 9; Donald L. Miller and Richard E. Sharpless, *The Kingdom of Coal: Work, Enterprise, and Ethnic Communities in the Mine Fields*, 5.

133 **Primrose or Peach Orchard:** Susan Campbell Bartoletti, *Growing Up in Coal Country*, 28.

133 **Squibs:** Thomas Foster, *Coal Miners' Pocketbook* (New York: McGraw-Hill, 1916), 677, 679.

134 **Firedamp:** Descriptions of gases and dangers, Miller and Sharpless, *Kingdom of Coal*, 105–09.

134 **In 1901:** All employment and injury figures, Report of the Bureau of Mines of the Department of Internal Affairs of Pennsylvania, 1900.

134 **More than one billion:** Peter Roberts, *Anthracite Coal Communities: A Study of the Demography, the Social, Educational and Moral Life of the Anthracite Regions*, 12.

134 **Anthracite made possible:** Details from Miller and Sharpless, *Kingdom of Coal*, 63, 65.

135 **Fake birth certificates:** Francis Nichols, "Children of the Coal Shadow," *McClure's* 20 (November 1902); Miller and Sharpless, *Kingdom of Coal*, 125.

135 **About seventy:** Roberts, *Anthracite Coal Communities*, 111; other sources cite figures ranging from 40 to 90 cents a day.

135 **A dozen eggs:** "A Miner's Story," *Independent*, 54 (1902) 1407–10.

137 **By 1874:** Robert J. Cornell, *The Anthracite Coal Strike of 1902*, 12.

137 **Men who:** Roberts, *Anthracite Coal Communities*, 127.

137 **"Mining the miners":** Robert Reynolds, "The Coal Kings Come to Judgment," *American Heritage* 11, no. 3 (April 1960).

137 **At least half:** Roberts, *Anthracite Coal Communities*, 20; fourteen languages, "Documents Relating to the Anthracite Strike of 1902," 154, Clarence Darrow

Collection, University of Minnesota Law Library, moses.law.umn.edu /darrow/trials.php?tid=12.

137 **Shopping there:** This account is from "A Miner's Story," *Independent*, 54 (1902) 1407–10.

138 **Explosive powder:** Details from Roberts, *Anthracite Coal Communities*, 133, 135.

138 **Many didn't:** Calculations of the average yearly salary for miners varies across sources. Philip S. Foner (*History of the Labor Movement in the United States*, vol. 3) says mean annual earnings were $375. Roosevelt's Commissioner of Labor reported the average to be about $560. The anonymous author of the piece in the *Independent* seems to have earned a bit more than that.

138 **They'd spend:** Details from "A Miner's Story," *Indepentent*, 54 (1902) 1407–10.

138 **John Mitchell first:** Two biographies of John Mitchell were invaluable in creating this account of his personal and professional lives, Craig Phelan, *Divided Loyalties: The Public and Private Life of Labor Leader John Mitchell*, and Elsie Glück, *John Mitchell, Miner: Labor's Bargain with the Gilded Age*.

140 **He cast his:** Glück, *John Mitchell*, 22.

141 **His first:** Miller and Sharpless, *Kingdom of Coal*, 248.

141 **"the most dangerous":** Quote from a U.S. district attorney, *The Autobiography of Mother Jones*, 51.

141 **Many of them:** Glück, *John Mitchell*, 78–79.

142 **"My personal interests":** Phelan, *Divided Loyalties*, 50, citing John Mitchell to John P. Reese, September 16, 1899, John Mitchell Papers, Cornell University Library.

142 **"Have just returned":** Phelan, *Divided Loyalties*, 54, citing John Mitchell to Robert Mitchell, February 23, 1899, John Mitchell Papers, Cornell University Library.

142 **Six railroads:** Miller and Sharpless, *Kingdom of Coal*, 243.

143 **"Cared nothing":** Phelan, *Divided Loyalties*, 101–02.

143 **"Extreme nervousness":** Phelan, *Divided Loyalties*, 53.

144 **"The coal you dig":** Glück, *John Mitchell*, 72.

144 **Hadn't received:** Glück, *John Mitchell*, 75; "Documents Relating to the Anthracite Strike of 1902," Clarence Darrow Collection, University of Minnesota Law Library, 47.

144 **At least:** Phelan, *Divided Loyalties*, 104.

144 **"Equal rights":** William Jennings Bryan speech August 8, 1900, at Democratic National Convention, voicesofdemocracy.umd.edu/william-jennings -bryan-imperialism-speech-text/.

144 **"I have had":** Roosevelt to Corinne Robinson, September 25, 1900, Morison, *Letters* 2: 1406.

145 **"That if the":** Phelan, *Divided Loyalties*, 113.

145 **Mitchell Day:** Glück, *John Mitchell*, 83.

145 **A national figure:** Details from Phelan, *Divided Loyalties*, 117–19, 121–22.

146 **A desperate note:** Cornell, *Anthracite Coal Strike of 1902*, 65–67.

146 **He suggested:** Phelan, *Divided Loyalties*, 131.

146 **But by summer:** Cornell, *Anthracite Coal Strike of 1902*, 70–71.

147 **As Mitchell recalled:** Philip S. Foner, *History of the Labor Movement in the United States*, vol. 3: 90, citing John Mitchell to Mark Hanna August 15, 1902, John Mitchell Papers.

147 **Ralph Easley:** Cornell, *Anthracite Coal Strike of 1902*, 79.

147 **Radicals accused:** Phelan, *Divided Loyalties*, 146.

147 **"I fear":** Michael Knies, "I Have Dreamed of It at Night," *Canal History and Technology Proceedings* (March 15, 2008).

147 **"We will endeavor":** George Baer letter to John Mitchell, February 18, 1902, "Documents Relating to the Anthracite Strike of 1902," Clarence Darrow Collection, University of Minnestoa Law Library, 3 5.

147 **"Always willing to meet":** George Baer telegram to John Mitchell, March 24, 1902, "Documents Relating to the Anthracite Strike of 1902," Clarence Darrow Collection, University of Minnestoa Law Library.

148 **A restaurant:** Knies, citing "Adjourned," *Scranton Times-Tribune*, April 29, 1902.

148 **"Anthracite mining":** John Mitchell telegram May 8; George Baer reply May 9, cited in "Documents Relating to the Anthracite Strike of 1902," Clarence Darrow Collection, University of Minnestoa Law Library 16.

148 **"I am of the":** John Mitchell to Mother Jones, May 10, 1902, cuexhibits.wrlc .org/exhibits/show/mother-jones-collection/letter-index/may10.

CHAPTER 10: ON STRIKE

149 **"Our boys":** "A Miner's Story," *Independent*, 1902.

149 **Playing golf:** Elsie Glück, *John Mitchell, Miner: Labor's Bargain with the Gilded Age*, 99.

149 **"Foolish and inconsiderate:** Quotes from coal executives, Robert J. Cornell, *The Anthracite Coal Strike of 1902*, 97 citing *New York Journal of Finance*, May 16, 1902 and *Philadelphia Public Ledger*, May 16, 1902.

149 **"These men":** "Report to the President of the Anthracite Coal Commission," 1902.

150 **Fourth generation:** Details of Baer from John Hepp, "George Frederick Baer," (working paper, Wilkes University, 2012).

150 **Pennsylvania prohibited:** Gustavus Myers, *History of the Great American Fortunes*, vol. 3, *Great Fortunes from Railroads*, 245.

150 **Five thousand:** Scott Connelly, "The Greatest Strike Ever," Spring 2010, Pennsylvania Center for the Book at Pennsylvania State University Libraries.

151 **"We are slaves":** Glück, *John Mitchell*, 102.

151 **Mother Jones:** Mary "Mother" Jones, *The Autobiography of Mother Jones*, 89.

151 **The men received:** Details about the Coal and Iron Police from Lance E. Metz, "The Role of Intimidation and Violence in the Great Anthracite Strike of 1902," in *The "Great Strike": Perspectives on the 1902 Anthracite Coal Strike*, Robert A. Janosov et al. eds. (Easton, PA: Canal History and Technology Press 2002), 47 and 52, citing *Allentown Morning Call*, June 4 and July 9, 1902.

151 **Miners who tried:** Details about the violence, Donald L. Miller and Richard E. Sharpless, *The Kingdom of Coal: Work, Enterprise, and Ethnic Communities in the Mine Fields*, 269.

151 **Charles McCann:** "Young Boy Shot at Wilkes-Barre," *Scranton Republic*, June 6, 1902.

152 **Effigy of Morgan:** "Effigy of Morgan Hanged by Strikers," *Evening World*, June 7, 1902.

152 **chose to not:** Allen, *The Great Pierpont Morgan*, 222–24.

152 **Avondale, where:** Miller and Sharpless, *Kingdom of Coal*, 110.

152 **Colliery No. 5:** Details from "Strikers to Meet Other Workingmen," *Allentown Morning Call*, June 18, 1902, 1.

152 **"I view with":** Cornell, *Anthracite Coal Strike of 1902*, 100, citing Mark Hanna to John Mitchell May 20, 1902.

153 **"One thing at":** Frank Julian Warne, "John Mitchell: The Labor Leader and the Man," *American Monthly Review of Reviews* 26, no. 154 (November 1902): 556–60.

153 **Ninety-six companies:** Robert A. Janosov et al, "The Great Strike," *Perspectives on the 1902 Anthracite Coal Strike*.

153 **"I will say"**: Joseph P. McKerns, "The Faces of John Mitchell" in *Perspectives*, 37, citing *Atlanta Constitution*, May 20, 1902.

153 **"On Johnny Mitchell's train"**: Songs and Ballads of the Anthracite Miners, Archive of Folk Song, Library of Congress.

154 **George Perkins:** Glück, *John Mitchell*, 105–06; Cornell, *Anthracite Coal Strike of 1902*, 104–05, citing a note in Cortelyou Papers, June 4, 1902 with Perkins message and Roosevelt's reply.

154 **"There is no":** Carroll Wright, "Report to the President on the Anthracite Coal Strike," *Bulletin of the Department of Labor* no. 43 (November 1902), 1165.

154 **The anthracite miners:** "Report to the President on the Anthracite Coal Strike," 1166–67.

155 **"We can help":** "Documents Relating to the Anthracite Strike of 1902," Clarence Darrow Collection, University of Minnesota Law Library, 38.

155 **"I like its tone":** Cornell, *Anthracite Coal Strike of 1902*, 110.

155 **advised him not:** Anita Torres Eitler, "Philander Chase Knox," 18–19 citing Roosevelt to Knox, June 28, 1902, and Note on manuscript of the Wright report in Theodore Roosevelt Papers, Library of Congress.

155 **Violence erupted:** This account from "Blood Spouting in Coal Regions," *Atlanta Constitution* July 31, 1902, 1; "Big Trouble at Shenandoah, *Pottsville Republican*, July 31, 1902, 1; "Guns Cowed Miners," *Philadelphia Times*, July 31, 1902; Front page stories of *Pottsville Republican* August 1 and 2; "More Light on Beddall Murder," *Scranton Tribune*, August 8, 1902, 1.

156 **"Bloodshed and riots":** "Report of the Adjutant General of Pennsylvania for the period between May 31, 1902 and December 31, 1903," 8.

156 **"All along the":** Stewart Cullin, *A Trooper's Narrative of Service in the Anthracite Coal Strike, 1902* (Philadelphia: George W. Jacobs, 1903), 24.

156 **The commissary bought:** All details from "Report of the Adjutant General."

157 **"I am fully":** Glück, *John Mitchell*, 112–13.

157 **"The rights":** A copy of George Baer's letter is in Theodore Roosevelt Collection, Harvard College Library; Mark Sullivan, *Our Times: The United States, 1900–1925*, vol. 2: 425–26.

157 **A financial disaster:** Margo L. Azzarelli and Marnie Azzarelli, *Labor Unrest in Scranton*, 97, estimates the coal companies were losing at least one million dollars a month.

157 **A group of:** Metz, "The Role of Intimidation and Violence," 56, citing *Allentown Morning Call*, August 27, 1902.

158 **He cruised:** Jean Strouse, *Morgan: American Financier*, 468.

158 **"the beginning":** "Morgan Back, Sets Wall Street on the Jump," *Evening World*, August 20, 1902, 3. Parkin was also president of the University of Toronto.

158 **He brought aboard:** Herbert L. Satterlee, *J. Pierpont Morgan: An Intimate Portrait, 1837–1913*, 387.

159 **"There's one thing":** "Morgan Holds Out No Hope to End Coal Strike," *Evening World*, August 20, 1.

159 **"We did hit":** Correspondence between George Perkins and Pierpont Morgan, June 2, June 23, July 30, 1902, George W. Perkins Sr. Papers, Columbia University Libraries.

160 **But when he:** Satterlee, *J. Pierpont Morgan*, 388.

160 **"What is the":** Roosevelt to Knox, August 21, 1902, Morison, *Letters* 3: 323. Morison notes that Knox replied they would have to wait for the Supreme Court ruling on Northern Securities. The Sherman Act was drawn too narrowly.

160 **The trusts:** "Necessity of establishing federal sovereignty over 'trusts,'" *The Roosevelt Policy Speeches, Letters and State Papers, Relating to Corporate Wealth and Closely Allied Topics*, ed. William Griffith, speech begins page 31.

160 **"All law must":** Address to mayor and citizens of Lynn, August 25, 1902, Complete Speeches and Addresses of Theodore Roosevelt, www.theodore -roosevelt.com/images/research/txtspeeches/346.txt.

160 **"favorite formula":** Roosevelt to Ray Stannard Baker, August 27, 1904, Theodore Roosevelt Papers, Library of Congress.

162 **Hanna arranged:** Craig Phelan, *Divided Loyalties*, 181–82.

CHAPTER 11: "CATASTROPHE IMPENDING"

163 **It was just:** Account from "President in Crash," *New York Sun*, September 4, 1902; "Looked in the Face of Death," *Boston Daily Globe*, September 4, 1902; "President Near Death," *New York Tribune* September 4, 1902 and "Roosevelt Is Injured, One Party Dead," *Chicago Tribune*, September 4, 1902; "As Told by President," *Boston Globe*, September 4, 1902, 5.

164 **"This is the most":** "Looked in the Face of Death."

164 **The Brotherhood:** E. P. Sargent, "A Short History of the Brotherhood of Locomotive Firemen," *Fifth Annual Report of the Commissioner of Labor* 1890, 40–41.

165 **"rugged virtues":** September 8, 1902, Chattanooga, Tennessee address in *The Roosevelt Policy: Speeches, Letters and State Papers, Relating to Corporate Wealth and Closely Allied Topics*, ed. William Griffith, 1: 67–74.

165 **Theodore shook:** "Grasped 8000 Hands," *Boston Herald*, September 16, 1902, in Theodore Roosevelt Papers: Scrapbooks, 1895–1910; vol. 2, 1902, Library of Congress.

165 **Five senators:** The three others were Nelson Aldrich, John Spooner, William Boyd Allison.

165 **"I have grave":** Roosevelt to John Hay, September 18, 1902, *The Letters of Theodore Roosevelt*, ed. Elting Morison, vol. 3: 326–27.

166 **Hanna would have:** A New York dispatch to Chicago *Inter-Ocean*, reprinted in *Indianapolis Journal*, September 24, 1902, 4.

166 **"Tomorrow I take up":** Roosevelt to John Hay, ibid.

166 **"We do not wish":** "President on Trusts," *Indianapolis Journal*, September 21, 1902, 1–2.

166 **In Detroit:** "President at Detroit," and "President Here Today," *Indianapolis Journal*, September 23, 1902.

166 **A bruise on:** Details of the president's surgery from several articles in *Indianapolis Journal*, September 23 and September 24, 1902; "When Theodore Roosevelt Was Hospitalized at St. Vincent's," *Hoosier State Chronicles* (online); "President Operated On," *Washington Times*, September 24, 1902, 1–2.

167 **If passengers called:** Lawrence Tye, "Choosing Servility to Staff America's Trains," aliciapatterson.org/stories/choosing-servility-staff-americas-trains.

167 **"My leg was":** Roosevelt to Henry Cabot Lodge, September 25, 1902, *Selections from the Correspondence of Theodore Roosevelt and Henry Cabot Lodge, 1884–1918*, 1: 531.

167 **Five-hundred-thousand:** Details of renovation, Sylvia Jukes Morris, *Edith Kermit Roosevelt: Portrait of a First Lady*, 238, 246.

168 **Near his desk:** "Favorite Poems of Abraham Lincoln and Theodore Roosevelt," Sagamore Hill National Historic Site collection via Theodore Roosevelt Digital Library; William Bayard Hale, *A Week in the White House with Theodore Roosevelt*, 1908, 9–10; Theodore Roosevelt letter of thanks to Anne Louise Ingalls, November 28, 1902, Theodore Roosevelt Papers, Library of Congress.

168 **Roosevelt developed:** Details from "President Undergoes Second Operation," September 29, 1902, *Washington Times*, 1 and 5; "A Second Operation," *New York Tribune*, September 29, 1902, 1.

168 **Earlier that month:** Details from "Washington's Coal Famine," *New York Times*, September 22, 1902; "Hard-Coal Famine Faces Households," *New York Times*, August 5, 1902; "Coal $11 Wholesale," *New York Times*, August 20, 1902; "Chicago Hard Coal Famine," *New York Times*, August 21, 1902; "Coal Sells at $10 a Tone," *Cambridge Chronicle*, August 23, 1902; "Anthracite Coal Famine," *New York Times*, September 20, 1902; "Coal Price in Washington, *New York Times*, September 27, 1902; "Coal Situation Grows Acute," *New York Tribune*, September 27, 1902; "Horse Chestnuts as Fuel," *New York Times*, September 28, 1902; "*Greenwich's Coal Famine*," *New York Times*, September 30, 1902; "Beer Kegs Stolen for Fuel," *New York Times*, October 5, 1902.

169 **Hanna went to:** Details on Hanna's attempts to end the strike, Herbert David Croly, *Marcus Alonzo Hanna: His Life and Work*, 398; John K. Winkler, *Morgan the Magnificent: The Life of J. Pierpont Morgan, 1837–1913*, 239.

169 **Roosevelt would send:** Roosevelt to Joseph Bucklin Bishop, October 5, 1902, Morison, *Letters* 3: 341–41.

169 **"Slight concession":** Roosevelt to Hanna, September 27, 1902, Morison, *Letters* 3: 329–30.

169 **In New York:** "Mitchell Cheered in Madison Square," *New York Times*, September 21, 1902, 12.

170 **"There is literally":** Roosevelt to Lodge, September 27, 1902, Morison, *Letters* 3: 331–32.

170 **Prices increased:** Frank Julian Warne, *The Slav Invasion and the Mine Workers: A Study in Immigration*, 157–59.

170 **the Brooklyn Bridge:** "Smoke Clouds Shut out View," *New York Tribune*, June 13, 1902, 14.

170 **Families used:** "Bricks in Demand for Fuel," *New York Times*, October 12, 1902.

170 **The health commissioner:** Warne, *Slav Invasion*, 160.

171 **"as he always":** Roosevelt to W. Murray Crane, October 22, 1902. Morison, *Letters* 3: 359–66.

171 **"wake up":** Roosevelt recounting his message to Lodge, September 30, 1902, cited in Robert J. Cornell, *The Anthracite Coal Strike of 1902*, 175–76.

171 **"The strike will not":** "Mr. Baer Does Not Fear Winter Coal Famine," *New York Times*, October 1, 1902.

171 **"We have not":** "Tells the Miners' Side," *New York Tribune*, September 29, 1902, 1–2.

171 **"The operators do not":** Roosevelt to Albert Shaw, October 1, 1902, Theodore Roosevelt Collection, Harvard College Library.

172 **"The plan to":** "Operators Will Meet Roosevelt," *New York Evening World*, October 1, 1902, 1.

172 **Mitchell was the first:** Account drawn from *Washington Evening Star*, October 3, 1902; *Evening Times*, October 3, 1902; *Evening World*, October 3, 1902; *New York Times*, October 3 and 4, 1902; "Ringing Words," *Washington Evening Star*, October 3, 1902, 1; "At the Corner of 4 1/2 Street," *Washington Post*, December 8, 1979; Roosevelt's *Autobiography*, 256–66.

172 **He was wearing:** Morris, *Theodore Rex*, 155.

173 **"I speak for":** Transcript of meeting, *Report of Conference between the President of the United States, Representatives of the Anthracite Coal Companies, and Representative of the United Mine Workers of America*, Philander C. Knox Papers, Library of Congress; "Official Statement of the Meeting," *New York Times*, October 4, 1902.

175 **"What they will":** Roosevelt to Seth Low, October 3, 1902, Morison, *Letters* 3: 336.

175 **so loudly:** "Coal Conference Proves a Failure," *New York Times*, October 4, 1902.

176 **"I explained":** Roosevelt to Joseph Bucklin Bishop, October 5, 1902, Theodore Roosevelt Collection, Harvard College Library.

176 **"The coal operators have neither":** *The World*, October 4, 1902.

176 **"Mitchell behaved":** Roosevelt to Crane, October 22, 1902, Morison, *Letters* 3: 359–66.

177 **"The language used":** Roosevelt to Robert Bacon, October 7, 1902, Morison, *Letters* 3: 343–44.

177 **"Well, I have tried":** Roosevelt to Hanna, October 3, 1902, Theodore Roosevelt Papers, Library of Congress.

177 **"advise Mr. Mitchell":** Cornell, *Anthracite Coal Strike of 1902*, 197.

177 **"few miners":** Roosevelt to Crane, October 22, 1902; "10,000 Troops Do Not Cause Rush to Mines," *Evening World*, October 11, 1902.

177 **"I only wanted":** Cornell, *Anthracite Coal Strike of 1902*, 210–11 citing Roosevelt's deposition in case of Alexander D. Wales v. John P. White as President of the United Mine Workers of America, 1914; Roosevelt, *Autobiography*, 474–75.

177 **"I have been so":** H. W. Brands, *T. R.: The Last Romantic*, 457, citing Roosevelt's October 8 letter to Jacob Riis in Riis Collection, Library of Congress.

178 **"What about the":** Frederick Wood, ed. *Roosevelt As We Knew Him: Personal Recollections of One Hundred and Fifty of His Friends and Associates*, 111–12.

178 **Then he let:** Kathleen Dalton, *Theodore Roosevelt: A Strenuous Life*, 235, citing Roosevelt's October 8 letter to Jacob Riis.

178 **On Dundee Island:** "Raids on Loaded Coal Cars," *New York Times*, October 5, 1902.

178 **more than five thousand:** "Poor Besiege Coal Sale," *New York Times*, October 11, 1902.

178 **Fifteen hundred:** "Conference in Buffalo," *New York Times*, October 8, 1902.

178 **"We wish to":** Cornell, *Anthracite Coal Strike of 1902*, 202, citing *Buffalo Review*, October 8, 1902.

178 **"We will not accept":** Glück, *John Mitchell, Miner: Labor's Bargain with the Gilded Age*, 129.

178 **Mark Twain:** "Mark Twain's Joke," *New York Times*, October 22, 1902. Twain's "letter" is dated October 3, 1902.

179 **Morgan announced:** "Morgan Gives 50,000 Tons of Coal to Poor," *New York Evening World*, October 4, 1902, 1; Satterlee, *J. Pierpont Morgan*, 392.

CHAPTER 12: THE CORSAIR AGREEMENT

180 **Pittsburgh gloom:** "City Is Another Pittsburg Today," *Evening World*, October 11, 1902, 3.

180 **All the news:** All details from articles on page 2 of *New York Tribune*, October 11, 1902.

180 **The manager at:** "Trade Menaced by Coal Famine," *Evening World*, October 11, 2.

181 **"They seem to want":** "No Federal Troops to Guard the Coal Mines," *Evening World*, October 11, 1902, 1.

181 **tired and depressed:** "Mitchell Depressed but Still Confident," *Evening World*, October 11, 1902, 2.

181 **"standing firm as":** Craig Phelan, *Divided Loyalties: The Public and Private Life of Labor Leader John Mitchell*. 185.

181 **"It has been such":** Roosevelt to Herbert Putnam, October 8, 1902, *The Letters of Theodore Roosevelt*, ed. Elting Morison, vol. 3: 344–45.

181 **"Such insolence":** Henry Cabot Lodge to Roosevelt, October 11, 1902, *Selections from the Correspondence of Theodore Roosevelt and Henry Cabot Lodge, 1884–1918*, 1: 538–39.

181 **Secretary of War:** This passage is Root's recounting of events in Philip C. Jessup, *Elihu Root*, 275.

182 **Root arrived:** "Meet on the Corsair," *New York Tribune*, October 12, 1901, 1.

182 **Corsair docked:** Details of yacht from Jean Strouse, *Morgan: American Financier*, 371–72.

182 **"Root saw Pierpont":** Roosevelt to W. Murray Crane, October 22, 1902, Morison, *Letters* 3: 363.

182 **Eight-page document:** Original—eight pages with two pages of insertions—is in Pierpont Morgan Papers at The Pierpont Morgan Library; statement released by coal executives can be found in "Documents Relating to the Anthracite Strike of 1902," 125–26, Clarence Darrow Collection.

182 **"It was a damned":** Jessup, *Elihu Root*, 276.

183 **Commodore Morgan:** Movements of Morgan and Root captured in "Root Here to See Morgan," *New York Tribune*, October 12, 1902 and "Root Registers, On a Mission," *New York Sun*, October 12, 1902.

183 **Reporters called:** Details of that Sunday from "Sunday Conference on J. P. Morgan's Yacht," *New York Times*, October 13, 1902; "President Baer Called by Mr. Morgan," *New York Times*, October 13, 1902.

183 **"little memorandum":** Jessup, *Elihu Root*, 275.

183 **"I can now":** Roosevelt to Ted Jr., October 12, 1902, Morison, *Letters* 3: 348–49.

183 **to close their home:** Sagamore Hill "Coal Consumption, 1895–1905" document provided by Sagamore Hill National Historic Site.

183 **Full time residents:** "Cutting Fences for Fuel," *New York Tribune*, October 13, 1902, 2.

184 **Sand doused:** "A Correspondent Suggests Saturated Beach Sand Instead of a Brick," *New York Tribune*, October 11, 1902, 2.

184 **A newspaper cartoon:** *Evening World*, October 13, 1902, 2.

184 **Fanny Simon was:** "Cheap Coal Causes Death," *Evening World*, October 13, 1902, 2.

184 **"What do I":** "'What do I know of coal,' says J. Pierpont Morgan," *Evening World*, October 13, 1902, 1.

184 **"If the solution":** Robert J. Cornell, *The Anthracite Coal Strike of 1902*, 217 citing a letter from Root to Mark Sullivan, July 14, 1927.

185 **"troublesome insular":** Theodore Roosevelt to Anna Roosevelt Cowles, October 16, 1902, *Letters from Theodore Roosevelt to Anna Roosevelt Cowles, 1870 to 1918*, 252. Roosevelt is repeating a phrase he heard from a cabinet

member who he doesn't identify but who's likely Knox. The phrase is attrib-
uted to him in "How Trusts Expect to Beat Roosevelt," *Mitchell Daily
Republican*, February 12, 1903, 6.

185 **Instead of rushing:** Morris, *Theodore Rex*, 167.

185 **"It was a concession":** "Operators Tell Why They Agreed on Plan," *Evening
World*, October 14, 1902, 2.

186 **He appeared nervous:** Details from "Morgan Back, Hopes the Miners Will
Accept," *Evening World*, October 14, 1902, 1–2.

186 **"justice will be done":** Phelan, *Divided Loyalties*, 186, citing telephone
memorandum between Mark Hanna and John Mitchell, October 14, 1902;
Sargent quote, "May Modify Terms," *New York Sun*, October 15, 1902, 1.

186–187 **"under cover of":** John Hay to Henry Adams, October 19, 1902,
Letters of John Hay and Extracts from Diary, ed. Louisa Hay, 3: 257–58.

187 **"The operators were":** This and quote in next paragraph, Roosevelt to
W. Murray Crane, October 22, 1902, Morison, *Letters* 3: 359–66.

187 **"The mighty brains":** Roosevelt to Lodge, October 17, 1902, *Selections from
the Correspondence*, 1: 539–40.

187 **"These names are":** Roosevelt to Mitchell, October 16, 1902, Morison, *Letters*
3: 353.

187 **"Gentlemen, if you":** "Mitchell to Urge Plan of President," *Evening
Journal*, October 16, 1902, George W. Perkins Sr. Papers, Columbia University Libraries.

188 **Mitchell looked haggard:** Elsie Glück, *John Mitchell, Miner: Labor's Bargain
with the Gilded Age*, 133–34.

188 **"this proposal":** Phelan, *Divided Loyalties*, 187, citing Mitchell's *Opening
Address to Delegates of the Joint Convention of Districts 1, 7, and 9, UMWA*,
October 20, 1902, John Mitchell Papers, Cornell University Library.

188 **"I feel like":** Roosevelt was confident enough of the outcome that he wrote
these two letters before the miners had voted. Roosevelt to Finley Peter
Dunne, October 20, 1902, Morison, *Letters* 3: 357; Roosevelt to Joseph Bucklin
Bishop, October 18, 1902, Morison, *Letters* 3: 356.

188 **"Late last night":** Roosevelt to Hanna, October 16, 1902, Morison, *Letters*
3: 354.

188 **"My dear sir":** Roosevelt to Morgan, October 16, 1902, Morison, *Letters* 3: 353.

189 **Thirty thousand dollars:** "Little Doubt Miners Will Accept Arbitration,"
New York Times, October 19, 1902.

189 **seventy-four million and twenty-five million:** "Report to the President on
the Anthracite Coal Strike Commission," 37.

189 **"One great trouble":** Roosevelt to Anna Roosevelt Cowles, October 16, 1902, *Anna Roosevelt Cowles Letters*, 252.

189 **At a banquet:** Details of Mitchell's post-strike life and preparations for the commission's hearings in Phelan, *Divided Loyalties*, 189–97.

190 **"Flattery and homage":** Phelan, *Divided Loyalties*, 187, citing Mary "Mother" Jones, *The Autobiography of Mother Jones*, 59–61.

191 **Andrew Chippie:** "Proceedings of the Anthracite Mine Strike Commission, 1902–1903," 72, reprinted from the *Scranton Tribune*, Clarence Darrow Collection, University of Minnesota Law Library, moses.law.umn.edu/darrow/documents/Proceedings_Anthracite_Strike_Cropped_OPT_Fina_OCR.pdf.

191 **James Gallagher:** "Commission Asks for Information," *Scranton Tribune*, December 8, 1902, 7; *Proceedings*, 72.

191 **Henry Coll:** "Almost Every Bone in Body Broken," *Wilkes-Barre Times*, December 9, 1902, 1 and 7; *Proceedings*, 77–78.

191 **"have as much right":** "Strike Commission Taking Evidence, John Mitchell First Witness," November 14, 1902, *Wilkes-Barre Times* 1; *Proceedings*, 4.

192 **"If you demand":** *Proceedings*, 21.

192 **They named the dead:** "Partial List of Acts of Violence or Intimidation during the Anthracite Strike of 1902," 3, Clarence Darrow Collection.

192 **The men's stories:** Ray Stannard Baker, "The Right to Work: The Story of Non-Striking Miners," *McClure's* (January 1903).

193 **Baer gave the:** "Argument of George F. Baer Before the Anthracite Coal Strike Commission, February 12, 1903," http://moses.law.umn.edu/darrow/documents/Baer_Argument_Cropped_Opt.pdf.

194 **"a condition of":** Roosevelt to Crane, October 22, 1902.

194 **Coal presidents:** "Coal Commission Report Satisfactory," *Philadelphia Inquirer*, March 23, 1903, 8.

195 **Hanna reportedly:** *Wilkes-Barre Record*, March 30, 1903, 6.

195 **He invested:** Phelan, *Divided Loyalties*, 203–04.

195 **"Many a wealthy man":** Phelan, *Divided Loyalties*, 204, citing letter from Mitchell to Andrew Chippie, January 6, 1903, John Mitchell Papers, Cornell University Library.

195 **"When Knighthood":** Phelan, *Divided Loyalties*, 200.

195 **Hanna greeted him:** "Civic Federation Hold a Reunion. Mitchell Present," *Wilkes-Barre Times*, December 8, 1902, 1.

195 **Silk hat:** Phelan, *Divided Loyalties*, 200, 202.

196 **Hanna, who continued:** "Rot, All Rot, Says Hanna," *Wilkes-Barre Times*, December 8, 1902, 1.

196 **Coal soot:** "Soot on the National Monument," *New York Times*, December 16, 1902; "The Public Grounds," *Evening Star*, December 16, 1902, 22; "Washington Monument Damaged," *Daily Times*, December 18, 1902, 6.

CHAPTER 13: RICH MAN'S PANIC

198 **At midnight:** "Over Thousand Wires: Heralding the Beginning of the New Year," *Washington Evening Star*, January 1, 1903, 8.

198 **The Treasury:** "Greatest of Nation's Happy New Year to World Powers," *Washington Times*, January 1, 1903, 9; *Annual Report of the Secretary of the Treasury for the Fiscal Year Ended June 30, 1902*, 7, 182, https://fraser.stlouisfed .org/title/194/item/5548/toc/174377. The $80 million in gold was in addition to the required $150 million gold reserve.

198 **Broadway was bright:** Details from "Greeting the New Year," *New York Times*, January 1, 1903, 3; "Double Salaries to Morgan's clerks," *Washington Times*, January 1, 1903, 3; "JP Morgan & Co.'s Gift," *New York Sun*, January 1, 1903, 1.

198 **On January 1:** Details of reception and renovation from "Brilliant White House Reception Marks Dawn of the New Year," *Washington Times*, January 1, 1903, 1–2; "A Brilliant Scene," *Evening Star*, January 1, 1903, 1; "The New Year Reception at the White House," *Minneapolis Journal*, January 1, 1903, 1; "Its Electric Plant," *Evening Star*, January 1, 1903, 3; Theodore Roosevelt White House Renovation: 1902," White House Museum, www .whitehousemuseum.org/special/renovation-1902.htm.

199 **Michael Owens:** Bill Lockhart et al., "The Owens Bottle Co. Part 1—History," Society for Historical Archaeology, June 17, 2018, sha.org/bottle /pdffiles/OwensBottleCoPart1.pdf; tea bag patent, patents.google.com /patent/US723287A/en.

200 **"This week I":** Roosevelt to Kermit, January 17, 1903, *The Letters of Theodore Roosevelt*, ed. Elting Morison, vol. 3: 406, and to Ted, January 20, 1903, Morison, *Letters* 3: 408.

200 **The bill proposed:** Doris Kearns Goodwin, *The Bully Pulpit: Theodore Roosevelt, William Howard Taft, and the Golden Age of Journalism*, 342–43; Gabriel Kolko, *Railroads and Regulation, 1877–1916*, 95; 100–01.

200 **The Expedition Act:** Robert C. Bonges, "The Antitrust Expediting Act: A Critical Reappraisal," *Michigan Law Review* 63, no. 7 (May 1965): 1240–57.

200 **That sounded like:** *New York Herald*, February 2, 1903, Philander C. Knox Papers, Library of Congress.

201 **Roosevelt didn't like:** Descriptions of the back and forth in Morison's notes 3: 416–17; 420, 429, and recounted in articles in Knox's correspondence, 118 and 128, Philander C. Knox Papers, Library of Congress.

201 **James Dill:** Elizabeth Ann Schiller, "James Brooks Dill: Father of the Trusts," 45.

201 **"But as soon as":** Roosevelt to Lawrence Fraser Abbott, February 3, 1903, Morison, *Letters* 3: 416–17.

201 **He pressed his:** Roosevelt to Senator Charles Fairbanks, January 19, 1903, Morison, *Letters* 3: 406–07.

201 **Rockefeller himself:** Goodwin, *Bully Pulpit*, 345–46.

201 **"For heaven's sake":** Roosevelt to Mark Hanna, January 23, 1903, Morison, *Letters* 3: 410.

202 **Perkins got one:** Morris, *Theodore Rex*, 207.

202 **The Gridiron Club:** Account of the dinner comes from *The Gridiron Club, 1885–1905, Annals: Twentieth Anniversary Dinner*, January 28, 1905 (The Gridiron Press, 1905), 85; Arthur Wallace Dunn, *Gridiron Nights: Humorous and Satirical Views of Politics and Statesmen as Presented by the Famous Dining Club*, 134–36; "Capital Is Grilled," *Evening Star*, February 2, 1903, 11, includes account of Morgan's conversation with Hanna.

203 **Morgan stopped back:** Account of his time in Cuba and in Washington from "Morgan Wanted at White House," *Atlanta Constitution*, March 13, 1903, 2; "Morgan in Washington," *Charlotte Observer*, March 13, 1903, 1; "Morgan Calls on President," *Sioux City Journal*, March 13, 1903, 2; Jean Strouse, *Morgan: American Financier*, 493.

203 **The marshal:** Details from "Federal Court Will Hear the Great Merger Case in Saint Louis," *St. Louis Post-Dispatch*, March 15, 1903

203 **As governor of New Jersey:** Details about Griggs from "New Jersey Republican," *New York Times*, November 6, 1895; William Letwin, *Law and Economic Policy in America: The Evolution of the Sherman Antitrust Act*, 138–39; "Federal Antitrust Laws with amendments," Department of Justice, 1916, 49.

204 **He had dark:** "Roosevelt's Favorite 'Trust Buster' Is Suave, not Strenuous, in Manner," *St. Louis Post Dispatch*, March 22, 1903, 11; "James M. Beck Resigns," *New York Times*, April 13, 1903.

204 **Beck went:** Details of the government's arguments from "Government Fight Against Merger Is On," *St. Louis Post Dispatch*, March 18, 1903; "Beck's

Argument," *New York Times* March 19, 1903; "Argument Is Begun on Railroad Merger," *New York Times*, March 19, 1903.

204 **Griggs summed up:** Details of the defense from "Griggs Closes Case," *New York Tribune*, March 21, 1903; Circuit Court of the United States for the District of Minnesota, Third Division, No. 789, Transcript of Record, Harvard College Library.

206 **"Not only is":** "J. P. Morgan Is Bullish," *New York Times*, March 31, 1903, 1.

206 **stocks were "indigestible":** Alexander Dana Noyes, *The Market Place: Reminiscences of a Financial Editor*, 223; *Outlook* 74, no. 14 (August 1 1903): 774–75.

206 **Roosevelt left:** Details about his trip from "President to Tour West in Style," *Washington Times*, March 31, 1903, 1; "At the White House," *Evening Star*, March 31, 1903, 1; "The President Departs on His Long Western Journey," *Washington Times*, April 1, 1903, 1; "The President's Tour," *Minneapolis Journal*, April 3, 1903; "Gossip about the Presidency," *Missoulian*, April 10, 1903, 1; Edmund Morris, *Theodore Rex*, 214.

206 **"terrific strain":** Roosevelt to Corinne Robinson, March 31, 1903, Theodore Roosevelt Collection, Harvard College Library.

206 **"I did not 'divine'":** Carleton Putnam, *Theodore Roosevelt: A Biography*, 600.

207 **"How can I leave":** "The President Departs on His Long Western Journey," *Washington Times*, April 1, 1903, 1.

207 **"meant to do":** Roosevelt speech, "Trust Legislation," Jamestown, North Dakota, April 7, 1903, *The Roosevelt Policy: Speeches, Letters and State Papers, Relating to Corporate Wealth and Closely Allied Topics*, ed. William Griffith, 133–35.

207 **forty books:** "The President's Books," *Minneapolis Journal*, April 3, 1903, 2.

208 **The railroad's president:** "Livingston Is Ready for the Arrival of President Roosevelt," *Missoulian*, April 8, 1903, 1.

208 **"You might put":** "The Keynote: Preaches Co-Operation at Dry Farming Congress," Associated Press report in *Los Angeles Times*, October 27, 1909, 14.

208 **Roosevelt hoped:** Details of Roosevelt's visit from "President Roosevelt Reaches Livingston and Goes to the Park" and "'Billy' Hoffer, Famous Scout, Will be President's Guide," *Missoulian*, April 9, 1903, 1.

209 **"I am back":** Quote from Major John Pitcher's diaries, cited by Livingston-Lodge32.org.

209 **Hill returned:** "Mr. Hill's Arrival," *Minneapolis Journal*, April 9, 1903, 2.

209 **"in the hands of"**: "A Sweeping Decision against the Holding Company's Plan," *Minneapolis Journal*, April 9, 1903, 1.

210 **"The courts can be"**: Roosevelt to Philander Knox, April 28, 1903, Morison, *Letters* 3: 473.

210 **"reaffirms the right"**: "Merger Defeated," *Washington Evening Star*, April 9, 1903, 1.

210 **victory was "revolutionary"**: "Hill Wants Merger," *Evening World*, April 10, 1903, 4.

210 **"was like a thunderbolt"**: *Minneapolis Journal*, April 9, 1903, 2.

210 **"will not rest"**: This quote and "You will have," Herbert L. Satterlee, *J. Pierpont Morgan: An Intimate Portrait, 1837–1913*, 401.

210 **"We hear with"**: Telegram from Jack Morgan to Pierpont Morgan, April 11, 1903, Vincent Carosso Papers, The Pierpont Morgan Library.

210 **"is a crime"**: "The Northwestern Merger," *Independent*, April 23 1903.

210 **He and Morgan**: "Their Tears Mingle: Mr. Hill and Mr. Morgan in Each Other's Arms," *Minneapolis Journal*, April 10, 1903.

210 **"If this decision"**: *Boston Record*, April 11, 1903, in Philander C. Knox Papers, Clippings, Library of Congress.

210 **"The decision itself"**: James Hill to Charles E. Perkins, April 21, 1903, James J. Hill Papers, Minnesota Historical Society.

210 **"What the Northern Pacific"**: Edward T. Nichols, April 9, 1903, memo in James J. Hill Papers, Minnesota Historical Society.

211 **"will probably find"**: "Hill and Morgan: The Two Magnates Seem to Be Sparring for Wind," *Minneapolis Journal*, April 10, 1903, 13.

211 **Coal companies**: Details about investors' reaction from "Severe Drop in Stocks," *New York Times*, April 14, 1903.

211 **Morgan was forced**: Details about Morgan's birthday from Satterlee, *J. Pierpont Morgan*, 401, 403; Strouse, *Morgan: American Financier*, 493; "JP Morgan is 66," *New York Sun*, 11; poem from Pierpont Morgan Papers, The Pierpont Morgan Library.

211 **Injunction against**: David Gordon, "Swift & Co. v. United States: The Beef Trust and the Stream of Commerce Doctrine," *American Journal of Legal History* 28, no. 3 (July 1984): 244–79; April 1903 decision, 266.

211 **"My dear sir"**: Roosevelt to Philander Knox, April 24, 1903, Theodore Roosevelt Papers, Library of Congress.

212 **"I have certainly"**: Roosevelt to William Taft, April 22, 1903, Morison, *Letters* 3: 465.

212 **Roosevelt toured**: "Country's Executive Speaks Interestingly," "Young John Czolgosz Is Taken to a Prison," and "Federal and State Soldiery Will March as Escort to Chief of Nation," *San Francisco Call*, May 8, 1903; "Floral Display and Grandeur of Cities of the Southland Deeply Impress Chief Executive of the American Nation," and "Beautiful Parade in City of Angels Arouses Enthusiasm of the President," *San Francisco Call*, May 9, 1903.

212 **unwilling to contribute:** "Southern Pacific Will Not Contribute," *San Francisco Call*, May 9, 1903, 3.

213 **Golden Banquet:** Details from "Eloquence at a Golden Feast," May 13, 1903, *San Francisco Call*; May Golden Banquet illustrated program, Theodore Roosevelt Collection, Harvard College Library.

213 **"a roughing trip":** "Charlie Leidig's Report of President Roosevelt's Visit in May 1903," vault.sierraclub.org/john_muir_exhibit/pdf/leidig_report.pdf.

213 **"You know":** Henry Adams to Elizabeth Cameron, April 19, 1903 *Letters of Henry Adams*, 5: 487.

213 **Hanna said publicly:** Exchange of messages in Morison, *Letters* 3: 479–80; Hanna's statement to the Associated Press, Theodore Roosevelt Collection, Harvard College Library.

214 **"was everywhere accepted":** Roosevelt to Mark Hanna, May 29, 1903, Theodore Roosevelt Collection, Harvard College Library.

214 **"I decided that":** Roosevelt to Henry Cabot Lodge May 27, 1903, Morison, *Letters* 3: 481–82.

214 **two best speeches:** "Liberty Through Law," Spokane, Washington, May 26, 1903, Griffith, *The Roosevelt Policy* 1: 138–41 and "The Supremacy of Law," Butte, Montana, May 27, 1903, Griffith, *The Roosevelt Policy* 1: 141–44. Roosevelt proudly recounted them to Henry Cabot Lodge, Morison, *Letters* 3: 481–82.

215 **Roosevelt was among:** "The Hanna Wedding," *Evening Statesman*, June 10, 1903.

215 **He asked Hanna:** Lewis L. Gould, *The Presidency of Theodore Roosevelt*, 127.

215 **"back-action":** Editor's note, Morison, *Letters* 3: 479–80.

215 **state had been forced:** Details from "Millions Wiped Out by the Failure of Air-bubble Trusts," *Evening World*, April 10, 1903, 4.

215 **By early June:** Details from "The Financial Situation," *New York Times*, June 7, 1903; "Wall Street and the President," *New York Tribune*, August 29, 1903, 6.

216 **"infatuated millionaires":** Alexander Dana Noyes, *Forty Years of American Finance,* 311

216 **halved the value:** Morris, *Theodore Rex,* 261; which employed, Philip S. Foner, *History of the Labor Movement in the United States,* vol. 3: 78.

216 **reduced wages:** Morris, *Theodore Rex,* 299.

216 **"There is no crisis":** "Morgan Dodges Cameras," *Baltimore Sun,* June 25, 1903, 5.

216 **By July:** Details of the summer panic from "International Mercantile Marine," *Wall Street Journal,* July 9, 1903, 5; Morris, *Theodore Rex,* 299; Strouse, *Morgan: American Financier,* 565; Roosevelt to Leslie Shaw, July 22, 1903, Morison, *Letters* 3: 526.

216 **"The financial situation":** Roosevelt to Henry Cabot Lodge, August 6, 1903, Morison, *Letters* 545.

216 **"about as intelligent":** Roosevelt to Anna Roosevelt Cowles, August 26, 1903, Morison, *Letters* 3: 574–75.

216 **"Mr. Perkins tells":** Roosevelt to Pierpont Morgan, October 8, 1903, Morison, *Letters* 3: 627.

217 **"I should like":** Pierpont Morgan to Roosevelt, October 12, 1903, Theodore Roosevelt Papers, Library of Congress.

217 **"There is no hurry":** Roosevelt to Pierpont Morgan, October 13, 1903. Theodore Roosevelt Papers, Library of Congress.

217 **businessmen in New York:** Herbert David Croly, *Marcus Alonzo Hanna: His Life and Work,* 435–37.

217 **Morgan invited:** Details from Morris, *Theodore Rex,* 299–300; "Mark Hanna Says D—N with a Big D," *Evening World,* November 27, 1903; Gould, *The Presidency of Theodore Roosevelt,* 127.

218 **"when all business":** Noyes, *The Market Place,* 202.

218 **record a loss:** Vincent P. Carosso, *The Morgans: Private International Bankers, 1854–1913,* 614–15.

218 **Zodiac club:** Details from Satterlee, *J. Pierpont Morgan,* 406; November 1903 Zodiac Club Menu, Pierpont Morgan Papers, The Pierpont Morgan Library; Danielle Oteri, "Inside the Zodiac Club: NYC's 145 Year Old Secret Dining Society," *Gothamist,* May 6, 2013.

218 **On the evening:** "Mr. Murray Crane. He May Succeed Hanna for Chairman," *Washington Evening Star,* December 5, 1903, 1; "Roosevelt and Hanna Reach Agreement," *Washington Times,* December 5, 1903, 2; Roosevelt and Hanna notes, December 5, 1903, Theodore Roosevelt Papers, Library of Congress.

CHAPTER 14: "THE SUPREME LAW OF THE LAND"

219 **John Marshall Harlan:** Biographical details of Harlan and his half-brother from Tinsley E. Yarbrough, *Judicial Enigma: The First Justice Harlan*; Linda Przybyszewski, *The Republic According to John Marshall Harlan*; Frank Brown Latham, *The Great Dissenter: John Marshall Harlan, 1833–1911*; Allen Westin, "John Marshall Harlan and the Constitutional Rights of Negroes: The Transformation of a Southerner," *Yale Law Journal* 1957; Charles Thompson, "Plessy v. Ferguson: Harlan's Great Dissent," *Kentucky Humanities* 1996; Gilbert King, "The Great Dissenter and his Half-Brother," December 20, 2011, smithsonianmag.com.

220 **"Let it be said":** Westin, "Constitutional Rights of Negroes," 660, citing "General Harlan's Republicanism," *Louisville Daily Commercial*, November 1, 1877 in Harlan Papers.

220 **by compromise:** Tilden won an outright majority of the popular vote, but there was an argument about the electoral vote. The Democrats agreed to accept Hayes' presidency if he withdrew federal troops from the South. The Compromise of 1877 formally ended Reconstruction efforts, and soon local authorities and militias reestablished antebellum "home rule."

220 **"Is Harlan not?":** Rutherford B. Hayes to William Henry Smith, president of Associated Press, September 29, 1877, cited in Malvina Shanklin Harlan, *Some Memories of a Long Life, 1854–1911*, 99.

221 **"Today it is":** Peter Irons, *A People's History of the Supreme Court: The Men and Women Whose Cases and Decisions Have Shaped Our Constitution*, 215.

221 **"It was, I think":** Przybyszewski, *According to John Marshall Harlan*, 93, citing Harlan, *Some Memories of a Long Life*; "some surprise," ibid., 95.

222 **The Louisiana railroads:** Irons, *A People's History of the Supreme Court*, 224.

222 **Antagonistic claims:** Irons, *A People's History of the Supreme Court*, 231. Irons believes Harlan wasn't racist but did celebrate "pride of race." Others disagree: Philip Hutchison, "The Harlan Renaissance: Colorblindness and White Domination in Justice John Marshall Harlan's Dissent in Plessy v. Ferguson," *Journal of African-American Studies* (2015): 426–447.

222 **"The white race":** Plessy v. Ferguson, Harlan's Dissent, Supreme Court of the United States, U.S. Reports: Plessy v. Ferguson, 163 U.S. 537 1895, www.loc.gov/item/usrep163537.

222 **Seventy-eight people:** Eugene L. Meyer, "'A Shameful Affair': The Last Man Lynched in Montgomery, County, Md.," *Washington Post*, August 22, 2018.

222 **Melville Fuller:** Details from "Melville W. Fuller," Oyez, www.oyez.org /justices/melville_w_fuller; "Chief Justice Melville Fuller Dies Suddenly," *Los Angeles Herald*, July 5, 1910; Sheldon M. Novick, *Honorable Justice: The Life of Oliver Wendell Holmes*, 241, 243; William H. Rehnquist, "Remarks of the Chief Justice: My Life in the Law Series," 52 *Duke Law Journal* (2003): 787–805, scholarship.law.duke.edu/dlj/vol52/iss4/3.

223 **Stood close to:** Rehnquist, "Remarks," 797; Virginia Van der Veer Hamilton, "In Defense of Order and Stability: The Constitutional Philosophy of Chief Justice Edward Douglass White," *Reviews in American History* 10, no. 1 (March 1982): 105–08.

223 **Rufus Peckham:** *The Judges of the New York Court of Appeals: A Biographical History*, ed. Hon. Albert M. Rosenblatt (New York: Fordham University Press, 2007).

223 **"All that we":** Letwin, *Law and Economic Policy in America*, 95, citing Congressional Record 2461, 1890; "experimental": ibid.

223 **Tennessee was:** Details of early tests of antitrust law from Letwin, *Law and Economic Policy in America*, 69, 106–07, 114, 166–67.

223 **"The statute":** United States v. Trans-Missouri Freight Association decision.

224 **"This decision left":** Theodore Roosevelt, *The Autobiography of Theodore Roosevelt*, 427.

224 **Both had been:** Similarities between the two are detailed in Richard H. Wagner, "A Falling Out: The Relationship between Oliver Wendell Holmes and Theodore Roosevelt," 119; G. Edward White, *Oliver Wendell Holmes, Jr.*, 63; "Unraveling Oliver Wendell Holmes' 'The Soldier's Faith,'" *Tulsa World*, May 28, 2012; Novick, *Honorable Justice*, 179, 228.

225 **"Life is a roar":** Wagner, "A Falling Out," 120, citing 1911 speech in *Collected Works of Justice Holmes*, ed. Sheldon M. Novick, 3: 504–05.

225 **Holmes impressed:** Novick, *Honorable Justice*, 206.

225 **"to ride boldly":** Richard Posner, *The Essential Holmes: Selections From the Letters, Speeches, Judicial Opinions, and Other Writings of Oliver Wendell Holmes, Jr.* (University of Chicago Press, 1992).

225 **Holmes held that:** Novick, *Honorable Justice*, 204.

225 **"Free competition":** Vegelahn v. Guntner, October 27, 1896, http://moses .law.umn.edu/darrow/documents/Vegelahn%201896.pdf.

225 **more cynical:** Irons, *A People's History of the Supreme Court*, 251.

225 **"loathed most":** Wagner, "A Falling Out," 121, citing Holmes to Felix Frankfurter, December 23, 1921.

225 **wear black robes:** Novick, *Honorable Justice*, 231.

226 **told a cousin:** Ibid., 234.

226 **"I am glad":** Roosevelt to Lodge, July 10, 1902, Morison, *Letters* 3: 288–89.

226 **"said just":** White, *Oliver Wendell Holmes, Jr.*, 66, citing August 17 letter from Holmes to Nina Gray.

227 **Roosevelt offered:** Novick, *Honorable Justice*, 236.

227 **far-right end:** from the justices' point of view.

227 **"great constructive statesmen":** December 9, 1902, at the Willard Hotel, http://www.theodore-roosevelt.com/images/research/txtspeeches/35.txt.

227 **Justice Brewer teased:** Details about Harlan from Przybyszewski, *According to John Marshall Harlan*, 48, 54; 185–88; Stephen Budiansky, *Oliver Wendell Holmes: A Life in War, Law, and Ideas*, 269; Yarbrough, *Judicial Enigma*, 129, 164–69, and 170–73.

228 **"a position which":** Malvina Shanklin Harlan, *Some Memories of a Long Life*, 123; Przybyszewski, *According to John Marshall Harlan*, 185, 188.

228 **Holmes had become:** Bodiansky, 274, citing Holmes letter to Ellen Curtis, January 25, 1903; Novick, *Honorable Justice*, 260, states specifically that it was Edward White who left the reception; "Southern Senators Miffed," and "Negroes at Reception," *Evening Times-Republican*, January 24, 1903, 1, 8.

228 **"I do think":** Roosevelt to Taft, October 21, 1902, Morison, *Letters* 358. Other letters, October 25, 1902, Morison, *Letters* 3: 368; October 29, 1902, 3: 372; and November 26, 1902, 3: 382–83. On January 29, 1903, Roosevelt wrote to Taft that he had appointed William Rufus Day to the Supreme Court so Taft could stay in the Philippines, Morison, *Letters* 3: 413.

229 **"wards of the":** Edward Douglass White and Supreme Court of the United States, *U.S. Reports: Lone Wolf v. Hitchcock, 187 U.S. 553*, 1902. Periodical, https://www.loc.gov/item/usrep187553/.

229 **"Dred Scott":** U.S. Congressional Record 2028 (1903) cited in Angela Riley, *The Apex of Congress' Plenary Power Over Indian Affairs*.

229 **"from every part":** Novick, *Honorable Justice*, 247, citing Holmes letter to Ellen Curtis, December 12, 1902.

229 **"my lion-hearted friend":** Yarbrough, *Judicial Enigma*, 127.

229 **"powerful vise":** Ibid., 126.

229 **"that won't wash":** Novick, *Honorable Justice*, 254.

229 **"It seems as if":** Novick, *Honorable Justice*, 260.

229 **never read:** White, *Oliver Wendell Holmes, Jr.*, 84; Washington, D.C., residents won the right to vote in national elections in 1961.

230 **"Washington is full":** Novick, *Honorable Justice*, 260.

230 **"our only social".** Henry Adams to Elizabeth Cameron, March 6, 1904, *Letters of Henry Adams*, ed. J. C. Levenson et al., 558.

230 **"We are on top":** Novick, *Honorable Justice*, 261, citing Holmes letter to Ellen Curtis, February 7, 1903, and Holmes letter to Baroness Moncheur, September 9, 1910.

230 **"Surely you must":** Roosevelt to Holmes, June 11, 1903, Theodore Roosevelt Collection, Harvard College Library.

230 **eight thousand pages:** Novick, *Honorable Justice*, 269.

231 **By 1903:** "Depending on Northern Securities," *Wall Street Journal*, December 15, 1903, 1; Larry Haeg, *Harriman vs. Hill: Wall Street's Great Railroad War*, 6; *Historical Statistics of the United States, 1789–1945*, 202, 204.

231 **John Johnson presented:** Details about the lawyer from "John G. Johnson, Noted Lawyer, Dies," *New York Times*, April 15, 1917; "John G. Johnson," Oyez, January 8, 2019, www.oyez.org/advocates/john_g_johnson; "The Hearing in the Northern Securities Case," *Nation* 77, no. 2008 (December 24, 1903): 499–500.

231 **Knox spoke for:** "Knox Dissects Defense Set Up for the Merger," *Philadelphia Record*, December 16, 1903.

232 **Johnson argued:** Details of the original complaint and response from earlier testimony from J. P. Morgan, and the arguments before the Supreme Court from *U.S. Reports: Northern Securities Co. v. United States, 193 U.S. 197* (1903), https://www.loc.gov/item/usrep193197/; "Oral Argument of the Attorney-General for the United States, Northern Securities Company v. The United States," reprinted in *The Quarterly Journal of Economics*, 1903, Harvard College Library; *Landmark Briefs and Arguments of the Supreme Court of the United States: Constitutional Law*, eds. Philip B. Kurland and Gerhard Casper, provides briefs and oral arguments of Knox and, for the appellants, George Young.

232 **What was to be done?:** Contemporaneous details and accounts from "Merger Case Argued," *New York Times*, December 15, 1903, 1–2; "U.S. Brief in Merger Case Is Filed and Arguments are Begun," *Star Tribune*, December 15, 1903, 1–2.

233 **Knox reminded:** "Securities Co. Promoters Called Oriental Dreamers," *Washington Times*, December 15, 1903, 1; clippings from Knox Papers, Library of Congress; James Wilford Garner, "The Northern Securities Case." *The Annals of the American Academy of Political and Social Science* 24: The Government in Its Relation to Industry (July 1904): 125–47.

234 **"most sublime confidence"**: "JJ Hill Will Still Control," *Minneapolis Journal*, December 14, 1903, 1; "Hill Confident," *Cincinnati Enquirer*, December 15, 1903, 2.

234 **Hill announced:** "Cuts Out Calendar," *Daily Review* (Decatur, Illinois), December 16, 1903, 8.

234 **"Already I begin":** Roosevelt to Philander Knox, December 14, 1903, Philander C. Knox Papers, Library of Congress.

CHAPTER 15: THE RULING

235 **Mark Hanna was sick:** Details of Hanna's illness and travels from Herbert David Croly, *Marcus Alonzo Hanna: His Life and Work*, 433, 450–52; New York Central Railroad schedule.

235 **A group of railroad:** "Hanna Picks Parker," Walter Wellman in *Philadelphia Press*, December 15, 1903; "Hanna's Friends See Ray of Hope," *Minneapolis Star Tribune*, December 16, 1903, 1.

235 **"Stop making":** William Henry Harbaugh, *Power and Responsibility: The Life and Times of Theodore Roosevelt*, 220.

235 **On January 30:** Details of the dinner and days immediately afterward from Croly, *Marcus Alonzo Hanna*, 448, 453; Edmund Morris, *Theodore Rex*, 309; "Song and Mirth Mark Feast of Gridiron Club," *Washington Times*, January 31, 1904, 1; "The Gridiron Dinner," *Evening Star*, February 1, 1904, 3.

236 **"You touched a":** Roosevelt included the note from Hanna in his own letter to Elihu Root, February 16, 1904, Theodore Roosevelt Papers, Library of Congress.

236 **"Indeed it is":** Croly, *Marcus Alonzo Hanna*, 454.

236 **Doctors sent out:** "Hanna Is Slowly Sinking," *Evening Star*, February 15, 1904; "Hanna Dead," *Boston Globe*, February 16, 1904, 1, 3; "Senator Hanna Dead," *Sun*, February 16, 1904, 1.

236 **Trading was tentative:** "Finance and Trade," *Evening Star*, February 15, 1904, 2.

237 **Sixteen inches:** Details of city life from Washington, D.C., Monthly Snowfall, National Weather Service and National Oceanic and Atmospheric Administration; "Celebrate New Year," *Washington Evening Star*, February 15, 1904, 7; "At the White House," *Washington Evening Star*, February 15, 1904, 1–2.

237 **Roosevelt walked over:** "Hanna Sinking," weather report, *Evening Star*, February 15, 1904, 3.

237 **"well-nigh irreparable":** Craig Phelan, *Divided Loyalties: The Public and Private Life of Labor Leader John Mitchell*, 235.

237 **Morgan said:** "The Life Memorial of Pierpont Morgan," Joe Mitchell Chapple, *National Magazine* 38: 654.

237 **a colleague said:** James Ford Rhodes, *The McKinley and Roosevelt Administrations, 1897–1909*, 291.

237 **Hanna served:** Details of his estate from "Senator Hanna's Estate," *Evening Star*, February 17, 1904, 2; "Congressional Pay Since 1855," Chuck Taylor, HeraldNet.com, March 21, 2013, citing Congressional Research Service; "Estate Must Pay Tax," *Detroit Free Press*, July 3, 1904, 1.

237 **"Hanna's death":** Roosevelt to Elihu Root, February 16, 1904, Theodore Roosevelt Papers, Library of Congress.

238 **"I have missed":** Roosevelt to Ted, February 6, 1904, *Theodore Roosevelt's Letters to His Children*, ed. Joseph Bucklin Bishop, 89–91.

238 **"is the greatest man":** Walter Wellman, "Elihu Root: A Character Sketch."

238 **"I feel that":** Roosevelt to Philander Knox, December 20, 1903 in Philander C. Knox Papers, Library of Congress.

238 **He accepted:** Philip C. Jessup, *Elihu Root*, 432–33.

239 **"the Big Interests":** William Roscoe Thayer, *Theodore Roosevelt: An Intimate Biography*, 203.

239 **They whispered:** Sereno Pratt, "The President and Wall Street," *World of Work*, February 1904. Pratt was editor of the *Wall Street Journal*.

239 **Defend the president:** Speech and details come from "A Tribute to Theodore Roosevelt," Address at a Banquet in Honor of the Secretary of War, Union League Club New York, February 3, 1904, in *Miscellaneous Addresses by Elihu Root*, collected by Robert Bacon and James Brown Scott; "Defends His Chief," *Los Angeles Times*, February 4, 1904, 1; "Root Is Loyal," *Burlington Free Press*, February 4, 1904, 2; "Root Speaks Up for Roosevelt," *Chicago Tribune*, February 4, 1904, 1; "Root Champions Roosevelt," *Sun*, February 4, 1904, 1.

240 **"You want to":** Jessup, *Elihu Root*, 416.

240 **"The evil":** Roosevelt to Elihu Root, February 16, 1904.

241 **A jujitsu master:** Details about his training from "President Roosevelt Jiu-Jitsu Enthusiast," *Washington Times*, March 15, 1904, 3; "Professor Yamashita Goes to Washington," Joseph R. Svinth, *Journal of Combative Sport*, October 2000.

241 **"My right ankle":** Roosevelt to Ted, April 9, 1904, Morison rejected letters, Theodore Roosevelt Collection, Harvard College Library.

241 **Criticized his spending:** The charges and Roosevelt's defense in "Fads, Frauds and Follies Cripple Nation's Finances," *Brooklyn Daily Eagle*, March 13, 1904, 33–34; "Roosevelt Likes Extravagant Display," March 5, 1904, in unidentified newspaper in Theodore Roosevelt Papers, Library of Congress; Roosevelt to Lawrence Abbott, March 14, 1904. Morison, *Letters* 4: 751–53.

241 **"family circle":** Henry Adams to Elizabeth Cameron, March 13, 1903, *The Letters of Henry Adams*, 560–61; Sheldon M. Novick, *Honorable Justice: The Life of Oliver Wendell Holmes*, 267.

241 **"All I can do":** Roosevelt to Charles Mellen, March 12, 1904, Morison, *Letters* 4: 750. Mellen had left Northern Pacific to become president of the New York New Haven Railroad.

242 **"The moral effect":** Knox to Roosevelt, February 27, 1904, Theodore Roosevelt Papers, Library of Congress.

242 **The morning of:** Details from "The Merger Illegal," *New York Tribune*, March 15, 1904, 1; "Against Merger," *Evening Star*, March 14, 1904.

242 **Roosevelt remained:** Hay Diary entry March 14, 1904, William Roscoe Thayer, *The Life and Letters of John Hay*, vol. 2: 351.

242 **The evidence:** Full Text of "Decision of the United States Supreme Court in the Northern Securities Case," www.law.cornell.edu/supremecourt/text /193/197; Supplement to the *Railway Age* 37, no. 12 (March 18, 1904), in James J. Hill papers, Minnesota Historical Society.

243 **Brewer alone was:** Novick, *Honorable Justice*, 270.

243 **"Yours will hit":** ibid.

243 **"If such combination":** All quotes from the four opinions found in www.law .cornell.edu/supremecourt/text/193/197; Supplement to the *Railway Age* 37, no. 12 (March 18, 1904), in James J. Hill papers, Minnesota Historical Society.

244 **"When his voice":** Novick, *Honorable Justice*, 271.

245 **The only blow:** Henry Adams to Elizabeth Cameron, March 20, 1904 in *Henry Adams Letters*, 563–64.

245 **"I could carve":** Harbaugh, *Power and Responsibility*, 161.

246 **Knox drove straight:** "Knox on the Decision," *New York Tribune*, March 15, 1904, 2.

246 **"The danger of":** "Merger's Death Marks New Era," *Washington Times*, March 15, 1904, 1.

246 **Morgan puffed:** Morris, *Theodore Rex*, 316, citing *New York Herald*, March 15, 1904.

246 **"Northern Securities Co.":** Jack Morgan telegram March 15, 1904 from New York to London, Vincent Carosso Papers, The Pierpont Morgan Library.

246 **"The properties are":** "Properties as Good as Ever, Says Hill," *Minneapolis Star Tribune*, March 15, 1904, 1.

246 **"We have as much":** "What JJ Hill Has to Say," *Boston Globe*, March 15, 1904, 14.

246 **Headlines in papers:** *Evening Statesman* (Walla Walla, Washington), March 14, 1904, 1; *San Francisco Examiner*, March 15, 1904, 1; *St. Louis Post Dispatch*, March 15, 1904, 11.

247 **"People will love him":** Editorial from *The World*, reprinted in *St. Louis Post Dispatch*.

247 **"has practically renominated":** "Queer Move by the Democrats," *Evening World*, March 15, 1904.

247 **"The decision means more":** "Against Merger," *Evening Star*, March 14, 1904, 2.

247 **"The decision speaks":** "It Speaks for Itself," *Star Tribune*, March 15, 1904, 1.

247 **"The decision marks":** "President Will War on Combines," *Minneapolis Journal*, March 15, 1904, 1–2.

247 **"protective supporting orders":** "Finance and Trade," *Evening Star*, March 14, 1904, 2.

247 **"hireling of the plutocrat":** *Brooklyn Eagle*, April 16, 1904, in Philander C. Knox Papers, Library of Congress.

247 **"does not mean":** "Government Will Not Run Amuck, says Knox," *New York Times*, March 15, 1904, 2.

247 **"Would not it be":** Roosevelt to Knox, March 26, 1904, Theodore Roosevelt Papers, Library of Congress.

247 **a Gridiron dinner:** Arthur Wallace Dunn, *Gridiron Nights: Humorous and Satirical Views of Politics and Statesmen as Presented by the Famous Dining Club*, 149.

248 **"resolved itself":** "Merger's Death Marks New Era," *Washington Times*, March 15, 1904, 2.

248 **Republicans from all:** "At the White House: President Felicitated on the Merger Decision," *Evening Star*, March 15, 1904, 1.

248 **"Your opinion":** David K. Watson to John Marshall Harlan, March 15, 1904, in John Marshall Harlan Collection, Brandeis Law Library, University of Louisville.

248 **"I have had no"**: Novick, *Honorable Justice*, 272, citing Holmes to Ellen Curtis, April 8, 1904.

248 **"The merger business"**: Henry Adams to Elizabeth Cameron, April 3, 1904, *Letters*, 569.

248 **"Holmes should have"**: Roosevelt to Lodge, September 4, 1906, Morison, *Letters* 5: 1906.

249 **"arm in arm"**: "Northern Securities Will Dissolve," *St. Paul Globe*, March 23, 1904, James J. Hill Papers, Minnesota Historical Society.

249 **"absolutely fair"**: Roosevelt to Root, May 12 1904, Morison, *Letters* 4: 796.

250 **which critics said**: Alexander Dana Noyes, *Forty Years of American Finance*, 349.

250 **He sold his**: George Kennan, *E. H. Harriman: Railroad Czar*, 395.

250 **"A moral tonic"**: Balthasar Henry Meyer, "A History of the Northern Securities Case," 306.

250 **"You must have"**: Henry Pringle, *Theodore Roosevelt: A Biography*, 150.

250 **"I am having"**: Roosevelt to Ted, May 28, 1904, Morison, *Letters* 4: 807.

250 **"the stanchest of props"**: Roosevelt to Knox, June 11, 1904, Philander C. Knox Papers, Library of Congress.

250 **"President Roosevelt's"**: *Pittsburgh Gazette*, June 10, 1904, Philander C. Knox Papers, Library of Congress.

CHAPTER 16: A PRESIDENT IN HIS OWN RIGHT

251–252 **The letters**: All three are in *Theodore Roosevelt's Letters to His Children*, ed. Joseph Bucklin Bishop, 101–05.

252 **But they discovered**: Editorial in *New York Times*, June 24, 1904, 8 and Editorial in *Chicago Tribune*, June 24, 1904, 6.

253 **"In the enforcement"**: "Fight on Tariff Plank Is Averted," *New York Times*, June 23, 1904.

253 **"Certainty produces no"**: "New York Will Vote as a Unit on Ticket," *New York Times*, June 21, 1904.

253 **"It is difficult"**: "Tame Convention; Anxiety to End It," *New York Times*, June 22, 1904.

253 **He paid**: "Incidents and Humor in and out of Convention," *New York Times*, June 22, 1904.

253 **"men of small capital"**: "Root's Review of the Past Four Years," *New York Times*, June 22, 1904.

253 **He missed his:** "Tame Convention; Anxiety to End It."

254 **"All except the":** "Incidents and Humor in and out of Convention."

254 **"Here's to Roosevelt":** "Picked Up Here and There at Convention," *New York Times*, June 23, 1904.

254 **Some delegates:** "Urge that Convention Should Adjourn To-Day," *New York Times*, June 22, 1904; "Tame Convention, Anxiety to End It," *New York Times*, June 22, 1904.

255 **The National Committee:** Details from Charles Morris and Edward S. Ellis, *Our National Leaders of 1904: The Official Non-Partisan Handbook for the American Voter*, 35, 36.

255 **Frank Black:** "War the Keynote of Mr. Black's Speech," *New York Times*, June 24, 1904; William Allen White, *Masks in a Pageant*, 312–13.

255 **"hypnotizes obstacles":** Morris and Ellis, *Our National Leaders*, 59.

255 **"They tell us":** "Day of Speeches in Convention," *Chicago Tribune*, June 24, 1904, 4.

256 **Cannon did not:** "Roosevelt and Fairbanks Named," *New York Times*, June 24, 1904.

256 **"With a vision":** "Roosevelt and the Negro," *New York Times*, June 24, 1904.

256 **At the White House:** Details from "Surrounded by Family, Roosevelt Hears the News," *New York Times*, June 24, 1904; "President Gets News at Home," *Chicago Tribune*, June 24, 1904; Edmund Morris, *Theodore Rex*, 337.

257 **"human iceberg":** This and other details about Fairbanks from "Cannon's Ruse Keeps Convention," *New York Times*, June 23, 1904; Morris and Ellis, *Our National Leaders*, 119; "Roosevelt and Fairbanks," Editorial, *Chicago Tribune*, June 24, 1904, 6.

257 **"To be named":** "Surrounded by Family, Roosevelt Hears News."

257 **"No man should":** Roosevelt to Charles Warren Fairbanks, June 24, 1904 in *The Letters of Theodore Roosevelt*, ed. Elting Morison, vol. *Letters* 4: 844.

257 **"That wouldn't be":** "Fairbanks Shuns the Convention," *Chicago Tribune*, June 24, 1902, 2.

257 **the bars filled:** "The Rush from Chicago," *New York Times*, June 24, 1904.

257 **"The President was not":** June 24, 1904 entry, William Roscoe Thayer, *The Life and Letters of John Hay*, vol. 2: 377.

257 **Judge Alton Parker:** This portrait of Parker is drawn from two highly informative dissertations about an otherwise neglected historical figure. James Otis Wheaton, *The Genius and the Jurist: A Study of the Presidential*

Campaign of 1904, and Fred C. Shoemaker, *Alton Parker: The Images of a Gilded Age Statesman in an Era of Progressive Politics.*

258 "The judge at once": Theodore Roosevelt, *The Autobiography of Theodore Roosevelt*, 269.

258 who told Edith: Doris Kearns Goodwin, *The Bully Pulpit: Theodore Roosevelt, William Howard Taft, and the Golden Age of Journalism*, 261.

258 After his last one: "Hanna Picks Parker," Walter Wellman column reprinted in *Neenah Daily Times*, December 15, 1903, 2.

258 Morgan, who bailed: Jean Strouse, *Morgan: American Financier*, 535; even Roosevelt: Letter to Lodge, May 23, 1904, *Selections from the Correspondence of Theodore Roosevelt and Henry Cabot Lodge, 1884–1918*, 2: 17.

258 "I never saw him": H. H. Rodgers to Mark Twain, *Mark Twain's Correspondence with Henry Huttleston Rogers, 1893–1909*, ed. Lewis Leary, 556.

259 Cleveland announced: "'Don't Mention Me!' is Cleveland's Command," *St. Louis Post Dispatch*, July 6 1904, 5.

259 "Where does he": "Bryan Denounces Parker's Candidacy," *New York Times*, June 21, 1904.

259 Henry Gassaway Davis: Details from Morris and Ellis, *Our National Leaders*, 177.

259 "I regard": Shoemaker, "Alton Parker," 56; Morris and Ellis, *Our National Leaders*, 147.

260 "from a nobody": Lodge to Roosevelt, July 12, 1904, *Selections from the Correspondence*, 2: 88.

260 "He has become": Roosevelt to Lodge, July 14, 1904, Morison, *Letters* 4: 858.

260 Conservatives called: Shoemaker, "Alton Parker," 60, citing a *New York World* editorial.

260 "not in gloom": Shoemaker, "Alton Parker," 62, citing Lewis L. Gould, *Reform and Regulation: American Politics from Roosevelt to Wilson*, 59.

260 His acceptance speech: Details from "Enthusiasm Dampened," *New York Daily Tribune*, August 11, 1904, 1–2; "Parker's Speech of Acceptance," *Wall Street Journal*, August 11, 1904, 1; Shoemaker, "Alton Parker," 65, 67; *Harper's Weekly*, August 27, 1904.

261 financial backers: Morris, *Theodore Rex*, 360.

261 "If Parker should be": James J. Hill to Charles E. Perkins, July 22, 1904, James J. Hill Papers, Minnesota Historical Society.

261 Knox should: Series of letters from Roosevelt to Cortelyou, September 23, 1904, Morison, *Letters* 4: 951 and August 13, 1904; Morison, *Letters* 4: 892; to

Maine Senator Eugene Hale, August 4, 1904, Morison, *Letters* 4: 880; to Taft, September 29, 1904, Morison, *Letters* 4: 960.

261 **As campaign manager:** Morris, *Theodore Rex*, 348.

262 **"I wonder":** Roosevelt to Cortelyou, August 12, 1904, Morison, *Letters* 4: 889.

262 **He suggested:** October 1, 1904, Morison, *Letters* 4: 964.

262 **Roosevelt ordered:** August 11, 1904, Morison, *Letters* 4: 886.

262 **"by force":** Roosevelt to Lyman Abbott, July 26, 1904, Morison, *Letters* 4: 866–68.

262 **Party platform:** The 1904 Republican Party platform, American Presidency Project, https://www.presidency.ucsb.edu/documents/republican-party-pla tform-1904.

263 **He didn't involve:** Philip S. Foner, *History of the Labor Movement in the United States*, vol. 3: 395–400; Roosevelt to Wright, August 13 1904, Morison, *Letters* 4: 891.

263 **"I wish I were":** Roosevelt to Lodge, July 14 1904, Morison, *Letters* 4: 858.

263 **"While I am":** Roosevelt to Cannon, August 3 1904, Morison, *Letters* 4: 879–80.

263 **He worried, too:** Roosevelt to Lodge, July 22, 1904, Morison, *Letters* 4: 863–64.

263 **He begged Root:** Roosevelt to Root, August 2, 1904, Morison, *Letters* 4: 877.

264 **"The thing to do":** Roosevelt to Lodge July 22, 1904, Morison, *Letters* 4: 863–64.

264 **"To give any color":** Roosevelt to Cortelyou, August 11, 1904 in Morison, *Letters* 4: 886–87.

264 **"I think I have":** Cortelyou's response is included in Roosevelt's August 15, 1904 letter, as Cortelyou requested. He wanted a full record of the exchange. Morison, *Letters* 4: 893–94.

264 **"He was in honor":** Roosevelt to William Moody, August 15, 1904, Morison, *Letters* 4: 896.

265 **"regarded Father":** Alice Roosevelt Longworth, *Crowded Hours: Reminiscences of Alice Roosevelt Longworth* (New York: Charles Scribner's Sons; 1933), 63–64, notes in Theodore Roosevelt Collection, Harvard College Library.

265 **"Theodore!":** *New York Sun*, August 11, 1904.

265 **"I think he always":** *Campaign Contributions: Testimony Before a Subcommittee of the Committee on Privileges and Elections, United States Senate*, vol. 1, 482. Known as Clapp Committee, after Chairman Moses Clapp, https://babel.hathitrust.org/cgi/pt?id=nyp.33433075934673&view=1up&seq=7.

265 **"Relations with Mr. Bliss":** Clapp Committee, 442; other details about contributions from Clapp, 438, 440, 444.

266 *New York Times* **editorial:** "Buying the President," October 1, 1904, 8.

266 **quarter of a million:** Clapp Committee, 40.

266 **"Cannot our papers":** Roosevelt to Cortelyou, October 1, 1904, Morison, *Letters* 4: 963–64.

266 **"unhampered by":** Morris, *Theodore Rex*, 357, citing Roosevelt's presidential scrapbook.

266 **"I earnestly hope":** Roosevelt to Cortelyou, October 4, 1904, Morison, *Letters* 4: 970.

267 **"In view of":** Roosevelt to Harriman, October 10, 1904, Morison, *Letters* 4: 979.

267 **"practical men":** Roosevelt to Harriman, October 14, 1904, Morison, *Letters* 4: 983; Pringle notes, Theodore Roosevelt Collection, Harvard College Library.

267 **"They are in":** George Kennan, *E. H. Harriman: Railroad Czar*, 2: 192–93; Clapp Committee, 114.

267 **"Gratitude has been":** Clapp Committee, 451.

267 **Roosevelt later insisted:** Clapp Committee, 482.

267 **"We do not want":** Ibid., 123.

267 **"We cannot":** Roosevelt to Cortelyou, letters October 26–29, 1904, Morison, *Letters* 4: 995–98.

268 **apparently he did:** Robert E. Mutch, *Buying the Vote: A History of Campaign Finance Reform*, 79.

268 **"posterity letters":** Morris, *Theodore Rex*, 361.

268 **Cortelyou did return:** Arthur Wallace Dunn, *From Harrison to Harding: A Personal Narrative, Covering a Third of a Century, 1888–1921*, 401.

268 **gave and raised 70 percent:** Mutch, *Buying the Vote*, 29; almost $2.3 million: ibid., 209; less than one million: ibid., 30, 32. Mutch accepts Croly's $3.5 million figure for 1896 and the Republicans' own estimate of raising about $3 million in 1900.

268 **"Corporation cunning":** Mark Sullivan, *Our Times: The United States, 1900–1925*, vol. 2: 249–50, citing Roosevelt interview with journalist Lindsay Dennison in 1904 that wasn't published until 1909.

268 **"perpetual delight":** Roosevelt to Kermit, October 15 1904, Morison, *Letters* 4: 983–84.

269 **"The President talked":** Thayer, *Life and Letters of John Hay*, 356.

269 **"badly bunged":** October 23, Thayer, *Life and Letters of John Hay*, 356.

269 **"The President will":** November 3, Thayer, *Life and Letters of John Hay*, 357.

269 **"Well, old fellow"**: Alton Parker, Clapp Committee testimony, 899; Morris, *Theodore Rex*, 360 uses slightly different language for this exchange, based on notes from Parker's unpublished biography.

269 **"either indecent or immoral"**: "Democrats Claim Sure Parker Victory," *New York Times*, October 24, 1904, 5.

269 **Parker came down**: Details from "Parker's Throat Sprayed," *New York Sun*, November 1, 1904, 1; "Parker! At Last," *New York Sun*, November 1, 1904, 2; "Parker, the Orator, Cheered by Throngs," *New York Times*, November 3, 1904, 1–2; James Otis Wheaton, "The Genius and the Jurist: A Study of the Presidential Campaign of 1904," 513.

270 **"I should feel"**: Roosevelt to Cortelyou, November 2, 1904, Morison, *Letters* 4: 1009–13.

270 **"The statements made"**: "Roosevelt Speaks; Cortelyou Charges called Monstrous," *New York Times*, November 5, 1904, 1; full statement in *The Roosevelt Policy: Speeches, Letters and State Papers, Relating to Corporate Wealth and Closely Allied Topics*, ed. William Griffith, 221.

270 **Fifty or so**: Interview with William Loeb, April 14, 1930 in Pringle 1904 Campaign Notes, Theodore Roosevelt Collection, Harvard College Libarary.

270 **"Did you ever"**: Roosevelt to Knox, November 6, 1904, Philander C. Knox Papers, Library of Congress.

270 **Roosevelt left**: "How President Voted," *New York Tribune*, November 9, 1904, 3; "Mr. Roosevelt Votes and Goes to Capital," *New York Times*, November 9, 1904, 9.

270 **Parker drove**: "Judge Parker Voted No. 147," *New York Sun*, November 9, 1904, 5; James Otis Wheaton, "The Genius and the Jurist: A Study of the Presidential Campaign of 1904," 518.

271 **"a little feast"**: Sylvia Jukes Morris, *Edith Kermit Roosevelt*, 280.

271 **white light**: "Election Results by Times Building Flash," *New York Times*, November 6, 1904, 3.

271 **"How they are"**: Noyes, *The Market Place: Reminiscences of a Financial Editor*, 214.

271 **The Democrats won**: Wheaton, "The Genius and the Jurist," 526.

271 **The Republicans won**: Ibid.

271 **"Have swept the"**: Roosevelt to Lodge, November 8, 1904, Morison, *Letters* 4: 1018.

271 **"I am no"**: Sullivan, *Our Times* 2: 460.

271 **"The people"**: Roosevelt included the telegram from Parker in his own to Cortelyou, Morison, *Letters* 4: 1016–17.

271 **"I am glad":** Thayer, *Life and Letters of John Hay*, 359.

271 **The president received:** Roosevelt to Corinne Roosevelt Robinson, November 11, 1904, Morison rejected letters, Theodore Roosevelt Collection, Harvard College Library.

271 **Morgan's secretary:** Excelsior Diary 1904, Pierpont Morgan Papers, The Pierpont Morgan Library.

271 **Morgan was also:** Details of his various activities from "Erie Railway Deal," *Railway News* 84 (December 2, 1905): 928; "Morgan Pays $1,200,000 for House," *Baltimore Sun*, November 23, 1904, 10; Strouse, *Morgan: American Financier*, 539–40; "No Morgan Knighthood," *Sentinel*, November 12, 1904, 1; Morgan, J. Pierpont, *Collier's Self-Indexing Annual*, 1904, 444; "JP Morgan Returns Ascoli Cope to Italy," *New York Times*, November 4, 1904, 1; "Papal Cope Returned," *Houston Post*, November 4, 1904, 2; "No Morgan Knighthood," *Sentinel*, November 12, 1904, 1.

272 **Roosevelt called:** Details from "Joy at the White House," *New York Tribune*, November 9, 1904, 2; "Roosevelt Calmly Receives the News," *San Francisco Call*, November 9, 1904, 2; "Roosevelt's Pledge," *Washington Evening Star*, November 9, 1904, 8.

272 **When Edith heard:** Sylvia Jukes Morris, *Edith Kermit Roosevelt*, 280–81.

272 **cut off:** H. H. Kohlsaat, *From McKinley to Harding: Personal Recollections of Our Presidents*, 138.

272 **"Of all possible oligarchies":** Roosevelt to Cecil Arthur Spring Rice, December 27, 1904, Morison, *Letters* 4: 1082–88.

272 **wrenched his thigh:** Roosevelt to Michael Joseph Donovan, December 13, 1904, Morison, *Letters* 4: 1065.

273 **The dinner:** Strouse, *Morgan: American Financier*, 498–99; "Guest of Architects," *Washington Post*, January 12, 1905, 10.

273 **niece Eleanor:** Kathleen Dalton, *Theodore Roosevelt: A Strenuous Life*, 271; "White House Luncheon," *Washington Post*, March 5, 1905, 3.

273 **The same material:** "Theodore Roosevelt, Readying for His Inauguration, Complains of Bad Tailoring," www.shapell.org/manuscript/president-elect -theodore-roosevelt-suffers-bad-tailoring-job-for-inauguration/.

273 **heavy gold ring:** Roosevelt, *Autobiography*, 385; Thayer, *Life and Letters of John Hay*, 363.

274 **"Modern life":** Inaugural address, www.theodore-roosevelt.com/images /research/txtspeeches/121.txt.

274 **inaugural parade:** Details of various arrangements, whereabouts from "Trains All Crowded," *Washington Post*, March 3, 1905, 27; "Depew Pays

Top Price," *Washington Post*, March 4, 1905, 26; "Inauguration Hotel Trust," *Buffalo Evening News*, March 3, 1905, 2; "News of the Labor World," *Daily Independent*, March 3, 1905, 7; Simon Cordery, *Mother Jones: Raising Cain and Consciousness*, 117; Alice Wexler, *Emma Goldman: An Intimate Life*, 115; "Knox Goes to Florida," *Reading Times*, March 3, 1905, 1.

274 **turned down:** "Declines $100,000 Job," *Topeka Daily Herald*, March 4, 1905, 3; "Order Out of Chaos," *Panama Canal Review*, University of Florida George A. Smathers Libraries, https://ufdc.ufl.edu/UF00097366 /00191/4j.

274 **"It really touched":** "Passed in Review," *Washington Post*, March 5, 1905, 2.

275 **"everybody and everything":** Roosevelt to George Otto Trevelyan, March 9, 1905, Morison, *Letters* 4: 1132–35.

275 **The Inaugural Ball:** "Ball is the Climax," *Washington Post*, March 5, 1905, 3; "Rare Display of Gowns and Gems at Inauguration Ball," *Washington Post*, March 5, 1905, 4.

275 **Drank a toast:** Corinne Roosevelt Robinson, *My Brother, Theodore Roosevelt*, 225–26; Sylvia Jukes Morris, *Edith Kermit Roosevelt*, 284.

275 **nervous about his health:** Strouse, *Morgan: American Financier*, 540.

275 **"had accomplished":** Roosevelt to George Otto Trevelyan, March 9, 1905, Morison, *Letters* 4: 1132–35.

276 **He commissioned:** https://americanart.si.edu/artwork/theodore-roosevelt -presidential-inaugural-medal-79387.

EPILOGUE

277 **Dozens of men:** This account is based on Jean Strouse, *Morgan: American Financier*, 587–87, and Pierpont Morgan Library presentations and records.

277 **"It may well":** "There Will Be No Change in Policy," August 20, 1907 speech in Provincetown, Massachusetts, *The Roosevelt Policy: Speeches, Letters and State Papers, Relating to Corporate Wealth and Closely Allied Topics*, ed. William Griffith 2: 570.

278 **Morgan declined:** Strouse, *Morgan: American Financier*, 600.

278 **"Money Talks":** *Chicago Daily Tribune*, December 10, 1908, 1.

278 **"There may be times":** "Morgan Tells His Secret," *New York Times*, December 11, 1908, 1.

278 **"The men of swollen fortune":** Speech to the National Educational Association, Ocean Grove, New Jersey, July 7, 1905, www.theodore-roosevelt.com /images/research/txtspeeches/144.txt.

279 **Morgan's railroads:** Strouse, *Morgan: American Financier*, 563.

280 **The fight was really:** Roosevelt, *Autobiography*, 253.

280 **Morgan telegraphed:** Strouse, *Morgan: American Financier*, 601.

280 **"I have done my":** Roosevelt to Paul Morton, March 2, 1909, Morison, *Letters* 6: 1541.

281 **"the civilization":** "Division of State and Federal Powers," speech in Harrisburg, Pennsylvania, October 4, 1906, Griffith, *The Roosevelt Policy* 2: 421.

281 **"sense of having so lived":** "Conduct as the Ultimate Test of Religious Belief," speech to Christ Church Parish, Oyster Bay, New York. September 8, 1906, Griffith, *Roosevelt Policy* 2: 409.

281 **Top one percent:** "Distribution of Household Wealth in the U.S. since 1989," federalreserve.gov; Alexandre Tanzi and Michael Sasso, "Richest 1% of Americans Close to Surpassing Wealth of Middle Class," *Bloomberg News*, November 9, 2019.

IMAGE CREDITS

Page 161   Stereograph Cards collection, Prints & Photographs Division,
            Library of Congress, LC-DIG-stereo-1s01956 and
            LC-DIG-stereo-1s01976
Page 162   Farm Security Administration/Office of War Information Black-
            and-White Negatives collection, Prints & Photographs Division,
            Library of Congress, LC-DIG-fsa-8e03064
Page 165   Theodore Roosevelt Collection, Harvard College Library
Page 174   Granger – Historical Picture Archive
Page 186   Bain Collection, Prints & Photographs Division, Library of
            Congress, LC-DIG-ggbain-00552
Page 189   Stereograph Cards collection, Prints & Photographs Division,
            Library of Congress, LC-USZ62-95897
Page 196   Miscellaneous Items in High Demand collection, Prints &
            Photographs Division, Library of Congress,
            LC-DIG-ppmsca-35788
Page 208   Theodore Roosevelt Collection, Harvard College Library
Page 217   Miscellaneous Items in High Demand collection, Prints &
            Photographs Division, Library of Congress, LC-DIG-ppmsca-25752
Page 220   Miscellaneous Items in High Demand collection, Prints &
            Photographs Division, Library of Congress, LC-USZ62-40292
Page 226   Miscellaneous Items in High Demand collection, Prints &
            Photographs Division, Library of Congress, LC-USZ62-42363
Page 227   Granger – Historical Picture Archive
Page 252   Prints & Photographs Division, Library of Congress,
            LC-DIG-ppmsca-35756
Page 254   Theodore Roosevelt Collection, Harvard College Library
Page 256   Niday Picture Library / Alamy Stock Photo
Page 262   Johnston (Frances Benjamin) Collection, Prints & Photographs
            Division, Library of Congress, LC-USZ62-83121
Page 273   Stereograph Cards collection, Prints & Photographs Division,
            Library of Congress, LC-USZ62-38463

INDEX

Note: page numbers in italics refer to images.

A NOTE ON THE AUTHOR

Susan Berfield is an award-winning investigative reporter for *Bloomberg Businessweek* and Bloomberg News, where she has covered some of America's largest corporations. She has been interviewed on PBS *NewsHour*, NPR's *All Things Considered*, and *Marketplace*. Her research for *The Hour of Fate*, her first book, took her to archives in New York, St. Paul, Washington, D.C., and Cambridge, Massachusetts, and was supported by a Logan Nonfiction Fellowship. She lives in Brooklyn with her family.

BRITAIN
AT WAR

RICHARD EURICH. The Withdrawal from Dunkerque. 1940.

This painting of the most celebrated event of this war shows troops being ferried from the beaches to the drifter and the sidewheel naval tug in the right foreground. At the far right a destroyer is departing. At the extreme left motor trucks have been lined up to form a small subsidiary pier. Across the center may be seen the jetty from which many troops were rescued.

Eurich was born in 1903 at Bradford. He studied art at the Bradford Art School and at the Slade School. An amateur yachtsman, he has specialized in naval subjects.   (Oil on canvas, 30⅛ x 40 inches)

BRITAIN AT WAR

EDITED BY MONROE WHEELER. TEXT BY T. S. ELIOT,
HERBERT READ, E. J. CARTER AND CARLOS DYER

THE MUSEUM OF MODERN ART, NEW YORK

Reprint Edition 1972   *Published for The Museum of Modern Art by Arno Press*

094439

ACKNOWLEDGMENTS

The President and Trustees of the Museum of Modern Art wish to record their deep appreciation of the services of Sir Kenneth Clark, Director of the National Gallery, London, who has been in charge of arrangements in England for the exhibition upon which this volume is based. Grateful acknowledgment is also extended to T. S. Eliot for contributing his poem, *Defense of the Islands*, to E. J. Carter and Herbert Read for their articles, and to the following persons and institutions who have generously collaborated in preparing the exhibition and book:

For Loans to the Exhibition: Acme Newspapers, Incorporated; Associated Press; L. Berman; Bill Brandt; British Library of Information, New York; British Official Photographers; Bundles for Britain, Incorporated; Mr. and Mrs. John Carter; Central Press Photos, Limited, in arrangement with British Combine Photos of New York; Stephen C. Clark; Fox Photos, Limited; *Flight*; Alexander Gross; International News Photos; Victor Levy; London *Daily Sketch*; London News Agency Photos, Limited; London *Times*; Ministry of Information, London; The National Gallery of Canada, Ottawa; *Punch*; Peter Ray; James A. Sinclair of London; Richard N. Stone; Miss Jessica Stonor; Topical Press Agency, Limited.

For Information and Counsel: David M. Bailey; E. M. O'R. Dickey; Alan A. Dudley; H. S. Ede; Sir Angus Fletcher; Talbot Hamlin; Jan Juta; E. McKnight Kauffer; H. O. McCurry, Director of The National Gallery of Canada; Lieutenant I. T. Morgan; General H. S. Sewell; Mrs. Ala Story; Lieutenant L. S. B. Worrall; Gary Underhill.

For the Camouflage Section: The camouflage section has been prepared by Carlos Dyer, of the Museum staff, with the collaboration of Stanley William Hayter, Richard Bennett, Lt. Colonel Homer Saint-Gaudens and Captain Paul W. Thompson. The models and diagrams for the camouflage section have been made by the faculty and students of The Art School of Pratt Institute, Brooklyn, New York: James C. Boudreau, Director; Alexander J. Kostellow, Supervisor of Design and Structure; William L. Longyear, Supervisor of Advertising Design; Konrad Wittmann, Chief of Industrial Camouflage Program; Major Peter Rodyenko, Chief of Military Camouflage Program; James R. Patterson, Supervisor of Exhibits; Donald R. Dohner, Supervisor of Industrial Design; Robert Kolli, Design Instructor, Ivan Rigby, Design Instructor.

For Photographs: All photographs, with the exception of those by Miss Lee Miller, have been provided by the Ministry of Information, London, and were selected by C. H. Gibbs-Smith, Misha Black, Miss Mona Beardsley and Milner Gray. The photographs by Miss Lee Miller (pages 58, 68 and 73) have been reproduced through the courtesy of Charles Scribner's Sons, New York, publishers of *Bloody But Unbowed: Pictures of Britain Under Fire*.

For Films: The films shown in connection with the exhibition were acquired by the Museum of Modern Art Film Library from the British Library of Information, New York.

For Assistance in the Preparation of the Book: Miss Lenore H. Browning, Miss Betty Chamberlain, Miss Lee Francis and Mrs. C. S. Hartman of the Museum staff.

TRUSTEES OF THE MUSEUM

STAFF OF THE MUSEUM

Library of Congress Catalog Card Number 70-169301
ISBN 0-405-01560-7

Copyright 1941, The Museum of Modern Art, 11 West 53 Street, New York, N. Y.   Printed in the United States of America

CONTENTS

DEFENSE OF THE ISLANDS

Let these memorials of built stone—music's
enduring instrument, of many centuries of
patient cultivation of the earth, of English
verse

be joined with the memory of this defense of
the islands

and the memory of those appointed to the grey
ships—battleship, merchantman, trawler—
contributing their share to the ages' pavement
of British bone on the sea floor

and of those who, in man's newest form of gamble
with death, fight the power of darkness in air
and fire

and of those who have followed their forebears
to Flanders and France, those undefeated in defeat, unalterable in triumph, changing nothing
of their ancestors' ways but the weapons

and those again for whom the paths of glory are
the lanes and the streets of Britain:

to say, to the past and the future generations
of our kin and of our speech, that we took up
our positions, in obedience to instructions.

T. S. ELIOT
9. vi. 40

THE ARTIST AND NATIONAL DEFENSE

With admirable wisdom, in this war as in the last, the British Government has recognized the usefulness of art to enliven the idealism with which its people are united in self-defense, to ennoble the scene of their common suffering and to provide visual imagery of their great cause and their peril. This book and the exhibition which is its subject matter offer a necessarily limited survey of what the artist can do in time of war.

During such a war as this, the security of every nation—even a nation at peace—must be sustained with clarity and vitality of the civilian mind as well as by force of armament. Therefore the role of the creative artist in the national emergency is a decisive as well as a complex problem. The example of Great Britain in using its artists' talents in painting, drawing, cartoon, poster and camouflage may help us to find our own solutions.

1914–18; 1939–41

It was not until 1917 that the Ministry of Information made arrangements for the employment of artists to record the last war—notably Kennington, Nevinson, Wyndham Lewis, the two Nashes and the two Spencers—some of whom had already seen service and been invalided home. There was general satisfaction with their work, and just before the end of the war, or immediately after it, John, Orpen, Bone, Lavery and others were commissioned to complete the pictorial history with official portraits and retrospective paintings. In this way the collection in the Imperial War Museum was built up.

Meanwhile the Canadian Government also assembled a fine group of war pictures, a selection of which has kindly been sent to us through the courtesy of H. O. McCurry and the National Gallery of Canada, Ottawa.

Within two months of the declaration of the pres-

ent war, a committee was formed under the chairmanship of Sir Kenneth Clark, Director of the National Gallery, to draw up a list of artists qualified to record the war at home and abroad, and to advise government departments on the selection of artists from this list and on such questions as copyright, disposal and exhibition of work and the publication of reproductions.

The committee consists of distinguished men professionally concerned with art, and representatives of the Admiralty, War Office, Air Ministry, Ministry of Home Security, Ministry of Supply and Ministry of Information.

Artists are employed in two categories: salaried appointments for full-time work with one or another

AUGUSTUS JOHN. A Canadian Soldier, 1917 Oil on canvas, 32 x 24 inches. Lent by the National Gallery of Canada, Ottawa.

branch of the armed forces; or particular commission and purchase.

Recalling that many of the best pictures painted of the last war were by men who saw active service, the committee has arranged that painters already in the armed forces should have opportunity to do some work of art.

With the exception of the paintings from Canada and a few additional watercolors, all the paintings in the present exhibition have been selected in London by Sir Kenneth Clark.

It is worthy of note how little false optimism, exaggerated pathos or war-time hatred these pictures show. There are three main divisions of subject matter: portraiture and the common people at all their tasks; destruction by and of the enemy; and the awe-inspiring martial machinery of defense.

There is little or no trace of corruption of the artists' taste or integrity. Indeed, in certain instances

of the abstract school—Graham Sutherland, John Piper, Henry Moore—the tragedy of war and the beauty of its mechanism seem as appropriate and personal as anything they have undertaken to paint before.

The honor the British have done their artists in summoning them to a particular role in the national defense may provide for us an object-lesson at a time when our own government is beginning the various enrollment of its citizens. No one pretends any more that international political issues and armed conflict are none of the artist's business. Like another man, he may be required to fight, and if his country loses, he may lose all that makes art possible. It would be tragic neglect, on the other hand, for anyone to be indifferent to the arts and the fate of artists in these times.

In defending a civilization there should be as little dislocation or abandonment of the civilizing arts as possible, and as much continuance and preservation as we can possibly afford. The artist is an extreme specialist and sometimes, even with the best will in the world, cannot become a first-rate soldier. The necessity of his talent for such things as posters and camouflage is well understood. And the influence of painting as a fine art may also be enlisted in the common cause, as the British have shown us. We must admire their perspicacity and courage, in spite of a shortage of man-power, in keeping so many British artists at the work they do best.

Those whose work is shown here have fought well without guns.

MONROE WHEELER

SIR WILLIAM ORPEN. Major-General Sir D. Watson, K.C.B., C.M.G., 1918. Oil on canvas, 36 x 30 1/8 inches. Lent by the National Gallery of Canada, Ottawa.

THE WAR AS SEEN BY BRITISH ARTISTS

American visitors to London must often have found their way to the Imperial War Museum where they would find, perhaps to their surprise, one of the most interesting collections of contemporary British painting to be seen in the city. This was the result of a rather haphazard policy carried out during the last war. Encouraged by the success of this experiment, the newly formed Ministry of Information lost no time at the beginning of this war in enlisting artists in a scheme of similar scope. Leading painters and draughtsmen were appointed as official artists to the Navy, the Army and the Air Force. These artists wear uniforms, and live and work with the various units to which they are attached. They may, indeed, go into action with those units and see the worst—and the best—of the war with their own eyes. Other artists are commissioned to do special jobs on the civilian front—in the armament factories or the air-raid shelters; and any artist may submit work to a committee of the Ministry of Information who will purchase it for the nation if it is considered of sufficient interest. Already, after little more than a year of the war, a very impressive collection of war pictures has been built up, and the exhibition of these pictures at the National Gallery has attracted crowds of people. In fact the National Gallery, with this exhibition of pictures and its mid-day concerts of classical music, has become a defiant outpost of culture, right in the midst of the bombed and shattered metropolis.

It is a representative selection of these pictures which is now being exhibited in the Museum of Modern Art in New York. It includes the work of veterans like Sir Muirhead Bone and Sir William Rothenstein whose names will already be familiar in the United States; it includes the work of artists like Paul Nash and Eric Kennington who first made their reputation with their paintings of the last war; and it includes the work of several artists whose names will be unfamiliar because it is only now, in this war, that they are revealing their exceptional talent. All these artists have had one aim: to bring us a little closer to the reality—to the pathos, the humour and the tragedy of the war—aspects of the war which only the sensitive artist can see and record. This is best done by the rapid sketch, and in the drawings of Edward Ardizzone, Anthony Gross and Feliks Topolski you will find a keen and human observation quite beyond the means of the camera. Ardizzone was with the expeditionary force in France, and his drawings give a vivid impression of that confused phase of the war. He has now been transferred to the London front, and sketches like "Shelter Scene" and "A Pub in Silvertown" convey with the fidelity and realism of a Daumier the atmosphere in which the people of London are now living. Topolski is attached to the Polish forces in Great Britain, and he shows how a true artist can snatch beauty from

SIR WILLIAM ORPEN. Man Thinking on the Butte de Warlencourt. Lent by Stephen C. Clark.

the most trivial incidents. Particular interest attaches to the vivid sketches of Midshipman Worsley, for in this case it is not an officially appointed artist who is recording an aspect of the war, but a member of the fighting forces.

All these artists, and others whose names have not been mentioned, are engaged on what might be called "reportage." To represent the reality of some aspect of the war remains their chief object, and the work of art begins and ends within this sphere of reality. But other artists begin from the reality which is the war and try to achieve a new order of reality or vision. This has been successfully achieved in Graham Sutherland's picture of air-raid damage, but one may feel that Eric Ravilious, though he has painted pictures which are as esthetically satisfying as any in the exhibition, has not told us anything of particular value about the war. The transformation of reality begins already in paintings still so obviously realistic as the portraits of Eric Kennington; his "Leading Stoker Cloke" and his "Able Seaman Povey" are no longer individuals, but representative types, figures visualized from some immense epic of war. In his portrait of "Group Captain Sweeney" you have not merely the features of a famous American hero, but the very symbol of visionary enterprise. But it is not merely the personnel of war, but the actual scene that can thus transcend reality. I am referring particularly to Paul Nash's pictures of aircraft. Here the machine which is most typical of the war is animated, is made into a monstrous bird threatening humanity from the skies. Nothing could be more desolate than these same monsters when they lie broken and defeated at the foot of some cliff or in the shallow water of the Channel: symbols of the triumph of man's free spirit over the instruments of tyranny and aggression.

It is not for an Englishman to praise these pictures for the spirit they represent, but one final word of explanation. It may be that the general effect will strike the American visitor as tame or subdued, as too quiet and harmonious for the adequate representation of war. It must then be remembered that though the English are energetic in action, they are restrained in expression. Our typical poetry is lyrical, not epical or even tragic. Our typical music is the madrigal and the song, not the opera and the symphony. Our typical painting is the landscape. In all these respects war cannot change us; and we are fighting this war precisely because in these respects we refuse to be changed. Our art is the exact expression of our conception of liberty: the free and unforced reflection of all the variety and eccentricity of the individual human being.

HERBERT READ

EDWARD WADSWORTH. *Dazzle Ships in Drydock at Liverpool. c. 1918. Oil on canvas, 120 x 96 inches.*
Lent by the National Gallery of Canada, Ottawa.

PAINTINGS: LAST WAR

ERIC KENNINGTON. The Conquerors. 1920. Oil on canvas, 117 x 96 inches. Lent by the National Gallery of Canada, Ottawa. For biographical note on the artist see page 26.

Men of the 16th Canadian Scottish Battalion, First Division, marching from Arras to Amiens.

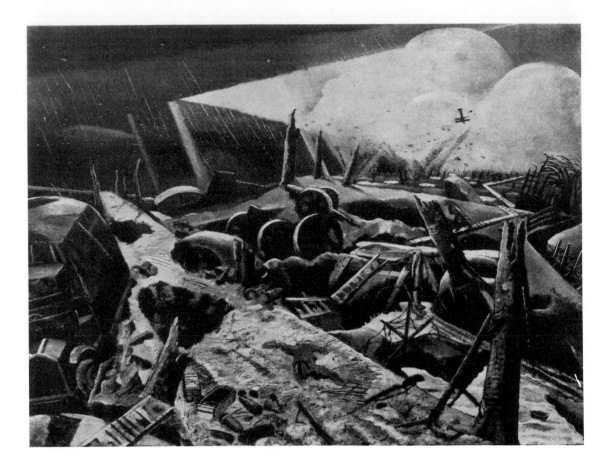

PAUL NASH. Void. 1918. Oil on canvas, 28 x 36 inches. Lent by the National Gallery of Canada, Ottawa.

A landscape of the Ypres salient.

    Paul Nash was born in London in 1889. Painter, wood-engraver, poster and stage designer and illustrator. Studied at the Slade School. Early member of the London Group. Served in the last war as an official war artist. Has taught at the Royal College of Art. Ex-President of the Society of Industrial Artists. Has held many exhibitions in London. In 1933 founded Unit One, a group of abstract artists. Air Ministry Artist, 1940.

EDWARD ARDIZZONE. *Priest Begging for a Lift in Louvain, May 1940. Watercolor, 9½ x 12⅛ inches.*

Ardizzone was born at Haiphong, French Indo-China, in 1901. Studied at the Westminster and Central Schools of Art. Previously a gunner in the Territorial Army, he was drafted to serve as an official war artist when the present war broke out, and went with the British Army to Flanders. Ardizzone has held several one-man exhibitions in London and is widely known as painter and illustrator.

EDWARD ARDIZZONE. A Pub in Silvertown. 1940. Watercolor, 9 x 12⅝ inches.

A devastated corner in London's East End.

PAINTINGS AND DRAWINGS: THIS WAR

JOHN ARMSTRONG. *The Elms. 1940. Tempera on canvas, 20 x 27 inches.*

Even before the war this artist delighted to paint ruins. Here he portrays an effect of bombing.

Armstrong was born at Hastings in 1893. Studied at the St. John's Wood School of Art. Designed scenery for the Lyric Theatre, Hammersmith, and for Charles Laughton's films. Painted classical compositions in tempera about 1927, later turned to abstract art. Member of Unit One, a group of abstract painters.

EDWARD BAWDEN. *The Quay at Dunkerque. 1940. Watercolor, 12 x 19⅜ inches.*

Soldiers are seen entering an air raid shelter.

    Bawden was born at Braintree, Essex, 1903. Studied at the Cambridge School of Art and at the Royal College of Art, where he later taught. Executed mural paintings at Morley College, London. Noted as water-colorist, book illustrator, and designer of wall- and pattern papers. Has executed posters for London Transport, and for Shell publicity in the famous "Shell-on-the-Road" series. Official war artist, British Army.

MAJOR SIR MUIRHEAD BONE. Dawn—from the Signal Station, Dover, 1940. Chalk, wash and pen, 17⅝ x 29⅝ inches.

Ships bringing the last of the rearguard from Dunkerque coming around the South Foreland and entering the Gate at Dover in June, 1940. Painted on the site.

Bone was born in 1876 in Glasgow. Studied at the Glasgow School of Art. Came to London in 1901. Member of the New English Art Club since 1902. Noted as draughtsman and etcher; especially of architectural subjects. Served as war artist in the last war; Admiralty Artist, 1940.

MAJOR SIR MUIRHEAD BONE. *The Exeter and Ajax Parade, 1940. Chalk, wash and pencil, 20¼ x 36¾ inches.*

The victory of the River Plate was celebrated by this review of the crews of the Exeter and the Ajax in the Horse Guards parade ground. At the table in the foreground are the King, Churchill and Chamberlain.

PAINTINGS AND DRAWINGS: THIS WAR

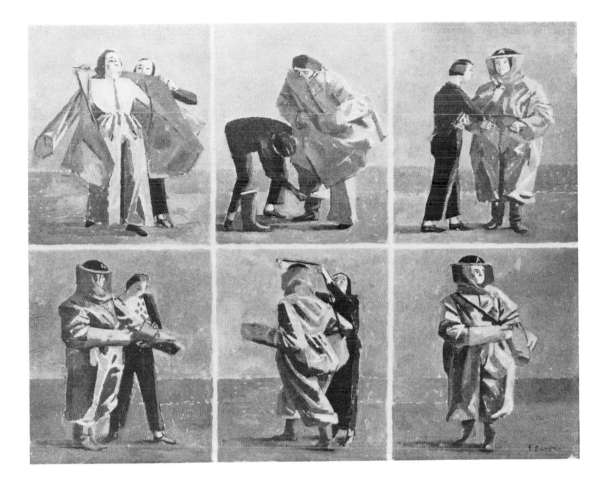

EVELYN DUNBAR. *Putting on Anti-Gas Clothes. 1940. Oil on canvas, 24 x 30 inches.*

Depicting the difficulties of getting into the special clothing worn by those exposed to mustard and other poisonous gases. This garment is so completely insulated that it can be worn only for a short time on emergency duty.

See photographs of gas masks, page 67.

BARNETT FREEDMAN. *The Gun. 1940. Oil on canvas, 23¼ x 36 inches.*

A 9.2-inch gun—one of many in readiness for the defense of the coast of Britain.

    Freedman was born in London in 1901. Studied at St. Martin's School of Art and the Royal College of Art. Has staged and produced plays. Has illustrated several books with color lithographs. Designed the George V Jubilee postage stamp in 1935, as well as many posters and book jackets. Official war artist, 1940.

ANTHONY GROSS. *The Watcher. 1940. Gouache, 7¾ x 12¾ inches. Lent by Dr. Alexander Gross, New York.*

One of those who wait on London roofs to extinguish incendiary bombs.

Gross was born in London in 1905. Studied at the Slade School, at Julian's and the Beaux-Arts in Paris, and for two years in Madrid.

KEITH HENDERSON. *Improvised Test of an Undercarriage. 1940. Oil on canvas, 30⅛ x 40 inches.*

A Lockheed General Reconnaissance plane is silhouetted against the open door of a hangar. This method of testing is contrary to all regulations but effective.

Henderson was born in 1883. Studied at the Slade School and in Paris. Exhibits at the Royal Academy and is represented in important public collections. Author of Letters to Helen, *1917,* Palm Groves and Humming Birds, *1924,* Prehistoric Man, *1927. Air Ministry Artist, 1940.*

ERIC KENNINGTON. *Able Seaman Povey of H.M.S. Hardy. 1940. Pastel, 29½ x 21⅝ inches.*

Povey was one of the heroes of the First Battle of Narvik.

Kennington was born in 1888 at Chelsea. Served in France and was invalided home in 1915. In 1922 went to Arabia with Col. T. E. Lawrence. Also noted for his sculpture. One of the foremost portrait painters of this war.

JOHN MANSBRIDGE. *An Air Gunner in a Turret—Sergeant G. Holmes, D.F.M. 1940. Oil on canvas, 30 x 25 inches.*

Mansbridge was born in 1902.

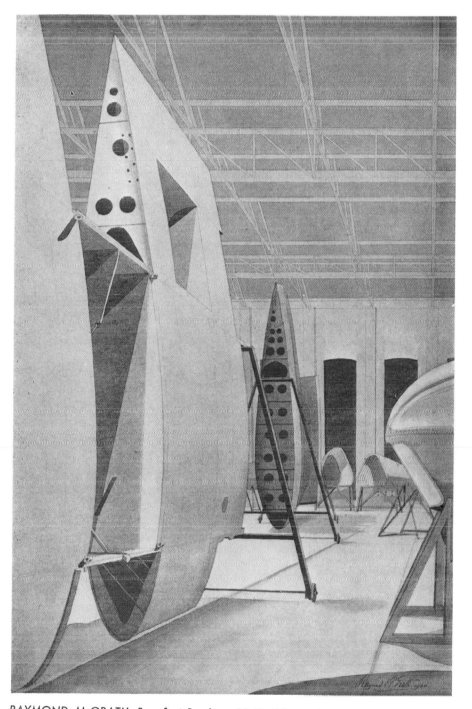

RAYMOND McGRATH. Beaufort Bombers. 1940. Watercolor on canvasboard, 14⅜ x 21½ inches. Wing sections awaiting assembly.

An Australian, McGrath is an architect by training and profession. At present he holds an important post under the Eire Government in Dublin.

PAINTINGS AND DRAWINGS: THIS WAR

HENRY MOORE. *Pale Shelter Scene. Drawing.*

Londoners sleeping in shelters and in the Underground have provided the subject matter for a series of drawings by this artist.

Henry Moore was born in Castleford, Yorkshire, in 1898. He studied at the Leeds Art School, in London, France and Italy. Influenced by the art of primitive peoples, by Arp and Picasso. Member of the Axis group and the leading abstract sculptor in England.

PAINTINGS AND DRAWINGS: THIS WAR   29

PAUL NASH. Under the Cliff. 1940. Watercolor, 15⅛ x 22⅜ inches.

The tail of a Heinkel bomber (HE-111K).

For biographical note on the artist see page 15.

JOHN PIPER. (See opposite page.)

Piper was born in 1903 at Epsom, Surrey. Studied at the Royal College of Art. He has been an archeologist, musician (once a jazz pianist), journalist, one of the founders of Axis (a magazine of abstract art), and art commentator for television. After an abstract period in which he employed collage, he has recently turned to architectural subjects. Commissioned to make drawings of North Buckinghamshire under the Pilgrim Trust Scheme for Recording England. Member of the London Group. Official war artist, 1940, for A.R.P. subjects.

PAINTINGS AND DRAWINGS: THIS WAR

JOHN PIPER. *Passage to the Control Room at S.W. Regional Headquarters. 1940. Oil on canvas, 29¾ x 20 inches. For biographical note see opposite page.*

A corridor in one of the nerve centers of the British Air Raid Precautions System.

ROLAND VIVIAN PITCHFORTH. Gravy Salt Factory, Birmingham. 1940. Watercolor, 21½ x 29⅝ inches.

The effect of German high-explosive bombs on a factory.

Pitchforth was born at Wakefield, 1895. Studied first at Leeds School of Art. Served in the last war (as a result of which he is gun-deaf) and then continued his studies at the Royal College of Art. Member of the London Artists' Association and the London Group.

PAINTINGS AND DRAWINGS: THIS WAR

ERIC RAVILIOUS. Norway, 1940. Watercolor, 18⅜ x 23 inches.

Ravilious was born in London in 1903. Studied at the Royal College of Art. Executed mural paintings at Morley College, London, with Edward Bawden, and at the L.M.S. Hotel, Morecambe. Has illustrated many books. Member of the Society of Wood Engravers. Instructor of Design at the Royal College of Art. Official war artist (Admiralty), 1940.

ERIC RAVILIOUS. *Ship's Screw on Truck. 1940. Watercolor, 17⅜ x 21¾ inches.*

A ship's screw en route from factory to shipyard. During the winter of 1939 40 Britain was under snow for an unusually long time.

PAINTINGS AND DRAWINGS: THIS WAR

SIR WILLIAM ROTHENSTEIN. *Air Chief Marshal Sir Charles F. A. Portal, C.B., D.S.O., M.C. 1940. Sanguine, 16 x 11½ inches.*

Sir Charles Portal, former Commander-in-Chief of the Bomber Command, has been appointed Chief of the Air Staff at the Air Ministry, the senior executive Air Member of the Air Council.

SIR WILLIAM ROTHENSTEIN. *A Sergeant Pilot of the Royal Air Force. 1939. Sanguine, 19 x 8⅞ inches.*

Rothenstein was born at Bradford in 1872. Studied at the Slade School under Legros, then in Paris, where he knew Whistler and Degas. Member of the New English Art Club since 1894. Visited India in 1910. Served as official war artist to the British Army in France and on the Rhine, 1917-18. Principal of the Royal College of Art, 1920-35. Published Men and Memories, *1931-32. Knighted in 1931.*

GRAHAM SUTHERLAND. *Devastation 1940: Farmhouse in Wales.* 1940. Gouache, 21¼ x 31½ inches.

For some time Sutherland has been hailed as one of the most gifted painters of his generation in England. While he is fond of abstract pattern, the solemn emotion and terror of war appear singularly in these new pictures.

Sutherland was born in London in 1903. He studied at Goldsmiths' College School of Art and later taught engraving at Chelsea Polytechnic. A member of the London Group. He has also designed posters.

PAINTINGS AND DRAWINGS: THIS WAR

GRAHAM SUTHERLAND. *Devastation 1940: Solicitor's Office in Wales. 1940. Gouache, 31½ x 21¼ inches.*

FELIKS TOPOLSKI. Scottish and Polish Soldiers at the Entrance to the Polish Camp. 1940. Line and wash drawing, 8⅞ x 11¾ inches.

Polish soldiers who had managed to get to Britain after the German advances through the Low Countries and France were re-formed and re-equipped at a camp in Scotland.

Topolski was born in Poland in 1907. Painter and caricaturist. He came to London in 1935 and is now an official artist to the Polish forces in Great Britain.

PAINTINGS AND DRAWINGS: THIS WAR

MIDSHIPMAN JOHN WORSLEY. *Part of a 6-inch Gun Crew in Action, the Shell Being Rammed Home.* *1940. Wash drawing, 11⅛ x 14¼ inches.*

Now only twenty years old, Worsley joined the Royal Naval Reserve at the beginning of the war, and during the long hours at sea enthusiastically records the activities of his shipmates.

PHOTOGRAPHS

The photographs reproduced in the section that follows are part of a large group selected in London by Mr. C. H. Gibbs-Smith and Mr. Misha Black. To them we have added a few by Miss Lee Miller, an American photographer resident in England.

They have been arranged in an impressive sequence of Civil Life, Activities of the Army and Navy, the R.A.F., and a group of significant forms of war-time objects, constructions and mechanisms. Perhaps in order to emphasize the collective and national character of all this pictorial evidence, the names of the individual photographers were not provided. Photography is, in fact, a somewhat anonymous medium. There are cameramen who are to all intents and purposes fine artists, but there are also cameras that have an eye of their own. But in the main its natural esthetic is documentary; it must usually be strained or tampered with to convey a private vision, and there is little or none of that here.

Although Americans have frequently surpassed the British in pictorial journalism, the esthetic and documentary effectiveness of these photographs is no less impressive than the work of the painters.

The present selection has been made on a basis of that odd or perhaps even accidental eloquence of mood that may be caught by the camera in bomb shelters, or at sea, or in the sky.

M. W.

DEPARTING SOLDIERS.

CAVALRY PATROL at dawn in the North of England. Constant watch for parachute troopers is maintained throughout the island.

PHOTOGRAPHS: ARMY

TANKS ON A COUNTRY ROAD. Once more, the contrast of tragic mechanism and the famous old-fashioned loveliness of Britain.

THE MANUFACTURE AND RELINING OF LONG-RANGE GUNS.

44

TANK. A Christie-type cruiser tank, as used in the Libyan desert.

BIOMORPHIC FORMS. Barrage balloons being towed from hangars.

PHOTOGRAPHS: R.A F.

REAR TURRET OF A WHITLEY BOMBER. *At the top may be seen four Browning machine guns, with flash eliminators, capable of firing 4,800 shots a minute. In the center bullets may be seen above the ammunition boxes. The chutes on either side discharge empty cartridge cases. The gunner is in a highly vulnerable position. His is a night vigil, and often he must maintain his watch for ten hours at a time.*

PHOTOGRAPHS: R.A.F.

R.A.F. GROUND CREW waiting for its planes to return. The return of a fighter plane is a grave and exciting moment. Damage inflicted by the enemy, though insufficient to prevent flying, may have crippled it so that it cannot land safely.

PHOTOGRAPHS: R.A.F.

WHITLEY BOMBER. See page 47 for rear turret.

SUNDERLAND FLYING BOAT. This plane, of which the power-operated rear turret is shown, is as large as a Pan American Clipper and is used principally as a convoy protector. It has been known to shoot down four-engine enemy bombers carrying two cannon as well as machine guns. The workman is polishing a red, white and blue cockade which prevents its being mistaken for an enemy plane.

BARRAGE BALLOON. To ward off Stukas, ships in convoy now also use barrage balloons. They must be shot down by enemy pursuit planes before dive bombers can be effective. The balloon in this photograph has been lowered; it usually floats at 10,000 feet.

PHOTOGRAPHS: NAVY

BATTLESHIP of the Nelson class, showing the nine 16-inch guns and, in the immediate foreground, the 4.7-inch gun used against high bombers. In the left foreground may be seen the "pom-poms," which the British call a "Chicago piano" because of their appearance.

SUICIDE SQUAD. Ships in a mine-sweeping flotilla. The casualty rate in this service is said to be the highest of all.

DESTROYER steaming into action.

CRUISER READY FOR LAUNCHING. *The youth's gesture is typical of the quickening of popular pride in Britain's defense effort.*

PHOTOGRAPHS: NAVY

NAVAL RESERVE SAILOR. This former fisherman, at the bow gun of a trawler, is setting the fuse on a twelve-pound anti-aircraft shell. The voice-pipes at his ears lead to the bridge.

From the start of this war the virtuosity of news photographers has shown to all the world the unfamiliar beauty of the British race.

AUXILIARY FIREMAN; NURSE; FISHERMAN; R.A.F. FIGHTER PILOT.

PHOTOGRAPHS

SOLDIER; R.A.F. FIGHTER PILOT; WOMEN'S AUXILIARY AIR FORCE PILOT; SAILOR.

INTERIOR. Park Crescent, Regent Park.

PHOTOGRAPHS: CIVIL LIFE

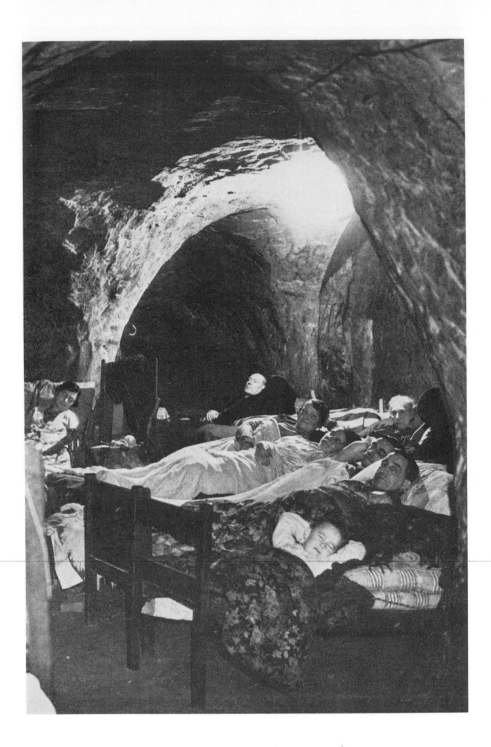

SOUTH COAST PREHISTORIC CAVE, near Dover, serving as a bomb shelter.

A HOP GARDEN IN KENT.

PHOTOGRAPHS: CIVIL LIFE

CONTRABAND. *Part of a consignment of rattan cane which fell into British hands.*

ST. JAMES' CHURCH, PICCADILLY.

PHOTOGRAPHS: CIVIL LIFE

THE HIGH ALTAR AT ST. PAUL'S.

MANNED BY WOMEN. Many lawns have been plowed to provide additional nourishment.

PHOTOGRAPHS: CIVIL LIFE

VEGETABLE-GARDENING in the moat of the Tower of London.

A BOMB-MADE PORTAL in the West End of London.

PHOTOGRAPHS: CIVIL LIFE

GAS MASKS. *Horse, man, child and dog ready for gas warfare.*

See photographs of anti-gas clothes, page 22.

HYDE PARK. Barbed wire and half-inflated barrage balloon amid familiar scenery in London.

PHOTOGRAPHS: CIVIL LIFE

THE NATIONAL GALLERY BY MOONLIGHT. Those who have seen London during the blackouts of this war all speak of the spectral beauty of its buildings by moonlight.

PHOTOGRAPHS: CIVIL LIFE

ST. PAUL'S. The night of the great fire, December 29-30, 1940.

DISASTER falling from the air grows more and more theatrical. Two heroines in a setting which Neher might have designed in Berlin in the twenties.

LONDON CHILDREN in an air raid shelter.

PHOTOGRAPHS: CIVIL LIFE

BURLINGTON ARCADE. *A shopping center familiar to all American visitors to London.*

ARCHITECTURAL RECONSTRUCTION AND WAR-TIME FORMS

It is a commonplace saying that omelettes cannot be made without breaking eggs—that one cannot create without some destruction. It is as true to say that civilized man cannot live among destruction without a desire to create.

In Britain now every bomb that falls is a stimulus to creation. No man, unless he is right down in spirit, can see his home crumble to dust before his eyes and his city made a ruin without dreaming of what that home or city may become when all this is over. That flash forward to a better future in the mind of the ordinary man is the point from which all planning and reconstruction starts.

For years there have been "planners" in Britain, far-sighted men and women who have talked and written and preached planning; and some of their talk has had effect. But whatever they have achieved here as yet has been won against the deadweight of the heaviest load of all—public indifference.

Now it is very different—a speaker or writer has only to mention "reconstruction" to excite response throughout the country from all those people, and that is all the people of Britain, whose physical need and ideals drive them to conceive this new New England which we must build on this side of the Atlantic. Planning has the headlines in Britain now in a way that we have never known before.

If all this is true, NOW, some may suggest, is surely the time for an exhibition of what planning means to Britain and what plans Britain has. If Britain is alive with ideas on reconstruction why can't they be shown both as a matter of pride and to encourage the others? Soon there will be much, but as yet there is nothing to show for our enthusiasms exactly because those enthusiasms are serious and have to be kept clear of meaningless utopianism. It would be magnificent if London could now, at this stage of the war, have a "plan" conjured from the brilliant mind of some new Christopher Wren, but it would be a magnificent distraction unless, which at this stage is almost certainly impossible, the plan could be conceived having inherent in it the means to its attainment. The plans we want must not be only the definition of an end, but must show the way to get there. This way can only be cleared by research, by education and the slow translation of enthusiasms into solid realization of the immensity and complexity of the problem. This is what we are up to in Britain now.

And so instead of plans for Britain and views of destruction and re-creation we show small symbols only of a sense of order. It is something in war time to have the machines of civil defense neatly designed. This neatness is a sign of order and of something clean and good which survives the inevitable disorder and mess of war. This is the folk art of 1941.

E. J. CARTER, B.A., A.R.I.B.A.
Librarian of the Royal Institute of British Architects.

MODERN BASTIONS. Road blocks like these have been built on all strategic highways.

GIANT CONDUITS in fields to prevent the landing of enemy aircraft.

WAR-TIME FORMS

BLOCKS like these have sprung up at strategic positions on English highroads. The British call them "dragons' teeth."

WAR-TIME FORMS

A.R.P. WARDEN'S POST.

CONVERTED TRUCKS. *A standard design is used for converting trucks into ambulances.*

HOODED LIGHT. One of these newly designed headlights must be carried by every vehicle during blackouts. Cars in government services are privileged to carry two.

WAR-TIME FORMS

CARTOONS

British cartooning, despite certain ups and downs, has been noteworthy for two centuries. The recent past has not been one of the high points; the greatness of Punch has diminished; Beerbohm and Belcher have done less, and nothing took their place. There is no Londoner to match our New Yorker.

But since the German enemy began to threaten, cartooning seems to have recovered the gusto of Hogarth and Cruikshank, and the violent intelligence of Rowlandson. The torch has been passed to a group of New Zealanders and Australians led by David Low, a merciless and combative idealist who will tolerate no timidity or delay of British statesmanship, while scorning but never underestimating Hitler and Mussolini. His polemical verve and grasp of current history reveal a literary as well as pictorial talent, and his cartoons have probably exerted greater influence upon the souls of the British people than any other art of this era.

But graphic oratory of this kind is not all the art of cartooning. It has always had, and still has, a legitimate aspect very near to mere entertainment. It can cheer and refresh and encourage mankind in its darker hours. This kind of humor is more important and valid now than ever, and for those who in time of war have scarcely an idle moment, it is often able to take the place of reading and theatre-going.

The cartoons which we show have been selected in London under the direction of Sir Kenneth Clark, save for a few provided by the Australian Newspapers Service in New York.

M. W.

WHERE NEXT, MEIN FÜHRER ?

DAVID LOW. "Where Next, Mein Führer?"

Low is the leading British cartoonist. He was born in New Zealand in 1891, has been cartoonist on important newspapers, and published several books. He is now political cartoonist to The Evening Standard, London.

HITALY

DAVID LOW. "Hitaly." From The Evening Standard, London.

DAVID LOW. "Hitler's Day." Cartoon from The Evening Standard, London.

GEORGE FINEY. "Doggo." February 15, 1941. Ink and crayon, 11½ x 18¼ inches. Lent by The Daily Telegraph, Sydney, Australia.

SAMUEL WELLS. "The New Order of the Boot—Germans Pouring into Italy." 10¼ x 14 inches. Lent by The Herald, Melbourne, Australia.
Wells served in the last war. Once cartoonist on the Manchester Daily Dispatch, he has returned to Australia.

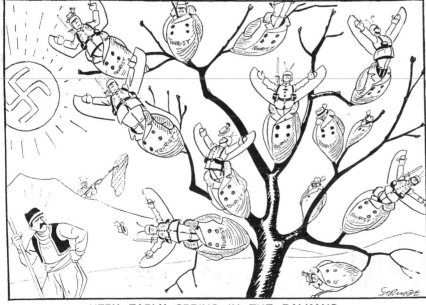

VERY EARLY SPRING IN THE BALKANS.

SYDNEY STRUBE, born in London in 1891, is cartoonist for The Daily Express.

HOW TO MAKE IT HARD FOR THE RAIDERS: THE SAFE WAY WITH DELAYED-ACTION BOMBS.

This "Safety first" method for coping with delayed-action bombs has been carefully thought-out by W. Heath Robinson. It is believed that the use of his device would eliminate practically all risk from the removal of those disagreeable souvenirs of Nazi visits.

DRAWN BY W. HEATH ROBINSON

WILLIAM HEATH ROBINSON. Cartoon from the London Sketch.

" I suppose, Captain, they do keep these files up to date ? "

" If I'd had my way, I'd never have let that fellow Tennyson give away all that highly confidential information about the Light Brigade."

" Hello, dear, it's Barnacle Billa speaking ! "

" It may sound caddish, Sir George, but 'pon my word, I don't care if it is the breeding season."

CARTOONS FROM PUNCH.

POSTERS

The art of the poster is always linked to a particular problem of salesmanship or persuasion, and it is therefore especially subject to changes in popular taste and emotion. When it is weak, the weakness is usually due to old fashion, to time lag, or to a mistaken adherence to reputations, a confusion between celebrity and popularity.

When one looks at the posters of the last war, one is strongly reminded that the historical situation is not the same. The mood of the masses has shifted. The melancholy hatreds of Brangwyn and the fine illustrative conceptions of Pryse and others now seem inappropriate.

The shift in feeling of the common people today has necessitated a change in the style of appeal addressed to them. Government agencies, anxious not to run ahead of those they represent, often hang timidly behind or fall badly out of step. This is what happened in England at the beginning of the present war. This was the more regrettable because between the wars poster art in England developed extraordinarily. British work equalled the best done by the French and was superior to any done in the United States. The influence of abstract modern artists across the Channel, of the French designers—Cassandre, Carlu and Colin—and of the able American, E. McKnight Kauffer, resident in London, was felt, and British enterprise was quick to avail itself of their talents and of those of a number of its own fine modern painters.

It was unfortunate that the British Government did not use the talents of its own best men at the beginning of this war. It now appears that it has realized and acknowledged this anomaly and shortcoming; and more work as good as the present small selection may be expected to follow.

M. W.

"KEEP IT UNDER YOUR HAT!" Poster, 15 x 10 inches.

"BE LIKE DAD—KEEP MUM!" Child's poster by Reeves for the "hush hush" campaign. 40 x 25 inches.

"POST YOUR LETTERS BEFORE NOON." Poster by Lewitt and Him, two Polish artists now working in England. 29 x 36½ inches. One of a series issued by the General Post Office to inform the public of the emergency schedule due to war conditions. (Ordinarily letters posted at night would be delivered early the next morning.)

"SAVE FOR THE BRAVE!" Poster by A. Brenet. 28¾ x 19 inches. Issued by the National Savings Committee. Lent by Bundles for Britain, Inc. Similar in its use of pictorial art to posters of the last war.

AIR RAID PRECAUTIONS POSTER by Ashley Havinden. 15 x 10 inches. One of the first posters used in this war.

"WE ARE VICTORIOUS — WINSTON CHURCHILL, PRIME MINISTER OF GREAT BRITAIN." Poster with Arabic inscription. Montage, 28⅞ x 19⅜ inches. Lent by Bundles for Britain, Inc. An example of the adaptation of photography to poster needs.

"FORM A SAVINGS GROUP NOW!" *Poster by Pat Keely, 1940. 8 x 20 inches. Issued by the National Savings Committee.*

"IN A RAID—" *One of a series of five posters by Tom Purvis. 10 x 30 inches.*

"DIG FOR VICTORY." *Poster to promote home production of crops. 28¾ x 18¾ inches.*

THE ROLE OF THE ARTIST IN CAMOUFLAGE

Because we in the United States shall soon be seeing strange new examples of camouflage, we have undertaken to explain the several types of camouflage now in use by the British. Photographs showing the concealments of military and industrial objects are necessarily subject to censorship, so we have been strictly limited in the matter of illustration. This may seem a difficult or dull subject to the general public; but it should interest artists, and may suggest to them further steps in this military science which has always depended upon their sensibility and skill.

As yet camouflage is in its infancy; there are many ideas yet untried; and there is still a wide divergence between its practice and its potentialities, which are still to be fully appreciated.

The methods of camouflage are essentially the same in all countries, for they are as old as nature. Camouflage as we know it, however, arose from the last war—a logical answer to the introduction of a new weapon, the airplane. The immensely increased speed, range and size, both of pursuit planes and of bombers, have extended the theatre of modern war to include all vital points within their

A WELL-CAMOUFLAGED ARTILLERY POSITION showing the use of overhead nets garnished with strips of painted canvas. The disruptive design on the canvas covering and the gun barrel conceal the form of the gun.

range, thus making camouflage today incomparably more important than it has ever been before.

The role of the airplane in reconnaissance, photography and bombing depends upon visual PERCEPTION. Camouflage, through visual DECEPTION, has become a major means of combating its efficiency.

Total concealment or a convincing disguise is the ideal of the camoufleur. Where total concealment is impossible, as with ships, tanks and planes, camouflage can at least diminish visibility or distract attention from the true form of the object to such an extent that the bomber will overshoot the mark. Camouflage cannot protect a city from indiscriminate bombings calculated to shatter citizen morale, but it can successfully conceal vital military and industrial sites from enemy observation.

The practice of camouflage requires the collaboration of the military strategist, the architect and the artist. The military strategist decides what should be camouflaged. The architect and the artist possess, each in his field, the knowledge and technical ability required to meet the problems of camouflage design—they understand the fundamental relation-

AN ANTI-TANK GUN concealed with fishnet. The gunners are wearing white. A few strips of white cloth tied into the netting imitate the sparse pattern of snow on the ground.

ships of plastic and graphic representation through the use of color, form and texture. The training of the artist, his sensibility to color, his instinctive sense of form and space, fit him for the role of camoufleur. For although in painting he may portray the appearance of three-dimensional form and space on a flat surface, in camouflage he must strive for an opposite effect. He must reverse optical effects and use the technique of contrast to cause three-dimensional objects to appear flat. He must use the principles of design to dissemble the appearance of form rather than to delineate it. It is known, for example, that the brain comprehends simple and regular forms and areas of color more readily than complex ones. Therefore, in order to render a simple form more difficult to recognize, the thing to do is to superimpose another, more complex and contradictory. This is precisely what nature does in the adaptive coloration of its more vulnerable creatures and what man is now learning to do in camouflage.

Camouflage has frequently been prepared to simulate protective coloring as found in nature, and it is true that the most effective examples are those based on nature's self-preservation techniques in the universal struggle for existence.

Whether in the realm of interspecific warfare between animals or in the sphere of international warfare between men, the fundamental aims of camouflage fall into two distinct categories: MIMICRY and CONCEALMENT, and the various stages of the life of the butterfly provide us with analogies for both.

MIMICRY is the imitation of an altogether different object, which conceals the true identity or whereabouts of the animal or military objective. The cocoon stage of the butterfly's development illustrates the camouflage principle of mimicry. In shape, color and even texture, the cocoon resembles a curled dead leaf or a remnant of debris not calculated to attract the attention of the hungry bird.

BRITISH SOLDIER weaving painted canvas strips into string net.

The simplest method of disguising guns is to cover them with branches making them, like Malcolm's army in Macbeth, appear as a forest. City roofs are covered over with gray-green shavings to make them resemble grass, with only a few bright red roofs in view to simulate houses in the country. The anti-aircraft gun is hidden in a rude hut.

In addition to making the object to be protected look like something else, the camoufleur distracts the attention of the attacker by making something else look like the object. Parallel furrows plowed at the proper distance apart will look to the aviator like railroad tracks. A makeshift structure built where little damage can result, to imitate the contours of a military objective, will confuse the attacker with an alternative and cause him to waste ammunition. Dummy guns, airplanes and even villages are erected and carelessly camouflaged, to be discovered and draw fire from a more thoroughly camouflaged objective nearby.

The camoufleur must take into account the bold, subtle distinctions and variations of the color, tone

BRITISH CAMOUFLAGE, WINTER. Two Bren gunners.

and texture; the light, shade and cast shadow; and the surface area and outline which make objects distinguishable.

CONCEALMENT is accomplished through modifications in the color, form or texture of the object, according to the following four basic principles:

1 Color resemblance
2 Countershading
3 Disruptive design
4 Shadow elimination.

COLOR RESEMBLANCE

To use an example from another phase of the butterfly's existence, a green caterpillar is indistinguishable by its color from leaves and grass. The camoufleur paints night bombers with lamp black.

Battleships are painted a gray which blends into the seascape.

COUNTERSHADING

In addition, the caterpillar derives safety from countershading; its back, exposed to highlights, is darker green than its underside, which is normally in the shade. As a result it appears flat, even in the full glare of the sun. For the same reason, dark paint is applied to the tops of guns exposed to the glare, light paint to the undersides in shadow.

DISRUPTIVE DESIGN

The bold, subtle patterns of the butterfly's wing serve to distract the eye from the significant outlines which make the total shape recognizable. The

camouflage of the mass and outline of a factory or battleship serves the same psychological purpose of delaying recognition, a factor of extreme importance in aerial warfare, which is carried on at such heights and speeds that the delay of even a second is of great value in preserving military objectives. For if a bomber overshoots his mark and has to return to a second attack, the chances for the success of anti-aircraft and pursuit planes are greatly increased.

Disruptive design, or "dazzle" painting, was used in the last war with disastrous consequences in some cases. This was the result of the use of purposeless lines which in no way simulated nature. "Dazzle" painting, if properly handled, can nevertheless be effective in its end. Many changes have had to be made in the technique employed in the last war. The camoufleur, with a frightening twenty-year record of lethargy in his field, is forced to make discoveries and improvements at a rapid pace in order to combat the results of a tremendous and steady development in aerial warfare over these years.

SHADOW ELIMINATION

The butterfly skillfully and frequently shifts its position, tilting its body according to the angle of the sun's rays, in order to eliminate betraying shadows. This principle may be applied to some extent in the concealment of guns by shifting them to the angle giving the smallest shadow. But shadow is, in general, the camoufleur's most serious problem. Despite

CAMOUFLAGE

CAMOUFLAGED SUIT to be used against a background of bombed buildings.

success in color resemblance and disruptive design, the shadow of an object may be identifiable at a greater distance than the object itself. This problem is somewhat relieved by the English climate. In new construction, shadows can be virtually eliminated by the architectural design of roofs which slope down to within a few feet of the ground, thus casting little shade. On existing buildings it is possible to break the solid shadow, so revealing to the aviator, by constructing irregular forms on the top edges of the building to break its sharp outline shadow.

Total concealment may sometimes be attained by the smoke screen, effective in both naval warfare and civilian defense. Entire cities can be hidden by smoke released from points selected to take advantage of prevailing winds.

By the methods enumerated above, the camoufleur can give the greatest measure of protection to objectives which must be recognized visually— legitimate military objectives such as men, guns, tanks, troop concentrations, matériel, munition dumps and factories. He cannot guarantee the immunity of anything, but any gains toward invulnerability are obviously justified economically, strategically and humanely.

CARLOS DYER

CATALOG OF PAINTINGS AND DRAWINGS

*Asterisk indicates that the picture is illustrated.

†Dagger indicates that the picture was still en route from England when catalog went to press.

Unless otherwise stated, items are lent by the Ministry of Information, London.

Due to exigencies of space not all the pictures listed have been hung in the exhibition.

LAST WAR:

GILMAN, Harold. 1878-1919.
Halifax Harbour, Sunset. 1918.
Oil on canvas, 77 ½ x 132 ½ inches.
Lent by the National Gallery of Canada.

JOHN, Augustus. Born 1878.
*A Canadian Soldier. 1917 (page 9).
Oil on canvas, 32 x 24 inches.
Lent by the National Gallery of Canada.

KENNINGTON, Eric. Born 1888.
*The Conquerors. 1920 (page 14).
Oil on canvas, 117 x 96 inches.
Lent by the National Gallery of Canada.

Mustard Gas.
Pastel, 24 ¼ x 18 ⅞ inches.
Lent by the National Gallery of Canada.

Colonel T. E. Lawrence.
Bronze, 16 inches high.
Lent by the Tate Gallery, London, through the courtesy of the British Pavilion, New York World's Fair.

LEWIS, Wyndham. Born 1884.
A Canadian Gunpit.
Oil on canvas, 120 x 142 inches.
Lent by the National Gallery of Canada.

MILNE, David B. Born 1882.
Seaford, South Camp from the Downs. 1919.
Watercolor, 13 ⅞ x 19 ⅞ inches.
Lent by the National Gallery of Canada.

The Belfry, Hotel de Ville, Arras. 1919.
Watercolor, 14 ⅛ x 19 ⅞ inches.
Lent by the National Gallery of Canada.

MUNNINGS, Alfred J. Born 1878.
Charge of Flowerdew's Squadron.
Oil on canvas, 20 x 24 inches.
Lent by the National Gallery of Canada.

NASH, Paul. Born 1889.
*Void. 1918 (page 15).
Oil on canvas, 28 x 36 inches.
Lent by the National Gallery of Canada.

Landscape, Year of Our Lord, 1917.
Mixed medium, 12 ⅞ x 17 ½ inches.
Lent by the National Gallery of Canada.

ORPEN, Sir William. 1878-1931.
Changing Billets, Picardy. 1917.
Oil on canvas, 35 ⅝ x 29 ½ inches.
Lent Anonymously.

*Man Thinking on the Butte de Warlencourt (page 11).
Oil on canvas, 35 ½ x 29 ⅜ inches.
Lent by Stephen C. Clark.

*Major-General Sir David Watson, K.C.B., C.M.G. 1918 (page 10).
Oil on canvas, 36 x 30 ⅛ inches.
Lent by the National Gallery of Canada.

ROBERTS, William. Born 1895.
The First German Gas Attack at Ypres.
Oil on canvas, 120 ½ x 144 ¾ inches.
Lent by the National Gallery of Canada.

ROTHENSTEIN, Sir William. Born 1872.
Houses at Peronne. 1918.
Mixed medium, 14 ½ x 20 ⅞ inches.
Lent by the National Gallery of Canada.

Ruined Houses at Chaulnes. 1918.
Mixed medium, 14 ⅜ x 20 ⅞ inches.
Lent by the National Gallery of Canada.

WADSWORTH, Edward. Born 1889.
*Dazzle Ships in Drydock at Liverpool. 1918 (page 13).
Oil on canvas, 120 x 96 inches.
Lent by the National Gallery of Canada.

THIS WAR:

ARDIZZONE, Edward. Born 1901.
Gunners of an Anti-Aircraft Regiment, August 1939. 1940.
Watercolor, 11 x 14 ⅛ inches.

Sleeping in a Shelter. 1940.
Watercolor, 10 x 14 ½ inches.

The Trek to the Shelters. Silvertown, September 1940.
Watercolor, 8 ¼ x 9 ⅛ inches.

Shelter Scene. 1940.
Wash drawing, 6 ⅞ x 8 ⅝ inches.

With the 300th—on the Move. 1940.
Watercolor, 11 ⅜ x 15 ½ inches.

Off to the Shelter. 1940.
Watercolor, 8 x 12 ⅛ inches.

With the 300th—Working Party in the Rain. 1940.
Watercolor, 8 ½ x 10 inches.

*Priest Begging for a Lift in Louvain, May 1940 (page 16).
Watercolor, 9 ½ x 12 ⅛ inches.

Louvain: Road to the Bridge, May 1940.
Watercolor, 12 ¾ x 8 ⅝ inches.

On the Road to Louvain, May 1940.
Watercolor, 14 ¾ x 22 ¼ inches.

The Bombing of G.H.Q., Boulogne, May 1940.
Watercolor, 14 ½ x 22 inches.

*A Pub in Silvertown. 1940 (page 17).
Watercolor, 9 x 12 ⅝ inches.

ARMSTRONG, John. Born 1893.
*The Elms. 1940 (page 18).
Tempera on canvas, 20 x 27 inches.

BAWDEN, Edward. Born 1903.
Halluin. 1940.
Watercolor, 17 ½ x 22 ½ inches.

*The Quay at Dunkerque. 1940 (page 19).
Watercolor, 12 x 19 ⅜ inches.

Carriers, M. T. Depot, Halluin. 1940.
Watercolor, 17 ½ x 22 ⅛ inches.

With the Quartermaster near Seclin. 1940.
Watercolor, 17 ¾ x 23 inches.

Factory at Armentières Burning after Being Bombed. 1940.
Watercolor, 12 x 19 ¼ inches.

BONE, Major Sir Muirhead. Born 1876.
The Deck Cabin of the *Campeador V.* 1940.
Pencil sketch, 6 ⅞ x 8 ⅞ inches.

*The Exeter and Ajax Parade, 1940 (page 21).
Wash drawing, 20 ¼ x 36 ¾ inches.

H.M.S. Victory in Wartime. 1940.
Wash drawing, 22 ⅛ x 30 ⅛ inches.

*Dawn—from the Signal Station, Dover, June 1940
(page 20).
Wash drawing, 17 ⅝ x 29 ⅝ inches.

COKE, Dorothy. Born 1897.
A.T.S. and Recruits Drilling. 1940.
Watercolor, 9 ⅞ x 15 ⅜ inches.

A.T.S. Air Raid Practice. 1940.
Watercolor, 9 ⅞ x 15 ⅝ inches.

CONOR, William.
Shipyard Workers Crossing the Queen's Bridge, Belfast.
1940.
Chalk drawing, 13 ½ x 18 ¼ inches.

The Evacuation of Children in Northern Ireland. 1940.
Chalk drawing, 13 ½ x 17 ⅞ inches.

CUNDALL, Charles E. Born 1880.
Return of H.M.S. Exeter. 1940.
Oil on canvas, 18 x 26 inches.

Tank Manufacture. 1940.
Oil on canvas, 19 x 30 inches.

DOBSON, Frank.
†Bristol, November 24th, 1940.

DUNBAR, Evelyn.
*Putting on Anti-Gas Clothes. 1940 (page 22).
Oil on canvas, 24 x 30 inches.

EURICH, Richard. Born 1903.
*The Withdrawal from Dunkerque. 1940 (frontispiece).
Oil on canvas, 30 ⅛ x 40 inches.

EVES, Reginald Grenville. Born 1876.
Brigadier H. Lumsden, D.S.O. 1940.
Oil on canvas, 19 ⅞ x 16 inches.

Lord Gort, V.C. 1940.
Oil on canvas, 20 x 16 inches.

FREEDMAN, Barnett. Born 1901.
*The Gun. 1940 (page 23).
Oil on canvas, 23 ¼ x 36 inches.

The Runway at Thelus During Construction by the 698 Co.
R.E. Air Component South. 1940.
Watercolor, 14 ⅜ x 21 ¾ inches.

GABAIN, Ethel. Born 1883.
The Evacuation of Children from Southend, Sunday 2nd
June, 1940.
Lithograph, 12 ⅞ x 20 ⅛ inches.

Evacuees in a Cottage at Cookham. 1940.
Lithograph, 13 ¾ x 12 ⅝ inches.

†Bombed Out, Bermondsey.

GROSS, Anthony. Born 1905.
Tank Practice on Training Ground. 1940.
Gouache, 13 ¾ x 21 ½ inches.

Sandbags in Bethnal Green. 1940.
Gouache, 12 ⅛ x 20 inches.

Medical Inspection of Recruits. 1940.
Gouache, 7 ¾ x 12 ⅝ inches.

Cleaning up after an "All Ranks" Dance. 1940.
Gouache, 7 ¾ x 12 ⅝ inches.

A.T.S. at Mess. 1940.
Gouache, 7 ¾ x 12 ¾ inches.

Recruits Waiting in Reception Room. 1940.
Gouache, 7 ⅞ x 12 ⅞ inches.

Rescue Party Clearing Up. 1940.
Gouache, 7 ¾ x 12 ¾ inches.
Lent by Alexander Gross.

Interior of Tunnel Shelter. 1940.
Gouache, 7 ⅞ x 12 ⅝ inches.
Lent by Alexander Gross.

Kensington Control Telephonists. 1940.
Gouache, 7 ⅞ x 12 ¾ inches.
Lent by Alexander Gross.

*The Watcher. 1940 (page 24).
Gouache, 7 ¾ x 12 ¾ inches.
Lent by Alexander Gross.

Barrage Balloon, 1940.
Gouache, 7 ⅞ x 12 ⅝ inches.
Lent by Alexander Gross.

Roof Spotters.
Gouache 7 ¾ x 12 ¾ inches.
Lent by Alexander Gross.

HARTRICK, A. S.
Seed Beds in King William's Garden, Hampton Court
Palace. 1940.
Watercolor, 8 ¾ x 11 inches.

HENDERSON, Keith. Born 1883.
*Improvised Test of an Undercarriage. 1940 (page 25).
Oil on canvas, 30 ⅛ x 40 inches.

KENNINGTON, Eric. Born 1888.
*Able Seaman Povey of H.M.S. Hardy. 1940 (page 26).
Pastel, 29 ½ x 21 ⅝ inches.

Leading Stoker C. Cloke of H.M.S. Exeter. 1940.
Pastel, 28 ⅝ x 20 ⅞ inches.

Leading Seaman Dove of H.M.S. Hardy. 1940.
Pastel, 31 x 20 ½ inches.

Squadron Leader W. E. G. Taylor. 1940.
Pastel, 26 ⅞ x 19 ¾ inches.

Group Captain Sweeney. 1940.
Pastel, 24 ¾ x 18 ⅝ inches.

†Group Captain B. E. Embry, D.S.O., A.F.C.

†Pilot Officer R. C. Dafforn, D.F.C.

†Sergeant F. W. Higginson, D.F.M.

†Sergeant J. H. Lacey, D.F.M.

MANSBRIDGE, John. Born 1902.
*An Air Gunner in a Turret—Sergeant G. Holmes, D.F.M.
1940 (page 27).
Oil on canvas, 30 x 25 inches.

McGRATH, Raymond.
    Assembling a Blenheim Main Plane. 1940.
    Watercolor, 14 ⅜ x 21 ½ inches.

    *Beaufort Bombers. 1940, (page 28).
    Watercolor on canvasboard, 14 ⅜ x 21 ½ inches.

    Wing Sections Awaiting Assembly, 1940.
    Watercolor on canvasboard, 21 ⅝ x 14 ⅝ inches.

MOORE, Henry. Born 1898.
*†Pale Shelter Scene (page 29).

    †Shadowy Shelter.

    †Brown Tube Shelter.

    †Woman Seated in the Underground.

MORLEY, Harry. Born 1883.
    †The Bombed *Toscalusa*.

MOZLEY, Charles.
    Kentish Lane, 1940.
    Watercolor, 11 x 14 ⅝ inches.

NASH, Paul. Born 1889.
    Flying against Germany. 1940.
    Oil on canvas, 28 ⅛ x 36 inches.

    The Raider on the Shore. 1940.
    Watercolor, 15 ⅛ x 22 ⅜ inches.

    Bomber in the Wood. 1940.
    Watercolor, 15 ⅛ x 22 ¼ inches.

    *Under the Cliff. 1940 (page 30).
    Watercolor, 15 ⅛ x 22 ⅜ inches.

    Down in the Channel. 1940.
    Watercolor, 15 ¼ x 22 ⅜ inches.

    Whitleys at Play. 1940.
    Watercolor, 15 ⅜ x 22 ⅝ inches.

    Wellington Bomber Drawn on the Day Hitler Invaded
       Belgium. 1940.
    Watercolor, 11 x 15 inches.

    Hampden Bomber. 1940.
    Watercolor, 11 x 15 ½ inches.

PIPER, John. Born 1903.
    *Passage to the Control Room at S. W. Regional Head-
       quarters. 1940 (page 31).
    Oil on canvas, 29 ¾ x 20 inches.

    †Coventry Cathedral, November 15th, 1940.

PITCHFORTH, Roland Vivian. Born 1895.
    A.R.P. Practice. 1940.
    Watercolor, 29 ½ x 21 ½ inches.

    A.F.S. Men at Practice with Trailer Pump, on the Banks of the
       Serpentine. 1940.
    Watercolor, 21 ½ x 29 ¼ inches.

    *Gravy Salt Factory, Birmingham. 1940 (page 32).
    Watercolor, 21 ½ x 29 ⅝ inches.

    Water Tank, Birmingham. 1940.
    Watercolor, 21 ⅝ x 29 ⅝ inches.

    Two Sheffield Steel Workers. 1940.
    Watercolor, 21 ⅜ x 29 ⅜ inches.

    Casting an Ingot. 1940.
    Watercolor and chalk, 23 ⅝ x 15 ⅝ inches.

RAVILIOUS, Eric. Born 1903.
    Passing the Bell Rock. 1940.
    Watercolor, 17 ¾ x 22 ½ inches.

    *Norway, 1940 (page 33).
    Watercolor, 18 ⅜ x 23 inches.

    Ark Royal in Action—No. 1. 1940.
    Watercolor, 16 ¾ x 22 ¾ inches.

    *Ship's Screw on Truck. 1940 (page 34).
    Watercolor, 17 ⅜ x 21 ¾ inches.

ROTHENSTEIN, Sir William. Born 1872.
    *A Sergeant Pilot of the Royal Air Force. 1939 (page 35).
    Sanguine, 19 x 8 ⅞ inches.

    An Officer Pilot of the Royal Air Force. 1940.
    Sanguine, 19 ¾ x 7 ⅞ inches.

    *Air Chief Marshal Sir Charles F. A. Portal, C.B., D.S.O., M.C.
       1940 (page 35).
    Sanguine, 16 x 11 ½ inches.

ROWNTREE, Kenneth.
    Foreign Service Men in Hyde Park—Early Summer 1940.
    Oil on canvas, 18 x 30 inches.

STONOR, Jessica. Born 1913.
    Raiders overhead.
    Charcoal, 11 ½ x 11 inches.
    Lent by the artist.

SUTHERLAND, Graham. Born 1903.
    Camouflaged Bombers. 1940.
    Gouache, 15 x 24 ¼ inches.

    Picketed Aircraft. 1940.
    Gouache, 15 x 24 ½ inches.

    Devastation 1940: Public House and Masonic Hall, Wales.
       1940.
    Gouache, 21 ¼ x 31 ½ inches.

    *Devastation 1940: Solicitor's Office in Wales. 1940
       (page 37).
    Gouache, 31 ¼ x 21 ¼ inches.

    *Devastation 1940: Farmhouse in Wales. 1940 (page 36).
    Gouache, 21 ¼ x 31 ½ inches.

    †City. Fallen Lift-Shaft.

TOPOLSKI, Feliks. Polish, born 1907.
    *Scottish and Polish Soldiers at the Entrance to the Polish
       Camp. 1940 (page 38).
    Line and wash, 8 ⅞ x 11 ¾ inches.

    Polish Camp in Scotland. 1940.
    Line and wash, 8 ⅝ x 11 ¾ inches.

    Polish Soldiers at Blackpool. 1940.
    Line and wash, 9 ⅛ x 15 ¾ inches.

    The Salvation Army in the East End. 1940.
    Watercolor, 11 ¼ x 15 ¾ inches.

    †Fire in Chiswick, October 1940.

WORSLEY, Midshipman John. Born 1920.
    Lieutenant Commander R. Daintree, R.N., Gunnery
       Lieutenant, Resting before Dinner. 1940.
    Pencil drawing, 10 x 12 ⅞ inches.

    *Part of a 6-in. Gun Crew in Action, the Shell Being Rammed
       Home. 1940 (page 39).
    Wash drawing, 11 ⅛ x 14 ¼ inches.

    Five Members of a Gun's Crew on Watch. 1940.
    Wash drawing, 11 x 12 ⅞ inches.

    Group of Figures in a Sailing Boat in the North Sea in War
       Time. 1940.
    Wash drawing, 10 ¼ x 10 ¼ inches.

    Smoke on the Horizon. 1940.
    Wash drawing, 9 ½ x 12 ⅞ inches.

TEN THOUSAND COPIES OF THIS BOOK WERE PRINTED IN MAY 1941 FOR THE
TRUSTEES OF THE MUSEUM OF MODERN ART BY THE PLANTIN PRESS, NEW YORK

Museum of Modern Art Publications in Reprint

Abstract Painting and Sculpture in America. 1951. Andrew Carnduff Ritchie

African Negro Art. 1935. James Johnson Sweeney

American Art of the 20's and 30's: Paintings by Nineteen Living Americans; Painting and Sculpture by Living Americans; Murals by American Painters and Photographers. 1929. Barr; Kirstein and Levy

American Folk Art: The Art of the Common Man in America, 1750-1900. 1932. Holger Cahill

American Painting and Sculpture: 1862-1932. 1932. Holger Cahill

American Realists and Magic Realists. 1943. Miller and Barr; Kirstein

American Sources of Modern Art. 1933. Holger Cahill

Americans 1942-1963; Six Group Exhibitions. 1942-1963. Dorothy C. Miller

Ancient Art of the Andes. 1954. Bennett and d'Harnoncourt

The Architecture of Bridges. 1949. Elizabeth B. Mock

The Architecture of Japan. 1955. Arthur Drexler

Art in Our Time; 10th Anniversary Exhibition. 1939.

Art Nouveau; Art and Design at the Turn of the Century. 1959. Selz and Constantine

Arts of the South Seas. 1946. Linton, Wingert, and d'Harnoncourt

Bauhaus: 1919-1928. 1938. Bayer, W. Gropius and I. Gropius

Britain at War. 1941. Eliot, Read, Carter and Dyer

Built in U.S.A.: 1932-1944; Post-War Architecture. 1944. Mock; Hitchcock and Drexler

Cézanne, Gauguin, Seurat, Van Gogh: First Loan Exhibition. 1929. Alfred H. Barr, Jr.

Marc Chagall. 1946. James Johnson Sweeney

Giorgio de Chirico. 1955. James Thrall Soby

Contemporary Painters. 1948. James Thrall Soby

Cubism and Abstract Art. 1936. Alfred H. Barr, Jr.

Salvador Dali. 1946. James Thrall Soby

James Ensor. 1951. Libby Tannenbaum

Max Ernst. 1961. William S. Lieberman

Fantastic Art, Dada, Surrealism. 1947. Barr; Hugnet

Feininger-Hartley. 1944. Schardt, Barr, and Wheeler

The Film Index: A Bibliography (Vol. 1, The Film as Art). 1941.

Five American Sculptors: Alexander Calder; The Sculpture of John B. Flannagan; Gaston Lachaise; The Sculpture of Elie Nadelman; The Sculpture of Jacques Lipchitz. 1935-1954. Sweeney; Miller, Zigrosser; Kirstein; Hope

Five European Sculptors: Naum Gabo—Antoine Pevsner; Wilhelm Lehmbruck—Aristide Maillol; Henry Moore. 1930-1948. Read, Olson, Chanin; Abbott; Sweeney

Four American Painters: George Caleb Bingham; Winslow Homer, Albert P. Ryder, Thomas Eakins. 1930-1935. Rogers, Musick, Pope; Mather, Burroughs, Goodrich

German Art of the Twentieth Century. 1957. Haftmann, Hentzen and Lieberman; Ritchie

Vincent van Gogh: A Monograph; A Bibliography. 1935, 1942. Barr; Brooks

Arshile Gorky. 1962. William C. Seitz

Hans Hofmann. 1963. William C. Seitz

Indian Art of the United States. 1941. Douglas and d'Harnoncourt

Introductions to Modern Design: What is Modern Design?; What is Modern Interior Design? 1950-1953. Edgar Kaufmann, Jr.

Paul Klee: Three Exhibitions: 1930; 1941; 1949. 1945-1949. Barr; J. Feininger, L. Feininger, Sweeney, Miller; Soby

Latin American Architecture Since 1945. 1955. Henry-Russell Hitchcock

Lautrec-Redon. 1931. Jere Abbott

Machine Art. 1934. Philip Johnson

John Marin. 1936. McBride, Hartley and Benson

Masters of Popular Painting. 1938. Cahill, Gauthier, Miller, Cassou, et al.

Matisse: His Art and His Public. 1951. Alfred H. Barr, Jr.

Joan Miró. 1941. James Johnson Sweeney

Modern Architecture in England. 1937. Hitchcock and Bauer

Modern Architecture: International Exhibition. 1932. Hitchcock, Johnson, Mumford; Barr

Modern German Painting and Sculpture. 1931. Alfred H. Barr, Jr.

Modigliani: Paintings, Drawings, Sculpture. 1951. James Thrall Soby

Claude Monet: Seasons and Moments. 1960. William C. Seitz

Edvard Munch; A Selection of His Prints From American Collections. 1957. William S. Lieberman

The New American Painting; As Shown in Eight European Countries, 1958-1959. 1959. Alfred H. Barr, Jr.

New Horizons in American Art. 1936. Holger Cahill

New Images of Man. 1959. Selz; Tillich

Organic Design in Home Furnishings. 1941. Eliot F. Noyes

Picasso: Fifty Years of His Art. 1946. Alfred H. Barr, Jr.

Prehistoric Rock Pictures in Europe and Africa. 1937. Frobenius and Fox

Diego Rivera. 1931. Frances Flynn Paine

Romantic Painting in America. 1943. Soby and Miller
Medardo Rosso. 1963. Margaret Scolari Barr
Mark Rothko. 1961. Peter Selz
Georges Roualt: Paintings and Prints. 1947. James Thrall Soby
Henri Rousseau. 1946. Daniel Catton Rich
Sculpture of the Twentieth Century. 1952. Andrew Carnduff Ritchie
Soutine. 1950. Monroe Wheeler
Yves Tanguy. 1955. James Thrall Soby
Tchelitchew: Paintings, Drawings. 1942. James Thrall Soby
Textiles and Ornaments of India. 1956. Jayakar and Irwin; Wheeler
Three American Modernist Painters: Max Weber; Maurice Sterne; Stuart Davis. 1930-1945. Barr; Kallen; Sweeney
Three American Romantic Painters: Charles Burchfield: Early Watercolors; Florine Stettheimer; Franklin C. Watkins. 1930-1950. Barr; McBride; Ritchie
Three Painters of America: Charles Demuth; Charles Sheeler; Edward Hopper. 1933-1950. Ritchie; Williams; Barr and Burchfield
Twentieth-Century Italian Art. 1949. Soby and Barr
Twenty Centuries of Mexican Art. 1940
Edouard Vuillard. 1954. Andrew Carnduff Ritchie

The Bulletin of the Museum of Modern Art, 1933-1963. (7 vols.)

DATE DUE

GAYLORD			PRINTED IN U.S.A.

Ihn suchen, den meine Seele liebt

Jeder, der sich halbwegs für einen Christen hält, weiß, daß er sich als Kind Gottes betrachten und deshalb Gott seinen Vater nennen darf. Jeder, der ein ganzer Christ sein will, weiß, daß das „kindliche" Vertrauen, zu dem ihn Gottes väterliche Liebe ermutigt, nicht Sache eines unmündigen Menschen sein (oder bleiben) darf.

Daß Gott den reifen Menschen als seinen Bundespartner sucht, spricht die Bibel unmißverständlich aus, wenn sie den Herrn als Bräutigam oder Ehemann darstellt, der um sein Volk wie um eine Braut oder Ehefrau wirbt: „Ich traue dich mir an auf ewig; ich traue dich mir an um den Brautpreis von Gerechtigkeit und Recht, von Liebe und Erbarmen." (Hos 2,21)

Ein ganzes Buch der Bibel, das Hohe Lied, läßt sich im Sinne dieses Bildes verstehen als poesievoll geformter Ausdruck des ebenso leidenschaftlichen wie innigen Verhältnisses von Gott und Mensch; und die Sehnsucht der Braut des Hohen Liedes als der Glaube eines Menschen, der mit allen Fasern seines Herzens seinen Gott sucht und alles von ihm erwartet, - eine Braut ist ja durch und durch Erwartung: „Des Nachts auf meinem Lager suchte ich ihn, den meine Seele liebt. Ich suchte ihn und fand ihn nicht. Aufstehen will ich, die Stadt durchstreifen, die Gassen und Plätze, ihn suchen, den meine Seele liebt." (Hld 3,1-2)

Maria, obwohl *Mutter* des Gottmenschen, darf durch das Lebende Bild sehr wohl mit dieser *Braut* verglichen werden, da ihre Sehnsucht nach dem Sohn ganz durchdrungen ist von erwartungsvollem Glauben, der nicht von ihm läßt, auch nicht angesichts des ihm drohenden Todes. So bewahrheitet sich in Maria beispielhaft das Wort des Hohen Liedes. „Stark wie der Tod ist die Liebe" (Hld 8,6). Denn der Tod (des Sohnes) vermag die Liebe (der Mutter) nicht zu brechen. Wie recht Maria hat, sich durch den Tod nicht beirren zu lassen, wird sich erweisen bei der Auferstehung, die die alttestamentliche Überzeugung noch überbietet: die Liebe ist *stärker* als der Tod.

I Looked for the One I Love

Anyone who considers himself more or less a Christian knows that he can regard himself as a child of God and that therefore he can call God his father. Anyone who wants to be a complete Christian knows that the "childlike" trust which is encouraged by God's fatherly love should not be (or remain) something for a person who is not yet an adult.

The Bible makes it perfectly clear that God seeks the mature person as his partner when it describes the Lord as a bridegroom or husband who courts his people as a man would court his future wife: "I will make you my wife; I will be true and faithful; I will show you constant love and mercy" (Hos 2,19)

An entire book of the Bible, the Song of Songs, can be understood as a metaphor of this kind, as a poetic expression of the passionate and intimate relationship between God and man. Likewise, the longing of the bride in the Song of Songs can be understood as the faith of a person who with every fibre of his or her being seeks his God and expects everything from him - a bride is full of expectation: "asleep on my bed, night after night I dreamt of the one I love; I was looking for him, but couldn't find him. I went wandering through the city, through its steets and alleys. I looked for the one I love" (Song 3, 1-2).

Although Mary was the Mother of the God-man, she can rightly be compared by the tableau vivant with this bride because her longing for her son is completely suffused with expectant faith which does not give up even when she sees him threatened by death. Mary, therefore, is a perfect illustration of the words of the Song of Songs: "Love is as powerful as death" (Song 8,6) because the death of the son cannot destroy the Mother's love. How right Mary is, not to be misled by death, will be proved at the resurrection, which even surpasses the assurance expressed by the Old Testament: love is *stronger* than death.

Hld 3;6
Song 3;6

Seht die Braut in Salomons Hohem Liede!
Wie sie klagt: „Der Bräutigam ist entschwunden!“,
Wie sie ruft und sucht, sich nicht Ruhe gönnend,
Bis sie ihn findet!

See the bride in the song of Salomon,
How she weeps for the missing bridegroom,
How she calls and seeks, allowing herself no rest
Until she finds him.

Maria: „O Simeon, Simeon, ehrwürdiger Greis! Jetzt wird sich erfüllen, was du mir einst geweissagt hast: ‚Ein Schwert wird deine Seele durchdringen!'" (Lk 2,35)

Maria: „Mein Sohn, wo werde ich dich wiedersehen?"
Jesus: „Dort, wo sich das Wort der Schrift erfüllt: ‚Er war wie ein Lamm, das zur Schlachtbank geführt wird und seinen Mund nicht öffnet.'" (Jes 53,7)

Mary: "O Simeon, Simeon, venerable old man. What you once prophesied to me will now be fulfilled: 'A sword will pierce your soul!'" (Lk 2,35)

Mary: "My son, where shall I see you again?"
Jesus: "There, where the words of the scripture are fulfilled: 'He was led like a lamb to the slaughter, and he opened not his mouth.'" (Is 53,7)

34

Jesu Rede über die Endzeit

Seine Jünger wiesen ihn auf die gewaltigen Bauten des Tempels hin. Jesus sagte zu ihnen: „Seht sie nur an! Wahrlich, ich sage euch: Hier bleibt kein Stein auf dem andern – keiner, der nicht niedergerissen wird!" Und sie fragten ihn: „Sag uns, wann wird das geschehen? Was ist das Zeichen deiner Ankunft und des Endes der Weltzeit?"

Jesus sprach zu ihnen: „Seht zu, daß keiner euch in die Irre führe! Denn viele werden unter meinem Namen kommen und sagen: ‚Ich bin der Messias!' Und sie werden viele in die Irre führen. Seid wachsam und habt keine Furcht, wenn nah und fern Kriege ausbrechen! Das muß geschehen, es ist aber noch nicht das Ende! Aufstehen wird Volk gegen Volk und Reich gegen Reich, und an vielen Orten wird es Hungersnot und Erdbeben geben, und dies ist nur der Anfang der Wehen.

Ausliefern wird man euch, quälen und töten. Die ganze Welt wird euch hassen, weil ihr euch zu mir bekennt. Dann werden viele zu Fall kommen und hassen werden sie einander und einander verraten. Aufstehen werden in Scharen die Lügenpropheten, Gottlosigkeit breitet sich aus, und die Liebe unter euch wird kalt. Doch ist gerettet, wer standhaft bleibt bis zum Ende.

Wenn aber der Menschensohn kommt in seiner Herrlichkeit und alle Engel mit ihm, dann wird er sich setzen auf den Thron seiner Herrlichkeit. Und alle Völker werden vor ihm versammelt sein, und er wird sie voneinander sondern, wie der Hirt die Schafe von den Ziegen sondert. Dann wird der König denen zu seiner Rechten sagen: Kommt zu mir, ihr Gesegneten meines Vaters! Nehmt das Reich zum Erbe, das euch zubereitet ist seit Urbeginn der Welt. Denn hungrig war ich – und ihr habt mir zu essen gegeben, durstig – und ihr habt mich getränkt. Fremdling war ich – und ihr habt mich aufgenommen, nackt – und ihr habt mich gewandet. Krank war ich – und ihr habt mich versorgt, im Gefängnis war ich – und ihr habt mich besucht. Wahrlich, ich sage euch, was ihr auch nur einem meiner geringsten Brüder getan habt, das habt ihr mir getan.

Dann wird er sich zu den anderen wenden und zu ihnen sagen: Weg von mir, ihr Verfluchten, ins unendliche Feuer! Wahrlich, ich sage euch, was ihr für einen meiner geringsten Brüder nicht getan habt, das habt ihr mir nicht getan! Und sie werden hingehen in unendliche Pein, die Gerechten aber in unendliches Leben."

Als Jesus all diese Reden geendet hatte, sprach er zu seinen Jüngern: „Ihr wißt, in zwei Tagen ist Pascha, und der Menschensohn wird zur Kreuzigung ausgeliefert."

Jesus speaks of the Endtime

His disciples pointed out to Him the buildings of the temple area. His comment was: "Do you see all these buildings? I assure you, not one stone shall be left on another – it will all be turned down." And they asked him: "Tell us, when will all this occur? What will be the sign of your coming and the end of the world?"

In reply Jesus said to them: "Take care that no one takes you astray. Many will come and say, 'I am the Messiah', and they will lead many astray. Be watchful and have no fear when wars break out near at hand and far away. This must happen, but it is not yet the end. People will rise against people and nation against nation, and there will be famine and earthquakes in many places, and this is only the beginning of the affliction!

You will be handed over, tortured and killed, the whole world will hate you because you believe in me. Then many will come to grief and will hate each other and betray each other. False prophets will arise in hordes, godlessness will spread and love among you will become cold. But those who remain steadfast until the end will be saved.

When the Son of Man comes in his glory, he will sit upon his royal throne, and all the nations will be assembled before him. Then he will separate them into two groups, as a shepherd separates sheep from goats. The king will say to those on his right: 'Come. You have my Father's blessing! Inherit the kingdom prepared for you from the creation of the world. For I was hungry, and you gave me food, I was thirsty, and you gave me drink. I was a stranger, and you welcomed me, naked and you clothed me. I was ill and you comforted me, in prison and you came to visit me. I assure you, as often as you did it for one of my least brothers, you did it for me."

Then he will say to those on his left: 'Out of my sight, you condemned, into the everlasting fire! I assure you, as often as you neglected to do it to one of these least ones, you neglected to do it for me.' These will go off to eternal punishment and the just to eternal life."

Now when Jesus had finished all those discourses, he declared to his disciples, "You know that in two days' time it will be Passover, and that the Son of Man is to be handed over to be crucified."

Mt aus Kapitel (from chapter) 24/25

„Man hätte das Öl teuer verkaufen und das Geld den Armen geben können." Jesus sagte: „Sie hat ein gutes Werk an mir getan. Die Armen habt ihr immer bei euch, mich aber habt ihr nicht immer." (Mt 26,9ff)

Judas ging zu den Hohenpriestern und Befehlshabern und beriet mit ihnen, wie er ihnen Jesus ausliefern könnte. Von da an suchte er eine Gelegenheit, ihn an sie auszuliefern – abseits der Leute. (Lk 22,4ff)

"This could have been sold for a good price and the money given to the poor". Jesus said: "It is a good deed she has done for me. The poor you will always have with you, but you will not always have me."

Judas went off to confer with the chief priests and officers about a way to hand him over to them. Then he kept looking for an opportunity to hand him over without creating a disturbance. (Lk 22,4ff)

Brot vom Himmel

Als einziger Evangelist überliefert Johannes bei seiner Darstellung des letzten Mahles Jesu mit den Aposteln nicht die Einsetzungsworte, die den Christen aller Zeiten und Konfessionen in ihrer Feier der Eucharistie - oder des Abendmahls, wie immer sie es nennen - gegenwärtig sind. Dafür bringt sein Evangelium im Anschluß an die wunderbare Speisung einer Volksmenge am See von Tiberias eine große „eucharistische Rede", in der Jesus ausruft: „Ich bin das Brot des Lebens. Eure Väter haben in der Wüste das Manna gegessen und sind gestorben. Ich bin das lebendige Brot, das vom Himmel herabgekommen ist. Wer von diesem Brot ißt, wird in Ewigkeit leben. Das Brot, das ich geben werde, ist mein Fleisch (ich gebe es hin) für das Leben der Welt." (Joh 6,48.49.51)

Da diese Worte und das Geschehen im Abendmahlssaal sich gegenseitig ausdeuten, stellt die Oberammergauer Passion der Spielszene des Abendmahls, sozusagen mit der Ermächtigung durch Jesus selbst, das Lebende Bild der Mannalese gegenüber.

Als Manna bezeichneten die Israeliten das „Brot vom Himmel" (Ex 16,4), Körner wie von Honigkuchen, die sie auf ihrem Auszug aus Ägypten ins gelobte Land jeden Morgen vom Boden der Wüste Sin auflesen konnten. „Sie aßen Manna, bis sie die Grenze von Kanaan erreichten." (Ex 16.35) Das Gottesgeschenk des Manna ließ sie die Furcht vergessen, ihre Reise könne in den Untergang führen; in seiner Kraft hielten sie durch bis ins gelobte Land der Freiheit. -

In Jesus ist die Liebe Gottes selbst vom Himmel herabgekommen, Fleisch geworden; sie bleibt uns zur Nahrung gegeben und wird an uns verteilt, bis wir unsere „irdische Pilgerfahrt" beenden - nicht im Tod, sondern in ewigem Leben.

Bread from Heaven

In his account of the last supper of Jesus with the apostles, John is the only Evangelist who does not hand down the words of institution which Christians of all times and confessions remember when they celebrate the Eucharist or Communion, whatever name it is given. On the other hand, following the miraculous feeding of the multitude by the Sea of Galilee, his gospel contains a great "Eucharistic" speech in which Jesus proclaims, "I am the bread of life. Your ancestors ate manna in the desert, but they died. I myself am the living bread come down from heaven. If anyone eats this bread, he will live for ever. The bread that I will give him is my flesh, which I give so that the world may live," (Jn 6,48.49.51).

As these words and the events in the room of the last supper must be explained by reference to each other, the Passion Play contrasts the enactment of the last supper with the tableau vivant of the gathering of the manna, so to speak with the authority of Jesus himself.

The "bread from heaven" (Ex 16,4) was described by the Israelites as manna, like grains of honey cake, which they gathered every morning from the ground in the desert of Sin when they left Egypt for the Promised Land. "They ate manna until they reached the land of Canaan". (Ex 16,35) The gift of manna from God made them forget their fear that their journey might lead to death. With the strength it gave they held out until they reached the land of freedom.

In Jesus the love of God himself came down from Heaven and became flesh. It is still there for our nourishment and is given to us until we end our "earthly pilgrimage" - not in death but in eternal life.

Ex 16
Mt 26,20-29; Mk 14,17-25; Lk 22,14-23; Joh (Jn) 13,2-Joh (Jn) 6,22-59

Mit des Mannas Genuß sättigte wunderbar
In der Wüste der Herr Israels Kinder einst.
Doch ein besseres Mahl
Bietet Jesus uns dar: aus dem Geheimnisse
Seines Leibes und Blutes
Quillt uns Gnade und Seligkeit.

Once long ago the Lord miraculously filled
Israel's children with manna in the desert.
But Jesus offers us
A better feast. Out of the mysteries
Of his body and blood
Mercy and bliss flow for us.

Wein - Verheißung der Lebensfülle

„Ich bin gekommen, damit sie das Leben haben und es *in Fülle* haben" (Joh 10,10), sagt Jesus über seinen Auftrag. Er vollendet ihn durch seinen Tod; am Kreuz gibt er sein Fleisch hin und vergießt sein Blut „für das Leben der Welt" (Joh 6,51). Um das Geschenk dieses Lebens sollen die Menschen nicht nur in der Erinnerung wissen, sie sollen es vielmehr nach seinem testamentarischen Willen jederzeit leibhaftig empfangen können: „Denn mein Fleisch ist eine wahre Speise und mein Blut ist ein wahrer Trank." (Joh 6,55)

Zu Gestalten seines Fleisches und Blutes bestimmt er bei seinem letzten Mahl mit den Aposteln Brot und Wein. Solange Menschen sein Gedächtnis begehen, werden diese Gaben ausgeteilt, bis er wiederkommt in Herrlichkeit. Brot und Wein - die jedem unmittelbar als Zeichen für das Leben und das Leben in Fülle verständlich sind; Brot, das den elementaren Hunger stillt, das die Lebensgrundlage schlechthin darstellt, und Wein, „der das Herz des Menschen erfreut" (Ps 104,15), der also - ein kleines Stück weit wenigstens - in die Fülle des Lebens hineinträgt; *ganz* auszukosten kann sie ja erst jenseits des rein Irdischen sein! Jesus selbst verbindet mit dem Wein ausdrücklich diesen Ausblick in die zukünftige Vollendung: „Ich sage euch: von nun an werde ich nicht mehr vom Gewächs des Weinstockes trinken, bis das Reich Gottes kommt." (Lk 22,18)

Die riesenhafte Traube, die Kundschafter aus dem Land der Verheißung zu den Israeliten in die Wüste mitbringen, um ihnen eine Ahnung davon zu geben, welcher Lebensreichtum jenseits der Grenze auf sie wartet, ist das naheliegende alttestamentliche Voraus-Bild für all das, „was Gott denen bereitet hat, die ihn lieben" (1 Kor 2,9). Wie die Rebe aus Kanaan dem ersten Gottesvolk auf seinem Zug durch die Wüste, so bietet dem neuen Gottesvolk auf seiner Wanderschaft durch diese Welt der eucharistische Wein einen „Vorgeschmack der kommenden Herrlichkeit" (Meßliturgie zum Fronleichnamsfest).

Wine - the Promise of the Fullness of Life

"I have come in order that you might have life - life in all its fullness" (Jn 10,10), says Jesus concerning his mission. He fulfills it by his death. On the cross he gives up his flesh and pours out his blood "so that the world may live" (Jn 6,51). Mankind should not only remember this gift of life, they should be able to receive it any time in the flesh in accordance with his testamentary will: "For my flesh is the real food; my blood is the real drink". (Jn 6,55)

At the last supper with the apostles he designates bread and wine as forms of his flesh and blood. As long as men and women celebrate his memory these gifts will be shared out until he comes again in glory. Bread and wine are directly comprehensible to everyone as a symbol of life and the fullness of life. Bread assuages elementary hunger and represents the basis of life, while wine, "which makes the heart of man happy" (Ps 104,15) contributes a little at least to the fullness of life. Of course, it can be tasted to the full only in the next world! Jesus himself expressly connects the wine with this prospect of future perfection: "I tell you that from now on I will not drink this wine until the Kingdom of God comes" (Lk 22,18)

The giant grapes which bear witness to the Promised Land to the Israelites in the desert in order to give them an idea of the richness of life awaiting them on the other side of the border are the obvious Old Testament prefiguration of all the things "which God prepared for those who love him" (1 Cor 2,9). The wine of the Eucharist offers the new people of God a "foretaste of the coming glory" (Liturgy for the Feast of Corpus Christi) on their journey through this world, just as the grapes of Canaan did for the first people of God in their passage through the desert.

Num 13,17-27
Mt 26,20-29 / Mk 14,17-25 / Lk 22,14-23 / Joh (Jn) 13,2

Gut ist der Herr, gut ist der Herr:	*Good is the Lord, good is the Lord!*
Dem Volke einstens hatte er	*Once He gave to His people*
Den besten Saft der Reben	*The best juice of the vine*
Aus Kanaan gegeben.	*From Canaan.*
Des neuen Bundes heil'ger Wein	*The holy wine of the new covenant*
Wird selbst das Blut des Sohnes sein,	*Will be His Son's own blood*
Der Seele Durst zu stillen.	*To quench the thirst of the soul.*

„Begreift ihr, was ich an euch getan habe?
Wenn ich, der Herr und Meister, euch die
Füße gewaschen habe, dann müßt auch ihr
einander die Füße waschen. Ein Beispiel
habe ich euch gegeben, damit auch ihr tut,
wie ich euch getan habe." (Joh 13,14f)

*"Do you understand what I just did for
you? If I washed you feet – I who am
your 'Teacher' and 'Lord' – then you must
wash each other's feet. What I just did was
to give you an example; as I have done, so
you must do." (Jn 13,14f)*

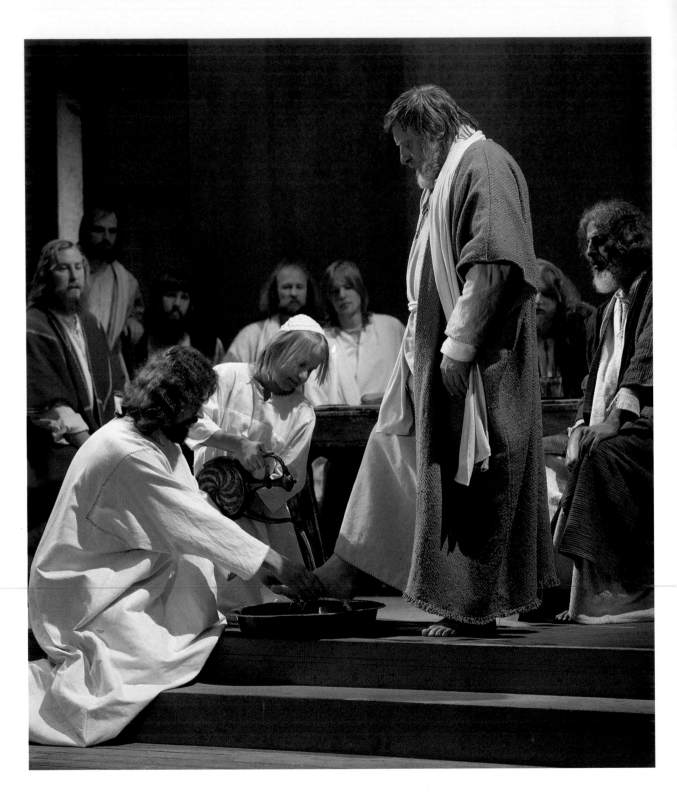

Dann kam der Tag der ungesäuerten Bro te, an dem das Paschalamm geschlachtet werden mußte. Jesus schickte Petrus und Johannes in die Stadt und sagte: „Geht und bereitet das Paschamahl für uns vor, daß wir es gemeinsam essen konnen." Und sie bereiteten das Paschamahl vor.
Als die Stunde gekommen war, begab er sich mit den Aposteln zu Tisch. Und er sagte zu ihnen·
„Ich habe mich sehr danach gesehnt, vor meinem Leiden dieses Paschalamm mit euch zu essen Denn ich sage euch: Ich

werde es nicht mehr essen, bis das Mahl seine Erfüllung findet im Reich Gottes."
Und er nahm den Kelch, sprach das Dank-gebet und sagte: „Nehmt den Wein und verteilt ihn untereinander. Denn ich sage euch: Von nun an werde ich nicht mehr von der Frucht des Weinstocks trinken, bis das Reich Gottes kommt." (Lk 22.6ff)

The day of Unleavened Bread arrived on which it was appointed to sacrifice the paschal lamb. Jesus sent Peter and John off with the instruction, "Go and prepare our Passover supper for us". And accordingly they prepared the Passover supper.
When the hour arrived, he took his place at table, and the apostels with him. He said to them:
"I have greatly desired to eat this Passover with you before I suffer. I tell you, I will not eat again until it is fulfilled in the king-dom of God".

Then taking a cup he offered a blessing in thanks and said: "Take this and divide it among you; I tell you, from now on I will not drink of the fruit of the vine until the coming of the reign of God". (Lk 22,6ff)

45

Und er nahm Brot, sprach das Dankgebet, brach das Brot und reichte es ihnen mit den Worten:
„Das ist mein Leib, der für euch hingegeben wird. Tut dies zu meinem Gedächtnis." (Lk 22,19)

Then, taking bread and giving thanks, he broke it and gave it to them, saying:
"This is my body to be given for you. Do this as a remembrance of me". (Lk 22,19)

Ebenso nahm er nach dem Mahl den Kelch
und sagte:
„Dieser Kelch ist der neue Bund in meinem
Blute, das für euch vergossen wird."
(Lk 22,20)

*He did the same with the cup after eating,
saying as he did so:
"This cup is the new covenant in my blood,
which will be shed for you". (Lk 22,20)*

47

Jesus sagte zu Judas: „Was du tun willst, das tue bald." Doch keiner erkannte, weswegen er zu ihm sprach. Als der nun den Bissen genommen, ging er sogleich hinaus. Es war aber Nacht. (Joh 13,27f)

Jesus addressed himself to Judas, "Be quick about what you are to do". Naturally none of those reclining at table understood why Jesus said this to him. No sooner had Judas eaten the morsel than he went out. It was night. (Jn 13,27ff)

49

Petrus: „Wenn alle an dir Anstoß nehmen, ich niemals!" Jesus entgegnete ihm: „Amen, ich sage dir: In dieser Nacht, noch ehe der Hahn kräht, wirst du mich dreimal verleugnen." (Mt 26,33f)

Lobet den Herrn alle Völker!
Preiset ihn, alle Nationen!
Denn mächtig waltet über uns seine Huld,
Die Treue des Herrn währt in Ewigkeit.

Peter: "Though all may have their faith in you shaken, mine will never be shaken!" Jesus said to him, "I give you my word, before the cock crows tonight you will deny me three times". (Mt 26,33)

Praise the Lord, all peoples,
Magnify the Lord, all nations,
For the power of His grace rules over us,
The faith of the Lord is eternal.

Verraten und verkauft

Wir „schätzen" unsere Freunde und „rechnen mit ihnen"; bei anderen sind wir im Zweifel, wie wir sie „einschätzen" sollen oder halten sie für „unberechenbar". Von manchen wissen wir, daß sie „ihren Preis" haben; über andere fällen wir das „abschätzige" Urteil, daß sie „nichts wert" seien. - Dasselbe Vokabular für Menschen wie für Geld und Waren! Überführen uns nicht die eigenen Worte einer Mentalität, mit der wir uns kaum über jene Zeiten und Gesellschaften erheben, in denen der Mitmensch - als Sklave - ganz selbstverständlich wie eine Ware behandelt und für Geld verschachert werden konnte?

Dies wäre zu bedenken, bevor wir selbstgerecht den Brüdern des Josef oder Judas ein Vergehen vorwerfen, für das es bei uns keine Parallele gäbe. Wir würden dann auch etwas tiefer blicken und erkennen: das Verwerfliche im Verhalten der Jakobssöhne, die ihren ungeliebten Bruder Josef an vorbeiziehende Sklavenhändler verkaufen, oder in dem des Judas, der, ihnen ähnlich, seinen Freund Jesus für einen Sklavenpreis verrät, ist nicht bloß die Empfänglichkeit für klingende Münze; bevor man Geld für einen Menschen nimmt, muß man ihm seine Menschenwürde abgesprochen haben.

Darin besteht das eigentliche Verbrechen der Jakobssöhne wie des Judas. Und das eigentlich Erschütternde: Wie konnten sie sich einem Menschen, der ihnen doch am allernächsten stand, so weit entfremden, daß ihnen am Ende ein paar Silberlinge mehr bedeuteten als der leibliche Bruder, mehr als der aufrichtigste Freund?

Den Weg der Entfremdung zwischen Josef und seinen Brüdern zeichnet die Bibel nach. Wie aber Judas dahin kam, die ihm zugesagte Seligkeit auszuschlagen - „Selig ist, wer an mir kein Ärgernis nimmt" (Mt 11,6) -, lassen die Evangelien weitgehend im Dunkeln. Vielleicht deshalb, damit wir uns erst gar nicht dabei aufhalten, empört auf *seine* Abwege zu starren, und uns stattdessen besser nach den Abwegen fragen, auf denen wir selbst unsere „erste Liebe" (Off 2,1) verlieren könnten.

Betrayed and Sold

We "value" our friends and "count on them". With others, we may not be sure how to "rate" them or we regard them as "unpredictable". We know that some of them have their "price", while we judge others scornfully by saying that they are "worthless". The same vocabulary for human beings as for money and goods! Do not prove our own words a mentality which shows that we have hardly progressed from earlier ages and societies where our fellow beings - as slaves - were treated as goods as a matter of course and could be traded for money?

We should consider this before we self-righteously accuse Joseph's brothers or Judas of an offence for which we would not have any parallel. Then we would see a little deeper and realise that the objectionable element in the conduct of Jacob's sons, who sold their unloved brother Joseph to passing slave-traders, or in that of Judas who, like them, betrayed his friend Jesus for the price of a slave, is not just their susceptibility to cash. Before someone accepts money as payment for another man, it is necessary to deny him his human dignity.

This is the real crime of Jacob's sons and Judas. The really disturbing question is how could they become so estranged from a person who stood closest to them that, in the end, a few silver coins meant more to them than their own brother or their truest friend?

The Bible traces the course of the estrangement between Joseph and his brothers, but how Judas came to reject the bliss he had been promised - "How happy are those who have no doubts about me" (Mt 11,6) - is not made clear by the Gospels. Perhaps because we should not spend time indignantly considering *his* mistaken reasons, but should instead ask ourselves about the mistaken reasons which could lead us ourselves to lose our "first love" (Rev 2,1).

Gen 37,12-28
Mt 26,14-16 / Mk 14,10-11 / Lk 22,3-6

„Was bietet für den Knaben ihr?"
So sprechen Josephs Brüder hier,
„Wieviel wollt ihr uns geben?"
Sie lassen bald um den Gewinn
Von zwanzig Silberlingen hin
Des Bruders Blut und Leben.

"What will you offer for this boy?"
Said Joseph's brothers there:
"How much will you give us?"
Quickly they give away their brother's
Blood and life for a profit
Of twenty pieces of silver.

54

Nikodemus aber, einer aus ihren eigenen Reihen, der früher einmal Jesus aufgesucht hatte, sagte zu ihnen: „Verurteilt etwa unser Gesetz einen Menschen, bevor man ihn verhört und festgestellt hat, was er tut?" (Joh 7,50f)

One of their own number, Nicodemus (the man who had come to him), spoke up to say: "Since when does our law condemn any man without first hearing him and knowing the facts?" (Jn 7,50f)

Darauf ging einer der Zwölf, namens Judas Iskariot, zu den Hohenpriestern und sagte: „Was wollt ihr mir geben, wenn ich euch Jesus ausliefere?" Und sie zahlten ihm dreißig Silberstücke. (Mt 26,14)

Then one of the Twelve whose name was Judas Iscariot went off to the chief priests and said, "What are you willing to give me if I hand him over to you?" They paid him thirty pieces of silver. (Mt 26,14)

Im Schweiß des Angesichts

Für ein schwaches Bild, für den allzu schwachen Widerschein der Todesangst Jesu muß man die Feldarbeit Adams halten, mag sie auch noch so schweißtreibend sein, wenn man sie nicht als Chiffre versteht für den Fluch, der auf der ganzen - gottfernen - menschlichen Existenz lastet.

„Im Schweiße deines Angesichts sollst du dein Brot essen, bis du zurückkehrst zum Erdboden!" (Gen 3,19), dieser Urteilsspruch steigert ja nicht einfach die Anstengung beim „Bebauen und Hüten" des Gartens, das schon dem „paradiesischen" Menschen aufgetragen war (vgl. Gen 2,15), ins Unerträgliche. Er stellt ihm vielmehr vor Augen, daß die Lebensaufgabe für den, der sich von Gott getrennt hat, unter völlig verändertem Vorzeichen steht: Der Mensch, der sein will wie Gott, muß folgerichtig auch gar alles von der eigenen Leistung erwarten: er bleibt allein mit seiner Sorge, allein mit seiner Angst. Die heillose Selbstüberforderung treibt ihm den Schweiß aus den Poren.

„In allem uns gleich außer der Sünde" nennt der vierte Meßkanon den Mensch gewordenen Sohn Gottes; kann er dann jene Angst des in Sünde gefallenen Menschen je gespürt haben? Er lernte sie kennen, da er „für uns zur Sünde" (2 Kor 5,21) wurde! Er, den die Evangelien bis hin zum Gang über den Bach Kidron als staunenswert angstfreien Menschen zeichnen, *fing* am Ölberg *an*, sich zu fürchten und zu ängstigen; Markus (14,33) und Matthäus (26,37) formulieren so, als wollten sie sagen, daß das Leiden Jesu mit einer für ihn neuen schrecklichen Erfahrung beginne, mit dem bewußten Nacherleben der inneren Verfassung Adams. Nicht anders sieht es der große zeitgenössische Theologe Hans Urs von Balthasar: Die „eigentliche" Passion beginnt im Innern: mit dem ,Grauen' und dem ,vereinsamenden Entsetzen'. Vereinsamung gegenüber dem sich entfremdenden, aber noch nicht entschwundenen Gott, an den Jesus sich wendet, mit dem es aber keine andere Kommunikation mehr gibt als den ins Leiden hinein stärkenden Engel."

In the Sweat of his Brow

Adams's work in the fields must be regarded as a weak image, a very pale reflection, of Jesus' fear of death, however much the work made Adam sweat, if it is not understood as a symbol of the curse on the whole of human existence far away from God.

"You will eat your bread in the sweat of your brow until you go back to the soil from which you were formed" (Gen 3,19). Of course, this judgement does not merely increase the effort of "cultivating and guarding" the garden which the man "in Paradise" was ordered to do (cf. Gen 2,15) to an unbearable degree. It also shows him that the life's work of anyone who parts from God is under totally different circumstances. A human being who wants to be like God must logically expect to achieve everything himself. He is left alone with his sorrow and fear. The terrible demands he makes on himself cause the sweat to pour from him.

"The same as us except in sin" is what the fourth Canon of the Mass says of the Son of God who became man. Can he then have felt the fear of the man who has fallen into sin? He came to know it because he "shared our sin" (2 Cor 5,21). He whom the Gospels describe as an amazingly fearless man even when crossing the river of Kidron, *began* to feel frightened and afraid on the Mount of Olives. The words used by Mark (14,33) and Matthew (26,37) seem to mean that Jesus' sufferings began with a terrible experience which was new to him, i. e. the conscious reliving of Adam's internal state of mind. This is how it is seen by the great contemporary theologian Hans Urs von Balthasar: the "real" Passion "begins inwardly: with 'dread and solitary terror'. Solitude as against the God who is drifting away but not yet disappeared and to whom Jesus turns, but with whom there is no communication other than the angel who gives him strength for his suffering."

Gen 3,16-21
Mt 26,36-46 / Mk 14,32-42 / Lk 22,39-46

Wie Adam kämpft mit drückender Lebensmüh',
An Kraft erschöpft, im Schweiße des Angesichts,
Um, ach, die eig'ne Schuld zu büßen,
So drückt den Heiland die fremde Sünde.

As Adam struggles, pressed down by life's burden,
With exhausted strength, in the sweat of the brow,
To atone, alas, for his own guilt, so likewise
The saviour is burdened by the guilt of others.

Er entfernte sich von ihnen ungefähr einen
Steinwurf weit, kniete nieder und betete:
„Vater, wenn du willst, nimm diesen Kelch
von mir, aber nicht mein, sondern dein
Wille soll geschehen!" (Lk 22,40ff)

He withdrew from them about a stone's
throw, then went down on his knees and
prayed in these words: "Father, if it is your
will, take this cup from me; yet not my will
but yours be done". (Lk 22,40ff)

Und er ging ein Stück weiter, warf sich zu
Boden und betete. (Mt 26,39)
Da erschien ihm ein Engel vom Himmel
und gab ihm neue Kraft. (Lk 22,43)

He advanced a little and fell prostrate in
prayer. (Mt 26,39)
An angel then appeared to him from
heaven to strengthen him. (Lk 22,43)

59

Der heuchlerische Kuß

Joab ist von David seines Feldherrnamtes enthoben worden, sein Vetter Amasa soll es übernehmen. Bei Gibeon (Gabaon) treffen der Abgesetzte und der Neuernannte zusammen. Das 2. Buch Samuel berichtet darüber: „Joab sagte zu Amasa: Geht es dir gut, mein Bruder? und griff mit der rechten Hand nach dem Bart Amasas, um ihn zu küssen. Amasa aber achtete nicht auf das Schwert, das Joab in der linken Hand hatte, und Joab stieß es ihm in den Bauch." (20, 9-10)

Das Lebende Bild dieser Szene ist vor mächtige Felsen gestellt. Sie charakterisieren gewiß zuerst einmal den Ort Gibeon. Der Gesang des Passionsspiels jedoch ruft sie darüber hinaus wie lebendige Zeugen der schändlichen Begebenheit an, damit sie mitklagen und sich entrüsten.

Wem nun freilich der wiederholte Anruf: „Ihr Felsen Gabaon!" als pure Theatralik vorkommt, sollte dies bedenken: Der Fels ist nicht nur ein unmittelbar verständliches Symbol der Beständigkeit und Treue, sondern - eben deshalb - geradezu Gottes selbst. „ER heißt: der Fels. Er ist ein unbeirrbar treuer Gott, er ist gerecht und gerade." (Dtn 32,4)

Wenn Joab seine Bluttat unter dem Deckmantel einer geheuchelten intim vertraulichen Geste *im Angesicht des Felsen* begeht, so höhnt er damit, schier für die leiblichen Augen sichtbar, Gott ins Angesicht. Vor dem Sinnbild des Felsens als Hintergrund tritt jeder Zug seiner Tat als völlige Verkehrung des göttlichen Willens ins Gegenteil hervor - statt Treue Verrat, statt Gerechtigkeit Verbrechen, statt Geradheit die denkbar „krümmste Tour".

Das ist so widergöttlich, daß Johannes für den Wiederholungsfall - Verrat des Judas - nur noch eine einzige Erklärung findet: der Satan, der Vater der Lüge, ist in Judas gefahren! (Vgl. Joh 8,44; 13,27)

The Hypocritical Kiss

David removed Joab from his post as leader of the army because he wanted his cousin Amasa to have it. The man who had lost his post and the one who replaced him meet at Gibeon. The account of the meeting is given in 2 Samuel: "Joab said to Amasa, 'How are you, my friend?' And took hold of his beard with his right hand in order to kiss him. Amasa was not on guard against the sword that Joab was holding in his other hand, and Joab stabbed him in the belly." (20,9.10)

The tableau vivant of this scene is set in front of huge rocks. They certainly characterise the place called Gibeon, but at the same time the song of the Passion Play calls upon them to lament and express their indignation as if they were living witnesses of the shameful deed.

Anyone who regards the repeated cry of "You rocks of Gibeon" as pure theatre should remember that the rock is not only a readily comprehensible symbol of steadfastness and loyalty, but also - and precisely for this reason - of God himself. "He is called the Rock. He is a steadfast and true God, he is upright and just." (Deut, 32,4)

When Joab carries out his bloody deed under the cover of a friendly greeting *in front of the rock* he derides God before his own face in a way which is visible to the eyes of the audience. With the symbol of the rock in the background, every element of his deed appears as the complete opposite of God's will - betrayal instead of loyalty, crime instead of justice, the greatest possible deceit instead of honesty.

It is all so contrary to God's will that John can only find one explanation for the similar act which was repeated later - the betrayal by Judas: Satan, the father of lies, had entered Judas! (cf. Jn 8,44; 13,27)

2 Sam 20,9-10
Mt 26,47-50 / Mk 14,43-46 / Lk 22,47-48

So Böses tat auch Joah an Amasa:
Er drückt zugleich mit heuchelnder Miene ihm
Den Kuß der Freundschaft auf die Wange
Und in den Leib des Dolches Spitze.

Joah was likewise treacherous to Amasa;
With a false expression he pressed
The kiss of friendship on his cheek,
And into his body the pointed dagger!

Judas kam gleich auf Jesus zu und sagte: „Sei gegrüßt, Rabbi!" Und er küßte ihn. Jesus erwiderte ihm: „Freund, das ist es, wozu du gekommen bist." (Mt 26,49f)

Da gingen sie auf Jesus zu, legten Hand an ihn und nahmen ihn fest. (Mt 26,50)

Judas immediately went over to Jesus, said to him, "Peace, Rabbi", and embraced him. Jesus answered, "Friend, do what you are here for!" (Mt 26,49f)

At that moment they stepped forward to lay hands on Jesus and arrested him. (Mt 26,50)

Der Schlag ins Gesicht

Unangenehme Wahrheiten hört niemand gern. Der eine verschließt vor ihnen die Ohren, der andere dagegen, zumal wenn er seine Stärke auszuspielen gewohnt ist, sucht den zum Schweigen zu bringen, der die „Frechheiten" äußert, die Einsprüche gegen bedenkliche Vorhaben, die Einwände gegen fragwürdige Vorstellungen.

Aus genau diesem Grund bekommt Micha (Michäas) einen Schlag ins Gesicht; er soll sich nicht unterstehen, mit Berufung auf einen prophetischen Auftrag - auch das noch! - seinem König das Kriegsglück zu bestreiten und die Weitsicht der Höflinge bezweifeln, die ihren Herrn schönrednerisch in seinen militärischen Plänen bestärken. Und ebensowenig soll Jesus wagen, mit seinem Messiasdünkel die Autorität des Hohenpriesters anzutasten, wie ein beflissener Gerichtsdiener meint - und ihm mit einer Ohrfeige die geschuldete Unterwürfigkeit beibringen will.

Beide Male soll das „schlagende Argument" den Inhaber der Macht wieder nach oben bringen, den ein prophetisches Wort, ein unbestechliches Urteil, eine beschämende Reinheit und Heiligkeit aus der unverdienten Höhe des Amtes herabgeholt hat. Und zugleich soll es den Anwalt der - göttlichen - Wahrheit *erniedrigen*.

Vor allem als Zeichen der *Erniedrigung* haben wir die Ohrfeige zu verstehen, die ein Gerichtsdiener Jesus versetzt (allein als körperliche Mißhandlung wäre sie den Evangelisten angesichts der Folter der Kreuzigung wohl kaum der Erwähnung wert gewesen). Nicht duckmäuserisch nimmt er sie hin, aber doch im Verzicht auf alle Überlegenheit, die ihm zu Gebote stünde - die „Engel-Legionen seines Vaters"!(vgl. Mt 26,53) Denn seine innerste Gesinnung steht so ganz im Gegensatz zu jener der gekränkten hohen Herren der Welt: „Er war Gott gleich, hielt aber nicht daran fest, wie Gott zu sein, sondern entäußerte sich und wurde wie ein Sklave. Er *erniedrigte* sich und war gehorsam bis zum Tod, bis zum Tod am Kreuz." (Phil 2,6-8)

The Slap in the Face

No-one likes to hear unpleasant truths. Some people refuse to listen, but others, especially if they are accustomed to show their strength, try to silence the person making the "insolent" remarks, raising objections to questionable plans or doubtful ideas.

This is precisely why Micaiah is slapped in the face. He should not have the impertinence to deny his King's success in battle on the grounds of his prophetic mission, which makes it worse, and to doubt the farsightedness of the courtiers who flatter and encourage their master in his military plans. In the same way Jesus is not supposed to impugn the High Priest's authority with the presumption that he is himself the Messiah. At least, this is what an eager court servant thinks and tries to teach him the due servility with a slap in the face.

In both cases the "argument" of force aims to restore the upper hand to the holder of power when he is challenged in his undeservedly high office by a prophetic word, an incorruptible judgement, a purity and holiness which puts him to shame. At the same time the slap is intended to *humiliate* the representative of God's truth.

We should regard the slap in the face given to Jesus by a court servant primarily as a sign of *humiliation* (the Evangelists would hardly have considered it worth mentioning as physical ill-treatment in view of the torture of the crucifixion). He does not submit to the slap in a servile way but he does refrain from calling on the superior forces which he could command - his father's "armies of angels" (cf. Mt 26,53) because his inner nature is such a complete contrast to that of the rulers of the world who feel offended: "He always has the nature of God, but he did not think that by force he should try to become equal with God. Instead of this, of his own free will he gave up all he had, and took the nature of a servant. He *was humble* and walked the path of obedience all the way to death - his death on the cross." (Phil 2,6-8)

1 Kön (Kgs) 22,1-28 / 2 Chr 18,1-27 / Joh (Jn) 18,19-23

Solcher schmähliche Lohn ward dem Michäas auch,   Micaiah also receives the same ignominious reward,
Da er Wahrheit enthüllt' Achab, dem Könige: For revealing the truth to Ahab, the King;
Von den Lügenpropheten   One of the lying prophets
Gibt ihm einer den Backenstreich.   Gives him a blow on the cheek.

Ruhelos

„Geschaffen hast du uns auf dich hin, und ruhelos ist unser Herz, bis daß es seine Ruhe hat in dir." Das berühmte Wort stammt aus der Einleitung zu den „Bekenntnissen", die der heilige Augustinus über sein bewegtes Leben ablegt. Man müßte schon ein arger Spießer sein, um nicht wie er diese Unruhe in sich zu spüren, diese Ruhelosigkeit des „homo viator", des Menschen, der seinem Wesen nach ein Wanderer ist.

Aber nicht jeder hat die gläubige Gewißheit des Kirchenlehrers, daß auch *sein* Leben nach aller Fahrt und Irrfahrt ans Ziel kommt, nicht jeder betet so vertrauensvoll wie er, daß Gott auch *ihn* einmal für immer in seine Arme schließt - in die Arme des barmherzigen Vaters, der seinen verlorenen Sohn schon längst erwartet.

„Rastlos und ruhelos werde ich auf der Erde sein", schreit Kain nach dem Mord an Abel; doch seine Ruhelosigkeit treibt ihn, ganz entgegengesetzt, - „fort vom Herrn" (Gen 4,14.16)! Nicht von der Anziehungskraft der Liebe Gottes läßt er sich ergreifen und wegholen aus der Sünde, wie die vielen, für die Augustinus spricht - oder Paulus: „Weißt du nicht, daß Gottes Güte dich zur Umkehr treibt?" (Röm 2,4) -, sondern der Fliehkraft des Bösen überläßt er sich, die ihn immer weiter von Gott und den Menschen fortreißt.

Aber noch viel weniger ist es zu fassen, daß einer der Zwölf, einer, der im innersten Bannkreis der Liebe gelebt hat, in der Ruhelosigkeit seiner Gewissensnot nur noch den Weg des Kain vor sich sieht; daß Judas, dem Jesus auch zuletzt die Anrede „Freund" nicht verweigert hat, - verzweifelter noch als Kain, selbstmörderisch - „winkend und rufend den Tod herbeiholt und sich nach *ihm* sehnt als seinem Freund" (Weish 1,16)!

Restless

"You have created us to be with you, and our heart is restless until it finds its peace in you." This famous saying is from the introduction to the "Confessions" written by Saint Augustine about his turbulent life. Anyone who does not notice this restlessness in himself, as Saint Augustine did, the restlessness of "homo viator", man who is by nature a wanderer, must be a very unimaginative person.

Not everyone has the devout certainty of the Doctor of the Church that *his* life will also reach its destination after all his wanderings, not everyone prays as trustingly as he that God will at some time embrace *him* also in His arms - the arms of the merciful Father who has been waiting for his lost son a long time.

"I will be a homeless wanderer on the earth", cries Cain after he murders Abel, but his restlessness drives him in exactly the opposite direction - "away from the Lord's presence" (Gen 4,14.16). He is not called away from sin and drawn by the attraction of God's love, like the many for whom Augustine speaks - or Paul: "Surely you know that God is kind because he is trying to lead you to repent?" (Rom 2,4), but he abandons himself to the centrifugal force of evil which drives him further and further from God and men.

It is even less easy to understand how one of the Twelve, one who lived in the innermost circle of love, in the restlessness of his own moral dilemma saw before him only the path taken by Cain. It is impossible to understand how Judas, whom even at the end taken Jesus called his friend, in greater despair than Cain and with thoughts of suicide, "beckoning and calling upon death to approach, longs for him as his friend" (Wisdom 1,16).

Gen 4,8-16
Mt 27,3-10 / Apg (Acts) 1,15-18

„Zu groß – zu groß ist meine Sünde!"
Ruft er mit Kain, dem Brudermörder.
Wie diesen – rastlos, ruhelos, unversöhnt –
So treibt zum Abgrund wilde Verzweiflung ihn.

"Too great, too great is my sin!"
Cries he with Cain, murderer of a brother!
Like him restless, agitated, unreconciled,
He is seized with terror and despair.

Der Hohepriester befragte Jesus über seine Jünger und über seine Lehre. Jesus antwortete ihm: „Ich habe offen vor aller Welt geredet. Warum fragst du mich? Frag die, die mich gehört haben!" Auf diese Antwort hin schlug einer von den Knechten, der dabeistand, Jesus ins Gesicht. (Joh 18,19f)

Als Judas sah, daß Jesus zum Tode verurteilt war, reute es ihn. Er brachte den Hohenpriestern und Ältesten die Silberlinge zurück und sagte: „Gesündigt habe ich, unschuldig Blut habe ich ausgeliefert." Sie sagten: „Was geht das uns an?" Dann ging er weg und erhängte sich. (Mt 27,3)

The high priest questioned Jesus about his disciples and about his teaching. Jesus answered: "I have spoken publicly to any who would listen. Why do you question me? Question those who heard me when I spoke". At this reply, one of the guards gave Jesus a blow on the face. (Jn 18,19f)

Judas seeing that Jesus had been condemned, began to regret his action deeply. He took the pieces of silver back to the chief priests and elders and said, "I did wrong to deliver up an innocent man". They retorted, "What is that to us?" He went off and hanged himself. (Mt 27,3f)

Falsches Zeugnis

Der Großgrundbesitzer, der den kleinen Campesino um sein Land und sein Leben bringt, das ist die heutige tausendfach praktizierte Variante des alttestamentlichen Falles Nabot.

Um seinen Besitz abzurunden, will der König von Samarien das Grundstück seines Nachbarn Nabot haben. Der aber beharrt auf seinem Recht und verweigert die Abtretung des väterlichen Erbes. Ärger als der entgangene Landgewinn erregt es den König, daß da einer seine Maxime nicht anerkennen will, die da lautet: Macht ist höchstes Recht. Die Königin weiß Rat: Am eigenen Leib soll es der Widerspenstige erfahren und mit seinem Tod aller Welt vorführen, daß die Maxime noch immer gilt!

Ein Exempel wird an Nabot statuiert, dessen Methoden sich seither kaum geändert haben: Falsche Zeugen treten auf. Falsche Anklagen werden erhoben. Aufrechte Haltung wird als ungesetzlicher Widerstand denunziert, Unbeugsamkeit gegenüber den maßlosen Ansprüchen der „staatstragenden Kreise" als Staatsfeindlichkeit und Volksverhetzung, Treue zur persönlichen religiösen Sendung im Konflikt mit den etablierten Ansichten als Gotteslästerung.

All das wiederholt sich in den Verhandlungen gegen Jesus. Eine zusätzliche Pointe liegt freilich darin, daß Nabots Grundstück, das ihm der König neidete und sich durch den ungerechten Prozeß verschaffen wollte, ein Weinberg war: Hatte sich nicht auch Jesus in einem Gleichnis (Mk 12,1-12) als den einzig legitimen Erben eines Weinbergs vorgestellt und damit die etablierten religiösen Führer herausgefordert, die recht gut herausgehört hatten, was Jesus da beanspruchte: „Ja, der Weinberg des Herrn der Heerscharen ist das Haus Israel" (Jes 5,7)?

Wie auch immer, - Jesus vor Gericht, das heißt: Jesus in der langen Reihe zwischen den Nabots und den Märtyrern unserer Tage. Und doch einsam aus dieser Reihe ragend: der einzige ganz und gar Schuldlose!

False Testimony

The large landowner who takes away the land and the life of the small peasant is the modern equivalent of the Old Testament case of Naboth.

To round off his property, the King of Samaria wanted to have the vineyard belonging to his neighbour, Naboth. However, Naboth insisted on his rights and refused to sell what he had inherited from his father. What annoyed the King more than losing the land was the fact that here was someone who did not wish to recognise the principle that might is right. The Queen told him what to do: the stubborn Naboth would learn firsthand what it meant, and with his death would show the whole world that the principle still applied.

Naboth's fate shows that these methods have hardly changed since then. False witnesses appear and false charges are made. An upright attitude is denounced as illegal resistance, refusal to comply with the excessive demands of state authorities is denounced as hostility to the State and incitement of the people. If someone's loyalty to his personal religious mission comes into conflict with established opinions this is regarded as blasphemy.

All this is repeated in the proceedings against Jesus. Of course, there is the additional point that the land owned by Naboth of which the King was envious and which he wanted to obtain by an unfair trial, was a vineyard. In a parable (Mk 12, 1-12) had not Jesus also described himself as the only lawful heir of a vineyard, thereby challenging the established religious leaders who realised perfectly well the claims which Jesus was making: "Israel is the vineyard of the Lord Almighty" (Is 5,7)?

However, the fact that Jesus stood trial means that he was one in the long line of martyrs from Naboth to those of the present day. And he is the one who stands out from all the others: the only one who is completely and utterly innocent.

1 Kön (Kgs) 21,1-13
Mt 26,59-63 / Mk 14,55-61

Wie einst Naboth schuldlos verfolgt, verurteilt   *As Naboth was once persecuted innocently,*
Ward durch falsches Zeugnis als Gottesläst'rer,   *Condemned as a blasphemer by false testimony,*
So auch Er, des einzige Schuld ist: Wahrheit,   *So He too, whose only offence is truth,*
Liebe und Wohltun.   *Love and acts of charity.*

Die Hohenpriester aber und der ganze Hohe Rat bemühten sich um Zeugenaussagen gegen Jesus, um ihn des Todes schuldig sprechen zu können. (Mk 14,55)

Der Hohepriester sprach zu ihm: „Ich beschwöre dich bei dem lebendigen Gott: Sag uns, bist du der Messias, der Sohn Gottes?" Jesus antwortete: „Das sprichst du. Ich jedoch sage euch: Von nun an werdet ihr den Menschensohn sehen: sitzend zur Rechten der Kraft und kommend auf den Wolken des Himmels." Da zerriß der Hohepriester sein Gewand und rief: „Er hat Gott gelästert! Wozu brauchen wir noch Zeugen? Seht, eben habt ihr die Lästerung gehört. Was meint ihr?" Sie antworteten: „Des Todes ist er schuldig." (Mt 26,63ff)

The chief priests with the whole Sanhedrin were busy soliciting testimony against Jesus that would lead to his death. (Mk 14,55)

The high priest said to him: "I order you to tell us under oath before the living God whether you are the Messiah, the Son of God". Jesus answered: "It is you who say it. But I tell you this; soon you will see the Son of Man seated at the right hand of the Power and coming on the clouds of heaven". At this the high priest tore his robes: "He has blasphemed! What further need have we of witnesses? Remember, you heard the blasphemy. What is your verdict?" They answered. "He deserves death!" (Mt 26,63ff)

Wo ist Gott?

Das Leid des Unschuldigen spitzt die Frage nach Gott zu äußerster Schärfe zu. Gott und das Leid zusammenzudenken, dagegen hat sich die natürliche Vernunft immer wieder gesträubt; und wenn sie es doch versuchte, sind ihre Erklärungen wenig überzeugend ausgefallen. Sind die beiden Größen überhaupt miteinander zu vereinbaren?

Dem Leidenden, so die einen, bleibe nur übrig, sich loszusagen von einem Gott, der ein so grausames Spiel mit dem Menschen treibe, – "das Leid ist der Fels des Atheismus" (Georg Büchner)! Die anderen dagegen meinen, die Überzeugung von einem guten und gerechten Gott zwinge den Leidenden, die Ursache seines Loses bei sich selbst, in der eigenen, allemal strafwürdigen Sündhaftigkeit zu suchen. Die einen wie die anderen können nur Spott übrighaben für jene „Unvernünftigen", die im Leiden sowohl an der eigenen Unschuld wie an Gott festhalten wollen.

Iob macht diese Erfahrung, als er, von einer Lawine von Schicksalsschlägen niedergeworfen, mit Berufung auf seine Unschuld bei Gott das Recht auf ein anderes Los einklagen will. Seine Freunde fertigen ihn ab: „Wie wäre ein Mensch gerecht vor Gott!" und seine eigene Frau: „Lästere Gott und stirb!" (Ijob 25,4;2,9) Für sie alle ist es eine ausgemachte Sache: am (Über-)Maß seiner Leiden läßt sich ablesen, wie weit der Abstand klafft, der ihn von Gott trennt.

Die Leute, die Jesus die ganze Passion hindurch mit Hohn verfolgen, denken nicht anders. Doch ihr Spott ist noch viel überheblicher! Über Jesus ist ja kein Verhängnis hereingebrochen, von dem sie, anmaßend genug, sagen könnten: Gott hat ihn geschlagen – oder verlassen; sie selber verhängen Folter und Kreuz, und tun dabei geradeso, als wäre *ihr* Verdammungswort der Spruch des Herrn und *ihre* schlagende Faust sein machtvoller Arm.

Und wo ist Gott wirklich? Die Antwort spottet der „Vernunft" der Spötter: „Im Inkognito des letzten Wurms" (J. Ratzinger, vgl. Ps 22,17), zu dem sie Jesus herabgewürdigt haben. - Bei der Auferstehung wird das Inkognito fallen!

Where is God?

The sufferings of the innocent raise in a very acute form the question of God's existence. Man's natural reasoning power has always resisted thinking of God and suffering together, and when it tried to do so its explanations were not very convincing. Can the two magnitudes be reconciled with each other at all?

According to some, all that a suffering person can do is to renounce a God who plays such a cruel game with mankind – "suffering is the rock of atheism" (Georg Büchner). On the other hand, others say that belief in a good and just God compels the suffering person to seek the cause for his suffering in himself, in his own sinfulness which in any case deserves punishment. The supporters of both views can only pour scorn on the "foolish" people who in their suffering hold firmly to their own innocence and to God.

Job experienced this when, overcome by a sea of troubles, he appealed to God for a different fate on the grounds of his own innocence. His friends dismissed his appeal, "Can anyone be righteous or pure in God's sight?" and his own wife said, "Why don't you curse God and die?" (Job 25,4;2,9). For all of them it is a foregone conclusion: the (excessive) measure of his sufferings shows how great is the distance separating him from God.

The people who pursue Jesus with mockery throughout his suffering think in the same way, but their mockery is even more presumptuous. No disaster has befallen Jesus which could cause them to say, arrogantly enough, that God has struck him down or abandoned him. They themselves inflict torture and crucifixion, acting as if their condemnation were the judgment of the Lord and *their* brute force his powerful arm.

So where is God really? The answer defies the "common sense" of the scoffers: "In the incognito of the last worm"(J. Ratzinger, cf. Ps 22,17) to which they have degraded Jesus. The incognito will be dropped at the resurrection!

Ijob (Job)
Mt 26,67-68 / Mk 14,65

Im geduldigen Job, dem in tiefster Trübsal
Selbst von seinen Freunden mit Hohn Belad'nen,
Seht ihr vorgebildet das Leid, das für uns
    Duldet der Heiland.

In patient Job who in his deepest affliction
Was covered with mockery, even by his friends,
You see prefigured our Saviour's sufferings
Borne for us.

Die Wächter trieben ihren Spott mit Jesus. Sie schlugen ihn, verhüllten ihm das Gesicht und fragten ihn: „Du bist doch ein Prophet! Sag uns, wer hat dich geschlagen?" Und noch mit vielen anderen Lästerungen verhöhnten sie ihn. (Lk 22,63ff)

In der Morgenfrühe faßten die Hohenpriester und die Ältesten des Volkes gemeinsam den Beschluß, Jesus hinrichten zu lassen. Sie ließen ihn fesseln und abführen und lieferten ihn dem Statthalter Pilatus aus. (Mt27,1f)

Meanwhile the guards amused themselves at Jesus' expense. They blindfolded him first, slapped him, then taunted him: "Play the prophet; which one struck you?" And they directed many other insulting words at him. (Lk 22,63ff)

At daybreak all the chief priests and the elders of the people took formal action against Jesus to put him to death. They bound him and led him away to be handed over to the procurator Pilate. (Mt 27,1f)

Pilatus sagte zu Jesus: „Von woher bist du?" Jesus aber gab ihm keine Antwort. Da sagte Pilatus zu ihm: „Mit mir redest du nicht? Weißt du nicht, daß ich Macht habe, dich freizulassen, und Macht habe, dich zu kreuzigen?" Da antwortete ihm Jesus: „Du hättest keine Macht, wenn sie dir nicht von oben gegeben worden wäre." (Joh 19,10f)

Pilate said to Jesus: "Where do you come from?" Jesus would not give him any answer. "Do you refuse to speak to me?" Pilate asked him. "Do you not know that I have the power to release you and the power to crucify you?" Jesus answered: "You would have no power over me whatever unless it were given you from above." (Jn 19,10f)

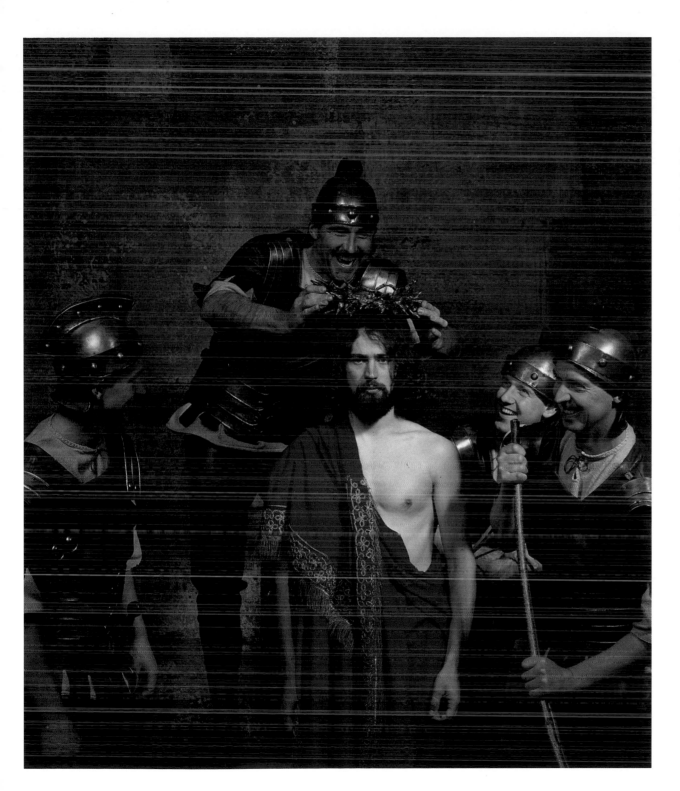

Dann nahm Pilatus Jesus und ließ ihn aus-
peitschen. Und die Soldaten flochten einen
Kranz aus Dornen, den setzten sie ihm auf
den Kopf. Auch mit einem Purpurmantel
gewandeten sie ihn, gingen auf ihn zu und
sagten: „Heil dir, König der Juden!" Und
sie schlugen ihn ins Gesicht. (Joh 19,1ff)

Pilate's next move was to take Jesus and
have him scourged. The soldiers then wove
a crown of thorns and fixed it on his head,
throwing around his shoulders a cloak of
royal purple. Repeatedly they came up to
him and said, "All hail, king of the Jews!",
slapping his face as they did so. (Jn 19,1ff)

83

Heil dir, König!

„Das Schwache in der Welt hat Gott erwählt, um das Starke zuschanden zu machen. Und das Niedrige und Verachtete hat Gott erwählt: das, was nichts ist, um das, was etwas ist, zu vernichten." (2 Kor 1,27.28) Es wäre unverständlich, wenn sich die Wahrheit dieses biblisch-christlichen Grundsatzes nicht am eindrucksvollsten an Jesus Christus selbst erwiesen hätte:

Da ist der mächtige Pontius Pilatus, der freilassen und kreuzigen kann (vgl. Joh 19,10), wie er will (das Kreuzigen gefiel ihm übrigens besser, wie die Historiker wissen!). Da ist ein lärmender Haufen, wie er sich zu jeder Zeit und an allen Orten zusammenzurotten pflegt, wo man im Schutz der Menge seine Aggressionen austoben kann. Und zwischen ihnen ein zusammengeschlagener Mensch, der amtlich erledigte, weil als Lügen-Messias entlarvte Zimmermannssohn.

Doch nun, was ist von dem einst mächtigen Pontius Pilatus geblieben? Kaum mehr als sein Name, und auch der haftet nur noch wie ein Schmutzfleck am Königsmantel des Jesus von Nazareth, der schon längst kein Spottgewand mehr ist. Denn diesen Jesus hat „Gott über alle erhöht und ihm den Namen verliehen, der größer ist als alle Namen" - und, tatsächlich, vor ihm „beugen sich die Knie", genau wie es der urchristliche Hymnus (Phil 2,5-11) sagt.

Der göttliche Umsturz von Hoheit in Niedrigkeit und von Niederlage in Sieg macht, vergleichbar der photographischen Umkehrung, aus dem „Negativ" der Szene vor dem Palast des Pilatus das „Positiv" der Erhöhung Christi; statt: „Seht, welch ein Mensch!" ist dann zu vernehmen: „Jesus Christus ist der Herr - zur Ehre Gottes, des Vaters." (Phil 2,11)

Die Auswahl des alttestamentlichen Vorbilds zu dieser Episode zielt denn auch auf den österlichen Glanz, in den Gott die Passionsdüsternis umwertet, das Lebende Bild zeigt einen Triumph: Josef, aus Sklaverei und Kerker zum ägyptischen (Vize-)König erhöht, nimmt die Huldigung der Volksscharen entgegen, die ihn als ihren Retter (vor drohender Hungersnot) erkannt haben.

Hail, o King!

"God chose what the world considers weak in order to shame the powerful. He chose what the world looks down on and despises, and thinks is nothing, in order to destroy what the world thinks is important" (1 Cor 1,27.28). It would be difficult to understand if the truth of this Christian principle of the Bible had not been shown most impressively in Jesus Christ himself.

There is the powerful Pontius Pilate, who can release people or crucify them (cf. Jn 19,10) as he thinks fit (but he likes crucifixion better, as historians know). There is a noisy mob of the sort which gathers at any place at any time, in which individuals can work off their aggressions under cover of the crowd. And between them a man is beaten up, officially disposed of because he is a carpenter's son who has been unmasked as a false Massiah.

But what remains now of the once powerful Pontius Pilate? Hardly more than his name clinging like a spot of dirt to the kingly mantle of Jesus of Nazareth, which has long ceased to be an object of mockery because God raised this Jesus "to the highest place above and gave him the name that is greater than any other name". Indeed, before him "all beings will fall on their knees", exactly as the old Christian hymn says (Phil 2,5-11).

God's reversal of individuals' positions so that those with power find themselves with none and those who were defeated find themselves victorious is rather like a photographic process whereby a negative becomes a positive. Thus the negative of the scene before Pilate's palace changes into the positive of the elevation of Christ. Then, instead of, "Behold the man" we hear "Jesus Christ is Lord, to the glory of God the Father" (Phil 5,11).

The choice of the Old Testament prefiguration of this episode looks forward to the Easter radiance into which God changes the darkness of the Passion. The tableau vivant shows a triumph. Joseph, after slavery and imprisonment is appointed governor of Egypt and accepts the homage of the crowds who recognise him as their saviour from the famine that threatened.

Gen 41,41-43
Mt 27,27-30 / Mk 15,16-19 / Joh (Jn) 19,2-5

Wie anders stand einst vor dem Ägyptervolk	*How differently before the people of Egypt once*
Joseph! Freudengesang, Jubel umbrauste ihn!	*Stood Joseph! Songs of joy surrounded him.*
Als der Retter Ägyptens	*As the saviour of Egypt*
Ward er feierlich vorgestellt!	*He was presented with all festivity.*

Seht den König!

Look at the king!

Der eine frei, der andere geopfert

Religiöse Opfer von Tieren oder gar von Menschen sind für uns fast unbegreifliche Erscheinungen aus einer anderen Welt. Doch unsere Sprache hält den Zugang zu diesen Dingen nach wie vor offen. Wir sprechen, auf der einen Seite, betroffen von den Opfern eines Krieges, eines Verbrechens oder eines Unfalls; auf der anderen Seite rühmen wir, wenn Menschen sich in der völligen Hingabe an ein Ideal oder für den Nächsten opfern. Die einen Opfer erregen unser Entsetzen über das Schlimme in der Welt, die andern wecken in uns Hoffnung auf eine bessere Welt.

Der dunkle und der lichte Aspekt des Opfers sind im Ritual des jüdischen Versöhnungsfestes aufs äußerste gesteigert, veranschaulicht an zwei Böcken. Nach einem Losentscheid wird einer von ihnen, seiner Fesseln ledig, in die Wüste geschickt, um dort nur umso elender dem Dämon Asasel zu verfallen, der andere dagegen endet, Gott wohlgefällig, sein Leben im heiligen Bezirk des Tempels.

Darin sieht das Passionsspiel die Entscheidung zwischen Barrabas und Jesus vorgebildet. Barrabas kommt frei, wie es die Priesterkaste und der Pöbel - keineswegs das ganze jüdische Volk! - fordern; ungestraft mag er, der Mörder, gehen, wohin er will, und dem Bösen verschrieben bleiben. Jesus aber wird ans Kreuz geliefert; die Prophetie des Jesaja geht in Erfüllung: *„Wie ein Lamm*, das man zum Schlachten führt, so tat auch er seinen Mund nicht auf". (53,7)

Aller - ohnehin vergebliche - kultische Opferbetrieb findet damit ein Ende, wie der Hebräerbrief herausstellt; denn Jesus, so heißt es dort, ist mit seinem Opfergang *„ein für allemal* in das Heiligtum hineingegangen, nicht mit dem Blut von Böcken und Stieren, sondern mit seinem eigenen Blut, und so hat er eine ewige Erlösung bewirkt." (9,12)

One Free, the Other Sacrificed

The religious sacrifice of animals or even humans is for us an almost incomprehensible phenomenon from another world. But our language still preserves this idea. On the one hand we speak with dismay of the sacrifices of a war, the victims of a crime or accident. On the other we speak highly of those who sacrifice their own lives in complete dedication to an ideal or for their fellow men. Sacrifices of the first kind make us feel shocked by the evil in the world, sacrifices of the other kind create in us hope for a better world.

The dark and the light aspects of sacrifice are intensified to an extreme degree in the ritual of the Jewish Feast of Atonement, symbolised by two goats. After lots are drawn the fetters are taken from one goat and the animal is sent into the desert where it will fall an even more wretched victim to the demon Asasel, while the other, well pleasing to God, ends its life in the holy precinct of the temple.

The Passion Play sees this as a prefiguration of the choice between Barabbas and Jesus. Barabbas is released because this is demanded by the caste of priests and the mob, but certainly not by the whole Jewish people. Barabbas, the murderer, can go unpunished wherever he wants and carry on doing evil. Jesus, however, is delivered over to the cross. Isaiah's prophecy is fulfilled: "He never said a word, *like a lamb* about to be slaughtered." (53,7)

This is how all religious sacrifices come to an end, and they are in any case futile, as the letter to the Hebrews emphasises. It says that, with his sacrifice, Jesus "entered *once and for all* into the Most Holy Place, He did not take the blood of goats and bulls to offer as a sacrifice; rather, he took his own blood and obtained eternal salvation for us." (9,12)

Lev 16,1-28 / Hebr 9,10
Mt 27,15-26 / Mk 15,6-15 / Lk 23,18-25 / Joh (Jn) 18,39-40

Des Alten Bundes Opfer dies,
Wie es der Höchste bringen hieß!
Das Blut der Böcke will der Herr
Im neuen Bunde nimmermehr,
Ein Lamm, von allem Makel rein,
Muß dieses Bundes Opfer sein!

This is the sacrifice of the old covenant,
As the Highest ordained.
In the new covenant the Lord
No longer requires the blood of goats,
A lamb, pure of all blemish,
Must be the offering of this covenant.

Pilatus ließ Wasser bringen, wusch sich vor allen Leuten die Hände und sagte: „Ich bin unschuldig am Blut dieses Menschen." (Mt 27,24)

Da lieferte er Jesus aus, damit er gekreuzigt würde. (Joh 19,16)

Pilate called for water and washed his hands in front of the crowd declaring as he did so, "I am innocent of the blood of this man". (Mt 27,24)

In the end, Pilate handed Jesus over to be crucified. (Jn 19,16)

Auf dem Weg zum Opfer

Zu den kaltherzigsten Zeugnissen diktatorischer Justiz gehören die Rechnungen, die den Angehörigen eines Hingerichteten auch noch die Kosten der Tötung, auf Heller und Pfennig aufgelistet, abfordern. Aus der Hinterlassenschaft des Delinquenten, also letzlich von diesem selbst, läßt sich die Obrigkeit ihr Henkersgeschäft bezahlen. Auch zur Zeit Jesu gab es schon die „Selbstbeteiligung" an der Urteilsvollstreckung; zur Kreuzigung mußte der Verurteilte auf dem eigenen Rücken sein Marterinstrument zur Todesstätte hinaustragen. Soweit der rein menschliche - nein, unmenschliche - Aspekt der Sache!

Um ihren religiösen Gesichtspunkt zu verdeutlichen, greift das Lebende Bild die Erzählung von der Glaubensprobe Abrahams auf; denn keine alttestamentliche Figur sieht dem kreuztragenden Jesus ähnlicher als Abrahams Sohn Isaak, der ebenfalls das Holz auf den Berg hinaufschleppt, wo er geopfert werden soll.

Die Übereinstimmung im Sichtbaren (dem in einem Schau-Spiel verständlicherweise für sich allein schon großes Gewicht zukommt) ist offenkundig. Aber gerade auch die Abgründe, die sich hinter der Schauseite der beiden „Prozessionen" auftun, sind einander ähnlich. Nach außen hin dieselbe ruhige Ergebenheit und Geduld eines gehorsamen Sohnes. Dahinter ein Drama: grenzenloses Bangen *und* Vertrauen, mit dem sich der Sohn dem Vater ausliefert, ungebrochene Liebe *und* Unerbittlichkeit, mit der der Vater den Sohn zum Opferaltar geleitet - schwindelerregend für den, der versucht, es begreifen zu wollen; es sei denn vom Ende her, wo die alles heilende und versöhnende Liebe Gottes triumphiert.

On the Path to the Sacrifice

Among the most cold-hearted aspects of dictatorial justice were the bills which the relatives of an executed person had to pay for the costs of killing him, listed down to the last penny. The authorities had the business of execution paid for out of the property left by the criminal, i. e. by the criminal himself. Also in Jesus' time the victim had to make his own contribution to carrying out the sentence. A man condemned to crucifixion had to carry, on his own back, the instrument of his martyrdom to the place of death. This is the purely human - or rather, inhuman - aspect of the matter.

To illustrate its religious point of view, the tableau vivant shows the story of the test of Abraham's faith. The Old Testament figure who most resembles Jesus carrying the cross is Abraham's son Isaac, who drags the wood up the hill where he is to be sacrificed.

The visual correspondence, which is understandably in itself very important in a stage play, is obvious. However, the depths of affliction which open up behind the outward appearance of the two "processions" are also similar. Outwardly there is the same serene resignation and patience of an obedient son, but behind is the drama: immense anxiety *and* the trust with which the son surrenders to the father, the unbroken love *and* pitilessness with which the father leads the son to the sacrificial altar. It is totally perplexing to anyone who tries to comprehend it, unless it is approached from the ultimate end, when God's healing and reconciling love triumphs.

Gen 22,1-18
Mt 27,31-33 / Mk 15,20-22 / Joh (Jn) 19,17

Einst trug Isaak willig auf seinem Rücken
Das Opferholz auf die Bergeshöhe,
Wo er selbst als Opfer bestimmt war nach dem
Willen des Herrn.

Isaac once carried upon his own shoulders
Wood for sacrifice to the montain top,
Where he himself was intended for sacrifice
By the will of the Lord.

Dann führten sie Jesus hinaus zur Kreuzigung. (Mt 27,31)
Maria: „Ach, so sehe ich ihn, zum Tode geführt, einem Missetäter gleich zwischen Missetätern!"

Afterward they led him off to crucifixion. (Mt 27,31)
Mary: "Alas, I see him led to death like a criminal between the other criminals".

Als sie Jesus hinausführten, ergriffen sie einen Mann aus Zyrene, namens Simon, der gerade vom Feld kam. Ihm luden sie das Kreuz auf, damit er es hinter Jesus hertrage. (Lk 23,26)

As they led him away, they laid hold of one Simon the Cyrenean who was coming in from the fields. They put the cross on Simon's shoulder for him to carry along behind Jesus. (Lk 23,26)

„Ihr Töchter Jerusalems, weint nicht über mich, weint über euch und eure Kinder! Denn es kommen Tage, da man sagt: ‚Selig die Unfruchtbaren und die Leiber, die nicht geboren, und die Brüste, die nicht gestillt haben!‘ Dann wird man zu den Bergen sagen: ‚Fallt auf uns!‘ Und zu den Hügeln: ‚Deckt uns zu!‘ Denn wenn das am frischen Holz geschieht, was wird erst am dürren geschehen?“ *(Lk 23,28ff)*

Sie teilen meine Kleider unter sich,
Und werfen das Los um mein Gewand.
(Ps 22,29)

"Daughters of Jerusalem, do not weep for me. Weep for yourselves and for your children. The days are coming when they will say, 'Happy are the sterile, the wombs that never bore and the breasts that never nursed.' Then they will beginn saying to the montains, 'Fall on us,' and to the hills, 'Cover us.' If they do these things in the green wood, what will happen in the dry?" *(Lk 23,28ff)*

They divided my garments among them,
And for my vesture they cast lots.
(Ps 22,29)

Rettender Aufblick

Dieses Bild geht nicht auf einen findigen Theologen zurück, Jesus selbst hat die Art seines Todes in ihm wiedererkannt: „Wie Moses die Schlange in der Wüste erhöht hat, so muß der Menschensohn erhöht werden." (Joh 3,14)

Als Strafe für ihre Auflehnung gegen Gott erleben die Israeliten am Ende ihrer Wüstenwanderung eine Schlangenplage. Doch Gott will nicht den Tod der Sünder. Jeder, der gebissen wird, bleibt am Leben, wenn er nur zu der Kupferschlange aufblickt, die Moses an einer Fahnenstange aufgehängt hat. - Eine seltsame Bedingung fürs Überleben, den Blick ausgerechnet auf das todbringende Wesen heften zu müssen.

Aus eigener Erfahrung wissen wir, daß es keine Aufarbeitung von Schuld gibt, wenn man sie nicht deutlich vor Augen hat. Das Übel nicht sehen wollen, es aus dem Bewußtsein verdrängen, heißt sein Zerstörungswerk ungehindert weitergehen lassen.

Darum müssen die Isrealiten den hilfesuchenden Blick auf die Kupferschlange richten. Nur über dieses Zeichen, das sie an den eigenen Ungehorsam, den letzten Grund ihrer Not, erinnert, - nicht in einem großen Bogen darum herum - läßt sich der vergebende, rettende Gott erreichen.

Wenn die Menschen aber gar erst „auf den blicken, den sie durchbohrt haben" (Sach 12,10/Joh 19,37), fällt ihr Blick auf beides in einem: auf die Sünde - denn sie hat Christus ans Kreuz geschlagen - *und* auf den Erlöser - denn „er hat unsern Schuldschein dadurch getilgt, daß er ihn ans Kreuz geheftet hat" (Kol 2,14). - Nirgends ist dieses unlösliche Ineinander von Schuld und Erlösung präziser gefaßt als in dem verwegenen Wort des Osterjubels, in den alle Passion mündet: „O glückliche Schuld, welch großen Erlöser hast du gefunden!"

The Sight which Brings Salvation

This tableau was not invented by an ingenious theologian, Jesus himself recognised that this was how he would die: "As Moses lifted up the bronze snake on a pole in the desert, in the same way the Son of Man must be lifted up". (Jn 3,14)

At the end of their wandering in the desert the Israelites suffer a plague of snakes as a punishment for their rebellion against God, but God does not want the death of sinners. Anyone who is bitten will not die if he looks up to the bronze snake which Moses hangs on a pole. Surely, to have to look precisely at the creature that brings death is a strange condition for survival?

We know from our own experience that we cannot purge ourselves of guilt unless we have it clearly before our eyes. To refuse to see evil, to dismiss it from our mind means allowing it to continue its work of destruction.

This is why the Isrealites seek help by looking at the bronze snake. The forgiving, saving God can only be reached through this symbol which reminds them of their own disobedience, the ultimate reason for their plight. They cannot reach God by trying to go around it.

But if "people will look at him whom they pierced" (Zech 12,10/Jn 19,37) they will see two things at once: the sin - because sin nailed Christ to the cross - *and* the redeemer - because "he cancelled the unfavourable record of our debts by nailing it to the cross" (Col 2,14). These interlocking concepts of guilt and redemption are summarised nowhere more accurately than in the daring words of rejoicing at Easter to which all suffering leads: "Oh happy guilt, what great redemption hast thou found!"

Joh (Jn) 3,14
Num 21

Denn wie aufgerichtet dort in der Wüste
Heilung brachte der Ehernen Schlange Anblick,
So kommt Trost und Segen und Heil auch uns vom
Stamme des Kreuzes.

For as the people were healed by the sight
Of the brazen serpent raised in the desert,
So also we receive consolation, blessing and redemption
From the tree of the cross.

PSALM 22

Mein Gott, mein Gott, warum hast du mich verlassen,
bist fern meinem Schreien, den Worten meiner Klage?
Mein Gott, ich rufe bei Tag, doch du antwortest nicht,
bei Nacht - und finde keine Ruhe.

Aber du bist heilig,
du thronst über dem Lobpreis Israels!
Auf dich haben unsere Väter vertraut,
sie haben vertraut und du hast sie gerettet.
Zu dir riefen sie und wurden befreit,
auf dich haben sie vertraut und wurden nicht zuschanden.

Ich aber bin ein Wurm und kein Mensch,
der Leute Spott, vom Volk verachtet.
Alle, die mich sehen, verlachen mich,
verziehen die Lippen, schütteln den Kopf:
„Er wälze die Last auf den Herrn,
der soll ihn befreien!
Der reiße ihn heraus,
wenn er an ihm Gefallen hat!"
Du bist es, der mich zog aus dem Mutterschoß,
mich barg an der Brust der Mutter.
Von Geburt an bin ich geworfen auf dich,
von Mutterleib an bist du mein Gott.

Sei mir nicht fern, denn die Not ist nah,
und niemand ist da, der hilft!

Viele Stiere umgeben mich,
Büffel von Baschan umringen mich.
Sie sperren ihre Rachen gegen mich auf,
reißende, brüllende Löwen.
Hingeschüttet bin ich wie Wasser,
all meine Glieder haben sich gelöst.
Mein Herz ist wie Wachs in meinem Leib zerflossen.
Trocken wie eine Scherbe ist meine Kehle,
die Zunge klebt mir am Gaumen,
du legst mich in den Staub des Todes.

Denn Hunde umlagern mich,
eine Rotte von Bösen umkreist mich.
Sie durchbohren mir Hände und Füße.
Zählen kann man all meine Knochen;
sie gaffen und weiden sich an mir.

Sie teilen meine Kleider unter sich
und werfen das Los um mein Gewand.

Du aber, Herr, halte dich nicht fern!
Du, meine Stärke, eile mir zu Hilfe!
Entreiße dem Schwert mein Leben,
mein einzig Gut aus der Gewalt der Hunde!
Rette mich vor dem Rachen des Löwen,
Vor den Hörnern der Büffel mich Armen!

Ich will deinen Namen meinen Brüdern verkünden,
inmitten der Gemeinde dich preisen.
Die ihr den Herrn fürchtet, preiset ihn,
ihr alle vom Stamme Jakobs, rühmet ihn;
erschaudert vor ihm, alle Nachkommen Israels!
Denn er hat nicht verachtet,
nicht verabscheut das Elend des Armen.
Er verbirgt sein Antlitz nicht vor ihm;
er hat auf sein Schreien gehört.
Deine Treue ist mein Lob in großer Gemeinde;
Ich erfülle meine Gelübde vor denen, die Gott fürchten.
Die Armen sollen essen und sich sättigen,
den Herrn sollen preisen, die ihn suchen.
Aufleben soll euer Herz für immer!

Alle Enden der Erde sollen daran denken,
und werden umkehren zum Herrn,
vor ihm werden sich niederwerfen alle Stämme der Völker.
Denn der Herr regiert als König;
er herrscht über die Völker.
Vor ihm allein sollen niederfallen die Mächtigen der Erde,
vor ihm sich niederwerfen, die im Staube ruhn.

Meine Seele, sie lebt für ihn;
mein Stamm wird ihm dienen.
Vom Herrn wird man erzählen dem Geschlecht der Kommenden,
seine Heilstat wird man künden dem künftigen Volk;
denn er hat das Werk getan.

My God, my God, why have you forsaken me,
far from my prayer, from the words of my cry?
O my God, I cry out by day, and you answer not;
by night, and there is no relief for me.

Yet you are enthroned in the holy place,
O glory of Israel!
In you our fathers trusted,
they trusted, and you delivered them.
To you they cried, and they escaped;
in you they trusted, and they were not put to shame.

But I am a worm, not a man;
the scorn of man, despised by the people.
All who see me scoff at me;
they mock me with parted lips, they wag their heads:
"He relied on the LORD;
let him deliver him,
let him rescue him, if he loves him."
You have been my guide since I was first formed,
my security at my mother's breast.
To you I was committed at birth,
from my mother's whomb you are my God.
Be not far from me, for I am in distress;
be near, for I have no one to help me.

Many bullocks surround me;
the strong bulls of Bashan encircle me.
They open their mouth against me
like ravening and roaring lions.
I am like water poured out;
all my bones are racked.
My heart has become like wax melting away within my bossom.
My throat is dried up like baked clay,
my tongue cleaves to my jaws;
to the dust of death you have brought me down.

Indeed, many dogs surround me,
a pack of evildoers closes in upon me;
They have pierced my hands and my feet;
I can count all my bones.

They look on and gloat over me;
they divide my garments among them,
and for my vesture they cast lots.

But you, O LORD, be not far from me;
O my help, hasten to aid me.
Rescue my soul from the sword,
my loneliness from the grip of the dog.
Save me from the lions mouth;
from the horns of the wild bulls, my wretched life.

I will proclaim your name to my brethren;
in the midst of the assembly I will praise you:
"You who fear the Lord, praise him;
all you descendants of Jacob, give glory to him;
revere him, all you descendants of Israel!
For he has not spurned nor disdained the wretched man in his misery,
Nor did he turn his face away from him,
but when he cried out to him, he heard him."
So by your gift will I utter praise in the vast assembly;
I will fulfill my vows before those who fear him.
The lowly shall eat their fill;
they who seek the LORD shall praise him: "May your hearts be ever merry!"

All the ends of the earth shall remember and turn to the LORD;
All the families of the nations shall bow down before him.
For dominion is the LORD's,
and he rules the nations.
To him alone shall bow down all who sleep in the earth;
Before him shall bend all who go down into the dust.

And to him my soul shall live;
my descendants shall serve him.
Let the coming generation be told of the LORD
That they may proclaim to a people yet to be born
the justice he has shown.

Über seinem Kopf brachten sie seine Schuld schriftlich an: DAS IST JESUS, DER KÖNIG DER JUDEN.

Mit ihm zusammen werden zwei Aufrührer gekreuzigt, einer zur Rechten und einer zur Linken.

Die Vorübergehenden lästerten ihn, schüttelten den Kopf und sagten: „Du reißt den Tempel nieder und baust ihn in drei Tagen wieder auf; rette dich selbst, wenn du Gottes Sohn bist!" Und: „Steig herab vom Kreuz!" Desgleichen höhnten auch die Hohenpriester samt den Schriftgelehrten und Ältesten. Sie sagten: „Andere hat er gerettet, sich selbst kann er nicht retten! Er ist doch der König von Israel! Er soll vom Kreuz herabsteigen, dann werden wir an ihn glauben. Er hat auf Gott vertraut, der soll ihn jetzt retten, wenn er an ihm Gefallen hat. Er hat doch gesagt: Ich bin Gottes Sohn." (MT 27,37ff)

Above his head they had put the charge against him in writing: "THIS IS JESUS, KING OF THE JEWS."

Two insurgents were crucified along with him, one at his right and one at his left. Peopel going by kept insulting him, tossing their heads and saying: "So you are the one who was going to destroy the temple and rebuild it in three days! Save yourself, why don't you? Come down off that cross if you are God's Son!"

The chief priests, the scribes, and the elders also joined in the jeering: "He saved others but cannot save himself! So he is the king of Israel! Let's see him come down from that cross and then we will believe in him. He relied on God; let God rescue him now if he loves him. After all he claimed, 'I am God's Son.'" (Mt 27,37ff)

Maria:„Einst zu Bethlehem - jetzt auf Kalvaria - erfüllt ist, was der Vater dir vorgezeichnet hatte. Mein Sohn, durch Hände und Füße haben sie dir Nägel getrieben, das Herz mit einem Speer durchbohrt! Dein Leiden und dein bittrer Tod durchdrang gleich einem Schwert meine Seele."

Joseph von Arimathäa nahm den Leichnam herab, hüllte ihn in Linnen und legte ihn in ein Felsengrab, in dem noch niemand bestattet war. Das war am Rüsttag, kurz vor Anbruch des Sabbats. Die Frauen, die mit Jesus aus Galiläa gekommen waren, gaben ihm das Geleit und sahen zu, wie der Leib in das Grab gelegt wurde. (Lk 23,53ff)

Mary: "Once before at Bethlehem, now at Calvary, the part with the Father marked out for you is at an end. My son, they have driven nails through your hands and feet and pierced your heart with a spear. Your sufferings and bitter death went through my soul like a sword".

Joseph of Arimathea took the body down, wrapped it in fine Linen, and laid it in a tomb hewn out of the rock, in which no one had yet been buried. That was the Day of Preparation, and the sabbath was about to begin. The women who had come with Him from Galilee followed along behind. They saw the tomb and how his body was buried. (Lk 23,53ff)

„Fürchtet euch nicht! Ich weiß, ihr sucht Jesus, den Gekreuzigten. Er ist nicht hier! Denn auferweckt ward er, wie er gesprochen." (Mt 28,5f)

"Do not fear. I know you are looking for Jesus the crucified. He is not here. He has been raised, as he promised". (Mt 28,5f)

Maria stand weinend am Grab. Wie sie da weinte, bückte sie sich ins Grab hinein. Sagt Jesus zu ihr: Maria! Die wendet sich um und sagt hebräisch zu ihm: Rabbuni! Das heißt: Lehrer! Sagt Jesus zu ihr: Halt mich nicht fest! Denn noch bin ich nicht zum Vater aufgestiegen. Doch geh zu meinen Brü-dern und sag ihnen: Ich steige auf zu mei-nem Vater und eurem Vater, zu meinem Gott und eurem Gott. (aus Joh 20,11ff)

Mary stood weeping beside the tomb. Even as she wept, she stooped to peer inside. Jesus said to her, "Mary!" She turned to him and said (in Hebrew), "Rabbuni!" (meaning "Teacher"). Jesus then said: "Do not cling to me, for I have not yet ascended to the Father. Rather, go to my brothers and tell them, 'I am ascending to my Father and your Father, to my God and your God!'" (from Jn 20,11ff)

Er ist erstanden! Jubelt, ihr Himmlischen!
Er ist erstanden! Jubelt, ihr Sterblichen!
Der Löwe aus dem Stamme Juda,
Er hat der Schlange den Kopf zertreten.
Jetzt zieht er ein zur höchsten Verherrlichung,
Dort, wo er alle um sich sammelt,
Die er erkauft hat mit seinem Blute,
Dort, wo ertönt das ewige Siegeslied:
„Lob sei dem Lamme, welches getötet war!"

He is risen! Rejoice you heavenly hosts!
He is risen! Rejoice you mortals all!
The lion from the tribe of Judah
Has trodden down the head of the serpent.
Now He ascends to the highest glory
Where He will gather round Him
All whom He has redeemed with His blood,
Where the eternal song of victory resounds:
"Praise be to the lamb who was slain!"

Der Weg

Das Lebende Bild folgt zuletzt nicht mehr seiner Regel, es gibt seine Starre auf und gerät in *Bewegung;* seiner „pädagogischen" Absicht bleibt es damit aber nur treu. Im Verlauf des Spieles wollte es immer wieder zu nachdenklichem Verweilen führen, am Ende aber zur Einsicht, daß alles Betrachten umsonst wäre, wenn es den Schauenden nicht *bewegte* - im wörtlichen Sinn:

Das ganze Spiel will doch letztlich nichts anderes, als seine Betrachter dazu bringen, sich, neu entschlossen und zielbewußt, *auf ihren Weg zu machen.* Die Schlußszene spielt deshalb auf den Theaterbrettern die *Bewegung* vor, die nach dem Ende des Stückes jedem Zuschauer auf der Bühne des wirklichen Lebens -„zum Schauspiel für die Welt, für Engel und Menschen" (1 Kor 4,9) - von neuem aufgetragen ist: dem Licht Gottes zuzustreben.

Der Christ weiß - und die Figuren auf dem Podium machen es augenfällig -, daß er dabei nicht an Jesus Christus vorbeikommt; denn dieser ist ja in persona *„der Weg"* (Joh 14,6). „Gebahnt wurde der Weg durch die Menschwerdung des Sohnes Gottes. Gewiesen durch sein liebendes Bei-uns-sein. ‚Weg' bedeutet, daß in Christus Gott zu uns gekommen; und wiederum, daß in Ihm die Menschennatur ganz und rein auf Gott gerichtet ist. ‚Den Weg gehen' kann infolgedessen nichts anderes heißen, als in den lebendigen Christus einzugehen und lebend, handelnd ‚in ihm zu bleiben'. Gangbar aber wurde der Weg, als Jesus im Heiligen Geiste auferstand und verwandelt, verklärt wurde:" (R. Guardini).

Mehr könnte das Oberammergauer Spiel demnach nicht erreichen, als wenn sich sein Betrachter das Apostelwort zu eigen machen würde: „Christus will ich erkennen und die Macht seiner Auferstehung und die Gemeinschaft mit seinen Leiden; sein Tod soll mich prägen. So hoffe ich, auch zur Auferstehung von den Toten zu gelangen. Ich sage nicht, ich hätte das Ziel schon erreicht und sei vollkommen. Aber ich jage ihm nach und greife aus nach ihm, da ich selbst von Christus Jesus ergriffen worden bin." (Phil 3,10-12)

Hermann Müller (Texte zu allen Lebenden Bildern)

The Way

The final tableau vivant does not follow the rules, it ceases to be immobile and begins to move. At the same time it remains faithful to its "educational" aim. The purpose of the tableaux vivants in the course of the play is to give constant pauses for contemplation, but the final tableau is to show that all meditation would be in vain if it does not *move* the spectator - in the literal sense of the word.

After all, the whole play really aims to persuade those who watch it to go on their way with new dertermination and awareness of a purpose. Therefore the final scene acts out on the stage the *movement* towards the light of God to which every spectator on the stage of real life - "as a spectacle for the whole world of angels and of mankind" (1 Cor 4,9) - should be impelled anew after the end of the play.

The Christian knows - and the figures on the stage make this manifest - that in doing this he cannot avoid Jesus Christ because he is "the way" (Jn 14,6) in person. "The way was prepared by the Son of God becoming man and shown by his being with us in love. 'Way' means that God came to us in Christ and, furthermore, that in Christ man's nature is directed purely and entirely towards God. Therefore 'to go the way' can only mean to enter into the living Christ and 'to stay in him' in one's life and deeds. But the way was opened when Jesus rose again and was transformed and transfigured in the Holy Spirit". (R. Guardini)

Therefore the most that the Oberammergau Play could achieve is for those who see it to adopt the words of the apostle: "All I want is to know Christ and to experience the power of his resurrection, to share in his sufferings and become like him in his death, in the hope that I myself will be raised from death to life. I do not claim that I have already succeeded or have already become perfect. I keep striving to win the prize for which Christ Jesus has already won me to himself." (Phil 3,10-12).

Hermann Müller (Texts to all of the Tableaux Vivants)

OBERAMMERGAU

Das Dorf an der Ammer

Die Anfänge

Ammergau - der Name steht für die Landschaft am Oberlauf der Ammer, deren Mittelpunkt erst im Laufe des hohen Mittelalters eine Siedlung gleichen Namens geworden war: das Dorf Oberammergau. Der Name des kleinen Flusses und der Name Kofel für den charakteristischen Felsabsturz hoch über dem Dorf weisen auf altes keltisches Siedlungsgebiet; Ammer bedeutet „kleines Wasser" und Kofel „Bergkegel". Auf die Kelten folgten die Bajuwaren, deren Spuren im Tal bis ins 6. Jahrhundert nach Christus zurückreichen. Noch im frühen Mittelalter wird der ganze Gau, den Lech hinauf bis ins Gebirge und der Ammer entlang bis zu ihrem Ursprung, welfisch. So ist es verständlich, daß die Welfengründung Rottenbuch (1073) die kirchliche Vorrangstellung im östlichen Teil dieses Welfenlandes einnimmt. Das Archidiakonat Rottenbuch, wie man den Sprengel nannte, umfaßte auch die Urpfarrei Ammergau, die bis Bayersoien und Kohlgrub reichte; die Pfarrei blieb rottenbuchisch bis zur Säkularisation der Klöster im Jahre 1803.

Beim Tod des letzten süddeutschen Welfen im Jahre 1191 wurde das Welfenland staufisch und kam 1269 als sogenanntes Konradinisches Erbe an das Haus Wittelsbach und somit an Bayern. Als dann Kaiser Ludwig der Bayer 1330 das Kloster Ettal gründete, schenkte er seine Güter im Ammergau, die aus diesem „Erbe" stammten, der neuen Stiftung. Dadurch wurde die Abtei Ettal zur unmittelbaren weltlichen Obrigkeit des Dorfes, während Rottenbuch das Kirchenwesen betreute. Ein halbes Jahrtausend blieb das so, bis zum Ende des alten Reiches und der alten Ordnung in den Jahren 1803 und 1806.

„Nur ein Dorf"

Keine ganze Autostunde von Oberammergau entfernt liegt draußen im Schwäbischen die *Stadt Markt*ober*dorf,* ursprünglich ein kleines Dorf, das 1453 zum Marktflecken arrivierte und 1953 zur Stadt erhoben wurde. Dieser „Werdegang" kommt in der Namengebung deutlich zum Ausdruck. Oberammergau ist dagegen Dorf geblieben, ja die Bezeichnung „Dorf", die etwas Ländliches, Kleines, Bescheidenes andeutet, ist eher zum Ehrentitel für diese Gemeinde von 5000 Einwohnern geworden, die doch so großes Ansehen errungen und fast in der ganzen westlichen Welt einen guten Namen hat. Es ist dieses Oberammergau also „nur ein Dorf", allerdings ein besonders.

Die wirtschaftliche Bedeutung des Dorfes Oberammergau beschränkte sich im Mittelalter auf das Niederlagsrecht für Waren, die von Augsburg über Schongau nach dem Süden geführt wurden. Die Verdienstmöglichkeiten waren jedoch eher bescheiden, und auch die Landwirtschaft war längst an ihre Grenzen gestoßen.

The village on the Ammer

Beginnings

"Ammergau" means the country around the upper course of the Ammer, the centre of which became a settlement only in the course of the High Middle Ages - the village of Oberammergau. The name of the small river and the name "Kofel" for the characteristic rocky precipice high above the village indicate an old Celtic settlement area. "Ammer" means "small river" and a "Kofel" is a cone-shaped mountain. The Celts were followed by the Bavarians, whose traces in the valley go back to the 6th century after Christ. In the Early Middle Ages the whole district upwards along the River Lech into the mountains and along the Ammer fell into the possession of the Guelphs as far as the source of the Ammer. This is why the Guelph foundation of Rottenbuch (1073) became the ecclesiastical centre in the eastern part of this land of the Guelphs. The Archdeaconry of Rottenbuch, as the region was called, also included the original parish of Oberammergau, which extended to Bayersoien and Kohlgrub. The parish remained under Rottenbuch until the secularisation of the monasteries in 1803.

On the death of the last in southern Germany Guelph in 1191 their lands fell to the Hohenstaufens and, in 1269, formed the so-called Conradine Inheritance which passed to the House of Wittelsbach and thereby to Bavaria. When Kaiser Ludwig the Bavarian founded the monastery of Ettal in 1330, he gave the new foundation his estates in Ammergau, which originated from this "inheritance". In this way the Abbey of Ettal became the immediate temporal authority for the village, while Rottenbuch looked after ecclesiastical matters. This remained the situation for 500 years until the end of the old Empire and the old order in 1803 and 1806.

"Only a village"

Hardly one hour's drive from Oberammergau is the town of Marktoberdorf in Swabia, originally a small village which became a market town in 1453 and was made a municipality in 1953. This historical development is clearly reflected in the name of the place. Oberammergau on the other hand remained a village, but the description "village", which indicates a small, modest, rural sort of place, has become more of an honorary title for this community of 5,000 inhabitants which, in spite of its size has gained such renown and is well-known in almost the whole of the Western world. So although Oberammergau is "only a village", it is rather a special one.

The economic significance of the village was limited to serving as a transfer point on the road from Augsburg via Schongau to the south. Making a living was difficult and agriculture had long ago reached its limits.

Blick auf alte Oberammergauer Häuser an der Dedlerstraße mit dem Turm der Pfarrkirche und dem Kofel.

A view of old Oberammergau houses in the Dedler Street, the parish church tower, and the Kofel.

Not macht erfinderisch

In dem Reisebericht des Florentiners Francesco Vettori von 1507, einem der ersten, der Oberammergau erwähnt, heißt es, das Dorf sei „ein sehr gesunder und ärmlicher Ort". Das herzhafte, frische Klima im oberen Ammertal galt also schon damals als gesund. Ärmlich aber war das Dorf trotz seiner Lage an einer Handelsstraße, die Einkünfte bot für Wirte, Fuhrleute und Wegmacher; ärmlich war es trotz der Verdienstmöglichkeiten im nahen Ettal; es war arm, weil die landwirtschaftlichen Gründe spärlich und diese wenigen mager waren. Das Dorf liegt zwar malerisch und behütet zwischen den Bergen, es hat gutes Wasser und einen bequemen Zufahrtsweg von Norden her, aber das Flußtal war zu eng für so viele Siedler, Selbstversorgung war nicht möglich. Doch Not macht erfinderisch. Die Menschen suchten eine Nebenbeschäftigung und fanden diese in der Schnitzkunst. Vettori berichtet auch als erster von den kleinen kunstvollen Schnitzereien aus Oberammergau, die er in Ettal und im Dorf selbst zu sehen bekam. Wann diese Fertigkeit ins Dorf gelangte, wer sie dorthin brachte, das weiß niemand mehr zu sagen. Sie hat jedenfalls neue Verdienstmöglichkeiten gebracht und so das Dorf verändert. Später kam noch anderes Kunstgewerbe hinzu, das Formen von Wachsfiguren, Bossieren genannt, und spätestens seit der ersten Hälfte des 18. Jahrhunderts vor allem die Hinterglasmalerei. Lange Zeit fanden die so entstandenen „Ammergauer Taferln" den Weg hinaus in die Welt zusammen mit den geschnitzten Kruzifixen, den Heiligenfiguren, Puppenköpfen, Pferdegespannen, mit Spielzeug aller Art und kleinen nützlichen Geräten. „Not macht erfinderisch".

In einem Reisebericht des gelehrten Botanikers Franz von Paula Schrank aus dem Jahre 1784 heißt es bereits: „Oberammergau ist nur (!) ein Dorf, aber ein schönes Dorf, dessen......Einwohner wohlhabend sind". Nicht, daß alle Not gebannt gewesen wäre, aber „ärmlich", wie 280 Jahre vorher, war Oberammergau damals nicht mehr. Alle Not gebannt? Wie oft kehrte Not ein im Dorf! Hungersnöte plagten die Menschen, Feuer fraß in jedem Jahrhundert einmal die schindelgedeckten Holzhäuser; am schlimmsten aber waren die Seuchen, wie die Pest des Jahres 1633. Damals gelobten die Gemeindevertreter und der Gemeindevorstand, alle zehn Jahre das Leiden und den Tod Jesu Christi zu spielen, wenn das Sterben ein Ende nähme. Tatsächlich hörte die Plage auf, und über 350 Jahre lang, bis auf den heutigen Tag, hat die Gemeinde das Versprechen gehalten. Vom Passionsspiel handelt der erste Teil dieses Bandes. Deshalb hier nur zwei Gedanken zu dem Thema. Es ist bezeichnend für die Oberammergauer, daß sie ein „Spiel" gelobten, kein Kerzenopfer, keine immerwährende Stiftung, sondern etwas Künstlerisches. Das paßt zu den Schnitzern und Malern, auch wenn beim Spiel auch andere Fähigkeiten gefragt sind. Das Zweite: Die Oberammergauer sind durch dieses Gelöbnis reich belohnt worden. Denn nicht die schöne Lage, nicht das gesunde Klima, auch nicht die besten Schnitzereien haben das Dorf berühmt gemacht, sondern dieses Spiel.

Necessity is the mother of invention

In the account of his travels by the Florentine Francesco Vettori in 1507, one of the first accounts to mention Oberammergau, the village is described as a "very healthy but poor place". So even then the brisk climate of the upper valley of the Ammer was regarded as healthy. However, the village was poor in spite of its situation on a trade route which brought income to innkeepers, carriers and road-makers. It was poor in spite of the opportunities to earn money in nearby Ettal. It was poor because there was not enough land suitable for agriculture and the little there was produced low yields. The village is situated in a picturesque, sheltered position among the mountains, it has good water and an easy road out to the north, but the valley was too narrow for so many settlers and self-support was impossible. However, necessity is the mother of invention. People looked for additional work and found it in the art of woodcarving. The above-mentioned Francesco Vettori is the first to report the elaborate, small carvings from Oberammergau which he saw in Ettal and in the village itself. No one knows when this skill first appeared in the village or who brought it there. In any case it was a new way of earning a living and it changed the village. Later on, people took up other handicrafts such as moulding wax figurines and, since not later than the first half of the 18th century, behind glass painting. Ever since this time the behind glass paintings of "Ammergau", carved crucifixes, figures of saints, dolls' heads, teams of horses, toys of all kinds and small wooden utensils have been taken all over the world. "Necessity is the mother of invention".

In 1784 the scholarly botanist Franz von Paula Schrank wrote about his travels and said, "Oberammergau is only (!) a village, but a beautiful village whose .... inhabitants are prosperous". Not that all distress had been banished, but Oberammergau was no longer as "poor" as it was 280 years previously. All troubles vanished? The village often suffered other forms of hardship such as hunger, and every hundred years or so fire raged among the shingle-roofed wooden houses.

Worst of all were the epidemics, such as the plague of 1633. This was the year when the village representatives vowed to perform the suffering and death of Jesus Christ every 10 years if no more people died. And indeed the plague ceased, and the village has kept its promise for over 350 years, right up to the present day. The whole of the first part of this book deals with the Passion Play so that it is sufficient to mention here just two points. It is characteristic of the people of Oberammergau that they vowed to perform a play, which was something artistic, and not to offer candles or set up an everlasting foundation. This is appropriate for woodcarvers and artists, even if acting requires words and gestures, i. e. skills of a totally different kind. The second point is that the people of Oberammergau have been richly rewarded by the vow because it is the Play, and not the beautiful landscape, the healthy climate or even the best wood carvings which have made the village famous.

Unter den freskengeschmückten Häusern Oberammergaus ist das Pilatus-Haus eines der schönsten. Der „Lüftlmaler" Franz S. Zwink (1748-92) bemalte es spielerisch-illusionistisch mit einer repräsentativen Scheinarchitektur, in die er zwei biblische Szenen hineinstellte: die Auferstehung (Ostseite) und die Ecce-homo-Szene (Süd-seite). Letztere zeigt die am Gericht über

Jesus Beteiligten: Pilatus auf dem Richt-stuhl (in orientalischem Gewand), zwei Soldaten, die Jesus vorführen, einige Prie-ster und Gelehrte, also alle – außer dem Volk. Doch es fehlt nicht, denn es ist – nach der Absicht der Bildinszenierung – im je-weiligen Betrachter vertreten. Er hat jetzt zu entscheiden, was er von diesem Jesus hält. – Historie wird zur Gegenwart.

The Pilatus House is one of the most beau-tifully fresco decorated houses in Oberam-mergau. The "Luftelmaler" Franz S. Zwink (1748-92) playfully painted upon the walls of the peasent house the illusion of a classical architecture which provides the setting for two biblical scenes: the resurrec-tion (east side) and "Ecce Homo" shown here. It presents the participants in Jesus'

trial: Pilate (in oriental costume) on the judgement seat, two soldiers holding Jesus, the priests and scribes, everyone except the crowd. But it is there. As intended by the artist – each one who views the fresco beco-mes a member of the crowd and has to de-cide what he thinks of this Jesus – history becomes the present.

Die kostbarste der historischen Weih-
nachtskrippen des Heimatmuseums wurde
1780-1800 gemeinsam von den Schnitzern
des Ortes für die Pfarrkirche gefertigt. Wer
in der Phantasie mit den Königen oder den
Hirten mitgeht, vergegenwärtigt - wie im
Passionsspiel - die Heilsgeschichte.

Zur Förderung der Schnitzkunst gab es in
Oberammergau ab 1802 gemeindlichen
Zeichenunterricht, ab 1856 eine Zeichen-
und Modellierschule, ab 1877 Schnitzkur-
se. Heute bildet die Staatliche Berufsfach-
schule in dem schönen Gebäude Franz
Zells (1909) junge Holzbildhauer aus.

The most splendid of the antique Nativity
Scenes collected in the local history museum was done jointly by the local woodcarvers for the parish church (1780-1800).
The viewer accompanying the Kings or the
shephards approaches the salvation history
- as in the Passion Play.

To promote the art of woodcarving, Oberammergau supported by 1802 drawing les-
sons, established in 1856 a school for drawing and sculpture and in 1877 courses in
woodcarving. Today the State Technical
School trains woodsculptures in the handsome building designed by F. Zell (1909).

„Ein schönes Dorf"

Dieses Lob des gelehrten und weitgereisten Franz von Paula Schrank aus dem Jahre 1784 gilt noch immer. Warum aber ist Oberammergau ein schönes Dorf? Nicht allein wegen seiner einzigartigen Lage im Gebirge, nicht allein wegen seiner gepflegten Anlagen oder der vielen malerischen Hausgärten, auch nicht wegen des reichen Blumenschmucks an den Häusern im Sommer - alles das gibt es auch in anderen Dörfern des bayerischen Oberlandes. Was Oberammergaus Schönheit ausmacht, ist sein Reichtum an kunstvollen alten Häusern aus dem 18. und 19. Jahrhundert und aus dem Beginn des zwanzigsten. Daß verhältnismäßig viel an alter Bausubstanz erhalten blieb, verdankt das Dorf auch dem Glücksfall einer Art Denkmalspflege, die von dem Münchner Architekten Franz Zell durchgesetzt wurde. Franz Zell, der Architekt von Schnitzschulgebäude und Museum, half viele alte Bausünden verbessern und neue vermeiden. Übrigens gibt es schon zwei Generationen früher Nachrichten von einer bewußten Bauweise in Oberammergau: Pfarrer Daisenberger berichtet in der Dorfchronik vom sogenannten „Sonnenbau" nach dem Brand von 1844, das heißt, alle Wohnhäuser wurden einzeln stehend und von einem freien Platz umgeben wieder aufgebaut.

Ein charakteristischer Schmuck des alpenländischen Hauses sind die Lüftlmalereien in Form von Umrahmungen gewisser Architekturteile oder von Medaillons auf den großen Wandflächen. Aber zur Schönheit dieser Häuser trägt auch ihre Form bei, die spezifische Dachschräge, die schön gestalteten Kreuzstöcke der Fenster und der kunstvolle Zierbund im Giebel der Schauseite. All dies findet sich heute noch an vielen Häusern des Dorfes und erhöht seinen Reiz.

Die Pfarrkirche St. Peter und Paul

Die Mitte des Dorfes, nicht nur optisch oder geographisch, ist die Pfarrkirche St. Peter und Paul, von 1736 bis 1741 errichtet, nachdem die gotische Kirche einzufallen drohte. Die Kirche ist ein mächtiger und doch gefälliger Bau, großzügig und vornehm. Dabei zählte die Gemeinde damals kaum 900 Einwohner! Als Architekt gewann das Kloster Rottenbuch den tüchtigen Joseph Schmuzer aus Wessobrunn, der viele Kirchen in der näheren und weiteren Umgebung errichtet hat: St. Anton in Partenkirchen, die Pfarrkirchen von Mittenwald und Garmisch, die Gotteshäuser und Klosteranlagen in Ettal, Rottenbuch und Schongau. Für Oberammergau finanzierten Rottenbuch und Ettal den Rohbau, zunächst ohne merkliche Hilfe der Gemeinde. Bei der Ausstattung der Kirche erwiesen sich die Oberammergauer dann umso großzügiger. Einzelne Familien übernahmen die Kosten von Figuren, von Teilen der Pflasterung, von Bildern, ja von ganzen Altären. Matthäus Günther wurden die Fresken zugeschlagen, Joseph Schmuzer sorgte zusammen mit seinem Sohn Franz für die Stuckierung, der angesehene Weilheimer Bildhauer Franz Xaver Schmädl wurde mit der Ausarbeitung der Altäre und des gesamten Figuren-

"A beautiful village"

This praise by the widely travelled and learned Franz von Paula Schrank in 1784 is true to this day. But why is Oberammergau a beautiful village? Not only because of its unique situation in the mountains, not only because of its well-kept public gardens and walks or the many picturesque gardens of houses, nor because of the profusion of flowers adorning the houses in summer. All of these things can be found in other villages as well in Upper Bavaria. What makes Oberammergau especially beautiful is the large number of ornate houses dating from the 18th and 19th centuries and the beginning of the 20th. The fact that a relatively large proportion of old buildings has been preserved is thanks to a stroke of luck in the form of a sort of building preservation scheme which was brought about by the Munich architect Franz Zell. He was the architect of the Woodcarving School and the Museum, and he helped to improve earlier architectural mistakes and to avoid new ones. Incidentally, there is mention two generations earlier of a deliberate method of building in Oberammergau. In the village chronicle the parish priest Daisenberger describes the so-called "Sonnenbau" after the fire of 1844. When the houses were rebuilt they were all detached, each being surrounded by an open space.

In Alpine regions houses are characteristically decorated with so-called "Lüftl" paintings which frame certain architectural elements or take the form of medallions on large wall surfaces. However, the shape is also part of the beauty of these houses, as well as the specific slope of the roof, the beautifully fashioned window frames and the elaborately decorated beams in the front gable. All these things can still be seen on many houses in the village and they all enhance its charm.

Parish church of St. Peter and St. Paul

The church of St. Peter and St. Paul, built 1736 - 41 after the Gothic church was about to collapse, is both the visual and geographic centre of the village. The church is a powerful but attractive building, spacious and noble. At the time it was built there were only 900 inhabitants in the village. The architect employed by the monastic authorities of Rottenbuch was the capable Joseph Schmuzer of Wessobrunn, who had built many churches and monasteries in the immediate locality and further afield: St. Anton in Partenkirchen, the parish churches of Mittenwald and Garmisch, monastic buildings and churches in Ettal, Rottenbuch and Schongau. The basic structure of the Oberammergau church was financed by Rottenbuch and Ettal, at first without noticeable help from the village. However, the people of Oberammergau were all the more generous in decorating and furnishing the church. Individual families paid the cost of sculptures stone flooring paintings and complete altars. Matthäus Günther was commissioned to paint the frescoes, Joseph Schmuzer and his son Franz carried out the stucco work, and the highly regarded sculptor Franz Xaver Schmädl of Weilheim was commissioned to design the altars and all the

schmucks beauftragt. Heute noch, nach 250 Jahren, überrascht diese Dorfkirche den Besucher durch ihre Weite und Vornehmheit, durch ihr theologisches Programm, das auch hier in echt barocker Weise das Ganze zu einer gedanklichen Einheit verschmilzt. Keine Einzelheit, die nicht durchdacht und bis ins Letzte geformt wäre. So gehört Oberammergaus Gotteshaus zu den Sehenswürdigkeiten des an schönen Kirchen wahrlich nicht armen Pfaffenwinkels, und es zeugt vom religiösen Sinn seiner Bewohner, von ihrem Kunstverstand und ihrer Generosität.

Die evangelisch - lutherische Kreuzkirche

Das evangelisch-lutherische Kirchlein ist Ende der zwanziger Jahre dieses Jahrhunderts aus einem Wohnhaus entstanden, einfach in seiner Ausstattung, aber würdig und einladend für die inzwischen durch Zuzug stark angewachsene Gemeinde und die vielen protestantischen Gäste aus dem In- und Ausland.

Von allerlei Künsten im Dorf

In Oberammergau fallen die vielen bemalten Häuser auf. Man nennt diese Kunst, wie schon erwähnt, „Lüftlmalerei", ein Wort, das vielleicht zusammenhängt mit „lüftig" in der Bedeutung von rasch, oder mit „Luft", weil im Freien gemalt. Diese so geschmückten Häuser bereichern das Ortsbild ungemein, heitern es auf und erfreuen das betrachtende Gemüt. Kunstverstand, Freude am Bildhaften allein genügen jedoch nicht für solchen Häuserschmuck; er setzt auch einen gewissen Wohlstand voraus, der - wie wir gesehen haben - tatsächlich gegeben war. In der zweiten Hälfte des 18. Jahrhunderts war es Franz Seraph Zwinck (1748 - 1792), ein Sohn Oberammergaus, der so viele Häuser mit solchen Fresken zierte, daß ihn sein Biograph den „Dekorateur seines Heimatortes" genannt hat. Das in jüngster Zeit vorzüglich renovierte Pilatushaus ist eines der schönsten Beispiele von Zwincks dekorativer Kunst. Viele Häuser in Oberammergau wurden auf diese Weise geschmückt, ihr Aussehen durch die Malerei veredelt, ihre Architektur gehoben. Zu Beginn dieses Jahrhunderts und noch einmal in den letzten Jahrzehnten blühte die Fassadenmalerei in Oberammergau neu auf, und zwar mit sehr erfreulichen, zum Teil sogar meisterhaften Arbeiten.

Es ist unübersehbar, welch große Rolle im Dorf die Künste spielen, die Literatur, wenn auch in erster Linie im Dienste der Passion, dann die Musik, die natürlich seit alters auch den Passionsspielen zu dienen hatte. Die größte musikalische Begabung des Dorfes war Rochus Dedler (1779-1822), der Messen und Kantaten komponierte, Hymnen und Lieder, vor allem aber die heute noch gespielte Passionsmusik. Es gibt im Dorf die Blaskapelle, früher „türkische Musik" genannt, ein Orchester für die Kirchen- und Passionsmusik, einen Kirchen- und einen Motettenchor, den Liederkranz und den Musikverein; aus Berichten von Passionsbesuchern im 19. Jahrhundert wissen wir, wie hochstehend damals schon die Haus-

decorative figures. Even today, after 250 years, this village church still surprises visitors with its noble spaciousness and its theological scheme which, in the genuinely baroque manner, blends the whole into a unity of concept. Every single element has been thought out and shaped down to the last detail. The church of Oberammergau is one of the examples of the many fine churches in the foothills of the Bavarian Alps and it is proof of the religious feeling of the people, their appreciation of art and their generosity.

The evangelical-lutheran Kreuzkirche

The small evangelical-lutheran church was converted from a house at the end of the 1920s. The furnishings are simple, but the church is dignified and inviting for the many Protestant visitors from Germany and abroad and the large number of resident Protestants who have moved to the community.

Of arts in the village

Many of the houses in Oberammergau are covered with paintings. As already mentioned, this is called "Lüftl" painting, a term which may be connected with "lüftig" meaning "fast" or with "Luft" meaning "air" because the painting was done in the open air. These painted houses enhance the appearance of the village enormously, they brighten it up and are a constant source of delight. However, appreciation of art and pleasure in the visual are not on their own sufficient for decoration on this scale. It also presupposes a degree of prosperity which, as we have seen, actually existed. In the second half of the 18th century Franz Seraph Zwinck (1748 -- 92), a son of Oberammergau, painted so many houses with frescoes that his biographer called him the "decorator of his home village". The Pilatushaus, which has recently been superbly renovated, is one of the finest examples of Zwinck's art. Many houses in Oberammergau were adorned in this way, their appearance enriched and the effect of their architecture brought out by the paintings. At the beginning of this century and also in recent decades wall-painting flourished again in Oberammergau and has produced some very enjoyable and, in some cases, masterly works.

It is impossible to overlook the importance of the arts of literature and music in the village, although literature primarily serves the Passion Play. Since very early times music has of course also served the Play. The greatest musical talent in the village was Rochus Dedler (1779 - 1822) who composed masses and cantatas, hymns and songs, and above all the Passion Music which is still played today. The village has a brass band, which used to be called "the Turkish Music", as well as an orchestra for church music and the Passion Play music, a choral society and a music society. We know from reports by English visitors to the Passion Play in the 19th century that amateur musicians reached a high standard even then. Of course, the theatre is the centre of artistic activity in Oberammergau, but

Die Oberammergauer Pfarrkirche St. Peter und Paul. An ihrer Gestaltung waren hervorragende Künstler des bayerisch-schwäbischen Rokokos beteiligt. der Bau meister Joseph Schmuzer (Wessobrunn), der Maler Matthäus Günther (Augsburg) und der Bildhauer Franz Xaver Schmädl (Weilheim). Es entstand ein glanzvolles Gotteshaus, ein festlicher Rahmen für die Eucharistie und die Feste des Kirchenjahres, ein Raum der Andacht und der Glaubensvermittlung in Bildern und Symbolen. Immer wieder stehen den Darstellungen des Leidens und der Bedrängnis Bilder ihrer Überwindung im Zeichen des Kreuzes gegenüber wie z.B. im Kuppelfresko, wo Martyrium und Glorie der Kirchenpatrone gezeigt werden.

Oberammergau's Parish Church of Sts. Peter and Paul. Outstanding artists of the Bavarian-Swabien Rococo took part in its creation: the architect J. Schmutzer (Wessobrunn); the painter M. Günther (Augsburg); and the sculpter F.X. Schmädel (Weilheim). A magnificent house of God was created, a festive atmosphere in which to celebrate the Eucharist throughout the liturgical year; a sacred space for devotion and the conveying of faith through pictures and symbols. Several presentations show suffering and afflication and their surmounting through the salvation of the cross, such as the martyrdom and glory of the church patrons depicted in the cupola.

121

musik war. Zentrum der musischen Beschäftigungen in Oberammergau ist freilich das Theater, und dies nicht nur deshalb, weil das Spiel auf den Brettern den Alpenbewohnern ohnehin viel bedeutet, sondern weil es hier notwendige Übung für die alle zehn Jahre wiederkehrende Passion ist. Doch damit ist die Pflege der Künste, ist das kulturelle Leben im Dorf nicht erschöpft. Oberammergau besitzt ein reiches Museum mit der großen Weihnachtskrippe, die früher in der Kirche aufgestellt war, mit einer umfangreichen, ja einzigartigen Sammlung von Hinterglasbildern, nicht nur aus der eigenen Produktion (s. oben), mit Ammergauer Schnitzereien und Volkskunst der besten Art. Da ist ferner das Pilatushaus als Zeuge der Wohnkultur im 18. Jahrhundert mit seiner qualitätvollen Fassadenmalerei und den „Lebenden Werkstätten", da lädt die Kirche ein zum gründlichen Betrachten, zu Stille und Besinnung.

Ausdruck des kulturellen Lebens im Dorf ist ferner das Brauchtum, übers ganze Jahr verteilt, mit den kirchlichen Festen als Höhepunkte, dem König Ludwig-Feuer am 24. August, dem Vorabend des Geburts- und Namenstages von König Ludwig II., dem die Gemeinde für sein Wohlwollen und seine Zuneigung dankt, oder dem großen Sternrundgang am letzten Tag des Jahres als Ausblick auf das neue Jahr unter dem Zeichen und unter dem sicheren Geleit des Heilandes. - Nichts davon ist bloße Routine, nichts bloße Schau für die Touristen, alles gehört noch zum Lebensrhythmus des Dorfes.

Sport und Natur

Rund um Oberammergau lockt eine vielgestaltige, abwechslungsreiche Landschaft von hohem Reiz, locken die Moore und Weiden mit ihrer kostbaren Flora, locken die Berge und das Tal der Ammer mit ihren Naturschönheiten. Doch Wanderungen und Radtouren sind nicht die einzigen Sportarten, die Oberammergau dem Gast und dem Einheimischen bietet. Das großzügig angelegte Schwimmbad „Der WellenBerg" macht Sport und Erholung im Wasser möglich, das Labergebirge gilt als Eldorado für Drachenflieger, im Winter sorgen Lifte, Pisten und Loipen für die Bedürfnisse der Skifahrer. Ein neuer, großzügiger Sportplatz bietet beste Voraussetzungen für viele Formen der Leichtathletik, und die überdachte Tennis- und Squash-Anlage macht die Ausübung dieser beliebten Sportarten von jeder Witterung unabhängig.

Die Oberammergauer

Wie aber sind die Menschen, die in Oberammergau leben, die das Dorf zu dem gemacht haben, was es heute ist?

Alois Daisenberger, der langjährige Pfarrer Oberammergaus im 19. Jahrhundert, auf den die heute gültige Textfassung des Passionsspieles zurückgeht, versucht eine Charakteristik seiner „Schäflein". Er beschreibt ihre Sprache, die altbayerische, schwäbische und tirolerische Elemente vereinigt. Er leitet ihre Geradheit und Freimütigkeit von

this is not only because acting means a lot to mountain-dwellers, but also because in this case it provides the necessary practice for the Passion Play which recurs every ten years. There is yet another facet to the cultural life of the village. Oberammergau possesses a richly endowed museum with the large Christmas Creche which used to stand in the church, an extensive and, indeed, unique collection of behind glass paintings not all of which are from Oberammergau itself, as well as Ammergau wood carvings and folk art of the best kind. In addition the Pilatushaus bears witness to the domestic decoration of the 18th century, with its fine wall-paintings and the "living workshops", while the church itself deserves close examination and invites passers-by to quiet meditation.

Customs and traditions are another expression of the cultural life of the village. They are spread over the whole year, with the church festivals as the high points and King Ludwig's mountain bonfires on 24 August, which is the eve of the birthday and name day of King Ludwig II, to whom the community will always be grateful for his goodwill and his attachement to the village. The "Starlight Walk" is on the last day of the year, when people look forward to the New Year under the sign and with the sure guidance of the Saviour. None of these is merely a matter of routine, none of them is just a show for tourists, all of them are part of the annual rhythm of the life of the village.

Sport and nature

The countryside around Oberammergau is very attractive and of diverse types. There are moorlands and pastures, with their precious plant life, and the natural beauties of the mountains and the valley of the Ammer. Walking and cycle tours are not the only kinds of recreation which Oberammergau offers visitors and natives. Swimming and water sports can be enjoyed in the spacious swimming centre "Der WellenBerg", the Laber Mountains are ideal for Hang gliders and in the winter there are lifts, trails and cross-country courses for skiers. There is a large new sports complex with excellent facilities for track and field athletics, while the covered tennis and squash courts enable these favourite games to be played irrespective of the weather.

The Oberammergauers

But what are the people like who live in Oberammergau and who have made the village what it is today?

Alois Daisenberger, who was the parish priest of Oberammergau for many years in the 19th century and who is responsible for the version of the text of the Passion Play which is used today, has tried to characterise his "flock". He describes their language, which unites Bavarian, Swabian and Tirolean elements. He derives their straightforwardness and openess from Bavarian influences, their wit and intelligence from the Tirolean influences and their cheerful disposition and liveliness from the Swabian in-

Die ausdrucksstarke und fast modern wirkende „Ecce homo"-Darstellung aus dem 18. Jh. gehört zur Hinterglasbilder-Sammlung des Oberammergauer Heimatmuseums (ca. 1000 Bilder). Sie enthält vor allem Arbeiten aus oberbayerischen Zentren dieser Volkskunst (Murnauer Raum, Oberammergau) und stellt die größte Sammlung von Hinterglasmalerei aus einem geschlossenen Gebiet dar. In Oberammergau blühte diese Kunst von Mitte des 18. bis Mitte des 19. Jh. Die „Taferln" – mit ihrer vorwiegend religiösen Thematik Andachtgegenstand und Hausschmuck zugleich – wurden in großer Anzahl in einer Art „Hausindustrie" hergestellt, bei der die ganze Familie zusammenhalf.

This 18th cent. representation of the "Ecce homo", expressive and almost modern, is part of the behind-glass painting collection in the local history museum. Most of the pictures (about 1000) were made in upper Bavaria. The museum represents the largest collection of this region (especially of Oberammergau and Murnau) where this folk art flourished from the middle of th 18th to the middle of the 19th cent. The "Taferln", as the pictures were called, were predominantly religious in theme, they functioned as objects for devotion and house decoration. Most were produced as a cottage industry involving a whole family.

Blick auf Oberammergau vom „Wies-mahd" aus. Ganz rechts das Passionsthea-ter, im Zentrum die Pfarrkirche, links – das größere Gebäude – die Schnitzschu-le.

Die Photographie verdeutlicht die Tallage Oberammergaus. Im Süden erheben sich die schroffen Felsformationen des Ammer-gebirges. Auf der Nordseite, von der man hier auf den Ort blickt, erstreckt sich der Aufackerzug mit seinen sanftgeschwunge-nen mittelgebirgsähnlichen Hügelformen, die der Zuschauer des Passiosspiels als na-türliche Kulisse im Hintergrund der Frei-lichtbühne wahrnimmt.

Der Standort der Photographie trägt den Namen „Wiesmahd", weil man hier, hin-auf bis zu einer Höhe von über tausend Metern, nach vorheriger Rodung des Wal-des die Wiesen bewirtschaftete und das Gras mähte. In mühseliger Arbeit mußte man das Futter für das Vieh ernten, das die Böden des Tales nicht in genügender Menge hergaben.

Die solcherweise kultivierte Landschaft ist Folge und Ausdruck der ursprünglichen harten Lebensbedingungen. Wie häufig in der menschlichen Geschichte bewies sich auch hier, daß eine Mangelsituation zum Ausgangspunkt einer schöpferischen Ent-wicklung werden kann. Weil die Natur nicht die Lebensgrundlagen bereitstellte, wandten sich die Oberammergauer dem Kunsthandwerk zu.

Neue Aufgaben erschlossen sich wieder, als Reisende die Schönheit dieser Landschaft und Erholungssuchende die gesundheitli-che Zuträglichkeit der Gebirgsnatur ent-deckten. Diese machen – zusammen mit den Kunstschätzen des Ortes und der Um-gebung – Oberammergau auch heute zu einem Ort, an dem man sich regenerieren und neue Anregungen finden kann.

View of Oberammergau from the "Wies-mahd". At the far right is the Passion Play theater, in the center the parish church and the larger building on the left is the wood-carving school.

The photo illustrates the character of the valley: To the south the rugged Ammer Mountain Range; in the north, from where the picture is taken, the Aufacker Range with its gently undulating highland hill forms. These the Passion Play visitor can see as a natural backdrop to the open air theater.

The location from which the picture was taken is called "Wiesmahd". From here on up to more than 1000 meters, the forest was cleared for meadows ("Wies") to be mowed ("-mahd"). Only through such arduous work would enough hay for cattle be produced. The valley floor could not fill this need.

The cultivated landscape is both a consequence and an expression of the original harsh conditions for survival. As so often in the history of humanity, here too the scarce resources acted as a stimulus for creative development. Nature could not provide the necessities for life, so villagers turned to handcrafts.

As the traveler discovered the beauty of the landscape and those looking for rest found a healthy mountain environment, new employment opportunities emerged. With the art treasures of the village, its natural beauty, Oberammergau is a place where one can seek renewal and find inspiration.

125

den baierischen, ihren Witz und ihre Klugheit von den tirolerischen, ihren heiteren Sinn und ihre Lebhaftigkeit von den schwäbischen Einflüssen her. Daisenberger erfährt seine Pfarrkinder als gelehrig und anstellig, als fleißig und als Freunde der Musik und des Theaters, als für alles Schöne und Gute empfänglich, aber auch als „störrisch und sehr empfindlich" - allerdings nur bei „übler Behandlung". Daisenberger ist klug genug, mit negativen Aussagen Zurückhaltung zu üben. Zweifellos rechtfertigt vieles im Dorf seine positiven Beobachtungen. Letztlich sind es wohl Ideale, die Daisenberger aufzeigt, und dazu gehört auch, daß das heilige Spiel, das im Leben eines Oberammergauers eine so hervorragende Stelle einnimmt, sein Leben beeinflusse, seinen Wandel bessere, seine Frömmigkeit vertiefe. Wieweit solch hochgesteckte Ziele erreicht werden, wer wollte darüber ein Urteil fällen?

Das Besondere an Oberammergau entstand aus einem Zusammenspiel vieler Faktoren, es ist nicht so sehr die Leistung einiger weniger Persönlichkeiten. Und doch ist die Geschichte Oberammergaus unverhältnismäßig reich an großen Gestalten: Franz Seraph Zwinck, der Lüftlmaler, müßte hier genannt werden und Rochus Dedler, der Komponist und Lehrer; auch Alois Daisenberger, der Pfarrer des Dorfes und Reformer des Passionstextes, gehört zu diesen Persönlichkeiten und Ludwig Thoma, der in Oberammergau geborene Dichter; tüchtige Verleger aus dem 18. und 19. Jahrhundert wären aufzuzählen, Männer von Unternehmungsgeist und sozialem Engagement und große, weithin berühmte Schauspieler und Spielleiter. Die Zeiten ändern sich, bringen neue Chancen und andere Gefahren. Wer wünschte nicht, daß die Oberammergauer die Herausforderungen sehen und bestehen und uns ihr Oberammergau erhalten.

fluences. Daisenberger sees his parishioners as clever, quick to learn and industrious, he considers them to be lovers of music and theatre, receptive to everything that is good and beautiful, but also as "stubborn and very sensitive", but only if "ill-treated". Daisenberger is intelligent enough to be sparing with negative judgments. Certainly there are many things in the village which justify his positive observations. After all, what he describes are ideals and one of these is that the holy Play, which has such a prominent position in the life of every inhabitant of Oberammergau, should influences his life, improve his way of life and deepen his piety. Who would wish to judge how far such high aims are achieved?

What is special about Oberammergau is the result of the interplay of many factors, and not so much the achievement of just a few individuals. And yet the history of Oberammergau is disproportionately rich in outstanding figures: Franz Seraph Zwinck, the painter, should be mentioned here together with Rochus Dedler, the composer and teacher. Alois Daisenberger, the village pastor and reformer of the text of the Play is another of these individuals, together with Ludwig Thoma, the poet who was born in Oberammergau. There would also be the names of efficient 18th and 19th century distributers, men with social commitment and a spirit of enterprise, as well as well-known actors and play directors. Times change, creating new opportunities and bringing different risks. Let us all wish that the people of Oberammergau see and overcome the challenges and that their Oberammergau is preserved for us.

Hans Pörnbacher

Dem interessierten Leser empfehlen wir:

Joseph Alois Daisenberger: Geschichte des Dorfes Oberammergau. In: Oberbayer. Archiv für vaterländische Geschichte Bd. 20. München 1859–1861 (Nachdruck Oberammergau 1988).

Oberammergau. Das Herz des Ammertales – das Land von Rottenbuch bis Linderhof. Ein Bildband von A. Buchwieser/V. Fenzl/F. Grawe. München 1988.

Die Pfarrkirche von Oberammergau. (Schnell Kunstführer Nr. 21), München 1990.

Further reading:

Joseph Alois Daisenberger: Geschichte des Dorfes Oberammergau. In: Oberbayer. Archiv für vaterländische Geschichte Bd. 20. München 1859–1861 (Nachdruck Oberammergau 1988).

„Oberammergau, Das Herz des Ammertals – das Land von Rottenbuch bis Linderhof". A picture book by A. Buchwieser/V. Fenzl/ F. Grawe. Munich 1988.

The Parish Church in Oberammergau. Munich 1990. (Schnell Kunstführer Nr. 21, English editions).

Brauchtum wird in Oberammergau in vielfältiger Form lebendig erhalten: im Zusammenhang mit den Kirchenfesten, aber auch z.B. in der Form einer Erinnerungsfeier für Ludwig II. Zum Jahreswechsel ziehen die Oberammergauer mit dem „großen" Stern durch den Ort und besingen in traditionellen Liedern das neue Jahr. Kindergruppen mit einem „kleinen" Stern bringen die musikalischen Neujahrswünsche von Haus zu Haus,. z.B. mit dem Lied:
„Ein Stern ist aufgegegangen
Aus Jakob hell und klar,
Am Himmel hoch zu prangen,
Er leuchtet so wunderbar.
Seht seine Strahlen funkeln,
Sie leuchten weit im Dunkeln!
Er hat die ganze Welt
Mit seinem Licht erhellt.
Geh milde uns zur Seite,
Mit deinem Licht begleite
Der Erde Pilgerschar
Durchs kommende neue Jahr."

Many customs live on in varied forms; for the Holy Days, but also, for example, the feast day in honor of King Ludwig II. On New Year's eve the Oberammergauers march through the village with a big illumined star and welcome the new year with traditional songs. Groups of children with a little star go from house to house singing New Year's wishes like this song:
"A star has risen
From Jacob bright and clear,
In the high heavens it sparkles,
It shines so beautifully.
Look at its glittering rays,
They penetrate the darkness.
It has illuminated
the whole world with its light.
Gently guide us along,
With your light to accompany
this earthly throng of pilgrims
through the coming New Year."

Die Fassade des Kölbl-Hauses zeigt – in der Gestaltung Franz Seraph Zwincks – das Motiv des Gnadenstuhls (Ettaler Straße 10). Fresken wie dieses erinnern auch im Alltagsleben an das Mysterium der Passion: „So sehr hat Gott die Welt geliebt, daß er seinen einzigen Sohn dahingab, damit jeder, der an ihn glaubt, nicht zugrundegehe, sondern unendliches Leben habe."
(Joh 3,16)

The Kölbl House (Ettaler Str. 10) was decorated by Franz S. Zwink with the motif of the "Gnadenstuhl" (God offers His Son). So even in the midst of everyday life one is reminded of the mystery of the passion; "God so loved the world that he gave his only Son, that whoever believes in him may not die, but may have eternal life." (Jn 3,16)

Impressum

Offizieller Bildband „Das Passionsspiel der Gemeinde Oberammergau 1990"

Konzeption des Bildbandes:
Passionsspielkomitee
Christian Stückl
Otto Huber
Thomas Klinger

Spielleiter: Christian Stückl

Bühnenbild: Georg Johann Lang (1889-1968, Spielleiter von 1922-1960; Entwürfe zu den Passionsspielen 1930)

Photographiert von Thomas Klinger

Texte
Otto Huber: Die Erlösung spielen, Chronologische Übersicht
Hermann Müller: Lebende Bilder
Prof. Hans Pörnbacher: Das Dorf an der Ammer

Textredaktion und Bildunterschriften:
Otto Huber

Übersetzungen ins Englische:
Translingua Frankfurt
Prof. Gottfried Lang PhD
Martha Lang PhB

Umschlaggestaltung und Layout:
Lorenz Meyboden & Thomas Klinger

Lithographie: Graphische Betriebe Zerreiss GmbH, Nürnberg

Satz und Druck:
Druckhaus Oberammergau GmbH
Schrift Garamond

Buchbindearbeit: R. Oldenbourg, Graphische Betriebe GmbH, München

2. Auflage 80000. – 120000.
© 1990 im Eigenverlag der Gemeinde Oberammergau (Gemeindliche Fremdenverkehrseinrichtungen)
Printed in Germany
Alle Rechte vorbehalten

Bildnachweis:
Alle Photographien incl. Titelbild von Thomas Klinger mit folgenden Ausnahmen:

Kreuzabnahme Passionsspiel 1900 (S. 7) von Leo Schweyer, Stuttgart; Eherne Schlange Passionsspiel 1870 (S. 11) von Hofphotograph Josef Albert; Dedlerstraße mit Blick auf den Kofel (S. 113) von Vitus Fenzl; Krippenfiguren „Die Heiligen Drei Könige" (S.116), Dorfstraße 1950 (S. 119), Sternsinger 1960 (S. 127) von Hans Kronburger; Blick auf Oberammergau (S. 124/5) von Ewald Haag. Die historischen Aufnahmen vom Passionsspiel (S. 7, 11) stellte das Gemeindearchiv Oberammergau zur Verfügung.